STATE AND LOCAL
GOVERNMENT
IN AMERICA

STATE AND LOCAL GOVERNMENT IN AMERICA

SIXTH EDITION

Daniel R. Grant
President Emeritus, Ouachita Baptist University

Lloyd B. Omdahl
Professor, University of North Dakota
Former Lt. Gov. of North Dakota

WCB Brown &
Benchmark
PUBLISHERS

Madison, Wisconsin • Dubuque, Iowa • Indianapolis, Indiana
Melbourne, Australia • Oxford, England

Book Team

Editor *Edgar J. Laube*
Developmental Editor *Sue Pulvermacher-Alt*
Production Editor *Marlys Nekola*
Photo Editor *Carol A. Judge*
Visuals/Design Freelance Specialist *Mary L. Christianson*

Brown & Benchmark

A Division of Wm. C. Brown Communications, Inc.

Vice President and General Manager *Thomas E. Doran*
Editor in Chief *Edgar J. Laube*
Executive Editor *Ed Bartell*
National Sales Manager *Eric Ziegler*
Director of CourseResource/Developmental Services
  Kathy Law Laube
Director of CourseSystems *Chris Rogers*
Director of Marketing *Sue Simon*

Director of Production *Vickie Putman Caughron*
Marketing Manager *Carla J. Aspelmeier*
Advertising Manager *Jodi Rymer*
Manager of Visuals and Design *Faye M. Schilling*
Design Manager *Jac Tilton*
Art Manager *Janice Roerig*
Publishing Services Manager *Karen J. Slaght*
Permissions/Records Manager *Connie Allendorf*

Wm. C. Brown Communications, Inc.

Chairman Emeritus *Wm. C. Brown*
Chairman and Chief Executive Officer *Mark C. Falb*
President and Chief Operating Officer *G. Franklin Lewis*
Corporate Vice President, President of WCB Manufacturing *Roger Meyer*

Cover illustration by Timothy James Heffron; Interior and cover design
by Design Graphics

Illustrations by Design Graphics unless otherwise noted

Library of Congress Catalog Card Number: 92–71004

ISBN 0–697–11116–4

Printed in the United States of America by Wm. C. Brown Communications, Inc.,
2460 Kerper Boulevard, Dubuque, IA 52001

10 9 8 7 6 5 4 3 2 1

Contents

9   THE LEGISLATURE: INSTITUTION AND PROCESS   **177**

10   THE EXECUTIVE BRANCH   **215**

11   THE GOVERNORSHIP   **246**

12   THE JUDICIARY AND CRIMINAL JUSTICE   **264**

Preface

Most students enter colleges and universities with only a vague concept of state and local government. In many institutions, courses in state and local government attract enrollees who are not majoring in political science but are seeking a general understanding of government. In this sixth edition, the needs of these students as well as the majors are addressed by a balanced combination of cutting-edge research in state and local government along with the more traditional historical and pragmatic perspectives. Students are given the basic structural outlines in an introductory fashion to help them think definitively about government.

With the text providing the basics of state and local government, the instructor can build on that foundation of reading with classroom lectures and activities that stress critical thinking about governmental interrelationships, policy analysis, political impacts, and philosophical issues.

The authors bring experienced insight to this edition, with 50 years of teaching state and local government between them, as well as years of academic and government administration. Grant taught at Vanderbilt University in the 'fifties and 'sixties, served as president of Ouachita Baptist University in the 'seventies and 'eighties, and teaches now at Ouachita in retirement. Omdahl has combined a career of teaching political science at the University of North Dakota, with service as a governor's chief of staff, a constitutional convention delegate, a state tax commissioner, a state budget director, a candidate for U.S Congress, and a lieutenant governor. This perspective has allowed the authors to focus the sixth edition on the dramatic cross-currents of American federalism in the final decade of the twentieth century—long-term centralization and the more recent politics of decentralization.

Topics given new or greater attention in this edition include: the results and implications of the 1990 census; the new politics of abortion in the "post-*Webster*" era, including the 1992 Supreme Court decision in the Pennsylvania case; the special urban impact of AIDS; trends in public coping with drug abuse, growing crime, homelessness, and environmental exploitation; policy politics of the crowded 1990s agenda of social and economic issues, as dramatized by the Los Angeles riots; the international networking of American cities; Professor Deil Wright's interesting "conceptual trilogy" in American intergovernmentalism; and a number of cross-current political developments such as "privatization" of governmental functions, increasing federal mandates to state and local governments with decreasing federal aid, the continued decline in party identification, the continued increase in the election to public office of women and minorities, the term-limitation movement concerning officeholders, the long-neglected concept of "judicial federalism," and the latest decisions of the Reagan-Bush Court on church-state relations, race and sex discrimination, obscenity and child abuse, criminal justice, the "right to die," and other areas with significant impact on state and local government.

We gratefully acknowledge the assistance of Shad Stastney in computations and tables, Marilyn Gerdon in copy preparation and permissions, Beverly Rosencrans in word processing, and Betty Jo Grant in proofreading and preparation of the excellent index.

We would like to thank the following people for their help in reviewing this text:

- Russell Ross, University of Iowa
- Bruce Caswell, Temple University
- Guy Clifford, Bridgewater State University
- William Binning, Youngstown State University
- David Folz, University of Tennessee
- Homer Williamson, St. Cloud State University
- Page Cubbison, Miami Dade Community College
- Charles Lasher, Notre Dame College, New Hampshire

D.R.G. and L.B.O.

FOUNDING FEDERALISM

CHAPTER 1

Developing a System of Government Commensurate to the Challenge

A funny thing happened on the way to the predicted downfall of state and local government and the federal system in the United States. The way was paved with eloquent and persuasive voices during much of the 20th century, citing the steady growth in size and power of the national government, numerous forces of centralization, and a succession of court decisions whittling down the concept of states' rights. The logical projection of these trends seemed to be, sooner or later, mere administrative province status (puppets on a string) for all the sub-national governments.

On the contrary, the decade of the nineties finds state and local governments alive and strong, charged with providing significant leadership in solving some of the most persistent problems ever to face American society:[1]

Issues of the nineties

- finding some kind of public-policy consensus on abortion in a nation and communities almost hopelessly divided;
- waging effective war against the pervasive drug abuse tragedy and against the closely related problem of runaway crime;
- finding answers to the ever-increasing array of frightening agents of environmental pollution;
- developing housing policies and programs that make a real difference for the homeless and others with inadequate shelter;
- coping with the medical and social dilemmas of the AIDS epidemic;
- rebuilding much of the nation's "infrastructure," said to be inadequately maintained and deteriorating;
- assuring opportunity for the good life for our nation's aging population;
- providing quality education that gives equal opportunity for all, yet produces a citizenry prepared to live and operate in the fiercely competitive tri-partite global economy of the 21st century; and
- numerous other issues old and new.

After decades of political pressures almost exclusively on Washington for action regarding society's problems, the decade of the eighties saw Washington turn an increasingly deaf ear and then "mandate" that states and localities must come up with

Deaf ears in Washington

Title photo: Architect of the Capitol. (Bob Coyle Photography)

their own creative ways and means for solving the problems. Not just the decision makers in Washington, but the majority of voters at the grass roots seemed to be saying they wanted less big government in Washington and more state and local involvement in solving these problems. Even the Los Angeles riots in the spring of 1992, said to be the worst in our nation's history, produced no consensus that a set of *national* answers will meet the diverse set of needs highlighted. The picture of American intergovernmental relations and federalism in the decade of the nineties, with all of its puzzling changes in directions, is discussed in chapter 2. It is important to begin, however, with a look at the onset of our American federal system. As we approach the year 2000, national-state-local relationships are unquestionably the product of this history. Governments are not designed, nor do they function, in vacuums. They are created and shaped by values, concerns, needs, and aspirations of the people they serve. This is especially true in societies in which democratic or republican mechanisms exist through the will of the people translated into public policy and institutional change.

Governmental institutions shaped by history

These mechanisms have been available, to one extent or another, since the colonists first set foot on American soil. Because American governmental institutions have been shaped by the tides of opinion and shifting needs, they have been subject to an evolutionary process from the Mayflower Compact into the 21st century. If history is any indication, this evolution will continue indefinitely.

Prelude to Federalism

Although the 1787 convention in Philadelphia is regarded as the landmark in the development of American government, historically the Constitution was not the first step—albeit a major one—in the evolution of government in America. In reality, the beginnings of the new Union antedated Edmund Randolph's presentation of the Virginia Plan to the newly convened assembly in Independence Hall.

Early Colonial Relationships

When the English government launched the American colonies through various forms of development companies, the purpose was to expand the economic base of the empire but not necessarily to create new political entities. The colonists were to produce goods that could enhance the economic power of England. To the government, they were vehicles in an economic system. Most colonists, however, saw America differently. For them, it was an escape from religious persecution, debtor's prison, and a variety of other hopeless futures. Nevertheless, the interests of the government and those of the colonists converged long enough to get settlers across the choppy Atlantic.

Mayflower Compact

While the colonists were extracting the products of commerce from the new land, they still had to live together—and that required order and law. Anticipating this need, they had agreed in the Mayflower Compact to abide by the will of the majority. While the Compact was a far cry from what would be called a "constitution" today, it was the first step in recognizing the political rights of Americans.

After the first colonists had established the beachhead, other similar economic enterprises were launched. Some colonies were begun by trading companies, such as the East India Trading Company; some were started under direct charter of the king; and some were launched by elite groups of proprietors. As a result of this diversity, and coupled with the poor intercolonial communications in the wilderness, the lines of accountability and communications ran from the individual colonies back to England rather than to each other.

Common Problems Arise

It wasn't long, however, before problems of common concern to the New England settlements began to develop. Relations with the Indians were erratic, with hostilities just frequent enough to require a loaded musket near at hand. Unfriendly white neighbors roamed the neighborhood as well, with the French competing for Indian trade and the Dutch resisting the westward movement of the English. In addition, differences developed among the Puritans themselves. Massachusetts quarreled with Plymouth over boundaries and everyone disliked the radicals of Narragansett Bay.[2] As the need for cooperation escalated, the colonists responded in 1643 by forming the United Colonies of New England, more commonly called the New England Confederation.

New England Confederation

At the onset, each settlement was guaranteed its continued independence. Then the Confederation dealt primarily with military defense, the extradition of criminals and fugitives, and a plan for resolving intercolonial disputes.[3] But the problems were not sufficient to bind the Confederation, and members eventually fell into disagreement. It survived long enough to assist in putting down the Indian uprising called King Philip's War and then faded into history, taking its place as the first significant venture in intercolonial government.

Problems persisted, however, varying in intensity from decade to decade. During this time, colonists and founders would postulate about the need for a central intercolonial organization. By 1754, England began to realize the need for greater intercolonial cooperation to protect its American holdings. It ordered the calling of a congress of colonial representatives in Albany, New York, to deal with the issue. Among those attending from seven colonies was Benjamin Franklin, who had argued for a continental organization for some years. The congress proposed an intercolonial government calling for a president-general appointed by the king and a council made up of representatives chosen by the colonial assemblies.[4] Apparently, the need for union was not seen as urgent, however, and hostility on both sides of the Atlantic killed the plan.

Consideration of Albany Plan

A Common Enemy Builds Common Bonds

Ten years later, events began to take a new turn. Now it wasn't the Indians, the French, or the Dutch that caused alarm among the colonials—it was England. In 1764, Parliament passed the Sugar Act to raise funds in America to help defray the cost of defense. This was followed in 1765 by adoption of the Stamp Tax. James Otis, early spokesman for the colonists, denounced the acts and declared them to be void because they were adopted against the principles of the British constitution—taxation without representation.[5] A special Stamp Act Congress, consisting of delegates from nine colonies, was convened in New York in October, 1765 to object to the adoption of colonial

Stamp Act Congress meets

tax measures without representation from the colonies. Thus, the idea of intercolonial assemblies responding to common problems that had begun in Albany became precedent-setting.

Continental Congress convenes

    The conflict with England escalated. The taxes were met with a determined boycott throughout the colonies: colonists dumped British tea into Boston Harbor; two regiments of British troops were ordered into Boston; bloodshed resulted from a confrontation between the troops and citizens; and the port of Boston was closed. As the crisis grew, so did the need for unified reaction. Colony after colony chose delegations to go to Philadelphia to meet as a Continental Congress in 1774—the third such meeting in twenty years. What the British government had started in 1754 as a tool for strengthening its holdings had now become a vehicle for colonists to oppose government policies.

The Shadow of a Government Appears

Even though there was great pressure for quick, unified action, the question of representation did not wait until the Constitutional Convention. It was a first order of discussion at the First Continental Congress. The large colonies favored representation proportionate to population while the small states stood firm for equality. The need for unanimity was so pressing the large states capitulated, only to renew the struggle thirteen years later.[6] Joseph Galloway of Pennsylvania offered a remodeled Albany Plan but found little enthusiasm for such a moderate approach. Instead, the Congress formed a network of committees, called the Continental Association, to enforce the boycott of British goods.[7]

    After the bloodshed at Lexington and Concord, the Second Continental Congress convened to become the nucleus of power for the colonies. Out of necessity, it assumed interim powers: supporting an army, appointing a commander-in-chief, issuing money, negotiating loans, and organizing several executive departments.[8] It was, in reality, a central government. Two weeks after the Declaration of Independence, the Congress started drafting the Articles of Confederation.

A League is Formed

Articles of Confederation

As finally approved by Congress and submitted to the states, the Articles of Confederation purported to create a "league of friendship" among equal partners. Each state had one vote in the unicameral Congress and unanimous consent was required for ratification and amendments. Drafted only to meet the contingencies of the day, the Articles empowered Congress to declare war, enter into alliances, make trade agreements, set the value of money, obtain loans, equip the military, make treaties with Indians, run postal stations, and appoint commissions to resolve boundary disputes.[9] There was no power to tax.

    While the Articles gathered dust in the legislative halls of the states, the Congress continued to oversee the war as an *ad hoc* government. Maryland refused to ratify the Articles until the other states gave up their claims to western lands. Its demands eventually met, Maryland gave its consent in March 1781 and the Articles went into effect. The war was almost concluded by the time the states had all agreed on a government.

The responsibilities and problems of independence soon weighed heavily upon the fragile central government, however. No longer a part of the British Empire, the states found certain trade privileges had vanished and new agreements were necessary. Some markets were closed to American ships. The money system was in chaos, with paper money being issued by the states as well as Congress. Thousands of soldiers who had won independence had not been paid and were restless. States levied discriminatory taxes on each other's shipping; Spain threatened to close western American traffic on *Problems multiply* the Mississippi; and British troops had not retreated from western forts. These and other problems beset a Congress that was rendered impotent by the states refusing to finance the central government or delegate authority equal to the challenge. Alexander Hamilton, surveying the problems arrayed against the anemic government under the Articles, observed in *The Federalist* No. 15 that "there is scarcely anything that can wound the pride or degrade the character of an independent nation which we do not experience."[10]

From a League of Friendship to a More Perfect Union

By 1787, it became apparent that the Articles of Confederation were not equal to the challenges. The convention that was called to consider revisions of the Articles was in session only a few days when the delegates turned to drafting a new document. Contrary to conventional wisdom, the Constitution, though innovative, was not a radical departure from past experience. Not only had the Articles of Confederation provided valuable insight upon which to build, but the state constitutions, with which most delegates were familiar, provided guidance in numerous ways. According to Walli Adams, "the basic structure of the Federal Constitution of 1787 was that of certain of the existing state constitutions writ large."[11]

Throughout the summer of 1787, the delegates struggled through the rending decisions involved in constitution-making. As soon as one issue was negotiated, another would appear to test their resolve. With each new controversy, new coalitions formed. Even though the large state–small state conflict pervaded the proceedings of the con- *Four phases of* vention, the coalitions were not this simple. Professor Calvin Jillson points to four phases *controversy* of convention controversy, each involving different coalitions of states.[12]

- •Phase I—Issue: Dominance of the new government. After nine weeks, Virginia and Pennsylvania succeeded in focusing on a strong national government.
- •Phase II—Issue: Scope and powers of the new government. Small states joined Virginia and Pennsylvania in giving extensive powers to the central government.
- •Phase III—Issue: Expanding role of large states in government. Pennsylvania and Virginia lost support of the small states by pushing a series of measures that threatened the roles of small states.

•Phase IV—Issue: Reasserting role of the small states. A coalition of small states and northern states shifted power away from the House dominated by large states to the Senate dominated by small states.

Throughout the course of the convention, according to Jillson, "each state participated in the core of a winning coalition that secured their dearest aims." As a result, the delegates could go home feeling that "their constitutional glass was at least half full as opposed to half empty."[13]

The Design of the New Federal System

Drawing on principles of government bequeathed to them by English traditions and experiences of governance on the American continent, the convention delegates were able to forge a federal design that would be commensurate with the problems facing the struggling states. Out of the deliberation and debate evolved new applications of old principles and a sharper focus for concepts of union. So the Constitution, though drawing together the diverse concepts and ideas, was not new. It was based on centuries of English tradition and decades of American experience.

The idea of equal privileges and immunities first appeared in the New England Confederation and was also a provision of the Articles of Confederation. The extradition of debtors and fugitives also originated in the early colonial proposals for union.

Constitution used old principles

Even though the Articles of Confederation were shunted aside in favor of a new document, the Constitution borrowed extensively from the Articles. Appearing in both documents were such clauses and phrases as "privileges and immunities," "full faith and credit," "freedom of speech and debate in Congress," "no titles of nobility," and a reference to spending for the "general welfare." Specific powers were also carried forward. The central government would continue to control foreign relations, determine standards for weights and measures, and run the post offices.

"If the new Constitution be examined with accuracy and candor," James Madison observed, "it will be found that the change which it proposes consists of much less in the addition of NEW POWERS to the Union than in the invigoration of its ORIGINAL POWERS."[14]

The Powers of the National Government

Delegated powers

The new national government was to be one of delegated powers. Many of these powers are identified in Article I, Section 8, and include the power to tax, to regulate commerce, to coin money, to declare war, to maintain armed forces, and numerous other specific authorizations. The drafters of the Constitution recognized that in order to exercise the delegated powers, the central government would need flexibility. To provide this flexibility the Constitution authorized Congress "to make all laws which shall be necessary and proper for carrying into execution" the enumerated powers. Thus, the national government became clothed with what is known as implied powers—powers implied by the existence of delegated powers. In *McCulloch* v. *Maryland,* decided by

Implied powers

the Supreme Court in 1819, the doctrine of implied powers was established as an integral part of national authority. In that case, the Court upheld the authority of Congress to create the Bank of the United States as implied (necessary and proper) by the delegated power "to lay and collect taxes; to borrow money; to regulate commerce; to declare and conduct war; and to raise and support armies and navies."[15] Eventually, another form of powers became apparent—the inherent powers. These powers are inherent in the very nature of a government, such as the power to receive foreign representatives.

Inherent powers

Being a government of delegated powers, the national government must constantly look to the Constitution for authority to act. On the other hand, the states must look to the document only for limitations because, with the exception of the delegated powers, the states are free to exercise all other powers. The powers reserved to the states were too numerous to list and are not classified in the Constitution. However, states limit their own governments through their own constitutions. A principal power reserved to the states is police power, which is discussed in chapter 4.

Some Powers are Exclusively National

A number of governmental powers are available to both the national and state governments, known as concurrent powers. Others are exclusively national government, such as for standing armies, foreign relations, foreign and interstate commerce, legal-tender money, patents and copyrights, tariffs, naturalization of aliens, maritime law, and the government of territories and colonies. Many of them were given exclusively to the national government because the lack of such power by the central government under the Articles of Confederation rendered the government impotent.

The neat allocation of exclusive powers to the national government has not foreclosed state or local forays into the forbidden territory. Although the conduct of foreign relations is delegated exclusively to the national government, the states and their local governments do participate, in effect, in American foreign relations in a variety of indirect ways. Resolutions of state legislatures or actions of officials have on many occasions complicated American relations with other nations. Examples include California restrictions on landholding by Japanese residents in the President Wilson administration; the removal of Italian citizens from a New Orleans jail by a lynching party; the snubbing of Soviet deputy premier Koslov by the mayor of Detroit; and the cancellation of the official reception by New York for King Faisal of Saudi Arabia because of anti-Jewish comments. When the Arab boycott was imposed against American companies dealing with Israel, several larger states, including New York and California, set up regulations to discourage companies from complying with the boycott. A number of states have taken steps to influence the race relations of South Africa by cutting back on state investment funds in firms doing business with that country. The growing role of state and local governments in international affairs was studied recently by the U.S. Advisory Commission on Intergovernmental Relations. It cites ten dimensions of their expanding international involvement, especially through state economic development programs.[16]

States in foreign affairs

Restrictions on State Powers

In addition to claiming some delegated powers as exclusive for the national government, the Constitution contains specific restrictions on state governments. Some are found in the original document, and others came in amendments adopted after the Civil War. Section 10 of Article I declares that no state shall "pass any bill of attainder, ex post facto law, or law impairing the obligation of contracts, or grant any title of nobility."

The Fourteenth Amendment specifies that citizens of the United States are citizens of the state where they reside. It goes on to declare that "No State shall make or enforce any law which shall abridge the privileges or immunities of citizens of the United States; nor shall any State deprive any person of life, liberty, or property, without due process of law, nor deny to any person . . . the equal protection of the laws."

Bill of Rights to Restrict the National Government

Even though the national government was construed by the authors of the Constitution to be one of strictly delegated powers, the state conventions called to consider the ratification or rejection of the Constitution were apprehensive. They had just finished fighting a war to protect certain rights held dear by all Englishmen and they didn't see any language in the Constitution safeguarding these rights. Responding to the clamor for a Bill of Rights, Alexander Hamilton asked: "For why declare that things shall not be done which there is no power to do?"[17] It was his argument that the central government was vested with only specific powers and since it had not been granted power to interfere in the rights of citizens, it could not do so.

Debate over Bill of Rights

But Hamilton's rationale was not sufficiently persuasive to allay widespread fears of governmental oppression. Consequently, a number of states ratified the Constitution on the condition that it be amended to include basic rights. Over 200 amendments were proposed.[18] Support began to build for calling a new convention to redo the Constitution.

James Madison, a member of the new Congress, moved quickly to head off a new convention by pushing through a series of amendments for submission to the states. Ten of the twelve proposed amendments were adopted and quickly became known as the Bill of Rights.[19]

States and People to have Reserved Powers

The Tenth Amendment put into words the concept of a national government with only delegated powers by stating that "the powers not delegated to the United States by the Constitution, nor prohibited by it to the States, are reserved to the States respectively, or to the people." The wording is not unlike that which appeared in the Articles of Confederation in which Article II stated that "each state retains . . . every power, jurisdiction and right, which is not by this confederation expressly delegated to the United States, in Congress assembled."

The Tenth Amendment was not seen by Federalist leaders as a grant of new powers to the states or as an obstacle to the exercise of national powers. To them, it was a statement of fact. However, the word *expressly* in the language of the Articles of Confederation was deliberately deleted from the Tenth Amendment to guarantee a greater degree of flexibility, according to Chief Justice John C. Marshall in his opinion in *McCulloch* v. *Maryland.*

Even though the Tenth Amendment was regarded as a mere confirmation of an understood principle, it has been cited often in confrontations between states and national leaders over the powers of state governments. It has long been a verbal weapon in the arsenal of the advocates of states' rights. Only rarely, however, has it served as the basis for judicial determinations in national–state disputes. One such rare occasion was in 1976 when the U.S. Supreme Court cited the Tenth Amendment to strike down an attempt by Congress to set minimum wages for the employees of state institutions.[20] The victory was short-lived, however. In five major Tenth Amendment cases between 1976 and 1983, the Supreme Court ruled for the national government.[21] Finally, the Court reversed its *Usery* decision early in 1985 in *Garcia* v. *San Antonio Metropolitan Transit Authority.*[22]

Dispute over Tenth Amendment

As the master architect of the Bill of Rights, James Madison had a direct influence in the exact wording submitted to the states for ratification. He was keenly aware of the implications for the Tenth Amendment with the inclusion of "the people" along with the states as possessors of the reserved powers. The substance and rationale of this inclusion can be found in the *Federalist* Papers authored by Madison and Hamilton.

One of the most dramatic changes occurring in the shift from the Articles of Confederation to the Constitution was the grant of authority to the central government to deal with the people directly. According to Hamilton, the people, as the source of governmental power, would have a definite role in the balance between the states and the national government.

Thus, while the Tenth Amendment does identify the states as the possessors of the reserved powers, it also recognizes that the people are the ultimate wielders of all authority, including the reserved powers. From the writings of Madison and Hamilton, it can be deduced that the people were expected to be an active political force in the balance of power between the states and the national government. As the people have exercised their portion of the reserved powers, the balance between the states and the national government has shifted with their aspirations and expectations, providing constitutional federalism with a dimension of political flexibility.

Constitution Extends Guarantees to States

The states received a number of guarantees in the Constitution, most of which are found in Article IV.

"The United States shall guarantee to every State in this Union a republican form of government. . . ."

1. Republican form of government

This guarantee was felt important because republican governments were a rarity in 1787 and the founding fathers felt it should be put on the list of endangered species immediately. It served notice on foreign countries that juntas overthrowing the republican governments of various states would be met with the resources of the entire Union. But James Madison also worried about the internal stability of states. He feared that ". . . the ambition of enterprising leaders" would cause states to depart from the republican ideal.

Although "republican" has never been clearly defined in official terms, Madison thought it to be ". . . a government which derives all its powers directly or indirectly from the great body of people, and is administered by persons holding their offices during pleasure for a limited period, or during good behavior."[23]

The courts have avoided giving a clear definition to "republican" on the ground that it was a political question outside their jurisdiction and thus to be determined by the legislative and executive branches of government. In the Dorr Rebellion in Rhode Island in the 1840s, the president gave assistance to the side he deemed the properly constituted authorities. His action was upheld by the Supreme Court.[24] Congress may pass on the question of what constitutes republican form by seating or not seating representation from the state involved. Some have attacked the initiative and referendum, techniques used for direct legislation by the people in some states, as being in violation of the republican form. However, the Court did not agree with that claim.[25] In summary, it may be stated that for the number of states and the length of our constitutional history, the need or demand for invoking this guarantee has been rare indeed.

2. Protection from invasion

"The United States . . . shall protect each of them (states) against invasion."

This guarantee, coupled with war powers granted the national government, makes the invasion of a state a matter of national defense. This was an important form of mutual security with the Spanish controlling the southwest and England eager to reestablish its power on the continent.

3. Help in domestic violence

"The United States shall . . . protect each of them . . . on application of the legislature, or of the executive (when the legislature cannot be convened) against domestic violence."

Recognizing that the states varied considerably in their abilities to cope with domestic violence or insurrections, the drafters of the Constitution felt that the availability of help from the national government would help dissuade perpetrators of disorder. After all, the uprising known as Shay's Rebellion had just occurred in Massachusetts and caused some alarm among the political leaders. However, neither was the national government to be a tool for interfering in the routine affairs of states, hence it was not authorized to act unless requested.

One of the more significant events involving this guarantee occurred in 1894 when, over the objections of Governor John P. Altgeld, President Cleveland ordered troops into Chicago during a railway strike. Cleveland claimed he had a national responsibility to protect the U.S. mail service, invited or not. In 1966, Detroit was in the throes of widespread rioting and because of the political implications in requesting federal troops, Republican Governor George Romney's initial contact with the federal government was not sufficiently direct to suit Democratic President Lyndon Johnson. President Johnson responded by asking Romney whether or not he was formally requesting federal help in domestic violence. With the city burning and looters running rampant, Romney capitulated and made his request clear and direct. Off the political hook, Johnson sent the troops.

4. Equality in Senate

Article V of the U.S. Constitution deals with the procedures for amendments and closes with the statement that *"no State, without its Consent, shall be deprived of its equal Suffrage in the Senate."* Thus, the Constitution guarantees all states an equal voice in the U.S. Senate in perpetuity. Or does it? Some political scientists wonder if states couldn't be deprived of their equal representation by repealing this guarantee and then proceeding to restructure the Senate.

> ". . . *no new state shall be formed or erected within the jurisdiction of any other state; nor any state be formed by the junction of two or more states, or parts of states, without the consent of the legislatures of the states concerned as well as of the Congress.*" *5. Territorial integrity*

This guarantee is probably of little significance today with a matured nation of fixed state boundaries. However, as of 1787, states had just ceded claims to western lands and a number of boundary disputes were still unresolved.

The promise of territorial integrity was conveniently overlooked during the war between the states when Virginia seceded from the Union. The state's northern counties remained loyal to the national government and were granted statehood as West Virginia in 1863. Congress was probably uncertain as to the status of the seceding states. It wasn't until 1869 that the Supreme Court declared that states could not secede.[26] That being the case, West Virginia was created without regard to the territorial integrity of Virginia.

Giving the Supreme Court original jurisdiction in cases between states was intended to reflect respect for the sovereignty and dignity of states. This respect was emphasized by the speedy proposal and adoption of the Eleventh Amendment which became effective in 1798. The amendment became necessary when the Court upheld a civil suit against the state of Georgia by a citizen of South Carolina.[27] This seemed at the time to be an undue restriction on state power, although there was clear language in Article III of the Constitution to support the decision. *6. Immunity in courts*

The Eleventh Amendment protects states from similar suits in the future by providing that *"the judicial power of the United States shall not be construed to extend to any suit in law or equity against one of the United States by citizens of another State, or of any foreign state."* This constitutional change was not necessary to protect a state against suit by its own citizens.

The Eleventh Amendment does not preclude action in lower federal courts by injured persons against state officials for violation or denial of rights provided in the Constitution. Furthermore, states and the national government may voluntarily permit claimants of official debts or damages to come into court for settlement.

Article V prescribes the procedures for proposing and ratifying amendments to the U.S. Constitution. Two methods were devised for proposing amendments: (1) Congress may propose an amendment by a two-thirds vote of its members, or (2) two-thirds of the state legislatures may petition Congress for a convention to propose amendments. The two methods were developed so that the Congress and the states would have an equal opportunity to propose amendments. The debates of the Constitutional Convention of 1787 reflected the intention that both methods for proposing amendments were to be on equal footing.[28] The states, however, have not been able to exercise their method for proposing amendments. One of the primary obstacles has been the lack of guidelines for the holding of a constitutional convention under Article V. The first serious effort in the development of procedures for holding a convention was begun in 1967 by Senator Sam Ervin of North Carolina, but the idea was greeted *7. Role in amending Constitution* *Lack procedure for convention* in Congress with little enthusiasm.[29] Governor Bruce Babbitt of Arizona observed that the lack of congressional enthusiasm was easy to understand. He said that ". . . there is a natural reluctance of anybody that has had control over a critical governmental process to surrender that perquisite."[30]

Article V vests the authority to call a convention for proposing amendments in the legislatures of the states. Citizens in California and Montana, eager for a convention to propose an amendment requiring a federal balanced budget, attempted to assume this authority in 1984 by placing measures on the statewide election ballot through the initiative process. The measures were designed to force the legislatures to join thirty-two other states in petitioning for the convention. However, the supreme courts in both states ruled that the procedure was unconstitutional and ordered the measures off the ballots. By refusing to accept jurisdiction of the question, the U.S. Supreme Court gave its tacit approval to the decisions of the two state courts.

Tactically unable to participate in the proposing process, the states are left with the role of ratifying. Ratification can be accomplished by either of two methods: (1) by the legislatures of three-fourths of the states, or (2) by conventions in three-fourths of the states. Congress prescribes which method is to be used. Of the present amendments, only the one repealing prohibition (Twenty-first) has been ratified by special state conventions.

Interstate Relations under the Constitution

While the U.S. Constitution focused on the national–state relationship, the experiences from the New England Confederation up through the Articles of Confederation suggested the need for some provisions for relationships among states.

1. Full faith and credit

"Full faith and credit shall be given in each state to the public Acts, records and judicial proceedings of every other state."

This "full faith and credit" provision, which traces its roots to the New England Confederation in 1643,[31] applies only to civil matters since no state is expected to enforce the criminal laws of another. A deed, mortgage, contract, will, property judgment, or other civil instrument executed and recorded according to the law in one state is recognized and accepted in other states. A marriage in one state is recognized in another, although marriage laws of the two states may differ.

2. Privileges and immunities

"The citizens of each state shall be entitled to all privileges and immunities of citizens in the several states."

To encourage free movement of people, the Constitution guarantees that the citizens of one state will be treated equally with the citizens of the home state. Visiting citizens are entitled to the full protection of the law, the use of the courts, and nondiscriminatory treatment.[32] In 1984, the Supreme Court held that a Camden, New Jersey, ordinance requiring at least 40 percent of the employees of contractors to be residents of Camden was a violation of the privileges and immunities clause. In 1986, the Alaska Supreme Court applied the privileges and immunities clause to strike down a state law giving job preferences to residents.[33]

The courts have not applied the privileges and immunities clause to every benefit provided by states, however. Certain privileges may result in a legitimate division of recipients into residents and nonresidents. For example, colleges and universities may charge a higher tuition for nonresidents than is charged residents; the same applies to hunting and fishing licenses.

The problem of fugitives fleeing from the administration of justice continues in the states just as it did in early colonial times. To deal with this recurring problem, the Constitution states that *"A person charged in any state with treason, felony, or other crime, who shall flee from justice, and be found in another state, shall on demand of the executive authority of the state from which he fled, be delivered up, to be removed to the state having jurisdiction of the crime."*

3. Fugitive rendition

Under this provision as supplemented by national legislation, fugitives to be extradited must be officially accused of committing a crime within the borders of the requesting state. For example, if a person commits a murder in Louisiana and is arrested as a fugitive in California, the governor of Louisiana sends a signed requisition, with a copy of the indictment and other papers, to secure the return of the fugitive. For more than a century, the Supreme Court held that even though the language of the Constitution appears to be mandatory, there is no provision for overriding the will of a governor refusing to honor a requisition. In 1984, for example, the governor of Utah was asked by the governor of Illinois to return a person indicted by an Illinois grand jury for the murder of an immigrant worker. The Utah governor refused on the grounds that the indictment involved an unprecedented attempt to hold a corporate officer liable for an unexplained workplace death.[34] In two 1987 cases, the Supreme Court ruled that there is no discretion for a governor or a state court to refuse rendition if the documents are in order on their face.[35]

Section 10 of Article I permits a state, with the consent of Congress, to enter into an "agreement or compact with another State." The "consent of Congress" requirement has been held by the Supreme Court to apply only if the compact tends to "increase the political powers of the states, which may encroach upon or interfere with the just supremacy of the United States."[36]

4. Interstate compacts

A compact is not only a statute in each participating state but it is also a contract between states. Consequently, when a state adopts a proposed compact, it is forbidden by the Constitution to impair the obligation of the contract or to alter its terms without a mutual agreement of other parties.

Today, compacts vary widely as to membership and authority. A compact may involve only two states for a single purpose, such as the Lake Champlain Bridge Compact between New York and Vermont, or it may be a regional compact, such as the Southern Growth Policies Compact, consisting of thirteen southern states, for regional planning and policy formulation. It may also be a national compact with all states as signatories, such as the Interstate Compact on Juveniles or the Interstate Compact for the Supervision of Parolees and Probationers.

One of the better-known compacts established the Port of New York Authority in 1921, with New York and New Jersey jointly tackling the construction and maintenance of port facilities, interstate bridges, tunnels, bus and truck terminals, and airports. Among the properties of this compact are the World Trade Center, Kennedy International Airport, the Lincoln Tunnel, Downtown Heliport, and the Bayonne Bridge, just to name a few. The budget and number of employees of the Port of New York Authority are greater than a number of states.

The purposes of interstate compacts vary widely, from the construction of a bridge, to health, crime control, planning, taxation, pest control, water conservation, transportation, and just about any subject falling within the "reserved" powers of states.

After the states have adopted a proposed compact by proper state legislation and congressional approval is obtained, if necessary, the compact moves into the implementation stage. Each of the member states names a delegation, which may consist of one or more persons, to serve on a governing board of commissioners. The commissioners develop the policy, hire the administrative personnel, and oversee the functioning of the compact. Some boards are made up of full-time members, whereas others may meet only once or twice a year.

Interstate compacts got off to a slow start with only 35 being negotiated during the period of 1783 to 1920, but 40 more were added from 1920 through World War II. Following the accelerating trend of intergovernmental relations, more than 100 additional compacts have been consummated to deal with interstate problems in the nearly five decades since World War II, with the biggest rush taking place in the 1950s and 1960s. The negotiation agenda in the early 1990s included a Midwestern Higher Education Compact, an Environmental Compact of the States, the Middle Atlantic Governors' Compact on Alcohol and Drug Abuse, an unusual seven-state Central U.S. Earthquake Consortium focusing on the New Madrid Fault, and a unique proposed compact for Alaska, California, Washington, and the Canadian Province of British Columbia, to deal with such common problems as oil spills, protecting fisheries, and better management of ocean resources. Interstate compacts are clearly staying on the cutting edge of public policy.[37]

The Supreme Law of the Land

Under the Articles of Confederation, there was no "supreme law of the land." It was a deficiency that resulted in innumerable problems for the states as they struggled to unify their response to the crises besetting them. Most of the delegates were convinced that the Constitution would be meaningless without vesting ultimate authority for national functions in the national government. Thus, they provided in Article VI that "this Constitution, and the laws of the United States which shall be made in pursuance thereof; and all treaties made, or which shall be made, under the authority of the United States, shall be the supreme law of the land. . . ."

To make the provision binding, the framers of the Constitution issued two mandates: (1) the judges of every state shall observe the supreme law of the land and enforce it, state constitutions and state laws notwithstanding; and (2) the legislative, executive, and judicial officers shall give an oath to support the Constitution.

Supreme Court as Arbiter

Of the three articles of the Constitution creating the branches of government, the shortest by far is the one providing for a federal judiciary. This brevity initially left some unanswered questions about the Court's jurisdiction and authority. One of the questions was: Is the Supreme Court the final authority in interpreting the Constitution?

During the debate over ratification of the new Constitution, Alexander Hamilton took the position that the Court and the power of judicial review were both necessary to give meaning to a limited constitution. He claimed that "limitations . . . can be preserved in practice no other way than through the medium of courts of justice, whose duty it must be to declare all acts contrary to the manifest tenor of the Constitution void."[38]

He argued that a constitution must be regarded by judges as a fundamental law and it "belongs to them to ascertain its meaning as well as the meaning of any particular act proceeding from the legislative body."[39] Apparently, the majority of the Supreme Court agreed with Hamilton. In 1803, the Court assumed the power of judicial review in the famous *Marbury* v. *Madison* case without a significant challenge from either of the two branches of government. With this assumption of the right to adjudicate federal questions, the existence of a Supreme Court means there can be no deadlock between state and national governments in the exercise of American sovereignty. Moreover, state courts are mandated to support the supreme law of the land as determined by the Supreme Court. And even though state supreme courts have not been unswerving in their obedience, they have a high rate of compliance with Supreme Court decisions. Only in questions of a disruptive nature have the state courts tended to stray.[40]

Assumes judicial review

The Constitution and New States

The Constitution provides that "new states may be admitted by the Congress into this Union. . . ." Following the pattern for admission of new states outlined in the Ordinance of 1787, the new Congress provided for the creation of territorial governments and their eventual conversion into states equal in standing with all of the other states. After a territory acquired sufficient population, Congress passed an "enabling act," outlining specific steps to be taken by the territory for statehood, including the drafting of a constitution and often requiring some key provisions. On occasion, Congress has opted to meddle in the internal affairs of the prospective state by mandating the location of the state capitol (as in the case of Oklahoma) or by ordering the elimination of an undesirable practice, such as the recall of judges (as in the case of Arizona). However, upon adoption of the resolution of statehood, Congress loses control of the new states and they can proceed to undo the mandates imposed as conditions of statehood—just as Oklahoma and Arizona did.[41] Upon achieving statehood, all states are constitutionally equal.

States on equal footing

Federalism: Defined and Summarized

In reviewing the grand design of federalism as prescribed by the Constitution, one scholar defined the essence of federalism as "a device for dividing decisions and functions of government."[42] According to James Madison, what happened in the 1787 Convention was merely a redividing of the decisions and functions. A researcher of early state constitutions agrees. Walli Adams posits that "the Constitution that replaced the Articles of Confederation in 1788 did not represent a counterrevolution or a restoration, as is sometimes claimed, but simply an extension of the centralizing tendencies that had existed since the beginning of the war for independence."[43]

The drafters of the Constitution made a determined effort to divide the decisions and functions of government in a workable manner. Even so, they foresaw the need for amendment, they anticipated the need for flexibility, and they expected the people to exercise an active role through the republican processes.

As stated in the beginning of this chapter, governments are not designed in vacuums. They are created and shaped by values, concerns, needs, and aspirations of the people they serve. American federalism was launched with an initial division of decisions and functions between two levels of government, with both levels interacting directly with the people. The values, concerns, needs, and aspirations of Americans in 1787 required such a government. And as they have changed with the generations, the

A changing federalism   initial shape of federalism has also changed within the flexible framework provided by the Constitution.

Endnotes

1. This dramatic reversal of the relative decline in the role of the states and their local governments is recorded and discussed with increasing frequency by political scientists and current historians. See, for example: Carl E. Van Horn, "The Quiet Revolution," in *The State of the States,* which he edited (Washington, D.C.: Congressional Quarterly, Inc., 1989), pp. 1–13; Deborah A. Gona, "The State of the States," in *The Book of the States, 1990–91* (Lexington, Ky: The Council of State Governments, 1990), pp. 1–17; Ann O'M. Bowman and Richard C. Kearney, *The Resurgence of the States* (Englewood Cliffs, N.J.: Prentice-Hall, 1986); Michael A. Pagano, Ann O'M. Bowman, and John Kincaid, "The State of American Federalism, 1990–1991," *Publius: The Journal of American Federalism* 21 (Summer, 1991), pp. 1–26; and numerous articles in *Intergovernmental Perspective,* a periodical of the U.S. Advisory Commission on Intergovernmental Relations, especially in the late 1980s and early 1990s.

2. Evarts Boutell Green, *The Foundations of American Nationality* (New York: American Book Company, 1922), p. 125.

3. Ibid., p. 126.

4. Ibid., p. 376.

5. Ronald E. Pynn, *American Politics,* 2nd ed. (Monterey, Calif.: Brooks Cole Publishing Company, 1984), p. 48.

6. Walli Paul Adams, *The First American Constitutions* (Chapel Hill, N.C.: University of North Carolina Press, 1980), p. 40.

7. Ibid., p. 40.

8. Greene, *The Foundations,* pp. 558–559.

9. Adams, *The First,* p. 282.

10. Alexander Hamilton, *The Federalist,* no. 15.

11. Adams, *The First,* p. 4.

12. Calvin C. Jillson, "Constitution-Making: Alignment and Realignment in the Federal Convention of 1787," *American Political Science Review* 75 (September 1981): 611.

13. Ibid., p. 611.

14. James Madison, *The Federalist,* no. 45.

15. *McCulloch* v. *Maryland,* 4 Wheat. 316 (1819).

16. John Kincaid, "State and Local Governments Go International," *Intergovernmental Perspective* 16 (Spring, 1990), pp. 6–9.

17. Hamilton, *The Federalist,* no. 84.

18. John C. Miller, *The Federalist Era* (New York: Harper & Row, 1960), p. 20.

19. Ibid., p. 22.

20. *National League of Cities* v. *Usery,* 426 U.S. 833 (1976).

21. Robert N. Roberts, "Federalism, The Tenth Amendment, and the Doctrine of State Sovereignty," paper presented to the Southern Political Science Association, Birmingham, Alabama, Nov. 3–5, 1983.

22. *Garcia* v. *San Antonio Metropolitan Transit Authority,* 105 S. Ct. 1005 (1985).

23. Madison, *The Federalist,* no. 39.

24. *Luther* v. *Borden,* 7 How. 1 (1849).

25. *Pacific States Tel. & Tel. Co.* v. *Oregon,* 223 U.S. 118 (1912).

26. *Texas* v. *White,* 7 Wall. 700 (1869).

27. *Chisholm* v. *Georgia,* 2 Dall. 419 (1793).

28. Elaine S. Knapp, "A Balanced Federal Budget and Constitutional Convention Controversy," *State Government* 52 (Spring 1979): 58.

29. Wilbur Edel, "Amending the Constitution by Convention: Myth and Realities," *State Government* 55, No. 2 (1982): 54.

30. Governor Bruce Babbitt, "A Constitutional Challenge to the States," *State Legislatures* 7 (April 1981): 18.

31. Greene, *The Foundations,* p. 126.

32. Pynn, *American Politics,* p. 106.

33. *United Building and Construction Trades Council of Camden County and Vicinity* v. *Mayor and Council of the City of Camden,* 79 L. Ed. 2d 249 (1984); *Law Week* 54 (January 28, 1986): 2375.

34. Associated Press report in Grand Forks (N.D.) *Herald,* September 5, 1984. The landmark case for a governor's refusing to honor a request for rendition is *Kentucky* v. *Dennison* 65 U.S. 66 (1861), in which Chief Justice Taney straddled an issue on fugitive slaves and states' rights. He ruled, in effect, that the governor of Ohio had a moral obligation, but not a legally enforceable obligation to return an escaped slave to Kentucky.

35. *California* v. *Superior Court of California,* 482 U.S. 400 (1987), and *Puerto Rico* v. *Branstad,* 483 U.S. 219 (1987).

36. *Virginia* v. *Tennessee,* 148 U.S. 503.

37. Benjamin J. Jones and Deborah Reuter, "Interstate Compacts and Agreements," *The Book of the States, 1990–1991* (Lexington, Ky.: The Council of State Governments, 1990), pp. 565–567, and Jones' sequel article in the 1992–93 edition.

38. Hamilton, *The Federalist,* no. 78.

39. Ibid.

40. For a discussion of this subject, see G. Alan Tarr, *Judicial Impact and State Supreme Courts* (Lexington, Mass.: D.C. Heath, 1977).

41. *Coyle* v. *Smith,* 221 U.S. 559 (1911).

42. Morton Grodzins, "The Federal System," *Goals for Americans* (New York: The American Assembly, Columbia University Press, 1960), p. 265.

43. Adams, *The First,* p. 290.

CHAPTER 2

INTERGOVERNMENTALISM

The Flexible Federal System Evolves with the Nation

The American federalism that approaches the year 2000 is quite different from that envisioned by Alexander Hamilton and James Madison as they penned their defense of a fairly neat division of powers in the Federalist Papers. Constitutional changes, historic developments, and a transformation of the social, political, and economic character of the nation have all changed the meaning of the term *federalism* in the U.S. context. What started as an effort to create a more perfect Union has evolved in the 1990s as a relatively integrated governmental system, at least by 1787 standards.

Federalism dead and alive

Federalism—old style—has been pronounced dead, yet federalism—new style— has been declared to be living and well in the United States under the name of *intergovernmental relations*.[1] To understand this transformation of federalism, it is necessary to look at the change that society has experienced over the past 200 years. As William S. Livingstone said: "The essence of federalism lies not in the institutional or constitutional structure but in the society itself. Federal government is the device by which the federal qualities of society are articulated and protected."[2]

Historically, new constitutions or charters have come into existence in response to recognized social, political, and economic needs—beginning with the New England Confederation up to and including the United States Constitution. But because those who were responsible for translating the Constitution into a working document found flexibility to respond to changing circumstances, it was not necessary for them to draft a new constitution every generation. They were able to adapt to changing circumstances within the Constitution's parameters. Adaptive changes in the neat layer cake of federalism perceived in the early decades have brought forth considerable debate among scholars of federalism as to what the term *federalism* means, if it no longer means a tidy division of powers between two levels of government. The classic definition of federalism includes the requirement that this state-national division of powers is defined in a fundamental law (constitution) that cannot be changed without the consent of both levels.

James Madison felt that federalism was a *state-centered system* with the states continuing to administer the scores of local programs and the central government han-

Title photo: President Bush with governors at Charlottesville. (White House photo by David Valdez.)

dling a specific few. However, Alexander Hamilton, along with such prominent Federalists as Chief Justice John Marshall of the Supreme Court, appeared to subscribe to the concept of a *national-centered system*. It wasn't long before a compromise idea came along, called *dual federalism*. Under the theory of dual federalism, the two levels of government are sovereign in their own assigned spheres of authority. It was fairly obvious, however, that the levels of government were engaged in too many joint ventures and activities to perpetuate the fiction of separateness. Hence, less doctrinaire observers began to describe federalism in practice as a system of cooperative governments. Out of this concept came the oft-repeated reference to federalism as a "marble cake," with the functions swirled throughout the levels of government.

Competing ideas of federalism

As though four theories weren't enough, President Lyndon Johnson invented "creative" federalism that included not only federal, state, and local governments but private foundations and corporations as well. Just about every president since Johnson has felt compelled to enunciate a "new federalism." Since they were not numbered, a simple reference to "new federalism" isn't very definitive. Like "creative federalism," they haven't been theories of federalism at all but merely catchy rhetoric to describe an administration's approach to federal–state relations.

Borrowing from these interpretations and synthesizing the theories with reality, one is forced to accept some form of "pragmatic federalism" that does not focus on the arrangement of power so much as the process involved in using the arrangement to solve problems. Pragmatic federalists see all levels of government cooperating extensively, as well as competing in many ways in the delivery of services in response to the democratic impulses of the electorate.[3]

Pragmatic federalism at work

Few would deny that current federal–state relationships are characterized far more by cooperation, coordination, and the sharing of power than by separation and competition. National, state, and local governments are involved daily in joint action—constructing highway projects, fighting drug rings, or dealing with a toxic waste accident. All three routinely share in providing county agents for farmers, assisting welfare clients, getting lunches to needy school children, and coping with high flood waters. There is hardly an agency of state or local government that isn't sharing functions with the national government. Even after the sharp drop off in federal aid in the 1980s, federal mandates, regulation, and preemption have continued into the nineties, but states have been given new policy and program initiatives in what some have called "fend-for-yourself federalism."[4]

"Fend-for-yourself federalism"

It is a fair inquiry to ask how the federalism of today was reshaped from the hazy theories of decades—almost centuries—ago. Instead of a central government with a few specified powers, we have a system in which the national government is the major governmental infrastructure of modern America. It is difficult to think of many things the national government cannot do today, assuming a reasonably strong consensus in the appropriate forces, in spite of what the Founding Fathers may have intended. How and why these changes have taken place, and some of the consequences, are the subjects of the discussion that follows.

A Changing America Changed Federalism

If institutions of government are shaped and reshaped by the society for which they exist, then radical changes in federalism must have been caused by radical changes in American society. The truth is that the United States has gone through dramatic, and sometimes traumatic, changes over the past 200 years to cause a transformation of its system of government.

Nationalization of the economy

Imaginative entrepreneurs, adapting to the rapidly changing modes of transportation and communication, quickly realized the limitless horizons for economic opportunity. Multistate corporations mass produced goods for national marketing, rendering state jurisdiction inadequate for coping with the new economy. Local commerce under the police powers of state governments became interstate commerce under the delegated powers of the national government. The inevitable next step—globalization of the economy—is adding international pressures to the national ones.

Urbanization and urban crises

As immigrants poured into the United States to provide the labor for the burgeoning economy, masses congregated in the centers of manufacturing, finance, and services. In 1790, only 5 percent of America was urbanized; by 1990, 75 percent lived in urban areas. Governmental services required to maintain viable communities outstripped the resources of the cities and the national government was rallied to cope with the urban crises.

Democratization of political institutions

The right to vote was extended to nonproperty owners, blacks, women, and youth in successive movements. At the same time, control of the electoral college was quickly wrestled from a deliberative elite and its powers transferred to voters, thereby making the presidency an office of the people. The United States Senate was converted from an assembly of delegates chosen to represent states, to a body popularly elected and responsive to people. The democratization of the presidency and the Senate, coupled with the spread of suffrage, resulted in a federal system that responded more quickly to the aspirations, fears, and wants of the people. Consequently, the development of public opinion polling sharpened the impact of voters on government decision making. Polls make policymakers constantly aware of the opinions and attitudes of the people on major issues. If forced to choose between a theory of federalism and winning the next election, presidents, senators, and representatives alike supported programs high in the polls, even though such programs may have violated the traditional distribution of federal responsibilities.

Television focus on national news

In 1963, television moved ahead of newspapers as the people's primary source for news, and it continues to dominate the news scene for most Americans today.[5] However, since gathering television news is expensive and time-consuming, comprehensive coverage of city halls, courthouses, and state capitols is beyond the resources of local television stations. Hence, America is exposed to the highly financed, star-studded national network reports that make Washington the center of the American governmental system.[6]

Nationalization of political parties

Once thought of as bastions of localism, political parties have been weakened and nationalized as their historic functions of candidate selection, campaigning, and fund raising have been stripped from them. Their candidate endorsements are constantly threatened and often defeated in primary elections. The professional campaign consultants freeze out party activists by relying on the techniques of mass marketing instead of the block worker; using interest groups, through political action committees, and by contributing millions of dollars to campaigns to wean office-holders from party programs and principles. As national campaign money pours into state races, as national party rules dictate state election laws, and as national strategists become more involved in state political campaigns, political parties are losing the capacity to preserve political pluralism based on state boundaries.

As new and better modes of transportation and communication battered the walls of pluralism, an America of local people became a national constituency. Whether they traveled by auto or observed television, Americans broadened their horizons to the whole of the nation. As a result, they developed a sense of national kinship and responsibility. They felt empathy for the homeless "bag ladies" on the cold streets of New York, for the poverty-stricken in Appalachia, for the bankrupt farm families in Kansas, for persons segregated by race, and for the crime victims in Los Angeles. And they asked: "Why doesn't the government do something?" So the national government did. *Nationalization of values and expectations*

For more than half a century the United States has been in an accelerated state of international military, political, and economic competition, first with the Axis Powers of World War II, then with expansionist communism, and more recently with economic rivals around the world. Since the national government is vested with responsibility for defense and foreign relations, fifty years of vigorous exercise of these powers has resulted in expenditures, programs, and policies that have expanded the scope of national power in a public mood of nationalism. The U.S. response to the 1990 Iraq invasion of Kuwait and the debate over the appropriate response to the 1992 Los Angeles riots only confirm this. *Impact of international crises*

The Evolution of Intergovernmentalism

National–State Relationship Changes

As the undying winds of change slowly shaped a new American society, the dialogue over the meaning of federalism was carried along. Those elected to power in the new government struggled to develop a working definition of a "more perfect Union." Because the forces of change were nationalizing in character, the role of states was most threatened and states' rights became the main skirmish line in most debates over the meaning of federalism.

States Assert Their Rights

Since the Constitution did not provide the last definitive word on the issue, and, in fact, left latitude for a flexible federalism, different interests and sections of the country have used the argument of states' rights to shape or limit the national government to their liking. As history will attest, the doctrine of states' rights has most frequently *The States' rights debate* been used by groups out of power on the national scene or by groups that felt they could press their points more effectively at the state level. History is replete with examples.

In Virginia and Kentucky
 The ink on the Constitution was barely dry when Madison and Jefferson found themselves drafting the Virginia and Kentucky resolutions to protest the Alien and Sedition Acts passed during the Adams administration. States ought to nullify the unauthorized acts of the national government, they argued in the second Kentucky resolution. So the idea of nullification of national laws was born early in the federal system.

In New England
 Soon the New England states took up the cudgel, smarting under the economic disruptions they were experiencing as a result of the War of 1812. Meeting in the Hartford Convention in 1815, they urged states to protect citizens against the acts of Congress not authorized by the Constitution.

In South Carolina
 When the Tariff of Abominations was passed in 1828, South Carolina adopted an ordinance nullifying the tariff. The theory of nullification of federal acts by state governments is incompatible with the existence of the Union, President Andrew Jackson told South Carolina.

Differences between the northern and southern states finally erupted into a war between the states and the question of a state's right to secede was put to the test. Military force, not necessarily logic, dictated that secession was not an acceptable right of states. Developing a legal rationale for the outcome of the Civil War, the U.S. Supreme Court said that the Constitution provided for an indestructible union of indestructible states.

Indestructible union

The Supreme Court may have resolved the particular question of secession but it did not mute the general question of states' rights. In fact, the high tribunal was destined in the years following to put the stamp of unconstitutionality upon a number of national regulatory measures because they encroached upon the reserved powers of states. So the states' rights argument was to remain a potent force, although many of the new champions would be corporation lawyers rather than spokespersons for state governments.

Interposition in the 1950s
 When the Supreme Court ordered the desegregation of schools in *Brown* v. *Board of Education of Topeka,* the doctrine of interposition was brought forward by a hundred southern congress members in a Southern Manifesto. This doctrine proposed that states may "interpose" themselves and their agencies between an improper national act and their citizens. Interposition was a useful political device for rallying massive southern opposition to desegregation but it was an ineffective legal argument before the Court. All hope for interposition evaporated in 1957 when Governor Faubus "interposed" the Arkansas National Guard between the court's desegregation order and the Little Rock Central High School, and President Eisenhower removed the "interposers" with units of the United States Army. Although interposition died almost as soon as it was born, its formal "last rites" may have occurred in 1990, at least symbolically, when Arkansas voters removed it from their state constitution.

States' rights is a durable doctrine and does not perish with a cause. For each advocate felled by the Court, another soon rises to snatch up the banner. The Southern

Manifesto may have been a futile gesture but it didn't dissuade a block of western states from pressing a Sagebrush Rebellion in the 1980s against the claims of the federal government on millions of acres of public lands within their boundaries.

States' rights moves West

Contemporary political leaders often enunciate their goals in terms of states' rights. Emphasis on returning governmental functions from the national government to the states has been in the rhetoric of just about every president since Eisenhower. Even so, a careful review of the records of their administrations can demonstrate that their use of states' rights is often a means to an end rather than just an end in itself.

Perhaps the most committed champion of states' rights in recent decades was President Reagan. Coming to Washington as a philosophical conservative and a former governor, he was determined to alter the federal arrangement by returning rights—and concomitant responsibilities—to the states. However, as in previous administrations, states' rights was only one value competing in an arena of political and constitutional conflicts. One observer pointed out, from the close-up vantage point of the Advisory Commission on Intergovernmental Relations, that despite its adherence to states' rights, the Reagan Administration supported nationalizing product liability, federal regulations of trucking, a twenty-one-year-old drinking law, premption of state involvement in coastal management, national education policies in state areas, and more federal authority in welfare administration.[7]

Competition from other values

That observer concluded that "it appears that virtually no one today—from the public at large to the public interest groups—believes that maintaining the integrity of the federal system is sufficiently important to justify sacrificing other important values to do so."[8]

A historic overview will verify that this has almost always been true. However, it is probably more true in the 1990s because of the national character of society.

The debate over the rights of states in the federal arrangement began in the Constitutional convention more than 200 years ago and has continued throughout our history. It will continue for decades into the future because it is an argument about an institution. As long as the institution of federalism continues, the debate will remain. Because it strives to define the meaning of that institution from generation to generation, the debate is a functional organism. It tends to shape our political institutions to an ever-growing synthesis of the ideas of such men as Hamilton, Madison, and Jefferson and their many subsequent counterparts. In the process, the system of states succumbs neither to prophesies of doom nor to blueprints of a national utopia.

Debate inherent in federalism

Federal Aid Changes the System

The authority granted Congress to tax and spend for "common defense and general welfare" (a term borrowed from Article VIII of the Articles of Confederation) in Article I, Section 8, of the Constitution slept, for the most part, during the first 150 years of the Republic. The tax base was limited substantially to "duties, imposts, and excises," meaning that the federal government was to have only lean means for defense and welfare. Nevertheless, federal aid was not unknown in the early years. In fact, it is older than the Constitution, having come to the fore in the Land Ordinances of 1785

Aid older than Constitution

which granted every sixteenth section of public lands in a township for the support of schools. During the Jackson administration, the federal treasury bulged with more receipts than were required for federal activities, so money was transferred to states and never recalled. Colleges and universities were given large blocks of public lands under legislation enacted during the Civil War to meet vocational needs. Later, Congress adopted plans for cash support for experiment stations and extension services at these colleges. The Smith-Lever Act of 1914 inaugurated further aid for agricultural education in the form of federal–state support for farm demonstration agents in hundreds of rural counties. Early federal aid for internal improvements and the huge land grants for railroads foreshadowed the federal–state highway program of the twentieth century.

Income tax fills coffers

Just as the supply of federal lands suitable for inducing development began to dwindle, the movement for a broader tax base culminated in adoption of the Sixteenth Amendment in 1913. Authorizing for the first time a tax on individual incomes, the amendment was launched just in time to catch the high wave of economic expansion. With its design of graduated rates, the revenue grew faster than the economy, resulting in the availability of vast new sums of money for activities directed by the national government.

People got roads, not theories

Soon the popularization of the automobile spawned the "good roads" movement on which many state leaders and national legislators founded political careers. Political pressure mounted to bring the federal government into the highway picture to shore up the financial inadequacies of states and to provide a system that could accommodate interstate traffic. There were no concerns about a "bloated bureaucracy," "creeping socialism," or "violation of states' rights." Government, at the behest of the people, was meeting a condition, responding to a need, and not following a theory. The Constitution was interpreted to mean that the highway program was a concurrent power held by both the states and the national government. Congress had express authority to "establish post offices and post roads" as well as the implied power to provide transportation facilities for defense and possibly other uses. The "post roads" power was more than a mere pretext for granting federal aid since the new system of rural free delivery of mail was rapidly spreading over all important roads. Thus, the Federal Aid Road Act of 1916 was passed.

Establish pattern for grants

A prototype of grant programs to come, the federal legislation established standards of cooperation for the state and national governments in the administration of joint projects, with Washington acting in an advisory, supervisory, and auditing capacity. Funding came from matching grants, with the two governments bearing a share of the cost. States were required to have central highway departments or agencies to execute their part of the venture. The Bureau of Public Roads was formed to manage national phases of the work and much local government responsibility for road construction and maintenance thus was central to state and national authorities.

The nationwide campaign to get America out of the mud and onto the pavement remained the principal joint venture of state and national governments until the Great Depression of the 1930s. State and local governments, paralyzed by state constitutional restrictions and a tax base of drought and economic stagnation, looked to Washington for help. Coincidental with the crisis was the election of a president who, uninhibited by traditional restraints, pushed for a series of government responses to the crisis. Using the untapped borrowing capacity of the national government, Franklin D. Roosevelt launched numerous relief programs, many of them calling for joint state–federal cooperation, without the requirement that states put up matching funds. Local units of government also shared in the intergovernmental struggle with the depression, building city streets, buildings, and sewers with the federal aid. A sweeping social security act was passed, encompassing characteristics of both welfare and insurance, with state and local governments sharing in the administration and finance. Many depression programs were made permanent as deterrents to future economic catastrophes.

Depression brings more federal aid

As the grant-in-aid programs began to emanate from the political branches of the national government, the judiciary broadly interpreted federal authority to act. In 1922, the Supreme Court upheld the authority of Congress to provide grants to states for programs that required the exercise of the reserved powers of the state, even though they were actually programs that Congress could not implement under its delegated or implied powers. The Court said that the reserved powers of the states were not invaded since the statutes merely offered states the option which the states could accept or reject.[9]

Court approves broad powers in aid programs

Then, in 1936, even the reluctant conservative court criticized by Roosevelt ruled that the power of Congress to appropriate (spend) for the general welfare was not limited to those purposes enumerated in the Constitution, where the exercise of spending power is appropriate, federal action was supreme over state action.[10] One year later the Court said that Congress was the sole interpreter of what was "necessary and proper" in carrying out the authority to tax and spend for the federal welfare.[11]

Congress to decide "necessary and proper"

The 1940s were committed to winning and recovering from global conflict. As America retrenched in the 1950s, Congress was not inspired to expand greatly the scope of national grants-in-aid. However, President Eisenhower proposed and Congress approved the National Defense Highway Act to build a network of four-lane highways across the nation, with the federal government putting up 90 percent of the money and the states providing the rest. Then, after the Russians successfully launched Sputnik, the first orbiting satellite, the national government rushed through an aid-to-education program focused on teaching the sciences and science skills in American schools.

The decade of the 1950s was the lull before the storm. John F. Kennedy was elected president in 1960 on the theme of getting America moving again. His rhetoric increased the tempo of national cadence. He began proposing government programs to deal with poverty, housing, education, pollution, medical care, and scores of other areas. The assassin's bullet in Dallas did not end the dreams of the "New Frontier," but instead accelerated the cause. President Johnson moved vigorously to carry the Kennedy proposals forward in his dream of a "Great Society." A virtual tidal wave of new grant programs poured out of the liberal Congress. Specific aid programs increased from 71 in 1950 to well over 400 in the 1960s. Federal aid tripled from $7 billion in 1959 to $20 billion by 1969. It became necessary for the government to publish a catalogue of federal aid so state and local officials could shop wisely for the programs they could effectively use.

The aid cornucopia of the 1960s

While the number and variety of newly authorized grant-in-aid programs in the 1960s were staggering, the majority of them were part of a two-pronged attack on poverty and urban problems. They all were founded on the premise that the ills to be solved were national problems and were to be dealt with as national priorities. To achieve these national objectives, then, the drafters of grant legislation structured the programs to obtain an application of resources across the nation in a uniform manner. This established federal standards and regulation as conditions for obtaining and using federal money. (See Figure 2.1.) As federal policymakers and administrators exerted greater and greater influence over state and local decision making and administration, the ardor of state and local officials for grants began to cool. They chafed under the regulations accompanying the federal funds. Political pressure began to build for a more flexible system of federal assistance.

National priorities bring regulations

In this environment, the idea of the federal government sharing income taxes with state and local governments, no strings attached, began to gain momentum. Alliances of the national organizations of state and local officials were formed and prepared to do battle. In spite of the federal funds siphoned off by the Vietnam War, the march of state and local officials could not be stopped. They prevailed upon Congress to authorize a revenue-sharing program.

States seek revenue sharing

The State and Local Fiscal Assistance Act of 1972 became a reality but not in the form contemplated by its supporters. Congress refused to make it a perpetual program with revenue coming automatically from a percentage of the federal income tax

Figure 2.1
"It's Washington. They say if we don't shorten our fishing season, they'll cut our highway funds by 10%."

receipts. Instead, Congress appropriated the money—roughly $6 billion per year—for fixed periods of time. Congress continued to renew the program into the 1980s, but in 1979, ironically, dropped the recipients for whom the program was originally intended—the states. The Reagan administration opposed further reauthorization of any revenue sharing because of the growing national budget deficit, and Congress finally killed the program in 1986.

Revenue sharing begun and ended

Even the general revenue-sharing program was not without its regulations. When first enacted, Congress identified fairly flexible categories for which the money could be spent. However, each renewal resulted in new restrictions. General revenue sharing was soon subject to sixty requirements that applied to all federal grants, such as nondiscrimination, environmental protection, health, welfare, safety, minority participation, labor standards, and access to information.[12]

In addition to general revenue sharing, other suggestions have been offered to reform the grant system. One common proposal was the adoption of "block grants" by combining the categorical grants in a functional area, such as health or education, and letting state and local officials decide priorities within that area. Local officials argued that block grants would make it possible for them to apply the money more effectively on the real problems to be solved. Resistance to block grants came from the interest groups that had managed to get Congress to create categorical grants to promote their particular objectives. If the money from several categorical grants was lumped together, the interest groups were concerned that "their" money would be diverted to other programs. Interest groups, consequently, opposed block grants. But if blocking must occur, they favored the inclusion of language that would require continuation of spending mandates for their particular programs. Under these circumstances, it is possible to understand how the combination of fifty-seven categorical grant programs into ten block grants by the Reagan administration resulted in very little flexibility for the state-level disbursers, with many of the old restrictions included in the blocks.

Seek block grants for flexibility

Passage of the Gramm-Rudman Act by Congress in late 1985, originally intended to force a balanced federal budget by 1991, signaled a retreat of the federal government in grant programs. But even with the cuts in state grants, the termination of general revenue sharing, and the persisting mood of austerity in Washington, federal grants will undoubtedly continue to be an important factor in federal-state-local relations in the years ahead.

In summary, the federal grant program has given great impetus to centralization and the intergovernmentalization of the federal system. Armed with the resources made available by the income tax, vested by the courts with wide latitude in designing grants, and buoyed by the nationalizing society, the federal government has not only initiated scores of shared programs under its delegated powers but it has also used grant money to induce states to use their reserved powers to achieve national objectives. The beneficiaries of the grant programs have become so numerous that it seems unlikely the system will be permanently impacted by different administrations in Washington, even though setbacks may occur.

Federal power grew with grants

Nationalization through Regulations

The intergovernmentalizing process has not been limited to grants. In recent years, the federal government has become more aggressive in the use of its regulatory powers to compel state action. These powers rest on four principal constitutional bases: (1) the "supremacy clause" which gives precedence to national authority over state authority; (2) the Bill of Rights, plus the Fourteenth and Fifteenth Amendments containing equal protection, due process and other individual and civil rights clauses; (3) the interstate commerce clause; and (4) the power to tax and spend for the general welfare, which is the basis of most grants.[13]

Types of regulatory
authority

Federal regulatory authority is manifested in a number of forms:

- *Direct orders:* Direct legal orders must be complied with under threat of civil or criminal penalties
- *Crosscutting requirements:* Standardized requirements may be attached to all grants to further basic national social and economic goals.
- *Crossover sanctions:* Threatening loss of federal money in one program can influence state policy in another. (See Figure 2.1.)
- *Partial or total preemption:* Use of federal authority can preempt certain state activities on the premise that "if you don't do it, we will."[14]

Case in point: Mining
Act

The scope and impact of federal regulatory authority may be seen in the case of the Surface Mining Control and Reclamation Act, a federal law relating to coal strip mining and reclamation of the mined land. Under the act, states could keep the federal government out if they would assume jurisdiction over surface coal mining under the conditions stated in the law. Among the requirements for retention of state control was submission of a state plan that included enactment of certain state laws, designation of a single controlling state agency, specific regulations concerning state administrative practices, description of past and present agency budgets, personnel information on state employees in the agency, and numerous promises to comply with federal regulations through virtually every administrative procedure.[15]

In addition, the Code of Federal Regulations contained another 350 pages of detailed standards to be applied to the surface mining operation.[16] Virginia argued against the constitutionality of the law as a violation of the Tenth Amendment, but the Supreme Court dismissed the claim.[17]

Researchers at the University of California (Riverside) estimate that there are 1,260 federal mandates bearing on state and local governments.[18] The pervading influence of these mandates throughout the intergovernmental system resulted in their reevaluation by the Reagan administration. One of the first executive orders issued by President Reagan was to reduce the number of regulations.

The Supreme Court Centralizes Power

Ever since the days of John C. Marshall, the intergovernmentalization of the federal system has been greatly facilitated by the decisions and interpretations of the U.S. Supreme Court. Given the flexibility of such terms as "necessary and proper" and

Court redefines
Constitution

"general welfare," the Court has been able periodically to reinterpret the meaning of the Constitution in the context of a changing society. New circumstances give new meanings to the old terms; new judges provide new perspectives for old powers. Woodrow Wilson once said that the Supreme Court was a "kind of constitutional convention in continuous session." Because the Court has been forced in recent years to make a number of controversial decisions, some of a highly emotional nature, Court appointments have become a consideration in presidential campaigns. The champions of the causes whose cases involve the Supreme Court openly speculate over the outcome of presidential elections in terms of the kinds and numbers of judges that would be appointed by one candidate as compared to another.

From the earliest times, questions about federalism found their way onto the Court's docket. The resultant decisions were always controversial since they affected the distribution of power. In 1937, the Court began to defer to the judgment of Congress in questions of appropriateness in the use of national power to meet national needs. But with the advent of the Warren Court in the 1950s and 1960s, a new era of activism ensued and the Court dealt with numerous national–state conflicts. More frequently than not, the Court ruled for the national government. According to a noted scholar of federalism, Daniel Elazar, the states were "best able to protect themselves . . . when the problems confronting them were handled through regular political channels and least able to do so when the Court was used."[19]

Court moves into conflicts

"Thus," Elazar observed, "the federal institution that has done most to limit the states' powers is the United States Supreme Court, which because of America's commitment to an independent judiciary, benefits extraordinarily from its position as the final judicial arbiter of the Constitution."[20]

Court limits states

Speaking at a conference on federalism, W. S. Moore agreed. He observed that in the 1960s and 1970s "the Supreme Court became a leader in centralizing power at the expense of the states and localities."

"The truth is, I believe," he continued, "that the prevailing wisdom in this country has been hostile to federalism and its values for the last thirty years or more."[21] Court watchers in the decade of the nineties will be seeking to determine whether the Reagan and Bush appointees slow down or stop this centralizing role of the Court, or add further evidence that the forces of centralization are above partisanship.

Many cases decided by the Supreme Court require the application of constitutional principles. However, many other decisions rendered by the Court are based on laws passed by Congress. In these cases, the Court is merely applying the policies promulgated by the nation's legislative body to specific circumstances. Many of the contemporary areas of conflict between the states and the national government originate in congressional acts—comparable pay for comparable work, sex discrimination in school programming, and applying anti-trust laws to local governments, to name a few. The decisions made by the Court could be changed by congressional action, provided the Congress were of a mind to make such changes. However, the Congress is often more than happy to let the Supreme Court assume the blame for policies the Congress has originated.

Congress could change laws

One aspect of federalism that is often neglected in the study of state and local government is the extent to which state courts operate independently of the federal court system. Although state supreme courts are ultimately dependent on the U.S.

Supreme Court in many matters, they overturn state statutes in numerous instances by relying on state grounds alone. In rare cases state courts have provided greater protection of individual rights than federal court interpretations.[22] Scholars' new interest in "judicial federalism" is discussed in chapter 12.

"Judicial federalism"

The division and redivision of power in the federal system has been wrought with conflict, so it should be no surprise to find controversy at each of the evolutionary benchmarks of nationalization. However, in reporting the transformation of federalism, the tendency is to focus on the conflicts without considering the positive results. Despite the conflicts and tensions, cooperation between the national and state governments is widespread and productive. Officials of federal and state governments cooperate in many kinds of activities, informally as much as through legal arrangements. Actually, just about every state agency has a federal counterpart cooperating in the delivery of common services to the public. On the whole, cooperation is probably more of a characteristic of federalism than competition or conflict.

Federal–state cooperation common

Cities in the Federal Relationship

In an urbanized society, it is no longer reasonable to view federalism only through the eyes of the states. The nature of intergovernmental federalism must also include a look through the eyes of cities. The rising tide of urbanism, suburbanism, and metropolitanism in the United States has thrust a third government into the arena of federalism and its magnitude is too great to ignore.

Constitutional Status of Cities

It is no accident that American history is filled with accounts of political, economic, and even military activity revolving around the doctrine of states' rights, with almost no corresponding activity including a doctrine of cities' rights. The federal Constitution simply does not recognize the rights of cities. In fact, it makes no mention whatsoever of cities. As far as the Constitution is concerned, the only existing subnational government is the state.

Constitution silent on cities

In sharp contrast to this rather amazing constitutional assumption of urban nonexistence is the actual picture of federal awareness of cities. As early as 1960, in their study of *The Federal Government and Metropolitan Areas,*[23] Connery and Leach described the staggering scale of some of the federal operations within the New York metropolitan area alone: fifty-two slum clearance and urban renewal projects involving federal grants of $120 million; commitments for 90,000 low-rent government housing units; $10 million to help construct ten airports in ten years; $120 million for highway and bridge construction in four years, not counting any funds for the new interstate expressway system; 16,000 home mortgages insured by FHA in one year, with an even larger number guaranteed by the Veteran's Administration in the same year; V.A. hospital construction exceeding $54 million in one year, with additional grants for hospitals by the Public Health Service and Defense Department; and thirty projects for port improvement in the New York area by the Army Corps of Engineers, totaling well over $100 million, with Corps commitment to maintain them at federal expense when completed.

Cities receive aid anyway

A decade later, Suzanne Farkas reported that a total of more than $1.3 billion of federal funds was in the budget of New York City for one fiscal year.[24] Although fiscal crises in New York and Cleveland in the 1970s dramatized the growing dependence on federal dollars, the condition was more widespread than in just a few major cities. When federal aid plateaued out in 1978, the Advisory Commission on Intergovernmental Relations reported that in nine northern cities, federal aid was 63 percent of the total city budget, while it was 52 percent in ten average southern cities.[25]

It is important to realize, therefore, that federal–city relations are characterized by a constitutional and political paradox. In spite of a growing network of direct and indirect communication lines between city governments and federal agencies, the city continues to be solely a creature of one of the fifty states, subject to such obligations, privileges, powers, and restrictions as the state sees fit to prescribe. The state may create or destroy cities, which are simply municipal corporations. When cities exercise power to collect taxes, regulate traffic, or enact city zoning ordinances, they are actually exercising the state's powers delegated to the cities by state constitutional or statutory provisions. The larger cities have increasingly complained of state restrictions and callous disregard for urban problems and needs. State officials, in turn, are equally critical and suspicious of city mismanagement and corruption. In many respects, the conflicts between state and federal governments are duplicated between the state and municipal governments.

Federal–city paradox

Because local governments are regarded as integral parts of state government, federal restrictions on states apply equally to cities. There are many such restrictions, but four will serve to illustrate.

Federal restrictions on cities

The "*obligation of contracts*" clause in the Constitution forbids any state to pass a law impairing the obligation of contracts. This has come to mean that a municipal corporation cannot normally withdraw from an agreement whether that agreement is a franchise permitting a transportation company to have a thirty-year monopoly on mass transportation service, or a simple contract to borrow money. On occasion, however, the state's police power takes precedence over the obligation of contracts.

1. Obligations of contracts

The "*tax immunity*" decisions of the Supreme Court have come to mean that post offices, arsenals, navy yards, and other federal property cannot be taxed by a city except where Congress gives its consent.

2. Tax immunity

The "*equal protection of the laws*" clause applies to the action of city officials and has come increasingly into the spotlight in civil rights cases where racial discrimination is charged against city schools, parks, buses, libraries, and similar services. It is this restriction that makes racial segregation of residential areas by city zoning regulations unconstitutional.

3. Equal protection

The "*due process of law*" clause becomes a federal limitation upon cities when an attempt is made to take the "life, liberty, or property" of a person (one's freedom of speech, for example) in a manner the courts have come to consider arbitrary, unreasonable, or unfair.

4. Due process

The Federal Government to the Rescue

There is obviously a discrepancy. On the one hand, the Constitution does not acknowledge the existence of cities; on the other hand, a cornucopia of federal programs and money has been pouring directly into cities, often bypassing states. The explanation can be found in three reasons: (1) a vigorous use of federal powers—especially the powers to tax and spend for the general welfare, commerce powers, and war powers; (2) the political muscle gained by cities as they came to constitute major blocks of voters commanding the attention of presidents, senators, and representatives; and (3) the weakness of cities as viable and unified political entities in state legislatures.

Reasons for federal–city relationships

1932 turning point

The turning point in federal–city relations was probably in 1932, even before the Roosevelt administration came to power. The year has been called "a sort of geological fault line in the development of the federal system."[26] It was in that year that Congress first mentioned the word *municipalities* in a federal statute and authorized the Reconstruction Finance Corporation to make loans to states and cities in economic distress because of the depression. It was a forerunner for a great deal more federal acceptance of direct responsibility for problems in urban centers previously thought to be purely a local responsibility. In 1933 and the years immediately following, the New Deal poured an avalanche of anti-depression programs through newly created agencies, and the city–federal contract mushroomed into use as a very common instrument in intergovernmental relations.

Between 1933 and 1939, the Public Works Administration made grants to states, cities, and other public bodies for approved public works projects, with up to 30 percent of the cost paid outright and the remaining 70 percent financed through federal loans. A different agency, the Works Progress Administration, was more exclusively an emergency work relief program aimed at immediate reduction of unemployment through massive construction of city streets, sewer lines, school buildings, hospitals, and airports. The states were bypassed by most of these programs and tended to lose face in the process; however, most cities were highly satisfied with this newly acquired recognition that had previously been denied them.

States bypassed

Direct federal–city relationships were continued and expanded during World War II, particularly in the fields of emergency defense housing and airport construction. Even the local jails came into direct relationship with the federal government, growing out of the overcrowded conditions of federal prisons and their need to transfer some of their prisoners. Local jails were eligible for this "extra business" only if they complied with rather rigid federal standards for facilities and operation.

Federal aid becomes permanent

As the relationships between cities and the federal government became more complex in the years after World War II, it became clear that these could no longer be considered merely "emergency programs." In an increasing number of federal aid programs, there was an open avowal of federal responsibility to assist in meeting certain urban problems, such as mass transportation, urban renewal, and the preservation of open spaces. Presidents and Congresses responded to the growing tendency of pressure groups and study groups interested in particular urban problems to speak of urban problems as national problems and to organize themselves on a national scale.

City officials have long contended, and with considerable justification, that they have been forced to go to Washington as a last resort, after exhausting all efforts to secure help from the rural-dominated state government in attacking the new problems on the urban scene. The cities became increasingly convinced that their plea for help received a more sympathetic ear in Washington than at their state capital and that their political leverage was weak at the state capital and strong in Washington. "Rural domination" through malapportioned state legislatures gave cities a made-to-order argument for bypassing the states and going directly to Congress with requests for financial assistance. Even after the fifty state legislatures were completely reapportioned so that both houses gave urban areas fair representation, cities continued to feel more welcome in Washington than in their own state capitals.

Cities felt welcome in Washington

As one big city mayor put it: "We depend on Washington far more than our own state government. . . . Matter of fact, we even have better rapport with the federal people than the state people—and the state house is right across the street."[27]

Urban frustration with state governments goes beyond the frugality of state legislatures that continued even after reapportionment. A political cleavage often existed between state government and the urban areas, with the major cities of the state controlled by Democrats and the state house by Republicans. Often, a Republican governor would feel politically threatened by a successful Democratic mayor. So partisan politics added a political dimension to state–city relations. Meanwhile in Washington, urban senators and representatives were building seniority and gaining positions of power on the committees controlling urban policies. They gave a sympathetic ear to their urban constituents and rushed to enact the programs that would continue their seniority. It is not by chance that four of the more important national associations of local officials—the National League of Cities, the United States Conference of Mayors, the National Association of Counties, and the International Association of Chiefs of Police—have their main offices in Washington, D.C.

Politics divided cities and states

Buoyed by public opinion in urban districts and pushed by the urban lobby in Washington, Congress responded with a wide range of programs. By 1966, the national government was administering between 75 and 100 separate programs involving financial assistance for urban development, depending on how narrowly urban development is defined. More than three-fourths of these new programs were authorized over the preceding fifteen years but many of them were enacted during 1965, the peak year for "The Great Society" legislation of the Johnson administration. Although some of the urban programs of the 1960s and 1970s have been renamed and/or combined into block grants, many of them continue to provide assistance in urban America.

1960s produce urban programs

One of the major federal–city partnerships has been in the area of housing. Beginning with the construction of some 16,000 housing units for shipyard workers during World War I, the federal government moved into additional housing programs in the depression of the 1930s, during World War II, and into the post-war era. The Housing Act of 1949 set forth a national goal of "a decent home and a suitable living environment for every American family" and provided assistance to cities for slum clearance and urban redevelopment. This was soon followed by the Housing Act of 1954, which introduced the broader concept of urban renewal. This program grew into a gigantic

Federal housing programs

effort to clear slums, provide new housing, and reinvigorate downtown areas in the nation's central cities. Another step in the ever-broadening federal involvement with cities was the enactment in 1966 of the demonstration cities program which went beyond housing. It called for the selection of sixty to seventy model cities to demonstrate how physical rehabilitation of slum areas could be combined with the social rehabilitation of the people living there. As federal appropriations dried up in the 1970s, partly due to the adoption of general revenue sharing, the remnants of model cities were absorbed by the Community Development Block Grant program.

Urban planning grants

Another program of federal assistance for cities that grew out of housing legislation was urban planning. Noting the helter-skelter fashion in which some of the federal funds were being spent in urban development projects, Congress provided for grants to state and metropolitan planning agencies, beginning with the Housing Act of 1954. By 1966, metropolitan planning agencies had been established in three-fourths of the nation's metropolitan areas with the help of "701" federal planning funds. The new federal requirements for planning as a prerequisite for receiving development funds practically spawned a new profession. Numerous colleges and universities started new majors and departments in planning to meet the great demand for personnel to work on federally funded planning programs. The federal requirement for comprehensive, metropolitan-wide planning was also the catalyst for greater cooperation among the governments making up metropolitan areas.

Urban mass transit

To cope with the deterioration of transportation systems in the bulging cities, the federal government moved into urban mass transit in 1961 with a relatively modest two-pronged effort. Grants were made available to public agencies for the demonstration of new transit methods, and low-interest loans were authorized for acquisition and improvement of mass transit systems in urban areas. The 1961 legislation was followed in 1964 by a more aggressive effort, providing funds for the capital costs of expanding and improving mass transit systems by public or private parties. This pioneering legislation was followed by additional, but limited federal mass transit assistance which continued in the 1990s.

Cities win share of highway funds

While federal funds were being made available for the research and development of urban fixed-rail and bus systems, ribbons of concrete and asphalt were wending across the plains and around the cities as the federal–state partnership was building the interstate highway system. Feeling that their needs were being neglected in this multibillion-dollar highway program, cities began to demand a greater share of the proceeds from the highway user funds, much of which was originating in cities, for urban transit projects. Urban political clout in Washington eventually resulted in the increased share of federal highway funds being earmarked for use in cities. Beginning in 1973, states were authorized to swap some of their interstate funds for urban transportation projects.

Airports

Federal–local relations in airport construction have been direct, bypassing states, from the beginning. The first federal assistance for city airport construction came as a part of the public works programs in the depression. This was followed in World War II with the improvement of some 550 airports as a defense measure. Then came the Federal Airport Act of 1946 which inaugurated a program of general assistance to local governments for airport facilities.

Environmental considerations came to the fore in the 1960s to spur federal funding of pollution control efforts in cities. At the time, many cities were slowly killing lakes and rivers with the uncontrolled dumping of raw sewage. In many cases, cities had failed to provide separated sewer systems for surface runoff and sewage. As a result, the undersized treatment plants were unable to clean the water before it was dumped into waterways, and pollution occurred. The federal government provided funds that could be used for increasing the sewage treatment capacity of cities and for separating sewer systems. At the same time, federal deadlines were established for terminating the contamination of lakes and streams. *Pollution control*

Other federal–city relationships have evolved out of the military preparedness required by the "cold war." The location of military installations and defense industries in or near urban areas has resulted in cooperative agreements for sharing the use and costs of municipal services. Federal funds have been used to upgrade the level of emergency preparedness of cities, including the purchase of warning sirens, civil defense equipment, and even construction of underground communications facilities. *Cities and defense*

In addition to the billions of federal dollars flowing into cities in the form of categorical and block grants was the money coming through the general revenue-sharing program beginning in 1972. Since these funds were available for city budgeting with very few restrictions, they could be used for making capital improvements or meeting routine operating expenses. Because Congress refused to accept the revenue-sharing concept on a perpetual basis, most cities used the money for capital improvements or separate programs during the first years of the program. Noting that revenue sharing had an expiration date, city officials were reluctant to commit the funds to programs that would require new city taxes should Congress refuse to renew the program. As a result, the need for fire stations, administration buildings, and equipment was met with general revenue sharing. But as revenue-sharing checks continued to arrive, more and more cities shifted their use into general budgets. *Cities cautious with revenue sharing*

As the urban programs and funds multiplied through the 1960s and 1970s, municipal dependence on the federal largess increased proportionately. Federal aid to the largest cities in the United States grew from $7.68 per capita in 1967 to $200 in 1981. The austerity budgets of Presidents Carter, Reagan, and Bush, caused federal aid to state and local governments to level off beginning in 1978, and to decline steadily into the 1990s, as shown in figure 2.2.

Problems in the Federal–City Relationship

As a price for this extensive federal assistance, the cities have been required to acclimate themselves to many of the same problems enumerated in the section on federal–state relations. Regulations, submission of acceptable plans, compliance with crosscutting requirements, and numerous other requirements have been an inseparable part of federal–city fiscal relations. Urban areas have also experienced other complications.

Federal officials came up with their programs to find that the ninety different governments making up the typical metropolitan area, ranging widely in duties and resources, were more than eager to participate. With few exceptions, federal agencies felt compelled to deal with these governmental units individually, rather than with the *1. Fragmented metropolitan areas and the federal government*

Figure 2.2
The Rise and Decline of
Federal Aid, 1958–88 and
projections through 1998
(as a percentage of state-
local outlays).
*(Source: Advisory
Commission on
Intergovernmental
Relations)*

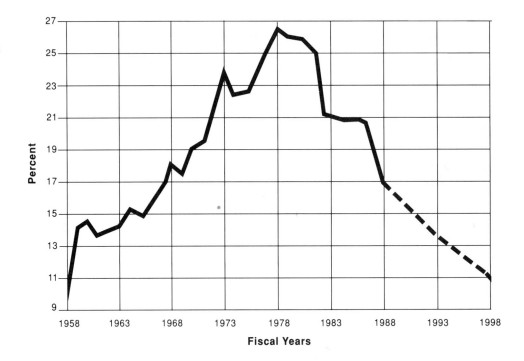

metropolitan area as a single political entity. This was necessary, of course, because there was no single political entity with which to deal. Because suburban votes were often as necessary as central city votes to secure passage of federal programs, Congress was unable to coerce fragmented governments to become more unified in applying federal funds. As a consequence, the result has been a case of failure to see the metropolitan forest because of focusing attention on the separate city trees.

There is also the dilemma of the federal government's uncoordinated urban programs. Urban programs have been created piecemeal over a span of years, each program embodied in its own piece of legislation and passed without due regard for other

2. Uncoordinated federal programs

urban legislation. This failure to fit the pieces of urban legislation into a coherent urban plan has resulted in conflicting goals. The federal highway program is often cited as a case in point. Urban highways are only part of the urban transportation problem that includes traffic, parking, and interaction with the other modes of transportation. Coordination has been lacking among the interstate highway program and public housing, urban renewal, and economic development. The fault cannot be laid solely at the federal door since fragmentation is a condition that state and local governments perpetuated for years before federal money became available.

When it came to urban problems, the federal government rushed in where

3. Lack of federal recognition

the states feared to tread. Because the urban "crisis" required the vast resources of the federal government, some urban spokespersons have begun to claim that many of the nation's cities have outgrown the traditional concept of being "creatures" of the state and thereby deserve a status somewhat equal to states. When populations of cities begin to exceed those of states and when budgets become larger than combinations of states, the point begins to gain legitimacy.

Overlooking the constitutional barriers involved in such a proposal, John Lindsay, then mayor of New York, proposed in 1971 that the federal government charter "national cities" with special powers that could deal directly with Washington on matters of trade, finance, and social welfare. "A 'national cities' charter," he said, "would free these cities from the restraints imposed by unresponsive state governments. . . . It would formalize the federal responsibility for the national scope of urban development."[28]

Propose national charters for cities

Even though the idea may have sounded like a good solution to residents of New York City, the policymakers in Albany could not bring themselves to consider seriously giving up the "Big Apple," and neither could policymakers in any other state boasting a major city within its borders.

Rejection of the concept of "national cities" does not resolve the question of whose responsibility it is to alleviate the blight, congestion, and sprawl found in the neighborhoods called "home" by three-fourths of the American population. Neither the states nor the national government have evolved with an urban policy that is coherent in goals or execution. The government most responsive to the pressures of the hour has assumed the challenge of the hour. Since the 1930s, the federal government has mustered more resources and more political will than the states to tackle the ills of urban America. Even so, the reapportionment of state legislatures and the growing professionalization of state policymakers are resulting in a growing awareness of urban needs.

4. No urban policy

Federal Relationships with Other Local Governments

The intergovernmentalizing process goes beyond the involvement of the national government with states and cities, albeit these are the two relationships of greatest salience in the federal system. Other local governments have been touched by the financial, regulatory, and judicial decisions of the national government.

While a variety of local governments have been eligible for various types of categorical grants upon application, general revenue sharing was the most universal funding program for local governments. For many of the 39,000 sub-national governments, general revenue sharing was the first direct contact with the national government. Receiving checks in the mail, with very little paperwork, was at first welcomed by counties and townships as well as cities. But with each renewal of the program, additional conditions were attached to the receipt and use of the funds. As indicated earlier, general revenue sharing became subject to some fifty-five crosscutting requirements. These requirements, representing a series of national goals, were incorporated into the functioning of all of the eligible political subdivisions across the country.

Revenue sharing first federal aid for many

School districts, the majority of which are operated as independent single-purpose governments, have become affected by national policy through the grant program. Regulations based on acts of Congress have been forthcoming on such matters as sex

Federal regulations reach schools

discrimination in school programming, the right to review records, security of student records, provision of access to the handicapped, and the "mainstreaming" of the handicapped.[29]

One-person, one-vote applies to local governments

As creatures of the state, local governments must comply with all requirements of the Constitution that apply to states. The Supreme Court has ruled that "equal protection of the law" in the Fourteenth Amendment requires that the apportionment practices of local governments conform to the one-person, one-vote principle if members of local governing boards are elected by subdistricts. If the board members are elected "at large" (i.e., by all the voters in the government), the one-person, one-vote requirement is satisfied although minority representation becomes more complicated.

Voting Rights Act affects many local boards

Sections of the country in which less than 50 percent of the eligible voters have registered or voted are required by the Voting Rights Act of 1982 to obtain the approval of the U.S. Attorney General before making changes that would affect the elective franchise. This act has become the foundation for challenging a variety of local elections. A proposal in Richmond, Virginia, to annex territory that was occupied primarily by whites was eyed suspiciously by federal courts, and the election of governing board members was held up for years before the issue was resolved. The election of "at large" representation on local boards has also attracted judicial attention. In 1982, the U.S. Supreme Court ruled that Burke County, Georgia, had to drop the "at large" system for electing county commissioners as discriminatory since blacks were unable to obtain representation under the system. The "at large" system had been used since 1911. Federal intervention on behalf of fair representation for minorities has continued into the 1990s, as discussed in subsequent chapters.

Consequences of Intergovernmentalism

Federalism has become synonymous with intergovernmentalism, and intergovernmentalism has become synonymous with the sharing of functions. Bringing the resources of all governments to bear on the needs of society has resulted in amelioration of many ills. However, intergovernmentalism has brought its disadvantages along with its advantages.

Loss of accountability

When functions are shared among three levels of government and three sets of policy-making systems have participated in shaping the programs, the taxpayers are hard-pressed to establish a line of accountability. Those who wish to protest or share in the service may contact their local government and be told that the policy about which they are complaining was determined by the state; at the state level, they are told the policy was made in Washington; and their representative in Congress says it is not being administered as Congress intended.[30]

Intergovernmental relations are dominated by specialists. The federal welfare administrators deal with the state welfare administrators who deal with the local welfare administrators. This vertical professionalism is often a more cohesive force than horizontal loyalty at any of the levels of government. As the specialists work with the complex rules and regulations that tie the three levels together, they become masters of the detailed information that is required to secure change or control. Hoarding this information gives them considerable power over the generalists among whom are the members of Congress, governors, legislators, mayors, commissioners, selectmen, and supervisors. Thus, the generalists—many of them just part-time novices at running governments—lose control.

Policymakers lose control

Intergovernmentalism tends to result in fiscal irresponsibility, with the lower governments feeling that tax money collected by higher governments is somehow less valuable than the dollar raised at home. Federal money, especially, has been treated lightly as it has been applied generously in undertakings that local officials would never finance with money raised through local taxes.

Fiscal irresponsibility

Money is power and the level of government distributing the money exerts power in the intergovernmental system. Categorical grants have demonstrated that Congress and the federal administrators can impose countless mandates as long as money is being provided. That is one reason both Congress and the administering specialists at all levels favor categorical grants over block grants. Categorical grants give Congress and the specialists control of the funds; block grants would give decision-makers at the lower levels of governments options not available in categorical grants.

Money shifts power

Because lower governments are directly affected by decisions made by the national government, they seek to influence directly the shaping of national policy. Twenty-five states, half of the organizations of state officials, and all of the major organizations of local officials have permanent offices in Washington to secure federal funds, to monitor legislation, to review regulations, and to inform constituents. Representing legitimate constituencies of their own, they constitute a powerful lobby. Their influence proved to be awesome when they forced a reluctant Congress to adopt a general revenue-sharing measure in 1972. Because the founding fathers sought to restrain a majority from abusing national power, the machinery of national government requires massive consensus before change can take place. Thus, changes in the intergovernmental system are relatively impossible until the representatives of all affected levels are in agreement. And if these representatives have mobilized great influence, change can be easily retarded.

Local governments become lobbyists

Intergovernmentalism has required an increasing role for the judiciary involving many decisions of a policy nature. Increases in interactions of governments result in conflicts, many of which must be resolved by the courts. Thus, the courts make decisions that some feel should remain in the jurisdiction of elected officials.

Enlarged role of the judiciary

Intergovernmentalism may be contributing to the decline in confidence Americans are feeling toward government. In its report, *A Crisis of Confidence and Competence,* the Advisory Commission on Intergovernmental Relations cites the rapid decline in the percentage of people who believe they can trust the government "to do what is right" as a possible consequence of the unresponsiveness of the monolithic governmental system that has evolved in recent decades.[31]

Decline in confidence

Reforming the Intergovernmental Maze

David B. Walker, long affiliated with the Advisory Commission on Intergovernmental Relations, has observed that "contemporary intergovernmental relations bear little resemblance to the comparatively simple Cooperative Federalism of a generation ago." He labeled the present intergovernmental arrangement as "dysfunctional federalism."[32]

The Eisenhower campaign

In the 1950s, President Eisenhower became concerned over the development of an unmanageable intergovernmental system dominated by the national government. After a two-year study by the blue ribbon Kestnbaum Commission, Eisenhower established the Joint Federal-State Action Committee made up of representatives of the states and the federal government, with hopes of beginning a transfer of certain federal functions to the states. However, after two years of work, the governors were unwilling to accept the financial arrangements for any significant changes. The committee concluded its business with the national government intact.

ACIR established

One tangible result of these efforts was the establishment by Congress, in 1959, of the Advisory Commission on Intergovernmental Relations. Its functions coincide in many respects with that of previous study groups on this subject, but it was structured to avoid domination by any one level of government. In the decade of the nineties, after 30-plus years of existence, this permanent bi-partisan agency had made significant contributions to monitoring the federal system and promoting balance, encouraging fiscal strengthening of state and local governments, and advocating accountability.[33]

In the sixties and seventies, political leaders devoted much rhetoric to federal–state relations, but it wasn't until the election of Ronald Reagan that the country found a president who would attack decentralization with a religious fervor. His initial proposals included reductions in federal spending and concommitant cuts in taxes so that states could levy the taxes and assume responsibility for the programs experiencing federal cuts. He pledged to reduce the number of federal regulations imposed on state and local governments; he proposed grouping categorical grants into block grants so state and local officials could influence spending priorities; and he promised preliminary consultations with state officials before federal action affecting them.[34] The president moved his version of New Federalism out of the realm of theory by proposing in his 1982 State of the Union message that the federal government and the states trade responsibility for specific welfare programs. Following that trade, which would have been of approximate equal cost to both governments, he proposed that the federal government give the states forty programs, costing about $30 billion yearly, in education, community development, health, social services, and transportation. To finance this new burden, the federal government would continue to pay states for the programs out of a trust fund that would eventually disappear as states imposed new taxes formerly used by the federal government.[35]

Reagan offers states a trade

The idea of assuming financial responsibility and raising taxes for the programs was a frightening prospect to state and local officials. They faltered in their zeal for a new deal in intergovernmental relations. By the time the president announced his detailed proposal, a year had passed since his budget cuts. A survey of the fifty state capitals by the *New York Times* found that most states were not moving to fill the coffers left short by fewer federal dollars.[36] It was already obvious that the fiscal flexibility of states was limited, so it was no surprise when governors and legislators protested that shifting financial responsibilities from the federal to the states as proposed would result in numerous inequities. They pointed out that the new burdens and taxes didn't match in many states. In addition, local officials protested the plan because they didn't feel they could trust the state governments to give them a fair deal in the new arrangement.[37]

States see fiscal problems

By 1983, state and local officials were coming up with counterproposals. Governor Richard Snelling of Vermont, chairperson of the National Governors Association, defended intergovernmentalism as inevitable and necessary.[38]

States make counterproposals

"Today," he wrote, "our economic and social fabric spans the continent and so requires every governmental level have some specific responsibilities for almost every public program. . . . In short, national, state, and local interests are interwoven, not neatly layered as the advocates of sorting out must presume."[39]

Snelling proposed that the federal government provide the broad policies and the revenue-raising capacity while the state and local governments apply the programs to local circumstances.[40]

By early 1984, Neal Peirce, a nationally syndicated columnist specializing in state and local government subjects, declared that the Reagan effort had stalled. He quoted ACIR Director David Walker as stating that "the game is lost for the foreseeable future."[41]

Federalism, Intergovernmental Relations, and Intergovernmental Management: Concepts, Actors, and Roles

In an attempt to help us understand the changes that have taken place, and continue to take place, in the complex maze of American intergovernmentalism, a "conceptual trilogy" has been developed. Professor Deil Wright suggests the utility of three concepts: (1) federalism (FED), (2) intergovernmental relations (IGR), and (3) intergovernmental management (IGM).[42] The concept of FED, emphasizing the vertical division of powers, has two centuries of much-studied U.S. experience behind it. The concept of IGR, emphasizing the increasingly complex relationships—horizontal, vertical, and at various other angles—between public "actors" at all levels of government, has little more than a half-century of experience on the American scene. The newest concept, IGM, made its appearance only recently—during the 1970s—and has been used in a tentative way to describe the heavy and even frustrating management responsibilities in implementing intergovernmental programs. Wright speaks of the mist and mystery surrounding the term IGM, indicating it is very much in the early stages of development, but identifies *problem solving, coping capabilities,* and *networking* as three terms commonly used in defining IGM.

The mist and mystery of IGM

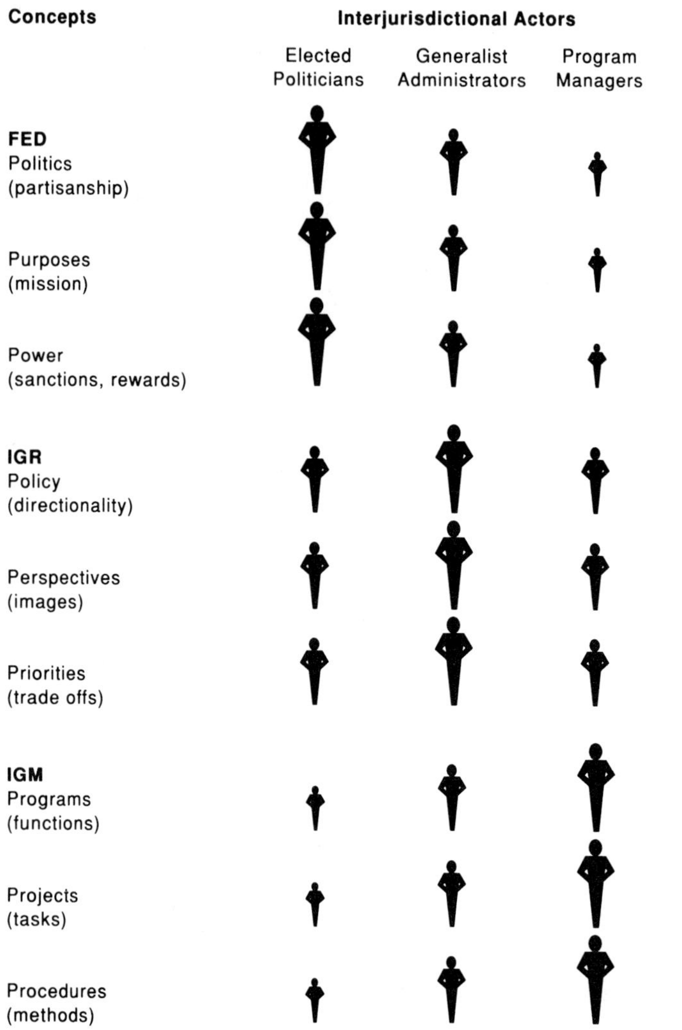

Figure 2.3
Federalism (FED),
Intergovernmental
Relations (IGR), and
Intergovernmental
Management (IGM):
Concepts, Actors, and Roles
(Source: Deil S. Wright,
"Federalism,
Intergovernmental
Relations, and
Intergovernmental
Management: Historical
Reflections and Conceptual
Comparisons," Public
Administration Review *50*
(March/April, 1990): 174.)

Concepts	Interjurisdictional Actors		
	Elected Politicians	Generalist Administrators	Program Managers
FED Politics (partisanship)			
Purposes (mission)			
Power (sanctions, rewards)			
IGR Policy (directionality)			
Perspectives (images)			
Priorities (trade offs)			
IGM Programs (functions)			
Projects (tasks)			
Procedures (methods)			

The varying size of the symbols indicates the differing degrees of role involvement.

One interesting use of Wright's analysis is the comparison of FED, IGR, and IGM, in terms of the various roles played by major types of public actors, as shown in Figure 2.3. Three types of actors are identified in the column headings: officials who are popularly elected, general administrators who are appointed, and program managers who are policy professionals. The resulting pattern of varying degrees of role involvement helps to indicate who will be prominent in shaping national–state–local relationships in the 1990s and beyond.

Prominence of three
types of actors

Despite its fissures, the intergovernmental system has evolved as a consequence of the nationalization of society. To assume that one or two presidents could alter in 4 or 8 years what took 200 years to develop, is to disregard the social, economic, and political underpinnings of the system. To change the system successfully, the political leadership would be required to rally a change in people's expectations and attitudes. Little is on the horizon of the computer age to suggest anything but further nationalization of American society and continued adjustment of the federal system to respond to the needs and aspirations of that society.

Endnotes

1. Michael D. Reagan and John G. Sanzone, *The New Federalism,* 2d ed. (New York: Oxford University Press, 1981), p. 3.

2. Quoted in Reagan and Sanzone, Ibid., p. 27.

3. Parris N. Glendening and Mavis Reeves, *Pragmatic Federalism,* 2d ed. (Pacific Palisades, Calif.: Palisades Publishers, 1984), pp. 62–63. In recent years many scholars have pointed to the salience of the model of "competitive federalism" with interjurisdictional competition for economic development, involving tax, regulatory, and service policies. See Thomas R. Dye, *American Federalism: Competition among Governments* (Lexington, MA: D.C. Heath, 1990); Daphne A. Kenyon and John Kincaid, Eds., *Competition among State and Local Governments: Efficiency and Equity in American* Federalism (Washington, D.C.: U.S. Advisory Commission on Intergovernmental Relations and The Urban Institute Press), 1991; and another ACIR publication: Inter-Jurisdictional Tax and Policy Competition: Good or Bad for the Federal System? (1991)

4. See: Joseph F. Zimmerman, "Regulating Intergovernmental Relations in the 1990s," *Annals of the American Academy of Political and Social Science* 509 (May, 1990), pp. 48–59, and also his *Federal Preemption: The Silent Revolution* (Ames: Iowa State University Press, 1990).

5. Surveys by the Roper organization as reported in *Public Opinion* 2 (August/September 1979): 30.

6. See William T. Gormley, "Coverage of State Government in the Mass Media," *State Government* 52 (Spring 1979): 46–51.

7. Timothy J. Conlan, "Federalism and Competing Values in the Reagan Administration," a paper prepared for delivery at the Annual Meeting of the American Political Science Association, Washington, D.C., August 30–September 2, 1984.

8. Ibid., p. 14.

9. *Massachusetts* v. *Mellon,* 1922.

10. *United States* v. *Butler,* 1936.

11. *Halvering* v. *Davis,* 301 U.S. 619 (1937).

12. Andrea Kailo, "Federal Mandates: What's the Problem?" *State Legislatures* 7 (February 1981): 18.

13. Cited by William G. Colman in "Intergovernmental Deregulation: Requisite for a Viable Federalism," *National Civil Review* 72 (January 1983): 25.

14. Joseph F. Zimmerman reports the growing exercise of partial and total preemption by Congress in new areas and in innovative ways in "Regulating Intergovernmental Relations in the 1990s," *Annals of the American Academy of Political and Social Science,* 509 (May, 1990), pp. 48–59. Zimmerman predicts that "Congress will rely less on grants-in-aid and more on preemption, supplemented by crossover and tax sanctions, to achieve its policy goals." (p. 48)

15. Jerome J. Hanus, "Authority Costs in Intergovernmental Relations," in *The Nationalization of State Government,* Jerome J. Hanus, ed. (Lexington, Mass.: D.C. Heath & Co., 1981), pp. 30–31.

16. Ibid., p. 31.

17. A. E. Dick Howard, "Judicial Federalism: The States and the Supreme Court," *American Federalism: A New Partnership for the Republic,* Robert B. Hawkins, Jr., ed. (San Francisco: Institute for Contemporary Studies, 1982).

18. Kailo, "Federal Mandates," p. 18.

19. Daniel J. Elazar, *American Federalism: A View From the States,* 3d ed. (New York: Harper & Row, 1984), p. 174.

20. Ibid.

21. W. S. Moore in "Response" to Howard, "Judicial Federalism," p. 240.

22. Craig F. Emmert and Carol Ann Traut, "A Quantitative Analysis of the New Judicial Federalism," a paper presented at the Annual Meeting of the American Political Science Association, San Francisco, August 30–September 2, 1990. See also: Sandra Day O'Conner, "Our Judicial Federalism," *Intergovernmental Perspective* 15 (Summer, 1989), pp. 8–12.

23. Robert H. Connery and Richard Leach, *The Federal Government and Metropolitan Areas* (Cambridge, Mass.: Harvard University Press, 1960), pp. 7–8.

24. Suzanne Farkas, *Urban Lobbying: Mayors in the Federal Arena* (New York: New York University Press, 1971), p. 6.

25. For a symposium on this subject, see Jerry McCaffrey, ed., "The Impact of Resource Scarcity on Urban Public Finance," a special issue of *Public Administration Review* 41 (January 1981).

26. Roscoe C. Martin, *The Cities and the Federal System* (New York: Atherton Press, 1965), p. 111.

27. Mayor Thomas Currigan of Denver quoted by Jules Loh in "Beleaguered Cities Turn to Washington for Aid," an Associated Press article in the Nashville *Tennessean,* January 16, 1966.

28. Remarks by Mayor John Lindsay at a meeting of the North Atlantic Treaty Organization Conference on Cities in Indianapolis, Ind., May 27, 1971.

29. U.S. Advisory Commission on Intergovernmental Relations, *Intergovernmentalizing the Classroom: Federal Involvement in Elementary and Secondary Education* A-81 (Washington, D.C.: Government Printing Office, 1981), p. 63.

30. For a more detailed discussion of this issue, see U.S. Advisory Commission on Intergovernmental Relations, *A Crisis of Confidence and Competence* A-77 (Washington, D.C.: Government Printing Office, 1980), pp. 19–25.

31. Ibid., p. 19.

32. David B. Walker, "Dysfunctional Federalism: The Congress and Intergovernmental Relations," *State Government News* 54, No. 3 (1981): 53.

33. For a variety of perspectives on the work of the ACIR, see: *Intergovernmental Perspective* 15 (Fall, 1989), which devotes much of the entire issue to the agency's accomplishments during three decades, as well as to the most important intergovernmental issues during this time.

34. Richard S. Williamson, "The Shape of Reagan Federalism," *State Legislatures* 7 (July/August 1981): 38–39.

35. Dan Pilcher, "Sorting Out the Federal System: The Prospects," *State Legislatures* 8 (February 1982): 8.

36. Ibid., p. 10.

37. Ibid., p. 12.

38. Governor Richard Snelling, "Decentralization Proposed as Alternative to New Federalism," *State Government News* 26 (June 1983): 8.

39. Ibid.

40. Ibid.

41. Neal Peirce, "Reagan New Federalism Initiatives Stalled," *Public Administration Times* (February 1, 1984).

42. Deil S. Wright, "Federalism, Intergovernmental Relations, and Intergovernmental Management: Historical Reflections and Conceptual Comparisons," *Public Administration Review* 50 (March/April, 1990), pp. 168–178. See also Robert W. Gage and Myrna P. Mandell, eds., *Strategies for Managing Intergovernmental Policies and Networks* (Westport, Conn.: Praeger Publishers, 1990), for a shift in emphasis from intergovernmental relations to intergovernmental management, and for a view of networks as separate and distinct levels of analysis, with different terminology, concepts, and emphases.

CHAPTER 3

STATE GOVERNMENT

A Vital Partner in a Dynamic Federalism

The 1990s picture of reduced federal aid should not obscure the reality of American intergovernmentalism's having drawn extensive powers into the national vortex. Federal legislators, administrators, and judges are making decisions that now permeate every state capitol, courthouse, city hall, and township center. Federal grants, with their proliferation of conditions and regulations, along with federal directives and preemptions have seemingly deprived state and local governments of their autonomy and vitality. However, to focus on the expansion of the national government during more than two centuries without keeping the total governmental picture in perspective provides a distorted view.

A political paradox

In truth, a political paradox pervades the study of state and local government. Any realistic analysis of what has been occurring in the governments of the fifty states and thousands of communities within them is complicated by two seemingly contradictory facts. First, it is relatively true that the power picture of national–state–local relations is characterized by what is often described as a trend toward "national domination," "centralization," the "eclipse of states' rights," the "decline of local autonomy," and the "movement of power to Washington," to name only a few of the descriptive phrases commonly used. Second, state and local governments are spending more money, employing more people, creating a greater impact, and, in short, are more vital in the federal relationship now than ever before in our history.

Few would deny the accuracy of the first statement, but many would be surprised by the audacity of the second. How valid is the assertion that the national government, victorious in most federal–state confrontations, has grown only at the expense of state and local governments? It is the thesis of this chapter that governmental powers are not quantitatively limited, that state governments command unprecedented importance in functions and services, and that states provide the vehicles through which the unique needs of their changing environments can be met in the 1990s.

Predictions of state decline

Close to sixty years ago, some political scientists were already delivering the funeral oration for state governments. The states were considered to be obsolete appendages, too small to handle regional or national problems and too large to handle

Title photo: The Pennsylvania state capitol and grounds at Harrisburg. (Photo: Harrisburg-Hershey Carlisle Convention Bureau.)

local problems. During the crisis of the Great Depression in the 1930s, as states floundered, one critic went so far as to say, with some logic in light of the times:

> Is the state the appropriate instrumentality for the discharge of these sovereign functions? The answer is not a matter of conjecture or delicate appraisal. It is a matter of brutal record. The American state is finished. I do not predict that the states will go, but affirm that they have gone.[1]

The political virility of the states was grossly underestimated, however, and new life has grown out of both old and new factors. In striking contrast to the "states are dead" theory is the surprising discovery that state and local governments have ranked with national defense and the federal government in growth.

Much of the explanation of the paradox referred to in the preceding paragraphs is found in the tremendous growth of government at all levels. The growth in power and functions of the national government has added more burdens and responsibilities to the states and their subdivisions than it has taken away from them. The flow of billions of dollars from Washington to state and local agencies and from state to local units calls for more government all along the line. It calls for extensive management of growing intergovernmental relations—for more government of government itself. This growth of state and local governments can be substantiated by two indices: expenditures and employees.

Growth at all levels of government

Fiscal observers who have focused their attention on the mushrooming federal budget have failed to note that state and local government expenditures have been growing with equal and even greater vigor. State and local spending grew more than 30-fold between 1950 and the early 1990's—from $25.5 billion to over $1 trillion. Federal spending during the same period grew 27-fold from $44.8 billion to $1.2 trillion. The scope of federal and local spending is even more impressive when it is kept in mind that over $134 billion of the federal figure is passed on to state and local governments in grant programs.

Budget increase

The skyrocketing costs of state and local governments can be attributed to accelerating costs in old programs, many of them under federal mandates, and the addition of new functions. Highway construction and maintenance costs have increased along with oil-related products such as asphalt, and the additional miles of roadways; welfare costs, particularly those involving medical services, the aging, and dependent children, have risen dramatically; and labor-intensive education expenses have grown with inflation. Thus, tremendous budgetary pressures have developed in the three major traditional functions of state and local governments. Corrections have also become very costly. Added to these are the newer functions of government such as the war on drug abuse, "mainstreaming" the physically and mentally handicapped, public housing, pollution abatement, urban renewal, and energy management.

Increases in old and new programs

The steady growth of state and local governments is reflected equally as vividly in the increase in number of employees, both numerically and proportionately. Federal employment of civilians leveled off at less than 3 million in 1970 (see figure 3.1) and state and local government has grown steadily into the 1990s to become, in combination, more than five times the size of the federal establishment.

Employment grows faster

Failure of state government to gain the recognition of the electorate may be attributed in part to its low visibility in relation to the national and local governments.

States lack visibility

Figure 3.1
Government
employment and
payrolls.
*(Source: Bureau of
the Census. Public
Employment in 1984.)*

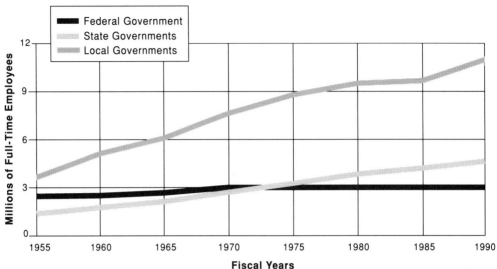

National events command the constant attention of network news and major newspapers while local government is on the immediate scene delivering daily services. When it comes to evaluating the three levels of government, local government receives the most positive evaluations. Only in recent years has state government begun to edge out the national government.[2] State government tends to be most salient to people raised on farms, living outside of metropolitan areas, southerners, and life-long residents.[3]

*Improved opinion rating
of the states*

Annual public opinion polls conducted by Gallup for ACIR revealed that the federal government dropped from the highest efficiency rating in 1972 to very nearly a three-way tie with the state and local government levels in 1988. In 1991, the survey showed Americans to be most satisfied with local government. State and federal governments tied for second in two measures of satisfaction: (1) Which government spends your tax dollars most wisely? (states), and (2) From which level of government do you feel you get the most for your money? (federal)[4]

Functions and Roles of State Government

In addition to quantitative evidence, the significance of state and local governments in American society can also be evaluated by the numerous indispensable functions they perform.

Functions in the Federal System

One of the major changes made by the U.S. Constitution was the creation of a national government with an existence independent from the consent of the states. This occurred when the government was vested with authority to develop direct relationships with the citizenry. Thus, it has an existence of its own. Even so, the states are required to perform a series of constitutional responsibilities without which the national government could not continue.

States provide for the designation and selection of the electors required to choose the president and vice president; states carve out the districts from which members of Congress are elected; states provide the electoral machinery for the choosing of electors, senators, and representatives; states consider amendments to the Constitution; and the state officials are sworn to uphold the supreme law of the land, thus giving them a critically important role in law enforcement.

State roles in federalism

Assisting in Achieving National Goals

Without the existence of state and local governments, the national government would be required to develop a massive administrative system for pursuing the national goals found in the hundreds of grant programs, mandates, and directives promulgated year after year. Grant-in-aid programs, particularly, give states the opportunity to participate administratively and decisionally in the provision of goods and services. State roles vary considerably from grant program to grant program. Norman Beckman has catalogued the wide diversity of state roles in federal aid programs: a "channel" in the "701" planning assistance to small communities; a "priority-setter" in sewage treatment and in hospital construction grants; a "planner" in the federal-aid highway program; a "partner" in river basin and economic development commissions; an "approving" party in the Land and Water Conservation fund; a "legislative enabler" for most of the programs of the Department of Housing and Urban Development; and a "non-participant" in the Farmers Home Administration grant and loan program for waterworks and sewage disposal plants.[5] As state and local personnel directors could affirm, these many roles in the administration of federal grants have inflated the numbers of state and local employees.

States have many roles in federal aid

Representing State Interests at National Level

Presidents represent a nationalized constituency, consisting primarily of the urban industrial states. Since 1913, U.S. senators have represented the residents of states but not necessarily states as entities. The majority of members of the lower house of Congress represent the people in substate districts with changing boundaries. Since these federal officials speak and vote primarily for the people, the responsibility for representing the federal character of the Union falls upon the officials of state government. These responsibilities divide into two major categories: (1) representing the economic, social, and political aspirations of the citizenry in the same manner as is done by the members of Congress; and (2) resisting the encroachment of the national government on the autonomy and integrity of states as states.

*Governors and
congressional hearings*

State officials assert the representative role by prevailing upon their congressional delegations for various causes, appearing before federal agencies and congressional committees, expressing policy preferences through legislative resolutions, and feeding information, albeit biased, into the national dialogue. A recent study of the frequency of participation by state governors in the congressional committee hearing process during the 1977–1988 period revealed interesting variations. Charles W. Wiggins examined three possible explanations of varying gubernatorial involvement: (1) personal and political characteristics of governors (age, tenure potential, party, power, electoral margins, etc.,); (2) state characteristics (region, economic stress, and tax effort); and (3) certain "intergovernmental relations" characteristics (era, party compatibility with president and congress, state dependence on federal revenue, existence of a state office in D.C., presence of federal land, etc).[6] The study showed a steady decline in gubernatorial testimony at congressional hearings during the 12-year period (corresponding to the trend in decreasing federal assistance) and identified Democrats from the western states, who enjoyed strong tenure potential and served during the Carter years, as the governors more actively involved in federal affairs.

*States resist national
power*

State officials fill the frontline trenches in resisting national encroachment and defending the concept of a two-tiered federal system. Though they may be motivated at times by the desire to retain, or even expand, their own power, they perform yeoman service in preserving diversity in a nationalizing system. Initially, a number of the founding fathers, including James Madison, felt that states were a greater threat to democracy than the national government. Madison's experience with the Alien and Sedition Acts, however, demonstrated to him how the states can play a positive role in safeguarding liberty. As constitutionally protected entities, states can resist—though not always successfully—the tendency toward nationalization.[7] Proposals to expand national power at the expense of state governments are constantly challenged by state officials. In the subsequent dialogue, advocates of nationalization are forced into the arena of public opinion where the people will "throw their weight," to use Madison's language, to the side they feel best represents the interests of the nation.

Solving Interstate Problems

Interstate compacts, discussed in chapter 1, represent the most formal of interstate relationships, but constitute only a small portion of the working relationships that exist between and among states. Most interaction occurs in other forms.

Uniform Laws

*Not all uniform laws
are uniform*

A common form of interstate relations is the uniform law. To draft proposals for uniform laws, the states select delegates to serve in a 250-person National Conference of Commissioners on Uniform State Laws. Joining the state delegates are lawyers, judges, and law school faculty members. Founded in 1892, the conference has developed some 150 uniform laws for the consideration of state legislatures. A major achievement has been the development of the Uniform Commercial Code designed to simplify interstate commercial activities. Almost all states have adopted the Uniform Commercial Code, but not one of the forty-nine approving states passed it without amendment. The Criminal Extradition Act ran the same gauntlet: of the forty-eight adopting states, forty-one amended it and seven adopted it as proposed. Thus, the general approach may have been uniform for all states, but the unique practices, or interest groups, have worked to make it less than uniform in detail. On the other hand, all states have adopted the Anatomical Gift Act in its proposed form, with the exception of minor revisions in California and Louisiana. Uniform laws are sometimes proposed as a maneuver to discourage federal action. The failure of states to resist internal pressures for preferential amendments has colored the success of uniform laws to a certain extent.

Organizations of State Officials

Over eighty interstate organizations of state officials maintain a dialogue among states on a regular basis through annual conventions, periodical publications, and conferences. An organization exists for just about every state administrative department head. In addition to the National Governors Association, the National Conference of State Legislatures, and the National Association of Secretaries of State, the list includes the National Association of State Boating Law Administrators, the National Association of Unclaimed Property Administrators, and the North American Association of State Lotteries.[8]

Indicative of the importance of national policy to state administrators, half of the secretariats for these associations are located in Washington, D.C. In fact, the Hall of the States was constructed in Washington to attract the state associations to one location for better coordination and communications.

State organizations in Washington

Of all the interstate associations of officials, perhaps the Council of State Governments is the most well known and most prestigious. Founded by Henry Toll, a Colorado state senator, the Council of State Governments held its first session in 1926 as the American Legislators' Association in Denver, and attracted representation from ten states. After a slow start, its name was changed to the Council of State Governments and it began to receive support through state appropriations. The council has become the secretariat of several of the state associations and is an affiliate with a large majority of them. It now serves as a repository for hundreds of research publications on state problems, conducts research projects of its own, and publishes a series of periodicals for state officials. The most important and well known of these publications is the *Book of the States,* a biennial encyclopedia of information about the structure and activities of state governments. For many years, the Council of State Governments was headquartered in Chicago but, at the invitation of the state of Kentucky, it moved in 1969 to a new building in Lexington.[9]

Council of State Governments

The National Governors Association, formerly known as the National Governors Conference, left the umbrella of the Council of State Governments in 1975 to establish its own main headquarters in Washington. The association already had a Washington office, organized in 1967, to exert influence on the federal government on behalf of the states.

National Governors Association

Also in 1975, the National Conference of State Legislatures evolved out of the merger of three legislative organizations: the National Legislative Conference, the National Conference of State Legislative Leaders, and the National Society of State Legislatures. The organization relocated in Denver and launched an aggressive program of researching contemporary issues confronting state legislatures and publishing research reports and periodicals.

National Conference of State Legislatures

The associations of state officials are communications systems that facilitate the sharing of common problems and the spreading of innovative administrative practices.

Commissions on Interstate Cooperation

Commissions to foster interstate cooperation have been used by states since colonial days, but they are often overlooked as mechanisms for resolving interstate difficulties. These commissions come into existence by the passage of resolutions or statutes of the participating states. Very often, only two or three states were involved, with the common example in the 1800s being boundary commissions.

Continuing commissions on interstate matters

In the 1930s, an effort was launched to create commissions that could represent states in interstate matters on a continuing basis. Following the lead of New Jersey, creator of the first such commission in 1935, forty-one states created such commissions by 1979. However, a survey by the Advisory Commission on Intergovernmental Relations discovered that only five of them were considered very active and cited four reasons for the atrophy of the continuing commission approach: (1) their national organizations assumed jurisdiction of problems before the commissions, (2) interstate compacts grew in number, (3) members often lacked interest or commitment, and (4) funds were not made available for research and travel.[10]

Special commissions for special problems

A fifth reason (not cited by ACIR) involves the manner in which most states respond to particular problems. Because states wish to involve state legislators, executives, and groups with a particular interest in a problem, they prefer to create a special interstate body to deal with a special problem rather than referring it to a general continuing commission. Maryland and Virginia provide an excellent example of two states using a commission to deal with a particular problem of mutual concern. The Chesapeake Bay shared by the two states appeared to be in serious environmental trouble. In 1978, the general assemblies of the two states passed concurrent resolutions creating the Chesapeake Bay Legislative Advisory Commission. In subsequent years, joint studies, with EPA supporting evidence, led to the formation of a Chesapeake Bay Commission, a Bi-State Agreement on Chesapeake Bay, a major Chesapeake Bay conference, and a Chesapeake Executive Council including the governors of Maryland, Virginia, Pennsylvania, the mayor of Washington, D.C., the EPA Administrator, and the chair of the Chesapeake Bay Commission. Neither the Commission nor the Executive Council had administrative or regulatory authority, but observers gave high marks to early results.[11]

Services across Boundaries

Countless state statutes have been adopted authorizing the provision of services by one state for residents of neighboring states. A common example is the authority granted for young people of one state to attend the schools of neighboring states. Cities in metropolitan areas are often authorized to disregard the state boundaries bisecting the area in the provision of certain municipal services, such as fire control, transportation, and planning. A common river boundary will often result in mutual agreements in water management and flood control plans.

Informal Exchange of Assistance and Information

Many of the interstate relations are informal. A state administrator is confronted with a particular problem for the first time and quickly places a telephone call to counterparts in neighboring states to find out how they tackled such a situation. Surveying other state officials to discover the best solution to a problem is a common practice, not only for legislative research committees but for executive agencies as well. Exchange of expertise is another form of informal cooperation. A state official with an outstanding reputation is frequently asked to visit another state to make an administrative review of the policies and practices and to offer recommendations for reform. Sometimes states dispatch a committee to visit other states on fact-finding tours.

Even with all of the mechanisms available for cooperation, proximity often generates interstate conflicts that continue unresolved for decades. Boundary disputes have been replaced by more contemporary disputes. Conflicts over water rights and management have been a source of never-ending friction for many states. In fact, over thirty of the interstate compacts were negotiated to resolve water problems of one kind or another.

Interstate conflicts arise

A variety of conflicts over taxation plague interstate peace. In some cases, states seek to develop tax systems that will import revenue from out-of-staters. In other cases, states use taxes as an economic development tool to attract industry. Almost all states now have exemptions and credits available for industries looking for places to relocate. States send out raiding parties to hold conferences with business and industrial leaders of other states. The conflict arising out of such ventures became so heated between South Dakota and Minnesota that it was featured on a national television program where the two governors sparred over which state was the better for industry. In the winter months, Texas ran television spots in New York touting the Texas business climate.

Send out "raiding parties"

The six New England states became embroiled in a disagreement over charges to out-of-state truckers in 1981. The dispute started when Vermont imposed a $15 entry fee to help the state's highway maintenance fund. In retaliation, New Hampshire, Maine, Connecticut, and Rhode Island also imposed fees. Massachusetts legislators threatened to follow suit. Reasonable heads prevailed and states began planning an interstate compact to formalize a settlement of the problem.

Providing for Conflict Resolution

Each of the fifty states may be regarded as an intricate conflict-resolving system, providing the institutions and ground rules for competing interests to enunciate their demands and negotiate their differences. Facilitating the "political" function of government is of crucial importance, according to authors Edward Banfield and James Q. Wilson.[12]

Because conflict must be managed before services can be delivered, it is imperative that the conflict-resolving institutions of state governments, particularly the legislative, executive, and judicial branches, be designed and staffed in such a fashion that the function can be performed equitably and expeditiously. Inadequate mechanisms can result in low levels of service.

Regulating Human Relationships and Providing Services

State and local governments encompass a wide range of human relationships and provide a plethora of services. They provide more material for realistic fiction than does the operation of the national government. Within their own borders, state and local units have the primary responsibility for regulating relations between the sexes, including marriage, divorce, alimony, property rights of wives and widows, and punishment for bigamy, rape, and other types of misbehavior. Most civilian murders are crimes against a state, not the United States, although national statutes may be violated simultaneously if, for instance, a murder was committed involving the postal service or a federally insured bank was robbed. Professional groups, such as lawyers, physicians, accountants, and public school teachers, are licensed under state laws. Making and recording land titles, issuing birth certificates, licensing motor vehicles, requiring dog tags, and administering many kinds of inspections fall within state and local jurisdiction. Every vote in a national election for president must be cast in a political subdivision of a state (or the District of Columbia) under the supervision of local officials. States rather than the national government provide for the routine chartering of private corporations, whether they are corner laundries or billion-dollar giants operating in interstate commerce under national regulations.

Intimate character of state functions

Directly and through local governments, states provide primary, secondary, and higher education, libraries, welfare administration, hospitals, health measures, highways, airports, water transport, law enforcement, corrections, parks, recreation, housing programs, and scores of other services too numerous and varied to catalogue in a general text.

Just as the national government has been assuming financial responsibility for some state services, state governments have been assuming responsibilities thought to be strictly local a generation ago. It was not long ago that poorly trained teachers provided education from one-room schools; unsurfaced roads, pocked with mud holes and sand traps, were a calculated risk for any Model A Ford; and welfare consisted of a county "poorhouse." States now provide more than 55 percent of the expenditures in most states in six functional areas: highways, public welfare, hospitals, health, natural resources, and corrections.[13]

States share local services

Training National Leaders

State and local politics have long been a testing arena for political gladiators en route to national leadership. Governorships are one of the four primary routes to the presidency, with the U.S. Senate, cabinet, and vice presidency making up the other three. Just when it appeared that the governorship was becoming the road to oblivion instead of to Washington, former governors Jimmy Carter and Ronald Reagan scored successive victories. Even so, governors have an uphill struggle to capture the White House. Their duties demand constant attention; they bear the direct mark of responsibility for their state's failures; they lack foreign service opportunities; they have only limited staff resources; and they seldom command nationwide television coverage. In the 1988 presidential campaign the efforts of Governor Michael Dukakis of Massachusetts to become the "environmental candidate" were apparently weakened by his difficulty in explaining the pollution problems of Boston Harbor. In 1992 Governor Bill Clinton of

Governors go to Washington

Table 3.1 State and Local Office Backgrounds of U.S. Senators

	Congress*			
	71st **1929–1930**	**81st** **1949–1950**	**91st** **1969–1970**	**101st** **1989–1990**
Governor	23%	26%	16%	16%
Other State Executive	10	14	16	17
State Legislator	42	36	42	34
State Judge	8	8	5	2
Local Official	42	34	27	23
No State or Local Office	27	29	32	38

Percentages do not add to 100 because some Senators held more than one state or local office. The table, therefore, shows the percentage of Senators who held the indicated state or local office prior to service in the U.S. Senate.
Source: ACIR Staff Compilation, May 1990, in John Kincaid, ed., "How Much Does Federalism Matter in the U.S. Senate?" Intergovernmental Perspective, 16 (Spring 1990), p. 37.

Arkansas faced a similar challenge concerning pollution of rivers by the chicken industry. Four-year terms, with most elections in off-presidential years, have improved gubernatorial prospects, however.[14] Lacking exposure on the Washington scene may usually be a liability, but in the cases of both Carter and Reagan, being an "outsider" was regarded by many political observers to be a distinct advantage in winning the presidency.

Greater evidence of state and local government as a "prep" school for federal service is found in the U.S. Congress. A 1990 compilation of the experience of U.S. senators in state and local offices reveals that well over one-half (62%) had held some kind of state or local office.[15] As shown in table 3.1, this percentage has declined slightly but steadily over a 60-year period, from a high of 73% in 1930. The state legislature is the most common place for this experience for U.S. senators—34% in 1990 had previously served there—and one out of six had served as governor. The long-term trend for members of the U.S. House of Representatives having previous state legislative experience has been steadily upward since 1950, increasing from about 30% to well over 50% in 1990. This seems to follow closely the trend toward modernization and professionalization of state legislatures. Figure 3.2 reveals that even the time spent in the state legislature by U.S. congressmen has steadily increased, and the time between leaving the state legislature and entering congress has actually decreased. Professor Michael B. Berkman believes this not only helps give the congressman an early start in legislative skills, but "those policy areas most active and innovative in the state may well become the areas most active in Washington, as careerist legislators continue their work on policies begun earlier."[16]

State, local experience for congress members

Laboratories of Government

For several decades, state government folklore invariably included the claim that one function of state government was to serve as a "laboratory of government" where innovations could be tested on a limited scale before being applied elsewhere in the nation.

Figure 3.2
Legislative Careerists' Time
in State Legislatures, 68 to
101st Congress
*(Source: Michael B.
Berkman, op. cit.)*

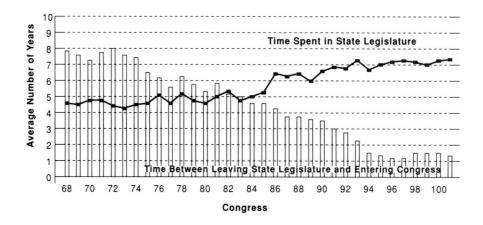

*Nebraska provides the
exception*

Substantiation of the claim is lacking, however, and the best of evidence suggests that the role has been exercised on a very limited basis. States have tended to be non-experimental in outlook toward features of governmental structure such as separation of powers, an elective governor, and the bicameral legislatures. The one exception that proves the rule is Nebraska's willingness to experiment with a unicameral legislature. Even then, it required a depression and a political giant, George Norris, to persuade the state that unicameralism was worth a try.

In matters of policy and legislation, several states have shown a willingness to pioneer. Consequently, a few programs in the national government in such fields as financial reorganization, labor regulation, and welfare legislation had the benefit of prior testing by at least a few states. Fair employment practice legislation at the national level was preceded by a variety of such programs in several states and cities. Other examples include no-fault insurance; electoral devices such as the initiative, referendum, and recall; and the presidential primary.

The recent use of states as the objects of studies of the "comparative policy outputs" of political systems has shed some light on the innovativeness of states. For example, in studying why some states adopt innovative policies more readily than others, Jack L. Walker has given each state an innovation score based on a state's record of early or late adoption (or nonadoption) of eighty-five different programs in such fields

*Large, urban states most
innovative*

as welfare, health, education, and conservation. The larger urban states, such as New York, Massachusetts, California, New Jersey, and Michigan, were the leading innovators. The smaller, rural states, such as Mississippi, Nevada, Wyoming, and South Carolina, tended to lag behind. Walker gives a note of caution, however, against rigid stereotyping. In spite of ranking last in the composite innovation score, Mississippi was the first state to adopt the general sales tax in 1936 and the first to authorize city and county governments to issue bonds for industrial plants leased to private firms.[17]

*Wealth, politics also
factors in innovativeness*

Using the Walker study as a point of departure, other researchers have probed the concept of state "innovativeness" and found that innovative states tend to be wealthier and politically more competitive than their lagging sister states.[18] However, being early adopters of one innovation did not necessarily mean that they would also be the early adopters of other innovations.[19] In his study of state health policy innovations as stimuli for federal action, William W. Lammers concluded that the strongest impact in the 1990s is likely to occur when there is (1) effective evaluation of state experiments, (2) broad-based political interest group activity, and (3) a strong ideological dimension with legislative coalitions.[20] Pointing out that Walker's research was limited by its focus on "diffusion" or spread of innovation, Dennis O. Grady and Keon S. Chi recently focused their research on how state government innovations originate in the first place.[21] Using Everett Rogers' evolutionary theory of innovation,[22] Grady and Chi study key variables and "external actors" in state government innovation development in three stages: (1) knowledge, (2) persuasion and decision—statutory or administrative, and (3) implementation. State innovators (chosen by the annual competition sponsored by the Council of State Governments), reported that their best sources of help in innovation development were their immediate colleagues in the agency and within their state government, and professional colleagues in other state governments, rather than federal government sources, interest group representatives, or higher education scholars.

Sources of innovation

The Uniqueness of Each State

The research on the innovativeness of states attests to the uniqueness of states despite the strong nationalizing trends they have been experiencing in recent years. This uniqueness can be attributed to the forces of history, geography, economics, demographics, and political culture that have worked to mold each state into an entity with distinct characteristics.

States Made Unique by Historical Experiences

State histories read like the stories of many different nations. Thirteen former British colonies entered the Union as states, ratifying the Constitution as provided by the Convention of 1787. Sixteen states are products of the eighteenth century, twenty-nine came into the Union in the nineteenth century, and three trans-Mississippi commonwealths and two noncontiguous territories acquired statehood in the twentieth century. Thirty states moved up to statehood from the status of organized territories. Vermont, Kentucky, Tennessee, and Maine were carved out of original claims or domains of other states, and West Virginia was admitted as the loyal part of Virginia during the Civil War. The republic of Texas, which had won a war of independence from Mexico, was annexed as a state by Congress in 1845. California, part of the Mexican cession of 1848, was the scene of a gold rush in 1849 and became a state the following year without any preliminary territorial step. Eleven southern states were involved in a bloody war of secession, which, in its failure, stirred up a temporary constitutional question as to whether these states as state entities had been out of the Union for the war period or had merely been interfered with by disloyal elements. Oklahoma has had a unique history as a combination of two territories, both before and since gaining statehood in 1907. One of these, the Indian territory, was established in 1834 for the relocation of

Network of history

five Indian tribes from states east of the Mississippi. Portions of this territory were thrown open in 1889 to individual homesteaders, and thousands rushed in at the scheduled noonday signal, finding, however, that many had evaded the guards and staked out choice claims ahead of them. These "sooners" provided a nickname for Oklahomans. The Territory of Oklahoma was created in 1890 and subsequently combined with the Indian territory to give the nation its most Indianized state, socially and politically. Louisiana is the most distinctive example of a state with a French–Spanish colonial background that continues to influence its civil institutions today.

The historical experiences of states still color the design of their political institutions, provisions in state constitutions, and responses to contemporary problems. Abusive royal governors and Jacksonian democracy are blamed for plural state executives; bankruptcies of speculating local governments in the 1800s account for restrictive constitutions; and exploitation by railroads, mineral developers, or other economic giants still make legislators apprehensive about corporate power. Every state has its own unparalleled experiences upon which to draw.

States Present a Geographic Mosaic

Ecosystems drift across state boundaries, linking each state to its neighbor, without regard to the imaginary line that has been drawn through them for purposes of civil government. Nevertheless, each state is geographically unique, harboring a distinct combination of land and resources that affects its policies and governance.

Alaska has 475 times Rhode Island's area of 1,214 square miles, and Texas is more than 200 times Rhode Island's size. California is nearly as large in area as Oregon and Washington combined. Pennsylvania could cover Delaware nineteen times. North Carolina is three-fifths larger than South Carolina, and Maine dwarfs the other New England states.

Problems caused by geography

Area is not the only geographic variation. Some states have problems of flood control; others are concerned with irrigation. There are twenty-four coastal states, a group of Great Lakes states, Mississippi River Valley states, mountain states, and so on. The large state of Texas or elongated states like Tennessee or California have enough sharp differences in their physical geography to give multiple-state characteristics to their public life. Amounts of rainfall, combined with a variety of soils, will dictate the ruralness and economic activity, both of which will bear on a state's innovativeness and policy interests. A state gifted with valuable minerals or energy resources will differ not only in economics but tax policies as well.

Natural barriers, such as mountains, deserts, rivers, and lakes will draw political boundaries within a state that will result in "upstate," "downstate," "plateau," "west river," or "slope" entities in state legislatures and elections. These cleavages usually have an economic dimension but pure sectionalism cannot be disregarded as a controlling factor in some state policies.

States Vary in Economic Activities

Economic activities vary among the states in spite of trends toward national standardization. The preeminent economic activity of a state is often singled out to emphasize the variety of the states—at times almost to the point of caricature. In agriculture there are wheat states, cattle states, corn and hog states, cotton states, tobacco states, and other groupings, although with considerable overlapping. West Virginia is important for coal, Louisiana for oil and natural gas, Florida for winter tourists, Maine for summer tourists, Wisconsin for dairy products, Kentucky for whiskey and horses, and so on. Thanks to Carl Sandburg's characterization of Chicago, Illinois is known as "hog butcher for the world." New York and New Jersey, between them, have the world's largest waterfront business. Pennsylvania leads in the iron and steel industry, Michigan in automobile manufacturing, California in movie productions, and Delaware in charters for corporations with operating establishments flung, empire-like, across the continent. Nevada and New Jersey are most conspicuous for legalized gambling.

Aside from differences in types of economic activity, the states show variations in the amount or extent of enterprise within their borders. Banking, for example, is less extensive in Ohio than in New York but greater than in Wyoming. Texas grows more cotton than any other cotton state, and Iowa raises more hogs than Virginia in spite of the reputation of Virginia hams.

Painful lessons from history and the terrain encompassed by the states' boundaries will affect a state's approach to the execution of its functions, but neither history nor geography will bear as heavily as the economic configuration of a state. James Madison saw economic activity as the most common source of differences among people.

"Those who hold and those who are without property have ever formed distinct interests in society," he wrote in *Federalist* No. 10. "A landed interest, a manufacturing interest, a mercantile interest, a moneyed interest, with many lesser interests, grow up of necessity in civilized nations, and divide them into different classes, actuated by different sentiments and views," he continued. "The regulation of these various and interfering interests forms the principal task of modern legislation . . ." he observed. Madison's use of the word *modern* in 1788 is still applicable more than 200 years later.[23]

Madison saw importance of economics

How politics of states take form will, in large part, depend upon the variety and size of the economic forces involved in the negotiation process. Because each state has a different mix of economic interest groups, the same policy proposed simultaneously in fifty state legislatures will evolve as a different statute. Evidence of this can be seen in legislative consideration of uniform state laws that have economic implications.

States Differ in Demographics

The distribution and composition of population among the states is far from uniform. California, at the top in 1990 with almost 30 million people, has sixty-five times the population of Wyoming, the least populous state. New York lost out to California in 1970 as the most populous state and has experienced only modest population increases in the succeeding years. Four of the five largest percentages gainers reported in the 1990 census were western states—Nevada, Alaska, Arizona, and California—with Florida being the non-western exception. Following California and New York in size of population are Texas, Florida, Pennsylvania, and Illinois. Four rural states—West Virginia, Iowa, Wyoming, and North Dakota—lost population in the 1990 census, with West Virginia's 8 percent loss being the highest. Illinois' gain was a squeaker—less

Table 3.2 States Reflect Wide Diversity in Area and Population

	Land Area in Sq. Miles	Rank in Nation	Population (1,000)	Rank in Nation	% Change 1980 to 1990	Density per Sq. Mile	Rank in Density
Alabama	50,767	28	4,041	22	3.8	79.6	25
Alaska	570,833	1	550	49	36.9	1.0	50
Arizona	113,508	6	3,665	24	34.8	32.3	37
Arkansas	52,078	27	2,351	35	2.8	45.1	34
California	156,299	3	29,760	1	25.7	190.8	12
Colorado	103,595	8	3,294	26	14.0	31.8	38
Connecticut	4,872	48	3,287	27	5.8	678.4	4
Delaware	1,932	49	666	46	12.1	340.8	7
Florida	54,153	26	12,938	4	32.7	239.6	10
Georgia	58,056	21	6,478	11	18.6	111.9	21
Hawaii	6,425	47	1,108	41	14.9	172.5	13
Idaho	82,412	11	1,007	42	6.7	12.2	44
Illinois	55,645	24	11,431	6	0.0	205.6	11
Indiana	35,932	38	5,544	14	1.0	154.6	16
Iowa	55,965	23	2,777	30	−4.7	49.7	33
Kansas	81,778	13	2,478	32	4.8	30.3	39
Kentucky	39,669	37	3,685	23	0.7	92.8	23
Louisiana	44,521	33	4,220	21	0.3	96.9	22
Maine	30,995	39	1,228	38	9.2	39.8	36
Maryland	9,837	42	4,781	19	13.4	489.2	5
Massachusetts	7,824	45	6,016	13	4.9	767.6	3
Michigan	56,954	22	9,295	8	0.4	163.6	14
Minnesota	79,548	14	4,375	20	7.3	55.0	31
Mississippi	47,233	31	2,573	31	2.1	54.9	32
Missouri	68,945	18	5,117	15	4.1	74.3	27

Source: U.S. Census Bureau, 1990 Census of Population.

than one half of one percentage point. The District of Columbia lost population between 1980 and 1990, fairly typical for the central city of a growing metropolitan area. Many states have densely settled metropolitan areas as well as wide-open spaces with few inhabitants. Texas has Houston and Dallas as well as sparsely populated cactus counties. A number of states have a considerable proportion of the total population concentrated in a single city or metropolitan area, such as New York, Chicago, Denver, Baltimore, Milwaukee, New Orleans, and Atlanta. Travelers would note differences in the immigrant stocks of the states as they moved from Massachusetts to Virginia, to Louisiana, to Wisconsin, and to states in the Southwest. (See table 3.2)

States Differ in Political Cultures

Historical experiences, geographic features, economic activities, and demographic characteristics all stirred into a state "melting pot" along with social, religious, and ethnic mores, will contribute to a political culture fairly unique to each state. A po-

Table 3.2   continued

	Land Area in Sq. Miles	Rank in Nation	Population (1,000)	Rank in Nation	% Change 1980 to 1990	Density per Sq. Mile	Rank in Density
Montana	145,388	4	799	44	1.6	5.4	48
Nebraska	76,644	15	1,578	36	0.5	20.5	42
Nevada	109,894	7	1,202	39	50.1	10.9	45
New Hampshire	8,993	44	1,109	40	20.5	123.7	18
New Jersey	7,468	46	7,730	9	5.0	1042.0	1
New Mexico	121,335	5	1,515	37	16.3	12.5	43
New York	47,377	30	17,990	2	2.5	381.0	6
North Carolina	48,843	29	6,629	10	12.7	136.1	17
North Dakota	69,300	17	639	47	−2.1	9.3	46
Ohio	41,004	35	10,847	7	0.5	264.9	9
Oklahoma	68,655	19	3,146	28	4.0	45.8	34
Oregon	96,184	10	2,842	29	7.9	29.6	40
Pennsylvania	44,888	32	11,882	5	0.1	265.1	8
Rhode Island	1,055	50	1,003	43	5.9	960.3	2
South Carolina	30,205	40	3,487	25	11.7	115.8	20
South Dakota	75,952	16	696	45	0.8	9.2	47
Tennessee	41,155	34	4,877	17	6.2	118.3	19
Texas	262,017	2	16,987	3	19.4	64.9	29
Utah	82,073	12	1,723	35	17.9	21.0	41
Vermont	9,273	43	563	48	10.0	60.8	30
Virginia	39,704	36	6,187	12	15.7	156.3	15
Washington	66,511	20	4,867	18	17.8	73.1	28
West Virginia	24,119	41	1,793	34	−8.0	74.5	26
Wisconsin	54,426	25	4,892	16	4.0	90.1	24
Wyoming	96,989	9	454	50	−3.4	4.7	50

litical culture will manifest itself in three ways: ". . . (1) the set of perceptions of what politics is and what can be expected from government, held by both the general public and the political actors; (2) the kinds of people who become active in government and politics . . . ; (3) the way in which the art of government is practiced by citizens, politicians and public officials. . . ."[24]

Daniel J. Elazar, the scholar of federalism who pioneered the study of political subcultures, suggests that there are three identifiable political subcultures in the United States that ". . . have emerged from historic interplays between the differences and similarities among the ethnic and socioreligious groups which settled the United States and the diverse continental environments they encountered over time."[25] The three subcultures described by Elazar are:[26]

- *Moralistic:* Politics perceived as seeking a good society; political participation is a duty, thus promoting "amateurism"; and government is an instrument for promoting the public good.

Figure 3.3
State political cultures.
(Source: American
Federalism *by Daniel J.
Elazar. Copyright © 1984
by Harper & Row,
Publishers, Inc. Reprinted
by permission of
HarperCollins Publishers
Inc.)*

M - Moralistic
MI - Moralistic-Individualistic
IM - Individualistic-Moralistic
I - Individualistic
IT - Individualistic-Traditionalistic
TI - Traditionalistic-Individualistic
T - Traditionalistic
TM - Traditionalistic-Moralistic

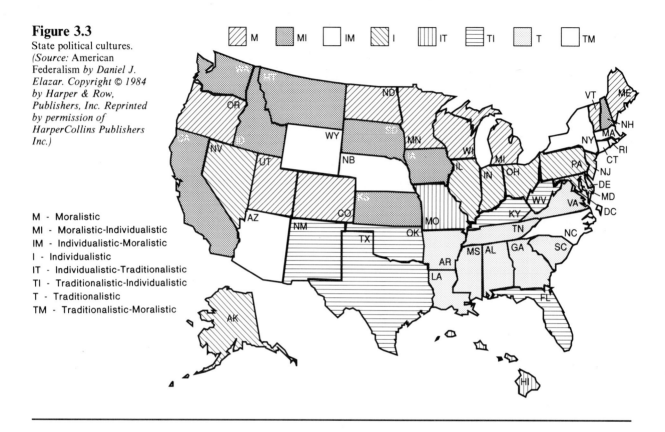

- *Individualistic:* Politics dominated by selfish interest; government restricted unless useful to promote private ends; party loyalty important and used for exchange of influence; politicians, often professional, expected to personally gain from participation.
- *Traditionalistic:* Paternalistic; politics dominated by closely knit elite families; government's task is to preserve traditional way of life; parties overshadowed by families and personalities; politics factionalized.

Summarize cultures   Elazar's subcultures can be summarized in terms of the proper scope of government as follows: "the moralistic culture supports expansive, activist government. . . . the individualistic culture promotes a more limited view of the role of government, particularly in regard to the economy, where the primacy of the market mechanism is emphasized . . . a still more limited governmental role follows from the traditionalistic culture."[27] (See figure 3.3.)

Mobility changes cultures   Whether or not the three subcultures can retain their identity in a mobile society is questionable, especially in such states as Florida where demographic facts are being radically changed by the influx of people from all other types of cultures and orientations. Nevertheless, the concept of subcultures provides a relative point of departure for analyzing and understanding the peculiarities of state institutions and behavior. As an example, the states of Michigan, Minnesota, and Wisconsin fall into the "moralistic" group and, according to one study, have a style of "issue-oriented" politics. On the other hand, Illinois, Indiana, and Ohio are classed as "individualistic" and have "job-oriented" politics.[28]

Several precautions are justified when applying the concept of subcultures. Each state consists of a mix of cultures competing for dominance and influence. Elazar has indicated which of the cultures he believes to be dominant but he, too, recognizes that each state is not a pure culture. The influence of culture can be modified and even overcome by dynamic leadership, economic crises, traumatic social upheaval, political institutions, reasonable application of new knowledge, or other factors that affect decision making.

The Changing Environment of State Government

Like people, governmental institutions are largely molded by their environment; when drastic changes occur in that environment, corresponding governmental changes may be expected in one form or another. The environment of state and local governments has been undergoing revolutionary changes in recent years and, while no exhaustive analysis is possible here, it is possible to identify briefly some of the mainstreams of change that have involved all state and local governments. In our increasingly mobile nation, almost 40 million people move to a new place of residence every year. Among the more important kinds of change are the four "isms" of population movement—urbanism, suburbanism, metropolitanism, and megalopolitanism.

Urbanism and Rural Decline

The growing tide of urbanism in the United States is demonstrated clearly by a few figures from past census reports on the proportion of the U.S. population living in cities of 2,500 or more.

The change from 5 percent to nearly 75.2 percent of our population living in cities, or from one out of twenty to three out of four Americans, explains many things about our government that are too often not understood. The multiplication of governmental functions, transfer of many local functions to the state or national capital, steadily rising taxes and expenditures, and the feeling that even local government has lost much of the personal touch that it once had—all may be attributed in large measure to the fact that we are now a heavily urbanized nation. The 1990 census revealed that the 200-year urban movement has concentrated three-fourths of the people on less *An urban nation* than three percent of the land. In the seventies and eighties, 30,000 square miles switched from rural to urban. Even in the "cowboy state" of Texas, four out of every five persons live in cities. California ranks highest in urbanization, with 93 percent of its population urban, and even the most rural state, Vermont, was 32 percent urban in 1990.

A prerequisite to understanding state and local governments is appreciating the change that urbanization has wrought in the demands made upon government. Where once the rural character of the population resulted in political concern for agriculture and good life on the farm, the urban chorus now cries out through pressure groups, party platforms, and elections for more and more attention to what has been called *urbiculture,* and the good life in the city. The steady decline of the farm population has resulted in an amazing drop from 15.6 million in 1960 to 4.8 million by 1990; less than 2 percent of the nation's population is now living on farms.

The focus of politics has been changing rapidly. Problems on the farm that were once the responsibility of the individual, such as waste disposal, water supply, fire protection, transportation, recreation, and even health, have become complex and costly group responsibilities in congested cities. States legislatures, long accustomed to a relaxed condition of noninvolvement in many of the more pressing problems of city government—blight, pollution of air and water, economic and racial ghettos, and snarled traffic patterns for the urban masses—were finally confronted with demands from urban majorities on a one-person, one-vote basis. The problem of the other side of the coin—rural fallout from urban demands on natural resources—has become a new battlecry in recent years. Renew America, a Washington-based environmental education organization, issued a report in 1989 criticizing degradation of the rural environment by urban pressures in six areas: water and air pollution, soil erosion, land misuse, pesticide contamination, and waste disposal.

Suburbanism and Central City Decline

Flight to suburbs
An added dimension to urbanism has been the flight to suburbia by close to 115 million Americans. Surburban population, metropolitan area residents living outside the central cities accounted for only 5.8 percent of the nation in 1900, but grew to 13.8 percent in 1930, and burgeoned to 46.2 percent in 1990. These are numerous reasons for this mass movement of population to fringe areas surrounding the major cities—the desire for more room, cleaner air, quiet surroundings, social status, lower taxes, and many more. Suburbanism constitutes a dynamic social revolution on wheels, with its peak still unreached, which is already dealing heavy blows to our traditional patterns of state and local politics. The suburbs of our metropolitan areas have now become the home of more people than our central cities, outnumbering them by more than four to three in 1990. Even those core cities with larger populations find themselves frequently outvoted by their suburbs.

In the early years of the growth of suburbs, it was quite common to refer to suburbs as look-alike "homogenized suburbs," implying that if you've seen one, you've seen them all. The new folklore suggested a stereotype of middle-class, white, business-oriented, and Republican population in all suburbs. More recent studies, such as the excellent analysis by Frederick Wirt and others, have dissected this modern mythology of suburban sameness and found a great diversity in political, economic, and physical characteristics.[29]

Central cities decline
Perhaps even more dramatic than the growth of suburbia has been the decline in population of many of our largest and oldest cities, starting in the 1950s and extending through the 1990 census. Of the ten largest cities in 1950 all but one (Los Angeles) were reported in the 1960 census as losing population. By 1990, Boston and St. Louis had suburbs containing over five times as many people as the area within their city limits. The nation's capital has not been spared; its population has declined,

while its Virginia and Maryland suburbs more than doubled in three decades. Many of the Sun Belt cities of the South and West have continued to have growth in their central cores, with the two principal exceptions of Atlanta and New Orleans, which showed losses in 1980 and 1990. Many of the larger cities of the Northeast and Midwest were so disappointed with the 1980 and 1990 census reports that they filed legal suit, alleging undercounts.

These two developments—the rise of suburbia and the decline of the core city—like urbanism and rural decline, have separate but related effects on state and local politics and administration. The centrifugal suburban pull is serving as a kind of shock treatment for sleepy, rural-oriented county governments in the United States. For counties that can survive the shock of sudden demand for the full gamut of urban services by thousands of demanding citizens no longer served by a core city, a new and vigorous local government may result. For others, a pathetic paralysis of ill-adapted political and administrative structures is inevitable.

Counties now have urban problems

The core city is also undergoing dramatic political change. Under the reapportionment shifts required by the one-person, one-vote principle, legislative seats have been following the outmigration to suburbia with each new reapportionment. The city–rural rivalries of yesteryear may well be replaced in the legislative assemblies by a core city–suburban cleavage[30] as central cities strive to obtain state assistance in coping with their most pressing problems—problems suburbanites moved to escape. Since most of the movement to the suburbs has been a "white flight," the balance of power in many major cities has been shifting to a black majority or a coalition involving a cross-section of minorities. This new political power can be seen in the election of a series of black mayors in some of the nation's largest cities. Black voters joined other minorities to elect women mayors in Houston and San Francisco.[31]

Central city politics changing

In the aftermath of the debilitating urban riots and civil disorder of the 1960s, *the urban crisis* became a household term. It came to mean many things to many people and bordered on a cliché or rhetorical formula in the language of politics, used to suit the purpose of the particular commentator of the moment. Most commonly, the term *urban crisis* was defined in the press and in political circles as a series of problems such as poor housing, crime, lack of public transportation, growth of drug use, riotous youth, and official corruption. From this viewpoint the urban crisis was the conglomerate threat and challenge posed by the physical deterioration of the city, the failure of its public services, and the decay of moral standards.[32] Some observers, particularly urban mayors and managers, have contended that this definition is too diffuse, and argue that many of these problems may be traced simply to a lack of money. They therefore define the urban crisis as basically a fiscal crisis.[33]

Defining the urban crisis

The difficulty faced by researchers on this subject is illustrated by the effort of the Kerner Commission to compare cities experiencing serious riots with those experiencing no riots. The data collected in 1967 became irrelevant in the spring of 1968 when three of the five cities chosen to represent nonriot cities experienced some of the most severe civil disorders of the 1960s.[34]

Before a national consensus could form on the causes of the urban crisis, the national government struck out in new directions, expectations declined, and the revolutionary fervor gripping the cities abated. The "changing of the guard" in many

New leadership takes over

cities, as a consequence of the rise of power of black majorities, helped give millions of urbanites a new perspective of their stake in preserving peace in troubled times. They found it easier to tolerate a shortage of amenities with a friendly face down at city hall.

When even more devastating riots occurred in Los Angeles in the spring of 1992— nearly 25 years later—many of the same debates took place with similar difficulties in reaching national consensus. The sequence of events was bizarre: a candid television camera showed a world audience shocking details of Los Angeles police beating a black man who had resisted arrest; in the police brutality trial that followed, the jury brought a not-guilty verdict; massive riots took place in L.A. almost immediately, involving violence against innocent people, mob brutality, arson, and looting, with television cameras transmitting it to the world; and public opinion had a field day placing the blame on a wide variety of culprits varying all the way from poverty and injustice to the slowness of police response and the breakdown of traditional American values and morality. One truth certainly emerged, that the explosive tensions of urban living have placed ever more awesome responsibilities on those making and executing public policy at all levels of government.

Metropolitanism and Governmental Fragmentation

Metropolitanism is not a precise technical term, but a word born out of necessity to describe the advent of a new creature on the political scene—the loose-jointed, often chaotic, yet interrelated mass of people in the larger cities and their suburbs. It is the product of an accelerated urbanism and suburbanism in the frozen context of horse-and-buggy local governments. The growth of metropolitan areas in the United States has compelled the Census Bureau to devise new schemes of reporting population to *Problem of definition* make it clear that the economic and cultural city of Boston (or Chicago or San Francisco) is a great deal larger than the legal city. The Census Bureau began reporting *metropolitan districts* in 1920 and changed to two terms in 1950: the *urbanized area* and the *standard metropolitan area.* The jargon grew further in 1960, with the SMA becoming the Standard Metropolitan Statistical Area, and in 1983 when "Standard" was dropped. As discussed in chapter 17, two other terms have been adopted in the efforts to analyze exploding metropolitanism: the Consolidated Metropolitan Statistical Area (MSA), a giant MSA in which two or more Primary Metropolitan Statistical Areas (PMSA) have been identified, each having a population of 1,000,000 or more. Even with the attempts at refinement of the definition, the Metropolitan Statistical Area is still not a precise term as used since it implies a congested urban area. Because the definition includes whole governmental units, such as counties, vast portions of some MSAs are rural. About one-half of the states of California, Florida, Michigan, Ohio, and Pennsylvania are included in MSAs.

The census reports in recent years have made it increasingly clear that the United States is not merely urban; it is distinctly metropolitan and becoming more so each year. The number of metropolitan areas rose from 168 to 353 between 1950 and 1990, including 262 MSAs, 71 PMSAs, and 20 CMSAs. The combined population of the areas grew from 89 million to nearly 193 million. Thus, 77.5 percent of the people of the United States live within the orbit of large cities; 50.2 percent of the U.S. population live in the 39 largest metropolitan areas—each with more than one million.

Advent of Megalopolis and Globalopolis

To complicate matters further, just when the *metropolitan area* began to make some headway toward acceptance in layperson's language, sociologists and political scientists began to talk about the developing *supermetropolitan area* or *megalopolis,* formed when two or more metropolitan areas grow together. The most publicized of these is a 600-mile-long Linear City on the East Coast, stretching from lower New Hampshire through Boston, New York, Philadelphia, Baltimore, Washington, and northern Virginia. This great metropolitan complex reaches into ten states and forty-five major metropolitan areas, and contains more than 40 million persons. A similar linear city on the West Coast is developing from Los Angeles to San Diego, and perhaps eventually up to San Francisco. Many metropolitan areas, even the small and medium-sized ones, have spilled across state boundary lines to become interstate cities.

Merged super-metropolitan areas

As if the burgeoning megalopolis is not enough to occupy the minds, energy and resources of American government officials at all levels, an even more complex urban phenomenon looms on the horizon as we approach the year 2000—the "globalopolis". In the global economic revolution that is taking place before our very eyes today—not merely looming on the horizon—it can be argued that it is city regions, not nations, that are the "relevant centers of economic prowess, competition, and advancement."[35] The growing economic interdependence of global cities like New York, Tokyo, London, and Hong Kong is accelerating rapidly as global business corporations engage in elaborate networking and make decisions that impact the fate and fortunes of communities, individuals, and other businesses without regard to national boundary lines. The number of cities in the world with over 5 million people has increased from only 7 in 1950 to 34 in 1990, with an estimate of 93 by the year 2025. The growing number of cities in the international arena is illustrated by the 830 U.S. cities that have established "sister-city" relations with 1,300 cities in 89 countries. American states, such as California and New York, and cities such as New York and Los Angeles, have larger budgets and production of goods and services than most nations in the world. This exploding global dimension is clearly changing the environment and the problems of governing American states and localities.

City as international entrepreneur

Other Migrations

Population changes in the United States have not been limited to the four "isms" just described. The last two census reports have revealed massive immigration totals for California and Florida, and several states and communities have been affected by special types of mass movements of population with racial, economic, and political overtones. The western movement of the "Okies" and "Arkies" during the depression of the 1930s, with its accompanying welfare problems, is familiar to us all. Blacks have moved in large numbers from southern farms and towns to cities outside the South; the total outmigration of nonwhites reached an all-time high of nearly 1.5 million during the 1950s. Continued migration of blacks from the South in the period from 1960 to 1970 (1.4 million) surprised demographers who had been reporting a slowing down of

Blacks leave the South

Table 3.3 Distribution of Blacks by Region

Region	1940	1950	1960	1970	1980	1990
North	22%	28%	34%	39%	38%	38%
(Northeast)	(11)	(13)	(16)	(19)	(18)	(19)
(North Central)	(11)	(15)	(18)	(20)	(20)	(19)
South	77	68	60	53	53	53
West	1	4	6	8	9	9
TOTAL	100	100	100	100	100	100

the outmigration. The destination states receiving the largest numbers of blacks through migration were New York, California, Illinois, Michigan, and New Jersey. More blacks (2.9 million) live in the state of New York than in any other state. Seven states outside the South—New York, New Jersey, Pennsylvania, Ohio, Michigan, Illinois, and California—have a black population of a million or more.

Racial tension is not a monopoly of the South. Black migration to the North and West accelerated to such an extent that the proportion of blacks living in the South dropped from 77 percent in 1940 to 53 percent in 1970, but leveled out between then and 1990. The regional distribution of blacks in the U.S. population between 1940 and 1990 is shown in table 3.3, which reflects a stabilization of movement.

A swelling tide of Puerto Ricans has migrated to New York since World War II. In the wake of the Cuban crisis, thousands of refugees from that nearby country flooded the city of Miami and other coastal cities. Hispanics account for 38 percent of New Mexico's population and more than 25 percent of Texas and California residents. A majority of Oriental groups—Japanese, Chinese, and Filipino—reside in western states, notably California and Hawaii, but totals of 10,000 or more in New York and Illinois for each of the three groups reflect sizable settlements in the New York and Chicago metropolitan areas. The American Indian population was almost 2 million in 1990, over 60 percent of whom were living in states west of the Mississippi River. These and other groups tend to live together as subcommunities within larger cities (or on Indian reservations), complicating the task of political, economic, and cultural assimilation. With the possible exception of Indian settlements, their more immediate impact is upon local and state governments, rather than upon the national government.[36]

Shift to National and International Economy

If population movements have been the most significant influence in the environment of local government, economic changes have undoubtedly been most significant in the changing role of state government. As pointed out in chapter 2, the simple term *economic bigness* hardly does justice to the revolutionary impact which this development has had upon state government and the federal system. Nothing even approaching the full extent of the impact of the growth of modern business and labor across state boundary lines was realized until the dark hours and years following the economic crash of 1929. The impact on the states came with devastating suddenness, as described by Luther Gulick:

> Where were the states when the banks went under? Powerless Maryland, hysterical Michigan, safety-first New York! . . . Where were the states in controlling blue sky securities? Where were the states in preventing destructive business competition and in protecting labor and the public? Where were the states in development of security through social insurance? In none of these fields affecting economic life was it possible for any state to do anything decisive without driving business out of its jurisdiction into areas where there was no regulation and no control.
>
> The same kind of sectional self-interest made it impossible for any state to go forward boldly with public improvement programs to offset industrial contraction.[37]

The growth and recognition of a tremendous national, and even international, economy, rather than fifty state economies as previously assumed, is a force to which state governments are still reacting and adjusting, sometimes rapidly but more often slowly or almost imperceptibly.

Impact of Mobility

Some aspects of the dynamic American society have been changing so fast in recent years that sociologists have been kept working overtime on analytical studies, and political scientists have hardly begun the task of relating these studies to politics and government in a meaningful way. The newfound physical mobility of the population, for example, is producing a variety of social and political changes—some good and some bad as judged by traditional values. Physical mobility provides greater opportunity for people to move away from economic or social "dead-end streets," and provides industry with a more flexible work-force situation. Yet this same mobility has produced a rootlessness and a breakdown of "primary controls," with a resulting higher rate of crime, increasing personal insecurity, lack of community identification, low political participation, and other social problems.[38] A later stream of analysis of modern society, with Erich Fromm[39] and David Riesman[40] as chief spokesmen, emphasizes the "lonely crowd" aspects of urban living and timid conformity to the expectations of the group.

Mobility produces new problems

Among the major characteristics of a mass society are a nationalized economy, an urbanized population, and declining ethnic and racial differences. Measured against these criteria, the United States has become a mass society. Nevertheless, state and local governments have a number of crucial responsibilities to shoulder, requiring to some extent the preservation of a political pluralism. Constitutionally and politically protected, states determine and administer policies in the context of their particular historic, geographic, economic, demographic, and cultural experiences. All the while, the contemporary environment is one of constant change, testing the flexibility and responsiveness of state and local governments alike.

Endnotes

1. Luther Gulick, "Reorganization of the State," *Civil Engineering* 3 (August 1933): 420–421.

2. James M. Penning and Corwin Smidt, "Citizen Evaluation of State Government Performance," a paper prepared for delivery at the annual meeting of the Midwest Political Science Association, Chicago, April 11–14, 1984.

3. M. Kent Jennings and Harmon Zeigler, "The Salience of American State Politics," *American Political Science Review* 64 (June 1970): 531.

4. Deborah L. Dean, "Closing the Gap: State and Local Governments Fare Well in ACIR Poll," *Intergovernmental Perspective,* 13 (Fall, 1988), pp. 23–24. The 1991 survey was reported in "Americans Most Satisfied with Local Government," *Public Administration Times,* November 1, 1991, p. 3.

5. Norman Beckman, "For a New Perspective on Federal-State Relations," *State Government* 39 (Autumn 1966): 270.

6. Charles W. Wiggins, "Gubernatorial Professionalism: Participation in the Federal Arena," a paper presented at the annual meeting of the American Political Science Association, San Francisco, August 30–September 2, 1990.

7. For a more detailed discussion, see Jean Yarbrough, "Federalism in the Foundations and Preservation of the American Republic," *PUBLIUS* 6 (Summer 1976): 43–60.

8. Council of State Governments and National Conference of State Legislatures, *National Organizations of State Government Officials,* Lexington, Ky., 1984.

9. For a complete history and review of the activities of the Council of State Governments, see the "50th Anniversary Edition" of *State Government News* 26 (December 1983).

10. U.S. Advisory Commission on Intergovernmental Relations, *State-Local Relations Bodies, State ACIRs and Other Approaches* (Washington, D.C.: Government Printing Office, 1981), pp. 41–42.

11. See Joseph V. Gartlan, Jr. (Virginia senator) and Catherine I. Riley (Maryland senator), "Interstate Cooperation To Save Chesapeake Bay," *State Government News* 27 (August 1984): 14–17.

12. See Edward Banfield and James Q. Wilson, *City Politics* (New York: Vintage Books, 1963).

13. A more detailed discussion is provided in U.S. Advisory Commission on Intergovernmental Relations, *The State and Local Roles in the Federal System* A-88 (Washington, D.C.: Government Printing Office, 1982).

14. Larry J. Sabato, "The Governorship as Pathway to the Presidency," *National Civic Review* 67 (December 1978): 512–518.

15. John Kincaid, ed., "How Much Does Federalism Matter in the U.S. Senate?" *Intergovernmental Perspective* 16 (Spring 1990), pp. 35–42.

16. Michael B. Berkman, "The New Professionals: Former State Legislators in Congress," a paper presented at the annual meeting of the American Political Science Association, San Francisco, August 30–September 2, 1990.

17. Jack L. Walker, "The Diffusion of Innovations among the American States," *American Political Science Review* 63 (September 1969): 880–899; revised in "Innovations in State Politics," *Politics in the American States: A Comparative Analysis,* 2nd ed., ed. Herbert Jacob and Kenneth N. Vines (Boston: Little, Brown and Co., 1971), pp. 354–387.

18. Virginia Gray, "Innovation in the States: A Diffusion Study," *American Political Science Review* 67 (December 1973): 1182.

19. Ibid., p. 1184.

20. William W. Lammers, "State Health Policy Innovations: A Stimulus for Federal Action?", a paper presented at the annual meeting of the American Political Science Association, San Francisco, August 30–September 2, 1990. See also Deborah A. Gona, "Innovations in State Government, 1990–91," *The Book of the States, 1992–93* (Lexington, Ky.: The Council of State Governments, 1992).

21. Dennis O. Grady and Keon S. Chi, "The Role of External Actors in the Formulation and Implementation of State Government Innovations," a paper presented at the annual meeting of the American Political Science Association in San Francisco, August 30–September 2, 1990. See also their "Innovators in State Governments: Their Organizational and Professional Environment," *The Book of the States, 1990–91* (Lexington, Ky.: The Council of State Governments, 1990).

22. Rogers, Everett M., *Diffusion of Innovations* (New York: The Free Press, 1983).

23. James Madison, *The Federalist,* no. 10.

24. Daniel J. Elazar, *American Federalism,* 3rd ed. (New York: Harper & Row, 1984), p. 112.

25. John Kincaid, "Introduction," *Political Culture, Public Policy and the American States,* ed. John Kincaid (Philadelphia: Center for Study of Federalism, 1982), p. 2.

26. Elazar, *American Federalism,* pp. 115–122.

27. David Lowery and Lee Sigelman, "Political Culture and State Public Policy: The Missing Link," *Western Political Quarterly* 35 (September 1982): 376.

28. The classifications of "issue-oriented" and "job-oriented" politics were developed by John Fenton, *Midwest Politics* (New York: Holt, Rinehart and Winston, 1966) and applied to the concepts of the moralistic and individualistic cultures by John S. Harrigan, *Politics and Policy in States and Communities* (Boston: Little, Brown & Company, 1980) p. 34.

29. Frederick M. Wirt, Benjamin Walter, Francine F. Rabinovitz, and Debora R. Hensler, *On the City's Rim: Politics and Policy in Suburbia* (Lexington, Mass.: D.C. Heath and Co., 1972).

30. See William J. D. Boyd, "Suburbia Takes Over," *National Civic Review* 54 (June 1965): 294–298.

31. Howell Raines (New York Times Service), "Victories Boost Clout of Women and Blacks," *Milwaukee Journal,* November 13, 1983.

32. This classification of definitions of the urban crisis relies heavily on the excellent analysis of Peter K. Eisenger in his paper prepared for the 1973 annual meeting of the American Political Science Association (New Orleans, September 4–8), "The Urban Crisis as a Failure of Community: Some Data." For other related studies, see his article, "The Conditions of Protest in American Cities," *American Political Science Review* 67 (March 1973): 11–28; and also Frances Fox Piven, "The Urban Crisis: Who Got What and Why," *1984 Revisited,* ed. Robert Paul Wolff (New York: Alfred Knopf, 1973), pp. 165–201; Gary Tobin, ed., *The Changing Structure of the City: What Happened to the Urban Crisis,* Vol. 16 of Urban Affairs Annual Reviews (Beverly Hills, Calif.: Sage Publications, 1979); and Edward C. Banfield, *The Unheavenly City* (Boston: Little, Brown and Co., 1970).

33. For related studies, see John V. Lindsay, *The City* (New York: Norton, 1970); Douglas M. Fox, "Federal Aid to the Cities," *The New Urban Politics,* ed. Douglas M. Fox (Pacific Palisades, Calif.: Goodyear, 1972); and Werner Z. Hirsch, Philip E. Vincent, Henry S. Terrell, Donald C. Shoup, and Arthur Rosett, *Fiscal Pressures on the Central City: The Impact of Commuters, Nonwhites and Overlapping Governments* (New York: Praeger, 1971).

34. See P. H. Rossi, R. Berk, and B. Eidson, *The Roots of Urban Discontent* (New York: John Wiley and Sons, 1974).

35. For the information and general thrust of this paragraph, the authors are indebted to Carwin C. Williams and Earl H. Fry, "Urban Opportunity in a Global Economy," a paper presented at the annual meeting of the American Political Science Association in San Francisco, August 30–September 2, 1990. *See* also Blaine Liner, "States and Localities in the Global Marketplace," *Intergovernmental Perspective* 16 (Spring 1990), and Earl H. Fry, Lee H. Radebaugh, and Panayotis Soldatos, eds., *The New International Cities Era: The Global Activities of North American Municipal Governments* (Provo: David M. Kennedy Center for International Studies, Brigham Young University, 1989).

36. For an early study of the Puerto Rican movement, see Oscar Handlin, *The Newcomers: Negroes and Puerto Ricans in a Changing Metropolis* (Cambridge, Mass.: Harvard University Press, 1959). For a recent study of American Indian tribes and governmental relationships, see Russel Lawrence Barsh and James Youngblood Henderson, *The Road: Indian Tribes and Political Liberty* (Berkeley: University of California Press, 1980).

37. Gulick, "Reorganization of the State," p. 421.

38. See, for example, R. E. Park and E. W. Burgess, *The City* (Chicago: University of Chicago Press, 1925).

39. Erich Fromm, *Escape from Freedom* (New York: Holt, Rinehart and Winston, 1941).

40. David Riesman, *The Lonely Crowd* (New Haven, Conn.: Yale University Press, 1950), and *Faces in the Crowd* (New Haven, Conn.: Yale University Press, 1952).

LIBERTY UNDER LAW

CHAPTER 4

Accommodating State Police Power to Individual Rights

The web of government developed by states and localities has two significant threads of thought and practice. One perpetuates the idea of liberty for the individual with respect to person, opinion, and property. It embraces substantive and procedural guarantees traceable to the Magna Carta, British common law and statutes of rights, doctrines of natural rights, and American prenational experience. The other thread, also a heritage from earlier times, is the concern for community interests and the recognition of citizens' responsibility for accommodating essential public interests. The twin threads of the individual's right and the public's power are roughly defined by the phrase "liberty under law." The public power is manifest in various forms, fundamental among them are the power to tax, the power of eminent domain (that is, power to take private property for public use), and the police power. It is the reconciliation of liberty with authority in the form of the police power that is the concern of this chapter.

Individual rights vs. public power

Historically, the states led the nation in emphasizing rights. When the state conventions assembled to ratify the Constitution and saw that there was no bill of rights, they demanded that a list of protections be added as a condition for ratification. By threatening to call a new constitutional convention to add a bill of rights, they forced Congress to quickly draft and submit a list of rights for their consideration. Thus, the federal Bill of Rights came into existence. States emphasize rights in their own constitutions as well. Every state constitution opens with an article on rights. When it appears that states have been remiss in providing such protection, the national government, through constitutional change or judicial interpretation, has buttressed or modified state protections and powers against discriminatory practices. The purpose or ultimate effect of the Civil War amendments, for example, was to place all persons, regardless of color, on the same basis with respect to rights and powers.

Police power should not be thought of as simply the authority of a uniformed officer with badge and pistol, although law enforcement is one manifestation of police power. Police power is the general power of state and local governments to provide for the public safety, health, welfare, morals, and convenience. Miscellaneous examples of its use are provisions for milk inspection, prevention of fire hazards, pollution control or abatement, fixing maximum interest rates, compulsory vaccination, compulsory

Scope of police power

Title photo: Police arresting protestors in front of abortion clinic in Fargo, North Dakota. (C. Hvidston III photo, *Fargo Forum.*)

school attendance, limits on child labor, enforcement of standards of weights and measures, zoning to exclude factories from residential areas, prohibiting or regulating the sale of liquor, and banning the sale or display of obscene pictures and publications. Police power is just about as broad in meaning as government itself. It is not a specific derivative from a constitutional clause or provision. It is inherent in the very concept of government. Its limits are found primarily through the interpretation of other constitutional or governmental features to which it must be adjusted.

Use of police power varies with states

As discussed in chapter 3, policies, including those relating to the use of police power, will vary from state to state depending on historical experiences, geographic features, economic preferences, demographic features, and political culture. Historically, a state may have witnessed an abuse of law enforcement in the 1920s and now has legislation restricting the use of force; geographically, regulations in the use of water will vary from a semi-arid state to one with ample water; economically, a state may wish to attract financial institutions by permitting a high interest rate while a neighboring state may restrict interest rates; demographically, an urbanized state may have annexation and zoning laws different from a rural state; and from the standpoint of political culture, an "individualistic" state may have fewer laws on political corruption than a "moralistic" state.

State police power in the federal system

In the American federal system the police power belongs to the states, with the exception of powers delegated by the Constitution to the national government or forbidden to the states. Thus, it is necessary to look at police power in terms of federalism. The police role of the national government within the states is distinctly limited, as will be subsequently explained. It may duplicate, reinforce, or complement the role of the states, as in prohibiting the shipment of liquor into a state for delivery and consumption contrary to state law. However, the average American has more day-to-day contact with the state police power, and has more opportunities to obey or violate state or local laws and ordinances than to make contact with national powers.

Challenge police powers in courts

As the states apply police power through their constitutions, statutes, and official acts, challenges are brought by parties injured by such application. Not only has there been extensive litigation in state courts but many of the challenges are taken to federal courts as violations of the U.S. Constitution. Through the decades, a series of judicial interpretations, weighing the police power against various provisions of the Constitution, has evolved to provide a general understanding of the scope of state police power. However, these interpretations have not always been clearly consistent since the particular circumstances in a case can tip the balance in favor of the police power in one case and in favor of a Constitutional provision in another.

State Police Power and the Obligation of a Contract

An important basis for challenge has been the provision in Section 10 of Article I of the Constitution that no state shall "pass any . . . law impairing the obligation of contracts." This prohibition was involved in the famous *Dartmouth College* case, decided in 1819 by the United States Supreme Court in an opinion written by Chief Justice John Marshall.[1] The legislature of New Hampshire had changed the Dartmouth charter, presumably making use of its police power by partly shifting the institution from private to public control without the consent of the trustees. Daniel Webster, a Dartmouth graduate, argued the case for his alma mater. The Marshall opinion declared that the corporate charter was a contract and held the act of the legislature was an unconstitutional impairment of the contract. The state was not allowed to use its police power to impair the obligation of a contract.

Dartmouth College case

Webster and legal colleagues, however, received a different opinion in arguing the same constitutional point in the *Charles River Bridge* case.[2] The Massachusetts legislature, after chartering the Charles River Bridge corporation to build a bridge and operate it for tolls, chartered another company to build and operate a bridge nearby in competition with the first company. The Charles River Bridge group claimed that this unexpected competition was an impairment of business and of contract. The Court rejected the claim, insisting that any doubt should be resolved in favor of the public or the community. In this case, the Court weighed the constitutional provision prohibiting impairment of contracts against the use of police power to protect the community interests, and decided that community interests should be uppermost. The case foreshadowed wider use of police power by state and municipal governments to protect community interests, particularly in connection with utility franchises.

Community rights considered

Almost a century after the *Charles River Bridge* decision, the Court further strengthened the police power in an opinion upholding a Minnesota mortgage moratorium law.[3] This law had been passed for the relief of debtors during the Great Depression of the 1930s. The act, providing for the postponement of foreclosures, was challenged by creditors as impairing the obligation of contract. To the layperson it would seem that this was a case in which the Supreme Court had no choice but to declare that Minnesota had used its police power improperly to change the terms of legally binding contracts. However, the Court ruled to the contrary. The Court said that the literal restraints of the Constitution could not stand in the way of the state's use of police power within the scope of "reasonable means" to save the state's economy in a time of economic crisis. In other words, the police power of the state could not be contracted out of existence. In 1965, the Court went one step further in *El Paso* v. *Simmons* when it approved what would seem to be a clear impairment of contract in a nonemergency situation.[4]

Police power in economic crisis

State Police Power and Interstate Commerce

The police power of the state is restricted by the power of Congress to "regulate commerce with foreign nations, and among the several States, and with the Indian tribes." The overlap of the state police power and the federal commerce power has provided material for discourse and decision by the Supreme Court in numerous cases since Marshall made their relationship important in *Gibbons* v. *Ogden* in 1824.[5] The broad opinion in this case interpreted "commerce" as including "navigation," and thereby invalidated a New York state law that granted a shipping monopoly in New York waters

Police power restricted by interstate commerce

to a group of steamboat operators. The state could not use its police power to interfere directly with navigation in interstate commerce as provided for by legislation of Congress.

The Supreme Court in 1886 put the stamp of unconstitutionality upon statutory provisions of Illinois prohibiting certain rate practices by railroads moving interstate freight originating in that state.[6] After Congress created the Interstate Commerce Commission and gave it authority over making rates, the Supreme Court upheld state rates. That national action was designed to prevent freight rate injury to Shreveport, Louisiana, near the eastern border of Texas, and curtailed the authority of the Texas railroad commission.[7]

Racial separation and interstate power

A still different use of the national commerce power to check the police power of the state is illustrated by the 1946 decision of the Supreme Court invalidating a Virginia requirement for racial separation of bus passengers insofar as applicable to persons traveling in interstate commerce. The opinion declared that segregation by state action was an undue burden on national commerce.[8] Similarly, a state may still require interstate trucks to comply with a variety of weight, height, width, and lighting specifications in the interest of highway safety. However, the Court has ruled that Arizona cannot limit the length of interstate trains and that California cannot keep indigent persons from moving into the state.[9] Many other examples might be cited of the problems in defining the border between the national commerce power and state police power, but that border is not definitely fixed in law or fact. It requires continuous reinterpretation and readjustment in the light of changing conditions.

State Police Power and the Fourteenth Amendment

Provisions of the Fourteenth Amendment

Since its adoption in 1868, the Fourteenth Amendment has provided the basis for hundreds of cases as well as extensive national legislation and investigation bearing on the scope of state police power. Its first section, after defining citizenship and determining that U.S. citizens are citizens "of the State wherein they reside," imposes three overlapping restrictions on the states:

- No state shall "make or enforce any law which shall abridge the privileges or immunities of citizens of the United States."
- No state shall "deprive any person of life, liberty, or property, without due process of law."
- No state shall "deny to any person within its jurisdiction the equal protection of the laws."

It should be noted that the shift from the term *citizen* to *person* expanded the coverage of the restrictions. A corporation is a legal person for many purposes, although it is not an individual citizen. Aliens, of course, are persons but not citizens. Thus, corporations and aliens have some standing under the Fourteenth Amendment.

Use by Private Corporations

Although the Fourteenth Amendment was an outgrowth of the Civil War and the emancipation of the slaves, it was used far more extensively by private corporations than by blacks during the first sixty years of its constitutional existence.[10] Business interests failed, however, in some of their early attempts to sidetrack state regulatory legislation under this portion of the Constitution. In deciding the *Slaughterhouse Cases*[11] in 1873, the Supreme Court upheld a Louisiana statute that provided for monopolistic private control of premises in New Orleans for slaughtering meat under public inspection and required all local butchers to use these facilities. Referring to the various provisions of the Fourteenth Amendment, the butchers complained that they were victims of abridgment of "privileges or immunities," of deprivation of "due process," and of denial of "the equal protection of the laws." The Court disagreed and emphasized the enduring regulatory power of the states in the federal system. It stressed the close but not exclusive connection of the Fourteenth Amendment with the rights of ex-slaves.

State Regulators versus Due Process

In the post-Civil War period, rapid expansion of railroads into the sparsely settled areas of the West led to transportation conditions that western farmers thought intolerable. The farmers banded together in the Granger movement to secure legislative regulation of the railroads in the interest of adequate service at reasonable rates. The farmers also sought state regulation of auxiliary services essential to movement of their produce to market. The state's regulatory power was soon challenged under the Fourteenth Amendment.

In *Munn* v. *Illinois,*[12] the first of the Granger cases, the Supreme Court upheld an Illinois statute fixing maximum charges for storing grain in warehouses in large cities. In delivering the opinion, Chief Justice Morrison R. Waite cited Taney and British authorities on police power and observed that the Illinois law was not violative of the "due process" clause of the Fourteenth Amendment since it applied controls to private property "affected with a public interest." *Regulating business having a public interest*

But just what is a business affected with a public interest? The Court subsequently stated that in the *Munn* case it had conceived the term "affected with a public interest" as the equivalent of "subject to the exercise of the police power."[13] This somewhat circular definition simply means that the scope of the state police power in this field is determined by the slow process of judicial inclusion and exclusion on a case-by-case basis.

Subsequent opinions of the Court showed a trend toward viewing the Fourteenth Amendment as the amendment of corporate business in a fashion highly disturbing to proponents of the police power. Broad clearance was set up in 1886 by the Supreme Court in a categorical statement that corporations were persons entitled to "equal protection of the laws."[14] In 1905, the high tribunal set aside a New York statute fixing maximum hours for employees of bakeries, holding it an unreasonable use of police *Due process and labor* power in violation of "due process" protection of the liberty of contract to sell and *regulations* purchase labor.[15] In 1937, the Court frankly reversed itself with respect to state power to regulate labor conditions, noting in the opinion that "the liberty safeguarded is liberty in a social organization."[16]

Support for narrowing the Fourteenth Amendment's protection of corporations came from such justices as Brandeis, Black, Douglas, and others. The constitutional history of the shift is one that would fill many pages. Suffice it to say with the Court in the *Nebbia* case, where it upheld New York's regulation of the price of milk, that:

> So far as the requirement of due process is concerned, and in the absence of other constitutional restriction, a state is free to adopt whatever economic policy may reasonably be deemed to promote public welfare. . .
>
> . . . The Constitution does not secure to anyone liberty to conduct his business in such fashion as to inflict injury upon the public at large, or upon any substantial group of the people.[17]

We had come a long way in the mid-1930s from the doctrine that the state's police power applied only to businesses "affected with a public interest."

Due Process in State Criminal Justice

Shield for human rights

The story of the Fourteenth Amendment as a shield for human rights is too long to be given here except as a summary of significant points. It has afforded the Supreme Court a new role as defender of humane democracy. The use of the amendment for protection of human rights, at ebb tide around the turn of the century, registered a genuine revival after 1930 when corporations were finding it a less useful weapon against state police power.

Right to fair trial in state courts

The "due process" clause of the Fourteenth Amendment has served more and more in recent decades to require state courts to exercise fair and proper procedure in criminal cases. For example, in 1923 the Supreme Court sent a case back to an Arkansas court for retrial on the ground that the jury had brought in a hasty verdict under the influence of a mob.[18] Some years later, the Court similarly interfered with the trial of a group of blacks at Scottsboro, Alabama, because the accused transients were shunted through proceedings to conviction without any advance provision for counsel.[19] A sequel to this case met similar treatment because blacks had been systematically and traditionally excluded from jury service in that Alabama jurisdiction.[20] Convictions in state courts have been set aside because they were based on a forced confession of guilt. Such methods of securing conviction, in the words of Justice Black, constitute "a denial of due process of law as guaranteed in the Fourteenth Amendment."[21]

Exclusionary rule

Unnecessary brutality to prisoners under arrest or in custody has subjected state or local officers to prosecution in federal court under civil rights legislation passed by Congress in conformity with the Fourteenth Amendment.[22] In 1961, the so-called federal exclusionary rule—making evidence obtained in violation of the Fourth Amendment inadmissable in court—was applied to the state judiciary as well.[23] Subsequent decisions require states to provide legal counsel for indigent defendants facing serious criminal charges;[24] to extend to defendants in state courts the same privilege against self-incrimination previously applicable under the Fifth Amendment to federal proceedings;[25] and to assure that protection against self-incrimination extended to questioning at the police station pursuant to the *Miranda* decision.[26] In 1984, however, the Court approved in *New York* v. *Quarles* the questioning of a suspect before warning him of his rights if the inquiry is prompted by concern for public safety. In 1985, the Court held in *New Jersey* v. *T.L.O.* that school officials could search students if there are reasonable grounds for believing that a search would produce evidence of violation of laws or school rules.

In the years following the controversial *Miranda* ruling, police have charged that it is an unreasonable barrier to solving crimes through confessions, while civil rights supporters have hailed it as a shield for human rights. The more conservative appointees to the Court have tended to moderate the more extreme applications of *Miranda,* however, and studies reveal relatively little impact, either on the confession rate or on police behavior.

In 1972, the Supreme Court refused to require uniform jury procedures for imposing the death penalty.[27] In another 1972 decision, *Furman* v. *Georgia,* the Court ruled that the death penalty as it had been imposed by the states was unconstitutional under the Eighth and Fourteenth Amendments. Many states thus revised their capital *Capital punishment* punishment legislation and, in *Gregg* v. *Georgia* in 1976, the Supreme Court ruled that the death penalty is not in and of itself unconstitutional. Court decisions since then have moved toward a more permissive position on the death penalty. A 1986 decision makes it possible to use "death qualified" juries in capital punishment cases—juries from which those who personally oppose capital punishment are excluded, even though this makes it less difficult to secure the death penalty.[28] The Supreme Court in 1987 rejected a claim that Georgia's new death penalty law was used in a discriminatory way,[29] and ruled in 1989 that applying the death penalty to the mentally retarded[30] and to juveniles[31] is not unconstitutional. Approximately three-fourths of the states now have death penalty legislation on the books—voters in California reinstated capital punishment after their own state supreme court invalidated it—and more than 2,300 waited on death row by 1991.

Fourteenth Amendment Protects Liberties

The Supreme Court has used the Fourteenth Amendment to protect basic freedoms against unreasonable interference from the use of police power by state and local governments. This has been achieved by broadening the definition of "liberty" in the Fourteenth Amendment. When the judges observed that the Fourteenth Amendment *Liberty in First* prohibited states from depriving any person of liberty, they pondered over the definition *Amendment* of liberty as it applied to states. Over time, the Court has included the liberties found in the U.S. Bill of Rights among those freedoms protected from state action in the Fourteenth Amendment. In effect, then, under the rulings of the Court, state and local governments must observe the restrictions of the First Amendment in respect to speech, press, assembly, and religion. Municipal regulations have been voided by the Supreme Court for interfering unduly with the liberties of religious, labor, and other groups wishing "to speak, write, print or distribute information or opinion." This was made clear by Justice Owen J. Roberts in a Court opinion in 1939 with numerous citations from other cases.[32]

Publications may not be suppressed by state action for obnoxious and derogatory remarks concerning public officers.[33] In two related cases in Alabama the Supreme Court further strengthened freedom of the press. It ruled that a public official cannot recover libel damages unless the statement was made with deliberate malice[34]. Four Montgomery city officials and Governor John Patterson sought damages from *The New York Times* and four black ministers for a full-page advertisement alleging racial oppression. In 1966, the Court held that state laws (in this case Alabama's 1915 statute barring publication of political editorials on election day) are a flagrant unconstitutional abridgment of freedom of the press.[35] The Supreme Court in 1979 ruled unconstitutional a West Virginia law requiring written approval from a juvenile court before the press could reveal the name of a youthful offender.[36] The Supreme Court struck down an Oklahoma ban of wine advertising on cable television systems in 1984 as a restriction of protected commercial speech.[37] In the same year, the Court upheld the right of Los Angeles to ban political advertisements and other signs from public property, ruling it not violative of free speech rights.[38]

When the U.S. Supreme Court ruled by a 5–4 decision in 1989 that burning the American flag as a form of political protest is protected by the constitutional right to free speech, an emotional outcry of popular opposition was almost instantaneous. Pollsters had a field day measuring the extent of the majorities disagreeing with the court and favoring a constitutional amendment to make it illegal. Moderates in Congress, opposing a constitutional amendment, passed the Flag Protection Act of 1989, only to have it struck down in 1990 by another 5–4 Supreme Court decision. Justice Brennan's majority decision stated, "Punishing desecration of the flag dilutes the very freedom that makes this emblem so revered." The U.S. House of Representatives quickly took up a proposed constitutional amendment stating that "Congress and the States shall have power to prohibit the physical desecration of the flag of the United States." The vote of 254–177 fell 35 votes short of the required two-thirds majority. There was irony in the failure of "super-patriotism" in this first instance, followed by the outpouring of flag-waving patriotism during and after the success of American military forces in the Middle East in 1990 and 1991.[39] In 1992 the Supreme Court ruled that the First Amendment also protects swastikas and cross burning saying that a St. Paul, Minnesota "hate crime law" was too restrictive of free speech.

Protection through the Fourteenth Amendment has invalidated the banning of movies under claims of their being sacrilegious or suggestive of crime and immorality,[40] and has served to limit state and local regulation of obscene literature. The *Roth* decision in 1957 required an obscenity test of whether the dominant theme of the material taken as a whole appeals to prurient interest, and whether the material has redeeming social value.[41] The decision in the *Ginzburg* case in 1966 gave censors an additional legal weapon—the obvious motive of the publisher—in controlling obscenity.[42] The trend of liberal Supreme Court decisions giving First Amendment protection to public portrayal of sexual conduct received a setback in the *Miller* decision in 1973. Chief Justice Burger wrote the majority opinion, holding that local community standards rather than national standards may be used to determine whether material is obscene, and that courts may determine whether the work "taken as a whole lacks serious literary, artistic, political, or scientific value to merit First Amendment protection."[43] In the years immediately following the *Miller* case, the courts were deluged with appeals of convictions for selling and displaying obscene motion pictures and printed materials, but they generally refused to hear the appeals and, in effect, supported local community standards. In a 1987 decision, the court backed up a little in its reliance on community standards, introducing a "reasonable person" test to determine whether disputed material on sale at a Rockford, Illinois adult bookstore had redeeming literary, artistic, or scientific value.[44]

Attempts by states to curb fund-raising abuses by charities ran afoul the Court's interpretation of the First Amendment when the Court banned state limits on the amount of money charities could spend on fund-raising. In the 1984 case, the Court expressed doubt that high solicitation costs could be correlated to fraud sufficiently to justify this restriction on protected First Amendment activity. The laws of twenty-two states were affected by the decision.[45]

State anti-subversion measures have had a checkered experience with the federal judiciary, with approval being given in the *Adler* case to the state's barring from employment in public schools persons holding subversive doctrines or membership in subversive organizations. The Court stated that the right of such persons to "assemble, speak, think and believe as they will" is not the "right to work for the State in the school system on their own terms."[46] Since 1960, however, the Supreme Court has struck down loyalty oaths required of public employees in six states—Arkansas, Florida, Washington, Maryland, New York, and Arizona. The Arizona law was said to be based on "guilt by association," making mere membership in an organization considered subversive the basis for discharge or suspension of salary. The ruling declared the law unconstitutional as a violation of "the cherished freedom of association protected by the First Amendment."[47] However, in 1972 the Supreme Court upheld a Massachusetts law requiring state employees and applicants not only to uphold the Constitution, but to oppose overthrow of federal or state governments by force.[48] The First Amendment right of "freedom of association" was upheld in 1984 by a federal circuit court against the refusal of Texas A&M University to recognize a gay student organization.[49]

Loyalty oaths

Religious Freedom and Separation of Church and State

The Fourteenth Amendment has protected freedom of worship in ways other than by safeguarding religious speech from interference by local authorities. With few exceptions, the Supreme Court has insisted rather strictly upon the separation of church and state in public education. Its insistence has extended to outlawing the release of time for religious activity or instruction on school premises even where such instruction is at the request of parents.[50] The school action was held to be contrary to the religious establishment clause of the First Amendment and, therefore, violative of the Fourteenth Amendment. Four years later, in the *Zorach* case, the Court reconsidered the problem of "released time" and approved the New York system of permitting students to go to religious centers not on public school property for instruction during the school day.[51] Reversing a former decision, the Court in 1943 overruled the action of a school

Religion in public schools

board that expelled children of the Jehovah's Witness faith for refusing to salute the national flag in school exercises because of religious scruples.[52] However, the practice of transporting school children in public buses to parochial schools has been upheld.[53] A 1972 decision affecting Amish parents and their children upheld their right to an exemption from compulsory school attendance laws on religious grounds.[54]

The landmark cases of the 1960s prohibiting prescribed prayers and Bible reading in the public schools have come under increasing attack.[55] Strong public opinion favoring prayer in schools has sustained a persistent effort to amend the Constitution or pass federal legislation to negate or modify the decisions. State laws requiring or permitting public schools to begin each day with a moment of silence for meditation or prayer have been passed by an increasing number of states. In *Wallace* v. *Jaffree,* decided in 1985, the U.S. Supreme Court struck down an Alabama statute providing for a moment of silence because it lacked a secular purpose. In 1989 the U.S. Supreme Court ruled out pre-game prayers carried over a public address system at Douglas, Georgia high school football games. In the Rhode Island case of *Lee* v. *Weisman* (1992), the court split 5–4 in prohibiting a public school sponsored prayer at graduation ceremonies.

In 1984 Congress passed the Equal Access Act in an effort to end what religious conservatives contended was widespread discrimination against religious speech in the public schools. The act provided that high schools permitting non-curriculum-related student groups (chess clubs, scuba clubs, etc.) to use school facilities could not deny the same use to other groups on the basis of "religious, political, philosophical, or other content of the speech at such meetings." While leaving the court decisions against prescribed school prayer and Bible reading undisturbed, the Equal Access Act takes a middle ground between the opposite extremes on the issue of separation of church and state. The Supreme Court approved the law in 1990 by a vote of 8–1 in *Westside Community Schools* v. *Mergens.*[56]

The First Amendment right of freedom of religion was sufficient in a U.S. circuit court to set aside a Nebraska law in 1984 requiring photographs on drivers' licenses. An applicant refused to have her picture taken because of the directive of the Second Commandment against making a "likeness." "The Free Exercise Clause requires a state to make reasonable accommodation of religion," Judge Myron Bright observed.[57] In 1985, the Supreme Court refused to hear an appeal, thereby affirming Bright's reasoning.

Teaching creation loses in courts

A growing movement of religious conservatives to secure state legislation requiring schools to balance the teaching of "evolution science" with the teaching of "creation science" achieved first success in Arkansas and Louisiana legislatures in 1981. Litigation followed and seemed destined to go to the U.S. Supreme Court with much of the same fanfare as the Scopes "monkey" trial. However, when federal district courts in Arkansas and Louisiana ruled against the teaching requirement, interest in pursuing the matter waned. A number of court cases have grown out of the claim by religious schools that they are exempt from state laws requiring private school teachers to be state certified. A majority of the state courts have ruled that the state has authority to impose such a requirement.

Two court cases in the 1970s (*Tilton* v. *Richardson* in 1971, and *Roemer* v. *Board of Public Works* in 1976) spelled out a grudging basis for approving public funds for church colleges. The *Tilton* case ruled that such aid must have a secular purpose, must not have the primary effect of advancing religion, and must not foster excessive government entanglement with religion. By a 5–4 margin, the *Roemer* case upheld a Maryland program of state grants to private colleges, as meeting the *Tilton* criteria.

In a break with traditional opposition to aid to religious schools, the Supreme Court upheld a Minnesota law in 1983 that allowed tax deductions for the costs of public and private education. In *Mueller et al.* v. *Allen et al.,* the Court said the law neutrally provided benefits for all parents and was thus permissible.[58]

Uphold Minnesota tax deduction

The relationship of police power to religion and religious freedom is somewhat flexible and not easy to define at any one time. Through the years, all levels of government have offered special concessions to churches, including tax exemption of church property and income, recognition of Sunday as a legal day of rest in every state, Sunday "blue laws," requirement of daily reading of the Bible in many public schools, and legal observance of such Christian holidays as Christmas and Easter. But what happens when one's religious freedom conflicts with a state or local government regulation for public health or welfare?

In recent years courts have supported the states' police power in a variety of unusual cases: despite religious objections of parents who were Jehovah's Witnesses, a court ordered that an Rh baby be given a blood transfusion; a compulsory chest X-ray requirement at the University of Washington was held to apply to all students, including one with religious objections; a nine-year-old girl helping her guardian aunt to sell publications of Jehovah's Witnesses was held subject to the child labor law in Massachusetts; and in 1989 and 1990 several Christian Science parents were convicted of involuntary manslaughter, felony child abuse, or child endangerment in California, Florida, Arizona, and Massachusetts, for rejecting medical care for their children. In such cases the courts are saying one's right to practice religion is subservient to a child's right to live. Another 1990 controversy revolved around the Supreme Court decision allowing the state of Oregon to prohibit Native Americans from using a banned drug, peyote, in their religious rituals, in spite of the First Amendment guarantees.[59] The 5–4 decision abandoned the long-standing "compelling interest" test for approving restrictions on religious freedom, in favor of the less stringent "reasonableness" test, causing strong protest from religious and civil liberties groups. The Religious Freedom Restoration Act was soon introduced in Congress to restore the compelling interest test, and by early 1992 had nearly 180 co-sponsors in the House.

Parents' rights vs. children's rights

The Supreme Court ruled in 1976 that civil courts have no right to decide internal ecclesiastical disputes in hierarchical churches, where resolution cannot be made without extensive inquiry by civil courts into religious law and policy.

Further illustrating the Supreme Court's tightrope walking on this issue, 1981 decisions approved specific references to Jesus Christ in Christmas programs in the Sioux Falls, South Dakota, public schools, but refused to allow North Carolina to publish a "Motorist's Prayer" on its official state highway maps. State payments to a chaplain to open the sessions of the state legislature passed Court muster in 1983 when the practice in Nebraska was challenged. A creche in a Pawtucket, Rhode Island, city Christmas display was not a breach of the Establishment Clause, the Supreme Court held in a 1984 case. The Court observed that the creche was only a portion of a larger

Keeping church and state separate

Christmas display that included a Santa Claus house, a Christmas tree, and a banner reading "Season's Greetings."[60] The *Pawtucket* decision affirmed a directional shift in the Court's interpretation of the Establishment Clause that was first noted in 1980 when the Court refused to reverse lower court decisions allowing Denver to include a Nativity scene in its Christmas display and allowing the Texas state capitol to continue Jewish holidays and Christmas displays.

Sunday "Blue Laws"

The perplexing relationship between the requirement of religious freedom and the state's police power, as manifested in Sunday laws, was considered by the Supreme Court in four cases in 1961. These cases challenged the constitutionality of laws in Pennsylvania, Massachusetts, and Maryland on the ground that they impose a Christian Sabbath on non-Christians. Orthodox Jewish merchants who close their stores on Friday evening and Saturday are then prevented by law from being open on Sunday. The Court upheld the Sunday closing laws, saying that such laws are legal if designed to promote a day of rest and recreation. The Court served notice, however, that such laws would be declared unconstitutional if they are found, on their face or by examining their legislative history, to be primarily designed to promote religious observance and church attendance.[61] The Court rejected at the same time an appeal to review South Carolina's law against commercial movies on Sunday. The state court decision, from which the appeal was made, upheld the state's power to enact such a law and concluded that if it was "out of step with the times" as alleged, it was the job of the legislature, not the courts, to change it. States are proceeding to abolish Sunday closing laws without pressure from the courts. In 1961, thirty-four states had general Sunday prohibitions; by 1981, this number had declined to twenty-four, and with the repeal of North Dakota's law in 1991, no state now has a general Sunday closing law. However, most states still have some restrictions on Sunday liquor sales.

Religious tests for holding office

In still another 1961 decision in the church–state area of the law, the Supreme Court struck down a Maryland requirement that each state officeholder must make a sworn statement of belief in a Supreme Being. In a unanimous opinion, the Court held that no religious test whatsoever may be applied by either federal or state governments to disqualify a person from holding public office.[62] The Supreme Court in 1978 also ruled unconstitutional an old provision of the Tennessee constitution prohibiting clergymen from serving in the state legislature.

Religious freedom and state constitutions

It is important to remember that religious freedom is protected by *state* constitutions and not merely by the U.S. constitution. Professor G. Alan Tarr points out that state constitutional provisions are often ignored because of the mistaken belief that state provisions merely repeat the content of the First Amendment. In fact, the state constitutions often reflect historical struggles over religion that led to more clear and explicit provisions for greater or less separation of church and state than the U.S. constitution provides.[63]

The Fourteenth Amendment Protects Right of Privacy

Abortion and right of privacy

With the advent of abortion as a major social and political issue of the 1980s and 1990s, the constitutional right of privacy has come into sharp conflict with state police powers. The right of privacy is the right of each person to live free of undue interference from the government or other people. The Constitution does not specifically mention or define a right of privacy, but the right is recognized and protected by the Third, Fourth, and Fifth Amendments, all of which apply to states through the Fourteenth Amendment. The Fourth Amendment, the most germane of the three in the case of abortion, protects the "right of people to be secure in their persons, houses, papers, and effects, against unreasonable searches and seizures." (The Fifth Amendment states that "no person shall be compelled in any criminal case to be a witness against himself." The Third Amendment prohibits the quartering of troops in private homes in peacetime without consent of the owner.)

Connecticut's eighty-six-year-old law prohibiting the sale or use of contraceptives or giving medical advice on birth control was invalidated in 1965. A test case was instituted following the closing by police of the Planned Parenthood Center of New Haven, Connecticut, and the Supreme Court ruled that it was an unconstitutional invasion of the right of marital privacy.[64] In another controversial area, the court ruled in 1973 that state governments cannot prohibit abortions during the first three months of pregnancy, or after this period if it is necessary to protect the health of the mother.[65] The issue became a politically volatile one, with opposing sides (right-to-life vs. freedom-of-choice) focusing on whether public welfare funds can and/or must be used to finance abortions. The Supreme Court shifted the decision arena away from the courts and toward the legislatures in 1977 by ruling that the Constitution does not require states and cities to provide such abortions.[66] In 1980, the Supreme Court ruled that the congressional ban of federal payments for most abortions (the Hyde Amendment) does not violate the constitutional rights of poor women.[67] The decision cut off abortion funds for an estimated 250,000 to 300,000 women a year, with only about 2,000 women continuing to qualify for allowable abortion—promptly reported rape, incest, or "where the life of the mother would be endangered if the fetus were carried to term."

States attempt to control abortions

At the same time anti-abortionists were cutting off federal funds for abortions, they were also lobbying state legislatures for laws that would curtail the breadth of the Court's 1973 decision. Passage of restrictive state laws resulted in another round of adjudication. In these cases, the Court held to its original opinion that abortion was shielded by the right to privacy. In 1983, the Court invalidated Missouri, Virginia, and Ohio statutes in which the states had adopted the provisions of an Akron, Ohio, ordinance that had become a model for the anti-abortionist movement. At the same time, the Court permitted some state legislation on the subject. In *Planned Parenthood Assn. of Kansas City* v. *Ashcroft* the Court upheld a Missouri law requiring unemancipated minors to have parental or judicial consent for abortions; in *Simopoulos* v. *Virginia* it upheld Virginia's requirement that the second trimester abortions be performed in licensed hospitals.[68]

Reflecting the growing impact of Reagan appointments, the Supreme Court began to chip away at *Roe* by partially reestablishing the states' right to restrict access to abortion, in *Webster* v. *Reproductive Health Services* (1989), and *Hodgson* v. *Minnesota* (1990).[69] *Webster* granted states more freedom to restrict abortions and *Hodgson* approved a state requirement that teenagers seeking an abortion must get parental consent.

The politics of abortion ushered in by the 1973 *Roe* decision zeroed in on the Supreme Court's use of judicial power and, more specifically, on its attempt to settle the dispute between pro-life and pro-choice groups on the issues of when life begins, whether or not the fetus is a person with rights, and the nature of a woman's right to privacy. The Court's compromise was accepted by pro-choice forces and rejected by pro-life advocates. Professor Malcolm Goggin has characterized this as the "old" politics of abortion and then describes the more proliferated and decentralized "new" politics of abortion that has developed following the 1989 *Webster* decision. The new politics is even more heated and divisive than the old, raging in all branches and levels of government, but the new politics of abortion makes all 50 states separate battlegrounds. Both sides attempted to apply abortion litmus tests to Supreme Court nominees Robert Bork and David Souter but the state legislatures, with gubernatorial vetoes and threats of vetoes, and state referenda, have moved into the political limelight. Many veteran state legislators feel they have no place to hide in what is essentially a "no-win" struggle between two almost equally balanced groups of rigidly polarized, zealous "ideologues."

The early 1990s in the post-*Webster* era found state legislatures, governors, and federal courts crowding the center of the abortion stage as the two extremes vied for their approval. Pennsylvania and Guam passed strong pro-life legislation and it promptly ended up in court. South Carolina's legislature required one parent to be notified before a minor can get an abortion, and West Virginia banned most Medicaid payments for abortions. Voters rejected pro-life issues on the ballot in Oregon, Nevada, and Texas, and governors vetoed strong pro-life legislation in Utah and Louisiana, but proponents continued the fight, achieving a new tough law in Utah and overriding the veto in Louisiana. Connecticut became the first state to make abortion legal by statute, making abortions available without regard to the future of *Roe* v. *Wade,* and the Maryland legislature passed what many have called the nation's most liberal abortion law in early 1991. The congressional prohibition against abortion counseling in federally funded family planning clinics was upheld by the Supreme Court in a 1991 decision (*Rust* vs. *Sullivan*), even though operated by state and local authorities. The boundary lines for the controversy were broadened even more by the development of the French abortion pill, RU-486, which induces miscarriages in the first seven weeks of pregnancy. A 1991 resolution of the New Hampshire legislature offered that state as an American testing ground for the pill.

State and local governments seem destined to remain at the heart of the new politics of abortion as we approach the 21st century, struggling almost hopelessly for a rational solution to this fiercely emotional conflict. Rather than overturning *Roe* v. *Wade,* as many expected, the Court divided 5–4 in favor of a middle-ground approach allowing restrictions on abortions unless they constitute an "undue burden" on a woman's right to choose. Specifically upheld were provisions requiring that a woman be told about the risks and alternatives to abortion; that they must wait 24 hours after receiving this information before having one; that unmarried girls under 18 get the consent of one parent or the permission of a state judge; and that doctors keep records on each abortion performed, some of it subject to public inspection. By a different 5–4 majority, the Court struck down the requirement that married women notify their husbands of their plans to undergo an abortion. In some, the decision reflected many of the sharp divisions of the American people concerning abortion, continued significant parts of the *Roe* decision by the narrowest of margins, and added fuel to the bitter battle at the level of the states.

Another state legislative and judicial struggle has been growing in recent years over the complicated legal and moral issues related to efforts to avoid lingering death. This was dramatized by the 1976 case of comatose Karen Quinlan,[70] whose parents obtained a court order from the New Jersey Supreme Court to remove the respirator after physicians refused to do so. Even after the respirator was removed she was fed artificially and lived for ten more years, but the ruling in the case, relying on the right to privacy and the right of parents as guardians, has been influential on court decisions in many other states. The Quinlan case has stirred many state legislatures to adopt "living will" legislation, beginning with California in 1976 and expanding to 41 states and the District of Columbia by 1991. The more recent case of Nancy Cruzan,[71] comatose since a 1983 car crash, was bounced back and forth between the Missouri and U.S. Supreme Courts, with the state court refusing in 1988 to allow removal of the feeding tube. On appeal, the U.S. Supreme Court ruled by a 5–4 vote in 1990 that an individual has a right to refuse medical care that prolongs life, but held that Missouri could prevent the withdrawal of treatment in the absence of "clear and convincing" evidence that Cruzan would have wanted to die. The parents came back to the state court with additional witnesses and removal of the tube was approved. Cruzan died 12 days later, three years after her parents sought court approval of her right to die. Henry R. Glick has studied extensively the politics of the right to die, and reports some of the same alignments as in the politics of abortion, with those states having larger percentages of Catholic population generally being the states that have not passed or have delayed passing living will laws. The prime mover in favor of such legislation has been the Society for the Right to Die. Glick was surprised to discover that the elderly as a group have not been significantly involved in lobbying on this subject.[72].

The politics of the right to die

The Fourteenth Amendment and Equal Protection

The Fourteenth Amendment's provision for "equal protection of the laws" has come to mean much more than the guarantee of fundamental freedoms against the unreasonable application of state or local police power. According to the highest judicial interpretation, it also means equality of opportunity in state-supported institutions of learning. With that principle assumed, segregation of races in the public assemblages and facilities of the states was to burden the courts with a weighty problem of interpretation in terms of sociological jurisprudence. In this American dilemma, was segregation in itself a denial of equal protection to the minority race? And, if not, what was essential to equal protection within the pattern of segregation?

Doctrinal guidance for half a century was set forth in 1896 by the Supreme Court in *Plessy* v. *Ferguson*,[73] a case concerning racial separation in railway travel in Louisiana. The Court held that the state requirement of separation was not contrary to the "equal protection" clause but was a reasonable use of police power in accordance with established "usages, customs, and traditions." "Separate but equal" accommodations were constitutional. A vigorous dissent by Justice John M. Harlan posed a point for the future with the observation that the "Constitution is color blind."

"Separate but equal"

After forty years the Supreme Court began to weigh the facts of segregation in state institutions. In 1938, it held that a black citizen of Missouri was "entitled to be admitted to the law school of the State University in the absence of proper provision for his legal training within the state."[74] State provision for his training in another state fell short of "equality of legal right." In 1950, the Supreme Court decided that the refusal to admit a black to the law school of the University of Texas was denial of equal protection, although he was offered training at a law school for blacks.[75] The opinion pointed out that the latter school was not equal to that for whites in faculty, facilities, recognition, and opportunity for contacts.

The Court next challenged segregation itself in the light of its sociological and psychological implications. In May 1954, in a unanimous opinion of the Court in *Brown* v. *Board of Education*,[76] Chief Justice Warren observed categorically that in public education "the doctrine of 'separate but equal' has no place. Separate educational facilities are inherently unequal." However, desegregation in the South and the North, like the building of Rome, was not to be achieved in a day. It soon became apparent that the Court requirements for "all deliberate speed" would be met with more deliberation than speed.

Separate "inherently unequal"

Token integration

Segregation by law first disappeared in the District of Columbia, with slower and more gradual desegregation beginning in the border states. Token integration took place in parts of Arkansas, North Carolina, Tennessee, Virginia, and Texas, with others following the Deep South pattern of hard-core resistance. Efforts of the Deep South to maintain segregated education have been described by Professor Robert J. Harris as follows:

> Many of the states in the South . . . pursued policies of aggressive defiance. Official resistance took such forms as public school closing and leasing laws, pupil placement laws, interposition resolutions, closing of schools by executive proclamation, and executive maintenance of segregated education by force in the name of law and order, as exemplified by the employment of state police by Governor Allen Shivers to maintain segregated education in Mansfield, Texas, and employment of the National Guard by Governor Orval Faubus in Little Rock to prevent nine children from entering Central High School.[77]

Shift in enforcement

Cracks in the segregationist armor of the Deep South appeared in 1960 and 1961 when token integration was carried out under court orders in the New Orleans public school system and at the University of Georgia. Because neither the president nor Congress had developed a policy or plan for meeting the constitutional crisis in race relations, the responsibility for implementing the Supreme Court decision initially fell on the federal judiciary, and primarily on the United States district courts. Some of the burden of overseeing and policing desegregation of the public schools was shifted away from the courts to the Congress and the executive branch by the passage of the Civil Rights Act of 1964. Under the law, the U.S. Office of Education was required to report within two years on progress of school desegregation at all levels, and to give technical and financial assistance, if requested, to school systems in the process of desegregating. The Attorney General was authorized to file suit for desegregation of schools and, where voluntary compliance had been sought unsuccessfully, federal agencies were authorized to cut off funds to discriminatory state and local programs. Passage of the precedent-breaking Elementary and Secondary Education Act of 1965 made this a potent weapon in federal acceleration of school desegregation.

The common pattern of racial desegregation of schools, white flight to the suburbs, and the resulting resegregation brought the courts back into the picture on the twin issues of racial balance and busing. In the *Swann* case in 1971, the Supreme Court unanimously ruled that courts have the power to require busing of students when school authorities fail to meet their obligations to desegregate.[78] The decision agreed that objections to busing may be valid if the time or distance of travel is so great as to risk the health of the children or significantly hamper the educational process. It also ruled that courts may alter school attendance zones, may group zones not having common boundaries, and may prohibit school boards from using future school construction or abandoning old ones to perpetuate or reestablish segregated systems. On racial balance, the Court said that every school need not reflect the racial composition of the system as a whole, but a court may use the racial ratio in the school system as a whole as a starting point to determine whether a violation exists.

Racial balance and busing

By the opening of school in the fall of 1971, federal judges had applied the principles of the *Swann* decision in cases involving more than forty school districts. The impact was immediate, and forced busing became very much a political issue. The controversy over busing caused a long stalemate on congressional legislation for aid to education, and caused Chief Justice Burger to issue an unusual opinion indicating misgivings about lower courts' interpretations of the *Swann* decision. While upholding extensive busing in Winston-Salem, he denied that a fixed racial balance is required in the schools. In 1974, the U.S. Supreme Court appeared to call a halt to required cross-district busing. In a 5–4 decision in the *Roth* case, the Court ruled that suburban school districts surrounding Detroit could not be forced into participation in metropolitan busing unless they were found guilty of helping to segregate schools in the metropolitan area. In 1979, however, the Court upheld massive busing in Dayton, Ohio, to "eradicate the effects" of segregated schools; in 1980, it refused to set aside Cleveland's court-ordered systemwide busing plan to achieve racial balance; and in 1981, it allowed a halt in mandatory busing in Los Angeles, the nation's second largest school district, following California voters' adoption of a constitutional amendment permitting busing only in cases of "intentional segregation." In 1991, one decade later, the Court made a decision interpreted by civil rights leaders as easing up on an earlier requirement that Oklahoma City schools maintain racial balance indefinitely.[79] See figure 4.1 for one cartoonist's unfavorable interpretation of the decision. The inconsistency of the Court points up the complexity of the desegregation issue.

The busing backlash

As affirmative action programs and quota systems by educational institutions became increasingly common, aimed at correcting years of racial discrimination, some people began to charge reverse discrimination. In 1978, the U.S. Supreme Court had to decide whether the University of California Medical College at Davis had discriminated against white applicant Allan Bakke in denying him admission. Bakke argued that his being white caused sixteen less-qualified blacks, Hispanics, and other minorities to be admitted instead of him. In a 5–4 decision, the Court ruled that Bakke must be admitted because this particular affirmative action program was inflexibly biased against white applicants, but it continued to uphold college admission programs that give special advantage to minorities to help remedy past discrimination.[80] The two-sided decision left many unanswered questions, but stayed away from extremes on either side. For a brief period at the end of 1990, an education official of the Bush administration announced that most minority scholarships are race-based and therefore il-

Reverse discrimination and Bakke

Figure 4.1
One interpretation of the
Supreme Court's easing up
on busing requirements.
*(Reprinted by permission of
the* News and Observer *of
Raleigh, N.C.)*

legal. The political fire-storm this precipitated led to a quick retraction and assurance of a four-year period in which current scholarship programs would be safe from government scrutiny. By 1992, Education Secretary Lamar Alexander had announced enough exceptions to the policy that it was expected to have "no practical effect" on minority students.

The logical extension of the desegregation decision in the *Brown* case to other areas of public activity has been taking place slowly but steadily since 1954. Federal courts invalidated segregation by law in publicly supported parks, golf courses, swimming pools, and other recreation facilities; publicly operated eating places; public transit facilities; public libraries, and other state and local activities involving service to all citizens. The use of state and local authority to preserve segregation and to make other racial distinctions in a hundred and one ways has now been clearly established as unconstitutional. Although segregated swimming pools were ruled unconstitutional, blacks were turned down in 1971 by a 5–4 Supreme Court decision in efforts to force Jackson, Mississippi, to reopen pools on an integrated basis. Justice Burger reminded critics that "all that is good is not commanded by the Constitution and all that is bad is not forbidden by it."[81] Efforts to alleviate *de facto* segregation in housing, employment, and other areas of American life continue, but the emphasis has shifted more to economic and political pressures than to adjudication.

Governmental efforts to encourage minority business ownership and success by requiring "set-asides" in the award of construction or procurement contracts have received conflicting yes and no Supreme Court decisions in recent years. In the first case, *Fullilove* v. *Klutznick* (1980), the Court held that federal legislation requiring state and local governments to set aside 10 percent of public works projects for minority-owned businesses (blacks, Spanish-speaking, Orientals, Indians, Eskimos, and Aleuts), did not violate equal protection of the law. It was significant as the first federal statutory effort to use express racial quotas in the administration of public works contracts. After nearly a decade of apparent widespread acceptance of this concept for overcoming the continuing effects of past discrimination, with some 36 states and 190 localities adopting their own versions of the program, the Court ruled that a nonfederal set-aside program violated the equal protection clause. In *City of Richmond v. J. A. Croson Company* (1989), the Court spelled out strict criteria for approving set-asides (stronger demonstration of past and/or present discrimination, and more careful consideration of race-neutral methods), and held that the Richmond case, with its 30 percent set-aside requirement, did not qualify. These two cases demonstrate the zigzag efforts of the courts (and of our society) to find a middle ground between distasteful racial quotas and an idealistic color-blind public policy of equal protection of the laws.[82]

Set-asides for minority businesses

The equal protection clause and an increasing number of statutory prohibitions on sex discrimination constitute limitations on state and local policies and actions that have traditionally treated women differently from men. A more sweeping elimination of sex discrimination was advanced by Congress in 1971 in the form of the Equal Rights Amendment, but only thirty-five of the thirty-eight required states had ratified by the original deadline of March 22, 1979. The legislatures in four of these states (Idaho, Kentucky, Nebraska, and Tennessee) voted to rescind their approval votes. Congress voted an unprecedented extension of the deadline (to June 30, 1982), but it was never clear whether three or seven additional states were required to ratify the proposed Twenty-Seventh Amendment. In any case, the new deadline passed without the required thirty-eight ratifying states.

Sex discrimination and ERA

While the proposal for a federal ERA amendment was being sidetracked in the ratification process, seventeen states did not wait for a change in the U.S. Constitution but adopted their own ERA. All but two of the adoptions occurred in the early 1970s when the fervor for the national ERA was at its peak. Utah and Wyoming had adopted equal rights amendments in the 1890s. The impact of the state ERAs has varied from state to state depending on the standards being used to enforce them. ERAs have had the most impact in states where officials have been supportive. In some ERA states, sympathetic attorneys general have simply ruled discriminatory laws unconstitutional. In an unusual 1991 case on sex discrimination, the U.S. Supreme Court unanimously struck down a company's exclusion of fertile women from hazardous jobs (the "fetal protection" policy), saying these decisions must be left up to the parents rather than the employers.[83] The court in effect concluded that equal opportunity begets equal danger, but left employers worried about the Catch 22 of "we're sued if we do and sued if we don't."

A relative newcomer to the civil rights political arena is the issue of statutory and constitutional equal rights for homosexuals. Laws enacted in the early 1970s as part of human rights ordinances often barred discrimination in housing, employment, and other fields because of "sexual and affectional preference." The issue mushroomed politically in Miami and Dade County in 1977 when singer Anita Bryant led a "Save our Children" group in a successful campaign to repeal a gay rights ordinance. Homosexuals experienced similar setbacks in Wichita (Kansas), St. Paul (Minnesota), and Eugene (Oregon), before defeating a statewide proposal in California that would

Homosexuals and civil rights

have provided broadly for dismissal of teachers who engage in homosexual conduct, defined as "advocating, soliciting, imposing, encouraging, or promoting of public or private homosexual activity." The U.S. Supreme Court has upheld state sodomy laws against homosexual attack (Virginia in 1976 and North Carolina in 1978), holding that they are reasonable laws for the protection of public decency, and not specifically for religious reasons, or in violation of the constitutional right to privacy. In 1992 a Vatican letter reaffirmed its stand that homosexuality is an "objective disorder" and that some measures discriminating against homosexuals promote common good. The courts will be busy throughout the 1990s in attempting to apply domestic, family, employment, and housing law to homosexuals.

To protect rights against the conflagrations of public opinion, the framers of the Constitution provided for a judiciary made independent by appointment for life and an assured salary. As a consequence, it is not uncommon to find public opinion supporting one course of action and the Supreme Court defending another. If courts were compelled to follow public opinion, rights would no longer be rights but merely licenses subject to revocation by the prevailing majority. Even though the federal courts are independent, changes in opinion occur as new appointments bring new philosophies and new perspectives to the bench. With the retirement of Chief Justice Earl Warren in 1969 and the gradual replacement of his majority, the activist era of the Court ended. His successors, Warren E. Burger (1969) and William H. Renquist (1986), were "strict *The Burger and* constructionists of the Constitution," and were soon joined by jurists of like mind ap- *Renquist Courts* pointed by Presidents Nixon, Ford, Reagan and Bush. The "Burger Court" as well as the "Renquist Court," did not overturn previous decisions so much as modify their impact by shifting away from emphasis on individual rights and toward law enforcement and traditional moral values. Even with the slowdown of the judicial trends of the 1950s and 1960s, there can be little doubt in the 1980s and 1990s that the state's police power was more than temporarily sensitized to the rights of previously unprotected citizens. The liberty aspect of "liberty under law" has new meaning to state and local governments as a result of its long day in court.

Federal Use of Quasi-Police Powers

The Constitution of the United States does not specifically delegate a "police power" to the federal government. However, several of the powers it does confer give Congress authority to exercise something very much akin to the power to regulate in the interest of the public safety, health, welfare, and morals—a kind of quasi-police power. Congress uses its delegated powers in various ways to supplement or even supersede the local workings of state police power. Broadly defined, this is notably true in the regulation of interstate commerce. Regulation of interstate trade in foods requires inspection, not at the state lines, but at places of processing and often brings federal "police power" to the local scene. The Interstate Commerce Commission in 1955 ordered an end to segregation of interstate passengers in southern stations. A decade *Policing interstate* later, the Supreme Court upheld the use of the interstate commerce power by Congress *commerce* to forbid racial discrimination in places of public accommodation.[84] The interstate commerce power is used to prohibit the shipment of prison products into states where the sale of such products is contrary to state law. There can be no practical differentiation at the state line for the regulation of aviation, radio, and television; consequently, national supervision of these activities applies to both interstate and intrastate operations. National legislation against interstate kidnapping, "white slave" traffic, and auto theft duplicates state jurisdiction and aids the states in punishing violators. State regulation of the issuance and marketing of securities, as in the case of railroad regulation, proved inadequate and, to close the gap, the national government entered the field through the commerce power.

Congress has constitutional police-like powers in addition to the commerce clause. Use of the mails for fraudulent purposes is punishable by legislation based on the postal power, regardless of whether or not it is interstate. Local narcotics peddling is violative of a federal tax law as is "wildcat" distilling of liquor. In the exercise of its spending power, the national government stipulated the conditions of labor working for contractors with government contracts, not a small item in the nation's economy. The war or military powers are used to regulate civilian activities around centers where armed forces are located, and certain practices are prohibited in the interest of military morals and morale. The national government protects its own property wherever that property is located.

Other national uses of police power

Hunting migratory birds is regulated under legislation that implements a treaty, which poses an interesting problem in federalism. Congress attempted to regulate the hunting of migratory birds in 1913, but the law was declared unconstitutional in the lower federal courts.[85] Power to regulate the hunting of migratory birds was not one of the powers delegated to the national government, the courts said. The United States subsequently entered into a treaty that provided for the protection of migratory birds by Canada and the United States. In implementation of the treaty, Congress passed a new migratory bird act and, on test in the Court, the constitutionality of the act was sustained.[86] Congress is empowered by the Constitution to "make all laws which shall be necessary and proper for carrying into execution the foregoing [listed] powers, and all other powers vested by this Constitution in the government of the United States, or in department or office thereof." The ability to make treaties is one of the other powers of the Constitution. The decision in *Missouri* v. *Holland* indicates that Congress may do something in implementing a treaty that it could not do under the Constitution prior to the treaty's existence, that is, regulate the hunting of migratory birds. The implications for the federal system are far-reaching indeed, and considerable controversy has ensued as to the proper scope of the treaty-making and treaty-implementing authority.

Treaties vs. state police power

Americans of this century have utilized national processes for important applications of police power as well as for many important determinations of civil rights. They have come to rely increasingly upon the functions of national and state governments, in coordination or in counterbalance, for the effective exercises of power and for the effective preservation of liberty. Thus, they recognize, in terms of a Toynbee synthesis of democracy, the twin principles of "Law and Freedom in History."

Endnotes

1. *Dartmouth College* v. *Woodward,* 4 Wheaton 518 (1819).
2. *Charles River Bridge* v. *Warren Bridge,* 11 Peters 420 (1837).
3. *Home Building and Loan Association* v. *Blaisdell,* 290 U.S. 398 (1934).
4. Cited by Martin Shapiro and Douglas Hobbs, *American Constitutional Law* (Cambridge, Mass.: Winthrop Publishers, 1978), p. 17.
5. *Gibbons* v. *Ogden,* 9 Wheaton 1 (1824).
6. *Wabash, St. L. and R. Rys. Co.* v. *Illinois,* 118 U.S. 557 (1886).
7. *Houston, East and West Texas Ry. Co.* v. *United States,* 234 U.S. 342 (1913).
8. *Morgan* v. *Virginia,* 328 U.S. 373 (1946).
9. Reported by Randy Arndt, "Supreme Court in 2 rulings limits state, local actions," *Nation's Cities Weekly,* February 27, 1984.
10. See C. W. Collins, *The Fourteenth Amendment and the States* (Boston: Little, Brown and Co., 1912).
11. 16 Wall 36 (1873).
12. 94 U.S. 113 (1876).
13. *Nebbia* v. *New York,* 291 U.S. 502 (1934).
14. *Santa Clara County* v. *Southern Pacific Railroad Company,* 118 U.S. 394 (1886).
15. *Lochner* v. *New York,* 198 U.S. 45 (1905).
16. *West Coast Hotel Company* v. *Parrish,* 300 U.S. 379 (1937).
17. *Nebbia* v. *New York.*
18. *Moore* v. *Dempsey,* 261 U.S. 86 (1923).
19. *Powell* v. *Alabama,* 287 U.S. 45 (1932).
20. *Norris* v. *Alabama,* 294 U.S. 587 (1935).
21. *Chambers* v. *Florida,* 309 U.S. 227 (1940).
22. 18 *U.S. Code Annotated* § 242; *see Screws* v. *United States,* 325 U.S. 91 (1945), and *United States* v. *Sutherland,* 37 F. Supp. 344 (1940).
23. *Mapp* v. *Ohio,* 367 U.S. 643 (1961).
24. *Gideon* v. *Wainwright,* 372 U.S. 335 (1963); *Argersinger* v. *Hamlin,* 407 U.S. 25 (1972).
25. *Malloy* v. *Hogan,* 378 U.S. 1 (1964).
26. *Miranda* v. *State of Arizona,* 384 U.S. 436 (1966). A 1981 expansion of the *Miranda* interpretation held that murder defendants must be warned before psychiatric tests if the results would be used after conviction to help choose life or death as a punishment.
27. *Apodaca* v. *Oregon,* 406 U.S. 404 (1972); *Johnston* v. *Louisiana,* 406 U.S. 356 (1972).
28. *Lockhart* v. *McCree,* 476 U.S. 162 (1986).
29. *McClesky* v. *Kemp,* 481 U.S. 279 (1987).
30. *Penry* v. *Lynaugh,* 57 U.S. Law Week 4958 (1989).
31. *Stanford* v. *Kentucky,* 492 U.S. 361 (1989).

32. *Schneider* v. *State (Town of Irvington)*, 308 U.S. 147 (1939).

33. *Near* v. *Minnesota*, 283 U.S. 697 (1931).

34. *New York Times Company* v. *Sullivan*, 376 U.S. 254 (1964).

35. *Mills* v. *State of Alabama*, 384 U.S. 214 (1966).

36. *Smith* v. *Daily Mail*, 443 U.S. 97 (1979).

37. *Capital Cities Cable, Inc. et al., Petitioners* v. *Richard A. Crisp, Director, Oklahoma Beverage Control Board* (No. 82-1795) *Law Week* 52 (June 19, 1984): 4803–4810.

38. Members of the *City Council of the City of Los Angeles et al.* v. *Taxpayers for Vincent et al.* (No. 82-975) *Law Week* 52 (May 15, 1984).

39. *Texas* v. *Johnson*, 109 S. Ct. 2533 (1989), and *U.S.* v. *Eichman*, 110 S. Ct. 2404 (1990).

40. *Joseph Burstyn, Inc.* v. *Wilson*, 343 U.S. 495 (1952). But a municipal or ordinance imposing prior restraint on showing motion pictures through censorship of the films by municipal authorities does not "on its face" violate the First and Fourteenth Amendment guarantees of free speech and press: *Times Film Corp.* v. *Chicago*, 365 U.S. 43 (1961).

41. *Roth* v. *United States*, 354 U.S. 476 (1957).

42. *Ginzburg et al.* v. *United States*, 354 U.S. 476 (1957).

43. *Miller* v. *California*, 93 S. Ct. 2607 U.S. (1973).

44. *Pope* v. *Illinois*, 481 U.S. 497 (1987).

45. "State lines," *State Legislatures* 10 (August 1984): 9.

46. *Adler et al.* v. *Board of Education of the City of New York*, 342 U.S. 485 (1952). A subsequent decision indicated, however, that a state violates due process of law when it discharges an employee on the sole ground that he has invoked the Fifth Amendment's safeguard against self-incrimination before a committee of the U.S. Senate. *Slochower* v. *Board of Higher Education of City of N.Y.*, 350 U.S. 551 (1956).

47. *Elfbrandt* v. *Russell et al.*, 384 U.S. 11 (1966).

48. *Cole* v. *Richardson*, 405 U.S. 676 (1972).

49. *Law Week* 53 (August 21, 1984): 2096–2097.

50. *Illinois ex rel. McCollum* v. *Board of Education*, 333 U.S. 203 (1948).

51. *Zorach* v. *Clauson*, 343 U.S. 306 (1952).

52. *West Virginia State Board of Education* v. *Barnette*, 319 U.S. 624 (1943), reversing *Minersville School District* v. *Gobitis*, 310 U.S. 586 (1940).

53. *Everson* v. *Board of Education*, 330 U.S. 1 (1947).

54. *Wisconsin* v. *Yoder*, 406 U.S. 205 (1972).

55. *Engel* v. *Vitale*, 370 U.S. 421 (1962); and *Abington School District* v. *Schempp*, 374 U.S. 203 (1963). See Robert H. Birkby, "The Supreme Court and the Bible Belt: Tennessee Reaction to the 'Schempp' Decision." *Midwest Journal of Political Science* 10 (August 1966): 304–319.

56. June 4, 1990. A broad coalition of 21 national educational and religious groups released in early 1991 *The Equal Access Act and the Public Schools: Questions and Answers*, providing consensus guidelines hammered out among varying points of view to assist school members, administrators, teachers, parents, students, and religious leaders, in understanding the meaning of the equal access law.

57. *Law Week* (March 27, 1984): 2533.

58. "Court Decisions Affect States," *State Government News* 26 (August 1983).

59. *Oregon Employment Division* v. *Smith* (1990), 494 U.S. 872 (April 1, 1990).

60. *Dennis Lynch et al., petitioners* v. *Daniel Donnelley et al.* (No. 82–1256) *Law Week* (March 6, 1984).

61. *McGowan* v. *Maryland*, 366 U.S. 420 (1961); *Braunfeld* v. *Brown*, 366 U.S. 599 (1961); and *Gallagher* v. *Crown Kosher Market*, 366 U.S. 617 (1961).

62. *Torcaso* v. *Watkins*, 367 U.S. 339 (1961).

63. G. Alan Tarr, "Church and State in the States," *Washington Law Review*, 64 (January, 1989), pp. 73–110, and "Church-State Issues and State Constitutions," *Intergovernmental Perspective*, 13 (Spring, 1987), pp. 27–30.

64. *Griswold* v. *Connecticut*, 381 U.S. 479 (1965).

65. *Roe* v. *Wade*, 410 U.S. 113 (1973).

66. *Beal* v. *Doe*, 432 U.S. 438 (1977).

67. *Harris* v. *McRae*, 100 S. Ct. 2671 (1980). For comprehensive consideration of this issue, see Maris Vinovskis and Carl Schneider, *The Law and Politics of Abortion* (Lexington, Mass.: Lexington Books, 1980).

68. "Court Decisions," *State Government News* 26 (August 1983): 13.

69. *Webster* v. *Reproductive Health Services* 109 S. Ct. 3040 (1989). *Hodgson* v. *Minnesota,* 110 S. Ct. 2926 (1990). This discussion of the politics of abortion follows closely the excellent analysis by Malcolm L. Goggin in his "The New Politics of Abortion," a paper presented at the annual meeting of the American Political Science Association at San Francisco, August 30–September 2, 1990.

70. *In the Matter of Karen Quinlan* (355 A.2d 647, 1976).

71. *Cruzan* v. Director, Missouri Dept. of Health (1990).

72. Henry R. Glick, "The Right-to-Die: State Policymaking and the Elderly," *Journal of Aging Studies,* 1991 (Greenwich, Conn. J.A.I. Press, Inc.) Glick reports in detail on litigative and legislative efforts on this issue in California, Florida, and Massachusetts.

73. *Plessy* v. *Ferguson*, 163 U.S. 537 (1896).

74. *Missouri ex rel. Gaines* v. *Canada*, 305 U.S. 337 (1938).

75. *Sweatt* v. *Painter*, 339 U.S. (1950).

76. *Brown* v. *Board of Education*, 347 U.S. 483 (1954).

77. Robert J. Harris, *The Quest for Equality* (Baton Rouge: Louisiana State University Press, 1960), pp. 154–155. For a more detailed account of state resistance measures, see "Race Relations Law Survey, May 1954–May 1957," *Race Relations Law Reporter* 2 (1957): 881.

78. *North Carolina State Board of Education* v. *Swann*, 402 U.S. 43 (1971). For an account of an effort to achieve racial balance by state legislation, see Frank Levy, *Northern Schools and Civil Rights: The Racial Imbalance Act of Massachusetts* (Chicago: Markham Publishing Co., 1971).

79. *Board of Education of Oklahoma City Public Schools* v. *Dowell*, 111 S. Ct. 630 (1991).

80. *Regents of the University of California* v. *Bakke*, 438 U.S. 265 (1978).

81. *Palmer* v. *Thompson*, 403 U.S. 217 (1971).

82. *See* Mitchell F. Rice, "Government Set-Asides, Minority Business Enterprise and the Supreme Court," a paper presented at the annual meeting of the American Political Science Association, San Francisco, August 30–September 2, 1991, for an excellent analysis of *Fullilove* v. *Klutznick* (448 U.S. 488, 1980), and *City of Richmond v. J. A. Croson Company,* 488 U.S. 469 (1989), and their impact on set-aside programs.

83. *United Auto Workers* v. *Johnson Controls* (1991). For an analysis of why individual states differ in laws and policies affecting women, see, "State Differences in Public Policies toward Women: A Test of Three Hypotheses," a paper delivered at the annual meeting of the American Political Science Association, San Francisco, August 29–September 1, 1990. Although abortion policies receive the headlines, Professor Hansen explored causes of differing policy effects in such matters as divorce, child custody or support, credit, insurance, community property, rape, battered women, inheritance, common-law marriage, fair employment, parental leave, comparable worth, and eligibility standards for welfare, Medicaid, and public housing. She discovered that political mobilization by women (proportion of women in the legislature, etc.), shows little independent impact on supportive policies for women, but that a generally liberal polity and political culture in a state leads to more feminist policies.

84. *Heart of Atlanta Motel, Inc.* v. *United States,* 379 U.S. 241 (1964).

85. *United States* v. *Shauver,* 214 Fed. 154 (1914); *United States* v. *McCullagh,* 221 Fed. 288 (1915).

86. *Missouri* v. *Holland,* 252 U.S. 416 (1920).

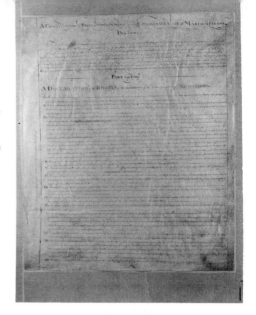

CHAPTER 5

STATE CONSTITUTIONS

Constituting the Permanent Foundation of State Government

Drafting the First Constitutions

The United States is a land of constitutions. Americans have an abiding faith in the idea of written documents to affirm the principle of "the consent of the governed" and to ward off abuses of governments. As early as 1620, a small group of "Americans" aboard a ship anchored off Plymouth Rock signed the Mayflower compact pledging:

Land of constitutions

> We . . . doe by these presents solemnly and mutually in the presence of God, and one another, covenant and combine our selves together into a civill body politick . . . and by vertue hereof to enact, constitute and frame such just and equall lawes, ordinances, acts, constitutions, and offices, as shall be thought most meete and convenient for the generall good of the colonie. . . .

Other forerunners of the modern state constitution were the charters granted by the kings of England for the management and governance of the various colonies. As American-English relations continued to deteriorate in the 1770s, the colonies asked Congress for direction. If the colonists were repudiating the authority of the king, shouldn't they renounce the charters under which they were being governed? However, a number of the colonial leaders were hopeful that the rift between the colonists and the Crown would not go so far as independence. If they proposed a standard state constitution, as was being suggested by some, it would be another move toward separation—and they were not ready for such a drastic step. Thus, the Congress left the states in limbo by suggesting that they deal with the problem of governance as best they could.

With no direction from Congress, the colonists proceeded to create governments, keeping in mind the abuses they had suffered at the hands of the Crown, the representative systems of government that they had already developed, and the contents of their existing charters. In January of 1776, six months before the Declaration of Independence, New Hampshire became the first state ever to adopt a written constitution

New Hampshire leads the way

Title photo: Pictured is the first page of the 1780 constitution of the Commonwealth of Massachusetts, the first state constitution ratified by a direct vote of the people. (Photo courtesy of the office of the Archivist of the Commonwealth.)

drafted by an English colony without consultation with either the Crown or Parliament.[1] Connecticut and Rhode Island found their charters very acceptable and adopted them as constitutions after only minor revision.

The first state constitutions were written primarily by special conventions or existing legislative assemblies, either of which ratified them without a vote of the people. Finally, a public outcry forced Massachusetts to submit a state constitution to the voters for approval or rejection. A conservative constitution was proposed as the first effort, but the Massachusetts voters rejected it. On the second effort, a much improved constitution was ratified by a wide margin and, in 1780, Massachusetts became the first state to have a constitution ratified by the people.[2] The Massachusetts action affirmed the theory that legitimate governments rested on the consent of the governed, and this consent was best obtained by a direct vote of the people on the basic law of the state—the constitution.

Some states had constitutions drafted and ratified by legislatures; others had constitutions drafted and ratified by special conventions; Massachusetts had a constitution ratified by the people. In all cases, the constitutions were regarded as the fundamental written law guaranteeing certain fundamental rights that could not be taken away by ordinary acts of legislatures. New state courts began to test laws against these constitutions, thereby exercising the power of judicial review. By 1787, the authority of judges to declare laws invalid that were contrary to constitutions seemed to be supported by the best legal opinion.[3] Thus, the drafters of the U.S. Constitution, many of them experienced in state government, probably anticipated a similar role for the federal judiciary.

People decide in Massachusetts

After 200 years, the concept of a constitution as the fundamental law remains the foundation of state government, and state courts continue to determine the validity of legislative acts by the process of judicial review.

Constitutions fundamental

The State Constitution in the Federal Arrangement

Even though state constitutions are the "supreme law of the state," they are framed within the limits of the powers delegated, implied, or inherent in the national government. In other words, state constitutions are subordinate to the "supreme law of the land" as defined in Article VI of the U.S. Constitution and as interpreted by the federal courts. Thus, the provisions of state constitutions may not be contrary to any provisions of the U.S. Constitution, acts of Congress passed in accordance with the Constitution, or treaties properly made "under the authority of the United States." Even though these national restrictions have been growing in recent decades, a great vacant space in the field of government is still left by the U.S. Constitution, and each state fills this space with a constitutional structure, using its own methods for establishing and changing this structure. A state constitution is the supreme law of the state for all matters that fall outside the national jurisdiction or that are not forbidden to the states. It also may duplicate the jurisdiction of the national government in significant areas over which both the states and the nation have concurrent powers, as in taxation or liquor regulation. In the final analysis, the citizen will find more overlappings than gaps in this constitutional duality.

Subordinate to "supreme law"

Figure 5.1
"Now, you try to get a fire
started while I draft a
constitution."
(From the Rotarian. *By
permission of the
publisher.)*

How State Constitutions Differ from the U.S. Constitution

*State constitutions limit
legislature*

Though they are all called constitutions, the U.S. Constitution and state constitutions
are based on very different premises. Since the national government is one of limited
powers, it must look to the Constitution for authority to act. If it can find no authorizing
language, it is unable to act. On the other hand, state constitutions are considered to
contain restrictions that limit the authority of state government, primarily the legislative assembly. Unless a constitutional provision exists that limits the authority of a
state legislature in a given field, the legislature is free to act. So the federal Constitution
delegates powers that may be exercised by the national government while the state
constitution identifies the powers that may not be exercised by state government.

While the basic concepts of the two kinds of constitutions may differ, ordinary
statutes of both Congress and the state legislatures are similar. They both authorize
the use of power within the framework of constitutional authority. Of course, Congress
can authorize only what the Constitution permits. At the state level, legislatures—the
custodians of the powers reserved to the states and the people—dole out all power not
restricted by the state constitution.

The Political Nature of Constitutions

State constitutions should be recognized at the outset as political documents. This is true even though they may have gained reverence through age or theoretical neutrality from a convention of nonpartisan delegates. Governmental power is inherently political. And since a constitution dictates the configuration of power to be exercised by governmental institutions, proposals to alter the power structure are wrought with political struggle. Philosophical conservatives may strive to minimize the role of state and local governments with a constitution full of restrictive language; liberals may want government vested with generous grants of authority to carry out numerous programs. In addition to a confrontation between conservatives and liberals, there are scores of battles among interest groups, all asserting influence to win a constitution framed to enhance their particular endeavors. Even when the processes of constitutional revision are supposed to be nonpartisan, political parties are drawn into the fray by constitutional provisions dealing with legislative apportionment, rules governing voting rights, or the allocation of power to a branch of government that is constantly dominated by one party or the other. Partisan politics may also erupt when an interest group allied with one party is being affected by amendments. Political bickering all through the constitutional convention of 1967 in New York resulted in a vote of "no confidence" in the convention by a 3–1 defeat of the proposed constitution at the polls.[4] It is not uncommon to have the best of efforts at constitutional revision destroyed by the politics involved in change.

Political struggles over constitutions

When the first states decided to frame governments with written constitutions, they set a pattern that was to become a standard for new states. Before a new territory could be considered for statehood, Congress passed an "enabling act" that required, among other things, a constitution as a condition for membership in the Union. From time to time, Congress would even specify language or principles to be included in the document before it would be acceptable.

Enabling acts require constitutions

The enabling act for Colorado, for example, dictated that "the constitution shall be republican in form . . . not be repugnant to the constitution of the United States" and provide for "perfect toleration of religious sentiment." Congress required the state of Nevada to prohibit the institution of slavery, to endorse "perfect toleration of religious sentiment," and to disclaim rights to unappropriated public lands. California was told it could not tax "nonresident proprietors" at a higher rate than residents; that all navigable waters shall be common highways; and that it couldn't tax the public domain of the United States.

Even though states have had constitutions for over 200 years, less than half of the people are aware of their existence. In a survey conducted by the U.S. Advisory Commission on Intergovernmental Relations, only 44 percent of the respondents said their state had its own constitution, and five percent ventured that the state had its own but also relied on the federal constitution. Nineteen percent said states relied on the federal constitution and 32 percent didn't know or gave no answer.[5]

Many people unaware of constitutions

State Constitutions Serve Four Functions

1. States provide bill of rights

Chapter 4 outlined the process whereby the U.S. Bill of Rights has become the bill of rights for every state through the Fourteenth Amendment. However, interpreting "due process" and "equal protection" in the Fourteenth Amendment to mean protection for citizens against abuses of state governments is primarily a twentieth century development. Prior to such interpretation, people had to look to their own state constitutions for protection of rights. As a consequence, the first article of most state constitutions is a "declaration of rights" or a "bill of rights." For the first 150 years of the nation's experience, these provisions were the primary barriers against state abuses. Many of the rights guaranteed in state constitutions were the same as those found in the national bill of rights, addressing such subjects as freedom of speech, press, religion, assembly, protection in criminal procedures, quartering of troops, and equal protection. As long as the U. S. Supreme Court was liberally interpreting the federal Bill of Rights, it could have been argued that the states' bills of rights were largely unnecessary. However, with the evolution of a more conservative philosophy on the Court in the 1980s and 1990s, the states' bills of rights become more significant. As one scholar put it: ". . . the conservative majority on the U.S. Supreme Court of the 1980s has caused civil libertarians to question that court's capacity to provide adequate protection for individual rights."[6]

The U. S. Supreme Court paved the way for state action in 1980 when it unanimously agreed that a state had a sovereign right to go beyond the federal Bill of Rights in protecting citizens' rights as long as the decisions were clearly based on state constitutional provisions.[7] With this authority, state courts in the 1980s ruled in more than 350 cases in such a manner that their constitutions gave more protection to individual rights than the U.S. Constitution.[8] As examples, 18 states have their own equal rights amendments to prevent sex discrimination; Pennsylvania citizens have a right to a clean environment; New York, Mississippi and other states have stricter rules of evidence than the U.S. Supreme Court.[9]

2. Structures government

The constitution prescribes the state's form of government, within the federal requirement that it be republican in character. All state constitutions provide for the separation of powers into the legislative, executive, and judicial branches of government, with separate articles describing the form and procedures of each. They often specify the creation and continuance of certain agencies of government deemed permanently essential to the state, such as a land board, a fish commission, or a board of higher learning. Local governments are also structured in the state constitution, often to the extent of identifying the local offices to be filled by election.

3. Allocates power

Not only does the constitution structure the government but it also assigns the powers to be exercised by the various branches, agencies, and levels of government. Often the constitution will mandate procedures to be followed in the exercise of power. For example, all state constitutions carefully specify the route to be followed by bills moving through the legislative assembly. A number of state constitutions contain provisions for exercise of home rule powers by cities and counties, written in sufficient detail to make them self-executing without additional legislation.

Since the legislative assembly has authority to act on all state and local matters not restricted by constitutional language, state constitutions serve to limit power. The constitution's very existence is a barrier to legislative action. Limitation of power is most readily seen in state legislative articles where drafters included lists of subjects on which legislatures may not pass local legislation. Another common limitation is found in the finance articles of constitutions where legislatures are prohibited from imposing certain kinds of taxes, bonding the state, or taxing certain properties. As a matter of fact, if the constitution addresses any subject, the legislature must accept that as the final word.

4. Limits legislatures

Features and Contents of State Constitutions

Despite a wide variety of detail and language, state constitutions have been cut from a common cloth when it comes to basic design. This similarity can be traced to the functions to be served by state constitutions—functions that are important in every state. Essentially, constitutions start with a preamble, commence with a bill of rights, and then move to the three branches of state government. Prescriptions for local government follow next, with articles on revenue, restrictions on corporations, and finally a section on miscellaneous matters. Constitutions are divided into major portions called articles, which are in turn subdivided into sections (Figure 5.2).

Constitutions divided into articles

Most constitutions start with a preamble, stating broad purposes and, in many cases, invoking divine guidance: "We the people of Alaska, grateful to God. . . ." Hawaii's constitution takes note of its unique heritage in the preamble: "We the people of the State of Hawaii, . . . mindful of our Hawaiian heritage, . . . and with an understanding heart toward all the peoples of the earth. . . ." As in the national Constitution, the preamble is the introduction to provisions of rights and powers, and is usually a collection of glittering generalities, rather than an actual statement of rights and powers.

Preamble: a general greeting

Usually following the preamble is the bill or declaration of rights substantially duplicating the provisions of the first ten amendments of the national Constitution. Its provisions are designed, in part, to prevent state and local authorities from interfering with the individual freedoms of worship, speech, press, assembly, and petition; to safeguard private property rights; and to ensure fair or proper trial and treatment of accused persons. Some older bills of rights, as in the constitutions of Kentucky and Tennessee, provide superfluous sermons on popular sovereignty and natural rights, even asserting or implying a right to revolt against abusive and arbitrary exercises of governmental power. There are also examples of modern additions to bills of rights, as in the Montana provision that "laws for the punishment of crime shall be founded on the principles of reformation and prevention." Many state constitutions place the article on voting rights immediately after the bill of rights, apparently regarding that as a logical sequence.

Bill of rights

Every state constitution provides for a structure or framework of government by outlining three branches of government: legislative, executive, and judicial. It sets forth powers, functions, and limitations for these branches and authorizes ways or means for

Articles on structure

Figure 5.2

The order and titles of the various articles in state constitutions may vary from state to state but this montage of articles of the Pennsylvania constitution depicts the general pattern.

CONSTITUTION
of the
COMMONWEALTH OF PENNSYLVANIA

PREAMBLE

We, the people of the Commonwealth of Pennsylvania, grateful to Almighty God for the blessings of civil and religious liberty, and humbly invoking His guidance, do ordain and establish this Constitution.

Article I
DECLARATION OF RIGHTS

That the general, great and essential principles of liberty and free government may be ... established. WE DECLARE THAT —

Article II
THE LEGISLATURE

Legislative Power

Section 1. The legislative power of this Commonwealth shall be vested in a General Assembly, which shall consist of a Senate and a House of Representatives.

Election of Members; Vacancies

Section 2. Members of the General Assembly shall be chosen at the general election every second year. Their term of service shall begin on the first day of December next

Article III
LEGISLATION

A. Procedure

Passage of Bills

Section 1. No law shall be passed except by bill, and no bill shall be so altered or amended, on its passage through either House, as to change its original purpose.

Article IV
THE EXECUTIVE

Executive Department

Section 1. The Executive Department of this Commonwealth shall consist of a Governor, Lieutenant Governor, Attorney General, Auditor General, State Treasurer, and Superintendent of Public Instruction and such other officers as the General Assembly may from time to time prescribe.

Article V
THE JUDICIARY

Unified Judicial System

Section 1. The judicial power of the Commonwealth shall be vested in a unified judicial system consisting of the Supreme Court, the Superior Court, the Commonwealth Court, courts of common pleas, community courts, municipal and traffic courts in the City of Philadelphia, such other courts as may be provided by law and justices of the peace. All courts and justices of the peace and their jurisdiction shall be in this

Article VI
PUBLIC OFFICERS

Selection of Officers Not Otherwise Provided for in Constitution

Section 1. All officers, whose selection is not provided for in this Constitution, shall be elected or appointed as may be directed by law.

Article VII
ELECTIONS

Qualifications of Electors

Section 1. Every citizen 21 years of age, possessing the following qualifications, shall be entitled to vote at all elections subject, however, to such laws requiring and regulating the registration of electors as the General Assembly may enact.

Article VIII
TAXATION AND FINANCE

Uniformity of Taxation

Section 1. All taxes shall be uniform, upon the same class of subjects, within the territorial limits of the authority levying the tax, and shall be levied and collected under

Article IX
LOCAL GOVERNMENT

Local Government

Section 1. The General Assembly shall provide by general law for local government within the Commonwealth. Such general law shall be uniform as to all classes of local government regarding procedural matters.

Home Rule

Section 2. Municipalities shall have the right and power to frame and adopt home rule charters. Adoption, amendment or repeal of a home rule charter shall be by refer-

putting persons and money to work to carry on their functions. The constitution also provides for separation of powers combined with a system of interbranch checks.

Articles on local governments

Following the articles that structure the state government are those providing for local governments. In some constitutions, these matters may be inclusively covered by a single article on political subdivisions or local governments. In others, such as Arkansas, Article 12 addresses municipal governments, Article 13 covers counties, and Article 14 deals with local school districts. Articles on local government vary widely in detail. Some constitutions have one or two paragraphs on key issues of local government and leave the rest to action by the state legislature; others will ramble through several thousand words, protecting county boundaries, county seats, elected officials, and townships.

Limitations and mandates

Correction of the negative historical experiences of states can often be found in constitutions. As a result of the reckless financial practices of local governments during the 1800s, almost all state constitutions have articles that limit the taxing, bonding, and spending practices of local as well as state governments. Building on this broad base of restrictions, voters in the 1970s and 1980s imposed additional restrictions on the legislatures' control of finances. Beyond the financial restrictions, the mandates and limitations of state constitutions tend to reflect the peculiar experiences of each state. As an example, if the influence of railroads jeopardized the integrity of state government at some point in history, the state will have constitutional provisions prohibiting members of the legislature from accepting free passes for riding the railroads.

Miscellaneous articles

Other common articles in state constitutions include education, the elective franchise, legislative apportionment, initiative and referendum, public lands, and provisions for amendments. Some articles reflect the particular interests of the states. For example, Wyoming has an article on "mines and mining"; Colorado on "mining and irrigation"; Mississippi on "levees"; South Carolina on "alcoholic liquors and beverages"; Hawaii on "Hawaiian affairs"; California on "usury"; Arkansas on "railroads, canals and turnpikes"; and New York on "conservation" and "canals." The constitutions of states boasting large cities, such as New York, Pennsylvania, and Illinois, have been required to include special provisions on local powers, or the organization of the judiciary for the urban centers. Most constitutions include a "general" or "miscellaneous" article to catch all of the unclassified items not included elsewhere. Included in the miscellaneous article will be specifications of the "Great Seal" of the state, delineation of boundaries, regulation of lotteries, requirements for oaths, location of the state capitol, control of alcohol, continuity of governments in case of enemy attack, and other subjects otherwise left unaddressed.

Length of State Constitutions

Because they reflect a variety of political cultures, state constitutions vary in length. They are longer than their forerunners of the Revolutionary period, when Virginia based its government on a constitutional document of 1,500 words. Professor Alfred de Grazia has graphed the trend toward longer state constitutions in American history,

Table 5.1 Estimated Length of State Constitutions: 1951 and 1991

State	1951	1991	Increase	Percent	Decrease	Percent
Alabama	39,900	174,000	+134,100	336%		
Alaska	——	13,000	——			
Arizona	15,600	28,900	+ 13,300	85%		
Arkansas	20,200	40,700	+ 20,500	101%		
California	72,000	33,400			−38,600	−54%
Colorado	23,100	45,700	+ 22,600	98%		
Connecticut	6,700	9,600	+ 2,900	43%		
Delaware	13,400	19,000	+ 5,600	42%		
Florida	15,000	25,100	+ 10,100	67%		
Georgia	25,000	25,000	0			
Hawaii	——	17,500	——			
Idaho	13,500	21,500	+ 8,000	59%		
Illinois	13,800	13,200			−600	−4%
Indiana	7,800	9,400	+ 1,600	21%		
Iowa	8,000	12,500	+ 4,500	56%		
Kansas	8,100	11,900	+ 3,800	47%		
Kentucky	16,500	23,500	+ 7,000	42%		
Louisiana	63,200	51,400			−11,800	−19%
Maine	10,300	13,500	+ 3,200	31%		
Maryland	22,100	41,300	+ 19,200	87%		
Massachusetts	16,500	24,100	+ 7,600	46%		
Michigan	13,200	20,000	+ 6,800	52%		
Minnesota	15,400	9,500			−5,900	−38%
Mississippi	15,300	24,000	+ 8,700	57%		
Missouri	30,000	42,000	+ 12,000	40%		

From 6,600 to 174,000 words

demonstrating a marked increase in length for the period from 1776 to 1910. Constitutions adopted thereafter have generally been much shorter, although the longest for the entire span from 1776 to the middle of the twentieth century was adopted in 1921.[10] The constitutions vary in length from about 6,600 words for Vermont to 174,000 words for Alabama. Also notable for length are the constitutions of New York with 80,000 words, Oklahoma with 68,800, and Texas with 62,000. Alaska and Hawaii each came into the Union with relatively brief constitutions of approximately 12,000 words. However, age is not directly correlated to length. Vermont's 1793 constitution is the oldest and shortest with 6,600 words while the Louisiana constitution of 1975 has over 50,000 words. Over the past 40 years, constitutions in most states have increased dramatically in length. (See table 5.1)

Table 5.1   continued

State	1951	1991	Increase	Percent	Decrease	Percent
Montana	17,400	11,900			−5,500	−32%
Nebraska	11,700	20,000	+ 8,300	71%		
Nevada	12,700	20,800	+ 8,100	64%		
New Hampshire	10,900	9,200			−1,700	−16%
New Jersey	12,500	17,100	+ 4,600	37%		
New Mexico	15,200	27,200	+ 12,000	79%		
New York	19,000	80,000	+ 61,000	321%		
North Carolina	8,900	11,000	+ 2,100	24%		
North Dakota	17,600	20,600	+ 3,000	17%		
Ohio	15,400	36,900	+ 21,500	140%		
Oklahoma	35,600	68,800	+ 33,200	93%		
Oregon	12,600	26,100	+ 13,500	107%		
Pennsylvania	15,100	21,700	+ 6,600	44%		
Rhode Island	5,800	11,400	+ 5,600	97%		
South Carolina	30,100	22,500			−7,600	−25%
South Dakota	19,300	23,300	+ 4,000	21%		
Tennessee	8,200	15,300	+ 7,100	87%		
Texas	23,700	62,000	+ 38,300	162%		
Utah	13,300	11,000			−2,300	−17%
Vermont	5,800	6,600	+ 800	14%		
Virginia	23,100	18,500			−4,600	−20%
Washington	14,700	29,400	+ 14,700	100%		
West Virginia	14,900	25,600	+ 10,700	72%		
Wisconsin	10,500	13,500	+ 3,000	29%		
Wyoming	14,600	31,800	+ 17,200	118%		

Source: Calculations by authors based on wordage reported in Book of the States 1950–51 *and* Book of the States 1990–91 *Council of State Governments. Lexington, KY.*

Criticisms of State Constitutions

As the basic law of state government, constitutions dictate the style and substance with which states tackle the reserved powers left in their domain by the national Constitution. Many scholars and researchers have criticized state constitutions as major barriers to a more vigorous state response to the problems evolving from the changing environment discussed in chapter 3. However, the practice of identifying defects of constitutions is a highly subjective exercise. After all, what one researcher may regard as an impediment to progress, another may praise as a valued protection against irresponsible action. Nevertheless, consensus seems to have developed over a few major criticisms that warrant discussion.

Around 40 years ago, the Kestnbaum Commission reported to President Eisenhower that ". . . many state constitutions restrict the scope, effectiveness, and adaptability of state and local action. These self-imposed constitutional limitations make it difficult for many states to perform all of the services their citizens require, and consequently have frequently been the underlying cause of state and local pleas for federal assistance. . . ."[11] In his book *Storm Over the States,* former Governor Terry Sanford called state constitutions ". . . the drag anchors of state progress. . . ."[12]

The most common and most devastating provisions that restrict state governments from a vigorous exercise of reserved powers are in the areas of finance. As a result of irresponsible bonding practices in the 1890s, almost every state included language in its constitution to limit the bonded indebtedness of state and local governments. Unable to function within these restrictions, states were then compelled to adopt amendments to grant specific exemptions for special bonds. As an example, the Ohio constitution authorized a general debt of $750,000, a totally unrealistic level for a large urban state. To overcome this restriction, the voters were called upon to approve $300 million for a World War II veterans' bonus in 1947; up to $500 million for highways in 1953; $150 million for highways and public buildings in 1955; $90 million for a Korean War bonus in 1956; $250 million for classrooms, universities, recreation, conservation, and state buildings in 1963; $500 million for highways in 1964; $290 million for capital improvements in 1965; and $300 million for a Viet Nam bonus in 1974. Wyoming also restricted its flexibility by requiring a two-thirds approval of the electorate to engage in internal improvements. Unable to muster the two-thirds, the constitution was amended four times to exempt various improvements from the rule.

Tax limitations

Even more crippling than the bonding provisions spawned in the 1800s are the new shackles stemming from the tax revolt of the late 1970s and the 1980s. Beginning with Proposition 13, which imposed a variety of constitutional restraints on the California legislature in 1978, the fever for cutting taxes and restraining state budgets has continued unabated. In the 1990 general election alone, eleven states voted on propositions aimed at tax reduction or fee limitations.[13]

Fiscal restraints are not limited to a handful of states. Over half of the states earmark certain tax revenues, thereby limiting the legislature's budgeting flexibility; eighteen states require approval of the people or unusual legislative majorities to approve taxes; most states include tax exemptions in their constitutions; and some states, such as Illinois and Michigan, dictate nongraduated income taxes.

A majority of states restrict the capacities of their governments to function by constitutionally restricting their legislative procedures. Some of the restrictions on legislatures are innocuous procedures that consume valuable time, but many, such as limitations on the length of legislative sessions, have a great impact on the deliberative capacity of the assembly.

As long as states see fit to limit their own exercise of the reserved powers through restrictive constitutional provisions, the federal government will continue to move in to fill the vacuum.

Restrictions on bonding

When citizens are unwilling to delegate authority to the government created by the constitution, then they must assume a role of greater involvement in the decision-making processes. For example, if the state constitution requires a vote of the people to impose taxes or float bonds, then the citizenry must become informed on state and local finances to make learned judgments. Or if the constitution will not entrust appointment powers to a governor and requires election of six state executive officers, the citizenry must commit the time to make those "appointments" with intelligence. Or if the constitution outlines a procedure for citizens to initiate laws or refer acts of the legislature, then voters must be prepared to judge wisely the implications of all measures upon which they are called to vote.

2. Require too much of citizens

The lack of knowledge about candidates and issues has been documented by a variety of surveys and polls taken before and after elections. Faced with some twenty to twenty-five decisions in a single election, unprepared voters resort to random voting on candidates and measures. The names that look familiar and the measure titles with the friendliest phrases receive the votes.

In theory, constitutions should contain only the fundamental principles of government while legislative statutes should deal with the changing, contemporary problems arising from the changing environment of state and local governments. Constitution writers, however, have not been able to restrain themselves from wandering into the statutory. As a member of the 1870 Illinois constitutional convention said to his colleagues:

3. Confuse fundamental and statutory

> It is assumed that when we depart from this hall all the virtue and all the wisdom of the state will have departed with us. We have assumed that we alone are honest and wise enough to determine for the people the ordinary, and in many instances even the most trivial, questions affecting the public welfare; as if the mass of people of the state of Illinois were not as competent hereafter to select others that are honest and capable as they were to select us.[14]

Despite the warnings, every state constitution contains statutory language.

Oklahoma's lengthy constitution is explained in part by the 6,400 words creating a corporation commission and regulating utilities; 2,000 words on the creation and management of emergency medical service districts; 350 words defining who may accept free passes from the railroad; 8,800 words providing for boundaries of counties; and 6,400 words on public debt. It required 3,000 words in Alabama to provide for voter registration, yet California covered the subject in twelve. California avoided brevity in most other articles, however, rambling 850 words on governance of the University of California; 1,140 words on insurance taxation; 1,900 words on liquor control; and well over 10,000 words on other items covered by statutes in other states.

Statutory language is also found in Missouri where the constitution deals with numerous departments of government; in Oregon where 4,000 words are used on debt limit and exceptions to it; in Louisiana where 5,780 words relate to revenue and finance and 4,760 words deal with civil service and personnel, but less than 350 words speak to suffrage and elections; in Maryland where 1,500 words prescribe procedures for handling the state budget; and in New York where 14,000 words are used on the judiciary, over 7,000 controlling local debt (followed by a "bill of rights for local government"), and another flare of rhetoric to delineate the boundaries of a forest preserve,

Poke-O-Moonshine Mountain

giving Poke-O-Moonshine Mountain constitutional status in the process. Because the forest preserve had constitutional status, New York required an amendment in 1979 to trade property with the International Paper Companies, giving New York the unique status of having a constitution that refers to a private company by name. Taken collectively, at least half of the language in state constitutions is statutory rather than fundamental, thereby limiting legislative response to changing times. The dramatic increase in the length of most state constitutions since 1950 can be blamed in large part on the addition of large blocks of statutory language.

4. Perpetuate the archaic

Because drafters of state constitutions were not content to leave statutory matters to legislatures, they created agencies, dictated levels of government, and required the continuance of archaic offices. By giving constitutional sanction to the election of township, municipal, and county offices, many state legislatures find it difficult to provide for the modernization of local governments. County offices, particularly, gained an eternal quality as constitution after constitution mandated their existence and the concomitant fragmentation of county governments. If county government is the "dark continent of American government," as was once said, constitutional provisions ought to be charged as accomplices. Many state agencies and elected administrators have also gained interminable existence in state constitutions, meaning that any state government reorganization must leave islands of power in the rechanneling of authority and accountability.

5. Provide haven for interests

If politics "is the study of influence and the influential," as Harold Lasswell has said, and the "influential are those who get the most of what there is to get,"[15] it is not too difficult to identify the "influential" within a state by the privileges and protections they have secured in their state constitution. Taxpayers' groups and property interests have been able to secure strict and detailed limits on state legislatures' taxing, borrowing, and spending powers. The strength of veterans' groups is revealed in constitutional guarantees of veterans' preference in public employment and even constitutional provisions for bonuses, pensions, tax exemptions, and other privileges. The influence of farm interests has been reflected in a variety of special privileges. Roscoe Martin notes the overwhelming concern most state constitutions express for farmers: "every time one turns a page, one stumbles over a milking stool or hears the distant whinny of the ploughmare—but not the cough of the tractor; that came later."[16]

Labor union influence, conversely, is reflected at a low level in most state constitutions. Only a few states specifically guarantee the right to join unions and to bargain collectively. More states have passed so-called "right to work" amendments to their constitutions, actions usually regarded by organized labor as anti-labor victories for coalitions of business and farm groups. Sometimes a small but powerful interest group wins special protection, such as in the New Mexico constitution where real estate brokers and salespeople are guaranteed the right to complete the instruments required in the exchange of property, an obvious victory over the legal profession.

Most provisions of state constitutions that are in violation of the U.S. Constitution have been adjudicated as unenforceable. In some cases, state attorneys general have issued opinions declaring sections unconstitutional. The largest body of unconstitutional language cluttering state documents violates the "one-person, one-vote" rule in reapportionment, or fails to acknowledge the federal court decisions pertaining to residence requirements for voting. Colorado, Montana, and North Dakota promise the right to bear arms to protect property, while the federal courts have frowned on use of deadly force for such purpose; Wyoming's restriction of employment of noncitizens on public works is of questionable validity. *6. Violate "supreme law"*

All state constitutions include some language that has no substantive meaning, that is, it does not accomplish any action or it is so vague as to be unenforceable. The most common use of meaningless verbiage is in permissive authority granted to the legislature when the legislature already has authority to act. Provisions that state "the legislature may" when no other provision of the constitution prevents such action are meaningless. However, they appear frequently, having been inserted to reassure interest groups or legislators that the legislature indeed will have authority to act. *7. Meaningless verbiage*

In addition to unnecessary "permissive" language, constitutions abound in meaningless generalities and unenforceable language. Many state constitutions declare the state to be an inseparable part of the Union and the Constitution to be the supreme law of the land. The Civil War and numerous court decisions have affirmed these truths whether the state constitutions concur or not. The North Carolina constitution declares: "A frequent recurrence to fundamental principles is absolutely necessary to preserve the blessings of liberty." Wyoming claims: "Absolute, arbitrary power over the lives, liberty and property of freemen exists nowhere in a republic, not even in the largest majority." In Virginia: "That no free government, nor the blessings of liberty, can be preserved to any people, but by a firm adherence to justice, moderation, temperance, frugality, and virtue. . . ." Montana: "The state recognizes the distinct and unique cultural heritage of American Indians and is committed in its educational goals to the preservation of their cultural integrity." Vermont: "Laws for the encouragement of virtue and prevention of vice and immorality, ought to be constantly kept in force, and duly executed. . . ." On the whole, claimants of the benefits of these generalities would be hard-pressed to find a court of law that could provide little more than comfort with these unenforceable provisions.

Modern-day advocates of state governments have scanned the horizon for hopeful signs that state constitutions have been revised sufficiently to master the responsibilities of a "new federalism," should one materialize. However, even after decades of effort, state constitutions, on the whole, may be poorer documents of governance than they were 100 years ago. Today, they are more restrictive of state authority, they demand a more unrealistic level of citizen participation, they contain more statutory language, they perpetuate more archaic structures, they protect more interest groups, and they include more meaningless verbiage. If this indictment could be limited to several smaller states, the health of the federal system would not be affected, but it applies to such states as New York, California, and Ohio. *State constitutions still lacking*

Consequences of Inadequate Constitutions

Impede state responsiveness

State constitutions that include more than the basic principles of governance can be an obstacle to responsive state government in the fast-changing 1990s. Talk of a "new federalism" with vigorous, responsive states becomes mere rhetoric when state constitutions prevent legislative action, especially in fiscal affairs. When vast sections of state constitutions are statutory in character, constant amendment is required. At the same time, the cumbersome processes for changing constitutions delay and prevent change. As a result, the constitutions—and the governments they constitute—suffer from a time lag, being more suited for the 1890s than for the 1990s. The processes of government continue impaired by fragmentation of power at both the state and local levels, defying modern concepts of effective administration. Restrictions on tax systems and dedication of revenues result in distorted fiscal programs and priorities. And because the entire process of constitutional change requires a higher level of citizen interest and understanding than is attainable, states seem permanently locked in the past. In summary, the evidence has persuaded the academic and governmental community that continuing revision of state constitutions is essential if state and local governments are going to cope with the growing challenges of the 1990s.

Methods for Revising Constitutions

State constitutions provide a variety of methods for proposing new constitutions or amendments. Three of the methods are fairly common, with the fourth unique to the state of Florida.[17]

Proposals by the Legislative Assembly

Legislatures propose most amendments

Legislative assemblies are the most common source of proposals for constitutional amendments. This method has proved to be more convenient and workable for making minor changes, or adding one or two amendments at a time, while conventions have seemed to be more suitable for overhauling whole constitutions. Figures from the 1980s attest to the dominance of legislatures in proposing amendments. Of the 1,125 amendments considered by the states in the last eight years of the 1980s, 1,030—or 92%—were proposed by legislative assemblies.[18]

All but one of the states provide for legislative proposal of amendments to the voters. (Delaware provides for passage by two successive legislatures with a two-thirds majority to put amendments into effect without a vote of the people.) The constitutional requirements in the other forty-nine states vary widely as to procedure and legislative majorities necessary to submit amendments to the electorate. About one-fourth of the states require passage of a proposal at two successive regular sessions of the legislature. The others permit submission of proposals by action at a single session, but

Require unusual majorities

more than half of them require a two-thirds or three-fifths majority of both houses. There are other restrictions, such as limiting the frequency of proposals or the number per session. In Florida, Georgia, and Oregon the constitution expressly authorizes the legislature to propose new state constitutions for consideration. Since the legislative body is the only route for changing the Virginia constitution, that state's general assembly proposed an extensively revised constitution which the electorate approved in 1970.

When the state legislatures originate proposals for amending constitutions, the process is started with the introduction of the proposed change as a concurrent resolution by a member or a committee of the legislature. It is then referred to an appropriate committee for hearings. The committee then makes its recommendations to the floor and the assembly votes whether or not to forward the proposal to the electorate. If passed by the required vote of both houses (by two consecutive legislative sessions in some states) it is then forwarded to the state's chief elections officer for inclusion on the election ballot.

Occasionally, for various reasons, the legislatures may not wish to assume responsibility for constitutional revision. Perhaps the revision requires more study than is available in a fast-moving session, or perhaps the participation of a "blue ribbon" committee of nonlegislators is desirable, or credibility for revision is sought by avoiding legislative politics. For these and other reasons, legislatures have resorted to the creation of special constitution study commissions. Since each state creates its commission to deal with its particular constitutional problems, the authority and makeup of commissions vary from state to state. As creatures of the legislature, their powers come from the assembly that created them, and they report back to the legislative assembly with recommendations for revision. These recommendations are then subject to the same process of the legislative system as if they had been introduced by a legislator or a committee of the legislature. However, since the commission concentrated its time on the subject of constitutional revision and is usually composed of "blue ribbon" members, its recommendations carry considerable weight in legislative deliberations. Even so, the legislature may still change the recommendations or bury them in committee for the duration.

Constitution study commissions

Proposals by Constitutional Convention

A constitutional convention usually begins when the state legislature submits the question of holding a convention to the voters in an election. (To guarantee that constitutional revision is not prevented by legislative inaction, fourteen state constitutions require that the question of calling a convention be put to the voters periodically.) The constitutions of most states outline the procedure by which the legislature is to call a convention. In states without such provisions, legislatures have exercised a sort of inherent authority over the subject and submitted the question to the electorate without specific authority. State courts have upheld such action. Legislatures are often restricted by the constitution, however, as to when and how a convention election shall be called, such as requiring a two-thirds vote to place the convention call on the ballot. The question of calling a convention may also be put to the voters in certain states by petition. This approach permits a certain number or percentage of the voters to propose an amendment or constitutional convention and requires action by the electorate to be approved or rejected.

Voters decide on "call" of convention

Delegates elected

If a constitutional convention is called, members of the convention are then elected, generally from legislative districts, but sometimes with the addition of a limited number from the state at large. Frequently, able people are more willing to serve in a constitutional convention than in a legislature, the rationale being that they can contribute to the formulation of the basic laws and yet not sacrifice the amount of time legislative service involves.

State constitutions are theoretically supposed to embody the fundamental principles upon which there is wide agreement in the state. A convention divided by partisan politics has difficulty in achieving consensus on mutually acceptable principles. Instead, interest in gaining long-term political advantages through the constitution causes party leaders to push a convention toward division rather than agreement. Anticipating the dangers of partisan politics, states have held conventions with equal numbers of delegates from both parties or bearing no political labels. Bipartisan conventions were held in Missouri in 1943 and in Connecticut in 1965. The nonpartisan election of delegates has become more common since 1968, with about half of the conventions using that method.

Problem of partisan politics

The much debated question of whether constitutional conventions are "above politics," especially party politics, was the focus of an interesting six-state study by Swanson, Kelleher, and English.[19] Convention delegates were interviewed before and after the convention session to determine which of the two conflicting views they held on convention operation: (1) the "idealized" view or the "statesman" model (decision making on the basis of rational, nonpartisan, disinterested choice, viewed as quite distinct from normal state politics), and (2) the "realistic" view or the "legislative" model (conventions as mere extensions of normal legislative politics, clearly and properly responsive to interest groups, political parties, and political leaders). As reported in table 5.2, the majority of delegates in the six states saw the convention in "idealistic-statesman" terms, and held to this view throughout the session. About one-third of the delegates, however, moved toward the "realist" position, especially in the New York and Illinois conventions. This shift probably resulted from the partisanship experienced by the different conventions. New York and Illinois conventions experienced crucial partisan divisions, but Maryland, New Mexico, Hawaii, and Arkansas appeared to avoid partisan conflicts for the most part.

Conventions are unicameral

Conventions are customarily unicameral and thus avoid the problems and delays of two-house deadlocks. Conventions have most often met in a legislative chamber of the state capitol at a time when the legislatures were not in session. Some have split their sessions into two periods with a recess to provide time for study and consultation. Conventions are financed by legislative appropriations and sit for an average of seven months.

Follow legislative pattern

A convention is essentially similar to a regular law-making body in methods of organization and procedure, with important committees performing much of the actual work. Convention deliberations normally stimulate less parliamentary maneuvering and fewer obstructive tactics than occur in a legislature, although these deliberations are

Table 5.2 Delegate Attitudes in Six States

	"Constitutional Conventions Are As Political As Anything Else."		"A Constitutional Convention Is Special and Above Party Politics."		"Party Loyalty Is a Strong Influence in Convention Voting."	
	Agree (Realist)	*Disagree (Idealist)*	*Agree (Idealist)*	*Disagree (Realist)*	*Agree (Realist)*	*Disagree (Idealist)*
New York						
Pre-convention	39%	61%	50%	50%	53%	47%
Post-convention	70	30	32	68	75	25
Illinois						
Pre-convention	45	55	46	54	41	59
Post-convention	69	31	13	87	75	25
Maryland						
Pre-convention	37	63	60	40	12	88
Post-convention	27	73	66	34	3	97
Hawaii						
Pre-convention	45	55	63	37	17	83
Post-convention	44	56	62	38	8	92
New Mexico						
Pre-convention	17	83	81	19	17	83
Post-convention	21	79	71	29	5	95
Arkansas						
Pre-convention	32	68	55	45	7	93
Post-convention	32	68	38	62	2	98

Source: Adapted from Wayne R. Swanson, Sean A. Kelleher, and Arthur English, "Socialization of Constitution-Makers: Political Experience, Role Conflict, and Attitude Change," The Journal of Politics 34 (February 1972): 189. By permission of the Southern Political Science Association.

nonetheless subject to the pressure of groups, parties, and sectional interests from within and without. The delegates to a convention are not likely to be swamped with details and local matters, which too often plague the members of legislative assemblies.

As a rule, the work of a convention is outlined in the language prepared by the legislature when the "call" was put to a vote of the people. The call may provide (1) for consideration of only a certain number of specified subjects, (2) for unlimited power to write a new constitution, or (3) for general power to revise or rewrite a constitution subject to specific reservations. Attempts to set limits in this manner may be ignored by the convention itself. Still, except in the case of a territory achieving statehood, every constitutional convention is primarily concerned with revision and modernization rather than with sweeping changes in the fundamentals of government. Any drastic break with constitutional traditions would only invite voters to reject the proposals. Thus, delegates are caught in a dilemma. Modest proposals that change very little are likely to be adopted while significant change will rally opposition. Faced with this reality of the ballot box, delegates are required to render a judgment as to how much change they can propose and still gain voter approval.

"Call" decides scope of work

The decade of the 1980s reflected a decline in the use of conventions for proposed constitutional changes. Only three conventions met—Arkansas briefly in 1980, New Hampshire in 1984, and Rhode Island in 1986. This compares to eight conventions in the 1970s and 14 in the 1960s.[20] None were convened in 1990–91.

Changing Constitutions by Initiative Petition

Citizens propose changes

The method of initiating proposals for constitutional change by petition is similar to the method of initiating legislation by petition. Oregon adopted this approach in 1902, and it has since spread to sixteen other states. To put a proposed amendment before the electorate in this manner, a petition must bear the signatures of a specified proportion or number of voters. Such a requirement might be as high as 15 percent of total votes cast for governor, as in Arizona, or as low as 3 percent of the vote cast for governor in the preceding biennial election, as in Massachusetts.[21]

The Florida Commissions

When Florida revised its constitution in 1968, it pioneered a new approach to constitutional revision with the creation of a 37-member revision commission empowered to submit amendments directly to the people. Members are appointed by the governor, legislative leaders and the chief justice to serve with the attorney general. It first met in 1977 and was then scheduled to reconvene every 20 years. In 1988, Florida added a second commission to assume control of amendments on fiscal matters. This 29-member body, called the Taxation and Budget Reform Commission and appointed by the governor and legislative leaders, first met in 1990 and will meet every 10 years thereafter.

Ultimately, the People Decide

People make final decision

Regardless of the method used for proposing changes in a state constitution, the people make the final decision on adoption in all states except Delaware. (Delaware permits the legislature to amend the constitution.) On very rare occasions, conventions have been authorized to ratify the constitutions, but the practice has become practically nonexistent in recent decades.

The final draft of a constitutional convention is usually submitted for acceptance or rejection as a whole at the polls. Through technical requirement or convention decision, however, proposals may be submitted to the voters separately. When amendments are offered separately, one may pass, while another may fail. A simple majority of the votes cast on the question is adequate for popular ratification of constitutional changes in most states. There are a few exceptions, however, as in Minnesota and Wyoming, where the majority for ratification of an amendment must be a majority of those voting in the election; in Illinois, where a proposed amendment is adopted if approved either by a majority of the electors voting in the election or by three-fifths of the electors voting on the amendment; or in Tennessee, where a legislative proposal must be ratified by a majority equal to the majority cast for governor. Such a requirement is an arithmetical handicap for the amendment, since voters are more inclined to vote for candidates than for constitutional propositions. Under such conditions, much more than a simple majority must be cast for a constitutional proposal in order to put it over.

Obstacles to Constitutional Revision

Amending state constitutions is not a simple task in most states. If they actually were fundamental documents, setting forth only basic principles, difficulty in amendment would be desirable to protect provisions from cavalier treatment at the hands of temporary majorities. Unfortunately, because of their length, constitutions require constant revision to keep pace with the changing environment of state and local governments, so procedures intended to safeguard enduring principles have become obstacles to needed changes.

Long constitutions require constant revision

None of the methods available for proposing amendments is without disadvantages. The legislative route requires the agreement of unusual majorities in over half of the states and the concurrence of two consecutive legislative sessions in twelve states. Because the legislature has a vested interest in the power arrangement in the constitution, it may refuse to propose measures that would alter its stature or performance. The major alternative to the legislature in most states is the constitutional convention, which is costly, often opposed by legislatures, time-consuming, and requires an informed electorate to judge its final product. One-third of the states can use the initiative, but the cost involved in securing signatures and waging a campaign usually requires the motivation of a selfish interest to activate. Only Florida has the special commission.

All methods difficult

Aside from the technical hurdles are the political problems of securing electoral approval. If revision involves a shift of power, those who stand to lose power become more violent in their opposition to the document than those who gain power become enthusiastic about the change. If the number of elected state or county officials is to be reduced, they rally against the proposal; if dedicated funds are to be "jackpotted," the champions of earmarked moneys come forth; if the legislature is to be given control over bonding and taxation, fiscal conservatives mount the charge; if the constitutional benefit of some interest group is removed, the group rises in opposition. Opponents will usually translate their selfish interests into a politically acceptable slogan. With limited financing and an obligation to uphold the truth, proponents find themselves at a distinct disadvantage in defending what has been conceived as the best interests of the state. Citizens, most of whom have been uninterested in the revision process from the outset, hear the predictions of rising taxes, oppressive government, and disappearing rights with alarm, and express their opposition by voting against revision.

Change brings out opponents

As delegates to constitutional conventions will attest, the road to constitutional revision is strewn with politics, lined with opponents, clouded by citizen apathy, and often leads to the abyss of defeat.

Alternatives to Amending

Because the amending processes have prevented change, constitutions have changed in ways other than formal amendment. Every state constitution is subject, more or less, to modification and development through judicial interpretation, statutory amplification, and official custom or usage. Like state statutes, state constitutions may become invalid through national action, as has happened with respect to questions of suffrage and issues of racial discrimination.

1. Judicial interpretation

A constitutional provision can be and sometimes is judicially interpreted to permit governmental action which, according to an earlier judicial interpretation, it prohibited; and for all practical purposes the constitution means what the judges say it means. Kentucky courts, for example, finally ruled that longstanding constitutional restrictions on salaries could be interpreted in the light of an increased cost-of-living. More often, however, the meaning of a provision is broadened by gradual interpretation to meet with the governmental needs of a developing community. The courts of our states and of the United States in dealing with matters fundamental in our governmental system constitute, in effect, continuing constitutional conventions.

2. Statutory amplification

Ordinary legislation is sometimes designed to supplement or even to circumvent the intent of the framers. In 1956, Oregon submitted to the voters an amendment designed to alter the constitutional prescription of a $1500 annual salary for its chief executive. The salary appropriated for the governor for 1955 was just ten times the constitutional limit, indicating legislative recognition that the salary set by the constitution was obviously out of keeping with current economic conditions. Statutory "amplification" is possible when statutes go unchallenged—and many questionable ones exist in states.

3. Custom or usage

Usage also has its impact upon the constitution, modifying its provisions or determining the way in which provisions will be applied or even judicially construed. An example of comingling forces for constitutional change is afforded by *Schardein v. Harrison et al.*[22] In that case, Kentucky's Court of Appeals, applying the principle that "legislative or executive construction of constitutional provisions adopted and acted upon with acquiescence of the people for many years is entitled to great weight with the courts," permitted an incumbent to succeed himself in office despite a constitutional question as to whether he was eligible to do so. Many analysts believe modification of a constitution by means other than formal amendment has been as important as change by formal amendment.

4. Ignore constitution

Unrealistic constitutional provisions are ignored in many states. The best examples are found in the conduct of the legislative assembly. In many states, the legislative procedures required by the state constitution are so cumbersome that, if followed, they would double the time required for legislative work. Constitutions often require three readings of bills in each house, with one reading at length. An assembly, with 1,500 bills and a limited 120-day session, would not be able to read the bills at length for final passage, so they ignore the requirement. Time restraints placed on some legislatures are so unrealistic that clocks are covered and the journals of the closing days all bear the same date.

Under the federal arrangement designed by the framers of the U.S. Constitution, citizens are the sovereigns of two governments—national and state. If constitutions obstruct the public will at the state level, citizens can turn to the federal government for action. Thus, state constitutions are often cited as one of the factors impairing state vigor in the federal parternership.

5. Turn to federal government

Reading over a state constitution will provide one with only a limited understanding of its meaning. As with the United States Constitution, it is necessary to have an acquaintance with a number of significant statutes, court opinions and practices of executive officials in order to know what the constitution means today. In other words, we must look at the state government both as a whole and in terms of its operating parts to get a valid view of its constitutional features. The foundation takes on meaning by looking at the superstructure that it sustains. Hence, all the chapters of this text throw light on the meaning of the living state constitutions, and the student should take care to treat this chapter more as an introduction than as a full explanation of the state constitutional system.

Endnotes

1. Walli Paul Adams, *The First American Constitutions* (Chapel Hill, N.C.: University of North Carolina Press, 1980). p. 5.

2. Ibid., pp. 88–93.

3. Evarts Boutell Greene, *The Foundations of American Nationality* (New York: American Book Company, 1922). p. 97.

4. Albert L. Sturm. *Thirty Years of State Constitution Making* 1938–1968 (New York: National Municipal League, 1970), p. 97.

5. U.S. Advisory Commission on Intergovernmental Relations, *Changing Public Attitudes on Governments and Taxes* (Washington, D.C.: Government Printing Office, 1988), p. 33.

6. Susan Fino (Wayne State University), "The Michigan Constitution." A paper delivered at the annual meeting of the American Political Science Association, Atlanta, August, 1989.

7. *Pruneyard Shopping Center v. Robins et al.,* 447 U.S. 74 (1980).

8. Elder Witt, "The Unassuming Architect of an Emerging Role for State Constitutions," *Governing* (July, 1989): 56. For a partial listing, see U.S. Advisory Commission on Intergovernmental Relations, *State Constitutions in the Federal System* (Washington, D.C.: Government Printing Office, 1989), pp. 79–81.

9. David McCormick, "States take charge," *State Government News* (December, 1989): 7. Also see Judith S. Kays, "Federalism's Other Tier," *Constitution* 3 (Winter 1991): 48–54.

10. Alfred de Grazia, "State Constitutions—Are They Growing Longer?" *State Government* 27 (April 1954): 82–83.

11. U.S. Commission on Intergovernmental Relations, *A Report to the President for Transmittal to the Congress* (Washington, D.C.: Government Printing Office, 1955), p. 37.

12. Terry Sanford, *Storm Over the States* (New York: McGraw-Hill, 1967), p. 189.

13. Rodd Zalkos, "Oregon officials strapped in tax straitjacket," *City & State* 8 (February 11, 1991): 13.

14. Quoted by Walter F. Dodd, *State Government*, 2d ed. (New York: Appleton-Century-Crofts, 1928): 96.

15. *Politics: Who Gets What, When, How*, quoted in *The Political Writings of Harold D. Lasswell* (Glencoe, Ill.: The Free Press, 1951), p. 295.

16. Roscoe C. Martin, *The Cities and the Federal System* (New York: Atherton Press, 1965), p. 49.

17. For a more thorough discussion of the amending process, see Janice C. May, "Constitutional Amendment and Revision Revisited," *Publius: The Journal of Federalism* 17 (Winter 1987): 153–179.

18. Janice C. May, "State Constitutions and Constitutional Revision: 1988–89 and the 1980s," *Book of the States* 1990–91 (Lexington, Ky.: Council of State Governments, 1990), p. 21. See also May's sequel article in *Book of the States 1992–93*, pp. 2–19.

19. Wayne R. Swanson, Sean A. Kelleher, and Arthur English, "Socialization of Constitution-Makers: Political Experience, Role Conflict, and Attitude Change," *The Journal of Politics* 34 (February 1972): 183–198. The data came from a comparative study of six state constitutional conventions (New York, Illinois, Maryland, Arkansas, Hawaii, and New Mexico), directed by Elmer E. Cornwell, Jr., and Jay S. Goodman. For a complete study of the Maryland convention, see Swanson, Cornwell, and Goodman. *Politics and Constitutional Reform: The Maryland Experience*, 1967–1968 (Washington, D.C.: Washington Center for Metropolitan Studies, 1970).

20. May, "State Constitutions and Constitutional Revision: 1988–89 and the 1980s," p. 21.

21. *Book of the States 1992–93* (Lexington, KY: Council of State Governments, 1992): 24. Janice May reports in the *Book of the States 1992–93* (p. 3) that an unusually high proportion of all proposals (12.8%) and adoptions (7.5%) were accomplished through the initiative approach during 1990 and 1991.

22. 18 S.W. (2d) 316 (1920).

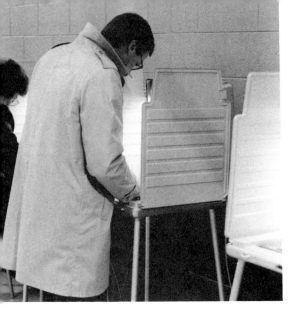

PARTICIPATION THROUGH VOTING

CHAPTER 6

Citizen Participation in Policy Development Through Voting

Voting is one form of citizen participation in the governing and policy-making processes in a democratic society. Political party activity and pressure groups are two other institutionalized systems of mass participation, and will be covered in chapters 7 and 8.

Objectives of Voting

Voting accomplishes a number of objectives. First, it chooses the executives, legislators, and, in many states, the judges who will actually hold the reins of government. Then, in a muted way, it directs the policies of government by relating issues to candidates. Voting also protects citizens from potential abuses of elected officials, since they will remain in office only so long as they command citizen confidence. Voting enhances the dignity of individuals by recognizing their equality as human beings and their right to affect their own destinies. Voting formally gives the "consent of the governed" to government, thereby making it legitimate.

The importance of the opportunity to participate in policy development through voting is reflected in the large number of elective offices in the United States—some 500,000. Only on rare occasions does a state or local government reduce the number of elected officials. On the other hand, with the creation of each new governmental entity, such as a city or a special district, the traditional array of elective offices appears (See table 6.1).

Many opportunities to vote

Voting as a Joint Federal—State Domain

For the first century of the Republic, voting was a right prescribed by state governments. Unable to agree on voter qualifications in the Constitutional Convention, the framers noted the variety of requirements among the states and agreed that voters casting ballots for members of Congress "shall have the qualifications requisite for electors of the most numerous branch of the state legislature." In other words, whoever would be qualified by state laws to vote for the state house of representatives would also be qualified to vote for members of Congress. The Constitution also provides that "The times, places and manner of holding elections for senators and representatives, shall be prescribed in each state by the legislature thereof; but the Congress may at any time by laws make, and alter such regulations. . . ."

Qualifications left to states, but . . .

Table 6.1 Elected Officials

	1977	*1987*	*Increase/ Decrease*
United States	542	542	
State	15,294	18,134	+ 2,840
County	62,922	55,500	− 7,422
Municipalities	134,017	137,542	+ 3,525
Townships	118,966	118,669	− 297
School Districts	87,062	86,772	− 290
Non-School Special Districts	72,377	80,538	+ 8,161
Total	491,180	497,697	+ 6,517

Source: 1987 Census of Governments, U.S. Census Bureau

Congress sets some rules

Beginning in 1842, a long process of nationalizing the right to vote began as laws, constitutional amendments, and judicial decisions limited the authority of states to control this vital function of democracy. In 1842, Congress passed legislation that required members of the House of Representatives to be elected from single-member districts. In 1872, a national law fixed the first Tuesday after the first Monday in November of even-numbered years as the day for electing members of Congress. Because conducting separate elections would be expensive for government and inconvenient for citizens, the practice of holding state and local elections at the same time as the federal elections became commonplace. This practice of holding joint elections subjected state elections to federal oversight. In a Maryland 1878 Congressional election, several people were arrested for illegal voting practices under state law. However, they were brought to trial and convicted in federal courts under a federal statute because federal elections were involved.[1] The Voting Rights Act of 1965 and its subsequent renewals in 1970, 1975, and 1982 intervened extensively into state control of elections in a selected number of states. (Since they were aimed at securing protection for the voting rights of blacks, they will be discussed later.) These acts added another dimension to federal control of elections by authorizing the U.S. Justice Department to provide guidelines as well as to approve or disapprove electoral changes and practices.

Constitutional amendments reduce state control

Constitutional amendments were also passed to reduce the jurisdiction of state governments over the elective franchise. Ratified in 1868, the provisions of the Fourteenth Amendment lay dormant for decades before federal courts began to realize that "equal protection" could be applied to the discriminatory voting practices of states. As interpreted today, "equal protection" means that states cannot create classifications of voters and nonvoters unless there is a compelling state purpose achieved by such distinction.

Apply "equal protection" clause

Interpreting constitutional amendments and acts of Congress, the federal judiciary moved the ball further into state territory. Using the "equal protection" clause, it struck down lengthy residence requirements for voting and literacy tests for state elections, while also addressing the impact of the vote by applying the one-person, one-vote principle to all state and local governments. The Court went on to give the national political parties authority to override state laws that prescribed the rules for choosing delegates to national nominating conventions. Federal intervention in state administration of elections has continued in recent years as Congress has considered legislation to require changes in state registration laws, to set standard hours for voting, and to regulate numerous other state election activities. At the same time, the Federal Election Commission has been promulgating voluntary standards for computerized voting systems.[2]

Extended federal involvement in state election procedures, especially registration, has prompted some state political party officials and political leaders to consider holding state elections separate from federal elections. Separate elections would insulate state procedures from unexpected consequences or Congressional changes.[3]

States may have begun as the wellsprings of voting rights but they are now circumscribed by constitutional amendments, judicial interpretations, federal laws, Justice Department guidelines, and national political parties. The right to vote has been nationalized to meet the needs of a national electorate. Many of the laws, amendments, and decisions have merely been the formal manifestations of America's expanding concept of equality and human dignity. The flowering of this concept may best be seen in four major movements toward universal suffrage.

Right to vote nationalized

The March of Universal Suffrage

Extending the Right to Vote to the Propertyless

In the eyes of early colonists, the argument for the property qualification consisted of five points: (1) owning property made a person free; (2) property, especially real estate, tied the owner to the community; (3) anyone who imposed taxes should have to pay them; (4) property and power in the same hands equaled political stability; and (5) property was subject to the majority decisions of only property owners.[4] As a consequence, standards of minimum property holdings were set to guarantee responsible voting by those with a stake in society. Property remained a major requirement for voting into the 1770s when the unpropertied urban residents became restless. Soon states began to accept payment of taxes in lieu of property qualifications.[5] The new western states were solidly against property qualifications, and by 1851 twelve states had eliminated them. As the nation continued to expand, states eliminated property requirements to attract new settlers as well as to reflect a changing view of rights. Today, the requirement for property ownership is not tolerated under "equal protection" by federal courts except in rare situations where the owners of property have a peculiar interest in the election, such as in the case of farmers in an irrigation district.

Western states against property requirement

Extending the Right to Vote to Blacks

Adoption of the Fifteenth Amendment in 1870 was intended to extend the right to vote to persons regardless of "race, color, or previous condition of servitude." Under the Amendment, white northern politicians moved into the South and used black votes to control many southern state and local governments. However, when the military was

Fifteenth Amendment

withdrawn from the South in 1877, control of southern states was regained by whites who promptly developed a number of mechanisms to disenfranchise black voters. Thus, the Fifteenth Amendment was effectively nullified and blacks were once again without voting privileges. While federal courts would occasionally invalidate a practice, such as the white primary for nominating candidates, they tended to reaffirm the view that states controlled the right to vote.

Abolish poll tax

One obstacle to black voters in several states was the poll tax. This tax was imposed on a per capita basis and proof of payment was required as a condition of voting. Either through negligence or poverty, blacks in large numbers failed to acquire their tax receipts and were thus disqualified from voting. In 1962, Congress proposed an amendment to the Constitution prohibiting the poll tax as a condition for voting for federal officials. The proposal was quickly ratified by thirty-eight states and the Twenty-Fourth Amendment became effective. The Supreme Court went one step further in 1966. Using the "equal protection" clause of the Fourteenth Amendment, it found no "compelling state purpose" for a poll tax and disapproved its use as a condition for voting in state elections.[6]

Voting rights war of 1960s

Prohibition of the poll tax was only a part of the federal effort to translate the Fifteenth Amendment into votes. Legislation was passed in 1960 and 1964 to attack the voting problems faced by blacks. The 1960 and 1964 legislation relied primarily on court action to eliminate racial discrimination in voter registration, authorizing federal judges to appoint "referees" to determine the voting qualifications of persons local officials refused to register. Title I of the 1964 Civil Rights Act further expanded the federal government's role, but continued to rely on court action to effect change. For federal elections, it prohibited denial of the right to vote because of minor errors or omissions on application forms—a device frequently used by some registration officials. Title I ruled out oral literacy tests; and it made a sixth-grade education presumptive of literacy. The U.S. Attorney General was authorized to request three-judge federal courts to hear voting rights suits, making possible immediate appeal to the Supreme Court.

Decide to bypass courts

The Voting Rights Act of 1965 was a major departure from the past practice of relying predominantly on the courts. It authorized direct action by federal executive officials without intervening court action. The 1965 act concentrated on several hard-core states, or subdivisions of states, in which fewer than one-half of the adult population were registered or voted in the 1964 presidential election, and which required a literacy, understanding, or good character test. In such areas, federal examiners were empowered to suspend literacy and other tests which had been used to discriminate against blacks and to proceed to register otherwise qualified voters and to protect their rights on election day. This act clearly involved federal displacement of state authority over voting in those areas where there was a long history of disfranchisement of blacks. A survey of black registration in six southern states[7] after the first full year of the Voting Rights Act revealed dramatic increases. Today, equal proportions of whites and blacks nationwide report that they are registered, with registration in the South being high enough to be considered normal in the context of the national figures.

Another barrier to minority voting was the literacy test, developed partly as a method for restricting certain groups from voting and partly to secure intelligent voting. By 1970, close to a third of the states had a literacy test. Instances where literacy tests were misused include passing uneducated whites and flunking college-trained blacks. Under the 1965 act, literacy tests were automatically suspended in areas where less than 50 percent of the electorate was registered or had voted. In 1970, Congress supplemented the 1965 law by suspending all literacy tests until 1975; this was upheld by the Supreme Court. In 1975, Congress extended the Voting Rights Act of 1965 for seven years, expanding its coverage to non-English-speaking citizens, and made permanent its ban on literacy tests.

Eliminate literacy test

In the 1982 amendments adopted with the renewal of the Voting Rights Act, Congress added an additional section, Section 2, that applied throughout the nation. According to this section, the act is violated when members of a protected class "have less opportunity than other members of the electorate to participate in the political process and to elect representatives of their own choice." Court cases through the 1980s and early 1990s clarified the meaning of this section in a variety of decisions affecting not only blacks but other minorities as well. "At large" elections in which a number of offices are filled by all voters in the jurisdiction have been successfully attacked under Section 2 as a means of preventing a racial or ethnic minority from electing representation. While many of the cases originated in the South where large pockets of minorities exist, states such as New York, Illinois, and California have also experienced legal action. Hispanics in Los Angeles county, for example, forced a change in the at large elections for county supervisors.[8] In Texas, at large judicial elections were found in violation of Section 2. As litigation continues in the 1990s, judicial decisions will result in a closer correlation of the number of minorities in the population and the number of minority officeholders.

Guaranteeing opportunity to elect

No longer fettered by restrictive laws, the newly enfranchised black voters quickly exerted their political power at the polls. Blacks were elected to offices in increased numbers. These electoral victories attest to the new meaning found in the Fifteenth Amendment for black voters in the twentieth century.

Extending the Right to Vote to Women

Winning the vote for women required several generations of intense campaigning, with a small meeting at Seneca Falls, New York, in 1848 identified as the campaign kickoff for women's suffrage.[9] This was followed two years later by the Women's Rights Convention in Worcester, Massachusetts, with Susan B. Anthony soon joining the campaign. In 1869, the National Woman Suffrage Association was formed. The association opposed adoption of the Fifteenth Amendment because it failed to include women. In 1890, the major organizations working for women's suffrage merged into the National American Woman Suffrage Association.

Campaign launched in 1848

The political mobilization of the "suffragettes" began to affect the voting laws. As early as the Civil War, Kansas permitted women to vote in school elections. The Wyoming territory accorded women full voting privileges in 1869, followed by Utah in 1870, and Washington in 1883. Congress and the Courts did not look favorably upon the extensions, however, and invalidated them. Nevertheless, the territories persisted and Wyoming entered the Union in 1890 as the first state giving women the right to vote. Suffragettes found the West to be the most hospitable section of the country, winning all of the states, to one degree or another, west of the Mississippi by the time the Nineteenth Amendment was adopted in 1920, some seventy years after the Seneca Falls gathering.[10]

Lowering the Voting Age

Adoption of the Twenty-Sixth Amendment was the latest, and most likely last, broad extension of suffrage, adding over 11 million voters to the qualified electorate in a single stroke. Prior to 1970, Georgia, Kentucky, Alaska, and Hawaii had a voting age under twenty-one, and in 1970 they were joined by Maine, Nebraska, Massachusetts, Minnesota, and Montana. Proposals to lower the voting age in ten other states were defeated in the 1970 elections. In a bold reach for authority, Congress, while reenacting the Voting Rights Act in 1970, extended the right to vote to all persons eighteen years and older in state as well as federal elections. The Supreme Court upheld the power of Congress to set the voting age for federal elections but denied it had that authority over state and local elections. Since states conduct state and federal elections simultaneously, the decision left states in an administrative quandary. At least two sets of registration records would be required under the Court's decision—one set for those voters age eighteen and older who would be eligible to vote for only the federal offices, and one set for those twenty-one years old and over eligible to vote for both state and federal offices. Two voting systems would also be required in each precinct to accommodate the two classes of voters. Anticipating inconvenience, new costs, and confusion, state legislatures meeting in 1971 quickly ratified the Twenty-Sixth Amendment to lower the voting age to a uniform age eighteen for all elections.

Congress moves to lower voting age

States forced to act

Changing the electoral ground rules is not a neutral activity. Advocates of change often see political gain in adding one group or another to the voting population. Republicans supported the Fifteenth Amendment because they felt that enfranchisement of the blacks would make the South a permanent bastion of political power for the election of Republican congressional delegations and presidents. Women rode to the polls on the tide of the reform movement, supported by citizens who expected women to help clean up the political corruption that was rampant in the early 1900s. Democrats, looking at statistics that indicated younger people leaned their way, were the staunch advocates of lowering the voting age, hoping to add political strength to their cause in future elections. Selfish motives aside, many supported the extension of the franchise strictly as a democratic ideal that had been rooted in American philosophy for some time.

Politics involved in suffrage

State Qualifications for Voting

Within the limitations imposed by federal authority, whether through the Courts, Congress, or the Constitution, the states are left to prescribe the remaining qualifications for voting.

All states require voters to be citizens of the United States. In the earlier days of the Republic, states sought to entice immigrants by offering liberal voting privileges. Citizenship was not a requirement, particularly in the frontier states, although some states required such persons to be in the process of gaining citizenship. As an example, Indiana allowed aliens to vote one year after declaring their intent to become citizens. However, as the land became settled and concern mounted over continuing immigration, states became more restrictive and citizenship eventually became the universal rule. *1. Require citizenship*

The rationale for the states' long residence requirements for voting came under heavy pressure as Americans became more mobile. The idea that new residents were unfamiliar with state and local political issues and should observe a one- or two-year waiting period eventually lost its validity in its application to national elections. Congress recognized this in the Voting Rights Act of 1970 by reducing to thirty days the residence requirement for voting in presidential elections, and by requiring states to make special provisions for absentee voting and for registering new residents. In 1969, 1970, and 1972 cases challenging residence and registration laws governing state elections,[11] the Supreme Court made it clear that only a "compelling state interest" justified the denial of the right to vote. The Court reaffirmed the power of the states to require their voters to be bona fide residents of the state, but denied the relevance of lengthy residence requirements as a test of bona fide residence. It finally settled on fifty days as the maximum residence requirement permissible. Thirty days is the most common residence requirement, that being the law in nineteen states, while fifty days is the longest, set in Tennessee and Arizona. *2. Residence*

Passage of the Twenty-Sixth Amendment enfranchising the eighteen-year-olds added new fuel to a long-time controversy in college communities over the question of residency for college students. Many states specifically stated that a person could not acquire residence for voting purposes while in the state as a student. Many also provided, either by statute or administrative ruling, that students who were already residents of the state were to vote at the residence of their parents. Taking a dim view of fettering the right of students to vote, the Court interpreted the word *abridge* in the Twenty-Sixth Amendment broadly and struck down many state and local efforts at restricting the meaning of "residence" for voting purposes. Nevertheless, states may require more than mere "presence" to prove residence. Now eligible to play in the electoral games, a smattering of students soon found themselves in state legislatures and on local governing boards, grappling with the problems of governance alongside the life-long residents. A few even became mayors. After a few elections, however, interest in extensive political forays disappeared among students and they became an accepted contingent of the resident electorate.

Passage of the Twenty-Sixth Amendment provides that a state may not set a voting age above eighteen; however, it does not preclude states from establishing a voting age of sixteen or seventeen. Political reality makes this such a remote possibility that the amendment, for all practical purposes, has preempted state action in determining voting age.

3. Voter registration

In the late 1800s, when the corrupt political machines rose to power in many of the nation's larger cities, corrupt voting practices became widespread. Claims were made that thousands of ballots were cast by nonexistent or unqualified voters. Out of this era came the practice of requiring voters to register before the day of election in order to establish their qualifications to vote. Deadlines, most commonly 30 days before election day, were set for receiving registrations, and the days between deadlines and elections were used to screen the registration lists for ineligible voters. When the polls opened on election morning, officials started the day with a list of qualified voters to be checked off as they appeared at the polls.

Each state designs its own registration system, sometimes through a detailed provision in the state constitution, but more often through acts of the legislature. As a consequence, the method for compiling lists of registered voters differs among the states and even within a given state. Traditionally, prospective voters were required to appear personally before a county, city, or town registration board or registrar to establish qualifications. Sixteen states still use this method. However, other states responded to the electoral reform sentiment prevailing since the 1960s by proposing innovative

Simplifying registration

methods for simplifying the registration process. Postcard registration was one such idea, which gained popularity in the early 1970s. By 1992, over half of the states permitted registration by mail.

In 1975, Michigan launched a new approach by using the 200 branch offices of the secretary of state's boat, auto, and driver's licensing system to register voters. Enjoying immediate success, some form of the Michigan "motor-voter" idea was adopted in half of the states by 1990[12] and was the centerpiece of Congressional election reform proposals in the early 1990s.

Election day registration is permitted in Wisconsin, Minnesota, and Maine. North Dakota is the only state that requires no registration.[13]

Apply modern technology

Using modern computer technology, states are developing statewide registration systems consisting of central files of all registered voters at the state level. Local governments send copies of registration forms to the central system for entry into the master file. The fully centralized systems provide counties or other local governments with updates, voter lists, poll books, and other information for conducting elections. In addition, the state is able to compile statistical information on registration rolls, including the total number of voters, by party (if registration requires that information), by precinct, or by legislative district.[14]

In addition to expediting the compilation of registration records, computers are now being used to cross check registration signatures utilizing the electronic capacity to "digitize." Signature digitization duplicates signatures for later recall on visual displays. Not only can the technique be used for verifying registration signatures but it saves months of work for validating signatures appearing on petitions.

Permanent vs. periodic

States use two general kinds of voter registration—permanent and periodic. All but a few states have the permanent system in which the voter remains registered as long as he or she votes periodically. Under the periodic system, used by only a few states, voters are required to reregister periodically. Both systems have their critics. The permanent system is criticized for failing to maintain a current check on eligible voters, thus opening the system to fraud. On the other hand, the periodic system is criticized for the inconvenience caused to voters, thus reducing voter turnout. It is rather obvious that the price of greater convenience is ballot security and the price of security is inconvenience for voters.

Conducting Elections

Though administered locally, elections are conducted under constitutional provisions, state laws, and, in some states, regulations developed by election boards. The chief elections officer in the majority of states is the secretary of state. Variations may be found in Alaska and Hawaii where election administration is vested in the office of lieutenant governor, in Delaware where a state election commissioner is appointed by the governor, and in Illinois where a state board of elections is provided by the constitution. Fragmentation of authority at the state level is not uncommon, even in states where the secretary of state is the designated administrator. Iowa, for example, not only has a secretary of state but also has a state registration board, a state registrar of voters, a state canvassing board, a state board of voting machine commissioners, and a campaign finance disclosure commission. Ohio has a secretary of state, a ballot board, a five-person elections commission, and an ethics commission.

State election officials

The most common level of election administration, below the state, appears in counties where the county clerk or auditor is usually designated as the chief elections officer. County boards of election supervisors or commissioners commonly participate in managing the elections by promulgating rules, naming precinct election officials, designating voting places and precincts, and canvassing votes after the election.

County elections staff

Under the counties are the wards and/or precincts where the votes are actually cast. Conducting the election is a local election board consisting of a chief elections officer aided by representatives of the two major parties and as many clerks as are dictated by the size of the precinct. In addition to the official paid staff, political parties are often entitled by law to have "poll watchers" or "challengers" in the polling area to observe the voting process.

Local election board

Precinct voting may be conducted in public buildings, such as schools, city halls, fire stations, and courthouses, but frequently it is necessary to rent polling places for the day. The hours for voting are determined by state law and most commonly begin at 7:00 A.M. and close at 8:00 P.M. After the polls close, the votes must be counted, certified, and reported. Local canvassing officials receive returns from the different voting places and report the results to the proper county or state authorities. The results are then officially announced, and certificates of election are issued to the winners. Several days may elapse before the final official results are announced, but, usually, unofficial results are reported to the public by the media within a few hours. Unhappy with the early projections of winners by the media before the polls are closed, Congress and several states have sought to protect election results by setting a standard time for closing the polls and regulating "exit polling" by media representatives. Occasionally, elections are too close to call on election night and the results are not known until the

Casting the vote

"Exit polling"

official canvass. Such was the case in the 1989 Virginia gubernatorial election in which Democrat Douglas Wilder defeated Republican J. Marshall Coleman by 897,000 to 891,000 votes. A special recount of the ballots was required.

The arrival of sophisticated electronic equipment has expanded opportunities for greater efficiency and service in the election process. As an example, Oklahoma was able to install a comprehensive registration and election system utilizing computers by 1992. The availability of electronic technology will likely lead to more state management of elections, primarily because the required expense and expertise will be beyond many local election units. By the year 2000, polling places may well consist of keyboards or touch screens through which the voters send their decisions to central computers for processing.

Ballots and Ballot Forms

The problems of voting have been gradually overcome since the Greeks applied the process of casting ballots, or small balls, to express choices. The spread of suffrage to the common people brought attention to ways of protecting the average voter from coercion by candidates, officials, political bosses, or employers. The first step was to end voting by voice. Voice voting was carried on in open meetings of electors who stood *Randolph denounces* and announced their choice of candidates as their names were called by the clerk. In *ballots* 1829, when voting by ballot was proposed as an alternative, John Randolph of Virginia exclaimed: "I scarcely believe that we have such a fool in all Virginia as even to mention the vote by ballot, and I do not hesitate to say that the adoption of the ballot would make any nation a nation of scoundrels, if it did not find them so."[15]

John Randolph to the contrary, ballots did come. However, they were first pro-*Secret Australian ballot* vided by factions or parties campaigning for their slates of candidates and the only *arrives* names appearing on the ballot were those of their own candidates. To insure party loyalty, the ballots were often prepared on colored paper so anyone watching the ballot boxes would know whether or not the voter cast a ballot for the "proper" candidates. In 1856, Australia started using a ballot that was furnished at the polls at public expense and bearing the names of all candidates, thus providing a secret ballot for voters. The Australian ballot first appeared in America in the February 1888 municipal elections in Louisville, Kentucky, but Massachusetts was the first to adopt the ballot statewide, doing so in May of the same year. An instant success, the Australian ballot was adopted by almost three-fourths of the states within three years.[16] The last states adopted it in the 1920s, except for South Carolina where it was successfully resisted until 1950.

The Australian ballot may have provided for secrecy, an important step in breaking up regimented voting by the corrupt political machines, but within a short period of time the political bosses found new ways to abuse the secret ballot, such as stealing ballots in advance for use on election day. Challenged to continue tightening the election process, reformers in the 1890s came up with the first voting machines.

Advantages of voting Among the advantages touted for voting machines were: (1) they could handle *machines* more voters at less cost, (2) they prevented spoiled ballots by not permitting voters to cast votes for more than one candidate per office, (3) they were more difficult to use corruptly than a paper ballot, and (4) they provided a faster, more accurate, and more honest tabulation of the votes than could be achieved by paper ballots. Critics of the machines pointed out that (1) they required a very high initial expense, limiting their use to heavy voting areas; (2) they intimidated older voters; and (3) they were difficult to operate for some of the handicapped.

Feeling that the advantages outweighed the negative features, state legislatures and/or state election boards approved their use. Initially, the machines were mechanical, with voters registering their preferences by moving marker levers. As voting machines became more popular and the size of the market increased, new companies entered the field, offering different voting devices. Today, around a dozen companies offer mechanical machines, ballot scanners, punch cards, and electronic systems.

Thousands of voters in modern and mobile America are absent from their city, county, or state on election days. To solve this problem, absentee voting has been widely established. The need was first realized during the Civil War, when steps were taken to accommodate the members of the armed forces in the matter of voting. The practice reached great proportions in World War II when Congress and the national government provided cooperative aid to the states in the task of returning ballots from the fighting fronts. Most of the states have arrangements for absentee voting, a few providing primarily for persons absent in the armed services. The Voting Rights Act of 1970 requires states to make special provisions for absentee voting in presidential elections for those who cannot vote at a new place of residence. The conditions and methods for absentee voting vary widely among the states.

Civil War brings absentee ballot

Though the absentee ballot may appear to be a politically neutral means of exercising the right to vote, it has become a partisan weapon used by political parties to wage electoral combat. Absentee ballot wars are becoming widespread in the United States, with both parties striving to win the close elections with a successful absentee ballot campaign. And some tight elections have been determined by absentee ballots counted days after the polls close. In his first race for governor of California, George "Duke" Deukmejian was trailing Tom Bradley by 20,000 votes on election night. But when the absentee ballots were counted, "Duke" was the winner by 90,000 votes. In a King County (Washington) contest, Republican Tim Hill trailed his opponent by over 2,000 votes when the polls closed. He and his party had spent $50,000 mailing 100,000 applications for absentee ballots. When 32,000 absentee ballots were counted, Hill took the majority and ended up winning by almost 4,000 votes.[17]

The battle of the absentee ballot

To be eligible for an absentee ballot in most states, a citizen must either be ill, handicapped, or absent from the precinct on election day. In May 1981, San Diego broadened the concept of absentee voting to the entire electorate by mailing each of its 430,000 registered voters an official ballot to vote on a special measure. More than 60 percent of the ballots were returned, considerably more than the 25 to 35 percent cast in such elections when conducted by personal appearance. The city felt it saved $175,000 while tallying a large vote. The San Diego experience prompted other states to authorize local governments to conduct elections by mail. Since the San Diego experiment, over 1,000 all-mail ballot elections have been conducted in Kansas, Oregon, California, Montana, Washington, Missouri and Nebraska. Popularity of voting by mail can be attributed to reduced cost, increased voter participation and convenience, and more time for voters to consider their decisions.[18]

Voting by mail

Party column vs. office group

Whether conducted on a machine or on paper, elections involve two forms of ballot for recording the decisions of the electorate—the party column ballot and the office group ballot. The party column ballot, used by twenty-six states and often called the Indiana ballot, lists the names of the candidates in columns under their party labels. Around twenty states permit voters to place a single mark at the top of the ballot that automatically casts their votes for all candidates in the column. Under the office group ballot, used by twenty-four states and often called the Massachusetts ballot, the candidates are grouped under the offices for which they are running.

Biases of ballot forms

Ballot design is not neutral. Partisan advantage exists in one ballot or the other. Since the party column ballot encourages straight party voting, it benefits the majority party of the state. On the other hand, the office group ballot forces voters to think through their selections as they vote on each office, giving candidates of the minority party an opportunity to get elected. Independent candidates—those not backed by a major party—also receive greater voter consideration under the office group since they receive equal recognition on the ballot with the candidates of major parties. Even though they may not have a chance to win, they can siphon enough votes to become the difference in close elections between the major party candidates.

Another consequence of the office group ballot is high "roll-off" or "voter fatigue"—the reduction in voting for the secondary offices on the ballot. As one would expect, if voters can vote for seven party candidates with the flip of one lever or one X on the ballot, more votes will be recorded for the whole ticket than if they were required to cast individual votes for each race on the long ballot.

In view of the benefits of each system, the battle lines are predictable in struggles over legislative or constitutional proposals to change ballot forms. Courts have begun to inquire into the equality of opportunity available to parties under each system. Requirements that the columns be alternated for parties and independent candidates and that names in the office group be rotated are becoming more commonplace. Both ballot forms must provide space for citizens to write in names of candidates in addition to those appearing on the ballot.

Minorities get right to representation

Section 2 of the Voting Rights Act passed in 1982 gives minorities a right to challenge the electoral systems in jurisdictions where they have not gained their proportionate share of seats in governing bodies. This requirement could lead to ballot forms that would enable minorities to elect proportionate representation.

Cumulative voting

One ballot designed to provide minority representation was the cumulative voting system used in Illinois until 1980 for the election of members of the state house of representatives. Originally, legislative districts were designed to elect three members each and voters were given three votes to cast in any combination they chose. Voters of the minority party in the district often chose to give all three votes to one candidate. If all minority party voters did likewise, they could—and did—elect at least one house member from the district. Voters of the majority, sensing they could get two seats, would cast one and one-half votes for each of two remaining candidates. While the system provided for minority representation from most Illinois house districts, practical politics required parties to limit the number of candidates to the number of seats they thought they could win. This eliminated meaningful competition in many areas of the state and became a principal reason for repeal of the system. Cumulative voting reappeared in Alamogordo, New Mexico in 1987 to give Hispanics a better opportunity to win a seat on the city governing board.[19]

Other schemes, mathematically more accurate, have been devised for achieving proportional representation (often called PR). Proportional representation has been used and abandoned in as many as twenty-five American cities for election to the council body, but never for higher legislative chambers as in Europe, Canadian provinces, and Australian states. PR is praised as a method of providing representation for minority and occupational groups and for checking local political machines. It is criticized as detrimental to the two-party system and as an encouragement to "splinter" parties. PR was abandoned by New York City not long after World War II because the Communists polled nine percent of the votes and received nine percent of the council seats. In 1969, the New York legislature provided for use of PR in New York City school elections to assure minority representation on the governing board. In 1973, 36 percent of the electorate was black, Chinese, or Puerto Rican, and 38 percent of the board members came from these groups. Apparently PR achieved its objective.[20]

Proportional representation

A device used by reformers to get rid of urban political bosses was the nonpartisan ballot. Reformers felt that voters ought to make deliberate decisions, unfettered and uncontrolled by political parties. Thus, they designed the "no party," or nonpartisan, ballot which listed candidates without party identification. Parties continued to function in many nonpartisan systems by putting up slates of candidates and then furnishing voters with "guidecards." Technically, however, the definition of a nonpartisan election is not the exclusion of party activity but the fact that a candidate's party identification is not shown on the ballot.

Nonpartisan ballot

Candidates found on nonpartisan ballots may include judges, education officers, state legislators (in Nebraska), county officials in a few states, candidates in special district elections, and candidates for municipal offices. Nonpartisan ballots are used in a majority of American cities, locale for the political machines against whom the ballots were initially directed.

Adoption of the nonpartisan ballot has not eliminated politics. It changed the players and redistributed influence. Civic associations, dominated by the business interests, tend to gain more power in the nonpartisan systems while the lower socioeconomic groups have a difficult time functioning in the system without party as a reference. Thus, the upper socioeconomic groups tend to have influence disproportionate to their numbers in nonpartisan electoral systems.

Politics of nonpartisan ballot

Some states and electoral districts confront the voter with more than one ballot at the same election. There may be one for state officers, one or more for local officers, and another for bond issues or constitutional amendments. States active in referring acts of the legislature and initiating proposals, such as California, may have ten or more substantive issues in addition to the slates of candidates. Voters may be called upon to make as many as twenty to thirty decisions in a single election.

Long ballot activates campaign

The short ballot was the goal of a reform movement of fairly long standing. Supporters of the short ballot have sought to reduce the number of state and local elective offices to a few of importance and responsibility. They emphasize the point that routine and technical positions in government can be better filled by appointment, particularly with the application of merit systems for the selection of civil servants. Research indicates that many voters, ill-prepared to make numerous deliberative decisions, resort to randomly checking boxes down the ballot, often voting for the first name on the list just to get the task completed.[21] In other cases, they vote for names with a friendly ethnic ring or names made famous by athletes, military heros, or politicians from the past.

In 1909, Woodrow Wilson became president of the National Short Ballot Organization, which exerted an influence for the next few years and later was merged with the more comprehensive National Municipal League. However, the long ballot continues to plague voters in most state, county, and local elections. It contributes to nonvoting and makes the outcome of elections more subject to the influence of trivial factors. The long ballot is locked in legal or constitutional provisions, staunchly defended by the elected officeholders, and widely supported by a citizenry concerned with accountability.

Types of elections   Not only must citizens deal with long ballots but they must also be familiar with the variety of elections in which they are expected to participate. The most common elections are the primary and the general.

Primary elections, to be covered more extensively in chapter 7, were implemented principally to take the nominating of party candidates out of the smoke-filled backrooms and place it in the hands of the rank-and-file of the party. However, primary elections are used for more than nominating party candidates. Primaries are now used in nonpartisan elections to reduce the field of candidates by screening off all but the top two for each position available in the general election. This screening process then guarantees that the winner in the general election will be chosen by a majority of the voters.

Whether partisan or nonpartisan, general elections are the "finals" for candidates who have been nominated in the primary. Many states have provisions permitting candidates to run in general elections as independents. Independents are candidates who do not choose to carry the label of either major party. Victories by independent candidates for major offices are rare.

Most cities and special districts conduct elections for their officials at times different from the statewide primary and general elections. In addition to these elections, special plebiscites are often required by state constitutions or state law to vote on raising tax limitations, approving bond issues, ratifying home rule charter amendments, and dealing with a variety of special issues and questions.

Canvassing the vote   As soon after the election as practicable, special boards are assembled first at local levels and then at the state level to review, or canvass, the vote. At the first level, usually a county, the board of elections, or some other statutory body, reviews the precinct-by-precinct vote as compiled by the county election administration unit. Errors will be corrected and the results forwarded to the state level where the state board of elections, or a specially constituted canvassing board, reviews the statewide results for error and correction. The board then certifies the winners to the appropriate official and certificates of election are issued.

Unsuccessful candidates frequently contest close elections. The laws for contests vary but ordinarily the defeated candidate or, in some cases, a qualified supporter may contest an election on claims of miscount, misconduct, fraud, or corruption on the part of election officials; ineligibility of the victorious candidate; illegal votes for the winner; rejection of legal votes for the loser; and bribery or intimidation in such a manner as to prevent a fair and free election. If an election is very close, state law may provide for an automatic recount, as was the case in the 1989 Wilder-Marshall election in Virginia. Contests may be heard by an election board or tried by a regular court, according to the law or constitution of the state, with possible appeal to the state supreme court. Denial of national constitutional rights in local elections may lead to cases in federal courts. The exposure of unsavory facts may lead to criminal prosecution of individuals. Legislatures may investigate elections, especially of their own members, and each house of Congress, of course, has full power to investigate state and local elections involving its seats.

Contested elections

The Vanishing Voters

In recent decades, a general decline in voter turnout has cast a long shadow across the democratic idea of "government by the people." Voter turnout has dropped almost 13 percent in presidential elections since 1960 and almost 12 percent in nonpresidential elections since 1966. This phenomenon of contemporary American politics has captured the attention of researchers and the concern of political activists. Because it suggests anemia in the body politic, nonvoting warrants serious consideration (Figure 6.1).

Voter turnout declines

Figure 6.1

(Reprinted courtesy of Larry Wright and the Detroit News.)

Table 6.2 Voter Turnout (1990 General Elections)

State	1990 Voting Age Population	Highest Number of Votes Cast for Any Candidates	Percent of Voting Age Population	Ranking
Maine	931,000	522,181	56.09%	1
Minnesota	3,249,000	1,806,777	55.61%	2
Montana	581,000	319,336	54.96%	3
Alaska	365,000	194,750	53.36%	4
Oregon	2,128,000	1,112,847	52.30%	5
Massachusetts	4,598,000	2,341,990	50.93%	6
Nebraska	1,181,000	593,828	50.28%	7
South Dakota	518,000	258,976	50.00%	8
Vermont	428,000	211,422	49.40%	9
North Dakota	478,000	233,973	48.95%	10
Wyoming	329,000	160,109	48.66%	11
Rhode Island	771,000	364,052	47.22%	12
Iowa	2,100,000	983,933	46.85%	13
Connecticut	2,516,000	1,141,101	45.35%	14
Idaho	710,000	320,610	45.16%	15
Louisiana	3,093,000	1,396,113	45.14%	16
Ohio	8,119,000	3,477,650	42.83%	17
Kansas	1,864,000	786,096	42.17%	18
Colorado	2,475,000	1,022,027	41.29%	19
Hawaii	854,000	349,666	40.94%	20
North Carolina	5,071,000	2,069,585	40.81%	21
Utah	1,084,000	442,213	40.79%	22
Alabama	3,060,000	1,215,889	39.73%	23
Arkansas	1,780,000	696,209	39.11%	24
Arizona	2,702,000	1,055,406	39.06%	25

Turnout varies with elections

Voter turnout varies considerably by the type of election. Election statistics have established the fact that the heaviest voter turnout occurs when the office of president is to be filled. Scoring second are state elections in the off-presidential years. Turnout is lowest for municipal and special district elections. Turnout figures fail to correlate with citizens' attitudes toward governments. Recent surveys indicate that citizens feel more positively about local governments than either the state or federal governments and yet local elections attract the fewest voters.

Voter turnout also varies widely by state. Utah, South Dakota, North Dakota, and Minnesota usually lead the nation with a high turnout, and Georgia, Alabama, Texas, and South Carolina generally have a low turnout (See table 6.2).

Decline puzzling

The decline in voter turnout that has occurred since 1960 has puzzling implications that seem to defy explanation. Ironically, this decline has been experienced while educational levels have been rising, more states have become politically com-

Table 6.2 continued

State	1990 Voting Age Population	Highest Number of Votes Cast for Any Candidates	Percent of Voting Age Population	Ranking
Oklahoma	2,337,000	911,314	39.00%	26
Wisconsin	3,617,000	1,379,727	38.14%	27
New Mexico	1,091,000	411,236	37.69%	28
Illinois	8,682,000	3,257,410	37.52%	29
Nevada	858,000	320,743	37.38%	30
Michigan	6,870,000	2,564,563	37.33%	31
Washington	3,597,000	1,313,217	36.51%	32
Indiana	4,164,000	1,502,687	36.09%	33
California	21,709,000	7,699,420	35.47%	34
Delaware	514,000	180,152	35.05%	35
Florida	10,150,000	3,530,871	34.79%	36
Missouri	3,893,000	1,352,552	34.74%	37
New Hampshire	861,000	294,819	34.24%	38
Pennsylvania	9,221,000	3,052,760	33.11%	39
Kentucky	2,778,000	916,010	32.97%	40
New Jersey	5,986,000	1,938,454	32.38%	41
Texas	12,156,000	3,892,746	32.02%	42
Maryland	3,622,000	1,111,088	30.68%	43
Georgia	4,827,000	1,449,652	30.03%	44
New York	13,582,000	4,056,896	29.87%	45
West Virginia	1,380,000	404,305	29.30%	46
South Carolina	2,621,000	760,965	29.03%	47
Virginia	4,755,000	1,152,854	24.24%	48
Tennessee	3,773,000	790,441	20.95%	49
Mississippi	1,877,000	368,502	19.63%	50

Source: The Election Center, *Washington, D.C.*

petitive, voting barriers have been reduced, and media coverage has increased. According to conventional wisdom, all of these trends should be bringing voters to the polls in droves, but just the opposite is occurring.

Historically, nonvoters have generally been urban, southern, young, less educated, of laboring occupations, lower class, lower income, female, and black. The decline in turnout since 1960 has not been occurring in all groups equally. The poor and less educated whites have been dropping out at greater rates than the more wealthy, highly educated whites.[22] That being the case, explanations must be sought that are applicable to that particular segment of the population.

1. Alienation

Alienation is characterized by high interest and low turnout. Voluntary alienation occurs when individuals with high interest choose not to participate in the electoral process; involuntary alienation arises in situations when a person with high interest is prevented from participating by external factors, such as difficult registration procedures or inconvenient polling circumstances.[23] Recent surveys support alienation as a partial explanation, reflecting as they do a growing disenchantment with political leadership and the institutions of government. In a Gallup poll, state political office-holders were given positive ratings by only 13 percent of the people; local political officeholders scored 16 percent; and U.S. senators and representatives fared just a few points better. In all cases, twice as many respondents gave negative as positive ratings.[24] Another pollster, Lou Harris, found a dramatic increase between 1966 and 1977 in the number of people who felt that "what you think doesn't count anymore."[25] Voter malaise is further substantiated by an American Broadcasting Company-Harvard poll in which the single most important reason people didn't vote was their belief that they had no stake in the election.[26] "Individuals with low levels of trust," observed William J. Crotty and Gary Jacobson, "those who can find little to be proud of in American government, who have little concern about the election outcome, and who either sporadically or rarely follow public affairs, have a depressed vote turnout."[27] Michael J. Robinson suggests that public dissatisfaction with government started to accelerate when the nightly news programs expanded from 15 to 30 minutes, providing more reports dwelling on political institutions as inept or corrupt.[28]

2. Barriers   Over the past twenty-five years, numerous barriers to voting have been reduced by federal legislation, court decisions, state laws, and election officials. The period of residence has been reduced, voter registration has been simplified, many states require time off for voting, voting hours have been extended, poll taxes and literacy tests have been outlawed, and absentee ballots have been made readily available. Nevertheless, political observers still harbor the idea that most nonvoting is attributable to mechanical and legal barriers, even though widespread removal of these barriers has failed to produce higher turnout. Some point to high turnout in the low barrier registration states of Minnesota, Wisconsin, North Dakota, Maine, and Oregon,[29] but this could be coincidental, and the moralistic political culture could explain the high turnout just as easily. One researcher reported that turnout does not seem to increase when registration is easy.[30] The U.S. Census Bureau reported that almost a third of the unregistered voters said they did not want to register and were not interested in registering.[31]

3. Costs of participation   Legal and technical barriers place "costs of participation" on all voters but there are other costs that impact the lower socioeconomic groups more than others. It is from this group of voters that the greatest defections are occurring. Many of these people are less educated, less adept at interactive skills, less exposed to public issues, less informed about the whole complex of issues and candidates involved, and have less free time to cope with the challenges of voting. The higher-status voter takes in stride what the lower-status person finds to be obstacles. It is easier for a college-educated voter to translate issues into a ballot decision. If American politics is becoming more issue-oriented, as some claim, the lower socioeconomic groups are going to find that system even more irrelevant unless issues can be translated into terms to which they can react electorally.

4. Parties lose appeal   Political parties have been declining in significance in the electoral picture since the reform movement at the turn of the century. Voters are less willing to declare party allegiance or vote a straight party ticket. With loyalties on the decline, party appeals "to come out and support the party ticket" fall on deaf ears. One group of researchers found that . . . "the weakening of party loyalties accounts for one-fourth of the decline in reported turnout between 1960 and 1980. . . ."[32] The researchers pointed out that younger voters are not developing the same party loyalties as held by older voters, suggesting a slow disappearance of party loyalty as older voters leave the scene.

According to Daniel Elazar, voting turnout may be explained to some extent by the dominant political culture in the state, with the moralistic and individualistic culture motivating voters and the traditionalistic stifling voting. To support his contention, Elazar points to the high voter turnout in presidential elections in the states with moralistic political cultures.[33] This claim has been corroborated by Russell Hanson, who correlated political culture with congressional elections over the period 1960 to 1976 and found that "states with the same political culture had similar turnout rates. . . ."[34] These findings may help explain the enduring differences in turnout among the states, but they cannot be used to explain declines in turnout unless evidence can be found that political cultures have been changing over the past twenty-five years.   *5. Political culture*

It could be argued that urbanization has contributed to the decline in voter turnout, but at best it could be only a peripheral argument since the number of urbanized people grew moderately between the 1960 and 1990 benchmarks of three decennial census reports. Nevertheless, some researchers have found that urbanites have a poor voting turnout, probably because of the numerous distractions involved in the urban lifestyle. A study of Illinois counties found a mean turnout in rural areas of 84 percent and a steady decline to 65 percent in metropolitan counties.[35] From studies of Montana, Mississippi, and Vermont, Frank Bryan concluded that " . . . rural areas are the most likely to generate high participatory habits when other factors are controlled. . . ."[36]   *6. Urbanization*

Mass marketing techniques have been spreading throughout the political process, displacing thousands of precinct workers, ward heelers, and headquarter volunteers who made up the backbone of the political process just two and three decades ago. Candidates are now packaged in television spots and speak directly to the voters in thirty-second segments without an army of intermediaries. The enthusiastic workers who used to pound the pavement for those exciting gubernatorial candidates are now asked for money rather than time. Some of them do door-to-door campaigning for local candidates but politics has taken on an impersonal hue since the populace acquired twenty-five-inch entertainment centers in living color. In fact, some of the electorate become downright belligerent if volunteers ring the doorbell and interrupt television viewing to leave literature or talk about candidates.   *7. Politics becomes impersonal*

It could be possible that apathy or indifference, much more than alienation, is a factor in the turnout decline. While alienation presupposes the existence of interest on the part of the voter, apathy involves little or no interest. One study indicated that nonvoters were much more politically ignorant than voters, suggesting indifference to the electoral process.[37] Evidence of apathy is witnessed in states that have lowered the barriers to voting. As indicated earlier, many of the technical and legal barriers that were once believed to stifle voting turnout have been removed with little or no impact on the number of voters. Some voters may not care about elections because they are not as threatened by the outcome as political activists and reformers believe. From an idealistic point of view, it is difficult to accept the fact that there could be millions of   *8. Apathy* people who really don't want to vote in a democratic society. Such an admission would violate the American ideal of participatory democracy and, therefore, is unacceptable. We feel compelled to find more substantial reasons than apathy to explain the absence of millions of voters on election day.

Responding to Nonvoting

Many factors involved

Only one conclusion can be drawn from the years of research, reams of reports, and hours of discussion devoted to dissecting the nonvoter: the decline in turnout is the result not of one but of many factors—alienation, barriers, decline of parties, culture, participation costs, urbanization, impersonalization of campaigns, apathy, and other factors yet undiscovered. Reformers and activists have already invested considerable time and effort in winning approval of changes that were at the time regarded as panaceas, but with experience have proven to be irrelevant. Cure should be related to the disease; it is common in public affairs to find this profound advice neglected. Nevertheless, if voter decline is occurring primarily among the lower socioeconomic groups, electoral reforms must be focused on these groups if the trend is to be turned upward. Until this is done, turnout will never regain the level of 1960 and most certainly never the levels of the late 1800s.

Endnotes

1. Earl R. Sikes, *State and Federal Corrupt Practices Legislation* (Durham, N.C.: Duke University Press, 1928), pp. 163–165.

2. *Election Administration Reports* (Richard G. Smolka, Ed.) (Maric, Inc., Washington, D.C.) August 21, 1989: 1.

3. Richard G. Smolka, "Election Legislation," *Book of the States* 1990–91 (Lexington, KY: Council of State Governments, 1990), p. 230. See sequel article in 1992–93 edition.

4. Walli Paul Adams, *The First American Constitutions* (Chapel Hill, N.C.: University of North Carolina Press, 1980), pp. 208–209.

5. William J. Crotty, *Political Reform and the American Experiment* (New York: Thomas Y. Crowell Company, 1977), p. 8.

6. *Harper* v. *Virginia State Board of Elections,* 383 U.S. 663 (1966).

7. Alabama, Georgia, Louisiana, Mississippi, South Carolina, and Virginia.

8. Janet Neiman, "Hispanic court victory boosts political power of minorities," *City & State* (June 18–July 1, 1990):1.

9. Crotty, *Political Reform,* p. 21.

10. For a contemporary review of the struggle for the right to vote by women see the Spring–Summer, 1990 edition of *Constitution,* a quarterly journal of the Foundation for the U.S. Constitution (New York, New York).

11. *Hall* v. *Beals,* 396 U.S. 45 (1969); *Evans* v. *Corman,* 398 U.S. 419 (1970); and *Dunn* v. *Blumstein,* 92 S. Ct. 995 (1972).

12. "CBS hot line," *State Government News* 34 (May, 1991):27.

13. See Richard G. Smolka, "Election Legislation," *Book of the States, 1990–91,* pp. 226–231 and Table 5–9 on page 261; pp. 258–264, 279 in 1992–93 edition.

14. Arthur Young and Company, *Statewide Registration Systems,* a report to the Federal Election Commission, Washington, D.C. (December 1977): 4–5.

15. Quoted by George Frederick Miller, *Absentee Voters and Suffrage Laws* (Washington: Daylion Co., 1948), pp. 81–82.

16. Howard R. Penniman, *Sait's American Parties and Elections,* 5th ed. (New York: Appleton Century Crofts, Inc., 1952), pp. 528–531.

17. Hugh A. Bone, "1989 Election in Washington," *Comparative State Politics Newsletter,* (Sangamon State University, February 1990):1.

18. Randy H. Hamilton, "American All-Mail Balloting: A Decade's Experience," *Public Administration Review* (September–October 1988): 860.

19. Richard L. Cole and Delbert A. Tarbel, "Cumulative Voting in a Municipal Election," *Western Political Quarterly* 43 (March 1990): 191–199.

20. Ruth K. Scott and Ronald J. Hrebenar, *Parties in Crisis,* 2nd ed. (New York: John Wiley & Sons, 1984), p. 85.

21. See H. M. Bain and D. S. Hecock, *Ballot Positions and Voter's Choice* (Detroit: Wayne State University Press, 1957).

22. Howard L. Reiter, "Why Is Turnout Down," *Public Opinion Quarterly* 43 (Fall 1979): 304.

23. William H. Flanigan and Nancy H. Zingale, *Political Behavior of the American Electorate,* 5th ed. (Boston: Allyn and Bacon, Inc., 1983), pp. 11–12.

24. *Gallup Report No. 214,* The Gallup Poll, Princeton, N.J. (July 1983).

25. "Lou Harris Finds Rising Alienation," *Public Opinion* (May/June 1978): 23.

26. "ABC-Harvard Analyze Voting," *National Civic Review* 73 (February 1984): 92.

27. William J. Crotty and Gary C. Jacobson, *American Parties in Decline* (Boston: Little, Brown and Company, 1980), p. 18.

28. Michael J. Robinson, "Reflections on the Nightly News," *Television as a Social Force* (New York: Praeger Publishers, 1981), pp. 313–366.

29. David Glass, Peverill Squire, and Raymond Wolfinger, "Voter Turnout: An International Comparison," *Public Opinion* 61 (December/January 1984): 53.

30. Robert S. Erickson, "Why Do People Vote? Because They Are Registered," *American Politics Quarterly* 9 (July 1981): 274.

31. Michael J. Malbin, "Election Day Registration—Can It Really Make A Difference?" *National Journal* (May 7, 1977): 719.

32. Paul R. Abramson, John J. Aldrich, and David W. Rhode, *Change and Continuity in the 1980 Elections* (Washington, D.C.: Congressional Quarterly, Inc., 1982), p. 87.

33. Daniel J. Elazar, *American Federalism,* 3rd ed. (New York: Harper & Row, 1984), p. 152.

34. Russell Hanson, "Political Culture, Interparty Competition and Political Efficacy in the American States," *Political Culture, Public Policy and the American States,* ed. John Kincaid (Philadelphia: Institute for the Study of Human Issues, 1982): 103–104.

35. Alan D. Monroe, "Urbanism and Voter Turnout: A Note on Some Unexpected Findings," *American Journal of Political Science* 21 (February 1977): 76.

36. Frank M. Bryan, *Politics in Rural States* (Boulder, Col.: Westview Press, 1981), p. 103.

37. Stephan Earl Bennett and David Resnick, "The Implications of Nonvoting for Democracy in the United States," *American Journal of Political Science* 34 (August 1990):787.

CHAPTER 7

POLITICAL PARTIES

Citizen Participation in Policy Development through Political Activity

Citizens participate in policy-making most extensively through voting, which brings millions of voters into the process. By comparison, participation through the structure of political parties ranks a poor second. Nevertheless, parties are still vital in the performance of functions that help translate democracy from an abstract ideal into a working system.

Functions of Political Parties

1. Resolve conflict

Each state is a composite of competing groups and interests making demands on the resources and authority of society. Since elections cannot be won by giving all groups everything they demand, parties negotiate with groups to reduce their demands until they become compatible with other interest groups in the state. By putting together a composite of five or six interest groups, and capturing support from the less organized, parties may be able to gain victory. Thus, in their quest for control of the government, political parties have helped reduce conflict in a pluralistic society by convincing interest groups that compromise is necessary.

The role of the politician in peace-making was well stated by Gordon S. Black, who observed that "In a 'pluralistic' political system, the politician is a principal broker in the process through which collective decisions are made. The person who is able to develop successful coalitions," he continued, "and who can work out acceptable compromises is critical to the decisional process where interest conflict abounds."[1]

2. Furnish public policy

As parties seek to win various groups, they propose programs designed to attract support. They may reach out for farmers by proposing overseas trade teams; they may reach out to workers by promising bargaining rights; or they may reach out to business executives by offering economic development programs. Often, the policies proposed by parties originate with the interest groups themselves. However, parties modify these policies to make them compatible with the demands of other groups. Policies of parties are most commonly articulated through platform planks and the campaign speeches of major candidates.

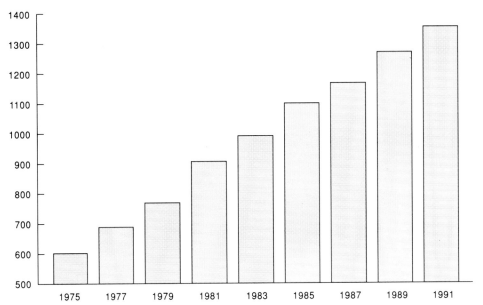

Figure 7.1
Female Legislators,
1975–1991
*(Source: Center for the
American Woman and
Politics, National
Information Bank on
Women in Public Office,
Eagleton Institute of
Politics, Rutgers
University. Copyright 1991.
Center for the American
Woman and Politics.)*

Voters seriously question the ability of parties to propose policy alternatives, seeing both parties as discussing the same policy in different words. In a nationwide survey taken to obtain the public's perception of party differences, respondents saw little difference between parties when it came to "reducing crime," "providing quality education," "providing health care," and "reducing waste in government."[2] Even though Republican and Democrat activists see themselves as being different,[3] many voters fail to see the distinction.

Except for offices elected on the nonpartisan ballots, parties assume responsibility for recruiting candidates to run for the thousands of positions filled by elections. Even in cases where the chances of success are remote, party activists feel an obligation to provide the public with a choice of candidates.

3. Furnish political personnel

Just a few decades ago, politics was regarded as a "man's game," but recent years have seen an upsurge of interest and participation on the part of women. This interest has not been fully translated into office-holding, since all politicians, men or women, are expected to demonstrate a civic or political track record as a qualification for higher office. State legislatures are frequently the first rung to statewide and national office. In 1969, women held only 300 of the 7,500 state legislative seats; by the early 1990s, this had increased to well over 1,300 (Figure 7.1).

In 1990, seven women ran in the 36 state general elections for governor, 14 ran for lieutenant governor, 13 for state treasurer, 12 for secretary of state and five for attorney general.[4] Even though women have been making significant strides in the electoral arena, their participation may still be impaired by their lower interest in politics than that of men.[5]

Figure 7.2
(Left to right) Governors
Joan Finney of Kansas,
Ann W. Richards of Texas,
and Barbara Roberts of
Oregon.

As they demonstrate electability, minorities are also being recruited by parties to fill political offices. Blacks have been making great gains, as cited in chapter 6. The number of Hispanic elected officials doubled during the 1980s.

Political parties also furnish personnel to conduct campaigns and encourage citizen participation in the election process. Party activists staff the storefront campaign offices, pass out leaflets, canvass door-to-door, run phone banks to support rallies, mobilize the "get-out-the-vote" effort, stuff envelopes, chauffeur candidates, and perform hundreds of menial tasks that make up campaign activity.

Staffing government

Once the election is over and the candidate has won, new officeholders look to the party to provide quality people who can help implement the political philosophy of the winning team. At one time, party victory would mean the replacement of administrative personnel and policymakers with the winning party's faithful supporters. However, looking at the First Amendment right of freedom of association, the U.S. Supreme Court has ruled that termination of employment must be limited to employees in positions requiring political affiliation for the effective performance of the office involved.[6] In 1990, the Court said federal, state and local governments violated the First Amendment when they based their refusal to hire, promote, or transfer employees on their party affiliation and activities. By restricting patronage, these Court decisions have stripped parties of one of their strongest incentives for getting candidates and volunteers to participate in the political process.

These decisions have been greeted with mixed reactions. The executive director of an organization promoting good government said patronage is despicable "because it takes our tax dollars and, instead of using them to hire the best people, uses them to hire political hacks." On the other hand, a state political party chairperson said that patronage was necessary for politicians to hire people who shared their beliefs. He also cited the fear that employees would cry patronage whenever they didn't get rehired or promoted.[7]

The impact of this loss varies widely among the states, depending on the role played by patronage in their particular governments. Many states had already limited patronage with extensive civil service systems.

In their quest for victory at the polls, political parties present a continuing barrage of information, propaganda, and interpretation of public policies being proposed or implemented. While much of the barrage is hardly accepted as educational by the citizenry, it does serve to alert public interest and make citizens aware of the implications of certain policies.

4. Educate on issues

Traditionally, political parties bore the brunt of raising funds to put candidates on the road for their campaigns. Banquets, raffles, auctions, button sales, receptions, and direct solicitations have all been tools used by parties to fill the war chests of candidates. However, the high cost of mass marketing candidates has outrun the financial capacities of political parties and has given rise to political action committees (PACs) formed by interest groups. These committees have challenged the financing function as they have rapidly become a major source of revenue for top state positions, legislative races, and the executive contests in large counties.

5. Finance campaigns

Through the years, many individuals have identified themselves with one party or another. Even though more and more voters claim to be independents, party allegiance is still an important factor in the electoral system. For many people who pay little attention to politics, their partisan identification helps guide them in their voting decisions. The party labels "Republican" and "Democrat" serve as voting cues and help rationalize voting for millions of voters.

6. Structure the vote

The separation of governmental powers into three branches may have been a good idea for preventing a majority from perpetrating evil on a minority, but, unfortunately, it also serves to prevent a majority from acting constructively. To act, a concurrence of opinion must be mobilized in all branches of the government. A political party can bridge the gaps between branches of government by providing a common ideology for the officeholders. Thus, when a Republican governor can secure the cooperation of a Republican legislature on the basis of their common political bond, a party philosophy of government can be implemented.

7. Bridge institutional gaps

Independent voting has been undermining this function, however, as the electorate has been choosing Democratic governors and Republican legislatures, or vice versa. In divided governments such as these, the political differences accentuate and aggravate the separation of powers. In any given year, approximately half of the states experience divided government where control of the governorship and the legislature is in the hands of opposing parties.

To the party out of power falls the responsibility of serving as the "loyal opposition" or the continuing critic of the party in office. Because the "out party" hopes to become the "in party," it is motivated to point out the failures and misadventures of the incumbents. To disinterested citizens, this watchdog role is often seen as petty politics when, in reality, it serves to keep the elected party accountable to the public.

8. "Loyal Opposition"

Party Organization

Defining party

A political party can be defined as a group of citizens loosely held together by an inner group of leaders and organizers for the purpose of putting its members in office, through election or appointment, with the goal of controlling the processes of government. Although this common definition describes all parties from state to state, the organizations they create to achieve their goals are neither common nor uniform. Party politics and party organizations are different between Mississippi and Minnesota, between New England and the Southwest, or between a rural and an urban area.

Abuses lead to laws

Initially, party organizations were regarded as private associations of individuals engaged in political activities. They had wide latitude in prescribing their own operating procedures, determining their organizational structures, and conducting their political affairs. Such informality led to abuses, and gradually forced states to enact laws prescribing basic organizational and procedural ground rules for parties. Consequently, almost every state has some legislation that regulates party organizations.

But these state laws on party organization have fallen under a judicial cloud since the U.S. Supreme Court ruled that sections of California law "burden the First Amendment rights of political parties and their members without serving a compelling state interest."[8] The Court struck down California laws dictating the organization of the political parties.

Political culture and access

A state's political culture may have an impact on the nature of its party organization. If those in control of political affairs strive to maintain a closed political system, such as found in traditionalistic states, the state laws may place the first organizational rung at a distant level to discourage new entrants. Some southern states use the county as the first level of organization. On the other hand, if control rests with people who invite open participation, as in the moralistic states, the first rung may be very localized and accessible. These states will provide for party organization in the smallest voting unit of the state, usually called the precinct.

Precincts

In states providing for precinct organizations, the party followers will choose a precinct committeeperson, or, in some cases, a committeeman and committeewoman. These officers may be chosen by the voters of their party in the primary election, elected at a party organizational caucus, or chosen by a precinct convention. If a precinct fails to name precinct representatives, the county committee may be authorized to fill vacancies by appointment. Since there are no elective public offices to be filled at the precinct level, organizations at this level tend to be anemic and sometimes nonexistent. Their duties are to serve as the doorbell ringers, poll watchers, and campaigners at the neighborhood level.

Counties most common level

In urban areas, precincts may be grouped into ward organizations or even into legislative districts. Most often, however, the strongest and most common level of party organization across the states is the county. Because officials of county governments are elected on the partisan ballot in most states, the availability of public offices and political patronage provides reason for political activity. At this level, there are candidates to endorse, campaigns to run, and offices to fill. Parties have reason and resources to exist.

A county committee is often made up of representatives of the precincts or wards, perhaps elected at a county organizational meeting, or chosen at a county convention. Heading the committee is the county chair, aided by the traditional officers and a few others who make up a county executive committee. It manages party business between general meetings or conventions.

Before the U.S. Supreme Court ruled that state legislators must be elected from districts of equal population, legislators were commonly chosen from districts made up of existing political subdivisions with existing party organizations. Following the Court decision, state legislatures (or other reapportionment bodies) sought to preserve the integrity of political subdivision boundaries in making up legislative districts, but they were not always successful. As a consequence, many legislative district boundaries meander aimlessly through counties, cities, and townships until they encircle the required number of people to meet Supreme Court requirements. Since legislative posts are important pockets of political power, parties must somehow adapt their traditional organizational boundaries to the strange geographic configurations furnished by reapportionment plans. If counties are large and heavily populated, they provide the campaign support required in the legislative races. However, if counties are small and/ or sparsely populated, legislative districts may include several towns, counties, and/or parts of other counties. This geographic anomaly requires an ad hoc coordinating organization through which the county parties can cooperate to recruit, nominate, and elect members of the legislature. To further confuse party organization in legislative campaigns, boundaries must be altered after every decennial census to keep up with the shifting population. By disassociating legislative candidates from a permanent political base, reapportionment may be forcing candidates to shift their reliance from party to personal organizations.

One-person, one-vote and party organization

Shifting legislative boundaries

The next level of organization in states with more than one congressman or congresswoman is the congressional district. Since the party unit exists at this level strictly for the purpose of facilitating the election of one public official, the organization is very tenuous. With Washington-based political action committees providing the bulk of the campaign funds for many incumbent members of Congress, the congressional district organization is more important to the challenger who must rely heavily on local resources to mount an effective campaign. In any event, it is transitory at best.

The congressional district

The state central committee or executive committee of a major party varies in composition, organization, functions, and extent of control by law. This diversity results partly from the fact that party rules and state statutes on the subject vary widely among the states. Custom and practice also affect the role and importance of the state committee. The membership ranges from about a dozen up to several hundred. The members are chosen through party primaries or through state party conventions, with a few exceptions or modifications. The Democrats of South Carolina pick the members by the county convention method. The unit of selection is frequently the county, but it may be a judicial district, state legislative district, or congressional district, sometimes with the addition of members from the state at large. The officers of the committee, such as chair, vice-chair, and secretary, are likely to be important cogs in the system, especially in states where the membership is exceedingly large. The committee chairperson is often selected on the basis of being satisfactory to the party's candidate for governor and may be chosen from outside the committee membership.

State organization

National party organization

Figure 7.3
Levels of party organization.

Parties not hierarchies

Informal power

Political machines

A state committee, which is unwieldy because of large membership, finds ways of facilitating its work by delegating much of its power to act to a small executive committee of its own creation. The important work of a large committee is also likely to be planned in advance by a caucus of leaders. Two important functions of the state committee are to serve as a central coordinating agency for election campaigns and to secure campaign funds. Through its officers, the committee also has duties connected with arranging and scheduling the state convention, if one is held.

States are authorized by national party rules to choose representation to serve on the national committees. Whereas the Republican National Committee is based somewhat on equal representation by states, the Democratic National Committee has moved toward a population base, giving urban states more power in the national party. At a minimum, both parties provide for a national committeeman and a national committeewoman. Selection of these representatives may be made under party rules or, in some states, under state laws.

Traditionally, the national parties have had little voice in state party organization. However, the U.S. Supreme Court recently ruled that national parties have the authority to prescribe the procedures for selecting delegates to the national convention, state rules and state laws notwithstanding.

From this description, party organizations may appear as hierarchies of authority, but observers should not be deceived into believing that they reflect a pyramid of power. Parties are merely layers of organizations with little more than influence moving vertically through the system. Authority is virtually nonexistent except in a rare instance in which a state law or party rules may authorize the state committee to exercise some specific supervisory power. The loose decentralized structure can be attributed in part to the nature of the personnel in the system. Local, county, and state committees consist of volunteers who contribute their time and money because they are interested in political objectives. Volunteers participate at their option and not on the order of some party leader at a level above. Consequently, communications from upper to lower levels of party organization tend to plead and persuade rather than command.

State laws or party rules may provide for the party organization but political power doesn't always accompany formal prescriptions. Strong personalities, or groups of politicians, outside the formal party organizations may actually develop such influence and control over political activities that they function as political machines.

Corrupt voting practices and wanton waste of public funds brought the wrath of the electorate down on the political machines in the late 1800s and early 1900s. Reformers rose up to destroy the environment that gave sustenance to these dinosaurs of corruption. Electoral reforms halted the stuffing of ballot boxes, civil service systems removed political jobs, competitive bidding wiped out favoritism in public contracts and purchases, welfare programs eliminated dependence on political machines, and mass media campaigns and primaries enabled candidates to bypass machines. These and other changes cut the lifelines on most political machines so that few continue to exist in the 1990s.[9]

Party Systems

The Australian ballot brought more than secrecy to the voting system; it also brought the problem of deciding which parties are entitled to have candidates listed on the official ballot. States passed laws to define political parties in order to legitimatize and organize the ballot. Since the Republicans and Democrats had long established themselves as functioning political parties, questions about definitions of parties relate more to third parties or new ones. A common procedure for a group to attain party status in a state is by fielding a slate of candidates and securing sufficient signatures on petitions, also prescribed by law, which requires election officials to place nominees on the general election ballot. If these slates win a certain number of votes, they automatically receive the right to function and be treated as an autonomous party in future elections. *State laws define party*

New parties are rare, with New York providing one of the most recent examples. Under New York election laws, petitions bearing the signatures of 20,000 independent voters, with at least 100 from each of 50 percent of the state's congressional districts, were required to get the names of candidates on the general election ballot. In 1978, the state "right-to-life" group secured the petitions and supported a candidate for governor who received 130,193 votes. This figure was well over the 50,000 votes required to gain permanent party status and an automatic spot on the ballot in future elections without having to circulate petitions.[10] *Starting a new party*

States with more than two legally recognized political parties are rare. Election laws, drafted by legislators from the two major parties, usually establish high entrance requirements for newcomers. Even if new parties overcome the legal barriers, the possibilities of winning elections are so remote that enthusiasm soon dies after one or two elections. New York persists in being an exception to the rule, having five legal parties. In addition to the Republicans and the Democrats, official party status belongs to the Liberal party, the Conservative party and the Right-to-Life party. Even though the election laws of New York may recognize the five-party system, the system still functions as a two-party system with the three lesser parties seeking to manipulate the outcome of the elections of the major party's candidates by throwing support to one or the other. Because New York statutes permit the parties to list the candidates of other parties on their ballots, this technique of cross-endorsement enables the minor parties to contribute or withhold votes from the major candidates and thus influence outcomes. If the New York election laws were changed to eliminate the cross-endorsement, the minor parties would disappear because their political leverage would be removed and there would be no political rewards in the system. The New York party system provides an excellent example of how state election laws may influence the nature of the political system. By winning over three percent of the vote in the 1990 gubernatorial election, the Green Party became a legal party in Alaska for 1992 and thereafter. *Types of party systems*

Multiparty systems

A two-party political system is considered the norm—even in states where one party has dominated elections for decades. Tradition has been credited as one of the reasons for the perpetuation of the two-party system. In fact, some people feel that the two-party system is as American as hotdogs and apple pie, and consider the idea of *The two-party system* creating third and fourth parties akin to treason. Buttressing tradition are the election laws that discriminate against the formation of new parties and give the major parties preferential treatment on statutory boards involved in administering the election process. The single-member electoral district also fosters the two-party system by limiting the prizes to one office. Since only one of the major parties has a chance of winning that prize, the third party seldom wins any rewards and, without rewards, support for third parties eventually disappears. The pluralism of the American melting pot also contributes to the perpetuation of the two-party system. Pluralism forces a negotiating and campaigning situation in which the parties compete to build coalitions of a variety of groups to constitute a winning majority. In this situation, the two major parties monopolize the campaign resources and the issues to such a degree that few are left for third and fourth parties. When a third party does develop an issue that attracts wide public support, the major parties quickly incorporate it into their platforms and thus absorb the third party's support.

Legally, there are no one-party states. Every state has at least two political parties organized under the laws of the state, although one of the parties may be too weak to mount successful campaigns. However, this becomes a matter of political competitiveness rather than a matter of law.

Faced with the massive task of running a campaign, candidates need the nomination of the party organizations required to appear on the ballot as the party's candidate. Nevertheless, states do provide for the listing of candidates who wish to run as "independents." While most such candidates have difficulty competing with the two organized parties, occasionally they win. In the 1990 gubernatorial elections, two "independents" won—Walter Hickel of Alaska and Lowell Weicker, Jr., of Connecticut. No doubt their "independent" candidacies were helped considerably by the fact that both had previously held high political office with party support.

Interparty Competition

The democratic ideal calls for two viable political parties in every partisan contest, with both parties within reach of the electoral prize. Because party dominance shifts from side to side in national elections, many people are under the impression that a competitive two-party system is the universal rule throughout American politics. As electoral districts become smaller and more homogeneous, genuine political competition declines, and in hundreds of counties, townships, and cities using the partisan ballot, one-party control becomes the rule rather than the exception.

With the aid of several measurements of strength, scholars have been able to rank the political competitiveness of states. The rankings in table 7.1 are based on the (1) proportion of successes at the polls in state elections, (2) duration of success in the executive and legislative branches of government, and (3) frequency of divided political control of the governorship and the legislature.[11]

As research and elections are proving, states have witnessed a significant shift away from the one-partyism that prevailed during much of the 1900s when whole re-

Table 7.1 States Classified According to Degree of Interparty
Competitiveness 1981–1988

One-Party Democratic	Modified One-Party Democratic	Two-Party	Modified One-Party Republican	One-Party Republican
Mississippi (.86)	Alabama (.84)	Iowa (.64)	Wyoming (.34)	(none)
	Louisiana (.81)	Minnesota (.64)	New Hampshire (.34)	
	Arkansas (.80)	Illinois (.64)	Colorado (.33)	
	South Carolina (.79)	Tennessee (.64)	Idaho (.30)	
	Kentucky (.77)	Missouri (.62)	South Dakota (.26)	
	Hawaii (.77)	Oregon (.60)	Utah (.25)	
	West Virginia (.77)	Connecticut (.58)		
	Georgia (.76)	Ohio (.54)		
	Maryland (.76)	Vermont (.53)		
	Texas (.75)	Michigan (.52)		
	Virginia (.74)	Nebraska (.52)		
	Massachusetts (.74)	Montana (.51)		
	Florida (.74)	New Jersey (.51)		
	Oklahoma (.74)	North Dakota (.50)		
	Rhode Island (.72)	Delaware (.50)		
	Maine (.70)	New York (.49)		
	North Carolina (.70)	Nevada (.49)		
	Wisconsin (.68)	Alaska (.47)		
	Washington (.67)	Pennsylvania (.47)		
	New Mexico (.67)	Arizona (.39)		
	California (.66)	Kansas (.39)		
		Indiana (.36)		

*Source: Politics in the American States: A Comparative Analysis, 5/e by Virginia Gray, et al. Copyright
1990 by Virginia Gray, Herbert Jacob, and Robert B. Albritton. Reprinted by permission of Harper-
Collins Publishers.*

gions of the country were in the iron grip of one party or the other. By comparing party
strength in the 1951 and 1991 legislatures, it is possible to observe the dimensions of
the change to a two-party system (See table 7.2).

The most striking changes occurring in recent times are in the South, where
Democrats have dominated for over 100 years. With Republican candidates for president, governor and U.S. senator gaining victories, more officeholders, party activists,
and voters are moving to the Republican party.[12] In one year, 60 elected Democratic
officials in Mississippi switched to the Republican party.[13] Generally, the decline of
one-partyism can be attributed to the growing independence of voters; the impact of
mass communications, especially television, on politics; and a national gravitation toward
common social, economic, and political values.

Decline of one-partyism

Political competitiveness may have moved from the national to the state level but
it still has not permeated all local governments. Smaller electoral units tend to represent concentrations of similar social, economic, or political expectations. The homogeneity of these electoral districts results in homogeneity of party—meaning one-party
domination.

When the political system does not provide legitimate competition, or one party
dominates politics, factions develop within the majority party to represent the competing interests. Factions may be based on ideological differences, such as liberal versus

*Factors perpetuating
two-party systems*

Table 7.2 Political Makeup of State Legislatures 1951 and 1991

	1951 Senate		1991 Senate		1951 House		1991 House	
	%Dem	% Rep	% Dem	% Rep	% Dem	% Rep	% Dem	% Rep
Alabama	100	0	80	20	99	1	78	22
Alaska	50	50	50	50	79	21	60	40
Arizona	100	0	57	43	88	12	45	55
Arkansas	100	0	89	11	99	1	92	8
California	35	65	65	35	44	56	61	39
Colorado	37	60	34	66	63	37	42	58
Connecticut	64	36	56	44	34	66	59	41
Delaware	47	53	71	29	49	51	41	59
Florida	100	0	58	43	100	0	62	38
Georgia	100	0	80	20	100	0	81	19
Hawaii	33	67	88	12	33	67	88	12
Idaho	55	45	50	50	41	59	33	67
Illinois	35	63	53	47	53	47	61	39
Indiana	42	56	48	52	60	40	52	48
Iowa	14	86	56	44	27	73	55	45
Kansas	15	85	45	55	24	76	50	50
Kentucky	76	24	71	29	75	25	68	32
Louisiana	100	0	85	15	100	0	83	17
Maine	15	85	63	37	17	83	64	36
Maryland	62	38	81	19	71	29	82	18
Massachusetts	50	50	60	40	51	49	75	25
Michigan	28	72	47	53	39	61	55	45
Minnesota	Nonpartisan		69	31	Nonpartisan		60	40
Mississippi	100	0	83	17	100	0	85	15
Missouri	56	44	66	32	61	39	60	40

conservative; economic conflict, such as wage-earners versus business; geographic differences, such as rural-urban, upstate-downstate; or ethnic or religious conflicts. Occasionally, the factions are personality cults that come into existence to promote certain candidates. In some states, factions may be content to battle for their interests within the confines of party meetings; in other states, they will field opposing candidates and run full-scale campaigns in the primary elections. Since factions exist even in healthy two-party systems, the movement of more states toward the two-party norm will not completely eliminate factions in state politics.

Recruiting and Nominating Candidates

A major goal of political parties is to gain control of the governmental processes. To achieve that objective, parties must recruit and nominate candidates for the offices that control those processes. The recruiting and nominating process for state and national politics has changed along with the political environment. The unexpected development

Table 7.2 continued

	1951 Senate		1991 Senate		1951 House		1991 House	
	%Dem	% Rep	% Dem	% Rep	% Dem	% Rep	% Dem	% Rep
Montana	41	55	58	42	61	39	61	39
Nebraska	Nonpartisan		—	—	Nonpartisan		—	—
Nevada	35	65	52	48	58	42	52	48
New Hampshire	29	71	46	54	36	64	34	66
New Jersey	29	71	58	43	27	73	55	45
New Mexico	75	25	62	38	61	39	70	30
New York	45	55	43	57	42	58	63	37
North Carolina	96	4	72	28	89	11	68	31
North Dakota	4	96	51	49	2	98	45	55
Ohio	11	89	36	64	12	88	62	38
Oklahoma	86	14	77	23	81	19	69	32
Oregon	33	67	67	33	18	42	47	53
Pennsylvania	30	70	48	52	44	56	53	47
Rhode Island	50	50	90	10	64	35	82	12
South Carolina	100	0	72	24	100	0	63	34
South Dakota	17	83	49	51	15	85	34	66
Tennessee	85	12	58	42	80	19	58	42
Texas	100	0	74	26	100	0	63	37
Utah	52	48	34	66	68	32	41	59
Vermont	10	90	50	50	10	89	49	50
Virginia	95	5	75	25	93	7	59	39
Washington	41	59	49	51	68	32	61	39
West Virginia	63	38	97	3	83	17	74	26
Wisconsin	12	82	58	42	25	74	59	41
Wyoming	33	67	33	67	50	50	34	66

Computations by authors on basis of data in Book of the States 1950–51 and Book of the States 1990–91, *(Council of State Governments, Lexington, KY). Percentages do not always add up to 100 because of rounding and nonaligned legislators.*

of political parties, the extension of the right to vote, and the growing demand for opportunities to participate have contributed to this evolutionary process.

Caucuses

The caucus method of unofficial nomination developed naturally from the growth of towns and other large voting units. John Adams said of the meeting of the Boston Caucus Club in the roomy garret of Tom Dawes:

> There they smoke tobacco till you cannot see from one end of the garret to the other. There they drink flip, I suppose, and there they choose a moderator, who puts questions to the vote regularly; and selectmen, assessors, collectors, wardens, fire-wards, and representatives, are regularly chosen before they are chosen in the town.[14]

This club operated without legal restriction or regulation, and similar groups operated in this manner for decades afterwards. The congressional caucus for nominating candidates for president followed this plan of eighteenth-century Boston. Despite its popularity, however, the caucus came under popular criticism with the rise of Jeffersonian and Jacksonian politics and was denounced as unrepresentative and corrupt. Besides, caucuses of legislators for nominating nonlegislative candidates seemed to violate the principle of separation of powers. This method of selecting nominees for president continued into the 1820s, even though steps were taken earlier to eliminate it in the states.

Conventions   The delegate convention was adopted as a more democratic and representative method than the caucus for nominating candidates. It also facilitated the offering of platform issues to the voters. Delaware adopted the convention system during the presidency of Jefferson, and many other states in the North went over to this method by 1830. The nominating convention gradually spread over the entire country. Domination of convention procedures and nominations by bosses in "smoke-filled" rooms resulted in disenchantment of party adherents who wanted a more effective voice in political affairs. As they were searching for a nominating system that would break boss control, the concept of the primary appeared on the scene.

Nomination by primary   The primary is a method of making nominations by direct popular action. It is a preliminary election in which voters choose the candidates directly without the use of delegates or representatives in caucus or convention for such purposes. It presumably permits any voter to participate in selecting the candidates to be put on the ballot of his or her party in the general election. Its first use has been credited to Crawford

Origin of the primary   County, Pennsylvania, where both Democrats and Republicans adopted the practice before the Civil War. The primary spread to other Pennsylvania counties and was used in several states before 1900. Wisconsin established the first statewide primary election system in the country in 1903. Oregon followed in 1904, and then the movement spread rapidly to all states.

Primaries are now the most common nominating system used. Nevertheless, party conventions still linger in a few states. In some states the parties hold pre-primary endorsing conventions to recommend candidates to primary voters. Several southern states permit party state committees to opt for a convention instead of primaries; and a few states permit a "challenge" primary for nominees who receive minimum support in the nominating convention.

Closed vs. open primaries   When adopting the primary as a substitute for party conventions, states were confronted with the problem of determining the qualifications of persons allowed to vote in partisan primaries. Partisan primaries are of two types: open and closed. In two-thirds of the states, the closed type prevails. It is based on the theory that only Democrats should vote in Democratic primaries and only Republicans in Republican primaries. Under this method the participant, besides being a qualified voter, is supposed to meet a prescribed test of party allegiance before receiving a ballot at the polls. The test varies from a simple statement of party affiliation to proof by the voter that he or she has supported the party ticket and expects to support it in the approaching general election. The open primary prevails in 14 states.[15] The qualifications for voting in such a primary are the same as for voting in a general election, with no legal way of preventing a Democrat or Republican from voting to nominate a candidate for the other party.

Wide open primary   Washington has the most open of primaries, with no semblance of party regularity in the voting booth. This system utilizes a ballot listing all candidates for nomination and permitting the voter to switch freely from party to party in marking choices.

The person with the most votes of each party for each office wins the nomination. Because the entire electorate is free to vote in the primaries of both parties, the candidates are forced to wage more expensive campaigns to win the support of all voters and not just those of their own political persuasion.[16]

In 1975, Louisiana instituted a new concept by staging a primary with the general election serving as a second stage when and if needed. All candidates for an office, regardless of political affiliation, are listed in a single column. If no candidate receives a majority in the primary, the top two individuals—regardless of political affiliation—move into a general election. However, if one receives a majority in the primary, the election for that office is over.[17]

The Louisiana primary

Partisan primaries became instant successes in the one-party states where they offered a structure through which factional differences within the dominant party could find electoral expression. Because the dominant party had "the only game in town," candidates and voters flocked to its primary. Numerous candidates filed for each office, fragmenting the vote until the leading contender could garner only 25 to 30 percent of the vote. Feeling that primary nominees should go into the general election representing a majority of the party voters, ten states traditionally faced with large fields of primary candidates provided for a "runoff" primary. If none of the candidates received a majority in the regular primary, the two top candidates engaged in a second primary campaign in the runoff. Runoff primaries became a point of national debate when Jesse Jackson claimed that they should be abolished as discriminatory against blacks. Blacks could win primaries if only pluralities were required to win nominations, he argued. It was also claimed that the cost of running in two primaries was prohibitive for most black candidates because they lacked the funds to finance two successive campaigns for the nomination.

Runoff primaries

Direct primaries, as generally understood and conducted, are usually partisan, i.e., Republican, Democrat. However, nonpartisan primaries are held in a number of states for local elections and for choosing certain state officers, particularly judges. Nebraska uses this method for choosing members of the state's unicameral legislature. The nonpartisan primary is designed to make certain officials independent of party organizations. The candidates are listed on the primary ballot without party designation or emblem. In some areas, a majority vote is sufficient to win the office without a second election; in others, the two top candidates for each office move to the general election regardless of the number of candidates or votes cast in the primary. The primary is thus used as a preliminary to the general election. The nonpartisan primary does not always escape political pressure, for candidates may be politically identified with one party or the other without the fact being stated on the ballot.

Primaries for nonpartisan offices

Primaries are generally regulated by state law. Partisan primaries are usually held on the same day for both parties at designated polling places. In some states, administration and supervision of primaries is left in the hands of the party organization; in other states, primaries are run by the election officials of state and local governments.

Names of candidates for nomination are entered on primary ballots in a variety of ways, including (1) petitions bearing a specified number of signatures, (2) preprimary convention endorsements, and (3) individual declaration and filing of candidacy. Of the

Getting on the primary ballot

three, the petition process is the most common. Aspirants for nomination may be required to pay a filing fee, which varies for different states and offices but must not be so excessive that it bars legitimate candidates from running.

States provide presidential primaries

Initially, delegates to national nominating conventions were chosen under procedures prescribed by party rules. However, as a part of the sweeping attack on political parties, the reform movement at the turn of the century encouraged states to pass laws providing for primaries to choose delegates to national conventions. By 1992, two-thirds of the states were providing for presidential primaries designed to influence the action of the national nominating convention, either in the selection of delegates or in giving candidates moral victories. Selecting delegates through an open primary in which non-Democrats could vote, Wisconsin invited the concern of the National Democratic Party and a rule was adopted to bar delegates from states permitting non-Democrats to participate in delegate selection. Out of this conflict came a Supreme Court decision ruling that national party rules could supersede state law on delegate selection because the open primary violated the First Amendment right of freedom of association when it failed to exclude nonmembers. The decision dampened enthusiasm for presidential primaries and they declined in number, partly as a result of the decision.[18] Even so, southern political leaders successfully launched an effort to coordinate the presidential primaries of southern states into one "Mega-Super-Tuesday" in 1988, continued in 1992, as a means of increasing their political clout in presidential politics.

Campaigning for State Offices

"Television is the new political god."[19]

This succinct observation about the pervasive impact of television on American politics may sound like an exaggeration but, in reality, it understates how television has transformed the conduct of political campaigns. As recently as thirty years ago, candidates in the quest for votes loaded their vehicles with boxes of campaign supplies and headed off down the highways to a series of bean feeds, banquets, rallies, and other gatherings of potential supporters. The campaign was a 6:00 A.M. to midnight ordeal of handshaking, street canvassing, baby-kissing, and stump speaking. Political communication was personal, eye-to-eye, and hand-to-hand. But not any longer.

Running for office in studios

In the coolness of a production studio, thirty-second television scripts are carefully reviewed by candidates, campaign managers, and, most importantly, the eyes of hired "political guns" brought in from Washington or New York. The words of the script and the message it projects come from the lips of 500 respondents to a poll designed to analyze public opinions, to find out where the people were going so the candidate could lead them there. The older candidates are advised to speak gingerly and youthfully; the youthful candidates are told to speak slowly, deliberately, and wisely. Every gesture or shift of posture is practiced. Then the cameras roll to capture the exact image for which the voters yearn. Soon the thirty-second campaign is sandwiched between ads for a rich coffee blend and a new powerful pickup—plucking at the heartstrings of every voter, not once, but five and ten times a day for three weeks.

Consultants market candidates

Initially, the mass media campaign was confined to presidential races and the larger states where the financial resources and the "market" were large enough to support the expense. However, mass media victories became so common that no serious candidate could afford to be without consultants, polls, and effective marketing techniques. As a consequence, consultants with their modern marketing techniques are now used in all state campaigns and numerous state legislative races.

The widespread use of consultants, whose sole mission is to win at any price, has generated wholesale negative advertising that attacks opponents with any criticism that will be believed. One observer, John Herbers, called this negative campaigning a deadly virus generated by consultants and advertising hucksters who "have brought us negative ads, insatiable need for big money from special interests, the removal of issues from campaigns, manipulation of voters, and the transformation of candidates into milquetoasts fearful of taking any stand their constituents might not agree with." Herbers claimed that consultant-run campaigns were much worse at the state and local level because they don't respect the traditions of local electorates and leave such a poison behind that the victor has an impaired ability to govern.[20] Efforts to curb negative campaigning have run afoul of the First Amendment guarantee of free speech, since laws prohibiting false or misleading campaign advertising have been found to be unconstitutional.[21] Protected by the Constitution, negative campaigning has spawned another group of campaign tacticians for hire called "opposition researchers" who plot negative twists in campaigns.[22]

Consultants bring negative campaigns

Television's attributes of sight, sound, and motion are also exploited by candidates for news. Campaign managers and media consultants plan proper location and proper activities for candidates to use in illustrating the themes of their campaigns. Points are made by calling a press conference before a crumbling prison wall, in the heart of an urban slum, at a factory gate, or next to an example of government waste. Giving television visual "media events" to bring to its viewers on the 6 o'clock news is an integral part of a well-plotted campaign of the 1990s.

Making media events

The mastery of television advertising and news is not the only step into modern technology for campaigns. Computers have also been put to work for political gain. They generate mailing lists by occupation, age, residence, political preference, and by other useful categories, to be used in solicitation for funds or for directing special correspondence with a special message to a special group. Thus, groups of voters receive letters addressing the fears and hopes they expressed in polls taken by the consultants.

Computerized mailings

Consultants, polls, production, and computers all converge into the modern media campaign that can spell victory for many candidates, but they also spell skyrocketing campaign costs. A gubernatorial race 30 years ago may have cost $100,000; the same race today may cost $4 million or more. As a matter of fact, the 1989 gubernatorial campaigns in New Jersey and Virginia cost each of the finalists $7 million or more. In 1990, an incumbent governor spent over $10 million to lose in Florida and gubernatorial candidates spent $53 million in California.[23]

Campaign costs skyrocket

Other candidates for state offices have been forced by competition into utilizing the new campaign technologies and absorbing the mounting campaign costs. As an example, the average campaign cost per seat in the Oregon state house of representatives rose from $10,000 in 1974 to $36,000 in 1988. In Maine, election costs increased by 173 percent between 1986 and 1988, according to a study of senate races by a legislative committee.

Financing the New Campaign

With victory hanging in the balance, pressures to raise sufficient funds to capitalize on the new skills and technologies have mounted over the past decade. Political parties have been unable to keep pace with the financial needs of their candidates. Conse-

Interest groups buy in

quently, interest groups are, for good or evil, moving to partially fill the vacuum through political action committees, commonly called PACs. In an effort to retain public accountability after a court ruling that PAC contributions could not be limited, state laws were passed requiring candidates to disclose the sources of their funds so the voters could determine whether or not influence was being sold in exchange for campaign dollars. While public disclosure laws may provide a semblance of accountability, they do not generate new funds with which to conduct campaigns.

States try campaign financing

To fill the void, one-half of the states have followed the lead of the national government by implementing campaign financing programs to furnish funds to candidates. Twelve states permit taxpayers to direct $1 or $2 of their income tax to a campaign fund; seven states make the taxpayers add the amount to their tax liability as a surcharge; and nine states give income taxpayers a credit or a deduction for contributions. Some of the states distribute these funds to the parties; other states give the money directly to candidates.[24]

Public funds too limited

These limited state experiments with public funding of campaigns have been ineffective in coping with mounting costs. Except for New Jersey and Michigan, public financing has not had significant impact on the campaign process because the amounts of money involved were too limited and funds given to parties were spent on general party programs rather than on campaigns.[25]

Limitations and the 1st Amendment

Ten of the states providing public funds for campaigns have also used the program to put limitations on campaign spending. According to the U.S. Supreme Court, such limitations can be imposed only when candidates accept them as a condition for receiving public funds. However, referring to First Amendment rights, the Court said that "the limitations on campaign expenditures, on independent expenditures by individuals and groups, and on expenditures by a candidate from his personal funds are constitutionally infirm."[26] If the funds being made available from state funding are less than could be raised privately, candidates opt to refuse the state money in favor of private solicitation campaigns, thereby avoiding the limitations.

States opt for restrictions

Many states have chosen not to enter the thicket of political finance but have preferred to direct their efforts toward regulation and restrictions on campaign activities. In addition to requiring public disclosure of campaign receipts, they have enacted scores of statutes to prohibit corrupt practices. Many of the provisions of these statutes grew out of the era of political corruption in the late 1800s, while many others were added in the wake of the 1972 Watergate scandal that sent President Richard Nixon out of the White House.

Laws define corrupt practices

Corrupt practices acts adopted by states may define corrupt campaign practices as circulating unsigned campaign literature, giving deceptive speeches, making false accusations in advertisements, engaging in political espionage, giving voters items of monetary value, stealing campaign literature, charging higher advertising rates for political candidates than other customers, using public property for campaign purposes, and paying newspapers for editorials or news stories. State law may also prohibit certain contributions to campaigns, such as those from corporations and labor unions. It may also try to limit or regulate the role parties can play in political campaigns. The corrupt practices acts also list activities that are considered crimes against the elective franchise, among which are multiple voting, misrepresenting qualifications for voting, violating absentee ballot procedures, bribing election officials, and obstructing or intimidating voters.

Except for crimes against the election process, courts have been very restrictive in interpreting the power of state government to regulate campaign activities. The Supreme Court upheld a ruling that no state law can impose a fine on deceptive campaign speeches without adhering to a malice standard; neither can they impose criminal sanctions on candidates who publish defamatory political advertisements so late in the campaign that the opposition has no time to respond; nor can they deny a candidate victory because he or she made a campaign promise contrary to state law.[27]

Courts limit regulations

National Parties In Legislative Campaigns

With presidential campaigns financed from public rather than private funds, millions of campaign dollars became available for other contests in the political arena. Not only have these funds escalated the cost of congressional races, but much of it is now used in state executive and legislative races. Beginning in 1978, the Republican National Committee started directing campaign money to state legislative races. They were joined in 1984 by the American Legislative Exchange Council, a conservative organization of state legislators, whose political action committee targeted specific senate and house seats. By early 1986, both national parties had organized efforts to influence the control of legislative assemblies. Since state legislatures draw the boundaries for congressional districts after each decennial census, the two parties were vying for control of the 1991 state assemblies—the Republicans with their "1991 Plan" and the Democrats with "Project 500."

National parties enter state politics

Resources furnished by the national organizations to state and local parties and candidates included techniques, technology, cash, and consultants. National functionaries taught local volunteers to organize effective get-out-the-vote campaigns, to maximize computers, to capture critical information in polls, and to conduct effective advertising campaigns. As a result of the involvement of outside party consultants, negative campaigning escalated—especially in the 1990 elections—when battles for control of legislative bodies generated campaigns of innuendoes, half-truths, and misrepresentation.

Negative campaigns escalate

Overview

In recent decades, numerous scholars and political observers have questioned the viability of parties. Primaries now determine the nominations; interest group money has displaced party funds; electronic media have come to dominate mass communications, and citizens have become more independent. In the words of one scholar: "No longer is the political party the central political institution it used to be in many, but by no means all, states."[28] At the same time, other researchers cite data that suggest political parties are more active than ever before in staffing offices, assisting in campaigns, and demonstrating other characteristics of organizational vitality.[29]

Parties decline

Through the years, the political focus has shifted from the party organization to the political leader. With a direct primary to bypass party conventions, with mass media campaigns to communicate directly to voters, and with PAC funding to finance campaigns, the political leader has gained considerable independence from the party organization. Unable to command the loyalty of officeholders and candidates, parties are hard-pressed to carry out their traditional functions. They no longer have the authority necessary to negotiate conflict, furnish policy, control recruitment of candidates, or bridge institutional gaps. Much of the campaign financing has been taken over by interest groups; growing independence among voters has reduced the need for "structuring the vote." As we review the traditional functions of parties, we find that the new political environment has reduced the effectiveness of parties in favor of other actors. If they are to survive as viable entities, parties will be required to redefine their niche in the changing world of new and newer politics.

Endnotes

1. Gordon S. Black, "A Theory of Professionalization in Politics," *American Political Science Review* 64 (September 1970): 865.

2. Survey by Yankelovich, Skelly, and White, September 20–22, 1983, quoted by John Kenneth White and Dwight L. Morris in a paper for delivery at the annual meeting of the American Political Science Association, Washington, D.C., August 30–September 2, 1984.

3. "Opinion Roundup," *Public Opinion* 16 (October/November 1983): 34–37.

4. Susan Biemesderfer, "Political Women Give Even Cowboys the Blues," *State Legislatures* 16 (October 1990): 21.

5. Linda L. M. Bennett and Stephen Earl Bennett, "Enduring Gender Differences in Political Interest," *American Politics Quarterly* 17 (January, 1989): 105–122.

6. See *Elrod* v. *Burns,* 427 U.S. 347 (1976); *Branti* v. *Finkel,* 445 U.S. 507, 48 LW 4331 (1980); and *Reitan* v. *Republican Party of Illinois,* 496 U.S. 110 S. Ct. 2729 (1990).

7. Cheri Collis, "Cleaning up the spoils system," *State Government News* 33 (September 1990): 6.

8. *Eu, Secretary of State of California et al.* v. *San Francisco County Democratic Central Committee et al.,* 87–1269 U.S. Supreme Court syllabus, p. 1.

9. For a review of a modern political machine, see a series of articles on the Republican machine in Nassau County, New York in *NEWSDAY,* Aug. 21, 1989.

10. Robert J. Spitzer, "A Political Party is Born: Single-Issue Advocacy and the New York Election Law," *National Civic Review* 73 (July/August 1984): 321–328.

11. John F. Bibby et al., "Parties in State Politics," *Politics in the American States,* 5th ed., ed. Virginia Gray, Herbert Jacob, and Robert R. Albritton (Glenview, IL: Scott, Foresman and Company, 1990), pp. 90–92.

12. Dorothy Davidson Nesbit and D. D. B. Needham, "Changing Partisanship among Southern Party Activists," *Journal of Politics* 50 (May, 1988): 322–334. Also, see "The Two Souths," *National Journal* 18 (September 20, 1986): 2218–2220.

13. "Elected Democrats in Mississippi are switching parties," *Governing* 3 (July, 1990): 15.

14. Charles Francis Adams, ed., *The Works of John Adams,* vol. 2 (Boston: Little, Brown and Co., 1850), p. 144. The citation is from a diary entry of February 1763.

15. *Book of the States 1992–93* (Lexington, Ky.: Council of State Governments, 1992), pp. 273–274.

16. "Washington Primary Is No Wet Blanket," *National Civic Review* 70 (November 1981): 551. This is a summary of Richard C. Kelley and Sara Jane Weir, "Unwrapping the Blanket Primary," *Washington Public Policy Notes* (Seattle: Institute for Public Policy and Management, University of Washington).

17. Charles D. Hadley, "The Louisiana Open Elections System Reform: Elite Perceptions and Political Realities," a paper prepared for delivery at the annual meeting of the Southern Political Science Association, Birmingham, Ala. November 3–5, 1983.

18. See Malcolm E. Jewell, ed., *Comparative State Politics* (University of Kentucky, December 1983): 2–8.

19. William J. Crotty and Gary C. Jacobson, *American Parties in Decline* (Boston: Little, Brown & Co., 1980): 67.

20. John Herbers, "To Free Campaigns from Hucksters, Try Little Demagoguery," *Governing* 3 (May 1990), p. 10.

21. Susan Biemesderfer, "Campaigning Ad Nauseum," *State Legislatures* 16 (September 1990): 24–26.

22. Robert Guskind, "Digging Up Dirt," *National Journal* 22 (October 27, 1990): 2592–2596.

23. Thad Beyle, "The 1989 Gubernatorial Races," *Comparative State Politics* (Sangamon State University, April 1990): 32; T. K. Wetherell, "Florida Takes the Big Money Out of Political Campaigns," *State Legislatures* 17 (August 1991): 44; and Thad Beyle, "It costs a lot to get there," *State Government News* 34 (November, 1991): 10.

24. Richard G. Smolka, "Election Legislation, 1990–91," *Book of the States* (Lexington, Ky.: Council of State Governments, 1992), pp. 258–264, and a companion article by Keon S. Chi, "Financing State and Local Elections; Trends and Issues," pp. 283–293.

25. Karen J. Fling, "The States as Laboratories of Reform," *Political Finance,* ed., Herbert Alexander (Beverly Hills: Sage Publications, Inc., 1979): 257–258, as quoted by Alexander and Frutig, ibid., p. 8.

26. *Buckley* v. *Valeo,* 424 U.S. 1 (1976).

27. *Vanasco* v. *Schwartz,* 401 F. Supp. at 94 (1975); *Commonwealth of Pennsylvania* v. *Wadzinski,* 422 A2d 124 (1980); *Brown* v. *Hartlage,* 102 S. Ct. 1523 (1982). Cases by Candice Romig, *Fair Campaign Practices,* a monograph published by the National Conference of State Legislatures, Denver, April 1983.

28. Alan Rosenthal, *Governors & Legislatures* (Washington, D.C.: CQ Press, 1990): 17.

29. See *The Transformation in American Parties* (A 106) published by the U.S. Advisory Commission on Intergovernmental Relations (Washington, D.C.: Government Printing Office, 1986) and Cornelius P. Cotter et al., *Party Organizations in American Politics* (Pittsburgh, Pa.: University of Pittsburgh Press, 1989).

CHAPTER 8

INTEREST GROUPS

Citizen Participation in Policy-Making through Organizations

Chapter 6 discussed voting as one avenue available to citizens for influencing the policy-making process of government. Chapter 7 considered playing an active role in political parties by writing platforms, nominating candidates, and campaigning a second avenue. In Chapter 8, we look at a third avenue—participation through organizations that represent particular interests before legislative bodies and executive agencies.

Madison foresees interest groups

On the subject of interest groups, James Madison wrote cogently in *The Federalist,* No. 10 of "a landed interest, a manufacturing interest, a mercantile interest, a moneyed interest, with many lesser interests" and observed that the "regulation of these various and interfering interests forms the principal task of modern legislation," involving "the spirit of party and faction in the necessary and ordinary operations of government." Madison realized that factional interests are inevitable and cannot be abolished or prevented in any way short of destroying liberty itself.

Two extreme views

Just how important are these organized factional interests or "pressure groups"? The naive citizen may have a totally unrealistic impression of the governmental process as consisting principally of well-insulated activities of voting, lawmaking, administration, and court interpretation, and may be unaware of the continuous day-to-day struggle among groups for power and influence over governmental decision-makers. At the other extreme, however, perhaps a citizen may have arrived at a cynical view that pressure groups are all-powerful, with politicians and administrators acting as mere pawns in a game of power politics. The truth is probably somewhere in between these extremes. A more realistic view of state and local government will strike a balance that includes an understanding of the importance of both the official institutions of government and the nonofficial forces of interest groups. (This chapter will use the terms *interest group* and *pressure group* interchangeably.)

Define interest groups

Interest groups are associations of people, organized and unorganized, that seek to influence public policy and make their appearance at every point public policy is made. They may be national organizations with millions of members working out of Washington offices to influence the national government; they may be state associations that send officers to the state capitol to appear before legislative committees; they may

Title photo: Taxpayers constituted a formidable interest group when they appeared en masse on the steps of the New Jersey capitol to protest higher taxes.

Table 8.1 Lobbying Techniques Used by Utah Lobbyists

Technique	% Using Technique
Contacting government officials to present your point of view	97.4
Testifying at hearings	89.5
Alerting legislators to the effects of a bill on their district	89.5
Sending letters to members of organizations to inform them about activities	86.8
Engaging in informal contacts with officials	86.8
Having influential constituents contact their legislator	78.9
Talking to press and media	76.3
Presenting research results or technical information	73.7
Serving on advisory commissions and boards	68.4
Entering into coalitions with other organizations	65.8
Attempting to shape the implementation of policies	63.2
Mounting grass-roots lobbying efforts	57.9
Inspiring letter-writing or telegram campaigns	52.6
Making financial contributions to electoral campaigns	36.8
Attempting to influence appointments to public office	31.6
Doing favors for officials who need assistance	23.7

Ronald J. Hrebenar, Melanee Cherry and Kathanne Green, "Utah: Church and Corporate Power in the Nation's Most Conservative State," Interest Group Politics In the American West, *ed. Hrebenar & Thomas (Salt Lake City: University of Utah Press, 1987), p. 117.*

be community clubs that send members to the county commission meetings; or they may be neighborhood associations that work with municipal governing boards.

A pressure group may exert influence to secure favorable legislation or administrative decisions. It may be against a too rigid or too lenient enforcement of a law or regulation, as in cases of urban zoning, formulating traffic rules, or granting permits for selling and serving beer. It may be for or against expansion of city limits; a proposed administrative reorganization; proposed changes in a state constitution; the issuance of county, municipal, or state bonds, or the election of candidates because of their views on issues affecting group interests. A pressure group may have an educational, religious, racial, or economic purpose, or a combination of purposes.

Varying interests

The techniques being used by lobbyists to represent their constituents in the policy process has been well summarized by scholars researching the lobbying activities in Utah. The findings are very similar to lobbying activities found in other states (See table 8.1).

Functions of Interest Groups

To influence policy, interest groups express their interests before the government through representatives commonly called *lobbyists*. Depending on the nature of the organization and the issues involved, lobbyists may be lawyers or public relations people experienced in the processes of government who are hired on contract for specific periods of time or for specific appearances. Lobbyists may also be members of a permanent staff of an organization who take time to interact with government policymakers. Lobbyists could also include lay members or officers of organizations who are called in to give a "citizen's" touch to the lobbying effort. Technically, then, lobbyists may also be

1. Represent constituents in policy process

Figure 8.1

Appearing before legislative committees to present information and opinions is just one of the methods used by lobbyists to influence policy making. *(Photo courtesy of Minnesota House of Representatives, Tom Olmscheid.)*

individuals who appear to promote their own particular concerns. All types will be seen at a legislative session or interacting with executive agencies.

Lobbying peaks during legislative session

The most intense lobbying occurs during sessions of the state legislature when policy-making is at its peak. Representatives from scores of organizations are drawn to the state capitol by the hundreds of bills proposed to change policy in one way or another (Figure 8.1).

Contrasting parties and interest groups

Interest groups differ from political parties in several ways. Interest groups seek to influence government while parties seek to control it; interest groups are homogeneous in their makeup while parties are quite diverse; as private associations interest groups are free to organize as they choose while parties must follow state laws to a certain degree; and the members of interest groups may be required to meet certain criteria, pay dues, and belong to other interest groups while parties tend to be open organizations with members loyal to only one party.

Culture may shape lobbying ethics

The ethics of lobbying will vary with the political culture, customs, and configuration of power in the legislative process. What is perfectly proper in an "individualistic" state may be regarded as unacceptably corrupt in a "moralistic" state. If bestowing favors on influential legislators has been a common practice for decades, it will not raise eyebrows in the 1990s. If the legislative process gives committee chairpersons life or death control of legislation, the opportunity for corruption is created and may be utilized by unscrupulous lobbyists and legislators. On the whole, however, the tactics of lobbyists have become much more forthright and honest since the late 1800s, partly because of the growing sophistication of legislators and partly because of increased news coverage of the legislative process.

Lobbyists active with administrators

Lobbying does not stop when a legislative battle is ended. As table 8.1 indicates, whether that battle is won or lost, the effective lobbyists will shift their focus to the administrative arena, or perhaps to the courts or the voters.[1] With the growing importance of administrators in state and local governments, especially with increased discretionary powers, the lobbyist's initial legislative defeat may be turned into an administrative victory or vice versa. If an interest group feels that it is not getting a fair deal from a particular government agency, it may support legislation to take the agency "out of politics," usually by establishing an independent board or commission. This commonly means organizing an agency in such a way that members of the most interested pressure group will control the selection of personnel and the formulation of policy, or make it more difficult for a competing pressure group to gain control. Thus highway contractors want an autonomous state highway commission, sportsmen want an autonomous game and fish commission, education leaders want an autonomous board of education, doctors want an autonomous board of health, and so on. To the extent that interest groups succeed in such efforts to increase their access to state and local officials by pulling "pet agencies" away from the rest of the governmental structure, the result is a fragmented, uncoordinated government. Most interest groups would agree that this fragmentation is not proper for all state or local departments, but would insist that their function (or agency) is different.

Lobbyists favor fragmentation

While legislative bodies are made up of representatives chosen by geographic areas, interest groups bring a second dimension to the policy-making process by representing economic, social, religious, ideological, and other concerns. Many organizations have too few members to influence a party platform, secure the nomination of a favorable candidate, or influence the outcome of legislative elections. For their members, effective representation in the policy process can only occur through interest-group activities. For larger organizations that may already have influenced the political process, the interest group system provides a second opportunity for them to assert their demands. In fact, a public opinion poll taken in the 1980s revealed that a plurality of people felt that interest groups represented them better than either of the political parties.[2]

2. A second opportunity for representation

In some cases, this trust is misplaced. Critical evaluation of interest groups suggests the possibility that they do not always reflect the opinions of their members. In many organizations, there is no method available by which members may express or discuss views. In some cases, the full-time staff will assume the right to speak on behalf of the membership without consultation. If the interest group receives money from sources other than membership fees, the leaders may modify views of members to placate those contributing funds or grants.[3]

Constituents not always represented

Although some citizens are content to have their respective organizations represent their particular interests, others are highly motivated. They are not satisfied to restrict their involvement to merely paying membership dues or by voting for party candidates once every two or four years. Feeling strongly about an issue, such as health care or abortion, they can focus their money and efforts on a continuing basis through an interest group. Most interest groups are strengthened by this grass roots participation.

3. Afford opportunities to participate

Interest groups seek to inform the public about the problems and needs of their members. Consequently, many of them have continuous public information programs. Naturally, they seek to put their organization and its demands in the best possible light by building a favorable public image in the education process. A positive public image

4. Educate the public

can be converted into influence in policy-making circles because it gives the organization an aura of credibility and respect. A group respected by the public will be respected by the public's representatives.

Using propaganda

In their "education" campaigns, interest groups of all types are likely to rely heavily upon propaganda to support lobbying efforts. Propaganda may provide useful information on public matters and contribute to popular education, but it is not primarily designed to educate or stimulate objective thinking. Propagandists seek to utilize or manipulate words and symbols in such ways as to influence belief and action between predetermined ends. American propaganda pressure is greatest in the realm of politics and policy. At the same time, propaganda is subject to extensive check and scrutiny, thanks largely to pressure-group competition, increased news coverage, and the sophistication of legislators with growing seniority. After a session or two, legislators become quite adept at cutting through the propaganda to get to the unvarnished facts.

5. Facilitate the political process

Because politicians ultimately become the policymakers, pressure groups like to "get in on the ground floor" by influencing the selection and election of candidates favorable to their points of view.

a. Infiltrate parties

Many interest groups resort to "infiltration," the practice of getting members of the interest group to become active in the political party machinery and work on the inside. They are encouraged to attend precinct and party caucuses, hold party offices, serve as delegates to conventions, write party platforms, serve on campaign committees, and even become candidates for office. As an example, state education associations embarked on an aggressive infiltration campaign over the past 25 years with great success. Not only have many of their members become legislators, but their infiltration partially explains the rapid rise of state education associations as powerful state lobbies in the 1980s and 1990s.

b. Electioneer internally

Another technique interest groups have found effective is internal electioneering—rallying members to support certain political candidates or issues. After each legislative session adjourns, or just prior to an election, interest groups compile the voting records of legislators on issues important to the groups. These are circulated within the organizations and members are expected to vote against legislators with "bad" voting records. If the organization feels that it commands public support, it may publicize these voting records in the mass media to bring credit to supporters and defeat to opponents. Another internal electioneering activity of organizations with large memberships is the get-out-the-vote drive to get their members to the polls. This is a common practice among labor unions.

c. Provide campaign funds

Financing the campaigns of friendly candidates is a third method interest groups use to facilitate the political process. As discussed in chapter 7, political action committees, created specifically to solicit funds from within organizations, have mushroomed dramatically in the last ten years and are partially responsible for the skyrocketing expenditures in political campaigns. According to reports of the Federal Election Commission, the total number of PACs has grown from 600 in 1974 to over 4,000 in 1992.

Pressure group infiltration in partisan politics is designed to get party policy committed to their goals and to elect those candidates who favor their programs or those who are at least willing to lend a friendly ear when policy is being made. Because their primary objectives are self-serving, some of their activities impair rather than help the political parties. Many of the infiltrators have little party loyalty and readily sacrifice the interests of the party to serve their own ends. While PAC money is welcomed by candidates, it undermines the candidate-party relationship by diverting candidate loyalties away from party ideology. Thus, the aid of interest groups has not come to parties without some price.

Activities impair parties

In the realm of lobbying, information is power. Every proposal for action, whether in the legislative or in the executive arena, involves consideration of many facets and impacts. Legislators cannot know all of the implications of every bill. Lobbyists representing the various and competing viewpoints bring forth information and research to buttress their arguments. Without this input, many legislative and executive actions would result in unexpected consequences and embarrassment for the policymakers. Therefore, lobbyists with solid, well-researched information are not only tolerated but they are welcomed into the policy-making arena.

6. Provide research and information

After securing approval of a program or policy by the legislative branch, the interest group moves to the executive branch where administration occurs. Having a special interest in the results of its labors, the interest group will interact on a regular basis with the administering agencies to see that the programs or policies are being carried out to its satisfaction. As an example, the state beekeepers association may have spent the entire legislative session testifying before committees and "button-holing" legislators to secure passage of a law requiring proper spacing of competing beehives. After the bill is passed, association representatives appear at the department of agriculture, the designated administering agency, to propose the best methods for implementing the legislation. If the executive agency fails to meet expectations, the interest group will return to the legislature for amendments and directives that will force the kind of administration it desires. With many legislatures unable to exercise fully their responsibilities of overseeing executive performance, the monitoring activities of interest groups help in the execution of this legislative function by alerting legislators to deviations from legislative policy.

7. Monitor administration of programs

Aid legislatures in oversight

In theory, the economic, political and social makeup of most states is sufficiently diverse to produce a wide variety of interest groups able to neutralize the unreasonable demands of other groups. Neutralization occurs when groups of equal power joust in the legislative halls or executive agencies. While it is true that neutralization does take place in many instances, the theory breaks down when some groups have more resources than others, or when some groups have better combinations of resources, or when some interests are not represented at all. In the view of one researcher, the collection of lobbyists at the state capitol will not fairly represent the public interest until all groups are represented, all groups have equal access to decision-makers, all groups have equal resources, and group leaders accurately represent the views of their members.[4]

8. Neutralize other interest groups

Classifications of Interest Groups

The complexity of our pluralistic society is fully reflected in the variety of interest groups that includes the single individual with an eccentric cause, the multinational corporation seeking tax benefits, the religious group that seeks exemption from the teacher certification laws, and the environmentalists who want a nature preserve. Although all cannot be classified into neat groupings, four major categories will include the vast majority of them.

1. Economic interests

As Madison surveyed the field of interest groups (factions) in *Federalist* No. 10, he noted that " . . . the most common and durable source of factions has been the various and unequal distribution of property." Today the largest and most powerful interest groups are concerned with state policy in relation to property—its control and its redistribution. The corporate community pairs off with labor unions over the ground rules for collective bargaining; state tax policies draw out organizations that seek to shift taxes from one economic group to another, and economic interests appear to advocate government support for certain economic expansion and opposition to other economic activities, depending on the economic base of the state. In-state economic groups will seek state policies that will discriminate against out-of-state economic groups.

2. Public interest organizations

Because of the legal relationship between the state and its political subdivisions, local governments have always maintained a strong interest in legislative and executive policy. However, in recent years, states have escalated their financial assistance for local functions, increased their supervisory activities over local governments, and assumed more responsibility for administering local programs. As the state government enlarged its role in the state-local relationship, local governments have more at stake in each session of the legislature. Consequently, the states' leagues of cities, associations of county officers, mayors' conferences, organizations of township officials, school board associations, and the other representatives of local governments have all accelerated their lobbying efforts, representing the interests of their publics back home.

3. Professional and occupational groups

Professional and occupational groups are fully aware of the scope of state police powers. As explained in chapter 4, the police power can be used to enforce licensing requirements for numerous professions and occupations in the state. Doctors, lawyers, pharmacists, accountants, optometrists, real estate agents, veterinarians, and scores of others are either licensed by the state or seeking to enhance their field of endeavor by becoming a licensed occupation or profession.

4. Ideological groups

Falling under the classification of ideological interest groups are organizations seeking to improve the social, moral, environmental, political, or economic well-being of humans. For example, Common Cause embarked on a state-by-state campaign to guarantee open, accessible, and honest government; right-to-life organizations continually seek to curtail abortions; the League of Women Voters conducts studies and supports programs to improve the workings of democratic government; "ban the can" groups of environmentalists come forward in some states to halt litter of nonreturnable containers; the National Organization of Women and the American Civil Liberties Union seek to safeguard individual rights at the state level. These are just a few of the ideologically oriented pressure groups.

Sources of Group Strength

In a comprehensive 50-state study of interest groups, Professors Ronald Hrebenar and Clive Thomas reported wide variations among states in interest group structure and power.[5] For example, in Alaska, the oil and gas lobby ranked fifth in the number of lobbyists, first in expenditures for lobbying and yet wasn't ranked among the five strongest lobbies in the state.[6] In Idaho, the big spenders on lobbying were business and labor interests while the Idaho Education Association was regarded as the most powerful lobby.[7] These examples point out that the groups that spend the most money or have the most lobbyists are not necessarily the most influential. In fact, interest group strength is determined by a number of factors.

Money isn't everything

Perhaps the most obvious source of strength is the number of members the lobbying organization can claim. This should be expected in a democratic society in which all voters are equal and have the same clout on election outcomes. But size alone is not a guarantee of strength unless it is accompanied by unity of purpose. As the size of an organization grows, maintaining unity becomes a greater challenge. However, if large size is accompanied by unity and cohesion, a high degree of lobbying strength is assured.

1. Number of members

Geographic distribution is another factor of organizational strength, primarily because members of the legislature are chosen from districts throughout the state. An organization can benefit from having members located in as many legislative districts as possible since legislators are usually more sensitive to the wishes of their own constituents than lobbyists at the state capitol.

2. Geographic distribution

A less tangible but equally vital factor is status. Leaders of the medical profession, the banking association, or the bar association will usually enjoy easier access to the decision-making circles of state and local government than will representatives of migratory farm workers, "off brand cults," or other groups that society has generally branded as having low status. Those who are not committed to working "within the system" can hardly expect to be held in high regard by the leaders in the governmental system. Status is not a permanent condition nor is it the same from state to state or city to city with respect to similar pressure groups. Leaders of the NAACP may not enjoy the same access to the Mississippi legislature as they do to the legislatures of Illinois, Michigan, and New York. Support of the local Chamber of Commerce may well defeat a proposal in some city councils but it may guarantee easy passage in others. Reputations vary with circumstances, but a prestigious membership is generally a tremendous asset to a pressure group.

3. Status

Although status and wealth do not always coincide, wealth is often a contributing factor in the traditional American definition of success. Money is used to acquire political power for interest groups up and down the spectrum of social status and, if effectively used, it can help moderate the bad image of a low-status group. Money is an important factor because it makes possible expensive image-building campaigns, public information programs, articulate professional lobbyists, and it buys access when contributed through PACs to the election campaigns of policymakers.

4. Money

Organization and leadership are other factors that can make or break the power of a pressure group. A decentralized, loosely knit organization with diversified local power centers may find it difficult to act quickly, communicate effectively, and speak with a single voice at the time and place needed. A centralized, tightly knit organization that concentrates authority in the top leadership can take public stands quickly and is not easily outmaneuvered by opposition groups or by state and local decision makers. The degree of centralization or decentralization in a pressure group may well

5. Organization and leadership

be the result of the quality of leadership the group has had over several decades. Group members and public officials alike look to a strong leader as the legitimate spokesperson for the interests of the group. Thus, legislators will come to know that popular, able Lobbyist X is the State Trucking Association, whereas less popular, less able Lobbyist Y can't really speak for the League of Municipalities but must check back constantly with 200 mayors, while the battle lines and issues may change drastically.

6. Program   Another characteristic of a pressure group that affects its power position in the state or community is the ideological content of the group's program. A simple axiom exists that a program reflecting the prevailing system of values and beliefs of the public at large will have easier sledding than one that runs counter to community values, all else being equal. Granted, a good public relations campaign may make black appear to be white on occasions, but pressure groups cannot afford to put their trust in such manipulative miracles. If a group's program is seen as being in the public interest, it will be more readily accepted than if it appears to benefit a limited few at the expense of the many.

7. Political environment   Another factor is the political environment in which the pressure group must operate. This is a characteristic of the state or local community rather than of the pressure group itself, but it may be an important source of strength or weakness in the group. The separation of powers, federal system, and weak political parties all provide a variety of access points for interest group exploitation. In addition, such factors as the attitude of legislators and councilors toward lobbying, the relative strength or weakness of the governor or local executives, and the degree of autonomy or integration of the administrative agencies all affect the strength of pressure groups and will not produce the same pattern in any two states. Other interest groups are also a part of this political environment. If effective opposing interest groups are present in the system, they can hamper or neutralize the influence of other groups.

8. Legitimacy   Pressure group strength is affected by the legitimacy of the group in the eyes of the legislators. If the group is acknowledged by policymakers as representing a public that deserves consideration, its requests will be greeted with favor. As an example, an association of mayors has inherent legitimacy because it is made up of elected officials promoting the interests of their communities, with little or no motive of personal gain.

9. Membership loyalty   Finally, an interest group's strength will also be influenced by competition for the loyalty of its own members. Pressure groups have extensive overlapping of membership, and frequently an organization or its leadership lacks the support of important blocs of members. Many a citizen belongs to several organized groups serving different and even conflicting purposes. Physicians who are members of the American Legion and the American Medical Association cannot support both organizations when they clash over policies relating to public health or hospital services. Citizens may not be able to go along with their taxpayers' association on a program of economy and at the same time support their civic group's plan for an expensive civic auditorium. The National Women's Political Caucus, with membership close to 40,000 in 45 states and 250 local caucuses, illustrates an organization with diverse and overlapping membership, sometimes and in some places stronger than others, depending on the issue and the setting. It is possible to have strong sympathies for both the environmental and energy interest groups, but they can be expected to lock horns in serious combat when it comes to defining the public interest.

Interest Groups in the States

Three decades ago, it was possible for researchers to identify specific patterns of interest group power in the various states. In the early 1960s, L. Harmon Zeigler discussed the "emerging patterns of group activity"—an alliance of dominant groups, a single dominant interest, a conflict between two dominant groups, and the triumph of many interests.[8] However, much of the interest group research of the 1950s and 1960s on patterns has been rendered obsolete by a series of trends that have brought forth new patterns of state interest groups in the 1990s, with "the triumph of many interests" dominant.

Pattern consists of many interests

New groups have come into existence to reflect the changing interests of people and the sharpening focus of a maturing economy and society. Each new decade has added its organizations to the growing pyramid, with the 1970s adding environmental, equal rights, health care, and consumer protection groups, among others, and the 1980s adding groups driven by single-issue moral questions, such as abortion and the usage of alcohol, drugs and tobacco.

1. Variety of interests growing

Another trend, initiated in the Carter years and accelerated during the Reagan-Bush administrations, was the fiscal freeze in Washington that forced more decisions to the states. With growing responsibilities and diminishing funds, states witnessed an increase in lobbying at the state level. Not only did this mean more intense lobbying by traditional state organizations but it also meant the arrival of lobbyists whose primary scene of action had been Washington. In the late 1980s, a number of national lobbying firms reorganized to serve clients throughout the nation at state capitols.[9]

2. Lobbying at state level increases

A third trend has been the increasing intensity of lobbying activities, not only due to the shift of responsibility to states but also due to the growing competitiveness of political parties across the nation. As the one-party electoral districts have disappeared, the political activities of interest groups have become more decisive in campaigns. When only a few votes can change the outcome of an election, policymakers must be more responsive to more organizations than ever before. Adding to the intensity of lobbying is the growing sophistication of lobbying organizations in the use of lobbying techniques. Skillful use of PAC money, mass media campaigns, "grass roots" mobilization, and other techniques are now being managed by highly professional and experienced lobbyists.

3. More influence in politics

A fourth trend has been the gradual but persistent reordering of the interest group power structure as the factors of interest group strength, such as programs, environment, status, leadership and legitimacy, change with the times. Looking back over the last few decades, we have seen the passing of the giants that had historically dominated some states—Anaconda Copper in Montana, the Southern Pacific Railroad in California, DuPont in Delaware, oil in Texas, and sugar in Hawaii. In the 1990s, many states still have lobbies that are influential and prominent, but they must share the

4. Reordering of power

Table 8.2 Ranking of the 40 Most Influential Interests in the 50 States[1]

	Number of States in Which Interest Ranked Among:		
	Most Effective	**Second Level of Effectiveness**	**Less Effective**
1. School Teachers' Organizations (predominantly NEA)	43	5	2[2]
2. General Business Organizations (Chambers of Commerce, etc.)	31	17	5[3,4]
3. Bankers' Associations (includes Savings & Loan Associations)	28	14	10
4. Manufacturers (companies & associations)	23	15	18
5. Traditional Labor Associations (predominantly the AFL-CIO)	23	13	12
6. Utility Companies & Associations (electric, gas, telephone, water)	20	17	14
7. Individual Banks & Financial Institutions	20	12	19
8. Lawyers (predominantly State Bar Associations & Trial Lawyers)	15	15	22
9. General Local Government Organizations (Municipal Leagues, County Organizations, etc.)	15	18	17
10. General Farm Organizations (mainly state Farm Bureaus)	11	23	16
11. Doctors	14	16	20
12. State & Local Government Employees (other than teachers)	16	11	23
13. Insurance (companies & associations)	13	14	27
14. Realtors' Associations	12	8	31
15. Individual Traditional Labor Unions (Teamsters, UAW, etc.)	13	3	35
16. K-12 Education Interests (other than teachers)	10	6	35
17. Health Care Groups (other than doctors)	4	18	26
18. Agricultural Commodity Organizations (stockgrowers, grain growers, etc.)	9	7	34
19. Universities and Colleges (institutions and personnel)	7	11	33
20. Oil and Gas (companies & associations)	7	10	34
21. Retailers (companies & trade associations)	9	5	37
22. Contractors/Builders/Developers	8	7	36
23. Environmentalists	3	16	31
24. Individual Cities and Towns	7	6	39
25. Liquor, Wine and Beer Interests	5	10	36

power with scores of competitors. Table 8.2, compiled by Hrebenar and Thomas from their 50-state study, reflects the new order of interest groups in the states.

Interest groups vs. government

Another dimension to the study of interest groups in states is the collective power they possess in relation to other political institutions in the state. In other words, do interest groups dominate the legislature, the executive, the political parties in their drive to achieve their goals, or do the traditional political institutions keep them at bay? By sifting through their 50-state study, Hrebenar and Thomas have been able to create five classifications for assessing the overall impact of interest groups.

Table 8.2 continued

	Number of States in Which Interest Ranked Among:		
	Most Effective	Second Level of Effectiveness	Less Effective
26. Mining Companies & Associations	7	5	39
27. Truckers and Private Transport Interests (excluding railroads)	7	2	41
28. Public Interest/Good Government Groups[5]	0	16	34
29. State Agencies	5	2	43
30. Forest Product Companies	4	4	43
31. Senior Citizens	1	11	38
32. Railroads	2	6	42
33. Women and Minorities	1	7	42
34. Religious Interests	3	2	45
35. Sportsmen/Hunting & Fishing (includes anti-gun control groups)	2	4	44
36. Gaming Interests (race tracks/casinos/ lotteries)	1	5	44
37. Anti-Abortionists[6]	2	2	44
Tourist Industry Groups[6]	2	2	44
38. Newspapers/Media Interests[6]	1	4	45
Taxpayers' Groups[6]	1	4	45
39. Tobacco Lobby	0	2	48
40. Miscellaneous	0	3	47

[1]*Rankings were calculated by allocating 2 points for each "most effective" ranking and 1 point for each "second level of effectiveness" placement and adding the totals. Where a tie in total points occurs, where possible, interests are ranked according to the number of "most effective" placements.*
[2]*These two states are Maryland and South Dakota. Although teacher organizations are very active in these states they are not considered to be effective.*
[3]*The totals for some interests add up to more than 50. This is because specific groups within an interest category sometimes appear within both the "most effective" and the "second level of effectiveness" category in a particular state. For example, general business organizations are ranked in both categories in New Jersey. Therefore, they are counted once for each category.*
[4]*The five states where general business organizations are not ranked are: California, Nevada, New Mexico, Oregon and Missouri. However, business interests are well represented in all these states through more specialized business groups.*
[5]*A very broad category which includes: Common Cause, the League of Women Voters, Public Interest Research Groups, or "PIRGs," the American Civil Liberties Union, anti-nuclear groups, etc.*
[6]*Tied ranking.*
From Politics in the American States: A Comparative Analysis, *5/e by Virginia Gray, et al. Copyright 1990 by Virginia Gray, Herbert Jacob, and Robert B. Albritton. Reprinted by permission of HarperCollins Publishers.*

As table 8.3 indicates, interest groups are dominant in nine states, most of which are in the southeastern part of the United States. In 18 states, interest groups are somewhat dominant but must negotiate; in 18 states, interest groups are "complementary" and in five states they are largely subordinate to the other political institutions. In none of the states are they totally subordinate.

Interest-Group Power is Growing
It has become conventional wisdom among students of American politics that the power of interest groups is growing in the 1990s and will continue to grow into the unforeseen future. This wisdom is based on a number of factors.

Table 8.3 Classification of States According to Impact of Interest Groups

States Where the Overall Impact of Interest Groups is:				
Dominant (9)	**Dominant/ Complementary (18)**	**Complementary (18)**	**Complementary/ Subordinate (5)**	**Subordinate (0)**
Alabama	Arizona	Colorado	Connecticut	
Alaska	Arkansas	Illinois	Delaware	
Florida	California	Indiana	Minnesota	
Louisiana	Hawaii	Iowa	Rhode Island	
Mississippi	Georgia	Kansas	Vermont	
New Mexico	Idaho	Maine		
South Carolina	Kentucky	Maryland		
Tennessee	Montana	Massachusetts		
West Virginia	Nebraska	Michigan		
	Nevada	Missouri		
	Ohio	New Jersey		
	Oklahoma	New Hampshire		
	Oregon	New York		
	Texas	North Carolina		
	Utah	North Dakota		
	Virginia	Pennsylvania		
	Washington	South Dakota		
	Wyoming	Wisconsin		

From Politics in the American States: A Comparative Analysis, *5/e by Virginia Gray, et al. Copyright 1990 by Virginia Gray, Herbert Jacob, and Robert B. Albritton. Reprinted by permission of HarperCollins Publishers.*

1. Protected by First Amendment

Because interest groups come under the umbrella of the First Amendment, effective regulation or control of their activities by state government is virtually impossible. Registration and disclosure of activities constitute the extent of interest-group control in most states. Many abuses must go unchecked.

2. Government vulnerable

Since most legislatures consist of part-time laypersons, and many executive branches are greatly fragmented, state governments are vulnerable to the machinations of interest groups. It is an environment in which success is more easily attained than at the national level where the branches of government are highly professionalized.

3. Government expands

As government has moved into new sectors of human activity, it has triggered the interest and involvement of new groups. For those areas not now in the government domain, interest groups have come forward to ask for government involvement.

4. Parties diminishing

By committing the allegiance of policymakers to a common philosophy, political parties have been major deterrents to interest-group power. But as party loyalties diminish, interest groups enjoy success more frequently.

5. PACs buy influence

Political action committees have demonstrated the power of campaign contributions for pressure groups. In many campaigns, PACs are able to displace the political party as the chief source of assistance, and thus create a sense of obligation on the part of the recipients. Three-fourths of the state legislators feel that lobbyists who contribute campaign funds improve their chances to influence legislation.[10]

To win elections, the policies and platforms of political parties must approximate the public interest. The demands of particular groups within the parties must be modified to meet public approval. Interest groups, on the other hand, accentuate the particular demands of their groups with limited compromise. Being free to pursue their goals with unbridled militancy, interest groups can generate unity and enthusiasm unmatched by political parties. As a consequence, groups with determination and emotional commitment tend to see interest groups as the best vehicles for attaining their goals. This ability to focus on key issues has strengthened pressure groups.

A great deal of money is required to carry on the extensive lobbying in states today. Millions of dollars are spent annually for the purpose of influencing opinion and action in matters of government. The ability to raise money and mobilize support for political influence differs widely among pressure groups, being based largely on the expectations of returns. On such a basis, it is normally easier to arrange for work and money for special purposes than for the general good—for groups of manufacturers, laborers, farmers, and professionals than for all consumers or citizens, however important the interests of all consumers or all citizens. The idea that everybody's business is nobody's business often means that special interests outrank the general interest in financial support for pressure politics, at least in the day-to-day movement of public affairs between elections. Meeting this discrepancy is one of the challenges of state and local government in the 1990s.

Endnotes

1. See Clement E. Vose, "Interest Groups, Judicial Review, and Local Government," *Western Political Quarterly* 19 (March 1966): 85–100. Vose suggests that political scientists have neglected the important role of interest groups in agitating for judicial review of state and municipal public policy.

2. U.S. Advisory Commission on Intergovernmental Relations, *Changing Public Attitudes on Governments and Taxes* (Washington, DC: Government Printing Office, 1988): 71.

3. For an expanded discussion of this topic, see "Interest Groups: Pluralism or Mass Society," by Michael T. Hayes in *Interest Group Politics,* Burdett A. Loomis and Allan J. Cigler, eds. (Washington, DC: CQ Press, 1983), pp. 110–125.

4. Hayes, "Interest Groups: Pluralism or Mass Society," p. 111.

5. In the late 1980s and early 1990s, Hrebenar and Thomas arranged to have political scholars in every state prepare a narrative on interest groups in their respective states. The works of these 70 scholars were published in a series of regional reports, the first appearing on the western states in 1987.

6. Clive S. Thomas, "Interest Groups in Alaska: Oil Revenues, Regionalism, and Personalized Politics," *Interest Group Politics in the American West,* eds. Ronald J. Hrebenar and Clive S. Thomas (Salt Lake City: University of Utah Press, 1987), pp. 16–21.

7. Gary Moncrief, "Idaho: The Interests of Sectionalism," *Interest Group Politics,* Hrebenar-Thomas, pp. 69–71.

8. See L. Harmon Zeigler, *Politics in the American States,* 1st ed., ed. Herbert Jacob and Kenneth Vines (Boston: Little, Brown and Co., 1965), p. 117.

9. Randy Welch, "Lobbyists, Lobbyists All Over the Lot," *State Legislatures* 15 (February, 1989): 18–21, and Tom Watson, "A Lobbyist's Middleman Who Helps Business Navigate State Capitol Halls," *Governing* 2 (February, 1989): 32–38.

10. Ted Lee, "Report underscores ethical challenges facing legislators," *Midwesterner* (October, 1991): 1.

THE LEGISLATURE: INSTITUTION AND PROCESS

How the State Policy-Making Assemblies are Structured and Function

Origin and Evolution of General Assemblies

The charter granted to the Massachusetts Bay colony in 1629 by King Charles I provided for a colonial government by a "general court" consisting of all the freemen of the colony. As the population of the colony grew and settlements developed some distance apart, the gathering of all freemen for the general court became inconvenient. Soon representatives were selected by the freemen of the several settlements to serve as the "general court" and pass the laws.[1]   *Send representatives*

Maryland witnessed the same experience in the evolution of its representative assembly. Freemen met at St. Marys until the settlements became too scattered. At first, absent members were permitted to vote by proxy, but this method concentrated power in the hands of a few and was soon discarded in favor of elected representatives. The Maryland assembly was divided into two bodies, as it was in neighboring Virginia, with the governor and council in one chamber and the representatives of the communities in the other.[2] With this colonial origin, the state legislature is the oldest American instrumentality for the exercise of representative self-government.   *Origin of two chambers*

Colonial assemblies played an important role in the course of events leading up to the American Revolution, primarily because British interference with local legislative processes was a major complaint against the government and the king. The first half dozen specific grievances set forth in the Declaration of Independence concerned the disregarding of colonial laws and the disruption of legislative sessions and proceedings. America had already become a land of laws and lawyers and the idea of legislative supremacy was prominent in the minds of the revolutionists as they undertook to transform colonies into states. The legislatures, in fact, assumed the chief responsibility for these changes, as well as for providing for representation in the Congress of the central government.   *British interfere with legislatures*

It was only natural that the idea of supremacy of the legislature would prevail in the establishment of the Continental Congress and later of the Congress of the Confederation. The patriots entertained a strong desire to have a government of laws passed   *Favor legislatures*

Photo by Garry D. Redmann.

by legislatures, rather than orders issued by arbitrary executives. It required years of experience before they would accept as meritorious the Hamiltonian concept of energy in the executive branch of government.

State executive emerges

For several decades after the adoption of the U. S. Constitution, legislatures remained the dominant branch of state government. However, as time passed, state executives began to emerge, partly out of the need for a focus of leadership and partly to emulate the design of the executive branch in the federal government. During the so-called Jacksonian era, however, the power of the state executive was weakened by the creation of several statewide elective executive officers, once again giving the legislative branch the competitive edge. Toward the latter part of the 1800s, however, state legislatures fell into disrepute as political bosses and economic interests used legislatures to make self-serving deals at public expense. Broadside attacks by reformers at the turn of the century blackened the image of state legislatures, leaving the integrity of assemblies tarnished well into the 1900s. In recent decades, however, legislatures have slowly regained much of the lost ground.

Legislatures decline

Governor's role increases

The executive branch has emerged to share power and functions with the legislature in ways not anticipated in the simplicity of Jeffersonian days. As a daily newsmaker, the modern governor has ways of leading and influencing the legislature. Moreover, since laws are not self-executing, a vast amount of administrative machinery, partly or largely under direction of the governor, is required to implement the work of the legislature. Furthermore, administrative activity is continuous, not intermittent like the legislative process. Before the reapportionment revolution of the 1960s, executive-administrative leaders may have been more responsible and responsive than legislative bodies to the demands of urban citizens. City-dwellers in most states had a larger voice in choosing the governor and other administrative officers than in choosing the legislative majority.

Legislatures handle heavy workload

Although the legislature has lost a measure of its supremacy in relation to the executive branch, its decline has been more relative than absolute. Its functional role has expanded to meet the breadth of problems confronting a typical state in the 1990s. In a very limited period of time, the typical legislature may consider 1,500 bills, authorize an annual state budget of $5 billion, pass 90 resolutions expressing opinions to the federal government, propose five amendments to the state constitution, conduct 14 oversight investigations in the state executive branch, redraft "home rule" legislation for cities and counties, revamp the state's tax structure, and review 63 recommendations from interim study committees. Only through continued modernization and improved representativeness can today's legislatures process this demanding mountain of work fairly and expeditiously.

In 27 states, the house and senate together are called the *legislature;* in 19 states, they are jointly called the *general assembly.* North Dakota and Oregon call them the *legislative assembly;* Massachusetts and New Hampshire call them the *general court.* All states call the upper house the *senate;* 41 states call the lower house the *house of representatives.* The eight remaining states (Nebraska having only a senate) use *assembly, house of delegates,* or *general assembly.*[3]

The Legislature and the State Constitution

Chapter 1 has already established the principle that state governments must submit to the U.S. Constitution, acts of Congress, and treaties as the "supreme law of the land," not to be contradicted by state constitutions, state laws, or state officials. In determining policies for states, legislatures are also limited by the provisions of state constitutions. If a state constitution has addressed a matter, it falls outside the jurisdiction of the state assembly. However, if the constitution is silent, the legislature, as the body exercising the sovereignty of the people, is free to act. Thus, state legislatures have considerable latitude in policy-making, a contrast from the federal Congress which must find constitutional authorization to act for every exercise of power.

Legislatures have broad jurisdiction

Functions of State Legislatures

Making Policy by Passing Laws

Even though the state policy-making powers are broad, state laws are subject to several significant limitations. First, they must conform to provisions of the federal and state constitutions. Second, they must guard against gubernatorial veto or be prepared to override such a disapproval. Third, they must be acceptable to the people, something that is often more restrictive than either constitutions or vetoes.

The exercise of legislative authority within these limitations applies to such a wide range of subjects that it taxes the intelligence, wisdom and knowledge of the typical state legislator. Among the subjects before the assemblies are the large body of statutes defining crimes and punishment; another group of enactments dealing with civil property relations among persons; numerous laws defining the structure and powers of state agencies and local governments; another group of laws implementing the use of police powers, especially in the licensing of certain activities and occupations; and another major area is that of designing the tax laws and appropriating funds for the state budget. The work of passing laws on criminal, civil, and public matters is a continuing task. Every adjourning legislature leaves in its wake scores of additional statutes and, many times, numerous unanswered questions begging to be addressed by the next session. The laws of each session are usually first published as "session laws," which are later incorporated into the state code or statutes at large.

Legislate on many subjects

Serve as Conflict-Resolving Institutions

In the process of passing laws, the legislature serves as a conflict-resolving institution, where opposing groups can press their demands and negotiate their differences. Legislators strive to keep a societal peace by acting as referees and compromisers for the warring factions. Very little legislation passes through the legislative process without some give-and-take designed to pacify opposing groups. Unless the legislative institution and its members are equipped to cope with conflict and perform this crucial social function, the state will falter in the delivery or equitable distribution of services.

Negotiate compromises

Oversee Faithful Execution of Laws

Passing laws is only one part of the legislature's responsibility in policy-making. It must also see that laws are administered in accordance with the intent of the legislature through a series of processes involved in oversight.

Conduct oversight activities

Traditionally, a major facet of legislative oversight is the review of the postaudit reports on state agencies furnished either by the elected state auditor or by an auditor employed by the legislature. Another oversight mechanism is the special investigating committee. Informed about improper activity in an executive agency, the legislature will often create a special committee to make an in-depth inquiry into the matter and to report its findings to the legislative body for corrective action. Legislative appropriations committees tend to be continuing oversight bodies as they hear agency requests for new appropriations. To justify requests for more funds, agencies are asked by appropriations committees to defend their past expenditures. These routine inquiries tend to measure the faithfulness of the funded agencies in carrying out legislative intent.

Ombudsmen for citizens

During the 1960s and 1970s, state legislatures sought to sharpen their oversight functions by adding new weapons to the arsenal. The concept of a legislative office called the *ombudsman* appeared in several states. Created on a full-time basis in Nebraska, Iowa, Hawaii, and Oregon, the office of ombudsman was designed to receive and investigate citizen complaints about state agencies that were failing to perform up to expectations. Efforts to strengthen oversight functions also appeared in the budgeting and appropriations process by requiring agencies to submit performance budgets or zero-base budgets. In a performance budget, the agency was required to calculate

Budgeting techniques

the units of service that would be delivered for the funds appropriated. The zero-base budget was a response to the common practice of "incremental" budgeting in which agencies would defend only the requests for new money. The zero-base budget required them to defend every dollar being requested.

Sunset laws

Starting in Colorado in 1976, passage of "sunset" laws swept the country until two-thirds of the state legislatures were engaged in reviewing the functions of agencies to determine whether or not the "sun ought to set" on their existence. Initially, expectations ran high but only a number of minor entities were eliminated with little significant change in the executive branch. Disenchantment set in and states began to repeal or neglect the "sunset" process. By 1990 six states had repealed their sunset laws and six had permitted them to lapse into inactivity, leaving 24 states with active sunset programs.[4]

Review regulations

Concerned about red tape growing out of regulations adopted by state agencies, legislatures created regulation review committees to determine whether or not state agencies were adopting regulations in strict accordance to laws. By 1992, over 40 state legislatures had review systems in place, with the majority reviewing all regulations.[5]

Evaluate programs

Program evaluation has become a major component in the oversight function. Over 40 states have established some mechanism to assess the performance of state agencies and the programs they administer. In some states, the program evaluation unit is a part of the existing state auditing agency; in others, it is a separate unit within the legislature; in still others, the work is assigned to the legislative staff. In any case, the common question asked is whether or not the state is getting maximum performance for the tax money spent.[6]

Oversight functions are not attractive duties for legislators since they consume precious time without yielding much in the way of personal credit or concrete results, and at the same time creating additional trouble for themselves by antagonizing affected agencies and interest groups.[7]

A Bridge for Constituents

The legislature and its members consititute a bridge that links individual citizens to the workings of state government through direct constituent services, or *casework* as much of it is commonly called. The assistance legislators can give citizens in dealing with their problems varies considerably from state to state. Such service is most available when a field office is provided; when legislators are engaged in legislative activity on a full-time or near full-time basis; when legislators represent small districts or single-member districts; when legislators solicit citizen contacts through public meetings or publicity; when legislators are from a lower income district; or when legislators are known to have influence with state agencies as a result of holding key legislative positions or being of the party in power.[8]

Assisting citizens

Constituent services can consist of a wide variety of activities, such as contacting an agency about welfare payments, accompanying a community delegation to plead for highway improvement or rerouting, inquiring about the denial of a license, interceding in a workers' compensation case, giving a letter of endorsement to a college student for summer employment in a state agency, providing information to local groups about legislation, or serving as a public speaker for community events.

Types of casework

Constituent service is of growing importance, with legislators spending anywhere from one-fourth to one-half of their time helping constituents with problems. This growth can be attributed to a number of factors. Legislators are getting re-elected more often and increasing in visibility, meaning that citizens get to know to whom they can go for help. More legislators are being assigned staff aides and district offices so they have the resources with which to help. Also, government is becoming more complex, creating a greater need for citizen assistance. Legislators are also becoming more professional and are, therefore, more capable of handling casework. More legislators are running for re-election and casework is good politics.[9]

Reasons for growth of casework

Casework not only helps bridge the gap between government and constituents, but it also facilitates the oversight function of the legislature by increasing legislative awareness, on an individual basis at least, of the administrative procedures being used to carry out the intent of the legislature.[10]

Represent States in Federal System

Executives are more active than legislators in relations with the federal government, but the U.S. Constitution vests several responsibilities to be performed in the federal system by state legislatures alone. Perhaps the most important of these functions involves amending the U.S. Constitution. Here, state legislatures may pass resolutions to call for the convening of a national constitutional convention to propose amendments to the Constitution or they may consider amendments to the Constitution as submitted to them by the Congress.

Consider Constitutional amendments

In Article IV, state legislatures are charged with protecting the geographic territory of the state in the creation of new states and are also authorized to represent the state in asking for federal help in cases of domestic violence.

Adjudicatory Duties

Decide impeachment

Invariably, state legislatures are charged with the judicial functions involving the impeachment of members of the other two branches of government. Usually, the house of representatives is required to bring the charges of impeachment while the senate is to sit as the jury. Some states permit the legislatures to remove members of the judiciary by resolution, without the cumbersome process of impeachment. Both houses of state legislatures are empowered to adjudicate issues relating to the qualifications, seating, and disciplining of their own members.

Exercise Executive and/or Administrative Duties

Share appointing power

The most common executive function performed by the legislative branch involves the sharing of the appointing power through the requirement for confirmation of certain agency heads and other appointees by the senate or both houses of the legislature. In several states, major appointments are made by the legislature itself. In Maine, the legislature chooses the secretary of state, attorney general, and treasurer; in Maryland, it selects the treasurer; in Tennessee, the secretary of state and treasurer.

Keeper of the State Constitution

Propose amendments

As indicated in chapter 5, the vast majority of amendments proposed and adopted for state constitutions originate in the state legislature. Thus, by practice, state legislatures have become responsible for keeping the state constitution up-to-date by proposing amendments whenever they see need for change.

In addition to proposing constitutional amendments, the legislature serves as guardian of the constitution when it decides whether or not to submit to the voters the question of calling a state constitutional convention.

Powers Peculiar to the Houses

Houses may act independently

The two houses of the legislature have different nonlawmaking powers after the manner of the two houses of Congress. Each is judge of the election and qualifications of its own members and has disciplinary power over its membership. Each has independent investigative functions, although joint committees of the two houses may be created for such purposes. Each house controls its own organizational setup, according to constitutional provisions, and makes its rules of procedure. In impeachment proceedings, the lower house makes the charges, and the senate tries the case. Besides confirming important executive appointments, the senate in a few states exercises approval power over executive dismissals. Some state constitutions require that bills for raising revenue originate in the lower house.

The Design of the Legislative Institution

The formal institutional structure of the state legislature designed to perform the foregoing functions is important and deserves careful attention. However, the student must beware of a common tendency to conclude that structure is the major determinant of the policies of the legislature, or of state government in general. Research indicates that the legislative structure and machinery do not shape the outputs of a state government as much as do the economic base of the state, the interest group structure, or the political culture. Therefore, it is unreasonable to expect revolutionary changes in legislative performance or policy by converting from two houses to one house, increasing or decreasing the sizes of the assemblies, shortening or lengthening terms, or changing the number of legislative committees. It would be equally unreasonable to assume that structure is unimportant since it may affect opportunities for citizens to participate, representativeness of the body, and the efficient handling of the state's business.[11] *Impact of structure limited*

All American states except one have the two-house (bicameral) type of legislature comparable to the United States Congress. The exception is Nebraska, where the voters followed the advice of Senator George W. Norris and passed a constitutional amendment in 1934 to establish a unicameral legislature of 30 to 50 members. Since then, serious attempts to change to the unicameral system have been defeated in Arizona, Montana, North Dakota, Oklahoma, and Oregon. *Nebraska is unicameral*

Bicameralism is traditional with states and became firmly established once the federal Constitution provided for the two-house Congress. Most of the 13 original states came into the Union with the two-house system that had developed from the popular assembly and the governor's council. Georgia and Pennsylvania abandoned their one-house systems in 1789 and 1790 respectively, but Vermont kept its unicameral until 1836 when it became the victim of warring political factions.

There is little immediate prospect of unicameral expansion among the states, although the Nebraska experiment has won praise. Several editions of the Model Constitution issued by the National Municipal League endorsed the plan, and unicameralism has proved satisfactory among Canadian provinces, Swiss cantons, and American cities. Despite strong arguments for the one-house type, the bicameral legislature prevails in the United States for historical and other reasons, including the strong opposition from members of the present two-house systems. *Two-house legislatures prevail*

Every state legislature, with the exception of Nebraska's chamber of 49 senators, consists of two houses of different sizes. The senate varies from 20 members in Alaska to 67 in Minnesota. The lower house varies from 40 members in Alaska to 400 in New Hampshire, with a median of 100. The total number for the 99 legislative chambers runs close to 7,500 members.

The size of state legislatures, particularly the houses of representatives, has been under attack for some years. Following an analysis of state government in 1967, a committee of outstanding leaders from the private sector recommended that the total membership for legislatures in large states not exceed 100, with even fewer members in smaller states.[12] This call for smaller legislatures was echoed a few years later by the Citizens Conference on State Legislatures.[13] As of the early 1990s, thirty-one states still had houses with 100 members or more. *Propose smaller legislatures*

Critics of large houses fault them because they restrict the ability of states to provide individual legislators with sufficient staff, salaries, or accommodations; they result in large, awkward committees; they contribute to disorder and tumult in floor *Disadvantages of large assemblies*

Table 9.1 State Legislatures: Sizes, Terms, Population per Member—1950 and 1990

	Senate						House								
	Members		Terms		Population per Member		Members		Terms		Population per Member		Total Legislators	
	1950	1990	1950	1990	1950	1990	1950	1990	1950	1990	1950	1990	1950	1990
Alabama	35	35	4	4	87,478	115,428	106	105	4	4	28,877	38,476	141	140
Alaska	X	20	X	4	X	27,500	X	40	X	2	X	13,750	X	60
Arizona	19	30	2	2	39,452	122,167	58	60	2	2	12,914	61,083	77	90
Arkansas	35	35	4	4	54,557	67,143	100	100	2	2	19,095	23,500	135	135
California	40	40	4	4	264,656	744,000	81	80	2	2	130,691	372,000	121	120
Colorado	35	35	4	4	37,857	94,114	65	65	2	2	20,385	50,677	100	100
Connecticut	36	36	2	2	55,750	91,305	272	151	2	2	7,379	21,768	308	187
Delaware	17	21	4	4	18,706	31,714	35	41	2	2	9,086	16,244	52	62
Florida	38	40	4	4	72,921	323,425	95	120	2	2	29,168	107,808	133	160
Georgia	54	56	2	2	63,778	115,679	205	180	2	2	16,800	35,989	259	236
Hawaii	X	25	X	4	X	44,320	X	51	X	2	X	21,725	X	76
Idaho	44	42	2	2	13,364	23,952	59	84	2	2	9,966	11,976	103	126
Illinois	51	59	4	4	170,824	193,729	153	118	2	2	56,941	98,864	204	177
Indiana	50	50	4	4	78,680	110,880	100	100	2	2	39,342	55,442	150	150
Iowa	50	50	4	4	52,420	55,520	108	100	2	2	24,268	27,760	158	150
Kansas	40	40	4	4	47,625	61,925	125	125	2	2	15,240	19,816	165	165
Kentucky	38	38	4	4	77,474	96,974	100	100	4	2	29,448	36,853	138	138
Louisiana	39	39	4	4	68,795	108,179	100	105	4	4	26,835	40,181	139	144
Maine	33	35	2	2	27,667	35,057	151	151	2	2	6,046	8,126	184	186
Maryland	29	47	4	4	80,793	101,723	123	141	4	4	19,049	33,908	152	188
Massachusetts	40	40	2	2	117,250	150,400	240	160	2	2	8,362	37,600	280	200
Michigan	32	38	2	4	199,094	244,605	100	110	2	2	63,718	84,500	132	148
Minnesota	67	67	4	4	44,507	65,298	131	134	2	2	22,763	32,649	198	201
Mississippi	49	52	4	4	44,449	49,481	140	122	4	4	15,557	21,090	189	174
Missouri	34	34	4	4	116,294	150,500	154	163	2	2	25,675	31,393	188	197

proceedings; they force rigid control of floor debate; and power tends to move into the hands of a few. Reducing the size of legislatures is both a procedural and a political problem. The constitution would require amendment and this would have to be done over the objections of many incumbent legislators. As a consequence, significant reductions are rare, although in the early 1980s, Illinois and Massachusetts were able to reduce the sizes of their houses of representatives by one-third, from 177 to 118 in Illinois and from 240 to 160 in Massachusetts. In most states, the size of legislatures has been creeping upward rather than downward (see table 9.1).

All but four states have two-year terms for members of the house of representatives; about three-fourths have four-year terms for senators. A few southern states have four-year terms for both houses. In 1990, voters in Oklahoma, Colorado and California adopted term limitations and thereby ignited a campaign to limit the service of state legislators. Many additional state legislatures and citizen groups entertained

Term limitations spread

Table 9.1 continued

	Senate						House							Total	
	Members		Terms		Population per Member		Members		Terms		Population per Member			Legislators	
	1950	1990	1950	1990	1950	1990	1950	1990	1950	1990	1950	1990		1950	1990
Montana	56	50	4	4	10,554	15,980	90	100	2	2	6,567	7,990		146	150
Nebraska	43	49	4	4	30,814	32,204	UNICAMERAL							43	49
Nevada	17	21	4	4	9,412	57,190	43	42	2	2	3,721	28,595		60	63
New Hampshire	24	24	2	2	22,208	46,208	399	400	2	2	1,336	2,773		423	424
New Jersey	21	40	3	4	230,238	193,250	60	80	1	2	80,583	96,625		81	120
New Mexico	24	42	4	4	28,375	36,071	49	70	2	2	13,898	21,643		73	112
New York	56	61	2	2	264,821	294,918	150	150	2	2	98,867	119,933		206	211
North Carolina	50	50	2	2	81,220	132,560	120	120	2	2	33,842	55,233		170	170
North Dakota	49	53	4	4	12,633	12,038	113	106	2	2	5,479	6,019		162	159
Ohio	36	33	2	4	220,722	328,697	139	99	2	2	57,165	109,566		175	132
Oklahoma	44	48	4	4	50,750	65,521	118	101	2	2	18,924	31,139		162	149
Oregon	30	30	4	4	50,700	94,767	60	60	2	2	25,350	47,367		90	90
Pennsylvania	50	50	4	4	209,960	237,620	208	203	2	2	50,471	58,527		258	253
Rhode Island	44	50	2	2	17,977	20,060	100	100	2	2	7,919	10,030		144	150
South Carolina	46	46	4	4	46,022	75,783	124	124	2	2	17,073	28,113		170	170
South Dakota	35	35	2	2	18,629	19,886	75	70	2	2	8,693	9,943		110	105
Tennessee	33	33	2	4	99,727	147,788	99	99	2	2	33,242	49,263		132	132
Texas	31	31	4	4	248,742	547,935	150	150	2	2	51,407	113,240		181	181
Utah	23	29	4	4	29,913	59,379	60	75	2	2	11,467	22,960		83	104
Vermont	30	30	2	2	12,567	18,733	246	150	2	2	1,533	3,747		276	180
Virginia	40	40	4	4	82,950	154,675	100	100	2	2	33,187	61,871		140	140
Washington	46	49	4	4	51,696	99,306	99	98	2	2	24,020	49,653		145	147
West Virginia	32	34	4	4	62,656	52,735	94	100	2	2	21,330	17,935		126	134
Wisconsin	33	33	4	4	104,061	148,212	100	99	2	2	34,346	49,404		133	132
Wyoming	27	30	4	4	10,741	15,100	56	64	2	2	5,179	7,078		83	94

Computations by authors based on data from U.S. Census Bureau and Book of the States 1950–51 *and* Book of the States 1990–91 *(Council of State Governments, Lexington, KY).*

term limitations proposals in the 1991–92 sessions and elections. Generally, the proposals provided for limitations of eight to 12 years of service.

Proponents of the limitations argue that re-election of legislators is becoming too common, making legislatures less responsive, too professional, and too cozy with interest groups and governmental agencies. Opponents counter with the claims that forced turnover deprives legislatures of seasoned leadership, makes the legislative process more vulnerable to the influence of experienced lobbyists and bureaucrats, and deprives people of the right to vote for whom they wish to represent them.[14]

Arguments over limitations

Legal qualifications for service in the legislature usually relate to age, residence, and citizenship. For service in the house of representatives, 17 states require a minimum age of 18; 24 require an age of 21; and four go as high as age 25. For the senate, 15 states permit service at 18; 20 require 25 years of age; and five go as high as age 30. Residence requirements are generally the same for both houses, with a large majority requiring one year or less. Citizenship is required directly or indirectly in all states.

Age and residence requirements

Political requirements
more rigid

More rigid than the official requirements are the political tests imposed by the electorate, such as longer residence requirements, appropriate party affiliation, maturity, religious preference, and other qualities citizens think important in a "representative" legislator.

Legislative Districts

Districts originally
based on local
governments

Because the first representation in assemblies came either from towns or counties, the number of legislators in states tends to correlate somewhat with one form of local government or another. Senatorial election districts usually are larger than those for the lower house; but the same district may be used for electing members to both houses, with more members elected to the house than to the senate. In sparsely settled areas

Creating legislative
districts

of the nation, several counties may be combined to bring together sufficient population to warrant a legislative seat. In New Hampshire, for example, towns are combined to form legislative electoral districts. In many cases, parts of counties are joined with parts of other counties to reach the population requirement for a legislative district. In populous counties, the counties may be subdivided into several districts (Figure 9.1).

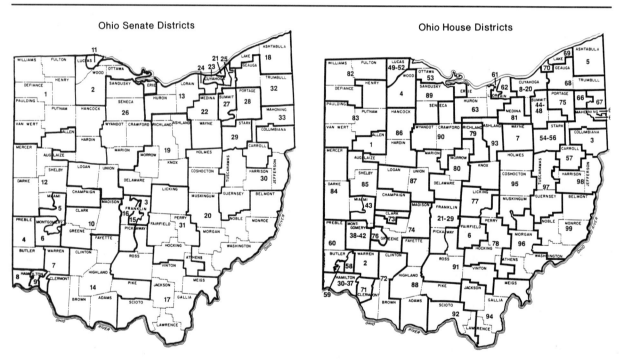

Figure 9.1

Since there are fewer senators than house members, senators represent larger districts. Larger districts make possible drawing district lines along the boundaries of existing local governments. The smaller house districts, however, force cutting through government boundaries in order to get within the 10 percent population range tolerated by the Supreme Court. The peculiar shapes of districts may result from following local government or geographic boundaries, reaching out to save an incumbent legislator, or gerrymandering a certain legislator out of strong territory.

(Source: Ohio Secretary of State.)

In a little over half of the states, members of the house of representatives are all chosen from districts electing only one representative; in three-fourths of the states, all senators are elected in single-member districts. That means a majority of the 7,500 legislators are chosen from single-member districts.[15] The remaining representatives and senators are elected from multimember districts. Multimember districts are often used as a form of gerrymandering because they can inflate the voting strength of the majority party or racial group in the district. As an example, if the Democratic party garners 55 percent of the vote in a three-member district, the party may win all three seats. However, if the district were divided into three separate electoral units, the party would likely get only two. Multimember districts have been on the decline for the past 20 years due partly to the suspicion that they deny minorities a rightful share of the legislative seats.[16]

Single-member districts prevail

Bias of multimember districts

Malapportionment has been a fact of American politics since colonial times when representatives were chosen primarily to represent towns and counties rather than equal numbers of residents. Population was sometimes taken into account and larger towns and counties were awarded additional seats to recognize the number of residents. Of course, the inequity of this system did not go unnoticed. Thomas Jefferson was one of the first to complain, noting that Virginia's county-based system gave the smallest county with 951 voters an equal voice with the county having over 22,000.[17] The Northwest Ordinance of 1787 prescribed a population base for territorial legislatures but upon adoption of the U.S. Constitution with a senate based on geographic units (states) and a house on population, many states began to copy this national design for their legislatures.

Jefferson notes malapportionment

As people poured into the urban areas, states made only minor adjustments in the allocation of legislative seats. By 1960, 70 percent of America lived in urban places yet the control of legislative assemblies remained in the rural areas. Only two states, Wisconsin and Massachusetts, had rural and urban representation coming close to the democratic ideal of "one person, one vote," according to Gordon E. Baker in his study of urban-rural imbalance.[18] The 1960 census indicated that urban underrepresentation was getting worse rather than better, especially in those states deliberately basing their representation on land area or something other than the number of people. In California, the 6,038,771 people in Los Angeles county were represented by one state senator, the same representation granted to the mountain peaks of the Sierra Nevadas and the 14,294 people living in that district. Across the country in Vermont, the town of Stratton, population 38, had one district representative as did Burlington, population 35,531. In Florida, a district of 9,543 people had one senator as did another district of 935,047. Translated into legislative control, 11 percent of the people in California could control the state senate; 12 percent of the people in Vermont could control the state house.[19]

Rural areas controlled legislatures

Malapportionment nationwide

Why was it so difficult to reapportion state legislatures to keep up with the changes in population? The answer is found in the vested interests of legislators and the economic and sectional interests that cut across urban-rural cleavages. The desire of legislators to preserve the status quo is well known and explains why the sizes of legislatures

Explaining politics of malapportionment

have remained the same for so many years. Professors Steiner and Gove report that legislators, when confronted with the need to reapportion, can be expected to work on behalf of several vested interests:

- *Individual preservation,* the desire to be in a "safe" district.
- *Mutual preservation,* the willingness of members to cooperate with each other in protecting incumbents against political challengers.
- *Political party preservation,* the desire of the leaders of each political party organization to maximize its strength in the legislature.
- *Bloc preservation,* the desire of members of voting blocs—whether based on geographic, economic, or ideological cohesion—to retain existing personnel and strength. Such blocs are often bipartisan, and their membership is relatively small.[20]

By 1962, the U.S. Supreme Court had had enough of malapportionment and decided in *Baker v. Carr* that voters may sue for relief on the grounds that malapportionment was a violation of the "equal protection" clause of the Fourteenth Amendment and fell within the jurisdiction of the Court. In 1964, the Supreme Court decided

Court orders both houses on population

to go all the way with "one-person, one-vote" in *Reynolds v. Sims,* and ruled, by a vote of eight to one, that both houses of legislatures must be apportioned on a population basis.

With self-preservation or party control at stake, many legislators were paralyzed by the challenge of redrawing legislative district lines. They crafted plans with minor changes, hoping to escape the scrutiny of the courts. But almost all of the reapportionment plans devised by legislatures in the 1960s wound up in the courts, challenged

States resist new apportionment

by urban areas whose citizens recognized a half a loaf when they saw one. Looking at the efforts in Pennsylvania, Justice Michael Musmanno observed that the plan was full of "marshes of inequality, swamps of uncompactness, bogs of invidious discrimination, and barren wastes of unconstitutional performance."[21] Recalcitrance and rebellion aside, the amazing reapportionment revolution took only two years to result in substantial compliance with "equal protection" in virtually all of the 50 states. During the 30 years following *Baker v. Carr,* answers were developed for the questions about the mechanics of apportionment and districting, such as the mathematical precision required to meet equal protection, the required frequency of reapportionment, the meaning of population, the acceptability of multimember electoral districts, and the age-old question of gerrymandering.

Eventually, the Supreme Court settled on the rule that variations in population may normally be ten percent from the largest to the smallest district in the state. Re-

Adopt 10% rule

apportionment every ten years was not specified as a rule of the Court, but it was endorsed as a rational approach to the task of adjusting legislative district boundaries to population changes. The Court has permitted variations among states in determining what population should be used as a base for equal representation. Census figures, citizens only, or registered voters have been permitted so long as they do not result in malapportionment. With few exceptions, states rely on the federal decennial census

Census data questioned

for reapportionment, overlooking the fact that it includes military personnel, aliens, college students, and institutional populations, many of whom do not vote where they are located, thereby giving overrepresentation to certain areas.

One of the last remaining techniques for malapportionment under attack in the courts is gerrymandering—the drawing of legislative district lines to maximize the influence of some voters while minimizing the impact of others. In 1986, after years of refusing to accept cases of partisan gerrymandering, the Court ruled in an Indiana case that legislatures could not draw boundaries to benefit one party at the expense of the other. Generally, to win a partisan gerrymandering case, the petitioners must prove that gerrymandering consistently reduced the party's chance to win and kept the party in a minority status.[22]

Court rules on gerrymandering

Despite the Court's admonition that partisan gerrymandering would be unacceptable, Republicans and Democrats continued to wage vigorous political campaigns in 1988 and 1990 to gain control of state legislatures and, subsequently, reapportionment. The national Republican and Democratic parties poured money into most states under the pretext that they wanted control to assure the people of a "fair" apportionment for both legislative and Congressional districts. Many of the legislative races became bitter negative affairs, primarily because the parties had completely opposite ideas of the meaning of "fair."

Parties fight to control apportionment

Even though the Court had indicated it would strike down partisan gerrymandering, the parties were undaunted and turned to every available vehicle for gaining the political advantage. A major vehicle was the computer that could utilize sophisticated programs to draw boundaries. To facilitate computerized reapportionment, the U.S. Census Bureau furnished states with a redistricting data program that offered population counts for every voting precinct.[23] With this program, some historic voting information, and a little ingenuity, majority parties were able to eke out political advantage in spite of the Court.

Computers help

As discussed in chapter 6, the 1982 amendments to the Voting Rights Act prohibited electoral practices that denied minorities the opportunity to elect representation. In 1986, the U.S. Supreme Court ruled that states must draw district boundaries with the goal of permitting minorities to win elections. As a result of this decision, states reapportioning after the 1990 census were particularly mindful of reapportioning to permit minority victories. This could perhaps be called "positive" gerrymandering.

Minorities must have opportunities to elect

When urban leaders first launched the charge against malapportionment, they expected that properly apportioned legislatures would finally address the critical problems of the central cities. But reapportionment did not become the panacea they expected. When the "spoils" were divided, the suburbs and not the central cities made the greatest gains in legislative representation.

Suburbs gain

After decades of waiting for "equal protection" to be translated into reapportioned legislatures, good government groups searched eagerly for indications of new progressive policies in state assemblies. Research conducted on the heels of the first wave of reapportionment suggested that malapportionment may not have been the critical element in major state policies after all. Thomas Dye concluded that a state's level of economic development was the key policy variable—not malapportionment.[24] When David C. Saffell asked 224 senators in 49 states about the effects of apportionment, they posited that policies had become more liberal, aid to urban areas had increased, Democrats gained more than Republicans, and that reapportionment did not greatly affect tenure.[25]

Effects of reapportionment

Table 9.2 State Legislative Turnover, 1979–1989

State	Upper Chambers			Lower Chambers		
	Total Mems	New Mems	Turnover	Total Mems	New Mems	Turnover
Alabama	35	26	74%	105	71	68%
Alaska	20	16	80%	40	35	88%
Arizona	30	19	63%	60	45	75%
Arkansas	35	24	69%	100	49	49%
California	40	21	53%	80	56	70%
Colorado	35	28	80%	65	58	89%
Connecticut	36	32	89%	151	124	82%
Delaware	21	13	62%	41	28	68%
Florida	40	35	88%	120	100	83%
Georgia	56	39	70%	180	120	67%
Hawaii	25	19	76%	51	42	82%
Idaho (1)	35	32	91%	70	57	81%
Illinois (2)	59	38	64%	177	87	49%
Indiana	50	33	66%	100	60	60%
Iowa	50	35	70%	100	76	76%
Kansas	40	27	68%	125	101	81%
Kentucky	38	24	63%	100	61	61%
Louisiana	39	26	67%	105	75	71%
Maine (3)	33	28	85%	151	132	87%
Maryland	47	32	68%	141	91	65%
Massachusetts	40	25	63%	160	110	69%
Michigan	38	19	50%	110	72	65%
Minnesota	67	53	79%	134	97	72%
Mississippi	52	49	94%	122	105	86%
Missouri	34	21	62%	163	120	74%

Many observers are convinced that properly apportioned legislatures demonstrate a greater willingness to grapple with urban and metropolitan problems than was true of previous legislatures, as well as greater willingness to levy the taxes required for such programs.[26]

Compensation and Turnover in Legislatures

Wide range of legislative salaries

Compensation for legislators varies widely among the states and continues to change from year to year. By 1992, thirteen states paid annual salaries of $25,000 or more, with New York's $57,500 leading all others and New Hampshire at the bottom with $200 for a biennium. The legislatures of California, Illinois, Massachusetts, Michigan, New York, Ohio, Pennsylvania, and Wisconsin have long sessions, fairly high legislator salaries, and many of their members now consider themselves to be full-time professional legislators.[27]

More legislators becoming full-time

As salaries are increased in additional states, more legislators will come to see their positions as full-time. This gradual change in status is not without political implications. It appears that increasing professionalization has been working to the dis-

Table 9.2 continued

State	Upper Chambers			Lower Chambers		
	Total Mems	New Mems	Turnover	Total Mems	New Mems	Turnover
Montana	50	37	74%	100	87	87%
Nebraska	49	38	78%	N/A	N/A	N/A
Nevada (4)	20	17	85%	40	34	85%
New Hampshire	24	21	88%	400	343	86%
New Jersey	40	28	70%	80	64	80%
New Mexico	42	31	74%	70	53	76%
New York (5)	60	23	38%	150	83	55%
North Carolina	50	38	76%	120	96	80%
North Dakota (6)	50	37	74%	100	72	72%
Ohio	33	25	76%	99	64	65%
Oklahoma	48	39	81%	101	86	85%
Oregon	30	25	83%	60	50	83%
Pennsylvania	50	31	62%	203	138	68%
Rhode Island	50	42	84%	100	80	80%
South Carolina	46	35	76%	124	89	72%
South Dakota	35	26	74%	70	57	81%
Tennessee	33	20	61%	99	61	62%
Texas	31	26	84%	150	122	81%
Utah	29	19	66%	75	65	87%
Vermont	30	25	83%	150	125	83%
Virginia	40	21	53%	100	62	62%
Washington	49	31	63%	98	88	90%
West Virginia	34	32	94%	100	90	90%
Wisconsin	33	25	76%	99	78	79%
Wyoming	30	26	87%	62	49	79%

Source: National Conference of State Legislatures

advantage of Republicans because people working in the private sector are finding it difficult to maintain a business or a profession while juggling a full-time challenge in the legislature.[28]

About one-fourth of the states do not pay an annual salary but instead compensate their legislators on a per diem (per day) basis, with no pay for days or periods when the legislature is not in session. However, the trend toward the salary basis is clear. In addition to salaries, legislators in 42 states are eligible for retirement benefits and in 46 states they receive various insurance benefits. *States offer fringe benefits*

Low salaries are rigidly determined in certain states by constitutional provision. In other states, legislators must make themselves politically vulnerable by passing legislation to set their own salaries. To defuse the explosive issue, several states have provided for legislative compensation commissions with the power to set legislative salaries. *Setting salaries*

With the exception of temporary deviations, the long term trend has been declining turnover in state legislatures. In the 1950s, turnover stood at around 40 percent; it now ranges between 15 and 20 percent. Some states, notably California, Colorado, Delaware, Illinois, Indiana, Michigan, New York, and Ohio, have reduced turnover to less than ten percent (see table 9.2). *Turnover declining*

Salary a factor in turnover

This dramatic decline in legislative turnover is explained in large part by the increased salaries and fringe benefits, both of which make legislative service more attractive—and more possible—for a larger number of people. Paverill Squire found a direct correlation between pay and tenure in a 25-state study of lower houses. He reported that an increase in salary of $1000 would result in an average increase in service of 0.12 years. Squire also found that another major factor in reduced turnover is the opportunity for career advancement. More legislators see career opportunities in the legislature or possibilities for attaining a higher office, which encourages them to remain in the system.[29] If the term-limitation concept becomes widespread, however, turnover will increase regardless of salary and career factors.

Incumbency important

Not only are legislators finding their jobs more attractive, but incumbency has made them better able to fend off challengers. A 14-state study by Malcolm E. Jewell and David Breaux revealed a significant increase in the margins by which incumbents win.[30] The importance of incumbency can probably be attributed to a number of factors—better press coverage, increased casework, and more articulate and sophisticated legislators, among others. Because of the power of incumbency, about two-thirds of the legislators who leave do so of their own choice. Less than one-third are defeated in re-election bids.[31]

Sessions of the Legislature

Most legislatures meet annually

Fifty years ago, only four states were holding annual sessions of the legislature—New Jersey, New York, Rhode Island and South Carolina. As the press of state business grew, the number of states holding annual sessions grew until 1991, when 43 states were meeting annually. Still meeting biennially were Arkansas, Kentucky, Montana, Nevada, North Dakota, Oregon and Texas. (In 1990, the voters in Oregon rejected annual sessions.)

Limit length of sessions

Only 13 states permit their legislatures to meet for unspecified lengths of time. Sixteen states limit sessions to 60 days or less; the remaining states have limits of 61 to 140 days. Eleven of the states with limited sessions permit the legislature to extend their deadlines provided an unusual majority (three-fifths, two-thirds) concurs. In most legislatures, such a majority would require bipartisan support.[32]

Circumventing time limitations

Time restrictions have become one of the most serious problems confronting legislatures as they try to approach their duties with research, deliberation, discussion, debate, and extensive interaction. Measures passed in haste to meet unrealistic time schedules sometimes conflict and require legal and judicial advice to unsnarl. Occasionally, the clock is turned back or stopped at the end of the session to provide time within the constitutional limit to dispose of the unfinished business. Another device for getting around time limitations is to meet officially for only one or two days a week toward the end of the session, thus leaving many days uncounted and free for clearing up matters through committees and informal adjustment. Another method used intermittently by some states with limited success is that of the split session, with a recess of at least 30 days and no bills introduced after the recess except as approved by a three-fourths majority.

Holding special sessions

The inadequacy of the prescribed number of legislative days has brought reliance on special sessions. All states permit governors to call special sessions and over half provide a procedure by which the legislators may call themselves into session. This latter method has developed in recent years as a move to make the legislative branch less dependent on the executive in determining whether or not a special session is warranted.

While most objective observers would agree that time restrictions impair the ability of the legislature to exercise its many functions, citizen dissatisfaction has spawned several recent efforts to limit sessions. In the 1980s, new session limitations were imposed in Colorado, Oklahoma, and Alaska.[33]

New session limitations

The makeup of the state legislative system extends beyond the elected membership. State legislatures employ more than 33,000 professional, clerical, and administrative staff, an 85 percent increase since 1979.

The last few decades have witnessed steps to establish systematic services to aid legislators. Three important types of aid are the legislative reference service, bill drafting service, and the legislative council. All states now provide in one way or another for reference service as an aid to lawmaking, and, in most cases, the bureaus are sections of the state library, law library, or archives. Almost all of the states provide formal assistance in the drafting of bills, which is particularly useful to members not versed in law.

Provide services for legislators

All but a handful of states have organized legislative councils to give continuous study to legislative problems. Councils may be divided into committees, with a supporting staff of research workers and advisers. Some states, with or without a formal legislative council, rely on interim committees of the legislature for research and planning.

Sharp contrasts exist among states in the working facilities provided for individual members of their legislatures. Members in the larger states, or states with smaller legislatures, have access to better personal facilities and services than legislators in the smaller states or states with large legislatures. In California, a wealthy state with a small legislature, legislators have individual offices staffed with secretarial and research assistance. Legislators in the large assemblies in small states are required to use pools of stenographers and researchers. They are also expected to manage their responsibilities from their small desks on the floor, their hotel rooms, or share off-the-floor general offices with a number of other legislators. Private conference rooms are scarce, and legislators must meet constituents at coffee shops or in the hallways.

Size influences facilities

Personal offices and staff assistance will not likely develop very rapidly as long as legislative sessions are limited to several months and the bodies consist of over 75 members. With tax revolts constantly in the air, frugal-minded citizens will not likely accept anything looking like unnecessary expenditures for the legislators. A case in point is an initiated measure adopted by the voters of California in 1990 to cut by 40 percent the money appropriated for the support of the state senate and assembly. Though its facilities are admired by legislators of other states and it ranked first in a national study, the California legislature was apparently seen as spending beyond its needs in the eyes of California constituents.

Public opinion limits facilities

Legislators have moved vigorously to harness electronic processing for systematizing the mass of information required for policy-making. A majority of states are using computers to speed bill drafting, track fiscal affairs, and generate projections of various kinds. Statutory retrieval is the most widely utilized computer application,

Legislatures using electronic technology

Figure 9.2
In legislatures all across the country, electronic technology is replacing the bulky billbooks seen in the background.

making possible a listing of all existing statutes on a subject by simply feeding the computer a key word. Thus, a legislator considering the introduction of a measure can review all related legislation, saving hours of research. Bill status and bill indexing furnish legislators with instant information on the status of bills in the legislature. Other uses include bill typing, revenue forecasting, revenue analysis, budget comparisons, budgetary effects of legislation, fiscal notes, journals, calendars, impact of salary and fringe benefits, legislative accounting, computer printing, mailing lists, and, most recently, reapportionment. Many states are installing computer terminals on legislators' desks to replace the bulk of bill books (figure 9.2). With terminals, legislators can call up the legislation under consideration, receive and send messages, access computer systems in their offices, draft correspondence, and perform numerous other activities.[34]

Legislative process open to public

Providing the public with information about the legislative process and day-to-day activities of the assembly is becoming more important for legislative staffs. Bearing the scars of corruption of years past and recognizing the declining confidence in political institutions, legislators are becoming keenly aware of the need for keeping the public informed. Legislative sessions and committee meetings have been opened to the public; recorded roll call voting is becoming more common; and space for reporters is being provided on the floor of the assemblies. Daily public television coverage of action on the floor is becoming more and more commonplace in legislatures.

Composition of Legislative Assemblies

Composition changing

Reapportionment opened up new opportunities for legislative service in urban and suburban areas; increasing legislative salaries have made service feasible for a wider diversity of people; the barriers to women in politics have been lowered; and pockets of racial and ethnic minorities have begun to assert political rights. As a result of these and other changes in the electoral environment, state legislatures have been scenes of changing demographics over the past 30 years.

Figure 9.3
The number of women serving in state legislatures has more than quadrupled over the past two decades. *(Photo by UND Bureau of Governmental Affairs.)*

Traditionally, lawyers have constituted the dominant occupational group in state legislatures, still holding around 16 percent of the seats. However, this is a marked decline from the 35 percent held just two and three decades ago.[35] Although farmers made up the second major block before reapportionment, the extensive one-person, one-vote redistricting mandated by the Supreme Court has diminished their 20 percent in the early 1930s to less than half that in 1991. If all business-related occupations, such as insurance and real estate brokers, bank officials, sales and corporate managers, and entrepreneurs, were grouped into a single business category, it would very likely be the most significant block in state legislatures, as it has been in years past. Making the greatest gains over the past two decades have been educators, who have doubled their four percent in the mid-60s to over eight percent in the early 1990s. Failing to elect representation anywhere near their numbers are people in the skilled and un-skilled categories.

Representation shifting

When legislatures are examined on the basis of sex, women held only four percent of the seats as recently as 1969. By 1991, this figure had more than quadrupled (figure 9.3).[36] Blacks and Hispanics have also been making gains. Even before the 1960s, blacks were found in a few state legislatures in non-southern states with large urban black concentrations. However, the breakup of the multimember legislative district into single-member districts has enabled concentrations of minorities to translate their numbers into legislative seats. In 1991, blacks held over 400 legislative seats and Hispanics had over 125.[37]

Women quadruple in number

Educationally, socially, and economically, state legislators tend to come from the middle and upper quadrants. Over three-fourths of the legislators have been exposed to a college education. Because legislative service requires a financial commitment under most legislative pay scales, legislatures consist of a disproportionate number of those

Legislators come from
upper classes

who can afford to serve. Since recognition of social status is a political requirement in many districts, persons of prominence tend to have great success at the polls.

Representational Roles of Legislators

Even though legislators may be wealthy, black, women, or young, they are all elected to represent a constituency that is usually pluralistic. If they expect to remain in office, they must consider the views of the poor, white, men, and aging in their districts. This brings us to the representational roles arising out of the question: What determines your vote—your conscience or your constituents? The three representational options are trustee, delegate, and politico.

Trustee

A legislator striving to serve as a *trustee* claims that personal conscience and judgment are the basis of decisions. Perhaps this role was best expressed by Edmund Burke, the English statesman who chastised his opponent in 1776 for promising to be subservient to the wishes of the people in his legislative voting. Burke pointed out the untenable nature of this position by noting that decisions will be made by constituents some miles distant from those who receive the information required to make the decision.

Delegate

The legislator playing the role of *delegate* follows the instructions and wishes of constituents, whether those instructions are contrary to personally held opinions or not.

Politico

The *politico* follows conscience on one issue and the dictates of constituents on another, depending on the circumstances that may require balancing one against another.

Trustee most common
role

A majority of legislators apparently perceive themselves as trustees.[38] Whether they have developed this perception as the product of a philosophy of representative government or as a reflection of self-efficacy makes little difference. The political reality of making hundreds of policy decisions in a short period of time precludes extensive interaction between constituents and representatives. As a consequence, legislators are forced by circumstances to make decisions on the basis of facts at hand and an assessment of how the folks back home want them to vote. On issues that have been involved in extensive debate, such as abortion or minimum drinking age, constituents may have telegraphed positions to representatives, but on the vast majority of measures, constituents have not had occasion even to consider the pros and cons, let alone provide the legislator with a coherent expression of opinion.

Constituents influence
decisions

Recognizing the volatility of some issues being forced into the legislative arena, trustees may find themselves playing the role of politicos on certain issues. As an example, legislators may have voted on the basis of their own judgment on 99 measures before encountering one prohibiting state aid for abortions for low-income women. Even though they may personally feel such aid should be continued, they know that a cohesive and vocal bloc of voters in their constituencies could endanger reelection. Thus, they play the politico by balancing the demands of their constituencies against their own judgment and bowing to the constituency.

Delegate role difficult

To play out the delegate role, legislators would first have to accept a theory of representative government that obligated them to follow the wishes of their constituencies. They would then require a constant flow of instructions from a mobilized and informed constituency.[39] Since both of these conditions raise a host of new questions and problems, the delegate role is unrealistic even for legislators who would like to believe that the voice of the people is the voice of God.

Even though unable to function effectively in the delegate role, many legislators have a strong interest in serving the people and interests of their legislative districts. In terms of the kinds of bills introduced and pushed by the great majority of legislators, William J. Keefe suggests that legislators seem to be preoccupied, not with statewide matters, but rather with solving local problems, meeting local pressure, conveying advantage to parochial interests, and satisfying pet peeves.[40] The major bills serving statewide purposes are more often the work of outsiders—the governor, administrative agencies, or private interest groups.

Legislators preoccupied with local matters

The Legislature as Process

Even though the legislature has a variety of duties, its chief function is to pass laws. Therefore, this section is concerned with the formal procedure, the institutional controls, the human behavior, and the political forces and techniques that constitute the state legislative process, especially the passing of laws.

An initial word of caution is in order for the casual observer who makes the trip to the state capitol to see the legislative process. The total legislative process is never on display because it is never confined to any one place or time. To *see* the legislative process, an observer would have to be in many places—a state administrator's office where information is being compiled for a legislator; in a hotel room where a business lobby is sponsoring a reception for a legislative committee; in a committee hearing while a bill is being discussed; in a cloakroom while senators are discussing strategy to stop a tax bill; in the gallery while the legislature grinds through its agenda; in the telephone center where calls are being received from constituents; or back in the legislative districts at public forums where legislators are making weekly reports. These are only a few of the scenes in the panoramic drama called the legislative process. As long as spectators realize that no matter which scene they are witnessing, it is only a part of the picture, a visit to the legislature can be a memorable learning experience.

Legislative process is everywhere

Uniqueness of Each Legislative Process

Like the human fingerprint, each state legislature is unique. It has its own formal and informal configurations of power and procedures. It may be similar to those in other states in some respects, but totally different in others. The legislature is only one part of the structure of power in the state's political system and is thus functionally interdependent with four other major political variables—the executive establishment, political parties, pressure groups, and the legislators' constituencies.[41] It is essentially this web of interdependent relationships, unique in varying degrees in each state, that explains much of the state's legislative decision-making process.

Each legislature unique

The amount of authority given a governor and the executive branch of government greatly affects the authority and role of the legislature in the scheme of government and politics. The state constitution may grant the governor a strong veto power, requiring a large majority of the legislature to override, or it may give the governor

1. Executive authority

control over special sessions, or it may delegate broad budgetary power. If the constitution provides for very few elected state officials, the chief executive will command the resources of numerous administrative agencies that can be used to influence the legislative process. As chief administrator, he or she can rally agencies for lobbying support, control the flow of information to legislative committtees, allocate programs to legislative districts, and use appointive powers to reward legislators.

Governor's personality important

Supplementing formal powers such as these are political and personal resources. As the titular head of his political party in most states, the governor shares a political future with fellow party members in the assembly. This mutual political bond becomes even more significant when his or her party controls the legislature. The personal qualities of the governor also affect the legislature. A strong-willed, imaginative, and articulate governor can convert a constitutionally weak governor system into one of dynamic executive leadership by sheer force of personality. Using the mass media, a governor can affect the legislature's agenda-building process by appealing to public opinion. The importance of personality cannot be overstressed when assessing the impact of the executive on legislative activity.

While governors may have considerable power, they seldom engage in extensive warfare with the legislative branch. Scores of other duties keep them occupied with responsibilities in the executive branch. Consequently, their interest in legislative matters usually extends to several key issues of particular interest. They seldom want sole political responsibility for the taxing and spending process; further, in a number of states, the political culture does not look favorably on an aggressive executive. One study of gubernatorial power found that the governor's office ranked third as a major center for legislative decision-making, greatly outdistanced by legislative committees and party caucuses.[42]

2. Role of political parties

It is one thing to know which party controls the state legislature and quite another to determine how important this control is to the legislative process. Political scientists specializing in the legislative process find it very difficult to generalize about the role of parties for all 50 state legislatures. Even making a statement about an individual state can be hazardous. The ascribed role of party in one legislative session may become unglued one or two sessions later by an internal squabble or desertion of the ranks by a few crossovers. In recent decades, legislators seem to be asserting more independence, meaning that squabbles and crossovers are occurring more regularly.

Factions in one-party legislatures

A number of state legislatures, most of them in the South, are predominantly one-party. In some respects, they become no-party states because there is no reason for tight party discipline to protect partisan control of legislation, such as may be necessary in competitive two-party states. The larger the majority held by the controlling party, the more difficult it is for party leadership to keep the party from breaking up into factions. Because of the large prevailing majorities in some legislatures, factions have become as permanent in some of those bodies as parties are in other legislatures. Even as late as 1991, ten states had Democratic majorities of over 75 percent in both houses.

Party-line voting varies

How often do most of the Republicans vote against most of the Democrats? The level of party voting varies widely among the states and even between houses of the same state. Looking at party cohesion where a majority of one party votes against a majority of the other party, Professors Jewell and Patterson found the parties voting against each other on 82 percent of the measures in the Pennsylvania senate but only 29 percent in the house. Parties in both houses in Massachusetts had strong party voting, running 74 percent in the senate and 72 percent in the house. The Utah senate recorded 98 percent party voting in the study.[43] Low party voting was found in the senates of New Mexico (24 percent) and Wyoming (24 percent). Party voting and intraparty cohesion are strongest in northeastern and midwestern states where two-party competition is healthy and where the parties represent diverse constituencies.[44]

Party activities in the legislative process are usually centered in the party caucus— a gathering of legislators of similar political persuasion, usually organized as Democrats and Republicans. Party caucuses are not used in some one-party states because they have such one-party legislatures that factions within the dominant party tend to displace caucuses. Among the items of business that may come before the party caucus are selection of leadership, establishing party policy on key legislative issues, disseminating information about bills, planning legislative strategies, coordinating release of public information on party positions, and providing staff assistance to legislators. While caucuses maintain a party spirit and cohesion on floor voting, only one-fourth of the caucuses resort to a binding vote that requires all party members to support a caucus decision on the floor.[45]

Parties function in caucuses

As discussed in chapter 8, the patterns of pressure groups vary widely from state to state. Consequently, their impact on the legislative process varies accordingly. While recognizing that lobbyists usually represent groups asking the government for special benefits and privileges, legislators nevertheless regard lobbyists as valuable sources of information and research. Unable to sound out constituents on a regular basis, legislators often obtain the views of their constituents through organizations and lobbyists that reflect constituent interests. As examples, a legislator from an agricultural district welcomes the views of farm organizations that include his or her constituents among their members, or a legislator from a labor district will obtain constituent opinions by what representatives of labor organizations say.

3. Pattern of pressure groups

Many times there are more lobbyists than legislators at a state capitol. Though mere numbers do not necessarily mean abused power, such conditions have provoked severe criticism for their alleged influence in corrupting the lawmakers. Some states became concerned about corrupt lobbying before the national government even seriously considered legislation. Important features of lobbying laws in most states require the registration of paid lobbyists, names of the sponsors, terms of compensation, total expenditures, and sources of income. Failure to comply with the requirements may subject the violator to fine, imprisonment, and denial of registration. The legislation has proved difficult to enforce, although it is said to have improved the practice of lobbying.

Regulate legislative lobbying

The fourth major variable that makes each legislative system different is the makeup of the legislative districts and constituencies that send legislators to the assembly. Admittedly, once elected, legislators are forced to become trustees and use their own judgment in voting for or against measures before the legislature. However, before getting elected, they must often demonstrate, through a record of experience and affiliations, that they are a "cut of the district" and that they represent the values and interests of the district. Suburbanites elect legislators who reflect the concerns and

4. Legislative constituencies

interests of the suburbs; farmers elect representatives who reflect an abiding interest in the agricultural society; and central city constituencies elect people who can speak about their problems with a sense of experience and insight.

Districts shape outlook

When the legislators arrive at the capitol from their various constituencies, they bring with them a variety of viewpoints—and that variety will vary from state to state. A legislature made up of representatives primarily from rural districts will be relatively conservative regardless of the party composition. On the other hand, a legislature with a majority from urban areas will be of a different persuasion. Thus, the nature of the constituencies from which legislators come will dictate, to a large degree, the nature of the legislative process and the output of that process. Out of this diversity in representation evolves the competing interests and demands that must be dealt with in the legislative process.

Leaders in the Legislative Process

Choosing legislative leadership

Except in the nonpartisan unicameral legislature of Nebraska and a few southern states where factions control, the leadership of the two legislative chambers is chosen by the political parties. In the house of representatives, the key position is that of *speaker*. Depending on the state, the speaker usually exercises considerable authority in naming committees, assigning bills to committees, recognizing speakers in floor debate, and applying rules of procedure. In the senate, 28 states provide in their constitutions that the lieutenant governor shall preside. In his or her absence, a president pro tempore chosen by the senate membership serves as presiding officer. In recent decades, legislatures have worked to remove the lieutenant governor, a member of the executive branch, from their chamber so the majority party can select its own presiding officer. At present, it is not uncommon to see a chamber controlled by one party under the gavel of a lieutenant governor of the opposite party. This situation can lead to political mischief, obstruction of the majority, and executive interference.

State traditions vary widely in the number of terms leaders may serve, with 17 states permitting one to two terms, 22 states permitting three or four terms and ten states with five terms or more.[46]

Roles of floor leaders

Both the majority and minority parties of each chamber choose floor leaders to guide party strategy, to represent the party in decisions on legislative assignments, to advocate the party position on legislation, and to serve as the loyal opposition. According to the Council of State Governments, selection of the party leaders is done by party caucuses in 70 percent of the legislative chambers.[47]

Leaders being challenged

Over the past two decades, the power of leaders has slowly diminished as rank-and-file legislators have gained a greater voice in decisions and as committee meetings and general sessions have been opened to the public. Not only has authority declined, but leaders are confronted with greater personal expenses, increasing demands for accountability, and an increasing number of single interest groups that resort to threats of political reprisals.[48]

In recent years, leaders have had to worry about another threat—rebellion from within. Members who are unhappy have formed coalitions with opposition party members on several occasions in recent years to overthrow leaders in North Carolina, Connecticut and Oklahoma. Discussing this rebellious spirit growing in legislative bodies, political scientist Alan Rosenthal blamed increasing decentralization of authority as a cause of the cross-party coalitions. "I think there is a trend toward people questioning power," he observed, "people wanting to share in power and doing what satisfies their immediate purposes. People are much more individually independent."[49]

The responsibilities of leadership have gone beyond merely serving in the legislative system. Leaders of today are finding themselves more and more involved in legislative election campaigns on a grand scale. California Assembly Speaker Willie L. Brown, Jr. highlighted this role in the 1980s and set the pace by raising over $2 million annually to dole out to legislative candidates worthy of his help. Other legislative leaders took his cue and formed their own PACs until leaders in a large majority of the states now play an important role in campaign financing. In some states, the party caucuses have formed PACs to help their candidates.

Leaders becoming fundraisers

The principal method for filling the PAC treasury is the big cocktail party or banquet featuring admission prices high enough to garner a heavy profit for the campaign. Among those paying the price are wealthy party supporters, generous friends, and droves of lobbyists. Heavy reliance on lobbyist money for legislative campaigns has raised questions about the integrity of the legislative process since most lobbyists expect to realize some sort of benefit from their contributions.[50]

Danger in fundraising

Procedures and Rules: Formal and Informal

Before business can be conducted in the legislature, a minimum number of legislators must be present. This number is called the *quorum.* Normally, the lack of a quorum is corrected by sending the sergeants-at-arms to scour hotels, committee rooms, and coffee shops to bring the wayward members to the floor so business can proceed. When attendance on the floor dwindles, some members may use the question about the presence of a quorum to force roll calls and a rounding up of members just to delay consideration of legislation.

Keeping a quorum

The passage of a bill, according to the state constitution, may require affirmative action by a majority of a quorum, or it may require a majority vote of the total membership. Kentucky requires an affirmative vote by two-fifths of those elected and a majority of those voting. In the New Hampshire house, a majority constitutes a quorum, but if fewer than two-thirds of the elected members are present, two-thirds of those present must assent to render any action valid.

Passing bills

Each state constitution has an article on the legislative branch that not only dictates the size of the legislature but also prescribes the basic rules to be followed in passing legislation. Constitutions invariably address such matters as quorums and majorities, introduction of bills, number of readings, referral to committees, deadlines for consideration, and other matters considered minimal in the process.

Constitution sets out procedures

Because state constitutions are brief and provide only the basic procedural guidelines, many of the activities and practices of the legislative bodies have been organized through rules of the house. Each house maintains a set of rules, usually adopted at the beginning of the session, to deal with subjects not covered by the constitution, such as controlling debate, referral of bills, types of calendars to be used, access to the floor, hiring of employees, design of the committee system, and scores of other matters crucial to the smooth functioning of the legislature.

Houses adopt rules

The unwritten rules

Legislative procedure involves far more than constitutional provisions, statutes, and formal rules, however. Some unwritten rules are more important than official ones and the consequences of their violation may be more serious to individual legislators. Many of the informal rules are peculiar to individual states, depending on practices that have become customary and were passed on from one legislative class to the next. Among some of the more common unwritten rules are to avoid personalities and focus on the issue; give notice if you plan to oppose; warn the presiding officer of unusual parliamentary moves; be willing to compromise; let the caucus leader know if you are not going along with a party vote; don't talk your bill to death; be a good apprentice before becoming a full practitioner; and be respectful of the leadership and your colleagues.

Punishing the rule breakers

Legislators who violate the rules are subject to a variety of punitive reprisals. By far the most popular punishment is obstruction of bills by bottling them up in committee, amending them, or voting against passage. Other forms of punishment include ostracism, distrust, loss of political rewards, and denial of special legislative privileges. Eventually, these political and social reprisals teach brash legislators that to "get along" in the system they must "go along," at least to a reasonable degree.

Launching the Legislative Process

Legislative assemblies are called into session in a variety of ways but the most common call is found in the state constitution. In almost all states, the constitution specifies that the assembly shall convene on a certain Monday, Tuesday, or Wednesday in January to commence the regular session. Seven states convene only every other year.

Most convene in January

Assemblies may also be called into special session by the governor; over half of the states provide for a procedure by which legislators can call themselves into session; some states have a flexible schedule that permits legislatures to be continuing bodies that reconvene according to a calendar adopted by the legislature itself; and several states have automatic reconvening of sessions to consider gubernatorial vetoes.

Introduction of Bills

The fodder of the process is the bills and resolutions. Some idea of the magnitude of the legislative load is afforded by consulting *The Book of the States,* which includes a biennial directory of the number of legislative introductions and enactments. A majority of states see over 1,000 new bills each regular annual session as well as 100 or more resolutions. At last count, New York led with an annual load of close to 18,000 bills while Wyoming had the fewest bills, averaging around 500 computed on an annual basis.[51] States with the largest number of bills do not necessarily pass the largest percentage of laws. New York passes around five percent of the bills introduced while Nebraska, North Dakota, and Utah may pass 40 percent or more. State legislatures witnessing the largest number of bills usually do not have the requirement that all bills be heard and/or reported out by committees. As a result, most of the bills are permitted to die in committees.

Rates of introduction and passage

All bills not intended to pass

Many bills are introduced without any intention by the sponsors of securing passage. Some measures are introduced only to please constituents, some to harass or threaten interest groups, some to serve as vehicles for amendments at the end of the session, some to serve as trading stock in the hard-bargaining sessions, and a few, regrettably, are introduced for the ulterior motive of personal gain in some way. Because these tactics delay the consideration of the serious legislation, some assemblies have been searching for methods to eliminate bills that are not designed for passage. Nebraska, Colorado, Indiana, and Tennessee have all experimented with limiting the number of bills a legislator may introduce during a session. About two-thirds of the legislative bodies set deadlines for the introduction of bills, thereby stopping the flow of new measures at some point in the session.

Prefiling has become a common practice in state legislatures to help assemblies get off to a quick start. A few decades ago, legislatures would convene, organize, and then stand idle until legislators could get bills drafted and introduced. By permitting members and interim committees to prefile bills before the legislature even convenes, a hefty workload can be ready for the committees as soon as they are organized.

No proposal becomes a bill for official consideration by a legislative chamber unless it is formally introduced by a member, group of members, committee of that house, or is received with a certificate of adoption from the other house of a bicameral legislature. Nonmembers, even high state officials, have no power to introduce bills, however much initiative and influence they may exercise in preparing drafts of laws or proposing legislation in the press. Usually a member introduces a bill by speaking from the floor, or by filing it with a designated legislative official.

Introducers of bills

The Readings of the Bills

On its trip through one house a bill is given three readings, actual or nominal, unless it gets "killed" along the way. A few states have reduced the requirement to only two readings. Separate readings on separate days are required in all states, either by constitutional provision or by rules of procedure. Full oral readings were essential in the days of simple government when convenient facilities for printing and distributing copies of pending bills were lacking. Today, full readings on the floor are neither necessary nor feasible for handling the mass of complicated proposals that pour into the process.

Referral to a Standing Committee

After the proposed law is introduced and given its first reading, the presiding officer refers the measure to the standing committee having jurisdiction of the subject matter involved in the proposal. Legislative bodies rely heavily upon committees for much of the actual work of investigation and lawmaking.

There are several types of committees and committee functions. At this point in the process, we are dealing with *standing* committees that are organized for the consideration of all bills and matters in a particular field of interest, such as revenue, appropriations, labor, or the judiciary.

In addition to standing committees there are several other types of committees. *Special, select, or ad hoc* committees look into temporary problems, such as election frauds, civil disorder, or administrative scandals; they make reports and recommendations; and then pass out of existence when the special task is completed. *Interim* committees make studies or investigations between sessions of a legislature. *Procedural* committees manage the various procedures involved in the legislative process, the most

Types of committees defined

important of which is the rules committee. *Joint conference* committees with members from both houses iron out differences when bills pass both houses but in different form or language, and the house of first passage will not accept the changes.

A number of states have many standing committees, with North Carolina leading all other states with 34 senate committees and 53 house committees. Rhode Island probably has the least with a total of 12 in both houses.[52] In Connecticut, Maine, and Massachusetts all standing committees are joint senate-house committees.

Creating conflicts of interest

Though the legislative committees are expected to capitalize on the occupational expertise and legislative experience of their members, this expectation raises two problems. In regard to occupational expertise, a common practice in making committee assignments is to permit legislators to serve on committees who have occupations related to the committee subject. For example, educators seek out the education committee, bankers ask for the banking committee, and so on. Thus, in order to utilize fully the expertise of legislators, potential conflicts of interest are created. Legislative experience is also difficult to capture because of the turnover among committee members. In one study, the average committee turnover in houses of representatives over a five-year period was over 75 percent. Arkansas and Virginia were the only two states with less than 50 percent turnover on standing committees.[53] Without the benefit of occupational expertise and legislative experience, committees are easier targets for professional lobbyists and seasoned bureaucrats.

The standard procedures of standing committees vary somewhat among legislatures and among the committees of any particular legislature. Committees are generally required to avoid conflict of time with the regular floor sessions, except for urgent reasons and with special house permission. They are expected to meet on a schedule that leaves the afternoons clear for attendance on the floor.

Figure 9.4
Standing committees are the real "workhorses" of the legislative process. Committees receive testimony and information, conduct studies, propose amendments, negotiate conflicts, and provide advice to the chambers through committee reports. *(Photo by Garry D. Redmann.)*

Committees are the heart of the legislative process. They perform the critical functions that make it possible for large deliberative bodies to function. First of all, they divide the legislative workload down to manageable proportions by accepting responsibility for specific substantive areas of policy. Second, they capitalize on the expertise of the legislators by utilizing them on committees requiring specialized knowledge. Third, they provide opportunity for citizen input by receiving testimony and information at hearings. Fourth, they conduct independent research and study to obtain factual insight into the issues being presented. Fifth, by proposing amendments. committees compromise the differences that may evolve in the debate and testimony. Sixth, they provide the main body of legislators with advice through the committee reports. In some states, acceptance of committee reports runs as high as 90 percent, indicating the degree of confidence and trust placed in the advice of committees (Figure 9.4).

Standing committees key to process

Just a few years ago, legislative committees were permitted to go into secret session to hold hearings, discuss legislation, or to decide the fate of bills in their possession. Today, however, all states require open committee meetings, with few exceptions. Two-thirds of the states require that advance public notice be given on legislation to be considered. Committee roll calls on final actions are also becoming more common as demands for legislative accountability grow.[54]

Open committee meetings

After receiving as many viewpoints and facts as obtainable within the limited time available, the committee is expected to provide the parent house with its best recommendation. Committees have a number of options in recommending action on a particular bill:

Define committee options

- *Do pass.* The committee recommends favorable action on the bill as referred.
- *Pass after amendment.* The committee recommends favorable action after its proposed amendments are adopted.
- *Do not pass or indefinitely postpone.* The committee does not concur with the legislation and recommends defeat.
- *No recommendation.* A rare committee report, this recommendation reflects a committee that doesn't know what to suggest. The issue involved may be so controversial the committee members want to avoid responsibility for it.
- *Amend and do not pass.* The committee does not favor the bill but if the body is determined to pass it amendments should be adopted to improve it.

Occasionally a minority of committee members may strongly oppose the recommendation proposed by the majority and draft a recommendation of their own for floor consideration. In the case of a divided committee report, when the reports are received on the floor, a member of the minority on the committee will move to substitute the report of the minority for that of the majority. Then the debate ensues and the entire body decides which report to put on the calendar for later action.

Minority may file report

Action on the Floor

Legislative bodies conduct floor activities in accord with orders of business and calendars. The calendars are really lists of bills completed by committees, to be taken up in order on designated days. There may be calendars for local bills, for general bills, for unanimous consent items, and for other matters. Urgent or favorite bills may be

Managing floor traffic

moved to the top of the calendar through unanimous consent, or through special rules of a powerful rules committee or majority leadership. In effect, this special treatment reduces the priority of other bills and also reduces the likelihood of their getting attention by the deliberative body. This discretionary treatment is part of the process of legislative politics, and it frequently is necessary for the passage of constructive legislation and avoidance of chaotic conditions near the end of a session.

Getting the floor

It is often necessary to limit debate in legislatures in order to get the work done. This requirement is more noticeable and necessary for assemblies of large membership than for the small bodies. The rank-and-file members of a lower chamber are likely to find it difficult to get the opportunity to speak at critical times. Also, they are likely to find their time limited to a few minutes when they finally do get the floor.

Making a decision

At the conclusion of debate, the measure comes up for final passage and the legislators are faced with the time of decision. By this time, they have received scattered communications from constituents, been dined by lobbyists, barraged by government agencies, reviewed articles and papers, consulted with colleagues, and advised by party leaders. Finally, they appeal to their own biases, experience and judgment. Each bill will bring a different mix of pressure and communications.

Legislators seek advice

A cursory glance at figure 9.5 may suggest that constituents are irrelevant in the legislative process, that they count so little in decision-making the legislature isn't even a representative assembly. To the contrary, constituents have great influence on legislators on those issues that are important to constituents. On most bills, however, legislators are left by the constituents to play the "trustee" role. Without guidance from constituents, legislators turn for advice and information to those who are available—primarily people who are in and around the legislative process, such as friends in the legislature, legislative specialists, interest groups, senior committee members, and legislative party leaders.

Voting on bills

Legislative houses cast votes in different ways. Over two-thirds of the states now use consent calendars to speed consideration of minor matters. On some actions, such as final passage of a measure, a roll call vote is required, with every member present responding to be recorded as voting for or against the motion or as being present but not voting. This is a slow process unless electronic devices are used. A majority of states have installed electronic voting systems, with push buttons at each member's desk and with a scoreboard to flash each vote as well as tally the results. This method also prints out a record of the vote for the daily journal.

To deal with unusual situations, the rules may be suspended by unanimous consent or by a two-thirds vote. Even if the rules and constitutional procedures were not followed to the letter, it is the practice of courts and attorneys general to accept the certified journals at face value, refusing to go behind them to check the process of a separate branch of government.

"The House Does Not Concur. . ."

If a bill is successfully passed in the first house, it is then sent to the second house where the entire process is repeated. When the second house considers the bill, it may suggest amendments. If the originating house does not agree with the amendments, each house then appoints members to a joint conference committee whose task it will

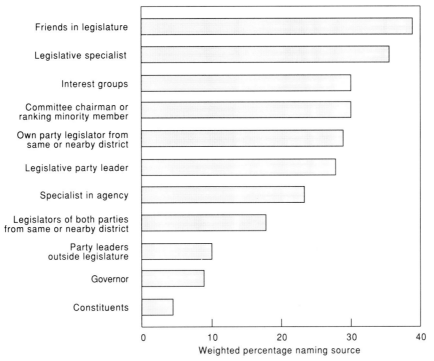

Figure 9.5
Whom Do Legislators Consult in Making Decisions?
(Reprinted by permission of Greenwood Publishing Group, Inc., Westport, CT from Patterns of Decision Making in State Legislatures *by Eric Uslaner and Ronald Weber. Copyright 1977 by Praeger Publishers.)*

be to iron out the differences between the houses. In most legislatures, the committee consists of three members from each chamber.[55] Appointments will usually go to members who have served on the standing committees that considered the legislation. If the conference committee is unable to resolve the differences, the membership may be changed on successive committees until the dispute is resolved. In one legislative session, a knotty tax measure required 23 successive conference committees before the differences could be resolved and legislators could adjourn.

Conference committees resolve differences

Governor as Legislator-at-Large

All states except North Carolina have given governors authority to veto acts of the legislature. Governors today have more extensive veto powers than the president. Not only are they empowered to veto measures outright, but 43 states permit governors to veto individual items in appropriation bills while leaving the main bill intact; 11 states permit governors to reduce items in appropriations bills; four states empower the governor to return bills with suggested amendments; and 17 states allow governors to send bills back for reconsideration.

Bills go to governor

While the item veto was given to governors to curb legislative spending, research indicates that there is little, if any, relationship between state spending and the item veto.[56] An in-depth analysis of 542 item vetoes occurring in Wisconsin between 1975 and 1985 demonstrated that they were used "primarily as a tool for policymaking and

Item veto and spending

partisan advantage rather than fiscal restraint."[57] New interest and research was generated on the gubernatorial veto when President Ronald Reagan proposed that the same power be given to presidents as a means of controlling spending.

Governors veto few bills

Having power and using it are two different matters. A review of the use of the veto revealed that governors are very restrained in their use of veto power. Through the decades, governors have vetoed only five percent of the bills. In some states, governors veto no bills while in other states, for unique reasons, they veto many bills.[58] Numerous vetoes suggest a divided government, with the legislature in the hands of one party and the governorship under the control of the other. In the late 1980s, a pitched battle occurred between the governor and the legislature in California and the governor vetoed over 20 percent of the bills. In the same years, the governor of Massachusetts vetoed none.[59]

Overriding vetoes

To override vetoes, almost all states require an unusual majority in both houses, with most requiring a two-thirds vote. Overrides are just as uncommon as vetoes, with only five to ten percent of the measures vetoed being successfully overridden by legislatures.

Governors usually have five or ten days to act on bills while the legislature is still sitting; however, a longer period is given if the legislature has adjourned. In a majority of states, bills become laws unless the governor vetoes them. This provision sometimes makes it possible for the governor to escape political liability for controversial legislation he or she may wish to see become law. The governor may just let it lapse into law without a signature. In about one-fourth of the states the measure dies unless signed.

When laws become effective

Upon being signed by the governor, bills go to the office of the secretary of state and normally become effective as laws 60 or 90 days after enactment or adjournment in a majority of states. Sometimes the legislation may provide for a later effective date. Emergency measures, passed by large majorities, can become effective sooner in most states. All laws adopted by the assembly during a session are then published as the "session laws" and later integrated into editions of the state "code" or "statutes at large."

Direct Democracy: The Initiative and Referendum

In three-fourths of the states, the legislature does not have a monopoly on proposing and considering legislation. In 19 states, legislatures are required to refer certain acts to a vote of the people. Most commonly, these tend to be bonding and fiscal issues. In 24 states, the people have the right to *referendum,* i.e., to refer acts of the legislature for a vote of the people by securing a fixed number of signatures on petitions circulated throughout the state. In 23 states, the people may exercise the *initiative,* i.e., the right to propose legislation through the petition circulation process.

People voting on laws

Participation of citizens in the law-making process, often called "direct democracy," has roots deep in history, with instances being recorded in Athens and other Greek city-states, Swiss cantons, and colonial New England.[60] The origin of direct democracy as found in states today was spawned in the later 1800s and early 1900s when public mistrust of state legislatures boiled over. Many citizens became convinced that powerful interest groups were dictating legislative policy to the detriment of the public.

Seek to bypass legislatures

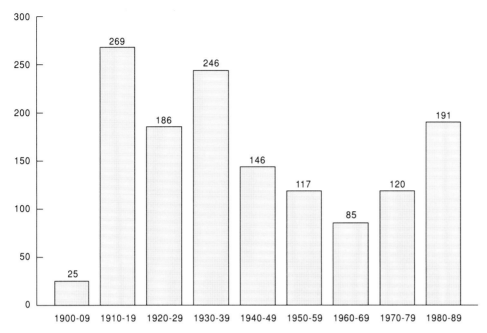

Figure 9.6
Statewide Initiatives on Ballot by Decade. *(Sources: Sue Thomas, "A Comparison of Initiative Activity by State."* Initiative Quarterly *3 (1984): 8–10; Virginia Graham, "A Compilation of Statewide Initiative Proposals Appearing on Ballots Through 1976." Washington, DC: Congressional Research Service; and David B. Magleby, "Taking the Initiative,"* PS: Political Science and Politics, Summer, 1988.)*

Both the Populist and Progressive parties rallied behind the tools of direct democracy as the only means of breaking the iron grip of political bosses and vested interests in legislatures.[61]

Just as direct democracy was founded by those effectively excluded from the legislative process, so has it been used and supported by those who could not get their way in the legislature. In states where Democrats control the legislature for a period of years, Republicans will espouse the use of the initiative and referendum. In states where Republicans control, Democrats see direct democracy as their avenue to action.

Figure 9.6 indicates the importance of the statewide initiatives through the decades. After peaking in the 1930s, the use of initiatives declined, bottomed out in the 1960s, and has been on the return in recent decades. Perhaps nothing stimulated recent interest in the initiative and referendum as much as a tax-cutting proposition that was adopted in California in 1978. The direct democracy fever struck California so hard that its citizens had to deal with 29 propositions in 1988—the highest in 46 years.

Direct democracy on increase

States vary in the number of signatures required to initiate legislation. Most require a percentage of the vote last cast for governor, with Wyoming appearing to be the largest with 15 percent of the vote cast for governor. A smaller number may be required for a referral.

Though direct democracy was created to facilitate the power of the people, modernization of campaigns has left the people out of the process in many cases. Polling, media production, direct mail, campaign management, gathering signatures, and legal

*Direct democracy
requires money*

services have all contributed to escalating direct democracy costs, according to Professor David B. Magleby.[62] Observers of the California 1988 general election ballot estimated that the battles over the 29 propositions cost over $125 million, with most of it going for and against five insurance measures.

Seek to curb abusers

Attempts by states to curb abuses in the exercise of direct democracy have not always been successful. While some of the corrective procedural steps have won approval, attempts to limit corporate spending and paying for signatures have run afoul of the federal courts as violations of the First Amendment. To protect the process, some states require statewide distribution of the signatures, i.e., fixed percentages by congressional district or county. States may also require authentication of signatures by a notary public and then random sample verification of signatures by contacting alleged signers.

*Arguments for use of
direct democracy*

After some 80 years of usage, the initiative and referendum are still matters of considerable debate, especially with the increased use to dictate state fiscal affairs and to wage environmental and consumer wars. The direct democracy crusade was initially launched as an effort to return control of the government to the people. "The people are sovereign and possess the ultimate right of government," advocates argue. In addition, supporters claim that direct democracy reduces apathy and alienation, keeps the legislature sensitive to the public interest, permits citizens to overrule legislators on single issues without turning them out of office, and encourages citizens to become more civic-minded and informed about government.

*Arguments against "I
and R"*

Those who have opposed the expansion of the initiative and referendum counter with the argument that direct democracy has not lived up to its expectations. Deliberativeness has been removed from the policy-making process when people vote on sketchy information and slogans. The opposition further argues that the ignorance of the people is often exploited by slick, well-financed advertising campaigns, with many of the less educated being duped into voting contrary to their own interests. In addition, they claim that most citizens don't understand the implications of many measures, resulting in serious disruption of government, and they further claim that direct democracy provides special interests the opportunity to circumvent representative government and use big money to overcome the public good. Finally, the opposition points out that the process has been used to abuse minorities by making it possible for citizens to vote their prejudices in the secrecy of the voting booth.

Because of the persuasive arguments on both sides of the issue, the tools of direct democracy have not spread significantly since the early 1900s. More significantly, in states without the tools of direct democracy, the legislatures control the proposal of amendments to the state constitution and are generally hostile to sharing legislative powers through the initiative and referendum.

Conclusion

The state legislature, as an institution and as a process, has been transformed and modernized over the past 50 years. As an institution, legislatures have become better organized and more representative than at any time in history. Compensation has been increasing and turnover has been declining, resulting in more professional, more competent legislative bodies. Almost all meet annually to tend to the pressing affairs of state government. Professional staff and computers are commonplace. In most states, legislators exercise and manage the functions assigned to the legislative branch with as much efficiency as is possible in a deliberative, representative assembly. As a process, the legislature has become a branch equal to the executive. Leadership has been emerging, with women, blacks, Hispanics, and Native Americans appearing more regularly in its ranks. In most states, the legislative process has been streamlined to move into the 1990s. Even though legislatures have improved dramatically in recent decades, public confidence in them has been declining. In 1968, 50 percent of the people in a six-state survey gave legislatures positive ratings. By 1991, this had fallen to 28 percent in seven states.[63]

Endnotes

1. Donald Levitan and Elwyn E. Mariner, *Your Massachusetts Government,* 9th ed. (Newton Centre, Mass.: Government Research Publications, 1980): 1–2.

2. Evarts Boutell Greene, *The Foundation of American Nationality* (New York: American Book Company, 1922): 72.

3. *The Book of the States 1992–93* (Lexington, KY: Council of State Governments 1992): 136.

4. Richard C. Kearney, "Sunset: A Survey and Analysis of the State Experience," *Public Administration Review* 50 (January/February 1990): 49–51.

5. Lanny Proffer, "Legislatures Review Alternatives," *State Legislatures* 10 (January 1984): 24. Also see Rich Jones, "Legislative Review of Regulations," *State Legislatures* 8 (September 1982): 7–9; Marcus E. Ethridge, "Consequences of Legislative Review of Agency Regulations in Three U.S. States," *Legislative Studies Quarterly* 9 (February 1984): 161–178, and *Book of the States 1992–93* (Lexington, KY: Council of State Governments 1992): 199–200.

6. Rich Jones, "Keeping an Eye On State Agencies," *State Legislatures* 13 (July 1987): 20–21.

7. Alan Rosenthal, "Legislative Behavior and Legislative Oversight," *Legislative Studies Quarterly* 6 (February 1981): 117–121.

8. For a more detailed description of casework, see Malcolm E. Jewell, "Legislative Casework," *State Legislatures* 5 (November 1979): 14–18.

9. See Alan Rosenthal, "The Consequences of Constituency Service," *State Government* 59, No. 1 (1986): 25–30.

10. Richard E. Elling, "The Utility of State Legislative Casework as a Means of Oversight," *Legislative Studies Quarterly* 4 (August 1979): 373.

11. See Herbert Jacob, "Dimensions of State Politics," *State Legislatures in American Politics,* ed. Alexander Heard (Englewood Cliffs, N.J.: Prentice-Hall, 1966): 36; Leonard G. Ritt, "State Legislative Reform: Does It Matter?" *American Politics Quarterly* 1 (October 1973): 499–511; "The Impact of Legislative Reform: A 50 State Analysis," ed. Susan Welch and John Peters, *Legislative Reform and Public Policy* (New York: Praeger, 1977); Albert K. Karnig and Lee Sigelman, "State Legislative Reform and Public Policy: Another Look," *Western Political Quarterly,* 28 (September 1975): 548–553; and Joel A. Thompson, "State Legislative Reform: Another Look, One More Time, Again," *Polity* 19 (Fall, 1986): 27–41.

12. *Modernizing State Government* (New York: Committee for Economic Development, 1967): 38.

13. The Citizens Conference on State Legislatures, *State Legislatures: An Evaluation of their Effectiveness: The Complete Report by the Citizens Conference on State Legislatures* (New York: Praeger Publishers, 1971).

14. For a pro and con discussion of term limitations, see "How long is long enough?" *State Government News* 33 (December 1990): 18–19.

15. Samuel C. Patterson, "Legislators and Legislatures in the American States, *Politics in the American States,* 4th ed., ed. Virginia Gray, Herbert Jacob, and Kenneth N. Vines (Boston: Little, Brown & Company, 1983): 140–141.

16. See Bernard Grofman, Michael Miglaski and Nicholas Noviello, "Effects of Multimember Districts on Black Representation in State Legislatures," *The Review of Black Political Economy* 14 (Spring 1986): 65–78; Gary Moncrief and Joel Thompson, "Electoral District Characteristics and State Legislators' Backgrounds," prepared for delivery at the Midwest Political Science annual meeting, Chicago, April 13–15, 1989.

17. Leroy Hardy, Alan Heslop, and Stuart Anderson, "Introduction" to *Reapportionment Politics* (Beverly Hills: Sage Publications, 1981): 18.

18. Gordon E. Baker, *The Reapportionment Revolution: Representation, Political Power, and the Supreme Court* (New York: Random House, 1966).

19. For more documentation of malapportionment in the early 1960s, see the *Compendium on Legislative Apportionment,* 2nd ed. (New York: National Municipal League, 1962).

20. Gilbert Y. Steiner and Samuel K. Gove, *The Legislature Redistricts Illinois* (Urbana: University of Illinois, Institute of Government and Public Affairs, 1956): 71.

21. Quoted by Sidney Wise in "Pennsylvania," *Reapportionment Politics,* p. 278.

22. For a more complete discussion of partisan gerrymandering, see *Davis v. Bandemer,* 106 S. Ct. 2797 (1986); Bill Waren, "The Gerrymander Puzzle," *State Legislatures* 12 (October, 1986): 21–24; Charles H. Backstrom and Leonard Robins, "The Supreme Court Prohibits Gerrymandering: A Gain or a Loss for the States," *The Journal of Federalism* 17 (Summer, 1987): 101–109; Harry Basehart, "The Seats/Vote Relationship and the Identification of Partisan Gerrymandering in State Legislatures," *American Politics Quarterly* 15 (October 1987): 484–501; Robert X. Browning, "Partisan Gerrymandering from Baker v. Carr to Davis v. Bandemer," *Comparative State Politics Newsletter* 9 (October 1988): 25–39; John D. Cranor, Gary L. Cawley, and Raymond H. Scheele, "The Anatomy of a Gerrymander," *American Journal of Political Science* 33 (February 1989): 223–239; Gerard S. Gryski, Bruce Redd and Euel Elliott, "The Votes-Seats Relationship in State Legislative Elections," *American Politics Quarterly* 18 (April 1990): 141–157.

23. Ed Schneider, "1990s Redistricting: High Stakes, High Tech," *State Legislatures* 16 (September, 1990): 20–22.

24. Thomas R. Dye, *Politics, Economics, and the Public: Policy Outcomes in the American States* (Chicago: Rand McNally and Co., 1966): 294.

25. David C. Saffell, "Reapportionment and Public Policy: State Legislators' Perspective." Paper presented at the Midwest Political Science Association Meeting, Chicago, April 1980.

26. See Kenneth T. Palmer, "Legislatures Seen Helpful to Cities," *National Civic Review* 59 (May 1970): 262–263; and Michael A. Maggiotto et al., "The Impact of Reapportionment on Public Policy," *American Politics Quarterly* 13 (January 1985): 101–121.

27. Rich Jones, "The State Legislatures," *Book of the States 1992–93* (Lexington, KY: Council of State Governments 1992): 130–131.

28. John F. Bibby, "Electoral Change in the Midwest: Presidential Republicanism and Counter Realigning Forces," paper prepared for presentation at the annual meeting of the American Political Science Association, Atlanta, August 31–September 3, 1989.

29. Paverill Squire, "Career Opportunities and Membership Stability in Legislatures," *Legislative Studies Quarterly* 13 (February 1988): 65–82.

30. Malcolm E. Jewell and David Breaux, "The Effect of Incumbency on State Legislative Elections," *Legislative Studies Quarterly* 13 (November 1988): 495–514.

31. Karl T. Kurtz, "Life After the Legislature," *State Legislatures* 15 (July 1989): 45–49.

32. *Book of the States 1992–93* (Lexington, KY: Council of State Governments, 1992): 137–140.

33. Ibid., 129.

34. See Andrea Paterson, "Automating the State Legislatures," *State Legislatures* 11 (May 1985): 9–16 and *Book of the States 1992–93,* 132–133.

35. *Modernizing State Government* (New York: Committee for Economic Development, 1967): 33. For research on the relationship of political culture to legislators' occupational status and diversity, see John D. Baker, "Exploring the 'Missing Link': Political Culture as an Explanation of the Occupational Status and Diversity of State Legislators in Thirty States," *Western Political Quarterly* (September, 1990), 597–611.

36. See *The Journal of State Government* 64 (April–June 1991): 46.

37. *Book of the States 1992–93,* 130. Iva Ellen Deutchman surveyed 400 male legislators in six Northeast states and interviewed 87 of them in depth, and constructed an interesting five-fold typology based on their attitudes toward their female colleagues: (1) Angry Idolators, (2) Dancing Dog Legislators, (3) "What's the Fuss" Legislators, (4) Good Ole Boys, and (5) Legislative Feminists. *See* "Ungendered but Equal: Male Legislators' Attitudes Toward Their Female Colleagues," a paper presented at the American Political Science Association meeting in San Francisco, August 30–September 2, 1990.

38. See John C. Wahlke et al., *The Legislative System* (New York: John Wiley & Sons, 1962): 272–286.

39. See Donald J. McCrone and James H. Kuklinski, "The Delegate Theory of Representation," *American Journal of Political Science* 23 (May 1979): 278–300.

40. William J. Keefe, "The Functions and Powers of the State Legislatures," *State Legislatures,* ed. Alexander Heard (Englewood Cliffs, N.J.: Prentice-Hall, 1966): 38–39.

41. Wahlke et al., 245.

42. See Eric M. Uslaner and Ronald E. Weber, "Changes in Legislative Attitudes Toward Gubernatorial Power," *State and Local Government Review* 9 (May 1977): 40–43.

43. Malcolm E. Jewell and Samuel C. Patterson, *The Legislative Process in the United States,* 3d ed. (New York: Random House, Inc., 1977): 384–385.

44. David E. Price, *Bringing Back the Parties* (Washington, D.C.: Congressional Quarterly, Inc., 1984): 82.

45. See Alan Rosenthal, "If the Party's Over, Where's All That Noise Coming From?" *State Government* 57, No. 2 (1984): 51; *State Legislative Report* of the National Conference of State Legislatures, Denver (January 1981); and Robert Harmel, "On the Importance of State Party Caucuses: An Empirical Study," a paper prepared for delivery at the annual meeting of the American Political Science Association, Washington, D.C., August 30-September 2, 1984.

46. Malcolm E. Jewell, "The Durability of Leadership," *State Legislatures* 15 (November/December 1989): 10.

47. Cited by Harmel, APSA paper, p.5.

48. Janet Beardsley, "Legislative Leadership: Is Everybody Leaving?" *State Legislatures* 7 (May 1981): 17–18.

49. Karen Hansen, "Are Coalitions Really on the Rise?" *State Legislatures* 15 (April 1989): 11.

50. For a more complete discussion of the role of legislative leadership and caucus PACs, see Anthony Gierzynski and Malcolm Jewell, "Legislative Party Campaign Committee Activity: A Comparative State Analysis," a paper prepared for delivery at the annual meeting of the Midwest Political Science Association, April 13–15, 1989, Chicago, and their paper, "Legislative Party and Leadership Campaign Finance Committees: An Analysis of Resource Allocation," prepared for delivery at the annual meeting of the American Political Science Association, August 31-September 3, 1989 in Atlanta. Also see Alan Rosenthal, "The New Chamber Game," *State Government News* 31 (April 1988): 22.

51. *Book of the States 1992–93* (Lexington, KY: Council of State Governments, 1992): 183–185.

52. Figures based on the *Book of the States 1992–93:* 191–192.

53. James R. Oxendale, Jr., "Membership Stability on Standing Committees in Legislative Lower Chambers," *State Government* 54, No. 4 (1981): 126.

54. U.S. Advisory Commission on Intergovernmental Relations, *State and Local Roles in the Federal System* A-88 (Washington, D.C.: Government Printing Office, 1982): 78–79.

55. *Conference Committees,* a monograph published by the National Conference of State Legislatures, Denver (August 1978): 2.

56. David C. Nice, "The Item Veto and Expenditure Restraint," *Journal of Politics* 50 (May 1988): 486–487.

57. Tony Hutchison, quoting research by Prof. James Gosling in "Legislating Via Veto," *State Legislatures* 15 (January 1989): 20–21.

58. Charles W. Wiggans, "Executive Vetoes and Legislative Overrides in the American States," *The Journal of Politics* 42 (November 1980): 1112–1113.

59. *Book of the States 1990–91:* 160–161.

60. Daniel F. Ritsche, "*Let the People Decide—Initiative and Referendum in Wisconsin and Other States*" (Madison, WI: Wisconsin Legislative Reference Bureau, 1990): 2.

61. Thomas E. Cronin, *Direct Democracy* (Cambridge, MA: Harvard University Press, 1989): 38–54.

62. David B. Magleby, "Taking the Initiative: Direct Legislation and Direct Democracy in the 1980s," *P.S.: Political Science & Politics* 21 (Summer 1988): 605. Also see Magleby, *Direct Legislation: Voting on Ballot Propositions in the United States* (Baltimore: Johns Hopkins U Press, 1984).

63. Alan Ehrenhalt, "An Embattled Institution," *Governing* 5 (January 1992): 28.

CHAPTER 10

THE EXECUTIVE BRANCH

Coping with the Management Challenge in the Midst of Fragmentation

---

The Fragmented Executive

When the framers of the U.S. Constitution designed the three branches of the federal government and provided for the executive branch in Article II, they molded it around the single executive office of the president. "The executive power shall be vested in a President of the United States of America," they declared simply and directly. Since most people are familiar with the design of the national executive and the centrality of the president, they often think the same concept applies to the state executive and the governor. However, the executive branch in most states consists not only of a chief executive but a number of other elected executives, independent boards created by the state constitution, and additional agencies, boards and commissions created by state assemblies and often answerable to them.

State executives more fragmented than national

In creating the executive branch, the Oklahoma constitution states: "The executive authority of the state shall be vested in a Governor, Lieutenant Governor, Secretary of State, State Auditor and Inspector, Attorney General, State Treasurer, Superintendent of Public Instruction, Chief Mine Inspector, Commissioner of Labor, Commissioner of Insurance and other officers provided by law and this Constitution. . ."

State constitutions frame executive branch

In many states, the constitution may structure the executive to a greater degree by creating boards or agencies. For example, the Georgia constitution creates a state board of pardons, a state personnel board, a state transportation board, a veterans service board, and a board of natural resources. By providing for these boards, the constitution places them beyond the control of central executive management.

Commenting on the structure of the typical state executive branch, Woodrow Wilson, as governor of New Jersey, observed:

> The governor . . . is not the 'Executive'; he is but a single piece of the executive. There are other pieces coordinated with him over which he has no

---

Title photo: The executive tower of the Florida state capitol overshadows the old traditional capitol, symbolizing the growth of the executive through the decades. (Photo by Florida Department of Commerce, Division of Tourism.)

direct official control, and which are of less dignity than he only because they have no power to control legislation, as he may do by the exercise of his veto, and because his position is more representative, perhaps, of the state government as a whole, of the people of the state as a unit.[1]

State executives weaker

Wilson's description of the governor's constitutional position, made over 80 years ago, is still valid in many states, although the management authority of the average governor has grown in recent decades. Even so, the governor's legal position in most states continues to be much weaker than that of the president in the government of the United States, an ironic truth when some surveys reflect a greater level of trust in states than in the federal government. This trust is not reflected in the structure of the state government.

Functions of the Executive Branch

Before we can make judgments on the adequacy of the structure and makeup of the typical state executive branch for the 1990s, we must review its specific functions.

1. Execute policy

In the scheme of separation of powers, the prime duty of the legislative branch is to determine policy, and the chief responsibility of the executive branch is to execute policy. Therefore, most state constitutions charge the governor with the responsibility to see "that the laws are faithfully executed." For most governors, this charge is difficult to carry out because the same constitutions also provide for a number of independently elected officials who also execute laws. Many constitutions also create agencies, commissions, and boards with administrative authority of their own. Legislatures, then, add another tier of administrative units which may or may not be accountable to the governor. Thus, executive authority is vested in a diversity of administrative units, each authorized to "faithfully execute" its own part of the executive branch. Because of this fragmentation, we must bear in mind that a good many agencies are involved in the execution of functions and not the governor alone. In a number of states the constitutional mandate to the governor to see "that the laws are faithfully executed" thus becomes one of oversight rather than management.

2. Propose policy

Since the days when Secretary of Treasury Alexander Hamilton was the chief proposer of economic development policy in the Washington administration, the executive branch has been expected to bring forward suggestions for policy adoption by the legislative branch. In fact, "State of the State" messages are required by constitutions and governors are directed to "recommend such measures as he or she shall judge to be expedient." After all, the people working in the administering (executing) units of government are most familiar with the implications of existing policy and are thus knowledgeable about the needs for changes. The service delivery levels of state governments constantly feed suggestions to the upper echelons where they are reviewed in the context of broader objectives. Invariably many of these proposals for policies are brought to the legislature, often by the governor, but just as often by other elected officials and units of government.

Since legislative assemblies are unable to foresee every administrative problem in the application of policy, they are forced to delegate discretionary authority to administrators. Of course, legislatures may not give their legislative authority to executive agencies, but legislatures must still leave considerable latitude for administrators to make policy within guidelines furnished by the assemblies. One of the first steps in carrying out programs adopted by the legislature is the issuance of rules and regulations by the administering agencies to fill the gaps left by the general provisions of the law. To guarantee that this discretion is not abused by administrators, almost all state legislatures have developed procedures to review and control excess rule making.

3. Make policy

Legislatures are designed to bring together representation from across the state, using geographic subdivisions for electing members to the legislature. Being accountable to the people who elect them, legislators are expected to view state government from the perspective of their constituents. However, much of the state legislation is of such a general nature that legislative constituencies are not concerned about it. Nevertheless, on some pieces of legislation, the interests of various constituencies are very much at stake and legislators engage in determined struggles to maximize the benefits for their home districts. Out of these struggles may come legislation that is partial to one area of the state or another, depending on the power of the bargainers and the bargaining that occurred during the legislative process. As representatives of the state as a whole, the governor, elected officials and other state administrators interject the statewide concerns and thereby balance the parochial interests of legislators with the concerns of the state as a whole. The balancing of these different perspectives—legislators with parochial views and officials with statewide concerns—points out the genius of the principle of separation of powers. The good of the state and its constituent parts are all well-served when these two viewpoints must be compromised before action can result. If the statewide view is not reflected in the legislative process, the governor—as legislator at large—is vested with the authority to veto legislation in order to protect the interests of the whole state against the consequences of a bad bargain struck in the legislature.

4. Represent state as a whole

For a number of reasons, the executive rather than the legislative branch is primarily responsible for intergovernmental relations with the national government, with other states, and with the state's political subdivisions. A principal reason is that many state legislatures are in session and at the capitol for short periods of time. This means that most legislators have other occupational pursuits that require their attention when not in session. In other words, they do not have time to become deeply involved in intergovernmental activities.

5. Conduct intergovernmental relations

a. Limited sessions

Secondly, while some intergovernmental activities involve policy formulation, the larger share relates to problems of day-to-day administration, with federal and local administrators interacting with state administrations in developing regulations and in implementing delivery of services.

b. Day-to-day administration

Another reason for executive leadership in intergovernmental relations is the familiarity of executive branch personnel with the facts and problems involved in intergovernmental problem-solving. Working with administrative problems on a day-to-day basis, the executive branch is more informed and better equipped to carry out intergovernmental policy and administration.

c. Better informed

Federal laws have also enhanced the role of executives in intergovernmental matters. In many programs formulated by the federal government but requiring state administration, the governor is empowered to designate the agency to administer the program.

d. Federal authorization

Other executives involved

As the chief executive, the governor plays a significant role as an intergovernmental representative, but his or her presence does not preclude federal-state interrelationships between numerous other members of the executive family. The elected state agriculture commissioner may interact with the federal agricultural officials on farm policies; the state highway board and administrators may work with federal transportation officials on programming; and the autonomous state education officer may work with the U.S. Department of Education.

e. Structure of executive

Finally, structure alone favors executive dominance in intergovernmental relations. Legislative leaders generally do not command constant majorities sufficient to give them authority to act on behalf of the whole legislature, and legislative committees are too awkward to interact systematically with other governments. On the other hand, authority in the executive branch is somewhat more focused, facilitating negotiation and discussion.

6. Check on legislative branch

The concept of separation of powers requires that each of the three branches be equipped to check the power of the other two branches. The legislative branch checks the executive branch through a variety of oversight activities, approval or disapproval of appointments, controlling appropriations, and passing legislation to order changes in policies. Likewise, the executive branch is charged with checking the legislative branch and does so in a number of ways.

Veto

Probably the most formidable check held by the executive is that of vetoing acts of the legislature. Though used sparingly, the importance of the veto, or the threat of a veto, should not be taken lightly. On those issues in which the governor has expressed an interest, legislators are fully aware of the veto power in every committee decision and floor action.

Special session

Another executive check on the legislature is the threat of a special session. With the constitutional authority to call a legislature back into session, governors are able to embarrass the legislature with a public scolding for its action or its inaction.

Informal checks

In addition to formal powers, all state executives have informal avenues for checking the legislature. They can hold ill-advised legislation up to public disdain and ridicule at press conferences. Another informal check used by state administrators is found in the style of administering laws. Using their discretion, executives can overadminister laws that are too weak to be meaningful and underadminister laws that they find repugnant. This behavior gives legislators time to reassess their action and perhaps modify or reverse it.

7. Resolve conflict

Administrative resolution

While the legislative session is the primary battleground for resolving conflict among competing groups, the executive branch is involved in conflict resolution before and after legislative sessions. Because agencies function in just about every facet of state activity, proposals to change state policy invariably affect some administering agency in the executive branch. This being the case, agency personnel are aware of most problems and conflicts involved in the programs they administer. In fact, they are the lightning rods that attract the first sparks of conflict among the clients they serve or between their constituencies and those of other agencies. As a result, they strive to minimize such conflicts by holding fact-finding conferences to determine the nature of the conflicts and methods for resolving them. When legislation is required to resolve differences, they are often in the forefront in drafting legislation that will be acceptable to the competing parties. Thus, during the course of their normal operations, executive agencies and administrators are either resolving conflicts or shaping conflicts for legislative resolution.

Once the conflict moves into the legislative arena, executives serve as resource advisers for the legislative committees and leadership. Holding positions of public trust and often, though not always, representing neutral points of view, their advice is given considerable weight in the legislative process.

Legislative resolution

Many conflicts resolved during the legislative process are handled in haste, sometimes leaving unanswered questions and unresolved conflicts. Occasionally, the implementation of a new law generates conflicts that were unanticipated. These conflicts must be dealt with by the administrators as they apply general legislative intent to specific situations. Postlegislative conferences of affected interests are common vehicles for seeking social peace.

Because of the varying number of players in the executive branch of state governments, the performance of the foregoing functions will vary considerably from one state to the next. For those few states with strong gubernatorial powers, the functions will be exercised with a higher level of order and coherence than in those many states in which powers are strewn across the executive landscape. While it would be unwise to suggest that the performance of functions rests solely on structure, the fragmentation found in most states is a matter that merits attention.

Executive varies from state-to-state

Forces That Shape State Executive Branches

As students compare the federal executive branch with the typical state executive branch, they will be struck by the contrast in formal structure and speculate as to the causes of these differences. A number of forces have moved through history to cause the evolution of state executive branches that are decentralized, fragmented, and cumbersome.

Once institutional patterns are established, including the design of a state executive, they are difficult to change. Tradition follows closely on the heels of innovation. As a consequence, the initial design of state executive branches that grew out of colonial experiences still casts a shadow across executive branches as they exist today. Colonial governors exercised autocratic power on behalf of the English authorities. They called and adjourned legislatures at will; they held absolute vetoes over legislative acts; they appointed and manipulated the judiciary; and they enforced the unpopular edicts of their superiors. When conflict erupted between the colonists and England, the governors represented the king and suppressed opinions, throttled the opposition, and forcibly dealt with troublemakers. Because of their actions on behalf of England, they bore the hatred of the colonists. So when each new state shook off the yoke of domination, it designed the executive branch with haunting memories of royal governors. The office of governor was stripped of power. Executive powers were largely taken over by the state legislatures until the national Constitution restored credibility to the executive branch. Slowly, governors began to regain executive authority. The initial gains

1. Historical and traditional factors

Colonial governors oppressive

were shortlived, however, as Jacksonian democracy fostered the direct election of numerous state executive officers. This practice of electing multiple executives has continued to the present, though states have been forced by a modernizing society to focus more authority in the hands of the governor.

2. Anti-party bias of the public

The disdain for political parties expressed by George Washington in his farewell address set the tone of public opinion about partisan politics. His forebodings were realized when corrupt political machines emerged in the late 1800s and made a mockery of representative democracy. Riding a wave of disgust for political machines and parties, the reform movement at the turn of the century sought to restrict political parties through a series of statutory controls. With ample evidence that parties were corrupting the process, they scrawled a clear indictment of parties across the pages of recent history. Even today, surveys reveal an abiding distrust of politics and politicians. This attitude has caused people to be unwilling to permit "politicians" to gain too much power or to control too large a portion of government.

3. Legislative distrust

Separation of powers breeds a minimum level of suspicion among the branches of government. As a consequence, the legislative branch is fearful that power concentrated in the executive branch will surely be abused. In states where the length of legislative sessions are very limited by the constitutions, lay legislators may have a tendency to be excessively suspicious merely because the full-time officeholders have a threatening level of expertise and continuing control of the activities of the government.

Role of political parties

The legislature's appraisal of the executive's trustworthiness is important because most state agencies obtain their structure and authority from the state legislature. A highly suspicious legislature will tend to create agencies with greater independence from the governor than a legislature that has confidence in the executive branch. Partisan politics often becomes involved. A legislature in the control of one party will not enhance the power of executive offices controlled by another party. Thus, even the temporary division of power between parties will result in permanent structural oddities designed to limit the power of some governors. Many anomalies of state executive design can be traced to a divided government that existed generations ago.

4. Citizen distrust of power

Gubernatorial candidates may be able to convince the voters that they are worthy of election, but few of them can persuade the citizens that the office ought to be given greater control of the executive branch. At the suggestion of more authority, trust wanes and suspicions rise. Citizens who may express praise of the design of the federal executive may be the same ones who will not permit a restructuring of the state executive to copy the federal. This high level of mistrust is a contradiction of the old adage, believed fervently by many, that the government closest to the voter can be trusted most. Apparently citizens will trust the president with more power than they will trust with governors.

5. Public's idea of accountability

An idea coming from the Jacksonian era was that officials who are directly elected by the people are more accountable. Therefore, to make state and local governments more accountable, the number of offices filled by election should be increased.

Some of the autonomous agencies existing in state governments are the result of interest groups seeking government sanction and support of programs for their benefit. The interest groups not only seek the creation of state service for their benefit, but they also want to control the service after it is authorized by the legislature. Consequently, in their draft of the legislation, they direct that a controlling board be created, with appointments made by the governor only from lists of names submitted by the interest groups involved. Thus, agencies come into existence under the virtual control of the interest groups that first conceived them.

6. Interest groups want control

Let's assume that the creators of the agency involved in the preceding paragraph were wheat growers who sought an agency to promote the marketing of wheat at home and abroad. Their proposal was to have the function managed by a board of gubernatorial appointees chosen from a list of wheat growers provided by the State Wheat-growers Association. The state secretary of agriculture, whose agency included other agricultural functions, argued with the committee of sponsors that the function ought to be placed in the agriculture department. However, the sponsors opposed this suggestion because their unit would "get lost in the big bureaucracy" and it would suffer a lack of emphasis on the part of agricultural administrators. Thus, sponsors seek autonomy to preserve the prestige and importance of the function involved.

7. Isolate function for prestige

There is often more at issue than just prestige, however. Interest groups realize that the head of the agriculture department will be required to balance the demands of one group against those of other groups. This could result in a deemphasis of some programs to the benefit of others. Separateness also gives the creators a greater opportunity to deal directly with the legislature in securing amendments and money for their programs.

Structural Consequences

The forces, attitudes and ideas just discussed have created the environment within which the state executive branch has been framed through the decades. By keeping them in mind, we can begin to understand some of the structural consequences in executive branches today.

Although states have been slowly removing restrictions on terms of office for executives, over half still prohibit the governor from serving more than two terms or consecutive terms. Three states still cling to two-year terms. Only Alabama and Pennsylvania apply the term limits to all elected executives, signaling the fact that in almost all states the concern over executive power is centered primarily on the governorship. Very few states limit legislative terms, clearly meaning that it is the governor who cannot be trusted.

1. Term limitations

To guarantee accountability to the public, state constitutions provide for a series of elected executives in most states. Among the 50 states, over 500 officials are elected, affecting the management of well over 300 agencies. Only a handful of states have managed to limit the number of elective offices to less than four (see table 10.1).

2. Create elective offices

E. E. Schattschneider was not persuaded by the argument that election meant accountability, declaring instead: "The power of the people in a democracy depends on the importance of the decision made by the electorate, not on the number of decisions they make."[2]

Table 10.1 State Executive Officials Elected Statewide

State	Governor	Lt. Gov.	Sec. of State	Atty. General	Treas.	Auditor	Supt. of Pub. Inst.	Agriculture Comm.	Insurance Comm.	Comptroller	Other*
Alabama	E	E	E	E	E	E	0	E	0	0	0
Alaska	E -JT-	E	0	0	0	0	0	0	0	0	0
Arizona	E	0	E	E	E	0	E	0	0	0	Mine Inspector
Arkansas	E	E	E	E	E	E	0	0	0	0	Land Comm.
California	E	E	E	E	E	0	E	0	E	E	0
Colorado	E -JT-	E	E	E	E	0	0	0	0	0	0
Connecticut	E -JT-	E	E	E	E	0	0	0	0	E	0
Delaware	E	E	0	E	E	E	0	0	E	0	0
Florida	E -JT-	E	E	E	E	0	E	E	0	E	0
Georgia	E	E	E	E	0	0	E	E	0	E	Labor Comm.
Hawaii	E -JT-	E	0	0	0	0	0	0	0	0	0
Idaho	E	E	E	E	E	E	E	0	0	0	0
Illinois	E -JT-	E	E	E	E	0	0	0	0	E	0
Indiana	E -JT-	E	E	E	E	E	E	0	0	0	0
Iowa	E	E	E	E	E	E	0	E	0	0	0
Kansas	E -JT-	E	E	E	E	0	0	0	E	0	0
Kentucky	E	E	E	E	E	E	E	E	0	0	0
Louisiana	E	E	E	E	E	0	0	E	E	0	Elections Commissioner
Maine	E	0	0	0	0	0	0	0	0	0	0
Maryland	E -JT-	E	0	E	0	0	0	0	0	E	0
Massachusetts	E -JT-	E	E	E	E	E	0	0	0	0	0
Michigan	E -JT-	E	E	E	0	0	0	0	0	0	0
Minnesota	E -JT-	E	E	E	E	E	0	0	0	0	0
Mississippi	E	E	E	E	E	E	0	E	E	0	0
Missouri	E	E	E	E	E	E	0	0	0	0	0
Montana	E -JT-	E	E	E	0	E	E	0	0	0	0
Nebraska	E -JT-	E	E	E	E	E	0	0	0	0	0
Nevada	E	E	E	E	E	0	0	0	0	E	0
New Hampshire	E	0	0	0	0	0	0	0	0	0	0
New Jersey	E	0	0	0	0	0	0	0	0	0	0

In addition to the idea of accountability, people have seen the election of state executives as an internal check within the one branch of government. By dividing executive power, they feel that elected officials will tend to keep a governor from becoming "too powerful."

Lieutenant Governor

The office of lieutenant governor (or deputy governor) has its origins in colonial history, existing in the charters of Massachusetts, Connecticut, Rhode Island, Pennsylvania, and Delaware as early as 1701. Early charters authorized the lieutenant governor to preside over meetings of the governor's council which served both as an advisory body to the governor and an upper house (senate) in the legislative system. The creation of the office of vice president in the U.S. Constitution virtually guaranteed popularity and continuance of the office of lieutenant governor.[3]

Table 10.1 continued

State	Governor	Lt. Gov.	Sec. of State	Atty. General	Treas.	Auditor	Supt. of Pub. Inst.	Agriculture Comm.	Insurance Comm.	Comptroller	Other*
New Mexico	E -JT-	E	E	E	E	E	0	0	0	0	Commissioner of Public Lands
New York	E -JT-	E	0	E	0	0	0	0	0	E	0
N. Carolina	E	E	E	E	E	E	E	E	E	0	Labor Comm.
N. Dakota	E -JT-	E	E	E	E	E	E	E	E	0	Tax Comm. Labor Comm.
Ohio	E -JT-	E	E	E	E	E	0	0	0	0	0
Oklahoma	E	E	0	E	E	E	E	0	E	0	Corp. Comm. (3)
Oregon	E	0	E	E	E	0	E	0	0	0	Labor Comm.
Pennsylvania	E -JT-	E	0	E	E	E	0	0	0	0	0
Rhode Island	E	E	E	E	E	0	0	0	0	0	0
S. Carolina	E	E	E	E	E	0	E	E	0	E	Adj. Gen.
S. Dakota	E -JT-	E	E	E	E	E	0	0	0	0	Lands Comm.
Tennessee	E	0	0	0	0	0	0	0	0	0	0
Texas	E	E	0	E	E	0	0	E	0	E	Land Comm.
Utah	E -JT-	E	0	E	E	E	0	0	0	0	0
Vermont	E	E	E	E	E	E	0	0	0	0	0
Virginia	E	E	0	E	0	0	0	0	0	0	0
Washington	E	E	E	E	E	E	E	0	E	0	Lands Comm.
W. Virginia	E	0	E	E	E	E	0	E	0	0	0
Wisconsin	E -JT-	E	E	E	E	0	E	0	0	0	0
Wyoming	E	0	E	0	E	E	E	0	0	0	0
	50	42	36	43	38	25	16	12	9	10	

E - elective
O - non-elective
JT - governor and lieutenant governor elected jointly
**Fragmentation of the state executive branches can be seen in the separate election of numerous state officials. New Jersey is the only state with one executive - the governor. Tennessee, New Hampshire and Maine elect only the governor but the legislature chooses other executives. In almost half of the states, governors and lieutenant governors are elected jointly. Elected public utilities commissioners were excluded since they exercise legislative and judicial functions as well as executive duties. (Compiled by Shad Stastney from various publications of the Council of State Governments and direct verifications.)*

Duties of lieutenant governors

In 27 states, the lieutenant governors' sole constitutional powers are twofold: (1) serve as presiding officer of the state senate, and (2) stand first in succession to the governor. Nevertheless, some states have broadened the functions of the office either by constitutional or statutory provisions. Two-thirds of the states now authorize the governor to delegate duties to the lieutenant governor. Because governors are placed on numerous boards and commissions by law, the availability of the lieutenant governor has made it possible for governors to delegate many of these committee duties. For example, in the 1980s, Georgia's lieutenant governor was serving on 16 commissions, boards, and councils; Kentucky's served on ten; and Indiana's served on some 40 boards in addition to managing the full-time duties of director of commerce.[4]

Joint elections

The sharing of executive duties has been facilitated by the growing practice of electing governors and lieutenant governors jointly as teams. Beginning in New York in 1953, joint election of the governor and lieutenant governor has spread to half of the states, putting an end to the election of governors of one party and lieutenant governors of the other party. Joint election has reduced the political competition between the two officials. The extent to which governors share their duties is as dependent on the personal relationship with the lieutenant governor as it is on joint election. Even though of the same political party, lieutenant governors with political ambition may "crowd" governors in their eagerness to demonstrate their right to move up when the governor steps down. If yoked with a lieutenant governor—of the same party or not—who is constantly trying to upstage him or her, the governor may well limit assignments to innocuous duties that keep the lieutenant governor busy but not very visible.

Executives disagree

A case in point: In the 1980s, Alfred DelBello ran for lieutenant governor as a team member to New York Mayor Ed Koch who was running for governor. In the primary election, DelBello won and Koch lost, leaving DelBello to serve with Governor Mario Cuomo. Even though both were Democrats, Cuomo gave few responsible assignments to DelBello. One was to develop an emergency response plan for a nuclear plant in Rockland County. Under the plan, the lieutenant governor was assigned to be the first responder to the scene. DelBello, recognizing his limited role, resigned his office.[5]

Another duty delegated to lieutenant governors in states is that of serving as governor while the chief executive is out of state. In some states, this duty may be triggered only under certain conditions, such as length of absence from the state.[6]

Attorney General

The office of attorney general originated in English history and first appeared in America in Virginia where Richard Lee was appointed to the post in 1643. After the Revolution, the office was filled by appointment of the legislature; later the office was made elective in most states. In four states, the governor appoints the attorney general; in Maine, the legislature makes the choice; and in Tennessee, the supreme court selects.

Interprets laws

The office of attorney general wields considerable power, primarily because this is the office that interprets statutes and constitutional provisions for state and local officials. The interpretation is often issued as a formal opinion, which binds state and local officials until it is changed by a court or the legislature.

State legal representative

Another duty of the attorney general is to represent the interests of the state in legal matters. He or she files suit on behalf of the state and defends the state in other cases. He or she may join the attorneys general of other states in litigation in federal courts to protect the interests of the state in state-federal conflicts.

Chief law enforcement officer

In many states, the attorney general executes the role of chief law enforcement officer by supervising local prosecutors and assigning staff members in major criminal cases. Of the state constitutions, California probably outlines this responsibility most clearly:

> The Attorney General shall have direct supervision over every district attorney and sheriff and over such other law enforcement officers as may be designated by law, in all matters pertaining to the duties of their respective offices, and may require any of said officers to make reports concerning the investigation, detection, prosecution, and punishment of crime. . . .

Other duties vested in the attorney general may include conducting investigations of misconduct in government, managing consumer protection units, staffing a central criminal investigation unit for use by local governments, reviewing rules proposed by state agencies, assisting agencies in drafting legislation, and serving on numerous state boards and commissions.

Miscellaneous duties

Secretary of State

Elected in 36 states, appointed in 13 and nonexistent in Alaska, the secretary of state is usually the chief elections administrator in the state. Often working with one or more state election boards, the secretary of state provides election guidelines to local election officials, conducts informational or training procedures and materials, fields technical questions about election procedures, collects the election statistics from local administrators, and prepares reports for review by election canvassing bodies. These duties will vary from state to state, depending on assignments given to state election boards.

Chief elections officer

The secretary of state is the custodian of legislative records, perhaps the original copies of measures adopted by the assembly, keeper of the state seal, publisher of state documents, recorder of incorporations and administrator of a wide range of duties, depending on the functions assigned by the assembly. Secretaries of state commonly serve on a number of the state boards and commissions.

Custodian of records

State Treasurer

A fourth office commonly filled by election is that of state treasurer, whose primary duty is to oversee the receipt of state revenues, allocation of funds to political subdivisions, investments of funds until needed, and to record the disbursements pursuant to state law. Since the handling of public funds is rigidly controlled by state laws, little discretion is exercised in the routine duties of the treasurer. When the state involves the treasurer in its investment strategies, he or she may be called upon to offer advice and make judgments.

Manages state funds

One of the coveted duties of state treasurer in the past was that of determining which banks would become official depositories for state funds. Because this function is vulnerable to bribery, conflicts of interest, and other forms of corruption, states gradually restricted the options open to a treasurer and this function is now carefully controlled in most states. Only North Dakota escapes this problem because it has a state-owned bank that serves as the sole depository for state funds.

Deposits money

State Auditor

Half of the states fill the office of state auditor by election. Most state auditors perform what is called the *postaudit* function, which is a review of the financial records of units of state government to see that all appropriated money was disbursed according to legislative intent. Audit reports completed by members of the auditor's staff are usually made available to legislative committees designated to review audits. In some states, the auditor may review the audits with the committees, pointing out problem areas, if any.

Reviews expenditures

Education Boards and Superintendents

Another function voters feel should be separate from gubernatorial politics is that of education. To administer this function, some states elect the chief executive officer, often called the *superintendent of public instruction,* while others elect the boards that appoint the chief education officer. Under either method, education is theoretically insulated from politics.

Lose campaigns to abolish elective offices

Reducing the number of elected state officials is a virtual impossibility. With political friends and constituencies supporting them, elected officials can usually resist any effort to convert selection from independent election to appointment by the governor. In the 1980s, West Virginia Governor Gaston Caperton tried to abolish as elective the offices of secretary of state, treasurer and agriculture commissioner, while North Dakota Governor George Sinner tried twice to abolish the elective office of state treasurer. The attempts in both states were soundly defeated at the polls. California, on the other hand, added one—that of state insurance commissioner.

3. Limit governor with boards

Another method by which the power of the governor is limited is the creation of boards and commissions to manage state functions. The widespread use of boards in state government can be attributed to a number of the environmental factors discussed earlier: the ability of interest groups to isolate and control functions of government; the desire of the legislature to minimize gubernatorial influence; the wish to moderate partisan politics with board members serving staggered terms that overlap gubernatorial administrations; and the elevation of the civic-minded citizen over politicians.

Boards persist

As early as 1900, many state executive branches consisted of no less than 100 offices, boards, and commissions, most of them independent and uncoordinated. Though reformers have managed to reduce the role of autonomous boards in government, many of them survive major reorganization efforts in state government. Some state reorganization efforts, hailed as milestones of administrative progress, have really been simple regroupings of boards that continue to enjoy a high degree of independence.

4. Legislatures restrict appointments

To control gubernatorial power, legislatures often write detailed legislation in the creation of new agencies, boards, and commissions. For many of the appointments involved, the legislature may require confirmation by one or both houses of the legislature. For other appointments, the law may practically dictate the appointment by placing qualifications and requirements that can be met by only a handful of candidates. For example, the legislature may require that membership on a state transportation commission be made up of representatives of various geographic regions of the state to guarantee each section a fair share of the construction; or the legislature may prescribe interest group representation for the state social service board so that all of the nursing homes, hospitals, doctors, and other disbursers of services can influence policy; or, in the case of an occupational licensing board, the law may specify that the governor make appointments only from a list of nominees provided by the major state organization in the occupation involved.

5. Legislatures encroach on executives

In the language mandating three separate branches of government, state constitutions often specify, as in Florida, that "No person belonging to one branch shall exercise any powers appertaining to either of the other branches unless expressly provided herein." Nevertheless, in some states, legislators with a keen interest in certain state functions and lacking confidence in the executive, have created boards and commissions with positions to be filled by legislators themselves. According to a recent survey of states, 37 states reported advisory boards with legislative members, 24 states had legislators on policy-making boards and commissions, and 20 states had legislators on boards exercising management responsibilities.[7]

This extensive encroachment on the executive branch of government has been brought to the attention of state courts. Decisions in Colorado in 1912, Georgia in 1975, Kansas in 1976, North Carolina in 1982, Mississippi in 1983, and Kentucky in 1983 all rolled back legislative efforts to violate the principle of separation of powers in this manner. Many state constitutions prohibit legislators from holding dual offices in the two branches of government. The Ohio Supreme Court in 1944 and the Tennessee attorney general in 1983 cited this provision as basis for removing legislators from state boards and commissions.[8]

Courts protect separation of powers

The desire to reduce the influence of partisan politics on state government resulted in the widespread adoption of the civil service system to protect professional and technical employees. Under the system, employees are recruited for their professionalism and can be fired only for cause and then only after a hearing. Before adoption of the civil service systems, new adminstrations would fire the political cronies of the previous administration and replace them with political cronies of their own. This arbitrary hiring and firing resulted in poor service, incompetent employees, sale of public jobs, political shakedowns, waste in government, and political machines.

6. Civil service restrains governors

Relying on the First Amendment and the right of free association, the federal courts have extended job protection to almost all public employees by holding that they cannot be fired because of their political beliefs. Only policy-makers can be removed when a new administration is elected. Partisanship cannot be a consideration in the hiring, promoting, or transferring of employees.[9]

Courts protect employees

To eliminate partisan politics from certain functions or governments, the reform movement advocated the adoption of nonpartisan elections—the choosing of public officials on a ballot without party labels. The campaign for nonpartisan elections did not gain much ground in the election of state officials, but it did flourish in city governments where the most corrupt of partisan politics existed. Today, a majority of cities in the United States choose their mayors, governing boards, and other officials on the nonpartisan ballot.

7. Nonpartisan elections

Problems of the Decentralized Executive

Because of various historical factors, biases, lack of trust, vague ideas of accountability, and desires of interest groups, state executive branches consist of a number of elected officials, independent boards and commissions, numerous restrictions on gubernatorial appointments, and insulation of most civil servants from policy influences. Rather than an executive patterned after the national government, states have dispersed executive authority among hundreds of participants. With this structure, the executive branch is expected to rationally administer, propose policy, represent the state as a whole, conduct intergovernmental relations, check the legislative branch, and resolve conflict. Under these circumstances, the charge to the executive, found in most state constitutions "to faithfully execute the laws," is most difficult to accomplish for a number of reasons.

1. No unity of leadership

Performance of the functions assigned to the executive branch requires a reasonable unity in leadership. Unity is difficult to achieve when the constitution and the laws provide for an array of independent entities, each with authority to administer a portion of the executive functions.

Elected officials with political agendas

Most challenging to coherence and unity are the elected officials who compete politically with the governor for the leadership role. Many of these elected officials actually head departments of lesser significance than those directed by appointed officials. Thus, it may not be their administrative power that undermines the unity of the executive—it is their political power. In considering this point, it is necessary to keep in mind that the vast majority of the elected state officials are politicians first and administrators second. They win elections on the basis of their political skills and resources. As politicians, they recognize that they will stay in office only as long as there is a constant flow of publicity that reflects favorably on their activities and maintains their public visibility. As a consequence, many of their day-to-day activities are performed with one eye on their jobs and the other eye on the media. Thus, they are constantly competing with the governor for publicity and credit.

Party rivalry in Capitol

With the growing trend among voters to split their tickets, states often have executive officials of different parties serving in the state government. In these circumstances, the divisiveness of party competition adds to the divisiveness of independence, making it even more difficult to develop coherent state policy. Many of the elected officials see themselves as gubernatorial contenders at the next election, adding political ambition to the ingredients. As a result of these various factors, most state capitols are hotbeds of political competition and rivalries, with each elected official jockeying for a better position at the next electoral rail.

2. Loss of coordination

Independent politically motivated elected officials, constitutionally independent boards, statutory boards with long overlapping terms of office, and units of government controlled by interest groups all create a centrifugal force in state administration that requires Herculean effort to resist and overcome. Confronted with this disjointed array of semi-autonomous empires, the governor, unable to command, must resort to the less effective tools of persuasion and coordination. When government is fragmented into 50 or 100 units, each agency's function becomes narrowly defined and administrators may tend to develop telescopic views of their roles in government. Representing the general interests of the state, and also bearing the brunt of political accountability, the

Governor must persuade

governor must persuade these units to consider the general good of the state rather than pursue their own ends. However, governors are burdened with numerous non-administrative responsibilities that greatly limit the time available for dealing with administrative chaos. Faced with a governmental structure that will function only through time-consuming coordination, governors tend to coordinate the functions of particular personal interest or become involved only when a crisis erupts, leaving most agencies to perform their functions without the unity of gubernatorial influence.

3. Lack of accountability

Ironically, the one quality Jacksonians sought to achieve through direct election of state officials—accountability—has actually been lost with direct election of state officials. Politically, governors may sometimes be blamed for corruption or inaction in state governments but, structurally, they cannot be held to account for those officials and agencies over which they have no administrative control. Thus, the voters who would not trust the governor to fill the offices by appointment must be prepared to assume responsibility for those they have elected. However, before citizens can hold officeholders accountable, they must be sufficiently interested and informed so they know not only the names of the officeholders but the skill with which their assigned duties were performed. Many political scientists, supported by polls, will claim that voters have not demonstrated the level of interest required to make learned decisions on long ballots and, thus, render elected officials effectively accountable for their actions.

Voters lose control

When the lines of accountability are weak or nonexistent, administrators of governmental units have great discretion in establishing their own policy directions. Fortunately, in most cases, their own good judgment leads them to cooperate with other agencies, to respond to gubernatorial initiatives, and otherwise to conduct themselves in a responsible manner. However, the diffused system renders agencies vulnerable to interest groups. With high stakes involved in many decisions, interest groups are very interested in the performance of certain agencies. When agencies do not have to account to a higher authority for many of their discretionary policies, agency-interest group relationships can become very friendly, with both benefiting from the harmonious relationship. Interest groups can help administrators win favorable legislation and appropriations while the administrators can develop policies beneficial to the interest groups. In states with full-time legislators, this two-way arrangement can become an "iron triangle" that involves the cooperation and support of sympathetic legislators strategically located on important committees.

4. Interest groups exert influence

Agency-interest group alliances

These consequences of fragmented government have piqued the curiosity of researchers interested in their impact. Studies have produced data that substantiate the belief that many governors are not the masters of their executive "houses" and that legislatures have been relatively successful in warding off the evolution of a strong executive. One survey of 778 state department heads in 50 states indicated that legislatures ranked above governors in influence on programs and objectives of state departments. In only 16 states did administrators see the governor as more influential than the legislature.[10]

Governors not the "masters"

Alexander Hamilton once observed: "A feeble executive implies a feeble execution of a government. A feeble execution is but another phrase for bad execution; and a government ill executed, whatever it may be in theory, must be, in practice, a bad government."

A feeble executive

Movement for Reorganization

By the turn of the century, those close to state governments began to recognize that the "feeble executives" were resulting in feeble government. The movement for state administrative reorganization received its start about 1909 or 1910. In 1910, Governor Charles Evans Hughes of New York stated in his annual message to the legislature:

Early reorganization efforts

It would be an improvement, I believe, in state administration if executive responsibility were centered in the governor, who should appoint a cabinet of administrative heads accountable to him and charged with the duties now imposed upon elected state officers.

Recent reorganization efforts

The trend toward positive action in state administrative reorganization accelerated sharply in the late sixties and seventies but dropped sharply in the 1980s.[11] Of the 45 "substantial reorganizations" by states since Illinois in 1917, nearly half of them took place between 1965 and 1980, with only one occurring in the 1980s. All involved dramatic regrouping of agencies into major departments. In Maryland, 246 agencies were consolidated into 17 cabinet-level departments; Louisiana regrouped 300 agencies into 19 departments. Significant changes occurred in the other states.[12]

All reorganization is not reorganization

All reorganization is not reorganization, however. A case in point is a Connecticut reorganization that was widely touted by the press as an outstanding example of agency consolidation. Professor Douglas Fox found that while some effective reorganization was accomplished in Connecticut, it was not as grandiose as the press reported. Of the 210 entities that were supposedly consolidated into 22 departments, 32 boards and agencies were placed within departments for administrative purposes only and the department heads were not granted any control over them. Another 28 agencies remained outside the new departments in an unaffiliated status.[13]

On the other hand, the only major reorganization in the 1980s was genuine reorganization. It occurred in Iowa where 258 agencies were reduced to 22 departments, and 21 of those departments were made appointees of the governor.[14]

Governors appoint less than half

After several waves of reorganization, notably 1914, 1937, and 1965, progress has been made, but the administrative authority of governors still falls short of that exercised by the president. As of the 1980s, governors were still appointing less than half of the major administrative positions in state governments. A survey of almost 2,000 administrative positions covering up to 48 functional areas found that 47 percent were appointed by governors, 38 percent were appointed by others, and 15 percent were separately elected.[15] With only one major reorganization occurring in the 1980s, little has happened since to change these figures.

All cabinets are not cabinets

Another widely acclaimed reform has been the growth in the number of states using cabinets. According to one report, only 26 states had cabinets in 1969, whereas by 1982 this number had grown to 40 states.[16] The use of the term *cabinet* may be somewhat misleading in that it conveys the impression that it means the same as is used to describe the president and the department heads directly accountable to the president. In many of the state governments, the term *cabinet* merely means a coordinating body of officials, some of whom are accountable to the governor but many of whom are not. A case in point is the "cabinet" created for Florida by the state constitution. Serving on the cabinet with the governor are six independently elected state officials, none of whom are accountable to the governor.[17]

Some governors able to initiate change

Governors in some states have the authority to initiate the reorganization of the executive branch by executive order, subject to legislative veto. After several states had adopted such a procedure by statute, Alaska became the first to incorporate such a plan in its constitution. According to the Alaska constitution:

> The governor may make changes in the organization of the executive branch or in the assignment of functions among its units which he considers necessary for efficient administration. Where these changes require the force of law, they shall be set forth in executive orders. The legislature shall have

sixty days of a regular session. . . .to disapprove these executive orders. Unless disapproved by resolution concurred in by a majority of the members in joint session, these orders become effective at a date thereafter designated by the governor.

State reorganization has been ordered by a number of the recently revised state constitutions. Constitutional conventions, appalled at the fragmentation in executive branches, decided that if reorganization were left to the legislatures, little would be done. Thus, they included provisions in the executive articles directing that all agencies of government shall be grouped into a maximum number of major departments. As an example, the Florida constitution states: "All functions of the executive branch of state government shall be allotted among not more than twenty-five departments. . . ." *Try limiting departments*

Standards for Reorganization

The reorganization movement has been based on principles that are no longer theoretical, but are based on experience and are supported by actual practice in a number of states. Although no exact classification of these basic standards of reorganization has ever been agreed upon, probably the six most commonly accepted standards are the following:

- •functional departmentalization of administrative agencies
- •concentration of administrative authority and responsibility in the governor
- •the undesirability of having boards for purely administrative work
- •establishment of staff and auxiliary agencies responsible to the governor
- •provision for an independent audit
- •establishment of a governor's cabinet[18]

According to the principles of functional departmentalization, state agencies performing similar or closely related activities should be organized and operated within the same department. Such consolidation would eliminate overlappings and gain savings by reducing the number of employees needed. Moreover, reduction of the hundred-odd virtually independent agencies into a dozen orderly departments would remove one of the greatest obstacles to central administration by the governor. *Grouping agencies*

Probably the basic standard of the reorganization movement, and the one upon which most of the others rest, is the concentration of authority and responsibility in the governor. It is considered not only unwise administrative practice but also unjust to impose a duty upon the governor without giving him or her authority to carry out that responsibility. The proper way to hold the executive branch accountable is to center authority and responsibility at a single point, so that both deeds and misdeeds may be attributed to the proper place. This principle requires elimination of elective administrators, extension of the governor's appointing power to include all department heads, and provision of a governor's cabinet in fact as well as in theory. *Concentrating authority in governor*

Boards or commissions are deemed undesirable for purely administrative activities because they are generally inefficient. Boards are also difficult to hold accountable. The single-headed agency is preferred for greater initiative, professional competence, *Abolishing administrative boards*

Figure 10.1

Before reorganization. A dispersed executive consists of a number of elected state officials, who are independent from gubernatorial control, and a bureaucracy controlled by various boards and commissions. Numerous other autonomous committees and agencies (not illustrated) also function independent of the governor.

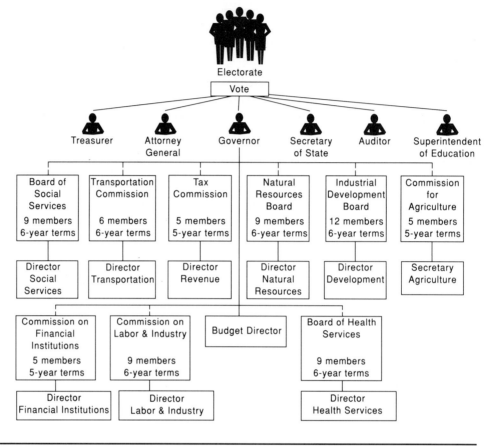

---

quicker action, and clear location of responsibility. It is conceded, however, that boards or commissions may be attached advantageously to departments that are required to perform duties of a policy-determining, quasi-legislative, or quasi-judicial character.

Strengthening staff agencies   In keeping with the expanded administrative role proposed for the governor, it is recommended that the various staff and auxiliary services of administration be co-ordinated and made responsible to the governor. Among these services should be a strong office staff, a planning agency, and central offices for the budget, accounting, purchasing, and personnel administration. During the 1960s, a trend developed in the direction of uniting many of these functions in a single state department of administration and finance.

Relying on post audits   Most of the state reorganization study groups have recommended a complete separation of the functions of financial control and accounting from those of independent auditing and review. This recommendation is based on the assumption that the financial control and accounting functions are executive in character and should be performed by an officer directly responsible to the governor, while the postaudit and review are oversight functions that belong to the legislature.

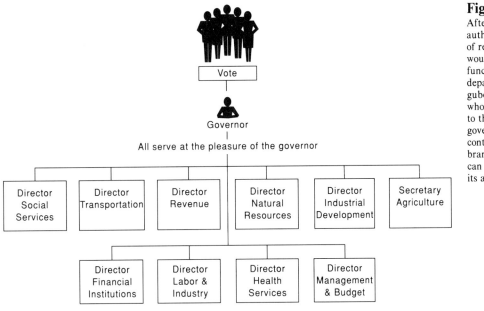

Figure 10.2
After concentration of authority. Under principles of reorganization, agencies would be grouped, by function, into major departments, headed by gubernatorial appointees who would be accountable to the governor. Thus, the governor not only has control of the executive branch of government but can be held accountable for its activities.

Reorganization Criticized

The reorganization movement has not been without its critics. Although most political scientists have generally agreed with the standards of reorganization and the movement as a whole, both the practice and theory of the reorganization movement have been criticized. Most of the criticisms come from those whose power and access would be reduced by a reshuffling of the administrative power structure.

One frequent criticism, which finds much popular support, is the contention that reorganization would concentrate too much power in the hands of the governor. Making the elected officials appointive is condemned as undemocratic, and the proposal to make the governor responsible for every administrative agency is said to stake too much on the ability of one person.

1. Governor too powerful

Many have criticized the efforts to abolish boards and commissions on the premise that the best work often comes from private individuals who feel an urge to serve the public on boards. Other arguments put forth in defense of boards and commissions are: a board will keep politics out of a department; it guarantees continuity when its members' terms overlap; group decision is frequently indispensable; and a board meets the need for group and sectional representation.

2. Boards beneficial

The contention is made that the spoils system is encouraged rather than eliminated by reorganization. According to this argument, the governor's control of the spoils system is consolidated by the increased appointing power over top administrative officers. Not only is the control of spoils, formerly scattered among independent agency heads, transferred to the hands of the governor, but the governor can more easily bypass civil service restrictions simply because of new powers under reorganization. This criticism will likely continue even though recent court decisions have eliminated the authority of elected officials to fire nonpolicymaking government employees.

3. Lead to spoils system

4. Governors not administrators

Another criticism, less frequently voiced but in many ways more serious, concerns the wisdom of compelling the governor to serve as chief administrator when the chief interest, capabilities, and constituents' demands all direct the governor toward political, legislative, and ceremonial leadership. The tendency of these nonadministrative functions to monopolize the governor's time casts some doubt upon the assumptions of a movement that undertakes to make him or her a general manager. Besides, some argue, many governors are not interested in administration.

Reorganization is Political

Most public administration consultants approach government reorganization with a professional neutrality, guided primarily by principles of effectiveness and efficiency. Consequently, many of their recommendations are warmly greeted at first blush but as they are exposed to the adoption process, their glitter is tarnished by the politics of change.

1. Reorganization changes power structure

The core principle of state government reorganization, as broadly suggested throughout this chapter, is the concentration of the authority that has been dispersed to a large number of officials, agencies, boards, and commissions. The concentration of authority proposes to rearrange the power structure by moving authority from present administrators to new adminstrators, primarily the governor. Proposals to shift power are inherently political in that the present possessors of power staunchly resist the loss of power or access to power. As an example, elected state officials are politicians who consider their offices as political opportunities as much as, if not more than, administrative responsibilities. Thus, proposals to abolish elective offices and make their departments accountable to the governor invariably result in a political conflict conducted by politicians seeking to protect their power.

2. Administrators resist change

Even administrators, often considered to be professionally neutral, resist the concentration of authority. Under a reorganized administration, their programs and policies would be subjected to broader considerations of the public good, something they presently avoid under their independent status. If they became accountable to the governor, they would not have sole charge of program emphasis or policy formulation since the governor would bring a broader context to bear. This broader context would likely result in compromising agency goals to accommodate the greater good.

3. Interest groups oppose reorganization

Interest groups will also join the fray when they observe that their ability to influence agencies would be reduced if agencies were required to answer to the governor. Being relatively immune from reprisals on the part of the governor, interest groups are at liberty to engage in freewheeling campaigns outside the government against any reorganization that would weaken their lines of influence. They can arrange negative media reports and orchestrate any number of ploys to taint the proposals and proponents. Agencies may not be free to oppose reorganization openly but they can provide valuable information and encouragement to the interest groups for use in resisting change.

Reorganization is also political when considered in terms of executive-legislative relations. The interbranch rivalry is a perennial tussle over which branch will control state policy. By design, the executive branch was dispersed by the legislature to limit the influence and power of the executive on state policy. Proposals to build authority and influence of the executive is often seen by legislatures as a threat to their authority. Observing that this legislative distrust has impaired state administration, some state constitutional conventions mandated limits on the number of state departments with the hope that legislatures would be forced to concentrate authority. In some cases, recalcitrant legislatures have merely rearranged the organizational boxes to comply with this requirement.

4. Strong executive threatens legislature

Partisan politics also becomes a factor when reorganization proposals are presented to a legislature controlled by one party by a governor of another party. Few organization efforts survive divided governments. For example, when Republican Governor John Volpe of Massachusetts proposed to concentrate the authority of several hundred agencies into a dozen departments, the proposal was greeted with considerable hostility by the Democratic legislature. Volpe's successor, Republican Governor Sargent, tried vainly to persuade the legislature to proceed with the proposal. Partisan politics was by no means the only cause of the defeat of reorganization in Massachusetts, but it was a factor.[19]

5. Political parties involved

Finally, governors themselves recognize the political costs involved in reorganization. As political creatures, they are sensitive to the qualities voters admire in political leadership, and no matter how legitimate, eagerness for power can be politically damaging to a governor interested in seeking reelection or promotion. If the governor is in the forefront of the undertaking, he or she will be tarnished by the attacks of officeholders and interest groups seeking to preserve the status quo. Terms such as *dictator, power-grabber,* and *autocrat* will be used freely to impugn the governor's motives and play upon the inherent distrust the people harbor for executive power. Many governors recognize that administrative organization, though necessary for effective, accountable government, is not a subject dear to the hearts of the electorate, and thus a loss may incur more political liabilities than a success could ever gain in assets. Hence, the political equation is not in the governor's favor under any circumstances.

6. Governors reluctant to lead charge

In reviewing the "hardball" politics involved in government reorganization, it is obvious that the reformer's centerpiece—concentration of authority—may start out as a neutral concept, but its implementation rapidly becomes a major political battle. Failure to recognize the impact of interest group, bureaucratic and partisan politics in government reorganization has resulted in the loss of scores of worthy efforts that would have improved government performance.

From the standpoint of management, a neat pyramid of executive power may be a desirable objective but it should not be regarded as a panacea when it comes to the quantity and quality of services. A number of researchers have raised doubts about the efficacy of governmental organization. After considerable study, Professor Thomas Dye has concluded:

Reorganization no panacea

> There is little evidence that a governor's formal powers significantly affect policy outcomes in the fifty states. While "strong" and "weak" governor states pursue somewhat different policies in education, health, welfare, highways, and taxation, these differences are attributable largely to the impact of economic development rather than to the governor's power.[20]

Table 10.2 Recent State Efforts to Improve Management

State	Program, Agency, Office, Executive Action	Year Begun	Reorganization	External Commission	Internal Efficiency Program
Alabama	Alabama Management Improvement Program	1987		■	
Alaska	Agency reviews by state management and budget office	1991			■
Arizona	State Long-term Improved Management Task Force (SLIM)	1991		■	
Arkansas	Total Quality Management program	1989			■
California	Creation of state environmental protection agency	1991	■		
Colorado	Commission on Government Productivity	1988		■	
Connecticut	Commission to Study the Management of State Government	1989		■	
Delaware	Maximizing efficiency and service quality (MAX)	1991			■
Florida	Commission for Government by the People	1991		■	
Georgia	Commission on Effectiveness and Economy in State Government	1991		■	
Hawaii	Advisory Committee on Excellence (ACE)	1988			■
Idaho	Accountability Measures Program	1980s			■
Illinois	Human Resources Advisory Council	1991		■	
Indiana	Government Operations Committee	1989	■		
Iowa	Committee on Government Spending Reform	1991		■	
Kansas	Director of Efficiency Management	1991			■
Kentucky	State Education Department restructured	1990	■		
Louisiana	Task Force on Efficiency and Effectiveness	1989		■	
Maine	The Restructuring Commission	1991		■	
Maryland	Management improvement studies	1991			■
Massachusetts	Program to restructure programs, streamline regulations	1991			■
Michigan	Agency reviews	1991	■		
Minnesota	Commission on Reform and Efficiency (CORE)	1991		■	
Mississippi	Executive Branch Reorganization Study Commission	1987	■		
Missouri	Advisory Council on Productivity	1985		■	

Although this sobering observation keeps expectations realistic, it by no means suggests that state administrations be abandoned in chaos and disorder. In a democratic society, organization may not greatly change the commitment or aspirations of people. Nevertheless, an efficient, accountable structure, headed by an executive empowered to lead, can greatly facilitate the initiation and implementation of policies acceptable to the state's political culture (see table 10.2).

Few states would turn back

In spite of criticism and opposition, few states that have experienced major reorganization now desire to return to the conditions existing before reorganization. It is generally agreed that responsibility can be more easily located in the reorganized

Table 10.2 continued

State	Program, Agency, Office, Executive Action	Year Begun	Reorganization	External Commission	Internal Efficiency Program
Montana	Transportation programs consolidated into new transportation dept.	1989			■
Nebraska	Internal reorganization studies	1991	■		
Nevada	Strategic planning	1989			■
New Hampshire	Management Review Task Force	1991		■	
New Jersey	Management Review Commission	1990		■	
New Mexico	Nine departments consolidated into four	1987	■		
New York	Two private section commissions (long-term and short-term)	1990		■	
North Carolina	Efficiency Study Commission	1985		■	
North Dakota	North Dakota Consensus Council, Inc.	1990		■	
Ohio	Operations Improvement Task Force	1991		■	
Oklahoma	Wide-ranging education reforms, tightened cost controls	1991			■
Oregon	Task Force on State Government	1991		■	
Pennsylvania	Department of Environmental Resources reorganization	1991	■		
Rhode Island	Rhode Island Public Expenditure Council	1990		■	
South Carolina	Commission on Government Restructuring	1991	■		
South Dakota	Commission on Tax Fairness and Government Cost Effectiveness	1989		■	
Tennessee	Department of Youth Development created	1989	■		
Texas	Blueprint for the New Texas; Texas Performance Review	1991	■		■
Utah	State Committee on Productivity and Excellence (SCOPE)	1986		■	
Vermont	Internal agency analyses	1991			■
Virginia	Project Streamline	1990			■
Washington	Commission for Efficiency and Accountability in Government	1987		■	
West Virginia	Restructuring of state government	1989	■		
Wisconsin	Reorganization of several state agencies	1987	■		
Wyoming	Commission on Government Efficiency	1988	■		

Experiencing serious fiscal pressures, all states are engaging in review of administrative structures and service delivery procedures.
Source: Rockefeller Institute of Government, State University of New York as reported in Governors' Weekly Bulletin, *September 13, 1991.*

administrative system, and many would cite this as the principal benefit attributable to reorganization. In terms of economies, it is difficult to show actual dollars and cents savings through reorganization, but there can be little doubt that reorganization has resulted in more and better service per tax dollar. Finally, the administrative work of the reorganized state is undoubtedly better planned than that of the unreorganized state. The credit for this rests with the governor's newfound executive leadership. The governor finds it easier to take an all-embracing view because of the more simplified structure of government and the assistance of new staff agencies. Information is more easily obtained, and long-range planning becomes attainable.

Benefits of reorganization

Management without
authority

Whether or not the governor has management authority over the executive agencies is of little concern to a majority of citizens. When something in state government goes awry, the governor is blamed. Knowing this, governors seek to maximize their oversight by keeping constantly informed about all agency operations, whether under direct control or not. They assign staff members to monitor and interact with agencies and with staff members assigned to general functional areas, such as social services, natural resources, environmental management, etc. These staff members are expected to give the governors early warning of trouble in the bureaucracy.

1. Staff monitor
agencies

A relatively new technique for enforcing accountability in the executive branch is the use of an office of inspector general. Created in the 1980s by the legislature in several states, the inspector general is a free-roaming investigator, vested with the authority to root out crime and corruption in executive agencies.[21] In other states, this task falls on auditors.

2. Inspector general

Another potent weapon for influencing independent units of government is the broad budgeting powers now in the hands of almost all governors. Since legislators tend to follow governors' budgets closely in their deliberations, the governors' initial budget proposals carry considerable weight. A recalcitrant agency can easily be penalized by stringent budget treatment in the executive agency. Funds may be restored, but only after a difficult struggle in the legislature.

3. Power of the budget

A governor's veto power can also be used to influence autonomous agencies. A good share of the legislature's workload consists of bills generated by agencies that are seeking enhancement of duties or corrective legislation. Agencies that have failed to maintain cordial relations with the governor may find their legislation vetoed.

4. Veto

This chapter has been devoted to discussion of the fragmented nature of state executive branches. While fragmentation has persisted through the decades, progress has been made toward the goal of strengthening the governor as chief administrator. By looking at such things as tenure, appointive power and budget-making authority, political scientist Thad Beyle has been able to measure the increase in the institutionalized powers of governor (see table 10.3).

Governor slowly gaining
authority

The oversight functions of legislative assemblies become more important in states with fragmentation. When governors are not given administrative authority, the legislature must utilize hearings, investigations, ombudsmen, sunset laws, and regulation reviews with greater vigor and diligence.

Recent Trends

For some 50 years, the civil service (merit) system was able to provide most public employees with a satisfactory system for job security, wage scales, promotions, and other work-related conditions. Beginning in the 1960s, however, state and local government salaries and benefits lagged behind those offered private and federal employees. Some employees concluded that action would be necessary to press the cause of state and local employees in the budgetary and appropriations processes. Low employee morale and discontent were fertile grounds for organization, and the unions, particularly the American Federation of State, County and Municipal Employees (AFSCME), began to organize state and local employees with vigor. Simultaneously,

Unions move into
government

Table 10.3 The Institutionalized Powers of the Governorship: 1965–1990, by State

1965

Very Weak				Weak		Moderate				Strong		Very Strong			
14	15	16	17	18	19	20	21	22	23	24	25	26	27	28	29
IN	IA	NH	AZ	RI	FL	AR	AL	DE	CO	AK	CA		NY		MD
VT	ND	MS	SC			MI	CT	IL	GA	HI					
		NC	WI			MT	KS	MN	KY	ID					
		OK				NV	LA	MO	MA	OH					
						NM	ME	NE		TN					
						TX	OR	NJ		UT					
						WV	SD	PA		VA					
								WY		WA					

1990

Very Weak				Weak		Moderate				Strong		Very Strong			
14	15	16	17	18	19	20	21	22	23	24	25	26	27	28	29
	RI	TX	NC	NH	AL	IN	AZ	CA	AK	AR	MN	NY	MA		MD
				SC	ME		FL	CO	DE	CT			WV		
				VT	NV		ID	GA	IL	HI					
					NM		KY	MS	IA	KS					
					OK		MO	MT	LA	NE					
								WA	MI	NJ					
								WI	ND	OR					
								WY	OH	TN					
									PA	UT					
									SD						
									VA						

Source: Thad Beyle, "Governors", POLITICS IN THE AMERICAN STATES: A *Comparative Analysis, 5/e by Virginia Gray, et. al. Copyright 1990 by Virginia Gray, Herbert Jacob, and Robert B. Albritton. Reprinted by permission of HarperCollins Publishers.*

legislatures in approximately half of the states were passing laws to give public employees the right to bargain collectively with their employers. During the past 25 years, AFSCME has been one of the fastest growing unions associated with the AFL-CIO. Going into the 1990s, AFSCME had 3,000 locals in 46 states.[22]

The presence of unions not only raises the usual questions about picketing, striking, and the other forms of confrontation, but it also affects the traditional role of the civil service. With unions, the government is divided into bargaining units that may be based on occupations or departments. Once the units are identified, the union negotiates with representatives of the government over wages, benefits, working conditions, grievance procedures, and a number of other facets of the workplace. However, many of the items to be negotiated have traditionally fallen within the purview of civil service. Where unions negotiate salaries from sheer strength, civil service supports a salary system based on systematic wage scales professionally developed. Where unions want to negotiate grievance procedures utilizing the union, civil service has established procedures for complaints, hearings, and reviews. Where unions want to control terminations through contracts, civil service has traditional steps for handling reductions in force.

Union bargaining vs. civil service procedures

*Unions use political
tactics*

Not only have unions been changing state and local personnel management systems but they have also brought a political dimension to public employment. Public unions have formed political action committees (PACs) to raise funds for candidates sympathetic to their demands at the bargaining table. By block voting in legislative and gubernatorial elections, they have been able to upset longstanding incumbents when government has failed to respond to their demands. The electoral power of public unions has unusual impact in local elections where turnout is small and union members constitute a large portion of the voters. Public employees in California contributed close to $2 million to campaigns in one year. Employee organizations are also endorsing candidates for public office.[23]

Unions voice concerns

The future of public employee unions in the 1990s is unpredictable due to a number of competing trends. Union growth in the 1980s slowed somewhat, suggesting perhaps that organizational opportunities are becoming limited. The nationwide trend to contract with private business to provide traditional governmental services may reduce the number of public employees—and union members. On the other hand, an anti-tax mood in the citizenry combined with declining federal grants to state governments is creating a fiscal crisis in many states. To respond to this crisis, states are reducing the number of employees and holding salary increases to a minimum. This will result in more discontent among employees and a greater willingness to join unions (Figure 10.3).

*Privatization escapes
"red tape"*

During the 1980s, *privatization* became a catchword in the provision of traditional governmental services. Initial impetus was given to the idea by the business-oriented administration of President Ronald Reagan. The idea of privatization was based on the belief that government was inept and, in many areas, unable to provide

Figure 10.3
As state budgets have tightened, proposals to cut benefits and employees have become commonplace in state government. As a result, employees are becoming more militant, with demonstrations on the increase.
(Tom Kelly, Pottstown, PA.)

public services as efficiently as the private sector. Public administrators also became frustrated with cumbersome governmental rules and regulations, such as competitive bidding, open meetings and records, employee work rules, and other time-consuming requirments and costly mandates.[24] Limited funds for capital investments increased the appeal of privatization. Governments in a fiscal squeeze could avoid initial capital investments in buildings, such as correctional institutions, by contracting for the services and paying for the capitol costs through periodic service payments.

While many governmental services do not lend themselves to private performance, a national survey indicated that state and local governments were contracting with private companies for correctional and detention services, food services, education, parks maintenance, human services, mental retardation facilities, and vehicle and highway maintenance, as well as scores of other activities.[25]

Privatization growing

As legislative assemblies continue to wrestle with budgetary constraints, the idea of privatization is constantly recurring as an alternative to direct service delivery. The concept will continue to be considered experimental in the 1990s as experience grows and provides a means of evaluating the technique. Even though the delivery responsibility may be transferred to the private sector, state policy-makers are still held accountable for the cost and quality of the services. Therefore, monitoring has become an integral expense in private contracting.[26] The trend will also be slowed by the resistance of public employee organizations who see private contracting as a means of undercutting employee salaries and benefits.

Privatization requires monitoring

Comparable worth gained national attention when a federal district judge ruled in 1983 that the state of Washington would be required to pay 15,000 employees close to $500 million in backpay for failing to recognize the principle of comparable worth. The judge based his decision on Title VII of the 1964 Civil Rights Act. As a result of the ruling, lawsuits were filed in Hawaii, California, Wisconsin, Illinois, New York, and other jurisdictions.[27]

File suits over comparable worth

The basic tenet of comparable worth is that classes of jobs having comparable worth should be rewarded with similar salary schedules. As an example, if the jobs of clerical supervisors were found to be of comparable worth with electricians, then both ought to be paid similarly. It has been argued that women have suffered most from failure to apply the principle of comparable worth because their jobs tend to be undervalued and underpaid.

Comparable worth defined

Even though a federal circuit court reversed the Washington decision in 1985, declaring that "the free market system is not a suspect enterprise," and a California suit on behalf of 60,000 female employees was dismissed in 1989 by a federal judge, the concept of comparable worth has become a part of the public agenda in states and localities. By 1992, a large majority of states had begun to implement new compensation plans reducing the gap between male and female jobs although only Minnesota had enacted a comparable worth law for all public employees.[28] Adjustments to the pay inequities will continue through the 1990s.

Adjust pay inequities

Until recently, state employees were clothed with immunity from liability for damages arising out of the performance of their duties as long as they were acting within the law and were not negligent. Recent U.S. Supreme Court decisions, however, have stripped away much of this immunity, leaving public employees vulnerable to lawsuits.

State employees lose immunity

State employees subject
to suit

Over the past two decades, the Court has entertained a series of cases that provided a thorough review of state sovereignty and immunities under 42 U.S.C. Section 1983 and the Eleventh Amendment. During the decade of the seventies, the Court declared that the Eleventh Amendment does not insulate states from injunctive relief in federal courts, that state officials could be sued under Section 1983, and that the Eleventh Amendment was no bar to claims for monetary damages against state officials. In 1980, the Supreme Court broadened the liability of state officials immensely by making them accountable not only for violations involving civil rights laws but all federal laws. Under this ruling, anyone who feels that a state official has denied him or her some direct or indirect right and/or privilege can begin action against the state official personally. Officials can become liable by misinterpreting the federal rules and regulations that implement federal laws providing benefits. The Court has also ruled that attorney's fees can be awarded for victorious litigants.[29]

Predict slowdown in
government

Assessing the impact of the new liability created for state officials by the Court decisions, Walter S. Groszyk, Jr., and Thomas J. Madden predicted that state administrators would likely introduce protective measures, such as elaborate procedures, extensive reviews, and shared decision-making. They suggest that administrators would follow the example of many doctors who, fearing medical malpractice suits, require every form of diagnostic testing to protect themselves. Groszyk and Madden also suggest that the practices of delegating responsibility may be altered, that states will be reluctant to accept responsibility for federal programs that incur liability, and that public administrators may simply tire of the nonproductive countermeasures and seek other employment.[30] While this greater exposure to liability did not have the degree of chilling effect predicted by Groszyk and Madden, state administrators in the 1980s and 1990s were demonstrating more caution and were consulting more frequently with their attorneys general.

States experience
technology revolution

As collector, retainer, assimilator, and translator of large volumes of information, state government has been a major beneficiary of the telecommunications technology revolution. Defined now as the transportation, switching and routing of voice, data, and video communications,[31] telecommunications are being used in a myriad of ways by state governments to control costs, speed delivery of services, and maintain accountability.

Technology facilitating
programs

Arkansas is using electronic technology to manage its food program for women, infants and children; South Carolina and numerous other states require major taxpayers to electronically transfer tax payments;[32] Georgia maintains a state paging system for caseworkers in the field; Kentucky uses it to provide an early warning system for floods; Florida has centralized information of child abuse and domestic violence; and several states are developing systems of automated teller machines to dispense welfare payments.[33]

In addition to these few specific examples, states have placed their entire fiscal systems on central management information systems. Following the lead of the federal government, many states have devised interagency systems for intercepting tax refunds, unemployment benefits and other government payments directed to parents who have failed to meet their obligations to support dependent spouses and children. States are moving money electronically to keep funds in interest earning accounts as long as possible. Reserve funds and investment portfolios are also being managed with telecommunications technology.

As states have been expanding the number of functions for which telecommunications technology is used, they are also developing intergovernmental networks with federal and local agencies as well as with private businesses and other entities. Extensive sharing of common data bases is occurring. The 1990s will see dramatic advances in the networking of all facets of telecommunications, and by the year 2000 the U.S. Postal Service will probably rank a poor second to telecommunications in message delivery.

Develop intergovernmental networks

Telecommunications has been transforming skill requirements and office procedures of state government, but there is yet more change to come in state employment. California pioneered "telecommuting" in the later 1980s and early 1990s to demonstrate that state employees could perform certain jobs just as effectively in their homes.[34] While not all employees or task assignments are suited to telecommuting, a number of advantages have been identified. Energy consumption and air pollution can be reduced; convenient job opportunities are opened for the handicapped and single parents; need for central office space is reduced; employees can save travel costs; productivity is improved; and jobs can be relocated to economically depressed areas.[35]

Working at home

Though great strides have been made, the full potential of telecommunications technology still has not been realized in government for a number of reasons. The fragmentation of government discussed in this chapter has been a deterrent, with independent agencies and institutions exercising their options to cooperate or to resist technological change. Fortunately for most states, this fragmentation is overcome to some degree by the centralization of staff services in departments of administration, among which are the components of telecommunications technology. Another deterrent to full utilization of technology is the limited capacity of many program managers to comprehend the array of possibilities available. Technology management is actually a new skill that must be learned.[36] A third problem encountered is provision of public access to government information. Programs have not always been designed to separate the confidential from the public records, thereby raising concerns among the media. Even the maintaining of central records on citizens raises red flags and slows decisions to fully utilize telecommunication technology. In the final analysis, however, the technology will prevail in the 1990s and rapid change in the governmental processes will take place in spite of the structural fragmentation.

Fragmentation will slow technology

Limited by capacity of managers

Access to information problems

Endnotes

1. Woodrow Wilson, *The State: Elements of Historical and Practical Politics,* rev. ed. (Boston: D.C. Heath and Co., 1909), p. 330. For a contrasting picture of the strong governorship some seventy-five years later, see Duane Lockard, ed., "A Mini-Symposium: The Strong Governorship: Status and Problems," *Public Administration Review* 36 (January/February 1976): 90–98.

2. E. E. Schattschneider, *The Semisovereign People* (New York: Holt, Rinehart & Winston, 1960), p. 140.

3. Deborah A. Gona, *The Lieutenant Governor: The Office and Its Powers* (Lexington, Ky.: Council of State Governments, 1983), p. 2.

4. Ibid., pp. 5–7.

5. Kathleen Sylvester, "Lieutenant Governors: Giving Up Real Power for Real Opportunity." *Governing* 2 (February, 1989): 48.

6. Gona, op. cit., p. 9.

7. Rich Jones, *Legislators Serving on Boards and Commissions* (Denver: National Conference of State Legislatures, 1983), p. 4.

8. Ibid., pp. 1–3.

9. *Rutan* v. *Republican Party of Illinois,* 496 U.S. 110 S. Ct. 2729 (1990).

10. Glenn Abney and Thomas P. Lauth, "The Governor as Chief Administrator," *Public Administration Review* 43 (January/February 1983): 40–41.

11. James K. Conant, "Executive Branch Reorganization of the States, 1965 to 1987," *Public Administration Review* 48 (Sept/Oct, 1988): 894.

12. Ibid., pp. 900–902.

13. Douglas M. Fox,: "Reorganizing Connecticut State Government," *State Government* 52 (Spring, 1979): 82.

14. Conant, p. 902, and James D. Carney, "Downsizing Government: Iowa's Challenge," *The Journal of State Government* 60 (July/August, 1987): 183–190.

15. Thad L. Beyle and Robert Dalton, "Appointment Power: Does It Belong to the Governor?" *State Government* 54, No. 1 (1981): 6.

16. Lydia Bodman and Daniel B. Garry, "Innovation in State Cabinet Systems," *State Government* 55, No. 3 (1982): 93.

17. Alan Rosenthal, *Governors and Legislatures: Contending Powers* (Washington, D.C., Congressional Quarterly, Inc., 1990): 23.

18. See A. E. Buck, *Reorganization of State Governments in the United States* (New York: National Municipal League, 1938).

19. Robert C. Casselman, "Massachusetts Revisited: Chronology of a Failure," *Public Administration Review* 33 (March/April 1973): 129–135.

20. See Thomas R. Dye, "Executive Power and Public Policy in the States," *Western Political Quarterly* 27 (December 1969): 926–939.

21. Cheri Collis, "The Watchdog Over State Agencies," *State Government News* 33 (April, 1990): 13.

22. John F. Persinos, "Can AFSCME Parlay Its Social-Issues Savvy Into Another Decade of Growth," *Governing* 2 (July, 1989): 45.

23. Charles Press and Kenneth Verburg, *State and Community Governments in the Federal System,* 2nd ed. (New York: John Wiley & Sons, 1983), p. 353.

24. Karen Torry, "Privatization: An antidote for ailing facilities," *City & State* 7 (March 26, 1990): 13–15.

25. See Joan W. Allen, et al., *The Private Sector in State Service Delivery: Examples of Innovative Practices* (Washington, D.C., The Urban Institute Press, 1989).

26. John Rehfuss, "Contracting Out and Accountability in State and Local Governments— The Importance of Contract Monitoring," *State and Local Government Review* 22 (Winter, 1990): 44–48.

27. Eric Wiesenthal, "Comparable Worth: Issue of the '80s," *Public Administration Times* (May 1, 1984): 12.

28. Michael Graham, "The Drive for Comparable Worth; Has It Sputtered Out?", and Bonnie Watkins, "Reassessing Comparable Worth: The Minnesota Experience," related articles in *Public Administration Times,* 15 (April 1, 1992), p.8. *See also* Sara M. Evans, Barbara Nelson and Nancy J. Johnson, "What Difference Does Comparable Worth Make." *Northwest Report* of Northwest Area Foundation, Minneapolis (September, 1989): 30, and Evans and Nelson, *WageJustice: Comparable Worth and the Paradox of Technocratic Reform* (Chicago: University of Chicago Press, 1989).

29. This brief summary is based on Walter S. Groszyk, Jr., and Thomas J. Madden, "Managing Without Immunity: The Challenge for State and Local Government Officials in the 1980s," *Public Administration Review* 41 (March/April 1981): 269–171.

30. Ibid., pp. 272–273.

31. M. J. Richter, "Telecommunications," *Governing* 3 (September, 1990): 6A.

32. Len Strazewski, "State sets places for computers in food program," *City & State* (February 11, 1991): 18.

33. Richter, ibid., 6A–14A.

34. Linda Wagar, "Coming home again," *State Government News* 34 (January, 1991): 12.

35. Simani Price and Karen Marshall, *TELECOMMUTING,* a special report (Lexington, Ky.: Council of State Government, June 1990).

36. Len Strazewski, "Government data specialists," *City & State* 7 (January 29, 1990): 11, 14.

CHAPTER 11

THE GOVERNORSHIP

Political Focus Point of the State

Governorship most difficult office

The governor holds the most difficult office in the American political system. Because the governor is charged with performance in a decentralized administrative structure, the office requires more managerial skills and persuasive abilities than the presidency. Because the governor is more accessible to citizens and organizations, he or she must display more perseverance, diligence, and tact than members of Congress. Because the governor is under the constant surveillance of television and news cameras, the position demands more accountability than any other state elective office. Because the governor is geographically situated at the scene of political and social conflict, the governorship requires steadfast courage and patience. Governors are given responsibilities far beyond their executive powers; their day-to-day schedules are crammed with unavoidable commitments that sometimes run into seven days and nights; and citizen expectations of the office far exceed available stamina and mental resources. One weary governor capsulized the burden when asked by an aide to accept two more "important" speaking engagements for the week. In refusing the commitments, the governor said: "Frankly, I don't see why I should die at 44 if there's a chance I can make it to 46."

Governors caught in middle

Governors first appeared on the American continent as representatives of the commercial and political interests sponsoring colonization and expecting gain. Their task was to see that the interests of the King or his benefactors were properly protected. As the demands of the colonists for greater independence grew in conflict with the homeland, governors were caught in the middle. They were expected to put out the fires of colonial resistance erupting along the road to independence. In desperation, they used force and autocratic suppression as the sound of battle neared. Finally, no longer able to hold back the flood, many of them were forced to abandon their posts, scramble aboard His Majesty's ships, and return to England.

Legislatures strip office

As the branch that represented the interests of the colonists in this clash with governors, legislative assemblies assumed many of the executive powers in the new states. The office of governor was stripped of its authority, given short terms of office, appointed by legislatures, limited in terms, denied veto powers, and was rendered wholly dependent on the legislative branches. Four states did not have a governor in the ordinary sense but preferred an executive council. Some states even feared the title "gov-

Photo by Garry D. Redmann.

ernor" and used the less sinister term "president." Only New York stood against the tide of fear and preserved the office, giving the governor a three-year term, veto power, pardoning authority, and various military duties.[1]

As states struggled with redesigning the office of governor to prevent future oppression, the U.S. Constitutional Convention convened and prescribed the features of the national executive. As in the case of other constitutional features, the states looked at the federal design as a model for remolding state institutions. During the years following the adoption of the Constitution, the states revamped their executive offices to conform more closely to the national model. As a result, governors began to reacquire powers lost in the Revolution. Just as the movement for a stronger state executive was emerging, however, it was waylaid in the first half of the 1800s by the idea that people ought to have a direct voice in state government by electing a number of state officeholders.

Constitution sets new model

As indicated in chapter 10, state executives still labor under the handicap of this divided executive. Nevertheless, through the decades, governors have slowly been regaining credibility and power. As the pressure for executive leadership has mounted with the transformation from a sedentary to a mobile society, the office of governor has grown. Not only has the office grown in stature within the various states, but it has constituted a milestone on the road to the White House for such leaders as Theodore Roosevelt, Woodrow Wilson, Franklin D. Roosevelt, Jimmy Carter, and Ronald Reagan.

Regaining credibility

Qualifications for Governors

The legal qualifications of governors are found in the state constitutions. Early constitutions, reflecting the suspicions of executive power, were full of restrictive clauses, some imposing property qualifications, others requiring certain religious beliefs. These restrictions have been removed over time and today the legal qualifications include a minimum age, U.S. citizenship, state residency, and qualifications as an elector. Age requirements run as low as age 18 in California and Washington and as high as age 31 in Oklahoma, with the vast majority of states requiring age 30. A large majority of states require the gubernatorial aspirant to have lived in the state for a period of time prior to serving. Kansas has no specific legal requirements, leaving qualifications to the good judgment of its voters.[2]

Legal qualifications in constitutions

Published in state constitutions, the legal requirements are generally known in the state and seldom provide a basis for removal of a governor. However, Governor Thomas Moodie of North Dakota lost his office in 1935 when it was discovered that he lacked the five-year residence requirement by five days. A residence requirement also prevented a prominent Iowa Democrat, Harold Hughes, former governor and former senator, from running for governor in 1982. He had voted and paid taxes in Maryland in 1980, thereby failing to meet Iowa's residence requirement of two years.[3]

Meeting the legal requirements set forth in the state constitution is usually much easier for gubernatorial candidates than meeting the "political" qualifications in the minds of voters. The voters have their own ideas of residence, gender, race, religion, experience, and origin requirements, even though most of these may not be mentioned in the constitution.

Voters set "political" qualifications

*Women winning
governorships*

One of the long-standing political requirements that still persists today is that the governor be a man. The 50 states have seen only eleven women governors, the first three of whom rode to victory on the reputations of their spouses. However, the last eight women governors successfully defied tradition by demonstrating the salient qualities required for the position. In 1974, Connecticut voters elected Ella Grasso, and Washington chose Dixy Lee Ray. In 1983, Kentucky promoted Lieutenant Governor Martha Collins to chief executive, and in 1984, Vermont elected Madeleine Kunin. In 1986, Nebraska elected Kay Orr, and in 1990 Kansas elected Joan Finney, Texas elected Ann Richards, and Oregon elected Barbara Roberts. It is safe to predict that as women continue to build credentials for the office, such as serving in other elective positions, more of them will be elected to the governorship.

Minority victories

Race has continued to be a more prohibitive political requirement than gender. Blacks have captured lieutenant governorships and positions on state supreme courts but have had less success with the governorship. The first African American to be elected governor was L. Douglas Wilder who eked out a narrow win in Virginia in 1989 (Figure 11.1). Hispanics have been more successful, with New Mexico electing Jerry Apodaca and Toney Anaya, and Arizona electing Raul Castro, all in the past two decades.

Figure 11.1
L. Douglas Wilder broke the race barrier by winning a close election for the governorship in Virginia.

Another political requirement is prior governmental experience, with legislative service being the most common. Of the 50 governors serving in 1992, over 60 percent had previous legislative experience. This was up considerably from the 37 percent who had legislative backgrounds in the 1930s.[4] Professor Samuel C. Patterson feels that the upsurge of gubernatorial candidates with legislative experience may be related to the reapportionment and professionalization of legislatures.[5] Other governmental experiences also appear in the records of most governors. Scores of them have served on school boards, city governing boards, county commissions, and other positions of responsibility. Other state executive positions, most commonly the lieutenant governorship, also serve as stepping stones for governors.[6]

Need governmental experience

Age does not appear to be a very restrictive political qualification, although the candidate's odds of election are improved in the 40 to 60 age bracket. This age bracket included 70 percent of those serving in the 1970s. Candidates in their thirties have to prove themselves, holding only one position in 1992.[7]

Age as a consideration

Other facts about governors may indicate characteristics voters seek in a governor: over half of the recent governors have been attorneys; almost all are family persons; over 60 percent have been veterans; and nearly all have attended institutions of higher learning.[8] Religious faith could be a factor in states with lopsided preferences, such as Mormons in Utah and Catholics in Rhode Island.

With the refinement of mass marketing techniques being used in television-dominated campaigns, personal qualities such as charisma, sincerity, and the ability to communicate are rapidly dwarfing the importance of other political qualifications. Articulate candidates who can come into living rooms appearing warm and credible are capitalizing on media politics and bringing a new breed of gubernatorial candidates to the fore. Since gubernatorial contests attract sufficient funds to utilize the expensive mass marketing techniques, attractive candidates can bypass some of the traditional political qualifications, such as prior governmental experience, and become qualified overnight by intensive public exposure through massive television campaigns. In states where party organizations still influence candidate selection, a question that presents a new political qualification has become familiar: "How does he (or she) come across on TV?"

Television sets new expectations

The ability to perform well and master the media are not only requirements for winning gubernatorial elections but they also have become requirements for effective leadership in the office. To retain popular support and to gain approval of programs, governors have been compelled to utilize the mass media to the maximum.[9] President Ronald Reagan's steady popularity was attributed to his performance as a television communicator.

Mastering mass-media

Over the past few decades, a number of trends have affected the terms of governors. Terms have been lengthened in many states. In 1950, 22 of the 48 states provided for only 2-year terms; by 1992, this number had been reduced to three—Rhode Island, New Hampshire and Vermont. At the same time, the number of terms permissible was limited in a number of states. Governors were limited to two terms in only a few states in the 1950s, but by 1992 half of the states had such a limitation.

Terms lengthened, limited

Forty years ago a majority of states were electing governors in the same elections as presidents. However, states have been moving gubernatorial elections to the non-presidential years and by the early 1990s three-fourths of the governors were being

Move to nonpresidential elections

elected in the non-presidential years.[10] This change has been occurring to reduce the influence of presidential politics on state elections, to increase the visibility and importance of state elections, and to spread the electoral workload of the citizenry.

As of 1992, the annual salary of governors ranged from $35,000 in Arkansas to $130,000 in New York, not including the governor's mansion and certain expense funds. Over half of the states pay their governors $75,000 or more. Forty-five states provide official residences for governors; almost all have access to automobiles; and four-fifths have planes.[11]

The size of a governor's staff tends to vary with the population of the state. By and large, political liability for increasing office expenditures has tended to keep the size of governors' staffs to a minimum. This translates into long, grueling hours for employees.

Campaigners get staff positions

Many staff members earn their positions by running the campaign gamut with the newly elected governor. Frequently, the chief campaign aide becomes the chief of staff; the campaign press director assumes a like position in the goverment; and even clerks and secretaries transfer from the campaign headquarters into similar positions on a governor's staff. Occasionally, governors find that employees who bear up well under the pressures and challenges of the campaign are not necessarily qualified for the administrative responsibilities involved in managing a governor's office. Nevertheless, campaigns create a kinship that cements a personal loyalty crucial for the survival of the governor. The loyalties of appointed department heads are eventually captured by the agencies and their clientele, so the governor must maintain a cadre of loyalists

Political experience helpful

in the office to protect his or her political and administrative interests. Campaign experience also broadens the political perspectives and acquaintances for staffers. They not only become astute at assessing sensitive and dangerous political situations, but they also become acquainted with the scores of supporters across the state who have given assistance to the governor. Many of these people will become social and political callers, deserving of particular courtesy from a staff who recognizes their friendship. An intensive campaign also impresses future staffers with the fishbowl experience of public life. They come to appreciate the piercing scrutiny of a critical press.

Governors' staffs tend to be young, capable, and often trained in law or communications. These tend to be the types of people willing to take short-term campaign jobs for frugal salaries on the chance that they can parlay the venture into a more permanent, exciting governmental position.

The Roles of the Governor

Prioritizing roles

Situated in the very center of state politics and policy-making, the governor's office is vested with numerous constitutional and statutory responsibilities and is also heir to countless informal and political expectations. Because a governor cannot conscientiously execute every role with thoroughness, time and resources must be prioritized and invested in the roles that are personally most important. For the business-minded governor, being an effective administrator may be the foremost role; for the ritualistic, the ceremonial and social responsibilities may be appealing; for the instinctive politician, the role of party leader may have the greatest attraction. While only two or three roles may be accentuated by an administration, they all must be performed to one degree or another. The breadth of skills required to deal with the variety of duties taxes the metal of the most competent governor.

Governor as Administrator

Although the governor's political and ceremonial roles have been emphasized since the beginning of our nation, it is only in recent decades that the office has been gaining strength in administration. The extraordinary expansion of governmental activities has made changes in the administrative role of the governor inevitable. The governor is recognized as the general manager of state government whether the role is sought or not. Based on the necessity for unity of command, effective coordination, internal responsibility, and administrative leadership, the state reorganization movement was undertaken to provide a general manager for the entire executive establishment in the person of the governor. Slowly but surely, states seem to be granting additional administrative power to the governor for performing this job.

Gain administrative authority

Although most state constitutions vest the governor with "the supreme executive power," little if any definite authority is conferred on the governor by this provision. State courts have applied the rule of strict interpretation to the powers of the governor. Only specific grants of authority are recognized. Differing court interpretations of seemingly equal grants of authority in the various states make it hazardous to generalize on the basis of constitutional and statutory provisions alone. Other variables of even greater importance, such as the effect of political strength, personal appeal, or custom, upon the administrative power of a governor make it obvious that no single pattern can describe the administrative powers of all governors. Nevertheless, three major administrative powers are possessed by every governor in varying degrees:

Courts strictly define powers

- the power of appointment and removal
- the power of fiscal management
- the power of supervision

These are the principal means by which the governor manages the administration of state affairs.

The power of appointment is one of the most important administrative powers possessed by the governor, affecting not only control of the executive branch but relations with the legislature as well. No governor can have complete confidence in subordinates selected by others, nor can a governor properly be held responsible for such persons' actions. Even though personal appointment of subordinates does not guarantee their accountability, it makes the probability considerably greater.

Importance of appointment

Exercise of the appointing power is not as simple as it might seem. There is the practical requirement that the winning candidate for governor must choose most of the people who will help operate the state government even before the oath of office is taken. A governor is also aware that although no appointee can make the administration a success, any one of the many persons appointed can seriously damage the administration by incompetence or dishonesty. There is seldom a shortage of applicants for the various positions, but salary limitations and insecurity of tenure make it exceedingly difficult to find capable people for the jobs. Few department heads can expect to serve longer than the limited tenure of the governor.

Salaries, tenure limit choices

Power to appoint not inherent

All states are generally agreed on a strict interpretation of their constitutions with respect to the appointing power; i.e., it is not inherently and exclusively an executive function. The history of court interpretation of the governor's appointing power reveals the predominant opinion that such power must be expressly granted in the state constitution or by statute. Since state constitutions generally have made little mention of a governor's power of appointment, recent increases in the use of this power result from legislative action creating new offices and boards. Furthermore, the state reorganization movement has increased a governor's power to appoint department heads.

Power of removal restrained

A governor's power of removal is the indispensable counterpart of the power of appointment. As a general rule, the power of removal must be specifically provided by the state constitution or statutes, since state governors are held not to acquire a power of removal from their general executive power or their power of appointment. There is no "Myers case for states" that gives to the governor extensive removal power over administrative officials in the way the 1926 Supreme Court case did for the president.

Removal for cause

The most common statutory and constitutional provision dealing with a governor's removal power is the requirement that removals must be *for cause only*. This undoubtedly serves to deter a governor somewhat, since courts have generally held it to require a definite statement of charges and opportunity for a hearing. In practice, a governor's removal power is frequently much stronger than the constitution, statutes, and court decisions indicate. In states where a newly elected governor is strong politically, there are always a number of holdover officials who voluntarily resign when the new governor takes office. Furthermore, a governor may ask an official to resign, whether appointed for a definite term or not and whether the governor has the removal power or not. Such a request may be honored in preference to the probability of an unhappy and prolonged "cold war" existence in the state government.

Executive budget expands powers

Because limited financial resources set a maximum on all that state government can do, the management of finance becomes a significant responsibility of a governor. Broadly conceived, fiscal management consists of budget making and budget execution. Since about 1920, there has been a steady movement in the direction of consolidation of fiscal powers. Probably the most significant development of all has been the increased role of the governor in budget making and budget execution. The executive budget, making the governor the budget-making authority, has been adopted in 41 states, and in the other states the governor shares the responsibility.[12] The importance of the governor's budget-making power cannot be overstated. By being authorized to present the legislative assembly with a budget, the governor sets the initial fiscal as well as the programmatic agenda. Because the time constraints on most legislatures prevent reconstruction of the budget, legislatures react by adding and subtracting from the governor's basic budget. At the end of the legislative session, most of it is still intact.[13]

Budget sets agenda

Duty to supervise

The supervisory power is as essential to a governor as to any business executive, but receives little formal recognition by state constitutions. Governors have the constitutional responsibility to "see that the laws are faithfully executed." This requires overseeing and directing the administrative process, fixing the major policies supplementary to legislation, and directing the operations of state agencies. Governors implement their supervisory power by requiring information, informal investigations, individual and group conferences, orders and directives, approval of administrative acts, and the use of staff agencies. While the constitutional and statutory provisions relating to the supervisory power of the governor are important, in the final analysis no amount of enabling legislation can make an effective supervisor out of a personally weak or disinterested governor. Individual case studies of governors reveal that such factors as personality, prestige, personal interest in administration, and political power are strong determinants of the supervisory power. *Personality important*

Simply to describe the administrative powers of a governor is not enough. When extra-legal powers are considered, one still does not have a realistic view of an actual governor, only of a potential governor. Whether the powers are utilized, how they are utilized, and the practical obstacles to their utilization are equally important parts of the picture of the governorship. Possession of formal powers alone does not make a governor a strong administrator.[14] The performance of the governor depends on such additional factors as political popularity, demands on the governor's time, abilities, personality, background, training, and interest in politics as compared with administration. *Performance depends on many factors*

Serving as the chief administrator is only one of the governor's duties. The other roles of the office demand constant attention. Lacking the time to assert full administrative leadership, a governor often is forced to be selective in performing managerial duties. Selective intervention then becomes a common style for chief executives, as pointed out by Martha Wagner Weinberg: *Selective administration*

> Governors do not manage in the customary sense of the word, that is, they do not direct or oversee affairs of agencies over some sustained period of time. Instead, management for elected chief executives usually involves sporadic intervention in the agencies' business, often only for a short period of time. This intervention is most often initiated because of a crisis.[15]

All of these are factors complicating, if not frustrating, the role of a governor in administration. Demands on a governor's time, preeminent concern for political matters and public relations, and the lack of previous experience in public administration make some analysts doubt whether an elective governor can perform effectively as the general manager of state administration. The most frequent proposals for improvement are to increase the governor's professional staff assistance to make time count for more in the administrative field, or to create the office of assistant governor. This official would essentially be a highly paid director of administration responsible to the governor. *Assistant governor?*

Governor as Legislator-at-Large

Under the doctrine of separation of powers, each of the three branches is assigned functions uniquely its own, but to be certain that they don't wander off in their own directions, each of the three is given "checks" to keep the other two on course. To check the legislative branch, the governor is assigned several legislative duties. In the performance of these functions, the governor provides a statewide perspective to the legislative process, acting somewhat as a legislator-at-large. *Checking the legislative branch*

By directing governors to present "State of the State" messages to legislatures, state constitutions give governors a formal role in the policy-making process. In these

Table 11.1 The Governor and Lobbying

Legislative Activities of Governor's Legislative Assistant/Staff	Often	Sometimes	Never
Lobby with individual members	31	4	1
Discuss legislative calendar with leadership	22	12	1
Recruiting witnesses to testify before committees	16	16	3
Encourage agencies and interest groups to lobby	15	14	6
Provide questions for friendly legislators	13	20	2
Prepare floor speeches	2	19	13

Source: Thad L. Beyle, "The Governor as Chief Legislator," State Government (Winter 1978); 6. Based on 37 responses to survey.

Formal presentation of policy

mandated messages, governors often attempt to set the policy agendas for legislatures. Not only do they propose policies but their agencies have already drafted proposed legislation to implement those policies. Furthermore, the governor's budget has been designed to finance the policies presented to the legislature. During the ensuing weeks of the legislative session, the governor's staff will spend long hours promoting the governor's program (see table 11.1).

Invariably, legislators will have different opinions, coming from the perspectives of their own legislative districts. If the legislature is controlled by the opposing political party, philosophical differences will result in counter proposals from the legislative branch.[16] In any case, the role of governors in policy development has been enhanced in recent decades. Today, citizens expect legislatures and governors both to play significant roles in policy leadership.[17]

Special sessions

Another common power granted governors is calling special sessions of the state legislature when an emergency or some contingency requires. In about one-fourth of the states, the governor can also limit the subjects to be taken up.

Power to veto bills

The most important formal legislative power vested in the governor is the veto, possessed by governors in all states except in North Carolina. When it comes to the veto, governors have more discretion than the president. While presidents must accept or reject whole measures submitted to them, most governors have the item veto—the authority to proceed selectively through appropriations measures and delete items. Around one-fifth of the governors also have authority to reduce appropriations and about one-fourth of the states permit the governor to "pocket" veto bills. Under a pocket veto, a bill fails to become law unless signed by the governor before a specified time after the adjournment of the legislature.

Legislature may override

Measures that are vetoed are returned to the originating house where the members decide whether or not to *override* the governor's displeasure. Because the governor is regarded as a representative of the whole state, constitutions require unusual majorities (usually two-thirds or three-fifths) to override a veto. If both houses muster the necessary votes, the bill becomes law in spite of the governor's action.

Veto 5%, override 5%

Few measures are vetoed—around five percent—in any given legislative year. Of those vetoed, only about five or six percent are overridden. These figures may lead some to believe that the veto is not a significant power. However, the very existence of the power to veto in the hands of the governor constitutes a beacon for legislative action.

Through press conferences, State of the State messages, and other public utterances, governors communicate to the legislature the policies they would greet with favor and those they would look upon with disdain. Being so advised, legislatures will usually avoid investing their valuable time passing legislation doomed by veto. If political gain is at stake in a divided government, the legislature may pass bills to force vetoes it deems politically embarrassing for the governor.

In the concluding days of a legislative session, scores of bills are passed and forwarded to the governor as the legislature adjourns. If the governor vetoes measures after adjournment, the vetoes becomes absolute because there is no legislature to reconsider the measures. A few states have moved to eliminate the absolute veto by scheduling automatic special sessions for the purpose of considering measures vetoed by the governor after adjournment.

Vetoes after the session

The formal powers of the governorship constitute only one facet of the influence the office may wield in dealing with the legislature. After proposing some favorite policies in the State of the State address, governors do not return to their offices and idly wait for the assembly—often under the control of the opposition party—to pass the necessary legislation. More likely than not, the governor will encourage agency heads to become executive lobbyists to persuade legislators to give serious consideration to the governor's program.[18]

Lobby for governor's program

Other influential methods may be found for throwing executive weight around for legislative purposes. The governor may come into office with a much publicized program and steadfastly insist upon translating it into law and fact. Effective appeals may be made to public opinion through speech and press for program support, particularly if the proposals meet recognized needs.

Appeal for public support

In addition to appealing to the public, the governor may appeal to political associates, in or out of the legislature, for assistance in pushing policies through the process. Usually regarded as the head of the political party, the governor can often rally some partisan support.

Appeal to party

Going beyond party or political factions, a governor may shrewdly manipulate pressure groups in order to attain objectives. The chief executive may also resort to the strategy of rallying the demands of different geographic regions of the state, since the constituents of a governor are not limited to one political subdivision as are those of a member of the legislature.

Rallying interest groups

Although majority control of the legislature is important to the success of a governor's legislation program, one study makes the surprising finding that it is not true that the more seats a governor has to spare, the more successful he or she will be.[19] Modest majorities are apparently more susceptible to gubernatorial leadership and influence than overwhelming majorities. Another study indicated that the party of the governor and the opposition both exhibited greater unity when the governor became a factor in the voting.[20]

Narrow majorities work best

Divided government, a situation in which the governor is of one party and at least one house of the legislature is controlled by the opposite party, is common. Only a handful of one-party states have avoided this predicament. Between one-third and one-half of the states experience this division of political control in any one year.

Divided government

Even in divided governments, a governor's cause is not lost. While a governor may lack some direct influence, his or her minority party in the legislature can still

*Bargaining from
minority position*

hard bargain with the majority. Rep. Marvin Barkis, a minority leader in Kansas, observed: "The opportunity to say, 'Look, if you don't do what makes sense here, we'll ask the governor to veto this,' gives us a powerful bargaining point."[21]

*Expect more divided
governments*

The dilemma of divided governments may become even more common. As voters continue to become more independent and as multimillion dollar gubernatorial campaigns present clear choices, party ranks will be disrupted with greater regularity when it comes to voting for governor. Thus, governors will be elected more frequently on personal appeal, and legislators will continue to be chosen on more traditional criteria, among which is party affiliation.

Governor as Party Leader

*Party leadership in
transition*

Generalizing about the role of governor as a party leader has become more difficult in recent decades as parties continue to decline in significance in the American political system. Not only have the voters lost their affinity for party loyalty, but legislators have also demonstrated growing independence. In some states, primarily in the South, the party has become relatively meaningless as a reference point because factions tend to become more important than party lines in the one-party systems. To further confuse the governor's role as a party leader, a number of governors have fought their way to office through the primary and general elections over the opposition of the party regulars and without party assistance. Following such an electoral ordeal, parties in some states may never close ranks to accept the leadership of the occupant of the governor's chair. All of these variables will cast the role of governor as party leader in a different hue from state to state. Consequently, this summary of the governor's role as party leader will consist of an enumeration of probabilities rather than a concise description appropriate to every state.

Making party policy

As the most prominent bearer of the party label and commander of considerable legal authority, the governor will often serve as the party policy-maker. The programs and policies espoused by the chief executive, either in the State of the State legislative messages or in press conferences, constitute guidelines for other officeholders of like political persuasion. To implement those programs, governors will often attend party legislative caucuses, conduct strategy breakfasts, and sponsor party social events.

Governors raise funds

Governmental favors and appointments also enable the governor to assert leadership in the party. Faithful party workers are rewarded, thereby strengthening the party as a whole and building personal loyalties. Mushrooming campaign costs have also given governors a party role as fundraisers, not only for their own campaigns but for the campaigns of other state executives, legislators, and even county administrators. This responsibility entails statewide tours of bean feeds, receptions, banquets, dances, and other fund-raising events.

Political strategist

The centrality of the governorship in future campaigns also permits the governor to wield considerable influence as political strategist for upcoming conventions and campaigns. In many states, party leaders will consult with the governor on ticket-slating, campaign issues, and organization building.

Other Gubernatorial Roles

Carrying out the scheme of checks and balances, governors are assigned certain ju- *Judicial duties*
dicial functions as a check on the judiciary. In some states, the governor will be granted
sole authority to change the decisions of the courts by granting pardons, paroles, com-
mutations, and reprieves to those convicted of crimes. Oregon is such a state, with the
following constitutional language in reference to the governor:

> He shall have power to grant reprieves, commutations, and pardons, after
> conviction, for all offenses except treason, subject to such regulations as
> provided by law.

In other states, such as Nebraska, constitution writers lacked confidence in the
governor and created a board to share the duties:

> The Governor, Attorney General and Secretary of State, sitting as a board,
> shall have power to remit fines and forfeitures and to grant respites, reprieves,
> pardons, or commutations in all cases of conviction for offenses against the
> laws of the state. . . .

In keeping with colonial tradition, a state constitution may charge the governor
with duties as "commander-in-chief of the military forces of the state, except when *Command military*
they are called into the service of the United States, and may call out the same to
execute the laws, suppress insurrection and repel invasion." Although Wyoming, from
whose constitution this was taken, may have little to fear from invasion, in the event
it happens state citizens will be properly on notice that the governor will be in charge.

Governors, at least thus far, have not used their military powers to engage in
hostilities with neighboring states but rather have used the power to employ National
Guard units in natural disasters and riots. In 1957, when Governor Orval Faubus of
Arkansas attempted to use the National Guard to prevent the integration of Little
Rock's Central High School, President Eisenhower simply called the Guard into national service. In one of the more controversial uses of military authority, Governor
Jim Rhodes of Ohio called on the Guard in 1970 to quell a riot at Kent State University. The ensuing debacle resulted in the death of several demonstrators and a law-
suit against the governor. After the tumultuous urban and college riots of the late 1960s
and early 1970s, Guardsmen were relieved with callouts as peaceful as floods, hurri-
canes, and blizzards.

As chief of state, the governor performs a number of ceremonial and ambassa- *Chief of state*
dorial duties. The governor represents the state not only at national and regional governors' conferences but also at special interstate meetings of executives to plan regional
strategies and coordinate interstate activities. Within the state, the governor serves as
chief of state by honoring state associations with his or her remarks at annual conventions; by welcoming distinguished visitors and delegations from other states, the federal
government, and other nations; and by issuing proclamations to recognize more important days and weeks than there are in the year.

Some governors enjoy the recognition and pomp of serving as chief of state; others
regard it as an encroachment on valuable time. In the words of one former Arizona

governor, ". . . being governor is a fascinating thing, but you just get sick and tired of going to formal affairs and listening to the honored speaker, listening to somebody else's promotions, and pretty soon you realize that everybody who has a cause would like to advance that cause by using the office of governor."[22]

Economic developer

As world competition in the marketplace continued to grow, the economic concerns of citizens rose rapidly on state agendas. Plant closings, job losses, and fewer dollars in circulation all contributed to a sharper focus on state responsibilities for economic development. For decades, governors have been heading delegations to visit economic decision-makers in neighboring states and even in neighboring nations. As early as 1959, Governor Hodges of North Carolina headed a state mission to Europe. However, the economic crunch of the 1980s and 1990s spurred governors on to stronger economic programs, including the development of overseas markets, romancing high-tech industries, enhancing tourist promotions, and pooling risk capital. By the early 1990s, all states had delegations roving the globe in search of economic opportunities.[23] Recognizing the political stakes in finding new jobs, governors commit days and weeks to keeping the lead in the prosperity parade.

Intergovernmental liaison

Chapter 2 covered the web of interrelationships that have developed among governments, vertically and horizontally. The federal-state relationship continues to be the most crucial even though the Reagan and Bush administrations attempted to disentangle the federal government from state affairs. As the chief budget officer of the state, the governor is directly concerned with the significant portion of state budgets still coming from federal sources and with the strings attached to federal dollars. Many of the federal programs recognized the governor as the state's appropriate decision-maker, delegating to the office authority to designate agencies to administer funds, certify state plans, and exercise a variety of controls over incoming federal dollars. A survey of former governors who had served during the period of 1960–1980 by Dennis O. Grady revealed the significance of the governor's role as intergovernmental liaison with the federal government.[24] The average governor invested almost one day per week to federal relations; close to 90 percent of the governors dealt with federal agencies weekly; over 60 percent called on congressional offices weekly; 81 percent considered federal-state relations to be important to the state's quality of life; and 97 percent would encourage new governors to spend as much time as they did on federal relations.

Work in federal-state relations

To facilitate their work as federal liaison managers, governors directed the opening of a Washington office of the National Governors Association in the 1960s to provide them with a constant flow of information on federal legislative and administrative decisions. To augment the NGA effort, 30 states opened their own federal liaison offices to gather information and lobby on programs of particular interest to them.

Utility player

Like the baseball utility player who is called upon to fill most fielding positions, governors have numerous other bases to cover as they play out their many roles. When labor-management impasses develop, the governor is called upon to be the chief negotiator; when the media wants a newsworthy opinion on a current subject, the governor is asked to be a chief newsmaker; when discouraged people encounter run-arounds with unsolvable problems, they appeal to the governor as the last resort; and, in the performance of all roles, the governor is constantly a chief agenda-builder and a chief opinion leader.

From the foregoing discussion of the various roles of the typical state governor, it is apparent that any one of them could easily justify the chief executive's full-time attention. Because of the immensity of the challenge, many factors make the actual role of governor different from the role prescribed by the legal powers found in the constitution and the statutes. None is more important than the personal qualities of the individual. Ability or lack of ability, forcefulness or weakness, political ambition or lack of ambition, and charisma or lack of charisma, all are important determinants of the governor's performance.

Personal qualities most important

Vacancy and Succession

Vacancies can occur in different ways before a governor's term expires. If the state has the office of lieutenant governor, that officer succeeds to the vacant governorship. In the states without a lieutenant governor, the presiding officer of the senate or the speaker of the house normally becomes the governor for the unexpired term.

Normal succession

Resignations may not be commonplace among governors, but positions of prestige in the federal government lure a few to Washington every decade. In the 1960s, Walter Hickel of Alaska resigned to become Secretary of the Interior; George Romney of Michigan resigned to become Secretary of Housing and Urban Development; and John A. Volpe of Massachusetts went to Secretary of Transportation. In the 1970s, Nelson Rockefeller of New York resigned to become Vice President; Cecil Andrus of Idaho became Secretary of Interior; Raul Castro of Arizona accepted an appointment as ambassador to Argentina; Richard Kneip of South Dakota resigned to become ambassador to Singapore; and Patrick Lucey of Wisconsin resigned to become ambassador to Mexico.[25] Neither President Reagan or Bush made extensive use of governors in cabinet or ambassadorial positions during the 1980s and early 1990s.

Resignations for appointments

Provisions for impeachment proceedings against the governor and other officials are found in the constitution of every state except Oregon. In most states the impeachment pattern is the same as is prescribed for dealing with officers of the national government. The lower house of the legislature adopts articles of impeachment, generally on the basis of a committee investigation and report. This adopted statement then goes to the senate, which conducts a trial, hearing testimony and argument from both sides. The lower house provides the prosecutor and the governor uses defense counsel. In the end, the senate decides the question, usually under the requirement of a two-thirds vote for a verdict of guilty. The punishment consists of removal from office and disqualification to subsequent holding of state office. Any conviction carrying a prison sentence must be decided through a separate trial in a regular court of law.

Removal by impeachment

There have been only 16 impeachment trials involving governors in United States history. Of course, governors served only two-year terms during most of that time so voters could readily turn unsatisfactory governors out of office before much damage could be done. The most recent brushes with impeachment occurred in the 1980s. In 1985, Governor Bill Sheffield of Alaska narrowly avoided impeachment proceedings after a grand jury accused him of improperly giving a state office lease to a political supporter.[26] In 1988, Governor Evan Mecham of Arizona became the first governor in 59 years to be impeached. He was convicted and removed from office for obstructing justice and loaning his own business funds set up to pay for state events.[27] His attempt to make a political comeback in 1990 failed.

Impeachments rare

In 15 states, the regular four-year terms of governors can theoretically be interrupted by the filing of recall petitions bearing the names of a specified number of signatures; such as 25 percent of those last voting for the office. The petition may provide a statement of reasons justifying the recall. A special election is held within a specified time and the results of the balloting determine whether or not the official relinquishes or retains the position.

Only one governor has been removed through a recall election. In a bitter factional fight among Republicans in 1921, Lynn J. Frazier of North Dakota was successfully beaten in a recall election. His political demise was brief, however, as he returned in 1922 to win election to the U.S. Senate. Governor Evan Mecham of Arizona barely avoided being recalled in 1988, saved only by impeachment. A committee had collected 388,000 signatures on recall petitions, well over the 216,000 required, and the recall election was set. However, after Mecham was removed by impeachment, the Arizona Supreme Court cancelled the election.[28]

The recall has been less effective at the state level than impeachment proceedings, probably because of the large number of signatures required to force an election. According to the *Book of the States, 1992–93,* California probably has the lowest, requiring 12 percent of the voters for the office in the last election, and Kansas probably has the highest, mandating 40 percent of the votes cast for the office in the last general election. In either case, only widespread discontent could fuel a recall effort.

Most state constitutions provide that in cases of gubernatorial disability, the lieutenant governor is to succeed to the office. However, few have defined the meaning of disability, and the method for peaceably determining that condition. After the adoption of the Twenty-Fifth Amendment providing for means of determining disability in the president, a number of states adopted constitutional amendments to fill this void. Several examples will demonstrate the variety of approaches used. Missouri provided for a nine-person disability board of state leaders, the majority of whom could determine the governor to be disabled. Colorado provided that the governor may declare himself or herself disabled or, if no declaration is forthcoming, a majority of the supreme court may make such determination that would become final upon two-thirds vote in the legislature. The Kansas constitution leaves the procedure for determining disability and the removal to legislative enactment. In Montana, the lieutenant governor and attorney general allege a gubernatorial disability to the legislature, and a two-thirds vote is required to declare the chief executive unable to manage duties. In Virginia, the attorney general, president pro tempore, and speaker of the house, or a majority of the general assembly may initiate disability proceedings.

For a number of reasons, governors have become particularly vulnerable from a political point of view. Faced with more duties than can humanly be performed, governors are forced to choose areas of emphasis and can be criticized for the areas of neglect. Governors are also newsmakers and, although constant exposure strengthens their visibility, it also makes possible that fatal casual comment. Perhaps the most important cause of political vulnerability is state fiscal policy.

As the states' chief budget officers, governors are unavoidably confronted with state fiscal issues. In recent years, volatility of state revenue and pressures for expenditures have taken their toll of governors. Fiscally, states have been on a virtual roller

Figure 11.2
"Easy does it!!! I think I've finally got control of this thing!"

coaster during the past decade, experiencing periods of feast and famine. Whenever a general fund surplus appears, political pressure mounts immediately for tax cuts and expenditure increases. Invariably, after the cuts and increases have been made, shortfalls have occurred, requiring the reimposition of tax levels. The credit for cuts, however, never seems to equal the blame for increases, resulting in political shortfalls for governors. State fiscal conditions have been exacerbated in recent years by the efforts of the national administration to reduce the flow of federal funds to state and local governments on the one hand and the dark clouds of tax revolt appearing on the other hand (Figure 11.2).

Fiscal issues critical

According to Professor Larry Sabato, ever since 1960 "governors have been faced with revenue dilemmas more complicated than the Gordian knot."[29] While governors may not have the authority to raise taxes by executive order, legislatures escape most of the political liability and leave the more visible governor to take the blame. The names on the political tombstones of governors whose demise was attributed at least partially to tax increases are numerous.[30] In a few cases, they were able to return to public office after a few years in exile. In summary, the sensitivity of voters to fiscal affairs will continue through the 1990s as state governments wrestle with their own revenue problems as well as those of the federal and local governments.

Hazard of the '90's

Political opportunities for governors are limited. Many have found the office a blind alley. Only a few can entertain hopes of candidacy for president. A governor may go to the United States Senate, but is likely to hold the seat for a long time, leaving little opportunity for another governor to move in this direction. A few former state

Nowhere to go

executives become judges, and a few are appointed to important administrative posts in state or nation. Some become lobbyists. Many return permanently to private life and enterprise, often in law or business. One was even rediscovered as a cab driver.

Endnotes

1. Thomas Schick, *The New York State Constitutional Convention of 1915 and the Modern State Governor* (New York: National Municipal League, 1978), pp. 2–3.

2. *Book of the States 1992–93* (Lexington, KY: Council of State Governments, 1992), p. 46.

3. Larry Sabato, *Goodbye to Good-Time Charlie,* 2d ed. (Washington: CQ Press, 1983), p. 20.

4. The figures for the 1930s were compiled by Joseph A. Schlesinger in *How They Became Governor* (East Lansing: Governmental Research Bureau, Michigan State University, 1957), as reported in *Comparative State Politics Newsletter,* ed. Malcom Jewell, February 1982 by Samuel C. Patterson, University of Iowa. The 1992 figures were by the authors from *Governors* (Washington, National Governors Association 1991).

5. Ibid., *Comparative State Politics Newsletter,* p. 17.

6. For a more detailed discussion, see Thad L. Beyle, "Governors," in *Politics in the American States,* 5th ed. Virginia Gray et al. (Glenview, IL. Scott Foresman & Co., 1990), pp. 201–208.

7. Compiled by authors from *Governors.*

8. Samuel R. Solomon, "Governors 1970–80," *National Civic Review* (March, 1981): 123–131.

9. See Paul West, "They're Everywhere! For Today's Governors, Life Is A Never-Ending Campaign," *Governing* 3 (March, 1990): 51–55.

10. Data from *Book of the States 1950–51* (Chicago, IL: Council of State Governments, 1950): 625; *Book of the States 1992–93* (Lexington, KY: Council of State Governments, 1992): 265–266; Beyle, "Governors," 30–43.

11. *Book of the States 1992–93,* p. 47.

12. *Book of the States 1992–93,* pp. 49–50.

13. For a fairly realistic scenario of the process, see Chapter 13 in Frank Trippett, *The States: United They Fell* (Cleveland: World Publishing, 1967). The research of Ira Sharkansky on agency requests in state legislatures (*American Political Science Review* 62: December, 1968) is still valid.

14. See Lee Sigelman and Nelson C. Dometrius, "Governors as Chief Administrators," *American Politics Quarterly* 16 (April, 1988): 157–170.

15. Martha Wagner Weinberg, *Managing the State* (Cambridge, MA: The MIT Press, 1977), p. 209.

16. For a detailed discussion see Alan Rosenthal, *Governors & Legislatures: Contending Powers* (Congressional Quarterly Press, Washington, 1990).

17. Report of Council of State Governments—Martin School of Public Administration, "Public Opinion and Policy Leadership In the American States," Savannah, GA: December 1–5, 1990.

18. Thad L. Beyle, "The Governor as Chief Legislator," *State Government* 51 (Winter 1978): 6.

19. Sarah P. McCally, "The Governor and His Legislative Party," *American Political Science Review* 60 (December 1966): 923–942. See also her related discussion in Sarah McCally Morehouse, "The State Political Party and the Policy-Making Process," *American Political Science Review* 67 (March 1973): 55–72.

20. E. Lee Bernick, "The Impact of U.S. Governors on Party Voting in One-Party Dominated Legislatures," *Legislative Studies Quarterly* 3 (August 1978): 441.

21. Sharon Sherman, "Powersplit: When Legislatures and Governors Are of Opposing Parties," *State Legislatures* 10 (May–June 1984): 10.

22. Comments of Governor Sam Goddard (1965–67) quoted in Bob Wischnia, "After They're Gone, What Do They Miss Most about the Governor's Job?" *Arizona* 5 (May 1974): 11.

23. Rodd Zolkos, "Jet-setting governors," *City & State* (June 4, 1990): 1, 27.

24. Dennis O. Grady, "American Governors and State-Federal Relations," *State Government* 57, (No. 3 1984): 106–112.

25. Solomon, "Governors: 1970–1980," pp. 144–146.

26. Clive S. Thomas, " 'The Thing' That Shook Alaska," *State Legislatures* 13 (February, 1987): 22–25.

27. Paula D. McClain, "Arizona 'High Noon': The Recall and Impeachment of Evan Mecham," *PS: Political Science & Politics* 21 (Summer, 1988): 628–637.

28. Paula McClain, p. 634.

29. Sabato, *Goodbye to Good-Time Charlie,* p. 105.

30. Researchers differ on the impact of economics and taxes on gubernatorial elections. See Robert M. Stein, "Economic Voting for Governor and U.S. Senator," *Journal of Politics* 52 (February, 1990): 29–53; Malcolm Jewell and David Olson, *Political Parties and Elections in the American States,* 3rd ed. (Belmont, CA: The Dorsey Press, 1988): 198–201; Susan E. Howell and James M. Vanderleeuw, "Economic Effects on State Governors," *American Politics Quarterly* 18 (April, 1990): 158–168; Elaine S. Knapp, "Taxes heat up campaigns," *State Government News* 33 (October, 1990): 18–21; Dick Kirschten, "Targets of Discontent," *National Journal* 22 (November 10, 1990): 2736–2741; and Susan L. Kone and Richard F. Winters, "Taxes and Voting: Electoral Retribution in the American States," a paper presented to the annual meeting of the American Political Science Association, San Francisco, August 30–September 2, 1990.

CHAPTER 12

The Judiciary and Criminal Justice

Resolving Conflicts between Individual Rights and Social Order

Understanding the court systems and criminal justice in the United States begins with remembering two kinds of divisions of power—the national-state division and the executive-legislative-judicial division. Loose reference to "the courts" often implies a kind of total state court subservience to the U. S. Supreme Court. This is misleading and even untrue for much of the operation of state and local courts. A state court still finds a significant amount of its authority in the state constitution and legislative enactments. One recent study of the "new judicial federalism" revealed that state supreme courts' rate of invalidating of state laws because of violating state constitutional provision is over twice as high as the rate of overturn because of violating U.S. constitutional provisions.[1] More conservative appointees to the U.S. Supreme Court in recent years, such as Justice Sandra Day O'Connor, have reminded us that, both quantitatively and qualitatively, state courts play a highly significant role in the judicial system of the United States. O'Connor cited sheer volume as an illustration: there were more than 27 million civil and criminal suits filed in state and local court systems in 1987 (excluding juvenile and traffic charges), and less than 280 thousand in the federal courts—approximately one percent of the total. In 1990 over 100 million cases of all kinds (including juvenile and traffic charges) were filed in state and local courts.[2] The crimes Americans fear most—mugging, burglary, rape, and murder—are almost entirely non-federal matters. It is the state and local officials that investigate and prosecute, the state and local courts that convict and sentence (or acquit), and overcrowded state and local prisons are where the convicted are punished.

Courts and the Political Process

Courts are politically distinct

Perhaps even more frequently misunderstood than the division of powers is the relationship of courts to the political process. The judiciary is cited in state constitutions as one of the three branches of government, and its unique mission in society requires it to manifest qualities that make it politically distinctive from the executive and legislative branches. When the courts in some states, or at some levels, fail to display these distinctive qualities, this failure is usually greeted with chagrin by a citizenry that

Photo by James L. Shaffer.

expects the judiciary to be politically unique. On other occasions, citizens and interest groups may be highly irritated when the judiciary refuses to respond to their demands in the same manner as the other two branches.

The courts themselves have nurtured the concept of political uniqueness. On some questions, such as whether or not a state has a republican form of government, the court has declined jurisdiction on the ground that this is a political question to be determined by the political branches of government, referring to the executive and legislative. Prior to *Baker v. Carr* in 1962, the courts held that legislative reapportionment was a political question to be resolved by the political branches. By citing certain questions as belonging in the political branches, the judiciary was affirming the idea that somehow the judiciary was a nonpolitical branch. The traditional case for political uniqueness of the judiciary in relation to the executive and legislative branches is built on a number of characteristics, as summarized in the discussion that follows.

Refuse political questions

Independence. In contrast to popular expectations of the executive and legislative branches, the first allegiance of the judiciary is not to public opinion but to the Constitution and the law. To shield this allegiance from the taint of oppressive public passions, courts are insulated from the ravages of politics. Writing in *Federalist* No. 78, Alexander Hamilton noted that ". . . independence of judges is . . . requisite to guard the Constitution and the rights of individuals from the effects of those ill humors which the arts of designing men . . . sometimes disseminate among the people themselves. . . ."

First allegiance to the law

To provide the judiciary with an environment conducive to withstanding attempts to trample the rights of minorities, the federal Constitution offers lifetime appointment. Among the states, only Massachusetts, New Hampshire, and Rhode Island have assured judges of this tenure. Most other states have limited terms of office with direct election to give an unhappy electorate the opportunity to apply political judgments to judicial decisions.

The Constitution, the Law, and Stare Decisis. While the political branches function with great flexibility, the judiciary is expected to confine its jurisdiction to the provisions of the federal and state constitutions, the statutes of the states, and case law consisting of previous decisions of judges on like questions. The latter is referred to as the principle of stare decisis, "let the decision stand." Occasionally, as in the desegregation case of *Brown v. Board of Education* (1954), courts will break away from stare decisis and strike out on new ground. However, judges feel a strong sense of obligation, barring unique and compelling circumstances, to follow established case law.

Decisions based on past

Formal Procedures. Constitutions may specify certain procedures for the legislative process but these constitute a mere shadow of the formality required in the judicial system. By established custom, participants in the judicial process are governed by rigid procedural standards, many arising out of the need to demonstrate to appellate courts that all rights of due process were properly accorded to the parties involved. Courtroom procedure and judicial practices have become extensively litigated and the judiciary is so compelled to adhere rigidly to numerous procedural requirements that participants in the courtroom could well be compared to actors playing out a carefully drafted script.

Assure due process

Objectivity. Executives and legislators are expected to reflect the political biases of their constituencies; judges are expected to reflect the alleged neutrality of the constitution and the law. The quality of independence and formality of procedures both

Should reflect neutrality

evolved to enable judges to maximize their objectivity. But as long as courts are staffed by human beings, objectivity is a goal to be sought rather than a quality that has been established. As the makeup of various courts changes, the orientations of the new judges bring new perspectives and new decisions to the bench. Studies of judicial behavior attest to the impact of the philosophical differences of Democrats and Republicans on judicial decisions. Nevertheless, most judges are still expected to strive, within their personal orientations, to achieve objectivity.

Rules of Access. Through determination and perseverance, most citizens can communicate with the governor and members of the legislature. Communication with

Not everyone goes to court

the court is quite a different matter. Three conditions must be met in order to gain access to the forum of the court: (1) A person must have "standing," i.e., he or she is personally aggrieved by a situation; (2) the issue involved must be justiciable, i.e., it is a proper question for judicial determination; and (3) the court must have jurisdiction to deal with the issue, e.g., it is a small claim that can be handled by the small claims court.

Legal training essential

Professional. Judicial issues are complex, demanding knowledge of constitutions, statutes, and case law, and a thorough understanding of the intricate rules of formal procedure. In addition, judges must be imbued with an unswerving commitment to recognized principles of law in a democratic society. To meet these qualifications, states require that judges have the education and experience to perform as professionals. In a few minor courts, untrained judges are still permitted to practice and often fail to meet public expectations of professionalism. Whereas judges are expected to be professional, governors and legislators come from a wide variety of occupational backgrounds and are not all expected to conform to one common set of professional standards. To execute successfully their assigned tasks, governors and legislators must be free to negotiate and compromise without the restrictions of certain professional expectations.

Unrepresentative. The policy-making mission of the state legislature requires that it be representative of the people. Two decades of reapportionment litigation attest to this requirement. The tradition of representativeness has not been so compelling in the executive branch but sentiment has been growing to make it reflective of women, blacks, Hispanics, handicapped, and other self-identified groups. In contrast to the legislative and executive, the judiciary is not expected to be representative because adjudication is to be based on the law rather than public opinion. Criteria for the selection

Not expected to represent views

of judges are expected to include issues of professional competence rather than group affiliations. Here again, a number of states have compromised this quality by providing for election of judges, thus making possible the evaluation of judges on political rather than professional criteria.

Lack of Self-Activation. The executive and legislative branches propose and initiate new policies and programs; the judiciary cannot issue opinions unless aggrieved parties come forward with an issue to address. Occasionally, judicial opinions may be written in such a fashion as to pique the curiosity of attorneys, thus inducing them to litigate unresolved issues. Such cases have the effect of inviting cases, thus making the court something other than inactive.

Must wait for cases

Addresses the Specific. Legislatures and executives pass laws and adopt standards that are usually applicable to everyone across the state; the judiciary is confined to resolving the issues involved in specific cases. Court cases sometimes involve resolution of questions of a general nature, such as malapportionment or rules of evidence. In many other cases, however, the specifics are so peculiar to the case that the decision has little or no application elsewhere, and it may be 40 years before the case can be used as a precedent for another situation.

Many cases unique

Decision Required. In a fairly unstructured political environment, legislatures and executives can deal with conflicts along a whole continuum of possibilities, from total inaction, to temporary compromises, to complete resolution. Courts do not have as wide a latitude in dealing with issues presented to them. They are expected to provide a solution of some finality, at least for the case involved. From time to time, they may also be reluctant to confront the issue and provide a less than satisfactory decision. Nevertheless, the courts do not enjoy the freedom to wait until the problem goes away.

More difficult to pass the buck

Depend on Others for Implementation. On one occasion, when the U.S. Supreme Court handed down a decision with which President Jackson disagreed, he said "John Marshall has made his decision, now let him enforce it." With this comment, he touched on a vulnerability of courts—they may issue opinions but implementation is vested in forces outside the purview of the court. The executive has people and funds to carry out its will; the legislature has oversight powers. Both of these branches can also wield political pressure to force compliance. The courts do have power to issue writs, subpoenas, and citations but these must always be appropriate to the nature of the institution.

Court rules: others act

Ideally, the foregoing characteristics provide a political distinctiveness to the judiciary. However, anyone who has observed judicial behavior can cite instances where judges have abdicated their independence to please an articulate pressure group, where the Constitution has been flaunted, where kangaroo proceedings were used in a speed trap, where all objectivity was lost as the judge orated about sexism and the innocence of rape, where professionalism became favoritism, or where the court split along party lines and made a patently political decision without a blush.

Ideal not always the real

Two recent studies of state courts in state politics (in Illinois and Arkansas) concluded that judges and courts are deeply rooted in the state's political system, and that all state court decisions have some political effect, from resolving conflicts to enforcing community norms.[3] One study of judicial behavior found that Democratic judges tend to favor the defense in criminal cases, claimants in unemployment cases, the government in tax cases, the divorce seeker in divorce cases, the tenant in landlord disputes, the labor union in management conflicts, the debtor in creditor cases, and the consumer in sale-of-goods sales. Republican judges tended to take the opposite view.[4] While the ideal judiciary strives to maximize its distinctiveness, from a realistic and practical point of view, it cannot become sufficiently disassociated from society to meet these criteria. Judges are themselves human beings who unavoidably reflect biases as they address issues pervaded by human difficulties.

To say that we have a government of laws and not of people often leaves the impression that courts and judges perform a cut-and-dried operation of applying unambiguous and impartial law to human situations in a way that completely avoids the political arena. Political scientists are increasingly studying the courts as a part of the political process rather than approaching them from the traditional concept of distinctiveness. This does not mean that there are no distinguishing features of the judicial process and judicial institutions, but it does mean that judicial decisions involving money, office, votes, service, life, and liberty determine in part who gets what, when, and how in society. No matter how hard they may strain to the contrary, courts are unavoidably

Cannot escape politics   enmeshed in the politics of society to a certain degree. As a consequence, maintenance of political distinctiveness is a constant challenge.

Jurisdiction and Functions of the Judiciary

State Courts Have Broad Jurisdiction

State courts have broad jurisdiction, stemming from constitutional and historical factors. In the American system of federalism, these courts are not restricted to delegated powers as is the federal judiciary. For instance, they have numerous functions and responsibilities in adjudicating issues involving police powers that are unique to state governments. To a greater degree than the federal courts, state courts have served as

English tradition   vehicles for perpetuating the principles of British jurisprudence in America, exemplified by the use of common law and equity. It is significant that the Revolution wrought no fundamental change in American judicial institutions and ways of justice. The state courts became direct heirs of the colonial courts and grand-heirs of the British judiciary. The origin and development of state systems of courts and jurisprudence cannot be understood without taking into account the growth, application, and meaning of the English common law, which has spread to the United States, Canada, and other countries. That body of law has vitally affected the legal commandments of all of our states except Louisiana, which was influenced by the Napoleonic Code and its antecedents. Even in Louisiana there has occurred a partial fusion of English and French doctrines, particularly in criminal law.

Common law   Elements of the common law came into vogue as early as the thirteenth century through the formulation by judges of rules based on recognized customs common to the British realm. These rules served for trying cases that involved points and issues not covered by the prevailing statutes. The decisions and their commentaries constituted efforts to apply established principles and common sense to civil and criminal matters. The system grew with time as judges relied upon former court opinions, thus adding precedent to precedent. This body of judge-made law had reached a high stage of crystallization when it became doctrinal baggage for export to America. But it had attained a wide scope, more suited to the functions of the state judiciaries than to the prescribed jurisdictions of federal courts.

As statutes come into existence, they take precedence over the common law in case of conflict or discrepancy. Statutory law may duplicate, amplify, modify, or displace common law. This statutory encroachment varies among the states according to the completeness or comprehensiveness of statutes and codes, but common law seems never to perish. A change in common law doctrine by state legislation is exemplified in the industrial era by the legislative requirement for compulsory compensation to workers for accidents incurred on the job. The statutes relieve the employee of much of the burden of proving damages and take from the employer much of the immunity handed down through the common law of a simpler society. Modern state constitutions also contain many provisions that deviate from the precepts of common law. The common law, however, has strongly influenced the applied meaning of state statutes and constitutions as interpreted by both state and federal courts. State laws and court opinions have been upheld by the Supreme Court of the nation on the basis of their accordance to the common law, and thus not violative of the federal Constitution. This point was set forth both before and after the adoption of the Fourteenth Amendment.

Statutes displace common law

Both state and federal courts try cases in equity, although state suits of this type are far more numerous. Equity applies to civil matters, not directly to criminal cases. It, too, originated in England, and arose through the crystallization of the common law by the judges. The rigidities of common law became inadequate for settling unprecedented disputes and for dispensing preventive or corrective justice not measurable in legal or monetary terms. For more flexible remedies the people of England turned to their king, who found it convenient to leave such matters to the royal chancellor, who thus became known as "the keeper of the king's conscience." The practice expanded into a separate system of jurisprudence and came under the administration of a chancery court.

Cases in equity

Equity proceedings in England and America today are circumscribed and regulated by statutory provisions, but nevertheless they serve modern needs flexibly. Equity hearings and decrees frequently offer the best or only means of satisfying the miscellaneous interests of a group of adult and minor heirs to an estate not covered by a will. Equity writs of injunctions serve definite purposes of preventing damage by one person to another. It might be said that the equity process is, in a sense, extra-legal, but in its flexibility, it may not become illegal or unconstitutional. Only Arkansas, Delaware, Mississippi, and Tennessee have separate chancery courts and chancellors. The others have law and equity jurisdictions in the same courts, as is true of the federal judiciary. Thus, equity has been considerably reduced as separate procedure in America.

Federal courts may issue the dramatic rulings that have sweeping impact across the nation but the state courts carry by far the largest burden in meting out justice. As pointed out earlier in this chapter the states' share of court cases in the nation amounts to close to 99 percent.

99 percent of cases in state courts

Functions of State Courts

Empowered to "pronounce the law," the judicial branch, consisting of a medley of courts, provides a variety of forums to which aggrieved persons and corporations can bring their differences with each other for resolution as civil cases. These same forums are

Handles civil and criminal matters

also used to entertain criminal cases, i.e., disputes that pit the governments against individuals and corporations for commission of acts contrary to the criminal statutes of state and local governments. Courts thus provide society with an institutionalized system through which conflicts can be modified, resolved, and contained by the application of established procedures and principles.

Principles are not necessarily established for resolving all disputes, however, so it is sometimes necessary for the court to interpret creatively existing principles to deal with the case at hand. Whereas the court may feel it is merely interpreting, others

Policy making?

consider many such interpretations as policy-making. Because of their visibility and impact, the best examples of perceived judicial policy-making are in the U.S. Supreme Court rulings on such issues as prayer in schools, desegregation, and abortion. From time to time state courts will elaborate on a constitutional provision to the point of policy-making but most such decisions are not widely publicized. Because state constitutions and statutes are written in greater detail than comparable federal provisions, they leave less to the discretion of state courts. Some state courts, such as New York and California, tend to be more vigorous in their policy-making orientations than others.

Check other branches

State courts also serve to check the other branches of government by entertaining challenges to the constitutionality of laws passed by the legislature, or the statutory basis of executive decisions made by governors. Courts may also be required to adjudicate questions arising out of the peoples' use of the legislative powers of initiative. As an example, in 1984 the state supreme courts in Montana and California invalidated initiated measures that would have forced state legislatures to ratify the federal balanced budget amendment. Many of the reapportionment plans passed by legislatures were reviewed by state courts, and found wanting.

Defend unpopular minorities

The independence and objectivity of state courts are put to the test when unpopular minorities invoke constitutional protection of their rights against the actions of oppressive majorities working through the legislature or the executive. Adoption of oppressive measures or policies, designed to deprive minorities of rights, often require the courts to assure cults, pornographers, and the like that their constitutional rights will be secure regardless of public passion. Minorities, lacking in political power, often find that the courts furnish the only means by which they can achieve corrective action.

May perform nonjudicial functions

Judges may also be called upon to perform nonjudicial functions. Several state constitutions require the supreme court to provide legal guidance in the form of advisory opinions. In some states, judges are asked to make appointments, such as in Tennessee where the supreme court appoints the attorney general, or in Pennsylvania where it may appoint a member of the legislative reapportionment commission. A number of states have the chief justice serving on the pardon and/or parole board, a continuation of judicial functions but with members of the executive branch involved.

Choosing Judges

Four Methods for Selecting Judges

To enable judges to defend the Constitution with independence, objectivity, and professionalism, the federal government provides for life-time appointment of judges by the president, with confirmation by the senate. For historical and political reasons, states shifted from appointment to methods designed to make judges more attentive to the political tenor of the times.

During the colonial era, judges were designated by the king. After the Revolution, this appointment power was assumed by the legislatures. But by the 1830s, the people sought a direct voice in the selection of judges and, in 1832, Mississippi became the first state to provide for election of judges. By the Civil War, 24 of the 34 states had an elected judiciary. Every state entering the Union thereafter provided for election until 1959 when Alaska came in with appointive judges.

Beginning of elected judges

Widespread corruption in the late 1800s resulted in a search for better methods of selection, and reformers seized upon the nonpartisan electoral system. Others felt that as long as the election method, partisan or nonpartisan, rested on an uninformed and disinterested electorate, the courts would always be subject to the manipulation of interest groups. They proposed a nominating commission that would receive nominations, interview applicants, screen candidates, and submit a list of three or five qualified persons to the governor for appointment to fill a vacancy.

This variety of preferences has resulted in a diversity of methods used by states to select judges. Methods not only vary from state to state but even within states, such as South Carolina where supreme court judges are chosen by the legislature, probate judges by partisan ballot, and magistrates by the governor. With a number of states using two or more methods, classifications become arbitrary so generalizations may serve accuracy best.

- *Election:* Around half of the states choose the majority of their judges by election, with more states using the nonpartisan than the partisan ballot.
- *Gubernatorial appointment:* Five states rely on direct appointment by the governor with confirmation by the senate or a commission.
- *Legislative appointment:* The legislative assembly names judges in four states. In Connecticut, the legislature selects from a list of nominees furnished by the governor.
- *Missouri Plan:* About one-third of the states use the Missouri Plan, which calls for a five- or seven-person nominating committee to submit a list of nominees to the governor for appointment. The nominating committee usually consists of laypersons, representatives of the state bar association, and a judge. It solicits applications, interviews top prospects, and provides the governor with a list of three or five names. After the appointment, the judge serves a fixed period of time and then the question of retention is placed on the election ballot: "Shall Judge ———— be continued in office?" If the people vote against retention, the nominating committee is reactivated to fill the vacancy. Thus, the Missouri plan permits voters to remove judges but not to elect a candidate of their own choosing.

Methods for choosing judges

Committee recommends for appointment

First promoted by the American Bar Association in 1937 as the "merit plan," the Missouri selection process has slowly gained in acceptance, usually in lieu of one of the electoral systems. Thus, the battle joined over selection methods usually becomes the merit plan versus an elective system.

Politics of elections   Judicial elections conducted on the partisan ballot are patently political. Non-partisan elections, though basking in an aura of neutrality, are also political. In some jurisdictions prescribing nonpartisan elections, parties may continue to put forth candidates and campaign for their election. Michigan is an excellent example of a state where political activity still occurs in nonpartisan judicial elections. Ohio has an unusual hybrid system of choosing supreme court justices that combines partisan primary elections with a nonpartisan general election ballot. A recent study by Lawrence Baum of partisan considerations and voter decisions in Ohio judicial elections confirmed two items of conventional wisdom: (1) partisan considerations are more influential in contests under a partisan ballot than in those under a nonpartisan ballot; and (2) partisan considerations can still be a significant influence on voting in judicial elections under a nonpartisan ballot.[5] When parties respect the nonpartisan character of elections and refrain from campaign activities, interest groups—particularly the members of the bar associations—become active, thus injecting a different style of politics into the process. Electoral politics in judicial selection is minimized, however, by the fact that many of the judicial positions are initially filled by gubernatorial appointment due to death or retirement. To minimize gubernatorial politics, a number of states have created judicial nominating committees to provide suitable candidates for the governor.

Qualifications, Terms, and Compensation

The state constitutions and statutes give rather limited attention to judicial qualifications aside from matters of age, citizenship, and residence. There are general indefinite requirements for professional expertise although such language as "learned in the law" will appear from state to state. In some states, this has been litigated to mean *Member of the bar* a law degree. Less than half of the states stipulate a minimum age and, for those states requiring it, that is most commonly thirty years of age. The most universal requirement is membership in the state bar.

Terms   Terms for the state supreme court tend to be longer than for lower courts, with almost half providing terms of ten or more years as compared to only ten states giving lower courts ten or more years. The shorter terms in the lower courts could make the judges more subject to public opinion, depending on the nature of the political culture of the state.

Salaries   Most judicial salaries are set by state law. Salaries are usually lower than is paid to federal judges. As of 1992, the highest paid judges were supreme court justices in California who drew $121,207; the lowest were in Montana with $62,452. More than half of the states were paying supreme court judges $90,000 or over. Judges in lower courts were paid less, but in most states not significantly less.[6]

Judicial training *programs*   While professional entrance requirements may consist only of membership in the state bar or "learned in the law," once on the bench judges are exposed to a number of opportunities to improve their judicial skills. The most notable of these is the National Judicial College founded in the early 1960s and located at the University of Nevada-Reno. The first month-long session was held in 1964 with 83 judges attending. Later, a three-semester system was established, the curriculum was broadened, and a 50,000-volume library developed. The college has its own classroom and housing facilities. In a little more than two decades it awarded around 15,000 Certificates of

Completion. The founding and expansion of the College has been credited to private sources, primarily the Max C. Fleischmann and W. K. Kellogg foundations.[7]

A majority of states still permit non-attorneys to preside as judges in minor courts with limited jurisdiction. As a matter of fact, only six states require that all judges have attorney status; several other states are requiring that all new judges be attorneys. The permissibility of using non-attorney judges was affirmed with certain parameters in 1976, when a defendant in a Kentucky justice of the peace court appealed his conviction to the U.S. Supreme Court.[8] Of the 20,000 judges on minor courts, it was estimated recently that over 13,000 were non-attorneys.[9] Most of the states using lay judges provide in-service training programs to help them master the basics of the judicial process.[10]

Still have many lay judges

Removal of Unfit Judges

In the electoral processes, incumbent judges are seldom turned out by the voters; the legislative impeachment process is seldom used; and in the few states having recall, the method is too cumbersome. With these traditional methods inadequate for realistically dealing with judges that are incompetent, temperamentally unfit, indolent, or alcoholic, judicial reformers have sought to develop alternative methods for removing unqualified judges from the bench. For some reformers, the best way to protect the bench is to assure quality in the initial appointments. For this reason, the judicial nominating systems, and particularly the Missouri Plan, have gained ground. However, it has not always been possible to predict judicial behavior and, invariably, a few gain office who lack in objectivity, professionalism, and the other qualities sought for a courtroom. Aside from impeachment, the most universal procedure available for dealing with incompetence in the courts are the judicial qualifications commissions now existing in almost all states. The commissions have tended to deal primarily with the most serious cases, such as alcoholism, mental disorders, and gross incompetence.[11] Usually the commissions make recommendations for corrective action to the state supreme courts which are empowered to act.

Judicial qualifications commissions

Rather than waiting for problems to develop, several states have formulated performance evaluations procedures. New Jersey and Colorado have evaluation systems in place, with the Colorado committee directed to "inform the public about judicial performance."[12] The perception of a good judge by the public, however, may diverge from standards of the judicial profession. The Alaska Judicial Council conducted a performance evaluation poll of the bar members and peace officers and recommended a "no" vote for a judge. A former state trooper, the judge had a "law and order" reputation that endeared him to the peace officers who rallied to his cause. The judge received more votes than those judges ranked "excellent" in the evaluation polls.[13]

Evaluating judges

The Judicial Structure

Except for the farrago of local minor courts, the state judicial system in most states consists of three tiers: the courts of first instance, often called the district courts; the intermediate appellate courts; and the supreme court. (See figure 12.1.)

Minor courts

Figure 12.1
State judicial hierarchy as
organized in most states.

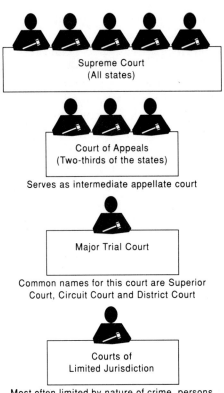

Supreme Court
(All states)

Court of Appeals
(Two-thirds of the states)

Serves as intermediate appellate court

Major Trial Court

Common names for this court are Superior
Court, Circuit Court and District Court

Courts of
Limited Jurisdiction

Most often limited by nature of crime, persons
involved, or subject. Includes courts for probate,
juvenile, county, municipal, police, small claims,
family, and many others, depending on state.

Local minor courts are presided over by justices of the peace, other local magistrates, or police judges, many of whom have no legal training. These courts function without juries and dispose of no major matters, either civil or criminal, although they may conduct preliminary hearings to determine whether an accused person shall be held in jail or placed under bond for a jury trial for homicide.

Justices of the peace   The justice of the peace (J.P.) once performed useful functions in rural neighborhoods and villages before the existence of speedy transportation and communication. This part-time officer has been subjected to criticism in recent years, sometimes for operating "marriage mills" at convenient points near a state line and sometimes for improvising a fee racket. There have been complaints of cooperation between justices of the peace and rural constables in "speed traps" for collecting advance fees and fines from passing motorists who could not tarry for court proceedings. The makeshift minor courts, rural and urban, have bred distrust for reasons of inadequacy, subservience to the fee system, and connection with unsavory politics. The dissatisfaction has led to their being supplanted or supplemented in a number of states and cities with more systematic courts and professional judges who exercise somewhat greater authority and serve larger territorial jurisdictions. These improved tribunals have such designations as municipal courts, general sessions courts, and courts of common pleas.

Above these minor courts is the first court of general jurisdiction, making up the bottom rung of the state judicial structure. These courts are courts of record, in that a transcript is made of the proceedings to provide a basis for appeal. With authority to entertain any and all criminal and civil suits, as well as appeals from minor courts, the work of these courts stands as the main component of the administration of justice. Officially, these courts are classified as *circuit, district,* or by other designations. Juries are used in these courts and each trial is presided over by a single judge. The geographical jurisdiction varies depending on the population density of the state and area. In the more densely populated areas, the court may encompass a single county or city; in the rural areas, the court may take in several counties, with the judges moving from one county courthouse to another, or riding "circuit," to take up the cases in the various parts of the assigned district.

First court of general jurisdiction

Two-thirds of the larger states with considerable court activity have established intermediate appeals courts as their second tier. These courts accept the first appeals from the courts of "first instance," thereby reducing the workload of the state supreme court.

Court of appeals

Every state has a highest court of appeals, generally called the supreme court, although other titles are used in New York, Massachusetts, and a few other states. This court consists of from three to nine judges, the number most often being five or seven. Most of its work is devoted to cases coming up from lower state courts, although it has original jurisdiction in special types of cases in a few states. It sits without a jury. In many states it has the responsibility of formulating rules of procedure for the whole judicial system of the state within the framework of constitutional and statutory provisions. In a few states, the supreme court may be required to render advisory opinions on vital matters, such as the constitutionality of pending legislation, if requested by the governor or the legislature. There is no appeal from this state court, except to the United States Supreme Court on federal constitutional grounds.

Supreme court

Special courts of different kinds are to be found on the fringe of the hierarchical system, notably in highly urbanized regions. These courts may handle such matters as domestic relations, juvenile delinquency, probation of wills, small claims, and the like. Much of their work is of an informal nature and partly free from battles by attorneys, although through proper channels it may be reviewed for possible reversal by higher courts.

Special courts

It is also true that in modern state government, as in the national government, there are administrative bodies with power to conduct hearings and render decisions that are binding in the regulation of civil affairs, unless invalidated upon review by a judicial court. Administrative tribunals and administrative laws are essential to all levels of government. This type of adjudication may be applicable to such problems as tax disputes, intrastate or local utility rates, urban zoning, licensing and location of liquor stores, enforcement of health and sanitary measures, abatement of pollution evils, and removal of fire hazards.

Administrative adjudication

Court reform was greatly stimulated by the outpouring of federal funds for improving the criminal justice system following the widespread urban and campus riots of the late 1960s. Having access to planning and implementation funds, judicial reformers created broad study and planning projects to review the judicial processes. Thus, a climate for change was created in many states. Finally, the criticisms of courts first expounded by such men as Roscoe Pound in 1906 and Arthur T. Vanderbilt in 1938 began to be addressed as the attention of state jurists turned to the concept of a unified court system. Under the unified court system, the trial courts would be unified while management, rule making, budgeting, and financing would be centralized in the office of the supreme court. Through the 1970s and early 1980s, state constitutions were amended to provide for this more orderly, pyramidal system, with the supreme courts receiving rule making and oversight jurisdiction over the lower courts.

Develop unified court systems

By the early 1990s the great majority of the states had in place a system to provide more uniform procedures to be used in all courts, to shift loads from court to court so that cases could be kept current, to redraw jurisdictional boundaries to better distribute work, to monitor the caseloads of lax judges, and to identify bottlenecks in the system.[14]

Court administration

To handle the increased administrative workload vested in the supreme court, the office of court administrator appeared in every state. Working under the court, the administrator was called upon to staff systems for a budget; rule making, advisory, and review committees; personnel management; and case management. Perhaps the most effective tool available was the computer, brought in for word processing, computerized legal research, automated jury selection, calendars, transfer of cases, workload monitoring, and sentence execution. Computer printouts furnish the supreme courts with case status reports on the entire judicial system, pinpointing overloaded courts and underworked judges.

States assume more costs

As states asserted leadership in restructuring their court systems, they were also required to assume a greater share of the court financing. Over half of the states have assumed full funding for the courts with several additional states giving serious consideration to relieving county and municipal governments of costs associated with state courts.

Crime—A Major Judicial Concern

Most cases moving through the publicly financed judicial system are cases between private parties—civil suits. However, courts interface with a major public responsibility in the other portion of its work—processing criminal cases in which the state seeks to deal judicially with persons who have violated the criminal laws. Thus, courts are a major institution involved in the preservation of an orderly society.

Criminal jurisdiction

Nature of Crime

Government, whatever its form, is not government unless it maintains law and order. Liberty, as emphasized in chapter 4, is always liberty under law. And liberty unrestrained becomes lawlessness which threatens the well-being of all in society. Hence, state legislatures and the governing bodies of local governments adopt statutes and ordinances defining the types of behavior that will not be countenanced in the jurisdictions. Violations of these statutes and ordinances are crimes. The less serious crimes

Defining crimes

Table 12.1 Major Crimes

Crime	Definition
Homicide	Causing the death of another person without legal jurisdiction or excuse.
Rape	Unlawful sexual intercourse, by force or without legal or factual consent.
Robbery	Unlawful taking or attempted taking of property that is in the immediate possession of another, by force or threat of force.
Assault	Unlawful intentional inflicting, or attempted inflicting, of injury upon the person of another. Aggravated assault is the unlawful intentional inflicting of serious bodily injury or unlawful threat or attempt to inflict bodily injury or death by means of a deadly or dangerous weapon with or without actual infliction of injury. Simple assault is the unlawful intentional inflicting of less than serious bodily injury without a deadly or dangerous weapon.
Burglary	Unlawful entry of any fixed structure, vehicle or vessel used for regular residence, industry, or business, with or without force, with the intent to commit a felony or larceny.
Larceny (theft)	Unlawful taking or attempted taking of property other than a motor vehicle from the possession of another, by stealth, without force and without deceit, with intent to permanently deprive the owner of the property.
Motor Vehicle Theft	Unlawful taking or attempted taking of a self-propelled road vehicle owned by another, with the intent of depriving the owner of it permanently or temporarily.
Arson	Intentional damaging or destruction or attempted damaging or destruction by means of fire or explosion of the property without the consent of the owner, or of one's own property or that of another by fire or explosives with or without the intent to defraud.

Sources: U.S. Department of Justice, Bureau of Justice Statistics, adapted from Report to the Nation on Crime and Justice (Washington, 1983), pp. 2–3. Based on BJS *Dictionary of criminal justice data terminology,* 1981.

are classed as *misdemeanors;* the more serious ones, usually carrying penalties of a year or more in a state institution, are called *felonies.* Many states subdivide each of the two major categories into subgroups, such as Misdemeanor A, Misdemeanor B, Felony A, Felony B, and so on.

 The definition of crimes will vary from state to state and locality to locality, depending largely on the political culture of the area. In some states, violations of property rights are more serious crimes than some violations of persons; and in some states, certain crimes warrant the death penalty while other states will reject such a philosophy. In some localities, being caught with a mind-altering substance will be a misdemeanor, yet in other areas this will constitute a felony. Taking a large saguaro cactus from public land in Arizona constitutes a felony, carrying one to ten years in prison. Occasionally, certain tough criminal laws can be traced to an incident in history. Arsonists may have caused great harm in several cities back in the 1920s, thus explaining why the state has a statute making arson a Class A Felony with a thirty-year sentence. Hence, crime is what the state or locality says it is. (See table 12.1.)

Crimes vary by state

Insufficient resources to fight all crime

A crime on the books may not be a crime on the streets. Public opinion has been much stronger in support of passing laws to declare acts to be crimes than it has been to fund the means to enforce the laws. One study of 396 cities revealed that crime had grown fourfold over a thirty-year period beginning shortly after World War II, but resources had grown only twofold.[15] Because of this mismatch between crime and resources, law enforcement and judicial agencies have been forced to choose when enforcing the criminal law. Weighing the consequences of each, they will often consider burglary more serious and leave prostitution for a later time. Also, if violent crimes continue to occur, they may seldom get to the so-called "victimless" crimes such as use of drugs, prostitution, drunkenness, and pornography. Some law enforcement observers, recognizing the futility of trying to enforce all criminal laws, have suggested decriminalizing some crimes and handling them in some other fashion so that enforcement personnel can commit their time to the more serious crimes. Some jurisdictions have followed this advice. However, as certain activities are being demoted from the level of "crime," new forms of behavior are appearing to challenge the criminal justice system. White collar crimes involving fraud in savings and loan institutions, dealings in securities, and computer tampering have moved in with the age of electronic technology.

Computer crime

Computers have been marvelous tools for business but they have been equally as dazzling as tools for crime. Computer tampering, initially regarded as harmless genius at play, has become serious as millions of dollars in damage and thefts has become commonplace. By the early 1990s, the majority of the states and the federal government passed legislation toughening the criminal penalties for the electronic larceny and tampering. New criminal statutes have also been placed on the books to deal with child pornography, child abuse, spouse abuse, and terrorist activities.

Women in crime

Not only has the definition of crime been changing and expanding but the circle of perpetrators has enlarged to include more women. Arrests of women for serious offenses rose 20 percent during the 1974–1984 decade, yet similar arrests of men went up only 13 percent. By 1990 the number of arrests of women in one year exceeded 2,000—18 percent of all arrests. The number of women in prison more than tripled during the decade of the 1980s, from 13,400 to more than 40,500. Though avoiding such violent crimes as robbery, women are claiming a rising share of property crimes such as fraud and embezzlement. Moving into a more equal status with men and holding high-level jobs, women are gaining "equal" opportunities to commit crimes. In addition, they are also feeling the impact of new mandatory prison sentences, making it more difficult for women to receive preferential treatment in the courts. One criminologist claims that the chivalry factor is disappearing. "In the old days," he said, "if a woman was arrested and started crying, the cops might let her go. That doesn't happen much today."[16]

Our inconsistent public policy toward drug use in the United States is now heavily intertwined with the dominant cause of crime in the 1990s. Although alcoholic beverages are legally advertised, sold, and consumed, automobile accidents caused by drunken driving result in close to the same number of deaths as caused by murder. The annual figure in each case has been close to 20,000 deaths per year, with a recent increase in drug-related violence and a decrease in drunken-driving deaths following the change in the legal drinking age from 19 to 21. The cancerous spread of drug use and drug trafficking, earlier with marijuana and more recently with cocaine, and especially the cheap but potent modification, "crack," has had a devastating impact on the personal safety and the physical and economic health of the American people. With about six percent of the world's population, the United States consumes about 60 percent of the world's illicit drugs. More than half of the males and 45 percent of the females arrested in 1990 tested positive for drugs.

Drug abuse as cause of other crimes

Even though there are hopeful signs in the 1990s of at least a modest decline in drug use, drug-related crime continues to be the toughest challenge on the law-enforcement agenda of all levels of government. This is especially true for the middle-size metropolitan cities that seem to have been attacked by the drug traffickers a little later than the largest cities. In Kansas City, Missouri, for example, their first black mayor, Emanuel Cleaver, spoke shortly after his 1991 election about the contrast between the enemy twenty years earlier (bigotry), and the enemy today. "Now our most diabolical opponent is crack," Cleaver said, "crack and the crime that comes with it."[17] The gang and drug violence that was once found primarily in the super-cities has become the number one crime problem in American cities of all sizes. A 1991 study by the U.S. Senate Judiciary Committee reported that the problems of drug abuse and crime have moved to small-town America, with violent crime increasing at a faster rate in 13 of 15 of the most rural states than in urban ones. One of every ten hard-core cocaine addicts was found to live in rural states.[18]

Pervasiveness of drug addiction

The Dimensions of Crime

When it comes to measuring the incidence of crime, the figures used to quantify its dimensions should be weighed cautiously. During the past few decades, crime has undoubtedly been on the increase but U.S. law enforcement has also become more professionalized and crime reporting has become more efficient. When the FBI Uniform Crime Reports revealed a doubling of crime in the decade of the 1960s, and another 38 percent increase during the 1970s, it is likely that at least some of the increase was the result of better reporting. In fact, the first ray of hope fell across the crime statistics in the early 1980s when reported crimes began to decline after peaking in 1980. Even so, violent crimes were at an all-time record in 1990 with 23,440 murders and more than 100,000 reported rapes in spite of a decline in the total number of personal and household crimes. The crime index (crimes per 100,000 population) turned back up in 1985 and by 1990 and 1991 had almost surpassed the 1980 rate (See figure 12.2). Some progress on the drug front occurred as surveys of cocaine and marijuana use by high school seniors showed a modest decline in 1990.[19]

Record violent crime rate

A growing overall crime rate is usually attributed to the consequences of a more urban society, crime on television, the decline in moral standards, breakup of the traditional family, and better crime reporting. With all of these factors still present, explanations for the decline in the early 1980s are difficult to find. Those who have advocated longer sentences and fewer paroles feel their programs have led to the decline. On the other hand, most academic experts have attributed the decline to the movement of the post-World War II baby boom past the crime-prone years of ages eighteen to twenty-five.

Efforts to explain ups and downs of crime rate

Figure 12.2
Crime index, 1980–1990.
*(Source: Bureau of Justice
Statistics.)*

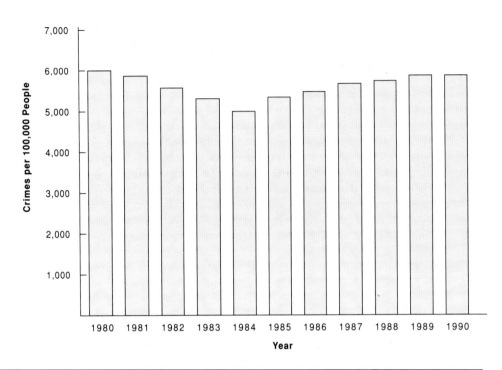

Responses to Crime

*Society supporting "get
tough" policies*

The constant bombardment of the American public with graphic news reports of violent crimes and drug abuse produced predictable political and psychological effects. In recent years public opinion has reflected a "get tough" attitude based on fear. Fear of crime runs relatively high, with 45 percent of the people reporting that they are afraid to walk alone in their neighborhoods at night, and even 13 percent afraid to do so in the daytime.[20] This fear translates into a demand for tougher measures to contain crime. California citizens initiated their own action against crime by introducing and approving a wide-ranging anti-crime law that limited plea bargaining, gave victims the right to restitution, prescribed longer sentences for chronic offenders, abolished some forms of bail, and guaranteed children the right to a "safe" school.[21] Other states have passed laws permitting householders to use "deadly force" to resist burglars. According to Cambridge Reports, Inc., 83 percent of the public favored mandatory prison sentences for persons using guns in crimes, and half of the states had enacted such legislation by 1982.[22]

*Volunteers fighting
crime*

Besides the tougher laws, people are more receptive to the idea of organizing volunteer anti-crime programs in their neighborhoods. In one Gallup survey, 17 percent said such activity was going on in their neighborhood and as many as 80 percent favored establishment of such an effort in their community.[23] Many citizens have indicated a lack of confidence in the criminal justice system by providing their own protection. Over 60 percent of the rural dwellers and over 40 percent of the urbanites have guns in their homes.[24] While arming themselves, citizens feel that laws governing handgun sales ought to be stricter. Of the 59 percent who felt this way, 47 percent were gunowners themselves.[25] Crime Stopper programs have been organized in 130 communities across the country, giving citizens the opportunity to provide law enforcement officers with leads in unsolved crimes. By the mid-1980s 500 Crime Stopper programs were operating in the United States and Canada, claiming involvement in solution of 60,000 cases (95 percent of them felonies) resulting in the recovery of $283 million in narcotics and stolen goods.[26] In 1991 Carl Horrowitz and the Heritage Foundation published a report recommending "An Empowerment Strategy for Eliminating Neighborhood Crime," that places strong emphasis on community involvement in the fight against crime, with closer cooperation between local public administrators and inner-city neighborhoods. This "empowerment" trend in urban management is receiving both local and national endorsement not only as the key to better law enforcement but to urban economic development as well.[27]

In the minds of some, when the criminal justice system has failed to protect a person from criminal activity, society has broken its contract to guarantee safety and therefore has an obligation to assist the victim. On this premise and for purely humanitarian reasons, over 40 states have established victim compensation programs. For many of the programs, the legislature simply appropriates funds to be granted to victims under the particular rules of the state. In 12 states, the programs rely entirely on penalty assessments levied on persons convicted of certain crimes. Restitution by the offender provides another source of funds. An increasing number of states take the profits from books and articles published by the offender and place them in an escrow account for reimbursement of victims, and in recent years, Congress has begun to appropriate funds to assist the victim programs of states.[28]

Victim compensation programs

The nationalization of society has not only led to a nationalization of the governmental processes but it has also fostered a nationalization of crime. Acknowledging the interstate—and even the international—character of modern crime, the federal government has invoked its delegated powers more vigorously in the 1980s and 1990s to fight crime. The Reagan administration launched an ambitious program to control the flow of narcotics through the use of diplomacy and enforcement. Congress passed the Comprehensive Crime Control Act of 1984 to toughen procedures involving federal crimes and, with obvious political overtones, has passed so much anti-crime legislation in every election year since then that judicial authorities have begun to worry about an overload of the federal court dockets with criminal cases. These laws have provided for holding persons without bail if they are a danger to the community, abolition of parole for federal crimes, creation of a commission to determine sentences, narrowing the scope of the insanity defense, and giving federal authorities power to impound the assets of persons convicted of drug violations or organized crime. Armed with this legislation, federal enforcement agencies can deal with certain crime without waiting for state or local invitations. The mood of the U.S. Supreme Court has also shifted away from concerns over the defendant to one of concern over controlling criminal activity.

Federal government expands activity

Structuring the Police Function

Central State Agencies

Every state has central agencies to facilitate or ensure the preservation of law and order in the commonwealth. The oldest of the state forces, or potential forces, is the *Militia*

1. National Guard as designated by the federal Constitution, or the National Guard as covered by later legislation by Congress. The states are forbidden to keep troops in time of peace except by the consent of Congress, and thus the national legislature has in various ways provided for the establishment and training of the state troops, as well as for calling them into federal service with federal compensation when necessary.

Members of the National Guard pursue their regular civilian occupations in normal times, but are subject to call by state or national authorities. They may be ordered by the governor or adjutant general to join their units in active duty to quell riots, to police communities visited by disaster, or to take over the whole law enforcement function in instances of complete breakdown of local administration.

2. State police With the rise of state police systems, state governments in modern times have been able to limit their use of the National Guard to more massive disturbances. Centralized state police systems have developed throughout the country in one form or another since the organization of the Texas Rangers in 1835 to patrol frontier regions harassed by lawless elements. Massachusetts provided for state constables in 1865, and Pennsylvania created a regular state police system in 1905. Several factors account for the growth and professional role of state agencies of public safety. Their routine performance stirs less curiosity or complaint than the sudden summoning of state troops. The universality of motor transportation on networks of superhighways requires enforcement of traffic regulations beyond the concern or capacity of local officers. State forces are likely to be best equipped to cope with intercity or intercounty operations of major criminals, not only to apprehend them, but also to procure or test clues and evidence through scientific methods. These central agencies may provide expert aid and service to local officers and, if they are called upon by the latter, no issue of local pride or prerogative is likely to arise. They may strengthen the hand of the law consistently in sparsely populated regions and, at times, in areas or centers of commercialized crime where local authorities may be subject to the subsidy of influential bosses of vice.

Most states have state police Every state except Hawaii has a general police force or highway patrol or both. Three-fourths of the states have central police systems with full authority of law enforcement, and the others have state highway patrols that are concerned with primarily or entirely with traffic violations, sometimes as units of the highway departments. There is no great degree of uniformity among the systems, but an increasing number of states select the personnel on a merit basis and also provide for training of the members.

The selection of the top officials usually is by gubernatorial appointment or at least with heavy gubernatorial influence and involvement. In a few states, the head or superintendent of the force is chosen by a board that may exercise substantial control over the activities of the agency. States with large or effective systems assign the officers on a more or less flexible basis to routes or geographical sections for adequate territorial coverage. The personnel is also likely to be organized in a military or semi-military manner, with companies, rank, and uniforms.

3. Special groups The states also have a miscellany of specialized officers or agencies for direct or indirect aid to security and law enforcement. These include such functionaries as fire marshals, game or fish wardens, liquor control officers, and different types of inspectors, who may be responsible to central regulatory agencies. There are state medical examiners to determine the cause of death in questionable or concealed circumstances. Central offices or bureaus, with professional staffs, make investigations with laboratory methods, including chemical and ballistic testing, establish evidence of crime, and identify criminals. This service is of invaluable aid to prosecuting authorities throughout the state. Such testing sometimes establishes the innocence of suspects since the methods are free from the bias or error of eyewitnesses.

4. Bureau of Investigation

County Law Enforcement

All officers of the law in a state, except those commissioned by the national government, are state officers, whatever their local functions, duties, and powers may be. They may be locally elected or appointed, occupy quarters furnished by local governments, and financed by local taxes, but they still have direct responsibility for enforcing state laws and apprehending violators of state laws within their respective jurisdictions. Federal courts and federal legislation hold them responsible as agents of the state for respecting the rights of persons as guaranteed by the Fourteenth Amendment. Because of their status as state representatives, the governors in many states have important powers of supervision, removal, and replacement over designated local officers to prevent neglect, laxity, or malfeasance in enforcement.

The American county sheriff historically embodies the combination of a medieval factotum with a kingpin of the wild western frontier. Sheriffs in most states are responsible particularly for three common functions: (1) enforcing the state criminal laws by apprehending and arresting violators; (2) serving as the executive agent of the state judicial courts by serving criminal and civil papers, subpoenas, and the like; and (3) maintaining a jail for prisoners awaiting trial or serving sentences. In some states, other duties are assigned to the office, such as collecting delinquent taxes or disposing of property for nonpayment of taxes.

Sheriffs' functions

In all states except Rhode Island, the sheriff is elected by the voters of the county, on a partisan ballot in most states. The Rhode Island legislature chooses the sheriffs for that state. The term of office is either two or four years, with many states limiting the number of consecutive terms a sheriff may serve. This restriction does not prevent a sheriff from winning the office for alternate terms, probably taking turns with a faithful deputy.

Sheriffs elected

The attractiveness of the office is enhanced in many states and counties by the retention of the antiquated fee system, with fees sometimes amounting to a fortune during one term in a large county. There may be a fee for every court order, process, or warrant served by the sheriff or a deputy, with additional compensation for capturing or handling prisoners. Sheriffs have been known to make handsome profits in the business of lodging and feeding prisoners, sometimes supplementing their gains by providing outside luxuries for prisoners having ample funds. The office thus tends often to become a desirable entrepreneurial undertaking, and some have been known to reap further gain by peddling lucrative protection to criminal interests. The incumbent is often enmeshed in the unavoidable business aspects of the office, whether for selfish or for unselfish motives, and thus tends to function merely as an amateur in the sphere of law enforcement. In addition to the regular staff, deputies may be commissioned on a nominal or honorary basis for political purposes or for authorizing privately employed guards to act in an enforcement capacity for their employers.

Sheriff has profitable sidelines

Criticisms of sheriff system

Critics have leveled three charges at the office of sheriff as operated in many states and counties: (1) the elective process results in politicization of law enforcement; (2) many of the extraneous duties are not related to law enforcement; and (3) personnel policies result in a high degree of amateurism in an office that requires professionals.[29] Some have suggested that the sheriff function as a process-server for the court and maintain the jail but surrender law enforcement duties to more expert agencies.

Constable

The constable is a sort of sheriff with duties inside the county. This officer is appointed in a few states but elected in most instances by the voters of a town, township, or precinct. The constable generally has duties or responsibilities within an electoral subdivision. As keeper of the peace, however, this officer has county-wide authority in some states and may act independently of other enforcement officers. Constables have actually undertaken raids on illegal establishments overlooked by urban police and sheriffs. The constable consistently acts as executive officer and process-server for minor courts or justices of the peace. Compensation is usually through fees. The constable is only a part-time public functionary, and, like the J.P., is tending to disappear from the civic landscape. A survey of nine states has demonstrated the trend toward disappearance of the constable. Of the 8,600 constable positions authorized, only 2,500 were filled.[30]

Coroner and jury

The coroner is also a local lay official, although somewhat more outmoded than the sheriff or constable. A popularly elected county officer in many states, the coroner investigates the cause of death occurring in the absence of witnesses and under circumstances indicating the possible use of unlawful means. The coroner may have the power of assembling a jury, usually of six laypersons, to conduct an inquest and render an official report on the testimony and findings. A few states, with Massachusetts as pioneer, have replaced the coroner with a local medical examiner, and the practice of choosing physicians for the office or adding medical personnel to the coroner's staff has been adopted as an improvement. Much of the work formerly performed by the local coroner is now handled by central state agencies or bureaus of analysis, investigation, and identification, as indicated earlier in this chapter.

City Police Department

Cities have most officers

Urban police departments constitute the most important instruments of law enforcement and public safety in the United States today. City police officers outnumber all other state and local enforcement officers combined. Urban protective vigilance must function around the clock, for its population is always on the move. Aside from directly combating crime and criminals, the city police must give constant attention to a moderate regimentation of the whole process of life, work, and play within its jurisdiction in order to prevent utter confusion. For example, multitudes of individuals leaving an auditorium or stadium require traffic direction, even if all the individuals should have the most saintly intentions. If fire damage leaves collapsible walls or buildings endangering life, the police must get on the job to protect the innocent and unsuspecting from jeopardy. The processes of urban civilization in the technological age make it necessary for the police to provide guidance and assistance for the obedient as well as force and compulsion for the disobedient.

Modern police departments are organized and operated through functional divisions in order to make use of specialized training and experience for efficient service. Traffic regulation as an expanding function calls for the concentrated attention of one branch or bureau of the force. Another task is performed by regular police patrols who move on foot or by motor to protect life and property and arrest lawbreakers. For every large or important city there is a separate division of detectives working quietly and in plain clothes to track down crime and criminals. Every such city must also have a headquarters staff that includes officers or employees for general records service, internal housekeeping, and other routine activity.

Operate in divisions

Federal Support Services

In recent years the federal government has become increasingly involved in efforts to improve the standards and performance of police personnel at the state and local levels. The Federal Bureau of Investigation has for many years conducted training courses for selected state and local officers. Its National Crime Information Center (NCIC), with highly sophisticated computer storage and retrieval of criminal information, provides a high-speed law enforcement communication and data-exchange network for the United States and Canada.

FBI offers aid

On an operational level, the federal agencies exercising quasi-police powers cooperate extensively with state and local authorities in combating crimes falling within the jurisdiction of all levels of government. A vivid example of this cooperation was a California-wide sweep by federal and local authorities in 1984 that netted some 2,000 fugitives. Detectives from local police departments were deputized as U.S. marshals to give them arrest powers throughout the state. Included in the net were 14 murderers, 10 people charged with murder, and 666 burglars and robbers. Similar joint federal-local operations were conducted in Miami, New York, Los Angeles, and Washington.[31]

All levels cooperate

Following the riots of the late 1960s, the federal Law Enforcement and Assistance Administration (LEAA) was formed to dispense federal grants-in-aid for the improvement of the state and local criminal justice systems, including law enforcement. Block grants were given to state governments and disbursed pursuant to a plan formulated by committees of representatives of all segments of criminal justice. In a number of states, LEAA funds were used as a "pork barrel" for all of the competing interests, sometimes to soothe politics rather than cope with crime. When crime rates continued to rise along with the federal anti-crime funds, the federal policymakers became disenchanted and the program was phased out. Only time will tell whether the Los Angeles riots in 1992 will stimulate another round of federal aid to local law enforcement.

Federal grants disappear

The Drama of Justice

The drama of justice begins when a police officer makes an arrest. Arrests can be made when a crime is committed in the presence of an officer or the officer has probable cause to believe that a crime has been committed by the person involved. Under other circumstances, the officer must obtain written authority (warrant) to arrest from a judge by setting forth facts personally known or substantiated by a complaint signed

Securing an arrest

by a citizen who alleges a crime. Only about 10 percent of all arrests are made on the basis of warrants; the remaining 90 percent are made by police officers using their discretion. Which acts will they overlook? Who will they arrest?

The answers to these questions were discovered in a three-state study conducted by Wayne R. LaFave. He found that police tend not to enforce laws based on vague statutes, laws that have a tradition of nonenforcement, offenses that are trivial, situations where the victim and the perpetrator are relatives, and crime in which the accused is willing to help the police solve other crimes.[32]

Adversaries: Prosecutor and Defender

Prosecutors   Responsibility for prosecution of crimes is vested in the local prosecutor, usually a county official, who is commonly chosen by the electorate for a four-year term. Local prosecutors have a variety of titles, including prosecuting attorney, solicitor, states attorney, district attorney, and county attorney. In larger jurisdictions, the prosecutor is a full-time employee; in smaller jurisdictions, it may be a part-time responsibility worked in with a regular legal practice. Among the motives attributed to attorneys who go into the prosecutor's office are the quest for higher office or an opportunity to augment a beginning or lean law practice.

Theoretically, public prosecution is supposed to serve at all times the ends of objective justice, not partisan injustice. However, a criminal case in court tends to become an adversarial game in which the prosecuting attorney seeks to win on his or her own terms, leaving the defense to look out for itself or take the consequences. Wealthy or professional criminals are able to meet the prosecution with equal or su-

Uneven competition in   perior legal talent, whereas many other defendants may be handicapped in this respect.
Courts   The constitutional requirements that defense counsel be furnished, at public expense if necessary, has often been inadequate since lawyers appointed by the court are often unequal to the opposition in ability or experience. Some convicts have won new trials on the ground that they did not have adequate counsel. To meet this dilemma, a number of jurisdictions have set up the office of public defender, putting this regular official on a par with the prosecuting attorney before the court. Connecticut and Rhode Island were the first states to require the public defender system on a statewide basis. Their example has been followed by a number of states. In jurisdictions lacking the volume for maintaining a full-time defense attorney, defense work has been obtained through annual contracts with regular law firms. However, many areas still rely on court appointments on a random basis.

Procedural Scenes

Preliminary hearing.

Following arrest, the accused is brought before a judicial officer who hears the evidence and decides whether or not the person should be formally charged by a grand jury or "information."

Bail.

If the person is to be held on the basis of the evidence, the judge sets bail, an amount stated in cash that must be posted with the court to assure that the accused will be available for further action. The amount of bail is usually determined by the serious-ness of the offense and the likelihood of the accused disappearing.

Making the charge.

The two most common methods by which states bring charges against alleged perpe-trators of crimes are the grand jury and information. In the grand jury method, a panel of citizens is called to hear the prosecuting attorney present the evidence and to decide whether or not an indictment ought to be made. Since members of grand juries are laypeople who may have never served before, they tend to follow the advice of the prosecuting attorney. Unknown to many jurors, they also have the authority to conduct investigations on their own. Under the information method, the prosecuting attorney brings the case before a judge who reviews the evidence and approves the charge.

Grand juries and information

Arraignment and plea.

Once the formal charges are made, the accused is brought before the judge and the formal charges are read. The defendant then pleads to the charges. If the defendant pleads guilty, the trial process is avoided and the court is then free to pronounce its judgment.

Plea bargaining.

As often as not, the next step in the process is plea bargaining, a negotiation between the prosecutor and the defense over the charge that has been brought. If neither side has an undisputed case, the defense will offer to plead guilty if the prosecutor will agree to reduce the charge. When an agreement has been struck, it will be brought to the judge for consent. Plea bargaining has become popular because it provides benefits for all actors. By pleading guilty to a lesser charge, the accused escapes the danger of being convicted of a more serious offense carrying a stiffer sentence, prosecutors are able to clear cases more rapidly and avoid the risk of losing, judges are able to prevent conges-tion in their courtrooms, and local governments are spared the expense of a long costly trial. The public remains skeptical of the system, however, suspecting that plea bar-gaining is merely following the course of least resistance to the benefit of the "criminal element." Although the Alaska Attorney General has banned plea bargaining between defense attorneys and prosecutors in criminal cases, Professor Otwin Marenin reports that plea bargaining in Alaska has not disappeared—"charge bargaining" continues.[33] Furthermore, the Alaska justice system differs from other states in important ways and Marenin urges caution in applying the Alaska experience in other states.

Negotiating for a guilty plea

Trial by jury.

If no plea bargain is made, the case goes to trial. At the option of the accused, the trial may be conducted before a judge or a jury. The right of trial by jury has been handed down for centuries. It is designed to ensure amateur and indigenous qualities in the performance of justice and prevent external or tyrannical professionalism. The trial jury, known as petty or petit jury, usually consists of 12 persons drawn from the juris-diction of the court. The Supreme Court in 1970 ruled that a jury of less than 12 members meets the Constitution's guarantee of a trial by jury. Both federal civil trials

Use of small juries

and a few states now use smaller juries. Potential jurors are selected from a large list of eligible voters, freeholders, or taxpayers, with some gaining automatic excuse or discretionary excuse from the judge for occupational or urgent personal reasons. Further screening is undertaken for a particular trial, eliminating those with a formed

Removing biased jurors

opinion or known prejudice in the case, as well as those with interest in the outcome through kinship or other close affiliation with a party to the suit. Finally, each side is allowed a limited number of peremptory challenges for disqualification. This prerogative is often exercised to the full extent by the counsel on each side in important criminal trials. Days may be required for the process of selecting and qualifying a jury for a highly publicized criminal trial.

The trial jury exercises the important role of passing upon the truthfulness and weight of evidence for the determination of the verdict, with guidance from the judge as to the meaning of the law and the significance of the evidence in so far as the jury finds it to be true. The jury, not the judge, establishes guilt or innocence and, in civil cases, grants or denies the claims of the plaintiff.

Traditionally the jury verdict must be unanimous, but unanimity has been re-

Nonunanimous verdicts permitted

moved in several states for civil cases and in a few for criminal cases. In a 5–4 decision in 1972, the Supreme Court held that unanimous jury verdicts are not required for state criminal convictions, except when the jury consists of no more than six persons. The two states involved in this decision were Louisiana, permitting 9–3 votes, and Oregon, permitting 10–2 votes for conviction. The opinion of dissenting justices pointed to the incongruity of the continued requirements of unanimous verdicts in federal courts to protect property rights, while permitting state courts to deprive a person of liberty with only a majority verdict.

A few states require a unanimous verdict only for sentence of death or life imprisonment. If a jury fails to reach a required unanimous verdict, the result is a mistrial, with choice to the prosecution of retrying or dropping the case.

Sentencing: The Judgment of the Court

Prior to the American Revolution, judges were free to determine sentences without legislative restrictions. Because of their cruel and arbitrary treatment of the convicted, sentiment grew to fix sentences legislatively so that punishment was related to the se-

Where twelve months is seldom a year

riousness of the crime. Fixed sentences soon filled the prisons, however, so the idea of reducing sentences for *good time,* a reward for being a good prisoner, became popular at the same time as the idea that prisons ought to rehabilitate prisoners. Since the degree of rehabilitation cannot be predicted by a judge at the time of sentencing, indeterminate sentences, such as five to ten years for robbery, were developed so that parole boards could fix sentences later when the prisoner's progress could be measured.[34] However, indeterminate sentencing became suspect in the 1970s and 1980s as

Fixed sentences returning

a mechanism by which judges and parole boards were letting criminals back on the street too soon. Beginning in 1976, Maine reinstituted fixed sentencing and by 1983 eight other states eliminated the discretionary releasing power of parole boards.[35] By 1990 mandatory prison sentences had been instituted in the great majority of states for violent crimes, habitual offenders, narcotics, and the use of gun in crime.[36]

A number of states have reduced judicial discretion by establishing sentencing guidelines for the court. Sentencing guidelines consider the severity of the offense along with the offender's criminal record and background.

In cases of capital crime, where the death penalty is a possibility, state courts are required to be particularly careful. As discussed in chapter 4, in 1972 the U.S. Supreme Court held that the death penalty was "cruel and unusual" punishment as it was being applied by states. To meet Supreme Court objections, three-fourths of the states quickly reenacted their capital punishment laws, removing factors of arbitrariness. Imposing the death penalty became a two-step process: first, the determination of guilt; second, the imposition of the death penalty. Even though state laws may pass U.S. Supreme Court interpretation of the Eighth Amendment, they still must meet the demands of their own constitutions. In 1984, the California and Massachusetts supreme courts invalidated death penalty legislation on the basis of provisions of state constitutions.[37] California voters quickly reversed this decision both by initiated constitutional amendment and by removing three state supreme court justices in their 1986 retention vote. The California court now has one of the highest rates of death penalty approval of any state.

Death penalty returns

Although the nation continues to be divided on the many emotional issues related to capital punishment, most political decisions during the 1980s and early 1990s have come down on the side of "getting tough" on criminals. In spite of arguments that capital punishment has not been proven to be a deterrent to crime and is administered with strong bias against minorities and the poor, popular majorities strongly support the position that murderers sentenced to life imprisonment are all too frequently back on the streets menacing society again after only a few years in prison. Even when the sentence is the death penalty, appeal after appeal and delay after delay in the actual execution have been cited by proponents of capital punishment as the reason it seems not to be a deterrent (See figure 12.3). With more than 2,400 prisoners living on death row in 1991, and an average of more than eight years' delay between trial and execution, it is no wonder that political support has grown for limiting judicial discretion in such matters as sentencing and repeated appeals.

Appeals and delays

Even though the sentencing parameters of judges have been reduced, judges still often have the option of incarceration or probation. For first offenders or minor infractions, judges may feel that incarceration would inhibit rather than aid rehabilitation. Consequently, they will refrain from sentencing the offender and impose a period of probation during which the offender is expected to behave in an exemplary fashion, avoiding associations and conduct of a criminal nature. If the offender violates the terms of probation, the judge can terminate probation and send the person to prison.

Appealing the Verdict

A disappointed party in a civil suit or a party convicted of crime may wish to appeal the case to a higher court in hopes of getting the decision of the lower court set aside. The state or prosecution cannot appeal a verdict of acquittal, although a chronic criminal may be held for another trial on a different offense. Before appeals can be accepted by an appellate court, justification must be furnished, such as errors or improper procedures in the conduct of the trial. If sufficient grounds for appeal can be furnished, the attorneys on both sides file briefs and argue the case before an appellate court of several judges that sits without a jury. After due consideration, the appellate court may uphold or reverse the original decision, or if it finds errors in procedure, it may send

Appealing cases

Figure 12.3
Appeals and delays in
carrying out the death
penalty have resulted in an
average lapse of eight years
between trial and execution.
*(Reprinted by permission:
Tribune Media Services.)*

the case back to the lower court for retrial. If the appellant loses at the intermediate
level, that may well exhaust use of the judicial hierarchy since most states with intermediate courts restrict the right of appeal beyond this point. It is then up to the state
supreme court to decide whether or not it wishes to consider the case. In states without
the intermediate tier of appellate courts, the state supreme court handles all appeals.

Incarceration

The prisons having the least concern with problems of human restoration are normally
the city and county jails, which serve primarily for the retention of accused persons
pending trial and sentence or other disposition of their cases. Such retention is not
technical punishment, however unpleasant it may be, and is not to be associated with
"hard labor." In many instances, however, short terms of punishment are served in such
jails, sometimes by persons who serve time for lack of funds to pay fines. Because most
juvenile court jurisdictions lack detention facilities other than city jails or police lockups,
thousands of children are held each year in these adult jails.

*Problem of constructive
employment*

The central state penitentiaries are often superior to local jails and workhouses
in scientific management and treatment of prisoners, although many state systems are
inferior to federal institutions in this respect. All have difficulty in providing useful and
constructive employment for those who are serving a sentence. Under various state and

federal statutes, prison labor must not be used for the direct production of merchandise for the channels of commerce. It is often utilized for turning out items for state purposes, such as equipment and supplies for government offices or for state institutions. Penitentiary farms may provide food for the prisoners, who cultivate the crops and attend the livestock. This activity competes only indirectly with free labor, and it serves to keep the prisoners from idleness. Prisoners also have limited opportunities for vocational training, reading, recreation, and entertainment. The best or largest of the penitentiaries are likely to have competent counselors, including chaplains, medical officers, and psychiatrists, as well as trained wardens. Serious cases of mental illness may be transferred to a special division of the state mental hospital.

The outbreak of bloody prison riots in Attica, New York (1971), and Santa Fe, New Mexico (1980), sharpened the social consciousness of the federal judiciary. Measuring the conditions in many local jails and state penitentiaries against "cruel and unusual punishment" in the Eighth Amendment, the U.S. Supreme Court found many incarceration facilities inadequate. With many facilities packed beyond their capacities by the tougher sentencing laws, by 1983 the courts had declared unconstitutional the entire prison systems of seven states and had ordered correction of one or more facilities in most of the other states.[38] A number of temporary steps were taken to prevent the issuance of judicial orders releasing prisoners en masse. In some states, prisoners were transferred to local jails; in a number of states, sentences of less serious offenders were shortened to make room for new prisoners; in other states, judges were putting prisoners on probation. However, the mood of the public seemed not of a nature to accept these as permanent policies, so prison construction was underway in earnest in states under court directives. State spending for prison renovation and expansion became the fastest growing part of state budgets in the 1980s, including state aid for local corrections programs. Virtually every state built new prisons during this decade.

Many jails in violation of Eighth Amendment

The prison population was growing faster than construction, however. By 1990, with record rates of violent crime and a tougher attitude on sentencing and paroling, the United States at all levels of government had more than one million people behind bars, an all-time record. The rate of imprisonment—426 of every 100,000 Americans in prison or jail—was even higher than South Africa (333) and the Soviet Union (268), and far above rates in Europe (ranging from 35 to 120) and Asia (21 to 140).[39] The U.S. Supreme Court set a much tougher standard in 1991 for prison inmates to prove that unfit prison living conditions are unconstitutional cruel and unusual punishment.[40] The decision in an Ohio case rested on an "intent requirement" specifying that prisoners must show that officials acted with "deliberate indifference" to create circumstances that violate the Eighth Amendment. This decision eases some of the pressure for massive new prison expenditures, but the growing prison population still constitutes heavy pressure (Figure 12.4).

Record prison population

Theories of Punishment

The 50 states have a wide variety of prisons and correctional systems, based on several theories of crime and punishment in relationship to the nature of people. These theories are not mutually exclusive but overlap slightly with varied emphasis when applied to the multitudinous jurisdictions. Four of them should be noted.

Figure 12.4

Many old, crowded state prisons have been found in violation of the Eighth Amendment protection against cruel and unusual punishment, leading to an extensive building program throughout the United States. Prisons in a majority of states were under court mandates to provide more room or release prisoners.

1. Revenge

There is the old theory that revenge should be visited by society upon the guilty persons, holding them solely and individually responsible for their errors and compelling them to pay their debt to society on the basis of an eye for an eye, a tooth for a tooth, a life for a life.

2. Deterrence

Closely related to the revenge theory is the general demand that punishment be sure, adequately severe, and sufficiently conspicuous to deter others from crime, regardless of inclination. This idea calls for a calculated matching of crime and punishment, with large penalties to check large crimes and small penalties to check smaller violations.

3. Protect society

There is the strong insistence that criminals be segregated behind walls in order to protect society from further violations by them until they learn their lesson.

4. Rehabilitation

There is a complex theory, with a modern socio-scientific bias, that assumes that society owes a debt of rehabilitation to lawbreakers who are socially maladjusted and victims of circumstances beyond their control. These circumstances may be physical, physiological, mental, economic, or social, and ultimately deny to the individual the role of free agent. The theory of reform or rehabilitation has been particularly applied in recent times to juvenile offenders, but it is also taken seriously by many authorities and institutional officers in the treatment of adults.

Most crimes by repeaters

Yet it must be said that penal institutions have only limited success in curing criminals of criminal tendencies, of checking the adage of once a convict, always a convict. More than 60 percent of the nation's federal and state convicts commit crimes after prison release, and 85 percent of all crimes in the United States are committed by repeaters. This cycle of crime has led some to describe jails as "factories of crime" and prisons as "colleges for advanced criminal education." Most recommendations for reform urge refocusing corrections on rehabilitation by more effective community-based treatment, expanded education and vocational training, and increased programs and facilities for work release.

The emphasis on the philosophy of correction rather than punishment has gained wider acceptance for the institutional treatment of juvenile offenders than of adult lawbreakers. For more than a century, leaders and organizations have urged sympathetic attention to delinquent children, matching the movement for more humane care of the mentally ill. State reformatories for boys and girls often function under the name of *training school, trade school,* or *industrial school,* and seek to measure up to the name. Their task is not easy, for many of the juvenile delinquents have mental limitations or emotional problems that cannot be overcome through institutional care. Furthermore, these institutions are not uniformly modern in methods and types of administrators.

Juvenile delinquency

Private and public agencies are attentive to methods of readjustment of problem children before the stage is reached for assignment to the reformatory. Through the development and training of social workers, many city school systems have visiting teachers to deal personally and individually with pupils who are falling down in work, attendance, or behavior. These professional workers have ways of getting to the root of the trouble, whether it be poverty, loneliness, a broken home, or other difficulties, and of providing help before it is too late. Probation officers attached to local juvenile courts may also provide constructive assistance. Different service groups and clubs aid in the work of reducing or preventing juvenile delinquency.

Though the federal government has indicated great interest in controlling crime in the 1980s and 1990s, over 90 percent of the personnel and money used to combat crime is in state and local governments. Courts and criminal justice have remained substantially state domains, even in the face of a nationalizing society. The burden carried by state, county, and municipal governments for criminal justice varies considerably among states. On the whole, 53 cents of every criminal justice dollar goes for police protection, most of it provided by municipal governments. Maintenance of the courts has been a state—county shared cost, with recent court reforms forcing states to assume a greater share of the costs. Corrections have been primarily a state burden.[41] With the increasing costs of law enforcement, courts, and corrections, the criminal justice system has become a major policy and budgetary concern for state and local governments in the 1990s.

Crime control a state, local function

Endnotes

1. Craig F. Emmert and Carol Ann Traut, "A Quantitative Analysis of the New Judicial Federalism," a paper presented at the annual meeting of the American Political Science Association, San Francisco, August 30–September 2, 1990.

2. Sandra Day O'Connor, "Our Judicial Federalism," *Intergovernmental Perspective,* 15 (Summer, 1989), pp. 8–12, and Kenneth G. Pankey, Jr., "The State of the Judiciary," *Book of the States, 1992–93* (Lexington, KY: Council of State Governments, 1992), pp. 210–226.

3. Samuel K. Gove and James D. Nowlan, "State Courts in State Politics: Illinois," and Diane D. Blair, "State Courts in State Politics: Arkansas," two papers presented to the

annual meeting of the American Political Science Association, San Francisco, August 30–September 2, 1990. Gove and Nowlan state that ". . . for many people, litigation is another way of waging a political battle."

4. Stuart S. Nagel, "Political Party Affiliation and Judges' Decisions," *American Political Science Review* 55 (December 1961): 845.

5. Lawrence Baum, "Partisan Considerations and Voting Decisions in Nonpartisan Judicial Elections," a paper presented at the annual meeting of the American Political Science Association, August 30–September 2, 1990. See also: David Moon, "What You Use Depends on What You Have: Information Effects on the Determinants of Electoral Choice," *American Politics Quarterly,* 18 (Spring, 1990), pp. 3–24; David M. Jones, "Ideology and Judicial Elections in Wisconsin," *Comparative State Politics,* 10 (August, 1989), pp. 6–8; and John T. Wold and John H. Culver, "The Defeat of the California Justices: The Campaign, the Electorate, and the Issue of Judicial Accountability," *Judicature,* 70 (1990), pp. 348–355.

6. Information on the qualifications, terms, and salaries of the judiciary was obtained from the *Book of the States 1992–93,* pp. 244–245.

7. Ernest J. Watts, "Judicial Education and Training," *The Improvement of the Administration of Justice,* pp. 99–101.

8. *North* v. *Russell* 427 U.S. 328 (1976).

9. Linda Silberman, "The State of the Art," *The Improvement of the Administration of Justice,* p. 256.

10. Ibid., p. 259.

11. Barry Mahoney and Harvey E. Solomon, "Court Administration," *The Improvement of the Administration of Justice,* p. 49.

12. James J. Alfine, "Judicial Evaluation Polls," *The Improvement of the Administration of Justice,* p. 86.

13. Ibid., p. 94–95.

14. Only three states are identified as "not reformed" (Arkansas, Tennessee, and New York) by Deborah J. Barrow, Gerald W. Johnson, and Robert S. Montjoy, in their study of "The Politics and Economics of State Court Reform: Alabama and the State Court Reform Movement," a paper presented at the annual meeting of the Southern Political Science Association in Atlanta, Georgia, November, 1988.

15. A study by Herbert Jacob and Robert Lineberry cited in the *National Civic Review* 71 (May 1982): 263.

16. Ted Gest, "Women Expand Their Roles in Crime, Too, "*U.S. News and World Report* (November 12, 1984): 62.

17. John McCormick and Bill Turque, "Big Crimes, Small Cities," *Newsweek,* June 10, 1991, p. 19.

18. Arkansas *Gazette,* June 19, 1991. The report, showing a continued increasing in violent crime in urban states, was released as Committee Chairman Joseph Biden (D - Del.) promoted the proposed Rural Crime and Drug Control Act of 1991.

19. William S. Sessions, Director, Federal Bureau of Investigation, "Law Enforcement and the Community: Illegal Drugs and Violent Crime," an address before the Annual Law and Society Banquet, Charlotte, NC, February 22, 1991.

20. *The Gallup Report No. 210,* The Gallup Poll, Princeton, NJ (March 1983): 3.

21. "StateLine," *State Legislatures* 8 (November/December 1982): 2.

22. Norm Sims, "Mandatory Prison Sentences," *State Government News* 25 (April 1982): 8.

23. *Gallup Report 210,* p. 3.

24. Debra Collins, ed. "Fear of Crime Afflicts America," *National Civic Review* 69 (November 1980): 572–573.

25. *The Gallup Report No. 215,* The Gallup Poll, Princeton, NJ (August 1983): 3.

26. Andrew Jones, "How Crime Stoppers Stop Crime," *The Readers Digest* 64 (January 1985): 7–8.

27. *Public Administration Times,* April 1, 1991.

28. See Mindy Haynes, "Compensating the Victim," *State Legislatures* 7 (November/December 1981): 11–77; and "Victim Assistance Changing Justice" in the *National Civic Review* 72 (July/August 1983): 387.

29. U.S. Advisory Commission Intergovernmental Relations, *State—Local Relations in the Criminal Justice System* A-38 (Washington, DC: Government Printing Office, 1975), pp. 159–161.

30. Ibid., p. 161.

31. Robert Lindsey, New York *Times* report carried by Grand Forks (ND) *Herald,* March 17, 1984.

32. Wayne R. LaFave, *Arrest: The Decision to Take a Suspect into Custody* (Boston: Little, Brown and Company, 1965), pp. 83–143.

33. Otwin Marenin, "The State of Plea Bargaining in Alaska," *Alaska Justice Forum* 7 (Spring, 1990), pp. 1, 6–10.

34. See *Definite Sentencing,* a report by the Council of State Governments, Lexington, KY, 1976, Jack D. Foster, project director.

35. U.S. Department of Justice, *Bureau of Justice Statistics BULLETIN* (Washington, DC: Government Printing Office, 1983), p. 2.

36. For annual update on this and other kinds of criminal justice statistics *see:* U.S. Department of Justice, Bureau of Justice Statistics. *Sourcebook of Criminal Justice Statistics* (yearly) (Washington, DC: Government Printing Office).

37. *Law Week* 53 (Washington, DC: Bureau of National Standards), November 27, 1984, pp. 1082–1083.

38. U.S. Department of Justice, *Report to the Nation on Crime and Justice* (Washington, DC: Government Printing Office, 1983), p. 80.

39. Based on a study by "The Sentencing Project" reported by Associated Press in the *Arkansas Gazette,* January 5, 1991.

40. *Wilson* v. *Seiter* 111 S. Ct. 2321 (1991).

41. U.S. Department of Justice, *Report to the Nation,* p. 89.

CHAPTER 13

LOCAL GOVERNMENT I

Sharing State Power Through Political Subdivisions

The illusion of three levels

In the minds of most citizens, the structure of the American governmental system consists of three levels—national, state, and local. This idea of three legally distinct levels, each somewhat supreme in its own sphere, is reinforced by the authority of the people to elect their own officials locally, the power of local governing boards to adopt ordinances, and the obligation to finance governmental functions through local taxes. Despite this extensive local policy-making, however, local governments are viewed quite differently in constitutions, statutes, and courts.

From the constitutional point of view, only two tiers of government exist and have standing—the national government and the state government. Theoretically, by establishing the national government through a written Constitution, the people of the United States have delegated their sovereignty in specific areas to the central government. All undelegated powers, not otherwise denied by the U.S. Constitution, reside in the states and the people. At the state level, the people, exercising their sovereignty, ordain a state government and outline the distribution of power through the state constitution. Even though most state constitutions provide for local governments, none of the sovereignty of the people is delegated to them and they remain as creations of the state. Local governments, with allowances for the real "de facto" power that some enjoy, are

Creatures of the state

"creatures of the state" that may be created and abolished by the state.[1]

The Rationale for Local Governments

The royal grants of land that eventually became the colonies preceded immigration. Therefore, the general authority was established before local governments came into existence. As colonists came, they brought the traditional forms of English local government and tailored them to function in the environs of the new frontier. With very little technology in transportation or communication, geography became a major factor

Geography shapes governments

in the initial design and use of local governments. In New England, where natives, land, and climate were all hostile, fearful immigrants huddled together and used the

Title photo: This majestic dual-towered structure in downtown Minneapolis is the Hennepin County Government Center. (Photo courtesy of the Hennepin County Public Affairs Department.)

town as the basic unit of governance. In the more friendly environs of the South, people could safely separate themselves by larger cuts of land and use the larger county as the basic unit of local government. By the end of the 1700s, the various forms of local governments in existence had substantially taken on many of the characteristics seen in them today. As people moved west in the 1800s and 1900s, they continued to adapt the eastern local governments to the demands of the west. Only in recent decades has urbanization forced a reanalysis of traditional forms of government, though most critics would say that little progress has been made in redesigning local governments for the unique needs of the 1990s.

The presence of native Americans, many of whom resented and opposed the invasion of the Europeans, forced settlers to think of local governments in terms of security. Thus, a major function of the local government for the first three centuries of the white man was defense. The eventual resolution of conflicts with Indians and with the colonial powers of Europe may have eliminated defense as a function of local government, but local governments continue to exist for a variety of other reasons.

Local governments serve many purposes

Local governments serve as vehicles for self-determination. Generally speaking, the American political culture nurtures a high level of citizen efficacy that requires opportunities for expression in governmental decision-making. Every jurisdiction includes people who feel strongly about influencing and controlling the governments that affect them. Local governments may be creatures of the state, but constitutions and legislatures recognize the rights of self-government at the local level by permitting election of officials whose duties include the administration of state laws. Locally elected means locally responsive; it also means applications of the state laws in conformance with local desires, traditions, and customs, within legal parameters. State law may require a local sheriff to enforce the criminal code but local opinions will influence the manner in which the sheriff carries out the responsibility. State laws requiring education of children are subject to similar local modifications.

1. Self-determination

Local governments provide optional governmental services. Local discretion in the provision of certain services will vary with the type of local government, with school districts and counties having fewer options than municipalities. Nevertheless, state laws include a plethora of options for general governments. Cities may be required to enforce the state criminal code but they may choose whether or not to have an ambulance service, a historical association, public transportation, or even a park system. Counties may be required to record the ownership of all tracts of property but they may choose to provide recreation, refuse collection, senior citizen services, or a rodent control program. By having these options available, local governments are able to respond to the particular interests and desires of their respective constituencies.

2. Provide services

Local governments mediate and resolve conflicts on a local level. As indicated in an earlier chapter, the institutions of government serve as forums in which competing groups can seek resolution of their differences. While state legislatures and executives deal with conflicts of statewide concern, local governments furnish the means of mediating conflicts of a more local nature. Differences arising out of political philosophy, religious beliefs, or economic circumstances creep into the debates in county commissions and city councils. Even when agreement is reached that roads ought to be hard-surfaced, the question of "whose road first" will require negotiation before any roads can be improved.

3. Resolve local conflicts

Local governments are strongly supported because they provide political, economic, or social advantages. Support is strongest and most vocal on the part of those

4. Enable some to keep advantages

who benefit most by those advantages. A major reason for separate incorporation of suburbs when municipal services are already available in a neighboring city is the desire of influential people to establish and retain control of government. Metropolitan reformers who seek a political unification of municipalities into one metropolitan government may provide irrefutable proof that the new system of government will be more efficient and more effective. However, suburbanites will resist, with their intransigence based primarily on the desire to retain political control. Likewise, county reformers are stymied when all evidence suggests that county consolidation is the only rational course for the future and yet the county power structure resists change. Even officials in townships and miniscule municipalities, decimated by shifting population, cling to governments that fail to meet any of the criteria for a viable government. A fatal flaw in most reform movements is the failure to recognize the intensity of belief by the beneficiaries of present governmental structures that their strong self-interest lies in preserving the status quo.

5. Laboratories of government

Local governments serve as laboratories of government. Municipalities and counties with home rule powers have opportunities to create new responses to old service problems. As examples, a city may decide to turn its fire-fighting function over to a private company on contract and thus become a test site for a new method of securing fire protection. Or perhaps a county will serve as an umbrella agency for managing the water systems for all cities and townships in the county. Other units, such as special districts, are too restricted to take on new approaches. On the basis of innovative experiences, local governments exchange information on the successes and failures of their experiments.

6. Train officials

Local governments are training schools for higher governments. Many state legislators and executives, not to mention large numbers of federal officials, began their political careers by serving as members of school boards, county commissions, city councils, or local executive agencies. Here, they first learned the intricacies of government under law, how to function with other officials, and the art of negotiation and compromise. After a term of apprenticeship, they moved up to state positions where they are required to apply their knowledge to the laws affecting local governments. If state service is the prep school for the federal government, then local government is certainly the grammar school for all levels.

7. Intergovernmental representation

Local governments are intergovernmental representatives of local interests. Just as state officials voice economic and social concerns for statewide interests at interstate and national forums, local officials reflect the aspirations and desires of their respective communities to officials at other levels of government. A county executive may prevail upon the state economic development agency for assistance in developing an industrial park for local businesses; a mayor may represent the city in securing federal grants or influencing national policies; or a township supervisor may appear before the county governing board to ask for a drainage system for his constituents. Local officials will use their offices to reflect nongovernmental interests, such as petitions to economic interests to locate in their jurisdictions, or expressions to legislatures pleading a case for senior citizens, or forming a delegation to a parent company in Chicago with the request not to close a plant in Northacres Township.

8. Provides base for parties

Local governments provide a base for the political party system. Many function with a nonpartisan ballot that uncouples party politics from their activities, but many others—especially counties—continue to nurture the party system through partisan electoral systems. With local offices and limited patronage available as rewards and stepping stones for political activity, local governments provide much of the foundation of the two-party system. As noted in chapter 7, the county is the strongest, most universal building block upon which political parties are built. The presence of political rewards gives parties vitality and vigor at the county level.

Local governments are an administrative convenience for the state. Just as the federal government relies heavily on state governments to provide the administrative machinery for implementation of federal programs, state governments look to cities, counties, towns, townships, and special districts to bring state programs to the people. State legislatures may define the crimes but it takes the local law enforcement officials to put teeth into the criminal laws. Both the federal and state governments may propose to bring welfare services to needy people, but county or city social workers actually knock on the doors and make the on-site determinations of need. States decide that children shall be educated, but the local school districts provide the buildings and much of the resources required to serve the children. Modern technology has made possible the centralization or consolidation of some administrative functions but the number of local employees engaged in delivering state and federal services is still significant. *9. Convenient for state*

Some local governments exist merely as the result of tradition. When measurements of viability are used to determine the legitimacy of continuing a local government, hundreds of "ghost" governments are found unable to furnish services or unable to provide a rational explanation for their existence. Even though they would never be able to come into existence under prevailing laws, they continue to exist because "we've always had a town," or "the township has been here for as long as I can remember." Perhaps, it is more than tradition. It may simply be the need of human beings for identification with a geographic place. At any rate, it is a place they will defend, and as long as they're willing to defend it, it will linger as a government. *10. Tradition*

A careful review of this digest of reasons for the existence of local governments will reveal that certain functions or reasons are more applicable to some types of local governments than others. In some governments, political control may be more important to the people concerned than the ability to deliver services. Some local governments exist more for the convenience of the state than to exercise local options or serve as laboratories for testing new procedures. A better application of these differences can be achieved once the different types of local governments have been discussed.

Types of Local Governments

A working definition of *government* is not so essential to the understanding of state governments as it is to local governments, because state governments clearly manifest the characteristics of government. However, in the jungles of local government, it is not always easy to distinguish the "creatures of the state" from the robots. Since each state government responds to changing governmental needs in its own way, legislatures design a variety of administrative forms, with one state using a local government and another creating an "authority." Because 50 mills are grinding out the local government designs, the U.S. Bureau of Census has been compelled to develop and apply *States grind out designs* some criteria for determining whether authorities or districts are in fact governments or merely administrative subunits of another government.

Census bureau defines government

According to the Census Bureau, to be counted as a government, local entities must possess three basic attributes: (1) existence as an organized entity, (2) governmental character, and (3) substantial autonomy.[2] To demonstrate existence as an organized entity, the unit must have some form of organization and corporate powers, such as a name, the right to sue, power to contract, authority to own property, and the like. Governmental character is reflected in officers who are popularly elected or appointed by public officials, responsibility to the public, power to levy property taxes, power to incur debt, and performance of a function considered governmental in nature. Substantial independence consists of considerable fiscal and administrative autonomy, especially authority to budget, set taxes, fix fees, go into debt, or conduct programs without review by another government.

By applying these criteria, it is possible to determine whether or not a government exists in an airport authority supervised by a board whose budget must be approved by a county budget committee before incorporation into the general tax levy of the county.

Two classes of local government

Local governments fall into two general classes—general governments and special governments. The class of general governments includes those entities vested with a number of governmental functions. This class includes municipalities, counties, townships, and towns. Special governments are commonly special districts and are usually created to perform a single governmental function. Districts for schools constitute the lion's share of this class but the category also includes numerous other functions, such as airport districts, health districts, park districts, transit districts, and water districts, to name just a few.

General Governments

1. Counties

Counties are found in all states except Connecticut and Rhode Island, although facsimilies are called boroughs in Alaska and parishes in Louisiana. Basic to understanding the role of counties in the families of governments is the legal premise that they are established primarily for the administrative convenience of the state and their basic functions are state functions administered on a local level. In recent years, however, states have given counties broader authority in the performance of state functions and in the adoption of options. Because the performance of state functions was expected in all portions of states, the subdividing of states into county units was completed some years ago and the number of counties has remained slightly over 3,000 for several decades.

2. Cities

Municipal[3] governments do not come into existence at the behest of the state for state purposes but rather are created when the residents of an area want services that can be obtained only through the existence of a city government. State laws prescribe the conditions under which an area may become an incorporated municipality. When these conditions are met, the city is created and citizens obtain the services they want. However, upon becoming a city, the entity automatically assumes certain responsibilities to the state, such as having its police personnel enforce the state criminal code, meeting certain health standards, and otherwise complying with the general mandates of the state that apply to cities. The growth in the number of municipalities in the United States has slowed along with urbanization and because a number of state governments have imposed more rigid requirements to slow incorporations in metropolitan areas.

Township and/or town governments are organized to provide for general government without regard to population concentration. The Census Bureau classifies the New England town, Maine plantations, New Hampshire locations, and the Midwest township into one class called *townships*. Township governments are found in twenty states. The type of services provided will vary considerably, with the New England towns furnishing some municipal-type services and the rural midwestern township providing fewer services suitable in a rural area. Townships in New Jersey and Pennsylvania are legally termed *municipal corporations* and may have many characteristics of a municipality.

3. Towns, townships

Special Districts

To meet special needs that could not be satisfactorily considered by the existing general governments, state legislatures authorized the creation of special districts as governments for the delivery of a single service. Occasionally, special districts have been empowered to perform several functions on the fringe of a metropolitan area and may be called *special service districts* or other appropriate descriptive titles. Not all single purpose entities are called special districts. They may be called *authorities, boards,* or *commissions,* forcing the development of criteria by the Census Bureau to determine whether or not they are genuine governments. School districts declined considerably in number during the twenty-year period between 1952 and 1972, dropping from 67,000 to 15,000. However, the change since 1972 has been minimal as the school consolidation movement has matured. While school districts have declined since 1952, the number of other special districts has been growing steadily—more than 150 percent—from 12,340 in 1952 to 29,532 in 1987, reflecting the inability of general government to meet many new needs, particularly in metropolitan areas.

Special governments for special needs

School districts decline; other districts grow

As graphically illustrated in figure 13.1, the number of general governments has remained fairly constant over the past 30 years. Counties have remained the same except for a few city–county consolidations; municipalities have grown slightly, reflecting continuing urbanization; and towns and townships have dropped slightly, due to the dissolution of rural townships. However, dramatic changes have been occurring in the special districts. Special districts seem to be the only politically feasible form of local government sufficiently flexible to adapt to urban and metropolitan demographic changes.

Metropolitan Areas

Though not qualifying under the definition of government, metropolitan areas must be considered in any discussion of local government because of their identity as places where people live, work, and interact on a regular basis. They are primarily areas of common interest but with uncommon governments, thus providing a dilemma in the normal delivery of governmental services and in the formulation of area-wide policy. Because metropolitan areas encompass a majority of the people, their governmental

Common interest but uncommon governments

Figure 13.1
Local governments,
1952–1987.
*(Source: Bureau of the
Census,* 1987 Census of
Governments.*)*

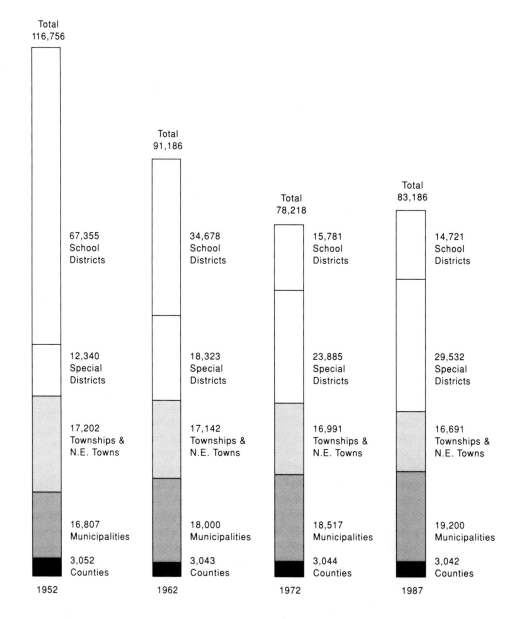

Total
116,756

Total
91,186

Total
78,218

Total
83,186

67,355
School
Districts

34,678
School
Districts

15,781
School
Districts

14,721
School
Districts

12,340
Special
Districts

18,323
Special
Districts

23,885
Special
Districts

29,532
Special
Districts

17,202
Townships &
N.E. Towns

17,142
Townships &
N.E. Towns

16,991
Townships &
N.E. Towns

16,691
Townships &
N.E. Towns

16,807
Municipalities

18,000
Municipalities

18,517
Municipalities

19,200
Municipalities

3,052
Counties

3,043
Counties

3,044
Counties

3,042
Counties

1952

1962

1972

1987

problems are of major significance in the study of state and local government, and are considered in more detail in chapter 17.

State–Local Relationships

The Federal–Local Context

State–local relationships must be considered in the context of other relationships, the most important of which is the federal–local relationship that has matured since the 1930s. Though creatures of the state, local governments and officials are answerable to federal administrators and courts, state policies notwithstanding.

In the delivery of services and performance of other governmental responsibilities, local personnel must recognize the parameters of the U.S. Constitution. Because local personnel implement the programs designed by federal and state governments, they are exposed to numerous possibilities of violations of constitutional rights on a daily basis. In apprehending a wrongdoer, a local police officer may not violate the due process clause; in conducting an election, a local inspector may not violate the equal protection clause; in arranging a Christmas display, a city manager may not violate separation of church and state. Local employees must also observe the latest interpretations of the Constitution as handed down by the Supreme Court. According to the U.S. Supreme Court, local employees may not deny certain welfare benefits without being personally liable, and local officials may not fire employees merely because of their political affiliations.

Local government and the constitution

Federal financial assistance to local governments has led to many of the same restrictions felt by state governments in federal–state fiscal relations. Federal aid resulted in extensive intervention in local government whether it came in the form of categorical grants or general revenue sharing. As a result of numerous federal guidelines, mandates, and policies bearing on local government activities, state officials have felt that the federal–local relationship was becoming somewhat illicit. To them it seemed that local governments may be creatures of the state but they were rapidly becoming "beasts of burden" for the federal government. The bypassing of states in federal aid allocations grew from eight percent of the aid direct to local governments in 1960 up to around 25 percent by the early 1980s. Where local governments were eligible for 132 grant programs in 1960, they could qualify for 537 programs in 1980.[4] To oversee the administration of funds and programs, federal employees communicated directly with counties, cities, towns, townships, and special districts regularly without regard to the legal state–local relationship.

Federal aid leads to restrictions

Bypass states

The attitudes of state policy-makers toward this budding romance were mixed. Unable or unwilling to develop and finance solutions to local problems, many state political leaders were pleased to see responsibility for local governments shared by the federal government. Others, however, feared for the long-term implications of the federal–local relationship and sought ways to permit the relationship to continue as long as it could be monitored and controlled by state government. Because of these differing views, state actions to neutralize growing federal power among local governments have been varied and difficult to generalize. State fears almost became moot in the late 1980s and early 1990s when the Reagan and Bush policies steadily reduced federal aid.

Politics of the State–Local Relationship

Political restraints on state control

Legally, local governments may be creatures of the state but politically they are not required to submit to unwarranted abuse. Local governments are staffed by officials and employees who constitute a political force that state government must respect for several reasons.

1. State officials started locally

In the first place, many members of the legislature and officials in the executive branch cut their governmental teeth with positions on county commissions, city governing boards, and town governments. In many states, local officials may also serve in the legislature while continuing to hold local office. So, whether applying past or present experiences, many state policy-makers have an empathy for the problems of local governments.

Another factor that gives local governments power in dealing with state government is the political influence and credibility local officials hold with the electorate. If local government's needs are not addressed at the state level, local officials will let local constituents know whom to blame. This fact is a matter of no minor concern to legislators and executives.

2. Influence with voters

3. Party ties

In states where local officials are elected on the partisan ballot, local government has an automatic bridge to like partisans at the state level. Lacking partisan kinship, a Democratic county commissioner can still approach a Republican senator from the same area because the Republican will readily understand the political implications in spurning the commissioner's concern.

4. Tradition of localism

Another weapon for local officials is the legitimacy of localism that prevails in almost every state. Whether justified or not, the prevailing sympathy of the American electorate lies with local government. In annual surveys conducted for the Advisory Commission on Intergovernmental Relations in the 1980s and early 1990s, the people gave their strongest vote of confidence to local government when asked which level gave them the most for their money.[5] This is merely one of many polls and surveys that reflect voter infatuation with local government. Backed by this widely acknowledged sentiment, local officials are in strong bargaining positions from the public point of view when asking the state for programs to strengthen local government. No legislator wishes to be billed as "anti-local government" in a society that reveres local government as the best level of government.

These factors, combined with others peculiar to various states, provide a political complexion to the legal theory that states can deal with local governments in a cavalier fashion. They force many state-local dialogues from the pedestal of mandate to the table of negotiation.

Policy-Making Over Shared Functions

Politics may be one of the most influential features of the state–local relationship but the sharing of functions is also an important characteristic that deters state absolutism. Many local functions are optional and the state policy-makers have little interest in whether City A runs a transit system or County B has a recreation levy. However, many other functions conducted by local governments are performed for the state, such as law enforcement, record-keeping, welfare administration, and education. The prescribing government depends on the cooperation of the administering government for the efficient delivery of the services. Because state governments must depend on a cooperative local spirit, state officials strive to accommodate local points of view in designing program delivery systems. Riding roughshod over local governments will only result in belligerent local administration that will seriously impair the effectiveness of the program involved.

States need local cooperation

Routine Oversight Activities

Unlike the national government, which must have a legal or financial basis for imposing mandates or requirements on lower governments, states may impose numerous regulatory and administrative requirements on local governments as a matter of normal procedure. Using this authority, states have developed numerous oversight activities. As a matter of course, local governments may be required to file regular reports with state agencies, to secure prior approval for certain activities, to conform to standards set by state law for the performance of a function, to notify an agency when it intends to engage in a service, and to submit to periodic inspection. These and similar requirements result in a constant pattern of communications between state agencies and counterparts in local governments.

States impose numerous regulations

How Much Local Autonomy?

The formal status of local governments vis-á-vis the state government was most succinctly stated by Judge John F. Dillon in 1868 when he said that local governments are "the mere tenants at the will of the legislature." His strict construction of local government powers came to be known as Dillon's Rule, which meant that local governments have no powers except those specifically granted by the state and, in cases of doubt, courts should rule against local governments. Dillon's Rule prevailed in most states through the 1900s. Under it, the state—usually the legislature—decided whether cities, counties, towns, townships, or special districts would have five- or nine-person governing boards, would be authorized to levy a property tax for recreational purposes, would be permitted to construct an airport, or whatever other functions would be performed, and the procedure for implementation. Under Dillon's Rule, states have determined the fiscal programs, structure, modes of election, and procedures for executing the public business. Pursuant to Dillon's Rule, when suits were brought before state courts questioning the authority of local government to act, any presence of doubt meant that local government lost the case.

Dillon's strict constructionism

Dillon did not stand alone in his interpretation, however. In 1903, the U.S. Supreme Court upheld his view by stating that local governments were "mere political subdivisions of the state for purposes of exercising a part of its powers. They may exert only such powers as are expressly granted to them."[6]

The movement to loosen the bonds began during the same era Dillon's Rule was born. State legislatures of the 1800s, exercising a tradition from the colonial period, were prolific in their enactment of special laws tailored to deal with specific local governments. These laws were often the result of a local petition by the officials of local government who sought authority to better meet the needs of their community. These laws were also sometimes forced upon unreceptive communities. This recurring behavior of state legislatures resulted in growing sentiment against legislative authority to pass abusive special legislation. Eventually, this sentiment was translated into constitutional amendments that deprived legislatures of this authority.

Seek home rule

Running concurrently with the anti-special legislation movement was the drive for granting local governments greater discretion in dealing with local matters. *Home rule,* local authority to control local affairs, became the watchword for local governments. Home rule for municipalities was born in Missouri in 1875 and slowly spread across the country until over forty states had joined the movement, to one degree or another, by 1980. The concept was soon expanded to counties, and today around half of the states permit counties to use home rule. Adapting the concept to counties was found to be somewhat more difficult—and some thought unwise—because counties were considered subdivisions for the convenience of the state whereas municipalities exist for the convenience of the local population. Many counties have been less than enthusiastic about home rule, with only half of the states with county home rule reporting use of the authority. By the mid-1980s, less than 100 counties had bothered to adopt home rule charters.

Fordham's rule

As another approach to vesting broader powers in local governments, Dean Fordham developed a concept of *devolution of powers.* Recognizing that local affairs could not be completely divorced from state affairs, Fordham proposed an amendment to state constitutions that would delegate to local government all powers capable of delegation and then require state legislatures to identify the specific powers that would be forbidden to local government. Under this proposal, legislatures would be required to take the initiative to deny powers, a reversal of the present situation where local governments must go to the legislature to obtain powers. Fordham's proposal would leave the legislature, rather than the courts, to decide on the extent to which discretionary powers were granted to local government.[7] Only Alaska, Montana, and Pennsylvania adopted Fordham's devolution of powers as proposed. However, many states amending their constitutions since 1953 have followed the principle, while reserving specific powers to the legislature.[8]

Few take advantage of home rule

In a study of the discretionary powers of local governments, the Advisory Commission on Intergovernmental Relations (ACIR) conducted an extensive survey of state officials and informed observers. On the basis of the survey, the ACIR reported that few eligible local governments take advantage of the authority to adopt home rule; only a fraction of the survey respondents reported increased use of certain local powers; twenty-seven states authorized general local governments to pass ordinances superseding general or special state laws but the power was not extensively used; constitutional prohibitions against special laws by legislatures are often avoided by creating classes of local governments; and over half of the respondents felt that federal grant restrictions impaired local discretionary authority.[9]

States vary in controlling local governments

The indices developed by ACIR for measuring local autonomy in major areas of activity indicated a wide range of control from one state to the other.[10] According to Daniel Elazar, political culture is one major factor in determining the division of authority between state and local governments.[11] New England has had a localistic tradition; the South has had equally as long a tradition of centralized state government. Elazar posits that political culture is still an influence in the state–local relationship in 31 states but its impact is declining as states are becoming more homogeneous.

Other factors influencing the state–local power arrangement, according to ACIR, include:

- The length of the legislative sessions, since it will determine the opportunity for legislative control of local governments
- The number of units of local government, since many units will skew the time available for local matters in the legislature
- The complexity and length of the state constitutions, and the difficulty of securing amendments
- The political strength of associations of local officials and of public employee unions and associations.[12]

Local autonomy in a nationalizing society

Preservation of local autonomy through devolution of powers or home rule becomes increasingly difficult in a nationalizing society in which people expect uniformity in governmental services to transcend the boundaries of political subdivisions. As each successive legislative session has convened, state policy-makers have been faced with resolving additional jurisdictional difficulties growing out of the governmental diversity. Responding to reality, they formulate laws to mandate more uniformity in the delivery of services through local governments. State administrators then give substance to laws by issuing implementing regulations. The laws and regulations constitute mandates that expand the preemptive authority of state government, even in states with a tradition of localism. Local governments resist state mandates, utilizing their political resources to maximize state grants and minimize state interference in local affairs. Nevertheless, one study of five states revealed that the states had issued 2,151 mandates since 1966, most by direct orders and 121 as conditions to receiving state funds.[13] The ACIR study, cited earlier, indicated that the exercise of local discretionary authority was found to be reduced by fiscal restraints in every state. Also, initiated measures approved by the people included provisions restricting the spending and taxing powers of local as well as state governments.

Five categories of state mandates

State mandates imposed on local governments fall into five categories: (1) dictating organization and procedures of local government, such as forms of government, conduct of elections, and designation of offices to be filled; (2) requiring services that enrich existing local government activities, such as special education, new health measures, additional welfare programs, and so on; (3) controlling interlocal activities that affect other local governments, such as land use regulations, property tax assessment, and so on; (4) reducing the local government tax base by giving property tax exemptions to new businesses or classes of citizens; and (5) establishing personnel practices, such as requirements to bargain collectively, local civil service, retirement benefits, and so on.[14] Mandates may be justified as necessary to assure minimum uniform statewide service levels, to develop professional standards for employees, to reduce the impact of local politics on service delivery, and to implement state policy objectives. Nevertheless, local officials resent state mandates that incur new costs in spite of limited revenues.

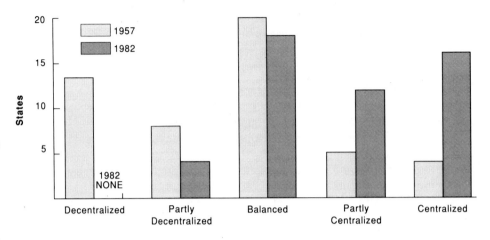

Figure 13.2
State centralization, 1957 and 1982. In his research, G. Ross Stephens ranked states on the basis of the division of state/local responsibility for personnel distribution, service delivery, and financial responsibility. During the period 1957–1982, Stephens found a dramatic shift from decentralization to centralization.
(Source: G. Ross Stephens, "State Centralization and the Erosion of Local Autonomy," Journal of Politics 36 (February 1974): 67 and G. Ross Stephens, paper delivered at American Political Science Association, New Orleans, September 1985.)

To make state officials aware of the fiscal impact of mandates, local governments have succeeded in forcing legislatures to compute fiscal notes (a statement of costs) for new mandates in a majority of states. (See figure 13.2.)

State–Local Fiscal Relations

Not only are state and local governments knotted together through state mandates, but fiscal relationships running back into the 1800s have resulted in an inescapable entanglement of the state with its political subdivisions. Perhaps the most restrictive *1. State constitutions limit local debt* are the provisions of state constitutions and statutes regulating the levels and procedures involving debt. Drafters of state constitutions may have reflected an abiding respect for brevity but when it came to the section on local debt, they cast aside restraint and wrote fiscal restrictions in painful detail. Restrictive fiscal policies in constitutions can be attributed to several factors. During the 1800s, many local governments abused their credit and were forced into bankruptcy. Constitution writers felt that legislatures could not always be trusted either, as control by bosses, railroads, or corporations was not uncommon in the 1800s. Finally, constitution drafters, as property taxpayers, shared the anti-property tax sentiments of their constituents. Common restrictions on local debt included a maximum limit on outstanding debt (often stated as a percentage of the assessed valuation of property); requirements for vote by the people of the political subdivision involved; maximum periods of time for debt maturity; maximum interest rate; and state approval of bond issues, among others.

Debt limits in the infrastructure crisis   State debt restrictions, especially those permanently imbedded in state constitutions, became an increasingly serious obstacle as local governments dealt with the infrastructure crisis of the 1980s and 1990s. As local governments celebrate centennials and bicentennials, the need becomes more pressing to replace water mains, sewage collection systems, streets, highways, bridges, and the other facilities required to keep society functioning. One study predicted that refurbishing municipal water plants alone will require from $75 billion to $110 billion during the 1980–2000 year period. Bridge surveys by state and federal agencies report that at least one-fifth of all bridges in America require major rehabilitation or reconstruction.[15] Federal funds for local capital construction have been on the decline since 1978. Thus, local governments face a real dilemma as they survey their infrastructure problems: declining federal assistance, tight state budgets, and constitutional restrictions on local debt. To evade the constitutional limitations, some subdivisions have created special districts to issue debt; others have turned to revenue bonds to be paid off with revenue gained from the project, such as toll fees; still others have contracted with the private sector either to furnish the service or construct-and-lease the facility to the local government.

Federal funds declining

Local budgeting and spending is also closely supervised by state governments. According to one study of fiscal management in nine randomly chosen states, states commonly require local governments to adopt a balanced budget, to hold public hearings, and to submit the budget to the state on prescribed forms. In monitoring expenditures, states require publication of an annual financial report, submission of annual report to states, and annual audits by professionals according to state standards.[16]

2. States restrict local budget process

Another facet of state–local fiscal relations is the control of the local revenue base by state government. Unless the local government is enjoying some form of fiscal home rule, it may impose only such taxes as are specifically authorized by the state constitution or state law. Because states themselves have been relying on income and excise taxes, they have been reluctant to delegate broader taxing powers to local governments. Consequently, many local governments are confined to property taxes—and those are rigidly controlled by constitutions and statutes.

3. States control local tax choices

Local governments have experienced three waves of property tax restrictions. The first occurred in the late 1800s when excessive bonded indebtedness and/or pressing developmental needs put considerable pressure on property tax rates. Limits were initiated, especially during the panic of 1870, to protect taxpayers from undue increases.[17] The next wave occurred in the 1930s when the depression decimated values at the same time as taxpayers found it practically impossible to pay their tax bills. A series of new limitations sprouted and grew—the only things that did in the years of the drought running through mid-America. The third wave began in 1978 with the passage of an initiated measure—Proposition 13—in California, aimed particularly at limiting the property tax rates. A dozen other states quickly followed with property tax limitations measures and amendments of various types.

Curtailing property taxes

The three waves have generated a variety of mechanisms for limiting property taxes—most states placed a ceiling on the amount of mills that may be levied; some, such as Massachusetts, limited property taxes to a percentage of market value; some required disclosure of tax facts to the public, thereby invoking political controls; and some limited the level of assessment to a percentage of the market value.

As state governments continued to foreclose property tax options on local governments, legislators recognized that new revenue sources were required to keep political subdivisions functioning. Reluctantly, states began to expand the number of taxes

Adopting nonproperty taxes

Table 13.1 Aid to Local Governments (billions of dollars)

	1970–71	1976–77	1979–80	1983–84	1989–90
Federal aid	3.391	16.637	21.136	20.912	18.449
State aid	31.081	60.311	81.289	105.819	172.274

State governments have demonstrated continued commitment to assist local governments while federal aid has declined in recent years. Source: Bureau of the Census, Governmental Finances in 1970–71, 1976–77, 1979–80, 1983–84, and 1989–90.

that may be used to meet local needs. With access to new sources, local governments saw a 435 percent increase in nonproperty taxes during the period of 1967–1980.[18] A brief inventory of taxes now available to local governments includes general sales and gross receipts taxes in 28 states; income taxes in ten states; franchise taxes on public utility bills in 37 states; motor vehicle licenses in 29 states; alcohol beverage taxes in eight states; tobacco products taxes in six states; motor fuel taxes in eight states; and miscellaneous excise taxes in 37 states.[19] In addition there are the states that permit local governments many tax options through home rule charters. Many states have compensated for the loss of property base by authorizing user charges for local government services. In fact, charges for services are an even more significant form of local revenue than many of the nonproperty taxes listed above.[20] Legislatures in 20 states have accepted responsibility for property tax exemptions and credits they have granted by reimbursing local governments for the revenue lost locally.[21]

4. State aid to local governments

The mounting needs at the local points of service delivery were met not only by authorization for new forms of revenue but direct state cash payments as well. By the early 1980s, the largest single component of state budgets was aid to local governments, accounting for more than one out of every three dollars spent by state governments. The increase during the 1970–1980 decade was dramatic, reaching over $80 billion—a threefold jump—by 1980.[22] School districts received 52 percent of this aid; counties 22 percent; municipalities 15 percent; townships one percent; special districts one percent; with nine percent combined and unallocable.[23] By 1990, this $80 billion had more than doubled to $172 billion while federal aid dropped from $21 billion to $18 billion. (See table 13.1.)

a. Grants

The largest portion of this $172 billion was distributed by states as direct grants-in-aid, which are transfers of funds on a formula basis from state revenue. In this category of aid, education receives over 62 percent of the funds, with public welfare receiving over 12 percent, general local government support ten percent, highways less than five percent, and miscellaneous close to ten percent.[24]

b. Shared taxes

Shared taxes make up another significant portion of state aid to local governments. Antedating federal revenue sharing by decades, states have developed a wide-ranging smorgasbord of shared taxes, some unrestricted and other dedicated to the financing of specific functions.

c. Reimbursement for costs

Another form of state aid has been the reimbursement for the costs of certain programs administered by local governments, such as tax collection, hospital care for the needy, and care of prisoners. Alaska has built the reimbursement concept into its

Table 13.2 State Aid to Local Governments (percentage of total local revenues)

Considerable (39% and Over)		Below Average (25%–20%)	
1. New Mexico	48	33. Florida	25
2. Alaska	47	34. Oregon	25
3. Kentucky	41	35. Rhode Island	25
4. North Dakota	40	36. Vermont	24
5. Wisconsin	40	37. Colorado	23
6. West Virginia	39	38. Texas	23
		39. Georgia	22
Above Average (33%–38%)		40. Michigan	22
7. California	38	41. Missouri	22
8. Mississippi	37	42. Montana	22
9. Delaware	36	43. Connecticut	21
10. Minnesota	36	44. Illinois	21
11. Nevada	36	45. Kansas	20
12. Oklahoma	36	46. South Dakota	20
13. Idaho	35		
14. North Carolina	35	**Minimal (19% and Under)**	
15. New Jersey	34	47. New Hampshire	15
16. Arkansas	33	48. Tennessee	15
Average Range (26%–32%)		49. Nebraska	13
		50. Hawaii	6
17. Indiana	32		
18. New York	31		
19. Louisiana	30		
20. Ohio	30		
21. South Carolina	30		
22. Utah	30		
23. Washington	30		
24. Arizona	29		
National Average	**29**		
25. Iowa	29		
26. Maine	29		
27. Alabama	28		
28. Maryland	28		
29. Massachusetts	28		
30. Pennsylvania	28		
31. Virginia	28		
32. Wyoming	28		

Source: Computations by authors from Governmental Finances in 1982–83, *Bureau of the Census.*

general aid for cities and boroughs by providing payments for specific services including police, fire, planning, parks, transportation, hospitals, and pollution control.[25]

Another step taken by many states to help local governments cope with their financial limitations is the assumption of all or a larger portion of the costs of delivering certain services. In recent years, state governments have assumed a substantial share of court costs, with one-third of the states paying over 80 percent and another six states funding between 50 and 80 percent. Welfare is another function in which states are shouldering a greater burden at the state level. By the early 1980s, two-thirds of the

d Assuming costs of services

states were paying the full costs of aid for dependent children; close to half of the states fully funded "general assistance." During the 1970s, half of the states made major changes in school finance, with the states assuming a significantly higher share of costs. In 28 states, the state share of nonfederal education costs increased five percent between 1970 and 1983.[26]

State Agencies For Local Governments

By the 1950s, state officials began to realize that state-local relations suffered for lack of coordination and management. Numerous state agencies were dealing with equally as numerous local agencies. Local officials were complaining about the bureaucratic confusion occurring when several state agencies were becoming involved in common functional areas. This was certain to occur in states with fragmented governments. Responding to the need for coordinating state activities with local governments, North Carolina, New York, and Colorado became the first states to launch state-level agencies for assisting local governments. The mid-1960s were the beginning of a nationwide interest in "departments of community affairs," as some came to be known. By the mid-1980s, every state either had a fully staffed agency or had designated an existing agency to play the lead role in coordinating state activities with local governments. Of these, close to 20 had organized community and economic development services into a major executive agency.

Departments of Community Affairs (DCAs)

Functions assigned to the departments of community affairs included, among others, encouraging intergovernmental relations; coordinating state service and assistance programs; assisting localities in obtaining state and federal aid; planning; economic development programs; research; policy and "how to do it" manuals; personnel training; financial management and technical assistance; home rule; information clearinghouses; and legal advisory services, including model ordinances.[27]

Small governments use DCAs most

As could be expected, agencies for local governments have been most utilized by units of government under 50,000, which often have part-time personnel and limited financial resources. Even so, they were still required to meet the same kinds of federal and state performance and reporting criteria as fully staffed larger governments. Impetus was given to the movement for establishing DCAs by the availability of numerous federal categorical grants, each with its own cluster of application, filing, and reporting requirements. Many local governments were unable to share in the programs without technical grantsmanship assistance from state agencies. The need for this kind of state technical assistance declined with the decline in federal aid.

Create intergovernmental advisory commissions

While staffing state-level offices to provide professional assistance and direction for local governments, states have also been institutionalizing intergovernmental advisory commissions to serve as continuing forums for state–local dialogue. When the U.S. Advisory Commission on Intergovernmental Relations recommended in 1974 that states create "little ACIRs," there were only four such panels in existence. By the late 1980s more than half of the states had established intergovernmental bodies, 18 of them following the ACIR pattern with representation of local officials, legislators, and state officials. (See figure 13.3.) Many other states created temporary commissions or committees to study state–local relations and to make recommendations to governors and legislators.

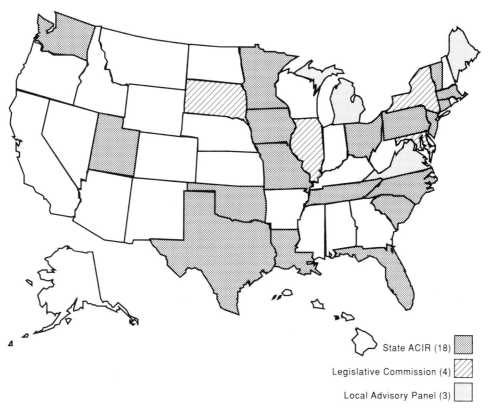

Figure 13.3
State-local
"intergovernmental panels"
have been established in
recent years by more than
half of the states. Of the
three structural categories,
the ACIR Model is the
most common, followed by
legislative commissions and
local advisory panels.
*(Source: Michael Tetelman,
"State Local Panels: An
Overview,"*
Intergovernmental
Perspective *13 (Fall, 1987),
p. 28.)*

State ACIR (18)
Legislative Commission (4)
Local Advisory Panel (3)

Many states encouraged local governments to consider intergovernmental service agreements to raise the effectiveness and efficiency in the delivery of local services. During the 1960s and 1970s, almost all legislatures followed the suggestion of ACIR to adopt intergovernmental contracting statutes that would grant all forms of local government broad authority to cooperate and contract in providing services. Fifteen states even permitted local governments to contract or share a service for which only one of them had responsibility, meaning that counties would contract with cities to provide a municipal service to other local governments.[28]

States permit interlocal cooperation

Generally, the more populous metropolitan and suburban jurisdictions tend to use the intergovernmental powers more extensively than the rural governments. Even so, relationships tend to be more intersuburban and urban–rural than central city–suburban. Jails and detention homes, police training, street lighting, refuse collection, libraries, solid waste disposal, water supply, and crime lab services tend to be the functions most affected by intergovernmental activities.[29]

Intergovernmental service agreements became a popular concept for several reasons. They provide the opportunity to obtain a service a local government cannot provide itself; they can lower service costs by achieving a better economy of scale; they can improve the quality of a service since a larger government most likely has better

Service agreements

equipment and expertise; they curb reformers who see local government consolidation as the answer to service delivery; they provide year-to-year flexibility to service delivery without impacting existing capital investments; they help some governments better amortize capital costs; and they can slow the proliferation of special districts.[30]

Local Government Evaluated

Common urban-rural problem: overgovernment

While millions of people have migrated from rural to urban America, the governmental structure of rural America has remained unchanged and the governmental structure of urban America has seen increasing proliferation and complexity. As a consequence, many observers are saying that the most urban and the most rural portions of the nation suffer from the same institutional malady: overgovernment. Diagnoses of the ailment began in the 1930s when the depression turned thoughts to reducing the burdens of government. World War II interrupted the dialogue, however, and the subject was not joined until the latter part of the 1940s when urban scholars began to assess the growing divergence of resources and problems in mushrooming metropolitan areas. During the 1950s and 1960s, the dialogue picked up tempo as the urban crisis grew. Perhaps the most sweeping proposals to be presented in the 1960s were included in the report on local government by the Committee on Economic Development, an organization bearing the names of around 100 business, government, philanthropic, and academic leaders of the country.[31]

Propose abolishing 80 percent of local governments

The report of the committee minced no words and withheld no worthy proposal: 80 percent of the local governments in America should be abolished; all towns and townships with less than 2,500 people should be dissolved and responsibilities transferred to counties; schools with less than 1,000 students should be consolidated; counties of less than 50,000 people should be merged; the potential for executive leadership must be institutionalized in local government; all local governments should be vitalized with broad home rule powers, including control of revenue; and state and federal funds should be used to induce local government reforms.

Proposals disregarded

Though issued in the mid-1960s, the recommendations are still applicable in the 1990s. Little has changed. In fact, special districts and municipal incorporations have continued to grow in numbers, especially in the urban areas. By and large, the recommendations were disregarded by policy-makers even though greeted as fresh fodder for round-table ruminators. Widespread neglect of the committee's recommendations can be attributed to the divergence of basic viewpoints between reformers and "influentials." CED recommendations were based on the premise that governmental services ought to be delivered as efficiently and effectively as possible within the context of a democratic society. Influentials in every political subdivision, on the other hand, give greater consideration to the political implications of government. The merging of two inefficient county governments disrupts the lines of communications and influence built by the power structure in both counties, not to mention the economic concerns of county seat cities, courthouse employees, and government suppliers. Given the choice between efficiency that saves tax dollars, and waste that perpetuates access and influence, those in position to decide have chosen waste as often as not. Hence, the political realities of reform constitute a formidable barrier for the most determined reformers—and the

Efficiency vs. political influence

reforms that have occurred, such as county–city consolidations in a few metropolitan areas, became possible only through the development of a political environment conducive to change. In the absence of scandal, obvious mismanagement, ominous alternatives, or other compelling evidence, the structures of general governments will remain of a late 1800 vintage. Structural gaps, created by a nationalizing and urbanizing society, are much more likely to be filled with stop-gap measures, such as special districts, intergovernmental agreements, and coordinating commissions, than by thorough-going reform.

Historically, the county, municipality, town, and township can be traced beyond the shores of colonial America to the medieval traditions in England. When they were brought to America, however, they were adapted to the needs of colonists as dictated by geography, climate, and other environmental considerations. In the westward movement, local governments came with the conestoga wagons—and were further adapted to the new frontier. As soon as local governments had been instituted across America, dramatic demographic pressures developed. Millions of immigrants crowded ungovernable cities; farming technology sent millions more into urban centers. Urbanization through the 1900s developed an insatiable demand for more and more services in urban areas while the need for many local governments in rural areas waned. Today, local governments constitute an institutional lag as reform proposals have failed to satisfy the political criteria of those in positions of influence. If fiscal pressures continue to mount in the 1990s as the federal coffers dry up and local tax revolts continue, the political concerns may become secondary to matters of efficiency and economy. However, local government reorganization and reform, even then, will be a slow, negotiated process.

Fiscal pressures may force action

Endnotes

1. *See* Richard Briffault, "State-Local Relations and Constitutional Law," *Intergovernmental Perspective* 13 (Summer-Fall, 1987), pp. 10–14, for a modified view of plenary state power. He argues that many *state* courts recognize a substantial amount of real power (local control) exercised by local governments in practice.

2. U.S. Department of Commerce, Bureau of Census, *1982 Census of Governments,* Vol. 1 (1983): 341.

3. In some statutes, the term *municipal* is applied broadly to include a variety of governments. In this text, however, the term shall apply only to its most common definition—the incorporated city.

4. David B. Walker, "The State–Local Connection: Perennial, Paramount, Resurgent," *National Civic Review* 73 (February 1984).

5. Randy Arndt, "Local Government Is Tops in Taxpayer Poll by ACIR," *Nation's Cities Weekly* (July 9, 1984): 2. *See also Public Administration Times,* November 1, 1991, p. 3.

6. *Atkins* v. *Kansas,* 191 U.S. 207 at 220–21 (1903).

7. U.S. Advisory Commission on Intergovernmental Relations, *Measuring Local Discretionary Authority* M-131 (Washington, D.C.: Government Printing Office, 1981), p. 17.

8. Ibid., p. 20.

9. Ibid., pp. 7–8.

10. Ibid., pp. 52–56.

11. Daniel J. Elazar, *American Federalism,* 3rd ed. (New York: Harper & Row, 1984), pp. 215–233.

12. *Measuring Local Discretionary Authority,* pp. 12–13.

13. Judy Heffner, "State–Local Relations in a New Era," *State Legislatures* 8 (May 1982): 7.

14. U.S. Advisory Commission on Intergovernmental Relations, *State Mandating & Local Expenditures* A-67 (Washington, D.C.: Government Printing Office, 1978), pp. 5–6.

15. See Pat Choate and Susan Walter, *America in Ruins* (Washington: The Council of State Planning Agencies, 1981).

16. John E. Peterson, C. Wayne Stallings, and Catherine Lavigne Spain, *State Roles in Local Government Financial Management* (Washington: Government Finance Research Center, 1979), pp. 29, 35.

17. U.S. Advisory Commission on Intergovernmental Relations, *State Limitations on Local Taxes & Expenditures* A-64 (Washington, D.C.: Government Printing Office, 1977), p. 11.

18. *How State Government Can Assist Local Governments to Raise More Money,* Legislative Finance Paper No. 25, prepared by the Intergovernmental Finance Project of the National Conference of State Legislatures, Steven D. Gold, director (July 1982), p. 7.

19. Ibid., pp. 7–9.

20. Ibid., p. 10.

21. Steven D. Gold, *State and Local Fiscal Relations in the Early 1980s* (Washington: The Urban Institute, 1983), p. 56.

22. *State Aid to Local Government,* a background paper prepared by the NCSL Intergovernmental Finance Project for a conference on New York's fiscal system in Albany, April 27–28, 1982.

23. Ibid., p. 8.

24. David Kellerman, "State Aid to Local Governments, Fiscal 1990," *Book of the States, 1992–93* (Lexington, KY.: Council of State Governments, 1992), pp. 633–635.

25. U.S. Advisory Commission on Intergovernmental Relations, *The State of State-Local Revenue Sharing* M-121 (Washington, D.C.: Government Printing Office, 1980), p. 65.

26. Gold, *State and Local Fiscal Relations,* p. 50.

27. *Book of the States 1978–79,* p. 595.

28. U.S. Advisory Commission on Intergovernmental Relations, *State and Local Roles in the Federal System* A-88 (Washington, D.C.: Government Printing Office, 1982), p. 326.

29. Ibid., pp. 330–331.

30. Ibid., pp. 27–28.

31. Committee for Economic Development, *Modernizing Local Government* (New York, 1966). For a 1992 perspective raising questions about traditional recommendations for local government reform, see Andree E. Reeves, "Enhancing Local Self-Government and State Capabilities: The U.S. Advisory Commission on Intergovernmental Relations Program," *Public Administration Review,* 52 (July/August, 1992), 401–405.

STUTSMAN COUNTY
COURTHOUSE

LOCAL GOVERNMENT II: THE COUNTY

CHAPTER 14

Townships and Towns

As we approach the 21st century the American county seems about to "come of age," or perhaps "come of new age," as many old "dark continent" images begin to fade. Recent research by Gregory Streib and William L. Waugh, Jr., concludes that county governments in the 1990s "have moved far beyond the unflattering characterizations" of textbook writers and reformers in the early 1900s.[1] Henry Gilbertson called the county the "dark continent of American politics"[2] and Richard Childs referred to counties as "formless" and "ramshackle," and "the plague spot of American politics."[3]

Although this orthodox view of the county does not die easily, and is an important part of understanding contemporary county problems, Streib and Waugh challenge it as not reflective of the many county changes that are coming fast.[4] The discussion that follows includes elements of the old and the new county, with the precautionary note that it is not wise to lump all counties exclusively in the old-fashioned or the modern category.

The County

Basics about County Government

The county is geographically the most universal jurisdiction of local government in America. According to definitions used by the U.S. Census Bureau, all states but Connecticut and Rhode Island have county or county-like governments. In Alaska, the comparable unit of government is the borough; in Louisiana, parishes serve the role of counties. The inhabitants of most cities are also inhabitants of counties and subject in various respects to county authority.

Counties most universal government

The origin of counties is traced back to the English shires created around the year 1000 A.D. Colonists brought shires to America where they first appeared in 1634 when Virginia was divided into eight shires or counties. Massachusetts followed in 1643, and soon most colonies had subdivided to provide local residents with judicial, military, electoral, and other services.

Counties formed in 1634

Table 14.1 County Sizes and Populations by State

State	Counties & County Equivalents	Average Sq. Mi.	Smallest Sq. Mi.	Largest Sq. Mi.	Average Pop.	Smallest Pop.	Largest Pop.
Alabama	67	758	542	1,589	60,307	10,153	651,525
Alaska	23	24,819	531	159,099	22,001	1,410	226,338
Arizona	14	8,108	1,837	18,608	244,348	8,008	2,122,101
Arkansas	75	694	516	1,053	31,343	5,826	349,660
California	58	2,695	46	20,064	513,104	1,113	8,863,164
Colorado	63	1,644	111	4,771	52,292	467	467,610
Connecticut	8	609	412	921	410,889	102,525	851,783
Delaware	3	644	396	942	222,056	110,993	441,946
Florida	67	808	280	1,994	193,103	5,569	1,937,094
Georgia	159	365	122	907	40,743	1,915	545,837
Hawaii	5	1,285	13	4,034	221,646	130	836,231
Idaho	44	1,873	405	8,497	22,881	727	205,775
Illinois	102	546	160	1,185	112,064	4,373	5,105,067
Indiana	92	391	87	659	60,263	5,315	797,159
Iowa	99	565	381	974	28,048	4,866	327,140
Kansas	105	779	149	1,443	23,596	1,774	403,662
Kentucky	120	331	99	785	30,170	2,124	664,937
Louisiana	64	696	194	1,417	65,937	7,104	496,938
Maine	16	1,937	257	6,721	76,745	18,653	243,135
Maryland	23	428	213	663	207,890	17,842	757,027
Massachusetts	14	559	47	1,513	429,745	6,012	1,398,468
Michigan	83	686	322	1,821	111,992	1,701	2,111,687
Minnesota	87	914	154	6,125	50,288	3,868	1,032,431
Mississippi	82	576	401	933	31,381	1,909	254,441
Missouri	114	605	379	1,180	44,887	2,440	993,529

Importance of counties varies

Although the term *county* is applied to a certain concept of government in virtually all states, the county is by no means a standardized unit of government. Its role in each state's family of governments varies considerably. In the South, counties constitute the very foundation of local government; in New England, the foundation consists of towns, with counties serving as auxiliary units. In rural America, counties command central importance while in urban America, the municipality overshadows the courthouse.

Not only have sections of the country affected the evolution of county government, but population density combined with geographic features have forced adaptation. Counties range in population from 107 people in Loving County, Texas, to some 8.8 million in Los Angeles County, California. Arlington County, Virginia, covers only 24 square miles; San Bernardino County, California, encompasses 20,131—almost as large as the five smallest states combined. The largest borough in Alaska is 159,000

Table 14.1 continued

State	Counties & County Equivalents	Average Sq. Mi.	Smallest Sq. Mi.	Largest Sq. Mi.	Average Pop.	Smallest Pop.	Largest Pop.
Montana	57	2,551	245	5,529	14,269	519	113,419
Nebraska	93	821	238	5,961	16,972	546	416,444
Nevada	16	6,868	264	18,155	75,115	1,344	741,459
New Hampshire	10	899	370	1,804	110,925	34,828	336,073
New Jersey	21	356	46	808	368,104	65,294	825,380
New Mexico	32	3,792	109	6,929	45,911	987	480,577
New York	62	764	22	2,728	290,169	5,279	2,300,664
North Carolina	100	488	182	949	66,286	3,856	571,433
North Dakota	53	1,307	634	2,754	12,053	907	102,874
Ohio	88	466	231	703	123,263	11,098	1,412,140
Oklahoma	77	892	372	2,265	40,852	3,301	599,611
Oregon	36	2,672	431	10,174	78,953	1,396	583,887
Pennsylvania	67	670	131	1,237	177,338	4,802	1,585,577
Rhode Island	5	211	26	416	200,693	48,859	596,270
South Carolina	46	657	380	1,143	75,798	8,868	320,167
South Dakota	66	1,151	409	3,481	10,546	1,324	123,809
Tennessee	95	433	129	772	51,339	4,548	826,330
Texas	254	1,032	128	6,169	66,876	107	2,818,199
Utah	29	2,830	299	7,725	59,409	690	725,956
Vermont	14	662	89	972	40,197	5,318	131,761
Virginia	95	418	26	989	65,130	2,635	818,584
Washington	39	1,705	179	5,281	124,787	2,248	1,507,319
West Virginia	55	439	84	1,040	32,609	5,192	207,619
Wisconsin	72	756	231	1,559	67,941	3,890	959,275
Wyoming	23	4,217	2,005	10,352	19,721	2,499	73,142
U.S.	3,092	1,145	13	159,099	80,437	107	8,863,164

In addition to the organized 3,041 counties, the Bureau of the Census 1988 County and City Date Book *included data for 51 geographic areas as "county equivalents."*

square miles—larger than all states except California and Texas. Delaware and Hawaii have only 3 counties; Texas has 254. (See table 14.1.)

Though counties in urban areas are metamorphically responding to the needs of an urban people, most counties are still rural. Over 70 percent of the 3,041 counties are primarily rural in character;[5] three-fourths of the counties have populations of 50,000 or less. As rural governments, counties reflect the rural cultures they serve. County government continues to reflect strong belief in the idea of political performance by laypersons or amateurs rather than experts and professionals. Much of its functioning is more personalized than systematized. Ministering to the public needs of a rural county differs from the governmental administration of a big city about as much as the management of an old-fashioned country store differs from the operation of Nieman-Marcus in Dallas.

Most counties still rural

*Administrative arm of
the state*

Counties have some unique legal distinctions not applicable to many other local governments. By the time colonists gathered on the docks in England, the traditional role of county in England had been established. It served as an administrative arm of the state. Counties were continued in this role in America and eventually case law confirmed that counties were mere extensions of state governments. In 1854, U.S. Chief Justice Taney wrote, "The several counties are nothing more than certain portions of the territory into which the state is divided for more convenient exercise of the powers of (state) governments." Taney's analysis was soon followed by the Ohio Supreme Court in 1857 which stated, "With scarcely an exception, all the powers and functions of the county organization have a direct and exclusive reference to the general policy of the state, and are, in fact, but a branch of the general administration of that policy." Then in 1872, Judge John F. Dillon made clear that plenary power resided in state government and that the county governments possessed only powers expressly granted them.[6] In the absence of special constitutional or statutory provisions, this strict constructionism of county authority prevails in most courts today.

Classify counties

This legal theory of state–county relations necessitates constant legislative activity to delegate powers, modify previous grants of authority, and pass other legislation essential for smooth functioning of county governments. Since many state constitutions prohibit special legislation (i.e., laws written for one specific county), legislatures have evaded the constitutional prohibitions by creating classes of counties so they can be more discriminatory in delegating authority. In Missouri, counties are classified into four groups based on total assessed valuation; in New Jersey, counties fall into six classes based on population and whether or not they border the Atlantic Ocean; and in Washington, counties are placed in 11 classes, all based on population. Using classifications of counties, state laws can be passed to apply only to certain counties of the state. Some states have gone so far as to create classes that fit only one county, thereby making special legislation possible.

Over 300 urban counties

Many rural-oriented county governments in recent years have been confronted with the perplexing fact that most of their citizens are city residents rather than country folks. Some 375 urban counties now govern more than two-thirds of the nation's population, and only 167 counties govern over one-half of the people.[7] (See figure 14.1.) The movement from rural to urban areas in recent decades has caused about half of the counties to lose population while the other half was increasing in population and becoming more urban. Since urban dwellers have different needs and expectations in terms of government services, urban and suburban demands for municipal-type services have caused many county governments to develop split personalities with a variety of symptoms of rural–urban cleavage. Although counties with 100,000 or more population constitute only 12 percent of the total number of counties, they have well over 60 percent of the county employees and three-fourths of all county payrolls. These statistics attest to the fiscal and administrative strain placed on heretofore rural institutions as they respond to an urbanizing constituency. The normal problems concomitant with dramatic growth are compounded by the numerous legal constraints evolving from the strict legal interpretation of county authority.

Figure 14.1
The St. Louis County
Government Center houses
the government offices for
one of America's important
urban counties. St. Louis
county has a population of
975,000, a density of 1,926
people per square mile, and
a jurisdiction of 504 square
miles. The county is 98
percent urban.
*(Reprinted with
permission.)*

Functions of County Governments

The functional role of county government varies, depending on the traditional patterns of local governments and expectations of each. In rural Maine, counties are expected to provide few services, priniapally the maintenance of the courthouse, the county jail, roads in unorganized areas, and limited police functions. Across the country in urban Los Angeles, the county probably provides as many as 100 different services, many of them municipal in nature.

Functions vary with ruralness

The principal functions of county government include the following:[8]

Land Records. The ownership of each legally severed and identified parcel of land in the state must be recorded to reduce conflicts over ownership, to simplify the obligations and benefits of clear ownership, and to provide accessible information for the public. Registration of property ownership is usually performed by a county recorder or register of deeds.

Election administration. Except in some New England states where election administration is performed by towns, counties generally serve as the primary local unit for administering federal, state, and many local elections. The county governing board, or perhaps a special county elections board, has the responsibility for establishing voting precinct or ward boundaries and the designation of certain election administration officials. A county official—the clerk, auditor, or elections registrar— will serve as the administrator for elections by sending election notices to newspapers, preparing ballots, distributing ballots, training local officials, and performance of other election functions.

Property tax assessment and collection. Over 90 percent of the counties are responsible for placing the taxable valuation on property through the employment of assessors, sending out tax bills based on those assessments, and collecting the property tax revenue.

Law enforcement. Through the office of the sheriff and the prosecuting attorney, county governments are responsible for enforcing the state criminal laws within their borders by apprehending and prosecuting violators.

Judicial administration. Though many state court systems have been streamlined through the judicial unification program in recent years, county courts with general jurisdiction still continue to be the base of the judicial system in many states. Counties provide courtrooms, office space, and secretarial services for their own courts, as well as for the circuit or district judges who conduct their judicial business by moving from one county to another. The county judicial services often include special courts, such as probate, small claims, family, juvenile, and others.

Disaster preparedness. Called civil defense in the 1950s and 1960s, over 90 percent of the counties maintain a disaster preparedness capability to deal with natural disasters as well as to plan for nuclear conflict.

Road maintenance. Almost 90 percent of the counties have designated a county highway system to supplement the state and federal highways transversing their borders. In many areas, counties will contract with smaller towns and townships to provide highway and street maintenance services.

Record vital statistics. Over 80 percent of the counties collect vital statistics on births, deaths, and other occurrences specified by state law.

Public health. Many counties maintain a staff of health professionals to monitor communicable diseases, control epidemics, provide health checks for children, render home health care for adults, and provide numerous other health-related programs. County health service may even include institutions, such as King County hospital in Seattle or Milwaukee County hospital.

Welfare. In approximately half of the states, county governments bear the responsibility for delivery of welfare services to the ultimate client, even though state and federal governments provide most of the money and policy guidelines. Over half of the counties provide some form of emergency financial assistance, administer food stamp programs, provide family social services and child welfare services, among others.

Education. Most education services are provided through independent self-governing school districts. Nevertheless, counties in states continue to be involved in a variety of ways. Some counties still elect school superintendents to assist small schools in the county. However, school district consolidation has changed the role and sometimes the need for such officials. In other areas, the county governments operate primary, secondary, and community college programs. Close to three-fourths of the counties operate or share in the operation of libraries.

Parks and recreation. The availability of leisure time and urbanization have both contributed to new pressures for county park and recreation programs. Close to half of the counties have responded with park and recreation programs.

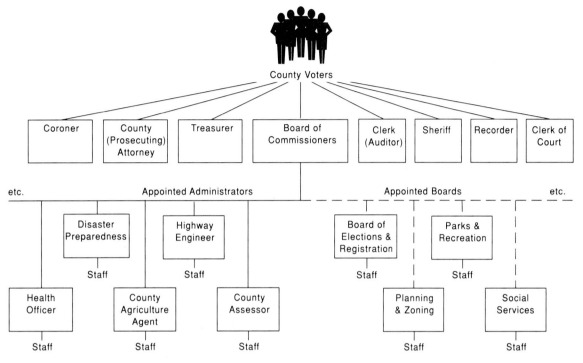

Figure 14.2
Structure of a typical county government.

Land use. A strong majority of counties have become engaged in land use planning, zoning, and subdivision control, practices that reflect the growing diversification of county functions to meet demographic changes.

Numerous other services can be found in county governments. Rural counties provide services related to an agricultural constituency, such as county extension programs, weed and rodent control, drainage control, and county fairs. Urban counties, on the other hand, will stress airports, mass transit, solid waste management, pollution control, convention centers, job services, housing development and management, and economic development programs.

Components of the Typical County Government

The structural configuration of county government will vary from state to state and even from county to county within states. However, approximately four-fifths of the counties have sufficient commonality in their design to substantiate some generalizations about most county governments. The "typical" county government is made up of four discernible components: (1) a governing board, (2) several elected administrators, (3) several appointed administrators, and (4) a variety of boards and commissions. (Figure 14.2).

The County Governing Boards

Thirty-four different titles

Almost universally the main governing authority of a county is a body of elected members with the official title of *board, court, commission,* or other title. Although some 34 different titles are used throughout the United States to identify county governing boards, the most commonly used title is *board of commissioners,* with *board of supervisors* running second. Other titles include: *commissioners court, county court, boards of commissioners and revenue, fiscal court, quarterly court, quorum court,* and a score of others. The size of the governing boards is three or five members in the case of more than two-thirds of the counties, but the average is seven, and it extends upward to 30 or more in some counties. The members hold such titles as *commissioner, supervisor,* or *magistrate,* and, in Louisiana parishes, *police juror.* The chair in a few states has the title of *judge of the county court,* as did Harry Truman when he headed the governing board of Jackson County, Missouri. The presiding officer has no regular veto, and the status as chair is decided sometimes by the members and sometimes by the voters. The chair has a measure of administrative authority in applying the decisions and orders of the body.

Five types of membership

County boards differ not only in title and size, but also in the type of membership. Any such classification of more than 3,000 governing bodies runs the risk of being arbitrary, but it is possible to suggest the following types, based on the official character of membership: (1) Boards of commissioners, or supervisors, whose primary function and accountability are as members of the county board; that is, this is their main job with the county. (2) Boards made up of township supervisors, who have dual functions and accountability as township officials and also county governing-board members. Some of these supervisors represent municipal governments as well. (3) Judges and justices of the peace boards, whose members serve both as board members and as judicial officers. (4) Judge and commissioner boards, with a mixed membership consisting of a presiding officer serving both as a board member and judicial officer, and others who function only as board members. (5) Other county governing bodies including such unusual types as the single-member "ordinary" in Georgia, and eight of the boroughs in Alaska where city officials serve with elected members of the board.

One-person, one-vote applies to county boards

In 1968, the U.S. Supreme Court ruled in *Avery v. Midland County* that members of county governing boards must be elected in accordance with the one-person, one-vote principle. For counties electing board members on an "at large" basis, the ruling had no impact. However, for counties using commissioner districts or township supervisors, the decision meant changing the method of election because many counties were choosing commissioners in much the same way as Midland county. The districts were grossly malapportioned, with perhaps 50,000 people in one district of the county electing one commissioner and another district with 1,000 people electing a commissioner. In many cases, commissioners sought to retain rural control over county governing boards even though the majority of the county's residents lived in urban areas. To comply with the one-person, one-vote principle, counties were forced to either redraw district boundaries so equal numbers of people were electing commissioners or change to an "at large" system where all of the people of the county voted for all of the commissioners. In counties having governing boards made up of representatives of townships, all varying widely in population, it was necessary to group townships and cities into districts of relatively equal population. In counties with a significant minority population, the courts have increasingly held that the at-large system of election is discriminatory and cannot be used.

County governmental structure reflects little regard for separation of powers. County boards often represent a merger of the executive, legislative, and judicial functions of government in the exercise of their responsibilities: *Duties of boards*

Pass ordinances. Legislative powers are exercised by the county board when it passes ordinances. Because of its legal status as an arm of the state, county ordinance-passing powers are limited to those granted by the state law. In some states, this may be limited to zoning or subdivision controls. In other states, especially those with home rule, counties may have ordinance-passing authority commensurate to that found in cities.

Fiscal management. Legislative powers are also exercised by the board when it reviews the budget requests of county agencies, approves the budget, levies the taxes to meet the budget, enters into contracts, and oversees the expenditure of county moneys. County boards are often required to approve bills before payments, thus performing the pre-audit function of government. The board is usually involved in questions of county indebtedness, capital improvements, and major purchases.

Staffing the administration. Except for the officials elected directly by the people, state laws usually vest county boards with the power to appoint administrators and the members of the county boards and commissions. Exercising executive powers, they select the county agent, the disaster preparedness director, the members of the social service board, the hospital board, the county librarian, and the numerous other administrators. As in the state government, many of the newer functions of counties are managed by appointed rather than elected administrators.

Issuing licenses. County boards exercise police powers when they are empowered to license rural liquor establishments, amusement activities, or business establishments of various kinds.

Administration. In urban counties, administrative duties are too complex and time-consuming for performance by the governing board. However, in the rural counties, the board may very well oversee bridge and highway construction, interview candidates for governmental services, or perform other duties of an administrative character.

Judicial responsibilities. In Southern states the judicial functions of key county officials were of paramount importance. Thus, the familiar judicial terminology of *judge* and *court* appear as a part of the reference to governing boards. In fact, the board may have a judge as chair.

To perform assigned functions, the governing board meets on a regular basis, with the volume of business dictating the frequency of meetings. In rural counties, the board may meet once a month whereas in an urban county the board may meet weekly in addition to performing a number of duties between meetings.

Elected Administrators

*Counties have long
ballots*

Counties did not escape the throes of the Jacksonian revolution which called for the direct election of public officials. Prior to the Jacksonian period, most county officials were appointed by the state. Hence, the era that produced many elective positions for the state ballot also brought counties the concept of accountability through direct election and the premise that any amateur can perform in a public office. County offices most commonly filled by popular election include the sheriff, prosecuting attorney, recorder, treasurer, county clerk, and clerk of court. In addition, auditors, assessors, superintendents of schools, county counsels, coroners, county engineers, and comptrollers are sometimes elected.

Clerk (Auditor). This official is usually assigned a wide variety of duties and may serve as somewhat of a "secretariat" for the county government. Responsibilities may include administering elections, serving as an administrative assistant to the governing board, centralizing certain staff functions (personnel, purchasing, budgeting, and computers), issuing vouchers for payment of county expenses, handling county correspondence, receiving bids, issuing licenses and permits, and maintaining county records.

Sheriff. The sheriff is the state's chief law enforcement officer in the county who enforces the state criminal laws in the county, serves as an officer of the court, and maintains the county detention center.

Prosecuting attorney. Called by many titles, the prosecuting attorney represents the state in criminal cases against persons arrested in the county. The county attorney also serves as a legal adviser to the county board, defends the county in civil suits brought against it, and initiates actions on behalf of the county.

Recorder. The recorder, sometimes called the registrar or register of deeds, is responsible for recording and keeping safe legal documents of various types required by state law. Very commonly this person is in charge of official state copies of land titles and deeds with all encumbrances placed against them.

Treasurer. As the title indicates, the county treasurer receives taxes, fees, and other moneys due the county, deposits money in local banks as dictated by state statute, and issues payments against the accounts on behalf of the county.

Appointed Administrators

*Administrators of newer
functions appointed*

Another segment of county governmental structure consists of appointed administrators. By the turn of the century, the county election ballot had become about as long as voters could reasonably manage. At the same time, the reform movement was touting the need for more professionalism in government. Thus, when new functions were being added to county responsibilities, legislatures provided for administration by appointed rather than elected officials. And many of the newer functions added to county government were the most important. As an example, the construction and maintenance of the county highway system has become the major function in many counties. To manage this function, the county engineer or road superintendent is almost always an appointed professional. In the 1930s, when the federal–state–local welfare program evolved out of the depression, counties assumed another major duty, headed by an appointed professional social worker. Other twentieth-century functions, such as public health, manpower, airports, utilities, planning, water management, pollution, zoning, housing, parks, facilities, and libraries are headed by appointed professional administrators. Professionalism may also be desirable in posts filled by the more politicized process but these positions became "grandfathered" into the administrative system.

Boards and Commissions

The fourth component of county government structure consists of the boards and commissions, many appointed by the governing board pursuant to state law and some ex officio, consisting of groups of elected and/or appointed officials. County boards may exist for overseeing public health functions, welfare administration, zoning and planning, housing, managing facilities, and other county duties. Often when a board exists, appointment of the full-time administrator is made by the board.

County Reform Efforts

Criticisms of County Governments

For decades, the county has been criticized as the scene of the most backward and most inefficient administration of government. As indicated earlier, it has been called "the dark continent of American government." From the foregoing discussion of county governments, several problems can be identified.

Many county governments no longer have sufficient population to provide basic county services. If 50,000 people are required to maintain an efficient county unit, as suggested by some,[9] then four-fifths of the counties today fail to qualify. The lack of population becomes crucial in the delivery of services by professionals. If too small a clientele is being served, the cost of professionalism becomes exorbitant. As an example, a county of 8,000 would hardly have enough users of social services to support a professional staff knowledgeable and expert in the numerous specialties that make up social services. Another example would be found in the sheriff's department. Small counties can support only a few officers, with very limited training and little time off. Small counties with few prisoners are hard pressed to provide jails that meet the new judicial standards for avoiding "cruel and unusual punishment." Unable to afford the cost of upgrading their jails, many counties abandoned local incarceration and opted for the new costs of driving prisoners to other county seats for holding.

a. Counties lack population, clients

Many counties no longer have the tax base to support a professional governmental staff. Stemming from the small populations of many counties, the problem of limited resources has become more pressing as personnel in the various service fields have become professionalized and the equipment they use has become costlier. Public opinion has practically frozen property taxes, the mainstay of local county taxes, over the past few decades. Much of the increase in county spending has been made possible by more extensive state and federal aid. Some counties have been authorized to utilize other taxes and fees but they have failed to keep pace with the modernization of government.

b. Small tax base

c. Lack authority

County governments lack the authority to respond vigorously to problems arising out of urbanization and modernization. Under the traditional legal views of county authority, local officials are in a virtual straightjacket in many areas of local concern.

d. No executive leadership

The structure of county government negates the possibility of political or administrative leadership. With an elected governing board, sharing executive and administrative responsibilities with several other independent elected officials, a number of appointed officials, and a plethora of boards and commissions, county administration lacks unity, coherence, and direction. Policy is erratic as numerous officials and bodies hopelessly seek to set the course for county government. While citizens may enjoy voting for a large number of county administrators and board members, the question of accountability is a serious one in county government.

e. County politics

County governments are highly politicized. Providing for the election of county administrators injects politics into issues that call for professional solutions. When sheriffs and prosecuting attorneys—both fields requiring professionalism in the 1990s—must secure office by election, they are judged by the electorate according to political criteria, sometimes to the exclusion of professional criteria. To keep their offices, they must continue to "play politics" and temper their professionalism with due consideration for "practical politics." Politicization not only threatens professionalism but it also may result in the delivery of services in conformity to the political power structure dominating the county, paving the way for preferred treatment for some citizens.

This is by no means a complete listing of the criticisms that have been directed at county governments. However, the few that have been presented are widely acknowledged and have stimulated interest in corrective measures through the decades.

Proposals to Reform County Government

For some reformers, the consolidation of counties has been the most rational approach

a. Consolidation

for dealing with the lack of adequate population. A few state constitutions permit consolidation but the results have been meager. In fact, the number of counties has remained around 3,040 for the past five or six decades even though more and more counties have been declining in population. Fear of counties becoming too large geographically, though enunciated by opponents, is not a consideration, especially since San Bernardino County, California, proves counties the size of Vermont and New Hampshire combined can function. Hence, consolidation is not a question of service efficiency or accessibility. It is usually a question of politics. Every direct beneficiary of the existence of individual counties, from the "courthouse gang" to the county seat businesses, opposes consolidation because it would jeopardize their benefits, whether in the form of material gain or political influence.

The duplication of services by county and city governments in the same geographical area raises many problems and stimulates many proposals in the fields of

b. Merge city-county

law enforcement, education, taxation, health, public utilities, and other matters. To eliminate costly duplication, proposals have been advanced to merge county and city governments. New Orleans has one administration for the city and coterminous parish of Orleans. In some states, especially Virginia, cities have been separated from county jurisdiction for governmental purposes. Major structural change is fraught with political implications and resistance, so duplication is most often eliminated through the

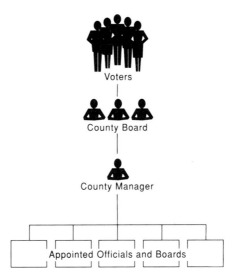

Figure 14.3
Manager form of county government.

merging of specific functions and offices. Thus, city–county health departments, and city–county solid waste disposal programs are more common than comprehensive city–county governments.

The most common suggestion for overcoming administrative fragmentation in county government has been to create a central management figure, either a professional manager appointed by the county governing board or an executive elected directly by the people. Since cities had observable experiences with the manager form, counties found it easier to implement. Thus, the manager form has been somewhat more popular in counties than the elected executive model. Under the manager form, the governing board employs a professional administrator to oversee the day-to-day management of county affairs, while the board confines itself to adopting policy and oversight activities. The administrators of various departments are accountable to the manager who, in turn, is answerable to the governing board for the entire county adminstration. (See figure 14.3.) The manager form may be found scattered throughout the nation, with the major concentrations found in Arizona, North Carolina, California, Florida, Louisiana, South Carolina, Virginia, and Maryland. The numerical extent to which county managers are being used is difficult to establish since the definition of *manager* may vary from state to state. Nevertheless, it appears that more than 600 counties have appointive administrators or managers.

Larger counties, recognizing a need for strong policy leadership, have been the users of the elected executive system (figure 14.4). Under this form, the doctrine of separation of powers is more pronounced, with the governing board serving as the legislative body and the elected administrator serving as the executive. This form sacrifices professionalism for political skills and direct accountability in the top administrator. By the early 1990s, close to 400 counties were using the system; however, more than half of these counties were located in three states—Arkansas, Kentucky, and Tennessee. Counties with the chief executive represented a little more than 10 percent of

c. Central manager

Manager form

Elected executive form

Figure 14.4
Executive form of county
government.

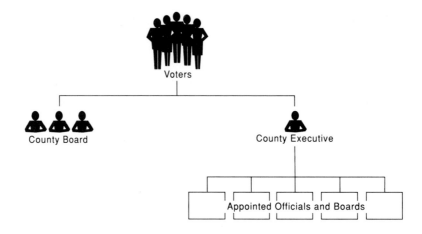

Voters

County Board

County Executive

Appointed Officials and Boards

the counties, a much higher percentage of the U.S. population, indicating usage in high population counties. Among the major counties using the elected executive are Nassau, Westchester, Suffolk, and Eric counties in New York; Milwaukee county in Wisconsin; Baltimore, Montgomery, and Prince George in Maryland; Atlantic, Essex, and Hudson in New Jersey; and Erie and Lehigh in Pennsylvania.[10] A number of the city–county governments in the United States use the elected executive. Approximately one-half of all counties of 250,000 or more have some form of appointive or elective executive.

This high usage in the urban counties suggests that where problems are pressing, counties cannot afford the luxury of administrative chaos. By the early 1990s three-fourths of all counties still had no chief administrator, with or without professional qualifications. In the absence of pressing problems, adoption of the central management forms is staunchly opposed by the courthouse power structure. The governing board may favor the manager system as a means of securing more control of government, but the elected officials and the various appointing boards and commissions see it as a system that will reduce their prerogatives if not their positions. Here again, political considerations take precedence over issues of efficiency and economy.

d. Home rule   To escape the problems involved in strict interpretation of county authority, and to allow more organizational flexibility the concept of home rule has been advanced for counties. Here again, with cities paving the way, counties have had the opportunity to observe home rule in action. Home rule is made available to counties either through constitutional amendment or legislative enactment. Either way, under home rule the state can authorize counties greater discretion in determining structures of government, fiscal policies, optional services, and other matters of local concern. Even though more than half of the states permit county home rule, very few counties have bothered to translate the state authorization into a working county charter, only eighty-five by 1987. Almost half of the charter counties have populations over 250,000, signifying that urban counties find home rule more useful than smaller counties.[11]

e. Intergovernmental
agreements   Numerous state constitutions and statutes authorize local governments to enter into intergovernmental agreements for the sharing of functions or for transferring

functions. In cases where counties have too few clients to justify professionalism in a certain function, many of them have entered into contracts with neighboring counties and cities to provide more effective delivery of services. Since the intergovernmental agreement usually solves the problems of a single service, it is politically more acceptable than some of the other reorganizational alternatives.

Amateurism in county leadership has resulted in the lack of appreciation for professionalism throughout the county bureaucracy. Often, county positions are seen as opportunities to provide jobs for political supporters, relatives, and others who may lack the professional qualifications to do a professional job. Adoption of the merit system, or civil service, has been proposed to minimize patronage and amateurism. Overall merit systems exist in only a small percentage of the nation's counties. What little progress there has been in this respect is to be found in the populous or urban counties or in administrative operations subject to state and federal standards. A few states have provisions for state assistance or supervision in administering local merit systems on a county optional basis. Among these states are New York, New Jersey, and California. An example of the merit system under special or local legislation is to be found in Jefferson County, Alabama, which contains the city of Birmingham. In many rural or isolated counties it would be impossible, even with full legal or constitutional power, to inaugurate a real merit or personnel policy without reliance upon imported experts and applicants. Rural folkways may prefer the development of rule-of-thumb competence that smacks neither of expertness nor of pure spoils. If the U.S. Supreme Court continues to hold that county employees cannot be fired by newly elected officials on the basis of partisan affiliation, the county spoils system may shrivel on the vine. Under these circumstances, counties may be more willing to adopt personnel systems that establish professional entrance requirements since employees will remain on the payroll regardless of election results.

f. Merit system

Historically, the property tax has been the workhorse for the county revenue system, but it has had limited potential. Public opinion is generally adverse to increases and the inequities inherent in the system. Diversifying local revenue sources has been hindered by the refusal of state governments to delegate authority and by the inability of many counties to gain jurisdiction of the mobile tax base involved in income and sales taxes. Organizing additional administrative machinery for new forms of taxes has also been a barrier. Because of these and other restraints, counties have been forced to rely more heavily on federal and state aid, running as much as two-thirds of some county budgets. In some functional areas, such as courts, counties have been able to get states to assume a greater share of the cost. Faced with limited local options and declining federal funds, counties are compelled to manage their finances with an air of flexibility. Every session of Congress and the state legislature threatens to alter the budget for the next year (figure 14.5).

g. Diversify revenue

Townships

The U.S. Census Bureau applies the term *township governments* to 16,691 organized governments in 20 states, located primarily in northeast and north central United States. Included by the Bureau in this broad classification are the towns of six New England

Towns and townships

Figure 14.5

Trends in county general revenue from selected major sources: 1980–1990. While intergovernmental revenue and property taxes doubled in the ten-year period, revenue from charges and miscellaneous tripled. This suggests that counties are imposing more user fees and service charges to recover the costs of delivering services. Nonproperty taxes are not a large part of the revenue picture, but they also almost tripled in growth. Stated in percentages, intergovernmental aid represented 39 percent of the county general revenue. Local taxes raised 36 percent, while charges and miscellaneous brought in 25 percent.

(Source: Bureau of the Census, County Government Finances in 1989–90.*)*

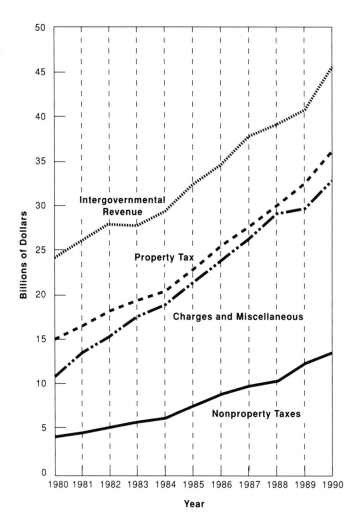

states, New York, Wisconsin, some *plantations* in Maine, *locations* in New Hampshire, and *townships* in the remaining states. These local governments are distinguished from municipalities in that municipalities are created to serve specific concentrations of population while townships exist to serve inhabitants of defined areas without regard to population concentrations. New Jersey and Pennsylvania describe their townships as *municipal corporations* but they are included in the Census township category because they function without regard to a concentration of population.[12]

Governments included in this township classification range widely in their scope of governmental services and operations. Those in New England, New Jersey, Pennsylvania, Michigan, Minnesota, New York, and Wisconsin have broad powers and provide services often identified with municipalities. In contrast, the rural townships in

Some townships provide municipal services

the North Central states perform a very limited number of functions.[13] New England towns often differ from their North Central cousins geographically. The boundaries of towns allow for the natural terrain while striking out with straight lines, thereby giving them 20 to 40 square miles of jurisdiction in an irregular shape unique to the town. Rural townships, on the other hand, are governments organized within the boundaries of the surveyed township, which is most often a standard square, six miles on a side, 36 miles in total.

Though counted as townships, New England towns and North Central townships possess sufficient numbers of unique qualities to be discussed separately.

New England Towns

Though some scholars credit early English parish meetings with the origin of New England towns, others claim it descended from farm meetings in ancient Germany. In either case, New England town government began just a few years within the founding of the settlements in the Boston area. Faced with an expanding population, the Massachusetts legislature decided that each settlement should be authorized to organize and govern as a town in the same fashion as the English parishes. Weekly or monthly meetings were held to dispose of business. Eventually, the agendas became too long, attendance declined, and decision-making was delegated to a committee of "select men" who would act between meetings. This interim committee made it possible to lengthen the periods between meetings until today town meetings are usually held once annually in March.[14]

Meetings and "select men"

Some days before town meeting day, a "warning" (notice) is issued of the upcoming annual session, stating the convening time and the items of business to be covered. At the appointed hour, all qualified voters are eligible to gather at the meeting house. Following the election of a moderator, business commences in earnest. Early town meeting agendas included a variety of subjects, some more fascinating and disruptive than others. They dealt with such issues as impounding stray animals, regulating the height of fences, punishment for Sabbath-breakers, care of the poor, laying out streets, granting pay raises, setting tax rates, approving the budget, electing officials, ad infinitum.

Town meeting

Among the officials elected at the town meeting are the selectmen who are empowered to make appointments, issue licenses, plan annual agendas, propose the budget, review bills for payment, arrange for elections, and otherwise conduct the business of the town between annual meetings. Other elective officers may include the town clerk, listers who review property assessments for tax purposes, a treasurer–tax collector, grand jurors to file charges involving minor crimes, a board of auditors, and a constable to enforce the laws. Some of the more quaint offices that have disappeared from the ballot are the sealer of leather, culler of hoop poles, staves and headings, the fence viewer, trustee of public funds, and a trustee of public money. Appointments available to the board of selectmen are the tree wardens, fire warden, pound keeper, inspector of lumber, shingles, and wood, and weighers of coal.

Town officials

Over the three centuries of their existence, town meeting agendas have changed as state governments have assumed greater responsibilities in law enforcement, highways, welfare, health, and education. Some towns have become so heavily populated

Town meetings change

that the eligible participants can no longer fit inside the meeting hall or have a meaningful role in the meeting. Attendance has declined. Less than 25 percent of the eligibles bother to attend, although that turnout is not too unlike the municipal elections in other parts of the United States.

Traditional town meetings have been on the decline, even though a strong majority of towns in New England still continue them. Some town meetings, especially in Connecticut and Massachusetts, now consist of representatives elected by the voters in district or precinct elections. The representatives, perhaps as many as 100 or 150, then convene and conduct the business of the town meeting. Other towns, especially in Maine, have gone to the town manager who works under the supervision of the selectmen. A form of town meeting is still held but the agenda is refined by the presence of a professional administrator in the community.

Representative town meetings

Townships

The structure and authority of townships in the 15 states outside of New England are contingent on the type of services required to meet the needs of the inhabitants. In states such as Michigan, New Jersey, Ohio, and Pennsylvania, the density of population varies considerably from one end of the state to the other, resulting in township governments that range from few services for the rural areas to scores of services for the populous areas. Pennsylvania even divides its township governments into two classes, with a density of 300 people per square mile as the point of division. In Michigan, townships provide police protection, emergency medical care, parks, recreation programs, water and sewer services, street lighting, libraries, solid waste disposal, zoning, planning, and many other urban services. Some urbanized townships have full-time board chairs or managers. In New Jersey, some urbanized townships have adopted regular forms of city government—commission, council-manager, or strong mayor-council.

Urban townships

Rural townships provide little in the way of services. Most assume responsibility for rural roads not maintained under the federal, state, or county highway programs; some may still serve as precincts for the conduct of elections under state law; some still have responsibilities in relation to the assessment and equalization of property for tax purposes. Other than the foregoing three functions, rural township duties will vary from state to state and include such items as fire protection, cemeteries, and weed control. Because rural townships lack the revenue base and the population necessary to support functions, counties and special districts are more important service units.

Rural townships

About one-half of the township states outside of New England require annual business meetings of the inhabitants to elect officers, approve budgets, and make other policy decisions. The remaining states provide for election of township officers who are charged with conducting the business of the township.

Township boards and officials

The governing board of the typical township is called the board of supervisors, the board of trustees, or simply the township board, and usually consists of three to five persons. While a majority of the boards are elected particularly for that function, some townships include other elected officials on their boards as ex officio members. Most townships also elect clerks and treasurers with assessors, constables, justices of the peace, and road commissioners becoming more rare. Over half of the townships, undoubtedly all rural, operate without employees. Nevertheless, almost 100 townships have 25 or more employees, with 25 of those 100 having 200 or more employees.[15]

Fifty years ago, Professor Lane W. Lancaster wrote that there wasn't a function being performed by townships that could not be better performed by other units of government.[16] Around thirty years ago, the Committee for Economic Development advocated the dissolution of townships with less than 2,500 people, which would have included the vast majority of them.[17] In spite of the questions raised about their viability, townships continue to exist in defiance of their detractors.

Townships defy prophets

Endnotes

1. Gregory Streib and William L. Waugh, Jr., "Facing the Challenge of County Governance: Examining the Policy Issues Facing Local Government from the Perspective of County Leaders," a paper presented at the annual meeting of the Southern Political Science Association, November 8–10, 1990, p. 1.

2. Henry Gilbertson, *The County: The Dark Continent of American Politics* (New York: The National Short Ballot Association, 1917).

3. Richard Childs, *Ramshackle County Government: The Plague Spot of American Politics* (New York: The National Municipal League, 1926).

4. Streib and Waugh, pp. 2–4. Streib and Waugh, together with nine other scholars, co-author a remarkable article assessing the literature on county government since the turn of the century and suggest a research focus for the future: Donald C. Menzel, Vincent L. Marando, Roger B. Parks, William L. Waugh, Jr., Beverly A. Cigler, James H. Svara, Mavis Mann Reeves, J. Edwin Benton, Robert D. Thomas, Gregory Streib, and Mark Schneider, "Setting a Research Agenda for the Study of the American County," *Public Administration Review,* 52 (March/April, 1992), 173–182. They recommend that county government research in the 1990s focus on: (1) The relationship between government structure and performance, (2) the role of leadership and professional management, (3) service delivery, administrative responsiveness and equity, (4) county responsiveness to changing environmental conditions, (5) county governments as democratic institutions, and (6) the role of counties in the American federal system.

5. Herbert Sydney Duncombe, *Modern County Government* (Washington: National Association of Counties, 1977), p. 5.

6. The Taney, Ohio, and Dillon observations are cited by Susan Walker Torrence in *Grass Roots Government* (Washington, D.C.: Robert B. Luce, Inc., 1974), pp. 6–7.

7. Bureau of the Census, U.S. Department of Commerce, *1987 Census of Governments,* Vol. 1, No. 1, 1989, p. vi.

8. The works of Herbert S. Duncombe, *County Government in America* (Washington: National Association of Counties, 1966), *Modern County Government* (Washington: National Association of Counties, 1977), and *Profile of County Government* (Washington: Advisory Commission on Intergovernmental Relations, 1972) have been helpful in this inventory of county functions. A more recent classification of functions incorporates the growing pressure for municipal-type services: (1) Administrative arm of the state, (2) traditional government, (3) local government, and (4) regional government. See John Larkin's discussion of Tanis Salant's classification of roles in "County Governments Redefine Themselves," *Public Administration Times,* August 1, 1992, pp. 1, 16.

9. See the discussion in *Modernizing Local Government* (New York, Committee for Economic Development, 1966).

10. "Chief Executive Plan Popular in Counties," a report in the County Government section, Thomas D. Wilson, ed., *National Civic Review* 68 (October 1979): 501–502. See also 1987 Census of Governments, *Governmental Organization: Popularly Elected Officials,* U.S. Department of Commerce, Bureau of the Census, Vol. 1, No. 1, 1988, p. 8.

11. "Michigan Council Studies Counties," in County Government section, Thomas D. Wilson, ed., *National Civic Review* (July 1981): 372. See also 1987 Census of Governments Vol. 1, No. 1, 1988, p. 8.

12. U.S. Bureau of the Census, 1982 Census of Governments, *Governmental Organization,* Vol. 1 (Washington, D.C.: Government Printing Office, 1983), p. VIII.

13. Ibid., p. IX.

14. Andrew E. Nuquist, *Town Government in Vermont* (Burlington, Vt.: Government Research Center, University of Vermont, 1964), pp. 3–4.

15. U.S. Advisory Commission on Intergovernmental Relations, *State and Local Roles in the Federal System* (Washington, D.C.: Government Printing Office, 1982), p. 235.

16. Lane W. Lancaster, *Government in Rural America* (Princeton, N.J.: D. Van Nostrand Co., 1937), p. 77.

17. Committee for Economic Development, *Modernizing Local Government* (1966), p. 42.

LOCAL GOVERNMENT III: THE CITY

CHAPTER 15

An Entity to Provide Local Services

Cities are as old as the human race. According to the book of Genesis, Adam's son, Cain, built a city that he named Enoch for his new son.[1] His motive may have been to pay tribute to a son, but most early cities—including many in the United States—were formed to provide protection for inhabitants. While defense may have been the earliest reason for the huddling together of families, tribes, and settlers, cities have come into existence for numerous other reasons—for human activity at points where changes of transportation occur (water to land, train to hoof, etc.), as service centers for commerce and manufacturing, as political capitols, as centers of religious worship, for military operations, as recreation facilities, and even as deliberately planned communities. Cities that conform to these various categories can be found throughout the United States, though some have matured into multipurpose municipalities.

Basics about City Governments

City government in America, born primarily to benefit its residents, supplements rather than supplants other governments. As an example, city government may provide local services, but these are normally in addition to those already provided by the county and the state. Not only are cities unique in their service characteristics, but they also differ from most other local governments because of their corporate character. They come into existence through a process of incorporation, thereby assuming the characteristics of a legal person for purposes of conducting business. They can sue and be sued; they can purchase, own, and sell property; and they can enter into contracts and agreements. In short, they can behave much like private corporations or persons and, consequently, enjoy considerable autonomy.

Cities have corporate characteristics

The U.S. Census Bureau defines a city as a municipal corporation that has been established to provide a general local government for a specific population concentration in a defined area. This definition includes all active governmental units designated as cities, boroughs (except in Alaska), towns (except in the six New England states, Minnesota, New York, and Wisconsin), and villages. Alaskan boroughs have been classified primarily as counties; in New England, Minnesota, New York, and Wisconsin,

Census gives definition

Photo by Eric K. Hylden.

the term *town* refers to an area subdivision that may be a municipal corporation but has no necessary relationship to a concentration of people and thus corresponds to townships in other states.[2]

Cities still increasing in numbers

Municipalities constitute the only class of general local governments that is increasing in numbers. Counties have remained around 3,040 for several decades, and townships are on a slow decline, but municipalities grew by 338 to a total of 19,200 over the decade of 1977–1987. Most of the new incorporations occurred in southern states and California. Illinois continues to lead the nation with 1,279 municipalities followed closely by Texas with 1,156. New England states tend to have few municipalities since the towns provide residents with municipal services. Hawaii has the fewest incorporated municipalities with one—Honolulu. Over 40 percent of the 150 million Americans now living in incorporated municipalities make their residences in cities of 100,000 and over. Almost half of all municipalities have less than 1,000 residents.[3]

Classifications

Although all cities of the state may exercise similar corporate powers, many states create classifications of cities. In some cases, classifications are created to evade constitutional restrictions against the legislature passing special laws for particular cities; in other cases, they are created so that states can delegate certain powers to classes of cities they deem able to handle the powers. Classifications are usually based on population, although a rare state, such as Utah, may base classifications on assessed valuation of property. In many cases, the state law creates a series of classes with each class including cities of a certain population. Sometimes the state will refer to the classes as cities, towns, and villages, each of which includes cities of certain population levels. To confuse matters, some states use these three labels even though all municipalities are treated alike.

City Charters

Origin of charters

Prior to the settling of America, the authority to govern cities in England was delegated to coteries of the King's friends through charters that specified powers to be exercised. When cities came into existence in America, governors represented the crown in granting the charters of governance to cities. Being somewhat more democratic, however, American city governance involved all people of property rather than a select few. It has been estimated that only about 20 cities were chartered in the 13 colonies during the entire colonial period.[4] After the Revolution, the chartering authority of the crown was assumed by state legislatures along with most royal gubernatorial prerogatives.

Three kinds of charters

Charters fall into three groups, classified according to the methods by which they are formulated and put into effect. They include special charters, general charters, and home rule charters. Different methods or combinations may be used in the same state. Furthermore, there is not necessarily any difference between one method or another when it comes to the actual form of municipal government resulting from the process. For example, a mayor–council form could exist under a special charter, general charter, or home rule charter.

1. Special charters

The special charter issued by the state legislature is the oldest of the chartering methods. Under this procedure, when the inhabitants of an area of concentrated population decided they wished to be incorporated as a municipality, a delegation would take the matter up with the local legislative delegation and/or the appropriate committee of the state legislature. A bill was drafted providing for incorporation, complete with an official name, boundaries, form of government, powers, procedures, and other pertinent matters. When it was passed by the legislature and approved by the governor, it went into the state statutes along with the other laws. Whenever the city encountered an unexpected problem with its special charter, its officials would reappear at the legislature to have the chartering act amended. While the special charter method permitted the tailoring of municipal government to fit the particular area, the need for amendments added greatly to the legislative workload. As the population of the country increased, more cities required chartering and more charters required amending.

Cities are still incorporated under charters, although the definition of the term has gone through extensive metamorphosis in many states. A charter includes provisions for defining the cities' boundaries, governmental powers, proprietory functions, methods of finance, election of officers, appointment of employees, and numerous other miscellaneous matters. Depending on the legal tradition of the state, these various components may be found in a variety of places—the governmental powers may be found primarily in state laws; the method of finance may be in the state constitution; proprietory functions, though in state law, may be modified by court cases; and a home rule charter may prescribe the appointment of employees. Thus, the term *charter* in most states no longer refers to a single act of the legislature but refers to all of the sources of municipal authority. Even cities that have adopted home rule charters must still look to the state constitution, state law, and court cases for powers not delegated by the state to home rule cities. Other problems of the special charter systems developed. Cities became pawns in state and local politics. If local legislators were displeased with local management, they could intimidate city officials with the threat that the next session would pass legislation to direct city management the way legislators thought best. Special charters also made cities vulnerable to the machinations of state-level politics. Political machines in the legislature could change municipal electoral systems or hold city charter amendments hostage until the local legislative delegations toed the political line. Even though imbued with the most altruistic of motives, legislatures were seen by reformers as unsuited for passing laws governing the particulars of city government. The report of a commission to devise a plan of government for New York cities charged that legislatures lacked the time, knowledge, and local accountability for such legislation. Of the 808 acts passed by the New York legislature in 1870, 212 related to cities and villages, 36 to the city of New York, and "a still larger number to the city of Brooklyn."[5]

Contents of charters

Sources of charters

Problems with special charters

The general act charters grew out of the dissatisfaction with special act charters, with some states (Ohio and Indiana as early as 1851) outlawing special legislation by constitutional amendment. Under the general charter approach, laws were passed to apply to all municipalities, thus becoming a standard charter for all cities. Instead of requiring individual areas to come to the legislature with hat-in-hand, the general laws would outline a general procedure by which new cities could become incorporated as they chose. Incorporation became greatly simplified, with the legislature no longer involved in the process.

2. General charters

It was soon discovered, however, that general laws covering cities of 250 to 500,000 proved inadequate for dealing with the variations in problems and needs. As a result,

a. General classified

the concept of a general act was subdivided to provide greater flexibility. One of the subdivisions could be called "general but classified," i.e., classes of cities were created and empowered to adopt the charter that was prescribed for their particular class. For example, Class A cities consisting of populations 100 to 10,000 were chartered as mayor–council forms of government with certain powers; and Class B cities consisting of populations 10,001 to 50,000 were chartered with council–manager forms of government with certain additional powers. However, some cities in Class A wanted the council–manager form and some in Class B wanted the mayor–council form, so another

b. General optional

division of the general charter was provided as "general but optional." Under this form of chartering, cities could choose which form of government and concomitant powers they wanted—commission, mayor–council, or council–manager.

To reformers, moving from special charters to general charters was a step in the right direction, but it was not quite adequate to escape the political machinations and meddling of legislatures. They wanted to be certain that local affairs were governed

3. Home rule charters

by local people and advocated home-rule charters as the ultimate escape. Home-rule charters may be made available to cities through an amendment to the state constitution or an act passed by the legislature. Of the two methods, cities have preferred the self-executing constitutional amendment to prevent future legislative sessions from tampering with powers as they can do if home-rule authority is based on a simple statute.

More than half of the states provide for some form of city home rule, and two-thirds of the cities with populations over 200,000 have home rule. The movement has

History of home rule

been rather intermittent since Missouri adopted a constitutional measure for home-rule government in 1875. Home-rule movements were most active at about the turn of the century and prior to World War I. Thereafter, interest declined until the period following World War II when it registered a strong upsurge. Several states, among them Georgia, Louisiana, Maryland, Rhode Island, and Tennessee, adopted constitutional amendments in the 1950s to permit or increase home rule in their cities. Cities with home-rule charters are found chiefly in the West, the Midwest, and the state of New York; New England and much of the South rely on the other methods of city chartering. Six states (Alabama, Indiana, Illinois, Kentucky, North Carolina, and Virginia) do not permit the adoption of a locally drafted charter.[6]

Restrictions on home rule

Some states have constitutional provisions making all cities eligible for home-rule charters; others have arrangements for applying the system to cities of specified population range, as over 3,500, or over 10,000, or over 50,000. Some states require gubernatorial or legislative approval to make the adoption of home rule effective for a municipality. Michigan authorizes a governor's veto of home-rule adoptions. Sometimes home-rule constitutional provisions are not effective without legislative action, which may not be forthcoming. This was discovered by Philadelphia, which had to wait 27 years for legislation implementing the "permissive" amendment.

Politics of home rule

The expansion of home rule is partly retarded by political considerations, and sometimes by political parties or pressure groups with more power in the legislature than in the city. An agrarian legislature may hesitate to reduce its power over a large city of a different political complexion. Urban legislators are often sent to the state capitol from counties rather than from cities. They may relish the continuous exercise of local power through special legislation, preferring not to grant home rule. Many cities may not feel threatened by the state legislature, particularly when the controlling local faction is a part of the controlling group at the state level.

Moreover, home rule, when granted, is never absolute and never establishes a "free city." It may stimulate local democracy, but it provides no necessary reduction of state administrative centralization, which may render any city financially dependent regardless of its type of charter. Other aspects and difficulties of home rule for cities and other units will be indicated in chapter 17, which deals with metropolitan problems.

Whether home rule is authorized by constitutional amendment or legislative enactment, it is meaningless until implemented by local initiative. The usual steps for adoption include: (1) an election on the question of implementing home rule; (2) an election of the local members of the charter drafting commission; (3) the charter commission drafts the specific charter, including such powers as it deems advisable for its city, within the parameters set by the constitution or law; (4) an election for the approval or rejection of the charter as proposed; and (5) the filing of the charter or other action as specified for completing ratification of the charter.

Steps for adopting home rule

Forms of Government

Every American city charter, however adopted, provides for one of three general forms of municipal government, although for each form there are adaptations or variations. The three, in chronological order of origin, are the mayor–council, commission, and council–manager forms. The first is the most widely used. It constitutes the only form in vogue for American cities with a population of a million or more, and it easily dominates the choice of small cities and towns that must rely largely upon part-time officials rather than full-time administrators. The other forms have been accepted for hundreds of large or middle-sized cities of less than a million population. After World War I, commission government, as strictly understood, ceased to make gains and, since World War II, has declined significantly, while the manager form has become widely attractive to cities of the middle bracket. The council–manager type rapidly supplanted mayor–council government in the second quarter of the twentieth century, becoming the form most widely used by cities between 25,000 and 250,000 in population. The number of adoptions of the council–manager plan stood at about 500 in 1940, doubled to approximately 1,000 by 1950, and more than doubled again by 1980, passing 2,000. The growth has continued, but at a reduced rate in recent years, with more than 2,800 by 1992, plus 133 in Canada. The trend has tended to match the growth or advancement of expert management in business and industry. (See table 15.1.)

Three basic forms of city government

Mayor–Council Forms

City government by mayor and council is the nearest approach to the separation of powers between legislature and executive in the old-fashioned way. It stems by title at least from cities of Britain or Europe, being an adaptation of the form the colonists knew in their native land. It is defended as suitable to American urban politics, whether for good or ill. It might be described as the most politicized type of urban government and, largely because of that characteristic, is not easily changed or replaced (Figure 15.2).

Table 15.1 Form of Government in Cities over 2,500

Population Group	Number of Cities	Mayor–Council No.	%	Council–Manager No.	%	Commission No.	%	Town Meetings No.	%
Over 1,000,000	8	6	75%	2	25%	—		—	
500,000–1,000,000	16	13	81%	3	18%	—		—	
250,000–500,000	36	16	44%	18	50%	2	6%	—	
100,000–250,000	125	42	34%	77	62%	6	5%	—	
50,000–100,000	313	105	34%	193	62%	10	3%	5	2%
25,000–50,000	668	247	37%	369	55%	29	4%	23	3%
10,000–25,000	1,602	745	46%	681	43%	54	3%	122	8%
5,000–10,000	1,789	999	56%	611	34%	35	2%	144	8%
2,500–5,000	2,125	1,472	69%	466	22%	34	2%	153	7%
All cities	7,130	3,805	53%	2,656	37%	174	2%	495	7%

Source: Adapted from *The Municipal Yearbook, 1991* (Washington, D.C.: International City Management Association, 1991), p. xiv. Percents may not total 100 because of rounding.

Figure 15.1

At one time, two-house city legislative systems were not uncommon. However, today Everett, Massachusetts, is the only remaining American city governed by a two-house system. Here in an unusual joint session are the seven-member Board of Aldermen and the eighteen-member Council. Most are elected from the city's six wards. The two bodies each elect their own presiding officers, meet on separate evenings, and independently consider ordinances.
Reprinted with permission.

Everett keeps bicameral council

Many cities that retain this form, however, have found ways of modifying and modernizing it. The bicameral council that once was in fashion has become virtually extinct; Waterville, Maine abandoned it in 1967, and Everett, Massachusetts is the only survivor of council bicameralism. (See figure 15.1.) Well over one-half of the cities with a population over 5,000 now have councils elected at large, and the percentage is much greater for the smaller cities. This poses a problem of minority and area representation and, to some extent, the citizens' feeling of loss of direct contact with "their" councilor. Proportional representation for council membership has been urged for some years by reformers for effective representation of minority groups and as a check to boss rule, but it has made little headway except in a small way with a few cities having council–manager government.

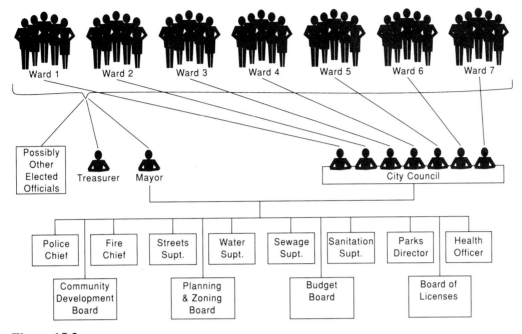

Figure 15.2
Mayor-council form.

Only in the largest cities are council members found who are devoting full time to the city's business, and even then many divide their time between being a member of council and a businessperson. A likely hypothesis concerning the kind of person attracted to the council is that the less time required for the councilor's job, the more likely it is that the community's most respected civic leaders will be found on the council. Generally speaking, smaller cities will have councils more nearly composed of leading citizens than will larger cities. But advocates of the council–manager plan contend that relief of council members from routine and time-consuming administrative detail is equally important in attracting community leadership to the council.

Most councilors part-time

It is customary for textbooks in local government to classify the various mayor–council systems in the United States as either the weak-mayor type or the strong-mayor type, some adding a third category called the hybrid type. To accept these categories uncritically is to run the risk of oversimplifying forms of city government and of neglecting the importance of the informal, "real power" picture of a city's government. Nevertheless, the classification is useful in differentiating the extremes of the power continuum for the mayor if these limitations are kept in mind.

Several types of mayor-council

The weak-mayor plan inherits the spirit of Jacksonian democracy that calls for the splintering of government into many small parts, none of which can do a great deal of good or evil. Strong reliance is placed on the council, not only for making policy, but for handling many administrative matters. The mayor is little more than a figurehead who competes with other elected city officials and a variety of independent boards,

1. Weak-mayor plan

Mayor lacks administrative authority

commissions, committees, and officials who look primarily to the council for administrative direction and control. Although the mayor is usually weak in policy-making, the greater weakness is in administrative power, being denied the important managerial tools of organization, finance, and personnel. Unless a mayor is able to change drastically the formal structure of power by such means as a strong political position or a forceful personality, the incumbent under the weak-mayor plan is doomed to the role of ceremonial head of the city. Chicago's mayors have often provided effective executive government, for example, through inherent political leadership or machine support while dealing with a council that is not only legally powerful but also large.

2. Strong-mayor plan

In many cities, administrative reorganization has strengthened the hand of the mayor as a genuine executive clothed with power as well as responsibility for the conduct of city affairs. An increasing number of weak-mayor cities have evolved into strong-mayor systems resembling a model of the national government that has the administrative departments clearly under the control of the president. Council surveillance over administrative details is diminished as the mayor is equipped with authority and staff assistance for administrative supervision. This includes extensive powers of appointment and removal, budget preparation and execution, day-to-day supervision, and veto power.

3. Strong mayor-CAO

More recently some of the largest cities have added a new feature to the strong mayor–council form by creating the position of *chief administrative officer,* a kind of deputy mayor in charge of many of the technical aspects of modern administration. The power of the CAO varies a great deal from city to city, but the general idea is to relieve the mayor of tedious administrative details so the political responsibilities can receive more attention. Some critics of the strong-mayor system in large cities felt that few mayors could serve as both politicians and administrators.

Hybrid type

Most mayor–council cities fall somewhere between the weak-mayor and strong-mayor plans, so that the most prevalent form might well be called the hybrid type. Neither the Jacksonian tradition of extreme dispersion nor the modern model of administrative integration can be said to dominate, although some elements of each can be found in most mayor–council cities today. Most cities have moved in the direction of central budgeting, purchasing, and personnel controls, but still remain a patchwork structure of independent boards and commissions not responsible to the mayor.

Commission Form

Commission born in Galveston tidal wave

The commission form of city government was born in a natural disaster. A tidal wave engulfed Galveston in 1900, entailing loss of life for thousands and property damage in the millions of dollars. Taxes could not be paid, city services were disrupted, and the city government was virtually helpless. In 1901, a group of businessmen tackled the task of reconstruction, and part of their work consisted of getting a new special charter from the state legislature to facilitate their emergency efforts. Commission government was the result, and the new form, although established for temporary purposes, became permanent and caught the attention of reformers looking for a new form to replace the mayor–council found in boss-ridden cities. For the first two decades of the 1900s, the commission form was promoted by reformers and adopted in many smaller cities, as well as a few larger ones like Birmingham and Des Moines.

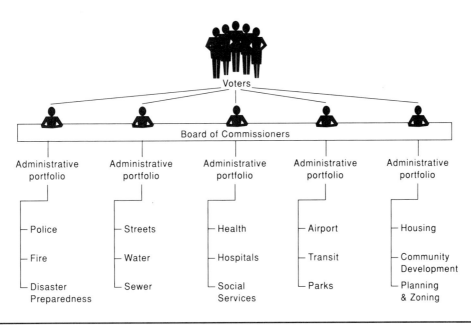

Figure 15.3
Commission form.

The city commission consists of three to seven members, most frequently five, who are elected at large, one of them serving as chairperson and nominally the mayor. (See figure 15.3.) The commission as a deliberative body formulates policy much in the manner of a council; each member is administratively responsible for the management of specific departments, such as finance, public works, or public safety. Thus, the same people make policy and execute it. As long as all are in agreement, government may run smoothly, but deadlocks can be unfortunate and disrupt leadership. Moreover, commissioners may tend to trade votes for the advantage of the departments over which they preside, with the result of extravagant budgeting or imbalance in overall program. It is sometimes observed that the membership of a city commission, which has both legislative and executive functions, is too small for the former and too large for the latter. These shortcomings became more noticeable as a newer form of municipal government began to attract attention. Reformers and reorganization experts turned from commission to city manager as a more efficient way of meeting the growing demands made upon the American city. Galveston, birthplace of the commission plan, abandoned it in 1960 in favor of the council–manager plan.

Make policy and execute it

Council–Manager

Something like council–manager government was established in Staunton, Virginia in 1908, but the plan was grafted upon the mayor–council form and retained a bicameral council. Sumter, South Carolina adopted a clear-cut council–manager form in 1912. The spread of the council–manager form dates from 1914, when Dayton, Ohio became the first large city to come under this form of municipal rule. Dayton, like Galveston earlier, had to meet sudden problems caused by a devastating flood. Civic leaders of the Chamber of Commerce, however, were already working on plans for municipal

History of manager plan

Figure 15.4
Council-manager form.

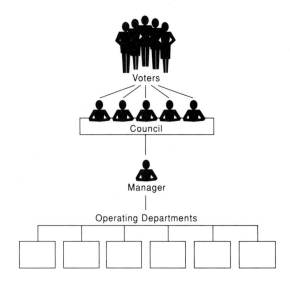

Voters

Council

Manager

Operating Departments

---

reorganization to remedy conditions of graft and inefficiency. The flood emergency intensified their effort and gave it national attention. The new charter and the new experiment lent popular impetus to the city–manager movement.

Council sets policy, manager administers

This form of government recognizes the separate but coordinate functions of politics and administration (figure 15.4). It provides for the setting of policy, approval of financial plans, and enactment of ordinances by a council, normally consisting of five to nine members elected at large on a nonpartisan ballot. The council chooses a manager who may or may not be a resident of the city at the time of appointment. The manager is responsible to the council, which controls his or her tenure and which, in turn, is responsible to the voters for the proper governance of the city. All or most of the branches and agencies of the city administration, except the board or department of education, operate under the general direction of the manager, who has power to hire and fire personnel within the scope and limits of a merit system. The council's role in administration is limited to selecting and dismissing the city manager; it is prohibited from exercising direct authority over city employees. A mayor is usually selected by the council to serve only as a ceremonial officer.

Advantages of manager plan

Many claims have been made to support adoption of the council–manager plan— so many, in fact, that over-enthusiastic proponents sometimes run the risk of serious disillusionment by the citizenry when all problems of a community are not actually solved. However, within the realm of reasonable expectation, two features of this form of government stand out above all others. One is its employment of a professionally trained, career-oriented administrator to the position of top management in municipal government, in contrast to nonprofessionalism in the other forms. Recent research supports the contention that city managers show greater respect (and awareness of the need) for professional training and assistance than do mayors.[7] The other outstanding feature is an institutional guarantee against stalemate since the manager serves only at the pleasure of the council. Many other features usually associated with the manager plan, and hotly debated in campaigns for adoption, are not exclusive features of the manager plan, and it is not unusual to find them incorporated in mayor–council charters. A few of these include the short ballot, administrative integration, nonpartisan elections, a small council elected at large, and a council freed from petty administrative routine and detail. These are not at all incompatible with the mayor–council plan.

Probably the most controversial part of the manager plan, both for governmental theory and practical politics, is the role of the manager in policy leadership. Statements made about the theory of the council–manager plan in the early years of the movement called for a manager whose role was strictly policy execution, not policy formulation. This raised a serious question concerning the source of policy leadership, no longer provided by an elective mayor, and many argued that councils could not be expected to lead themselves and that a political vacuum existed under the manager plan. This whole controversy has been modified by more systematic research that examines the council–manager plan in practice as well as on paper. A study by Professor Charles Adrian of policy leadership in three middle-sized council–manager cities in Michigan revealed that the manager and administrative departments are the principal sources of policy innovation and leadership—even though the manager avoids a public posture of policy leadership.[8]

Where is policy leadership?

The heavy involvement of city managers in policy-making is reported by Newell and Ammons, based on their survey of 527 city managers, mayors, and their assistants, with 56 percent of city managers indicating that the policy role was most important for success in their jobs. The provocative title of this report is "City Managers Don't Make Policy: A Lie, Let's Face It."[9] Some explain this policy-making involvement in terms of the steady changes in local governments' policy responsibilities in the second half of the century, moving from the more traditional "systems—maintenance policies" to the highly politicized "redistributive" programs.[10] James Svara has sought to develop a more realistic framework for dealing with this policy-administration dichotomy by identifying four components: *mission* (the broad goals and philosophy of the jurisdiction), *policy* (the mid-range decisions such as how to split the budgetary pie and who gets what services), *administration* (decisions and practices used to accomplish the policy objectives), and *management* (actions taken to support the policy and administrative functions). Svara argues for this as a model for dividing authority, with the elected council dominating mission and the city manager controlling management, but with the two sharing policy and administration.[11] The concept of "strategic decision-making" has been used by some to incorporate a rational approach to governmental effectiveness without worrying about the niceties of what is policy and what is administration. Gregory Streib commends this "systems approach" while conceding that it has many similarities to earlier experiments with "planning programming budgeting systems" (PPBS) and "zero-based budgeting" (ZBB).[12]

Any evaluation of the council–manager plan must recognize this ambivalent position of the manager with respect to political leadership. Some argue that the manager cannot be a strong leader, and for this reason, oppose the manager plan, particularly for the largest cities where policy matters loom so large. Others criticize the manager plan as primarily "businessmen's government," which is not responsive enough to the

Other criticisms of manager plan

"labor viewpoint." Minority groups and areas at times complain that their interests are overlooked by a small council elected at large and a manager responsible to such a council. Researchers have found a white middle-class protestant bias in the municipal reform movement, and also that such jurisdictions tax less and spend less, and are less responsive to the socio-economic characteristics of the community than the unreformed jurisdictions.[13] On the other hand, proponents of the plan can and do marshall an imposing array of arguments, usually centering on the idea that the proof is in the pudding—that, in fact, the manager plan has provided progressive leadership for cities and continues to meet with widespread public acceptance. Relatively few municipalities have taken steps to abandon it after trying it. City management as a career continues to grow, with an increasing number entering the field by way of graduate training and internship experience in municipal administration.

Governing Boards

Electing governing boards

During the full bloom of the corrupt political machines in the 1800s, members of governing boards were chosen by wards. The spoils of government were made available to them so each alderman could peddle city contracts, utility franchises, and public jobs for as much as the traffic would bear. During the days of Boss William Tweed of New York, aldermen quickly became wealthy by parlaying the city largesse into personal gain. The growing middle class chafed under these corrupt practices and developed a distaste for the ward system of electing the city governing board. In addition to the corruption, they felt ward elections resulted in short-sighted, parochial aldermen

Ward vs. at large

who would "logroll" away the general good of the city to satisfy petty demands of neighborhoods. When the reform movement swept to power, one of the electoral reforms it touted was the at large election of governing boards to provide a citywide perspective to policy-making. For this reason, both the commission and council–manager forms promoted by reformers carried the at large feature. However, extended use of the at large elections eventually revealed some weaknesses, including poor geographic distribution of board members, increased political distance between the government and the governed, alienation of citizens disassociated from understandable representation, increased costs of citywide campaigns, and discrimination against the political opportunities of minorities. In recent years the U.S. Department of Justice has been applying various provisions of the Voting Rights Act of 1965, and its successive acts, to force local governments in certain sections of the country to abandon the at large elections in favor of district elections in order to improve the chances of minorities to elect representation more proportionate to their numbers in the population.[14] Since Section Two of the 1982 Voting Rights Act applies all across the nation, the at large feature achieved by reformers after decades of struggle came under heavy attack during the 1980s. Changing electoral systems from at large to district may enhance the representation of minorities, but it tends to inhibit the election of women who do better in the at large systems.[15]

Using at large and wards

Some 800 cities have sought to capture the strengths of both the at large and district election methods by using a mixed system, with a portion of the board elected by each method. They hoped to produce a board that would be more representative than the at large system and still more cosmopolitan than the ward system. Kansas

City elects six members by district and six at large; New Orleans elects five by district and two at large; Buffalo has nine by district and five at large. These mixed elections appear to have provided for black representation somewhat proportionate to the black population.[16]

The Neighborhood Concept

The campus and urban riots of the late 1960s forced considerable soul-searching across the country. One of the conclusions arising from this introspection was that the riots were the result of a constituency alienated and frustrated by normal city politics. Unable to impact municipal policy, citizens turned to violence in the street to communicate their disenchantment with life in the city. In response to this conclusion, a number of cities created mechanisms designed to establish a positive relationship between the government and the governed. A variety of strategies was developed, ranging from walks through neighborhoods by mayors to establishment of mini-city halls throughout the city. Out of this quest for improved communications came the concept of neighborhood government, in many respects a modernized version of wards and aldermanic services.

Neighborhood concept advanced

At least four arguments were presented as justification for dividing large cities into neighborhoods and delegating authority to locally-controlled policymakers. Supporters of neighborhood governments argued that the highly centralized city governments with bureaucratized public services ignored neighborhood interests; that centralized control in large cities resulted in a sense of alienation and distance; that input from those being served could humanize and improve the quality of service; and that neighborhoods could serve as vehicles for improving the economic base.[17]

Though the concept was backed with millions of federal dollars, political and administrative resistance was formidable to decentralizing authority and inviting possible inefficiencies to the service delivery systems. Thus, acceptance of the concept and the degree of implementation were contingent on the political environment of each particular city.[18] Virtually all of the top cities with populations over 750,000 tested and considered some form of decentralization. Even smaller cities, such as Atlanta, Oakland, Dayton, and Pittsburgh created neighborhood administrative and advisory councils to share effectively in municipal policy-making. The most decisive action was taken in New York City where the city charter was amended in 1975 to divide the city into 59 community districts, ranging from populations of 100,000 to 250,000, each with a community board empowered to appoint a district manager. The boards hold public hearings, recommend priorities, review agency performance, assist in service delivery, provide information to the community, and have a formal role in land use development. The district manager presides over a district service cabinet composed of representatives from agencies delivering services—police, fire, parks, sanitation, recreation, streets, traffic, code enforcement, sewer maintenance, health, and social services.[19]

New York forms community districts

The Changing "Model" City Charter

One of the instruments of the municipal reform movement during much of the 20th century has been the Model City Charter, formulated by the National Civic League. Political scientists became increasingly critical of the idea of a model charter or a "one-best-way" approach to organizing city government, and the latest edition of the Model

City Charter reflects some of these criticisms, especially in the areas of leadership and representation. Perhaps because of this criticism, the 1964 edition went 25 years without revision, but the seventh edition (1989) reflects several changes in the municipal reform tradition in the United States: (1) Direct election of the mayor is provided as an equal option to election from within the council; (2) the mayor's role is enhanced over earlier editions by assigning additional responsibilities; (3) the council election issue was resolved by stating a number of options from which a city can choose, depending on its circumstances at-large, at-large with district residency requirement, mixed at-large and single-member district system, single-member district system, and proportional representation; and (4) a continuation of the movement away from independent commissions for civil service and city planning programs to more simple statements endorsing the merit system and planning as integrated staff services. Professor James Svara has described the new edition of the Model City Charter as "slimmed down and more flexible in some sensitive areas," with some of the "hallowed practices" once treated as integral parts of the municipal reform package now having lost their special status.[20]

Importance of Forms of Government

Impact of forms of government

The ferocity of some political struggles over changing the form of government suggests that large stakes are involved in the outcome. However, the answer to the question "Does the form of government influence municipal policy and services?" seems to be "Not as much as the combatants think." Research on the question thus far has failed to produce a consensus among scholars. The difference, if there is one, either has not been adequately researched or is not sufficiently momentus to be identified. This should be no surprise. After all, if the democratic processes are all functioning, the form of government serves only as a mirror through which the political culture of the city is reflected. If the political culture of the city is strongly oriented toward public services, this preference is likely to be implemented whether the government is mayor–council, commission, or council–manager. A change in governmental form does not change the foundation for policy-making—political culture. Many state laws and home rule charters guarantee citizens opportunities to express preferences through mandatory plebiscites on capital expenditures, as well as those twin tools of direct democracy, the initiative and referendum.

While forms of government may not result in radical departures in policy-making, they do alter the avenues of access and the quality of representativeness. In cities with geographically concentrated minorities, ward elections will increase their representation on the governing board and give them a sense of efficacy in the shaping of municipal policy. Garbage collection may still be poor, but it is easier for citizens to accept when a person they trust tells them that's the way it has to be.

Who Runs the City?

The discussion thus far in this chapter has dealt primarily with the legal roots of the municipal corporation and the more visible aspects of governmental structure commonly called the *form of government*. It is quite possible to be a master of these subjects and still be unable to answer even in general terms the question, "Who really runs your city? Do the duly elected officials really run your city? The bankers? The clergy? The newspapers? Is it the politicians or a single boss behind the formal officeholders? Is it a small group of wealthy oldtimers who own half of the property and have been 'calling the tune' on major community decisions as long as one can remember? Or is your city government of, by, and for all the people, as democratic theory would seem to suggest?"

The Reform Response to Boss Rule

One hundred years ago, there was little doubt about the answers to these questions in many cities. "Who really runs the city?" "The boss, that's who." The Jacksonian revolution paved the way for boss rule in cities by dispersing the executive authority among *Boss rule* a number of elected officials. As time passed, various boards and commissions were also created to participate in the urban montage. During the middle decades of the 1800s, immigrants poured into the country, many remaining to swell the population— and the problems—of America's cities. The need for municipal action was pressing, but the diffused governmental systems were not equal to the task. Politicians, endowed with a combination of ingenuity and greed, used the political party to informally centralize the power that was formally dispersed. The political machines took over city governments and wreaked incredible graft and corruption upon the taxpayers. Though wasteful and corrupt, they temporarily provided the means by which thousands of immigrants were sheltered and assimilated. As soon as the expanding middle class realized the cost of boss rule, they rallied to reform the structures and procedures upon which it rested. Most crucial to continuance of boss domination were decentralized city government, a dependent population, the availability of jobs and contracts, and political parties. So the agenda of the reformers included a systematic eradication of these tools of control. The civil service system was adopted to eliminate patronage; election reforms to end ballot box stuffing; business-like forms of government to professionalize administration; immigration laws to restrict the influx of dependent peoples; government welfare programs to reduce dependence on machines; and the nonpartisan ballot to negate partisan ties.

The Quest for Cities without Politics

Among the reforms eventually adopted by cities to end boss rule, the nonpartisan ballot has been foremost in impact on city politics. Though some of the larger cities have remained loyal to the partisan ballot, two-thirds of the American cities have adopted *Adopt nonpartisan* the nonpartisan system. Of course, in some cities tenacious political activists continued *ballot* to wage partisan wars even though the ballot carried no political identification of the candidates. In most cities, however, partisans retreated to other ground, such as the county courthouse.

Supporters of the nonpartisan system point out a number of advantages. After all, it did eradicate intolerable corruption; it enabled political minorities, such as Republicans, to share in city governance; it removed irrelevant state and national issues from the local campaigns; favoring incumbents, it stabilized membership on governing boards; and it neutralized state legislative politics in the adoption of municipal legislation.

Though these points have merit, experience has revealed that the nonpartisan ballot has had its tradeoffs. Because the party label is used as a point of reference for a majority of voters, its removal from the ballot casts many, especially the lower socioeconomic groups, adrift without a rudder. Unable to relate to such a system, many of them quit voting, and turnout for city elections declined.[21] Since the majority of them were Democrats by partisan measurements, Republicans were the beneficiaries of the nonpartisan system, often winning control of governments in cities that were voting heavily Democratic in state and national elections. Members of governing boards no longer divided along partisan lines and found it easier to avoid the collective accountability of a party label. Mayors found it difficult to assert leadership, lacking a stable following in both the electorate and the government.

Partisan politics of nonpartisan elections

With the mobilizing power of political parties removed, interest groups moved into the vacuum. Commissioners and councilors without loyalties to a party philosophy or platform were more vulnerable to the parochial requests of special groups. Without organizational support, it became more difficult to take unpopular positions or resist groups with political resources.

The Search for Power Structures

When political parties endorsed the candidates and rallied at the hustings, questions about who ran the city were easier to answer. At least every alert citizen knew whether the Republicans or the Democrats were making the decisions down at city hall. However, the mysteries enveloping the nonpartisan system have frequently hidden the identity of those who were really wielding the power. Thus, inquiries into the scope and nature of city power structures became more than academic curiosity. They became genuine quests for hidden actors who impacted municipal decisions.

Pyramidal elite versus pluralism

Probably the two best known power structure studies are the ones done in Atlanta by Floyd Hunter and in New Haven by Robert A. Dahl.[22] Hunter, a sociologist, reported that Atlanta was run by a pyramidal elite, whereas Dahl, a political scientist, ventured that New Haven decisions involved many centers of power. The findings challenged other researchers. Following Hunter in Atlanta, M. Kent Jennings studied three kinds of participants in community decision making: *prescribed influentials,* (those with formally defined political roles); *attributed influentials,* (those who are perceived to be influential); and *economic dominants,* (those occupying major economic positions). He concluded that the Atlanta power structure was not monolithic but midway between monolithic and an amorphous typology.[23] New Haven received a second review by G. William Dumhoff, who found a greater overlap between New Haven's economic notables and social notables and concluded that New Haven was more elitist than Dahl thought.[24]

Contest for prizes

Other studies of community power systems have produced other findings. Sayre and Kaufman found no single pyramid of decision-makers but rather a system of separate and numerous islands of power in a New York "contest for prizes" among party leaders, officials, bureaucrats, the electorate, and a whole host of nongovernmental groups.[25] In a comparative study of four communities, Agger, Goldrich, and Swanson found several kinds of power structures and regimes defined by such facts of political life as distributions of power, illegitimate sanctions, and leadership ideologies.[26] The diversity of findings suggests that methodology influences results and that each power structure is very probably unique to its own city, with some monolithic and others pluralistic.

At a time when many concluded that the community power structure dialogue and debate had pretty well reached a stalemate (Nelson Polsby called it a "scholarly morass"),[27] a new approach arrived on the scene in 1981 in the form of Paul Peterson's prize-winning book, *City Limits*.[28] Some have called it "perhaps the single most influential book on developmental politics in the urban field."[29] Peterson emphasized a political-economy perspective on urban politics, making two arguments: (1) cities are severely limited in policy choices because of economic competition with other cities (and thus are prevented from pursuing "redistributional policies" because they can be made only at the national level) and (2) city officials and business officials are close allies on economic development/growth policies (making for consensual politics with little vitality). Other than the latter, Peterson's analysis leaves for cities only allocational policies (decisions on delivery of services), and organizational policies (on the structure of decision making in the community), which he concludes are relatively insignificant.[30]

The city-limits perspective

As might be expected, this down-grading of urban politics by the "city-limits perspective" (CLP) has not gone uncontested, and has given new vitality to research and debate on power in the urban community. Robert J. Waste speaks of community power research as being "on the verge of a new era."[31] Among the heaviest counterattacks is one by Sanders and Stone, aimed at the assumption that development politics is consensual, with an overriding unitary city interest in growth. They point out that the politics of city development is often divisive, with winners and losers, advocates of no growth, slow growth, management of growth, and only the NIMBY kind of growth ("Not in my back yard!), all of which makes for a dynamic politics-policy relationship not suggested by Peterson's picture of the city as a kind of apolitical business firm driven by economic competition.[32] Other critics allege that: while economic constraints on cities are often powerful, cities have a non-trivial amount of discretion in the way they can respond;[33] rational economic interests of the city can be overridden by political coalition-building strategies of its elected officials;[34] equitable city policies often depend not so much on inevitable economic forces as on alterable features of the legal framework (organizational policies);[35] allocation policies are a more important source of human benefits than CLP allows;[36] and the mobilization politics of neighborhood, race, and ethnic background is overlooked in the CLP simple focus on city-level economic interests.[37] The sharp exchanges between CLP and its critics may seem at times to produce more heat than light but, as with the earlier community power debates, if they stimulate more researchers to explore the mystery of power and policies in our urban communities, the result should be constructive. Fulfillment of the democratic ideal of popular control of the decision-making process in cities continues to be dependant on greater knowledge and understanding.

Counterattacks on CLP

More research stimulated

The Changing Form of City Politics
Absorption of the changes wrought by the reform movement has not closed the chapter of change for city governments. Transforming trends continue to reshape municipal politics and governance.

1. Impact of chain store marketing

The nationalization of retailing that has occurred since World War II has altered the community power structures of many municipalities. Slowly but surely, chain stores have eroded the economic dominance of sole proprietorships and local corporations that prevailed in local retailing in the mid-1900s. Second- and third-generation entrepreneurs have been replaced by chain store managers who are in Omaha only until a larger store opens in Indianapolis or Louisville. Because their economic future was linked to the well-being of "their" city, local entrepreneurs took an active interest in municipal politics, usually in some role supportive of officeholders. On the other hand, the chain store manager is a professional merchandiser whose future is linked to the successful management of the present location, as usually measured by profits. She or he has little incentive for getting involved in municipal affairs. Thus, as the locally owned retail outlets gave way to the chain outlets in the shopping centers, sole proprietors not only disappeared from business but they also disappeared from local politics—and were not replaced politically by the new business interests of the city.

2. Intergovernmental programming

Intergovernmentalization has also altered local politics. With federal and state governments providing a substantial portion of the municipal revenue, city political leaders are compelled to share their decision-making authority with the other funding governments. In the case of categorical grants, cities may be forced to reorder priorities to become eligible to receive certain federal or state funds. In the case of block grants or revenue sharing, cities have been under constant pressure to continually justify their dependence on federal and state funds. In many cases, the availability of general revenue sharing has given cities more flexibility in moving money from one municipal pocket to another, holding local taxpayers at bay with the claim that this is "federal" or "state" money being spent on low priority items.

3. Municipal professionalism

Accelerated professionalism of the municipal bureaucracy has created a significant challenge for part-time mayors and governing board members. For various reasons, many cities have been determined to preserve the part-time status of policy-makers while the professional disciplines required to deliver services have continued to become more sophisticated and complex. For the decision-makers to promulgate sound policy, they must comprehend the implications of their decisions. Unless they are able to invest the time required to understand the ramifications of their policies, one of two consequences can develop: either they permit the professionals of the bureaucracy to make the decisions and reduce citizen control of government, or they can make uninformed decisions that will disrupt the smooth functioning of the city.

4. Municipal employee unions

Municipal employee unions have become a political force of considerable influence in city affairs. Using political clout at the state capitols, unions secured legislation in most states that recognize the right of municipal employees to organize and bargain collectively with city governments. Though prohibited from striking, police officers, fire fighters, sanitation workers, and other employees have walked off their jobs until the city fathers surrendered or at least came to terms. Employee unions have not been content to rely solely on traditional bargaining weapons. Like many other groups, they have become politically active, supporting candidates favorable to their demands with votes, money, and campaign assistance. The low voter turnout in most city elections gives them influence disproportionate to their numbers in the city electorate.

5. Judicial intervention

Judicial intervention has also become a factor in city politics. Forms of government and annexations have been particularly affected by U.S. Supreme Court decisions based on various Voting Rights Acts. Other decisions affecting employee performance and service delivery relate to such matters as control of cable television, authority to grant franchises, the immunity of city government and employees from lawsuits, and police practices in crime control. Though governing bodies have been held exempt from personal liability in almost all circumstances, policies they adopt must be tempered to conform to the constantly changing flow of court decisions.

Administering the City

The scope and cost of municipal administration continue to increase, both for cities that have stable populations and those that are still growing. Mounting costs are no longer being matched by increasing federal and state aid, primarily due to the huge federal deficits and cutbacks occurring in the 1980s and 1990s.

Costs mounting

Increasing costs result from the expansion of old functions as well as the demand for new services. Law enforcement is an old function, but it becomes more difficult and costly with the creation of more laws and ordinances, the need for more training, and the additional procedural requirements to guarantee due process. Mass transit and traffic regulation are old functions but have increased in cost due to the need for new equipment, the cost of fuel, the decline in ridership, and the requirements of expensive computer-directed traffic control systems. Old functions incurring new costs include a wide range of other municipal activities, such as water treatment and distribution, maintaining judicially acceptable jails, dealing with juvenile delinquency, regulating health and sanitary conditions, and many others. In recent decades, cities have also developed a social consciousness that has resulted in such new services and new costs as health programs, alcoholic rehabilitation, medical services, halfway houses, shelters for street people, and other help programs heretofore charged to national and state welfare programs.

Changing services

The Politics of City Services

The service delivery system of every city, regardless of size, requires an organization of agencies or departments that is more or less politically accountable to the mayor, manager, commission, or council. If the city is large enough to justify professional administrators at the heads of departments, the interfacing of professionals with the politicians is always an area of potential conflict. The elected officials have the duty of establishing municipal policy in harmony with the will of the people; on the other hand, professionals feel an obligation to pursue their work according to the standards of their profession. As an example, the governing board, responding to community pressures, wants the police department to arrest all the prostitutes on South Boulevard. The police chief feels that prostitution, involving a willing buyer and a willing seller, is a moral issue that ought to be dealt with from the pulpits rather than a police car. Coming from that philosophical position, he looks at his work force, the crime rate, and other objective criteria and, in his professional judgment, feels that pursuing prostitutes is not an efficient use of limited police resources. Thus, differing views—the political and the professional—result in friction.

Political vs. professional

Another common conflict between politicians and professionals may occur when the city street engineer develops the long-term street improvement plans on the basis of traffic counts and laboratory analyses of the condition of the asphalt. Using engineering standards, he rank orders streets in the improvement program. However, the mayor and two councilors, up for election, are getting considerable pressure from the Eastdale Neighborhood Association to move three streets in their area from Priority 7 in the program up to Priority 2. They propose reordering the street improvement program on the basis of political rather than professional considerations.

The "right" way vs. the political way

In both of these examples, the professionals feel strongly that there is a "right" way to provide municipal services and this "right" way is being subverted by politics. Most citizens, when they are not personally involved, espouse the principles of efficiency and effectiveness in municipal service delivery, thus creating a climate in which professionalism has political support. Thus, blatant politicization of municipal administration can become poor politics citywide. This forces the politicians to act with restraint, so they bargain with the professionals so as to preserve the professional integrity of service delivery while still being somewhat responsive to their constituents. The result is compromise—with the police working South Boulevard one night a week and the street engineer moving Eastdale's streets up only two notches. Thus, to keep both responsiveness and professionalism in city administration, compromises are made to approximate the requirements of both. In very large cities, several layers of politicians and administrators exist to absorb the conflicts; in small cities, however, the distance between politics and delivery is minimal, meaning that professionalism is always endangered by closeness of politics.

Delivering the Services

The heads of departments may be political appointees, career professionals, or, in a few cases, elected directly by the people. State law or the municipal charter provides for the selection of top administrators. Each department is organized from its head to

Administrative organization

its lowest rung of common labor and staffed by personnel usually selected by merit tests. While organization is complex for the larger cities, it is rather simple for villages and small cities and may consist of only two key administrative officers, sometimes known as *Inside* and *Outside*. The "inside" person may be the director of finance, or simply the city clerk, but he or she will be responsible for much of the housekeeping work related to finance, personnel, purchasing, and the routine details of administration. The "outside" person is usually named director of public works and will handle such matters as street maintenance, parks, water supply, sewers, and planning.

A large city is likely to have a personnel office or board to recruit, examine, and certify applicants for appointment by the employing officers and also to perform duties with respect to position classification, promotion, salary scales, tenure, and other employee relations. Such a city must likewise have administrative officers to conduct financial affairs, including budgeting, purchasing, accounting, auditing, and general treasury management. It must have officials and facilities for handling tax matters, such as assessment and collection of property levies, issuing licenses of various kinds and receiving payments for them, and sometimes gathering in city sales and income taxes. The management of financial and personnel matters vitally affects the scope and effectiveness of all the agencies of a city administration, for no unit of government can function without staff and money.

It is further recognized in city government, as in other governments, that effective operation, or line work, requires general staff work at the center. The central staff organization of an increasing number of large and medium-sized cities includes a full-time officer or agency for research, study, and advice in the wide field of city planning. The recommendations of the planning authority, insofar as they are adopted, affect both the work of the operating agencies and the trend of city development. As in other levels of government, the planning establishment is likely to be closely linked to the chief executive authority. State planning assistance may be available to urban communities, especially the smaller ones.

Planning

Closely related to planning is the process of zoning through laws or ordinances with administration by boards or officers. Zoning is really enforced planning to designate or preserve areas for residential, commercial, industrial, or other purposes, with modifications and combinations of these classifications. It affects both public and private enterprise, and zoning authorities are often subjected to strong conflicting pressures because zoning involves thousands and sometimes millions of dollars. A single zoning change, such as one from single-family units to multi-family units, can triple the value of lots and result in a huge windfall of profits to the developer. Once a city takes the step of seeking to regulate land and passes a comprehensive zoning ordinance, it then is faced with the never-ending task of "holding the line" against creeping blight by "spot zoning" amendments and the granting of variances and exceptions. Decisions or recommendations of planning agencies are sometimes reversed by higher authority, such as a city council. It is common for the tradition of "councilor courtesy" to exist in city councils, giving the individual councilors virtually complete control over zone changes in their own wards. Considering that zoning decisions involve large sums of money, councilor control of zoning changes creates the opportunity for payoffs, extortion, and other corrupt practices.

Zoning

Public safety is a function of major importance and becomes more crucial with the size of the city. (Municipal police services were covered in chapter 12.)

Fire protection is more completely a local responsibility than the maintenance of law and order. Fighting fire is different from fighting crime, even though a large fire creates problems for the police. Fire fighters, like police officers, perform miscellaneous services besides their primary task; they may answer calls for trapped persons or animals, flooded homes, storm damage, and the like. Normally there is no attempt to corrupt fire departments and to limit their effectiveness comparable to the kinds of pressure often brought to bear upon police departments; hence, American urban fire service is generally efficient, employing competent personnel as well as modern mechanized equipment. However, fire losses in American municipalities far exceed the losses in European cities, largely because of differences in the construction of buildings and in methods or habits of fire protection. Many American cities have antiquated building codes, sometimes with inadequate inspection and enforcement to avoid fire hazards. Political pull at times relaxes the administration of regulations.

Fire protection

Preventing fire, like preventing crime, is a large problem for urban America. Budget-conscious administrators who favor merging police and fire departments have succeeded to some degree in around 50 small and medium-sized cities. Such mergers are rare because they draw stiff resistance from the unions and uniformed employees who face new training for broader responsibilities, reshuffling of the hierarchy, perhaps

Merging police and fire services

fewer employees overall, and adaptation to new procedures. Scottsdale, Arizona caught the attention of many cities when it eliminated its municipal fire department and contracted with a private company for fire protection.

Operation of water distribution, sewage disposal, and solid waste disposal is most commonly done by cities and is often self-supporting through a fee schedule. However, private enterprise is most commonly used to provide heat, light, power, communications, and some forms of transportation. The private companies sell their services under state or local franchises or regulations which are supposed to safeguard the public interest and also permit a fair return for utility operations. However, federal courts have recently permitted the application of antitrust laws to cities granting certain exclusive franchises.

Mass transit   In the late 1800s, urban mass transportation systems were profitably managed by private enterprise. However, as widespread ownership of the automobile developed with improved highways, ridership fell off and mass transit operations began losing money. To keep transit services, many municipalities were forced to take them over, often with the aid of the federal government, and absorb the losses with general revenue, special tax levies, and federal subsidies. In metropolitan areas, transit operations may be vested in a "metro transit authority" administratively removed from municipal governments. Increasing demands for convenient air travel have also challenged cities. New construction is constantly underway to expand existing facilities, to build anew, and to escape the complaints of noise pollution in neighborhoods that have engulfed many airports. Financial support for airports has come from several sources—federal aid, state aid, local revenues, airport concessions, special levies, and assessments on airlines.

Housing   While private enterprise still provides most new housing for the regular market, many cities, aided by state and/or federal funds, have gone into housing programs for the low-income families.

Lack of funding at the federal level, along with increased federal finger-pointing at state and local government responsibilities, has coincided with the dramatic rise in homelessness in America. Cities are faced with not only the housing needs of the homeless, but with their multiple poverty-syndrome problems of physical disabilities, mental illness, unemployment, drug abuse, hunger, and crime. In the 1980s, a number of states *Enterprise zones*   borrowed from the British experience with "enterprise zones" in depressed areas. This approach sought (by means of tax breaks and regulatory relief) to retain existing businesses, foster new ones, and improve housing in designated blighted areas. In spite of extensive programs in the cities of such states as Ohio and Illinois, many have raised questions about the effectiveness of enterprise zones, charging that they have been caught up in the interstate competition for bringing in or keeping industry, and that few are targeted to minority communities.[38]

Whatever else can be said of the AIDS crisis and its tragic consequences, few would deny that its demand for services has overwhelmed America's biggest cities. In a 1991 report to the U.S. Conference of Mayors, its executive director stated that the cities simply "can't meet growing demands for health care, drugs, and prevention." A Conference study revealed that the 26 largest cities have over 50 percent of the 179,000 *Urban impact of AIDS*   AIDS cases in the nation, but only 17 percent of the nation's population; the rate of

AIDS cases per 100,000 population is much higher in the larger cities; up to one-third of AIDS cases are among people who have no public or private health insurance; and cities forced to choose between expenditures for AIDS prevention services and AIDS patient care services inevitably cut prevention services.[39] The municipal governments of urban America, especially its biggest cities, are clearly being hit the hardest by the AIDS epidemic.

Though most schools inside and outside of municipal boundaries are operated through special governments, education is the responsibility of municipal governments in a few sections of the United States. The function may be buffered to some degree from municipal politics by the appointment of a school board that oversees the education program. Aside from the public school systems, a number of cities support, or partly support, municipal colleges or universities. Most notable examples include New York, Cincinnati, Toledo, Louisville, and Omaha. Nearly every city has a public library, customarily administered by a trained librarian responsible to a lay board. *Education*

Adapting to Tighter Budgets

To reconcile limited revenue sources with unlimited service demands, municipalities are forced to reconsider priorities in virtually every budget session. While general consensus may exist in the importance of maintaining fire and police departments, most other service administrators must constantly justify their existence. New budgeting methods, such as zero-base and performance, have been tried to better magnify and detect lost efficiency and effectiveness. Consulting teams have been employed to bring a new perspective to city management and perhaps provide clues for cutting costs. *1. New budgeting systems*

The search for cost effectiveness led some cities, notably New Orleans, Akron, Oklahoma City, Kansas City, and Minneapolis, to test the efficiency of municipal operations against the private sector by creating competitive situations. The mixed private–public collection of refuse has increased efficiency, decreased vulnerability to employee actions, and provided yardsticks for comparing performance.[40] Private contracts for services have been common among municipalities for years, some negotiating for services from private companies, others buying municipal services from a neighboring government or county. Use of private enterprise to provide the traditional services became popularized with the call word *privatize* in the early 1980s and advocates recommended *privatizing* a broader spectrum of municipal services. A 1990 survey revealed the contracting out of at least one service to a private enterprise is widespread, and that local governments are most likely to contract out if they have: a council-manager form or strong mayor form of government, few unions, no well-entrenched power base, and/or a financial crisis.[41] *2. Seeking cost effectiveness*

Privatization

A number of cities have sought to fight rising costs by instituting productivity improvement programs. Kansas City, Missouri, applied engineered work standards to its streets division; Harrisburg, Pennsylvania, introduced the same flat rate pay in the vehicle maintenance center as used by private auto repair shops; Philadelphia introduced monetary rewards based on performance; Flint, Michigan, shared overtime and improved productivity savings with employees; and Orange, California, pegged increased wages for the police department to reductions in four major categories of *3. Productivity improvement*

crimes.[42] One effort to improve city government performance is called Total Quality Management (TQM), which grew out of American private sector efforts to respond to increasing global competition.[43] Holistic in its approach to management, and strongly "customer oriented," TQM is said to be easier to implement at the local government level and has had early success in council–manager cities.[44]

Revenue shortfalls that exist after the city policy-makers have turned every screw are being filled to a considerable degree by new reliance on user charges. According to the U.S. Census Bureau, user charges have grown faster than tax revenues, increasing by 213 percent from 1971 to 1981, as compared to a 126 percent increase for taxes. Some cities are more receptive to user charges than others. For example, user charges exceeded 50 percent of local taxes in Albany, Georgia; Galveston, Texas; Champaign, Illinois; and Tallahassee, Florida, while running less than 5 percent of local taxes in Peoria, Illinois; Providence, Rhode Island; and Pittsburgh, Pennsylvania.[45] Proponents argue that users ought to pay for services and charges to curb waste; opponents posit that user charges create new unfair burdens for the poorer citizens, especially on the elderly with fixed incomes.

4. Increasing user charges

With citizens virtually at their elbows, city fathers are on the very frontline of governmental service delivery. An irate citizen demanding to be heard at the city council meeting creates an aura of urgency that is lost in a phone call or a letter to the state capitol or Washington. The political challenges for municipal governments in the 1990s are unlimited as federal cutbacks, limited revenue opportunities, taxpayer revolts, and demands for middle-class quality all converge on city hall. Political ingenuity and professional creativity will be required to manage higher levels of conflict and deliver municipal services.

Endnotes

1. Genesis 4:17. Perhaps Jefferson's often quoted recriminations against the evils of cities stem from this Biblical account of who founded the first recorded city. It may also have been linked to the idea that people "go to town to raise Cain."

2. U.S. Bureau of the Census, *Governmental Organizations,* Vol. 1, *1987 Census of Governments* (Washington, D.C.: Government Printing Office, 1988), p. vii.

3. Ibid.

4. Thomas A. Flinn, *Local Government and Politics* (Glenview, Ill.: Scott, Foresman & Co., 1970), p. 8.

5. N. A., "Causes of Existing Evils" in *Current Problems in Municipal Government,* ed. Lamar T. Berman (New York: The H. W. Wilson Company, 1923), pp. 85–86.

6. Joseph F. Zimmerman, "Charter Reform in the 1990s," *National Civic Review,* 73 (September–October, 1989), p. 330.

7. James D. Slack, "Information, Training, and Assistance Needs of Municipal Governments," *Public Administration Review,* 50 (July/August, 1990), pp. 450–457.

8. Charles R. Adrian, "Leadership and Decision-Making in Manager Cities: A Study of Three Communities," *Public Administration Review* 18 (Summer 1958): 208–213. See also Robert Paul Boynton and Deil S. Wright, "Mayor–Manager Relationships in Large

Council–Manager Cities: A Reinterpretation," *Public Administration Review* 31 (January/February, 1971): 28–35. The issue contains a symposium on "The American City Manager."

9. Charldean Newell and David Ammons, "City Managers Don't Make Policy: A Lie, Let's Face It," *National Civic Review,* (March/April, 1988), pp. 124–132.

10. Tari Renner, "Appointed Local Government Managers: Stability and Change," *Municipal Year Book, 1990* (Washington: International City Management Association), 1990.

11. James H. Svara, *Official Leadership in the City: Patterns of Conflict and Cooperation* (New York: Oxford University Press), 1990, pp. 20+; see also his "Dichotomy and Duality: Reconceptualizing the Relationship Between Policy and Administration in Council–Manager Cities," *Public Administration Review,* 45 (January/February, 1985), pp. 221–232.

12. Gregory Streib, "Strategic Decision-Making in Council–Manager Governments: A Status Report," *Municipal Year Book 1991* (Washington: International City Management Association), 1991, pp. 14–23.

13. Samuel P. Hays, "The Politics of Reform in Municipal Government in the Progressive Era," Pacific Northwest Quarterly, 55 (October, 1964), pp. 157–189; William Lyons, "Reform and Response in American Cities: Structure and Policy Reconsidered," *Social Science Quarterly,* 59 (June, 1978), pp. 118–132; Thomas Dye and John Garcia, "Structure, Function and Policy in American Cities," *Urban Affairs Quarterly,* 14 (September, 1978), pp. 103–122; and Tari Renner, "Municipal Election Processes: The Impact on Minority Representation," *Municipal Year Book 1988* (Washington: The International City Management Association), 1988.

14. See "Local At-Large Election Systems Continue to be Struck Down" in Local Government section, ed. Joseph F. Zimmerman and Thomas D. Wilson, *National Civic Review* 73 (September, 1984): 408; Robert J. Mundt and Peggy Heilig, "District Representation: Demands and Effects in the Urban South," *The Journal of Politics* 44 (November 1982): 1035–1048.

15. Susan Welch and Albert Karnig, "Correlates of Female Office Holding in City Politics," *The Journal of Politics* 41 (May 1979): 490.

16. Francine F. Rabinovitz and Edward K. Hamilton, "Alternative Electoral Structures and Responsiveness to Minorities," *National Civic Review* 69 (July, 1980): 384. For a more recent summary see Joseph F. Zimmerman, "Alternative Local Electoral Systems," *National Civic Review,* 79 (January–February, 1990), 23–36.

17. Donna E. Shalala, *Neighborhood Governance,* a monograph (New York: National Project on Ethnic America, n.d.), pp. 4–6.

18. See John Mudd, "Beyond Community Control: A Neighborhood Strategy for City Government," *PUBLIUS* 6 (Fall, 1976): 113–135; Edward G. Goetz, "Beyond Pluralism," a paper prepared for delivery at the annual meeting of the American Political Science Association, Washington, D.C. August 30–September 2, 1984; and John M. Goering, "Towards A National Policy for Neighborhoods," *Public Administration Review* 40 (November/December 1980): 553–560.

19. Regina S. Axelrod, "Decentralized Service Delivery: Role of the District Manager," *National Civic Review* 69 (June 1980): 321–324.

20. James H. Svara, "The Model City and County Charters: Innovation and Tradition in the Reform Movement," *Public Administration Review,* 50 (November/December, 1990), pp. 688–692. See also: National Civic League, *Model City Charter* (Denver, CO: National Civic League, 1989).

21. See Albert W. Karnig and B. Oliver Walter, "Decline in Municipal Voter Turnout," *American Politics Quarterly* 11 (October 1983): 491–505.

22. Floyd Hunter, *Community Power Structure: A Study of Decision-makers* (Chapel Hill: University of North Carolina Press, 1953), and Robert A. Dahl, *Who Governs?* (New Haven, Conn.: Yale University Press, 1961).

23. M. Kent Jennings, *Community Influentials: The Elites of Atlanta* (New York: Free Press of Glencoe, 1964).

24. G. William Dumhoff, *Who Really Rules?: New Haven and Community Power Reexamined* (New Brunswick, N.J.: Transaction Books, 1978).

25. Wallace S. Sayre and Herbert Kaufman, *Governing New York City* (New York: Russell Sage Foundation, 1960).

26. Robert E. Agger, Daniel Goldrich, and Bert E. Swanson, *The Rulers and the Ruled: Political Power and Impotence in American Communities* (New York: John Wiley and Sons, 1964).

27. Nelson Polsby, *Community Power and Political Theory* 2nd ed., (New Haven: Yale University Press, 1980), p. x.

28. Paul Peterson, *City Limits,* (Chicago: University of Chicago Press, 1981).

29. Heywood T. Sanders and Clarence N. Stone, "Developmental Politics Reconsidered," *Urban Affairs Quarterly,* 22 (June, 1987), p. 521.

30. See Jeffrey R. Henig's "Defining City Limits," a paper presented at the annual meeting of the American Political Science Association, August 30–September 2, 1990. The authors have used his excellent summary and analysis in part of this discussion.

31. Robert J. Waste, ed., *Community Power: Directions for Future Research,* (Beverly Hills, CA: Sage, 1986), p. 204.

32. Sanders and Stone, pp. 521–538.

33. Clarence N. Stone, *Regime Politics,* (Lawrence, KS: University of Kansas Press, 1989), and Tod Swanstrom, *The Crisis of Growth Politics,* (Philadelphia: Temple University Press, 1985).

34. Susan E. Clarke and Anne K. Moss, "Economic Urban Growth, Environmental Quality, and Growth Services: Mapping the Potential for Local Positive-Sum Strategies," *Journal of Urban Affairs,* vol. 12 (1990), no. 1, pp. 17–34.

35. Judith A. Garber, "Law and the Possibilities for a Just Urban Political Economy," *Journal of Urban Affairs,* vol. 12 (1990), no. 1, pp. 1–5.

36. Rufus P. Browning, Dale Rogers Marshall, and David H. Tabb, *Protest Is Not Enough,* (Berkeley, CA: University of California Press, 1984). An important new book in late 1991, Ester R. Fuchs' *Mayors and Money* (Chicago: University of Chicago Press, 1991), takes a radical departure from dominant economic-centered approaches. Fuchs examines the fiscal policy-making process in New York and Chicago over the past 60 years and shows how policy choices resulted in different political structures that, in turn, affect the cities' fiscal stability to this day.

37. Jeffrey R. Henig, *Neighborhood Mobilization: Redevelopment and Response,* (New Brunswick, N.J.: Rutgers University, 1982).

38. "How Enterprising Are Enterprise Zones?" *Governing,* (November, 1987), p. 14.

39. Arkansas *Gazette,* June 14, 1991. *See* also: James D. Slack, "AIDS, The Local Government Workplace, and the Law," *The Municipal Year Book 1991* (Washington: International City Management Association, 1991), pp. 63–71, and his *AIDS and the Public Work Force: Local Government Preparedness in Managing the Epidemic.* (Tuscaloosa: University of Alabama Press, 1991).

40. E. S. Savas, "Intracity Competition Between Public and Private Service Delivery," *Public Administration Review* 4 (January/February 1981): 50.

41. For a discussion of privitizing, see John Larkin, "Privatization Holds Promises/Perils for PAs," *Public Administration Times,* December 1, 1990, pp. 1, 36; and E. S. Savas, *Privitizing The Public Sector* (Chatham, N.J.: Chatham House Publishers, 1982).

42. John M. Greiner et al., *Monetary Incentives and Work Standards in Five Cities* (Washington, D.C.: The Urban Institute, 1977).

43. John L. Larkin, "TQM Efforts Increase at All Levels of Government," *Public Administration Times,* 14 (June 1, 1991), pp. 1, 9.

44. David Carr and Ian Littman, *Excellence in Government: Total Quality Management in the 1990s* (Coopers and Lybrand, 1990). See also James E. Swiss, "Adapting Total Quality Management (TQM) to Government," *Public Administration Review,* 52 (July/August, 1992), 356–362.

45. James H. Ammons and Thomas R. Dye, "Marketing Public Services: Tests of Costs and Need," *National Civic Review* 72 (October 1983): 499–501.

CHAPTER 16

LOCAL GOVERNMENT IV: SPECIAL DISTRICTS

Creating Special Governments to Perform Special Tasks

Evolution of Special Governments

While researchers and scholars have been preoccupied with the problems, challenges, and impacts of general local governments, few have taken notice of the dramatic increase in numbers, employees, and expenditures of special governments—the special districts that have been multiplying faster than any category of local governments. Since 1962, the number of county governments has remained constant; municipal governments have grown a mere 7 percent; townships and towns have declined by 3 percent; school districts continued to plummet by 58 percent; but nonschool special districts have increased an amazing 61 percent. (While most schools are provided through special districts, this chapter is devoted primarily to nonschool districts.)

It is true that many of the 30,000 special nonschool governments now in existence are mere ciphers. They have no employees, very limited equipment or buildings, and perform a relatively minor service. However, at the other end of the spectrum are some governmental giants that simply dwarf most counties, cities, towns, townships, and even states, such as the bi-state New York–New Jersey Port Authority, the Metropolitan Sanitary District of Greater Chicago, the Chicago Transit Authority, and the Metropolitan Atlanta Rapid Transit Authority. These special governments employ more people and have larger budgets than some states. This growth of special governments has been a matter of serious concern to some scholars of public affairs. Heretofore, they had railed counties as being the "dark continent of American politics." Now they are beginning to label the special district as the "new dark continent of American politics."

Larger budgets than states

Defining the Special District

To be counted by the U.S. Census Bureau, special district governments must be independent, limited-purpose units that exist as separate entities with substantial administrative and fiscal independence from general local governments. One of America's

Title photo: Perhaps the most famous of the special districts is The Port Authority of New York and New Jersey. The Port Authority manages much of the transportation in the New York metropolitan area and has a payroll and revenue that approaches those of small states. (Photo by The Port Authority of New York and New Jersey.)

364

foremost researchers on special governments, John C. Bollens, defines special governments in greater detail as " . . . organized entities, possessing a structural form, an official name, perpetual succession, and the rights to sue and be sued, to make contracts, and to obtain and dispose of property." He also states that they require " . . . officers who are popularly elected or are chosen by other public officials. They have a high degree of public accountability. Moreover, they have considerable fiscal and administrative independence from other governments."[1]

Definitions of special districts are confused by the extensive use of other terms to refer to both special districts and entities that are not special districts. In some writings and laws, the term *authority* will often be used in reference to a special district, such as the case of the New York–New Jersey Port Authority. In some instances, however, an *authority* is simply an adjunct of a general government, created to isolate a function from city or county government while the general government still retains control. On the West Coast and in New England, special districts are often called authorities. To further confuse the definition, some units called districts are not autonomous governments but are dependent on the powers of general government for existence. For example, their members may be appointed by a county board and their budgets approved by the county board. With these features, they can hardly be termed *governments,* according to the definitions of either the Census Bureau or Bollens. The term *corporation* is also a troublesome word often used in the special district category. Here again, criteria must be applied to their autonomy and powers in order to determine whether or not they qualify for the title of *government.* Failure by states to be specific in legislation has resulted in widespread confusion over the status of special districts, authorities, corporations, boards, and other labels used in establishing special district governments.

Districts confused with other entities

Terminology is not the only problem when pursuing a systematic study of special districts. Few states have designated an agency to compile information about the special districts within their borders; many do not levy property taxes, so property tax administrators are unaware of their existence; new classes of special districts are created with very little publicity; and creative acts provide simple procedures for suspension and dissolution, with little record of their demise.[2]

Lack information on districts

History of Special Districts

As early as the 1600s, the traditional forms of local governments in England, such as the counties and parishes, proved too rigid and inflexible to solve problems in an urbanizing society. Hence, a system of ad hoc authorities was created to deal with the problems of paving, lighting, policing, and cleaning streets. Turnpikes with toll charges were trusts created to finance the demand for new roads and streets. After some decades of these ad hoc structures, municipalities assumed responsibilities for the urban services.[3]

In the United States, special districts were used in colonial times to care for the poor, build and repair roads and bridges, and maintain tobacco warehouses. As early as 1789, districts were established in Massachusetts to provide schools; in 1790, Philadelphia created special authorities to administer prisons, poor relief, port development, health measures, police, and education; in the early 1800s, toll road and canal

Districts in colonial times

Figure 16.1
Special districts by
function, nonschool: 1977
and 1978.
(*U.S. Bureau of the Census,*
1987 Census of
Governments,
Governmental Organization
Vol. 1 (Washington:
Government Printing
Office, 1988), p. xxiv.)

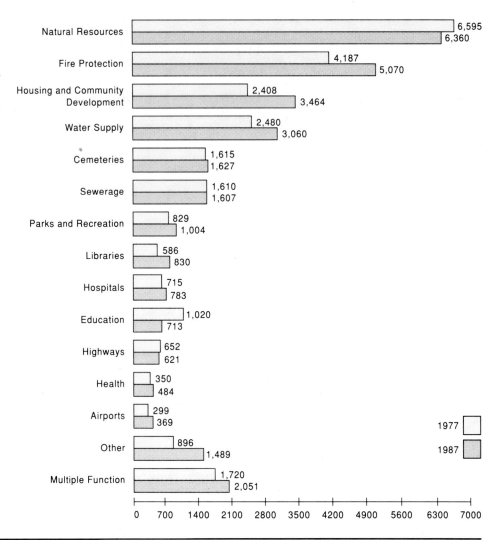

School districts become
popular

corporations were formed to manage these services.[4] Across the continent in California, special districts filled a pressing need in the gold rush by providing the authority for making and enforcing decisions on claims, filings, and operations.[5]

As states and communities developed during the 1800s, the use of the special district, especially for schools, continued to multiply. In some cases, they were used instead of a general government, because special districts were the traditional vehicles for providing education. In other cases, the new service was not suited to the local general government. In the settlement of the west, water management and irrigation programs gave birth to special districts. As fringes surrounding major cities became populated, the need for services beyond those provided by the local township mandated special districts. Thus, the number of special districts continued to rise through the twentieth century, with the exception of the school districts. During the decades fol-

Table 16.1 States with Largest Number of Special Districts

Illinois	2,783
California	2,734
Texas	1,892
Pennsylvania	1,805
Kansas	1,387
Missouri	1,217
Washington	1,177
Nebraska	1,119
Colorado	1,085
New York	978
Oregon	876
Indiana	836

Source: U.S Census Bureau, *1987 Census of Governments.*

lowing World War II, a concerted drive to reorganize the districts for delivering educational services reduced the number of school districts by some 80 percent. However, the other types of special districts continued to increase in number and importance. (See figure 16.1.)

Location of districts

The twelve states boasting 800 or more special districts account for 61 percent of all special districts in the United States. Curiously, none of the top twelve states come from the deep South, where counties are powerful, or from New England, where towns dominate. The five most heavily populated states in the nation are among the top twelve in special districts, but there is no relationship between the number of districts and population to explain the remaining seven states in the top twelve. (See table 16.1.)

Uses vary widely

General categories do not reflect the full gamut of uses to which special districts have been put, however. Among others, state laws authorize mine drainage districts in Colorado, beach-shore preservation districts in Florida, stadium authorities in Georgia, pest control districts in Arizona, fencing districts in Arkansas, memorial districts in California, television districts in Montana, weather control districts in Nebraska, convention hall authorities in New Jersey, regional arts and cultural districts in Ohio, geothermal heating districts in Oregon, regional railroad authorities in South Dakota, and predatory animal districts in Wyoming.

Creating Special Governments

Just as other local governments exist at the behest of the state, so do special districts draw their existence from the state constitutions and state laws, though most state constitutions are silent on special districts. Special districts have been created by special acts of the legislature or provided for through general statutes setting forth the organizational procedure. Except for California, districts created by special statute exist largely in the original 13 states where the practice of special charters for municipalities preceded the special district movement.

Created by special acts or general laws

Whether created by special or general laws, special districts came into existence when a group of citizens realized that they were in need of a service that could not be

Designed to meet special needs

conveniently obtained from the existing governmental structure. As an example, when Kansas farmers recognized that irrigation would increase and stabilize their productivity, they went to the legislature to secure passage of authorization for the creation of irrigation districts that could build water storage, distribution, and collection systems. The great Kansas flood of 1903 resulted in legislation authorizing the formation of drainage districts that could control water runoff and flooding.[6]

Procedures for creation

Whenever the legislature perceived that the function to be performed would be desired by people in various parts of the state, it passed a general statute that set forth the procedure by which local residents may create districts wherever they were needed in the state. Authorization was thus granted, but local initiative was required to trigger the procedure outlined in the law. In many cases, a petition signed by a considerable number of citizens was required and presented to a local governing board, very often the county board or, in some cases, a judge. Upon receipt of the petition for organizing a special district, the board or judge may have been required to call for a hearing on the question and then submit the issue to a special vote of the qualified electorate. If a majority voting on the issue approved, the district was created. The next step then was the selection of the members of the district governing board. The two most common methods were: (1) election by the electors within the district, or (2) by appointment by some board or person in authority. Depending on the nature of the district, the beneficiaries of the service, and the geographic size of its boundaries, the governing board consisted of members elected by the people, designated by mayors, designated by governing boards, or even appointed by the governor of the state.

Examples of governing boards

Of the ten-member board of directors managing the Metropolitan Atlanta Rapid Transit Authority, four are appointed by the Atlanta city council and the remainder by governing bodies of the counties in the authority. The New York City Housing Development Corporation has a board made up of three ex-officio officials plus two members (one appointed by the governor and one by the mayor). The Delaware River Joint Toll Bridge Commission, created by special acts of New Jersey and Pennsylvania, has a board consisting of five appointed by the governor of New Jersey, two appointed by the governor of Pennsylvania, and three ex-officio from Pennsylvania. When districts are created under general laws, selection tends to be more commonly by popular election and local appointment. However, the large size of the special districts mentioned here warranted special laws and special methods for choosing the governing boards (table 16.2).

Counties play key role

Once the general statute is on the books authorizing creation of a special district, the only discretion to be exercised in the process is found in the county government and only then in regard to the question of creating the district. Some 80 percent or more of the counties are authorized to control the formation of drainage, irrigation, flood control, air pollution, solid waste, water supply, housing, urban renewal, and sewage districts.[7] However, once the districts are created, counties lose a portion of this control, although about one-third of the counties are still involved in district fiscal affairs.

Most districts single-purpose

Most special districts are created with authorization to perform a single function, which is usually indicated in the name (e.g., Waterford Park District, Northland Fire District, Mosquito Abatement District). Of the 28,588 special districts in existence at the time of the 1982 Census of Governments, nine percent were multiple function; however, the majority of these involved only two services.

Table 16.2 Major Special Districts in the United States

	Revenue ($ mils)	Employees
Power		
1. New York State Power Authority	$1,620.0	3,300
2. Salt River Project, Arizona	1,210.8	5,026
3. Sacramento Municipal Utility District, California	713.1	2,200
4. Intermountain Power Agency, Utah	627.0	623
5. Municipal Electric Authority of Georgia	555.5	77
6. Omaha (Neb.) Public Power District	400.7	2,443
7. Nebraska Public Power District	390.9	2,128
8. Lower Colorado River Authority, Texas	352.4	1,780
Water & Sewer		
1. Los Angeles Department of Water and Power	$2,763.3	11,613
2. Metropolitan Water District of Southern California	638.7	1,715
3. Orange County Sanitation Districts, California	575.0	425
4. Metro Water Reclamation Dist. of Chicago	507.4	2,228
5. Milwaukee Metropolitan Sewerage District	494.3	693
6. Sanitation Districts of Los Angeles County	481.2	1,730
7. Washington (D.C.) Suburban Sanitary Commission	338.0	2,150
8. Massachusetts Water Resources Authority	300.0	1,707
Transportation		
1. Metropolitan Transportation Authority, New York	$6,423.8	65,000
2. New York City Transit Authority	3,562.9	49,866
3. Massachusetts Bay Transportation Authority	1,044.5	6,556
4. Washington (D.C.) Metro. Area Transit Authority	991.4	8,374
5. Los Angeles County Transportation Commission	919.5	383
6. Regional Transportation Authority, Chicago	897.3	70
7. Southeastern Pa. Transportation Authority	789.3	9,324
8. Chicago Transit Authority	745.7	11,646
Other		
1. Port Authority of New York and New Jersey	$2,800.0	9,200
2. Triborough Bridge and Tunnel Authority, New York	702.9	1,633
3. Municipality of Metropolitan Seattle	547.3	3,735
4. Alaska Housing Finance Corp.	437.8	145
5. Port of Portland (Ore.)	424.8	716
6. Port of Seattle	382.9	1,275
7. Chicago Park District	292.8	4,350
8. Dallas-Fort Worth International Airport	221.1	1,400

Source: City & State, *February 25, 1991.*

Geographically, most special districts have boundary lines that are peculiar to the particular government. As a part of the preliminary planning that goes into the creation of the district, planners prepare a map of the area to be included in the district. The boundaries are delineated to include those who wish to participate in the service delivery program. Because the boundaries are drawn to include an area with sufficient clients and resources to undertake the function, boundary flexibility has been one of the principal advantages of special districts.

Usually have special boundaries

Not all special districts are authorized to have boundary lines wandering across the landscape to include various and sundry settlements. Some special districts are only authorized to provide a service within the existing boundaries of counties, townships, towns, or municipalities. Thus, the boundaries of the special district are the same (coterminous) with the boundaries of an existing general government. Park districts and housing authorities commonly have the same boundaries as a general government.

Sources of revenue   Property taxes are a primary source of income for most local general governments. However, only 43 percent of the special districts have been given authority by
the state to impose a property tax to support their functions.[8] This means that a majority of districts must look to other forms of revenue. Initial financing of capital expenditures, such as buildings and equipment, is usually arranged by borrowing through
the issuance of revenue bonds which can be paid off by the revenue produced in the
service delivery. For example, a new sanitation district may need $4 million for garbage
trucks, a landfill site, and buildings. Revenue bonds are issued for the amount, with
the guarantee that charges for the sanitation services will be sufficient to pay off the
bonds over a period of years. Thus, the entire fiscal foundation of the new district consists of user charges for the services. User charges are also used to meet the need of
operating expenses, such as employee salaries, vehicle maintenance, and so forth. Thus,
unaided by general taxation, the special district is operated as a business of sorts that
sells its products and/or services at a price sufficient to recover all costs and, in some
cases, even make a profit.

Growth of Special Districts

As the population patterns have continued to splash randomly across the local governments and as people have sought government initiatives to meet their service needs, the
Special districts growing   number of special districts has continued to grow in urban and rural areas alike.
rapidly   Nationally, the rate of growth has slowed over the past three decades, dropping from
a growth rate of 52 percent in 1967, to 22 percent in 1977, to 14 percent in 1987.
Nevertheless, an average of 5,000 new special governments came into existence in each
of the past three decades. (See figure 16.2.)

Reasons for Growth of Special Governments

The shape and development of government is an institutional reflection of the aspirations of the people. Therefore, when special governments are rapidly growing, substantial reasons must exist for this sustained governmental change.

1. General governments   First, general local governments lacked the constitutional or statutory authority
lack authority   to perform the desired service. Since local governments are permitted to perform only
those functions delegated by the state, the function desired was not among those delegated to local governments. Therefore, people wanting a new service on a local level
went to the state legislature to secure authorization for the function. Why didn't the
legislature merely add authority to perform the function to that list of services permitted for an existing local general government, such as a county, township, or city?
Apparently, the citizens who wanted the service felt that the service ought to be provided in a predetermined manner and not in the manner some county or city may provide it. In some cases, there was no general government suitable for the peculiar service
being considered. Perhaps it involved several counties or even several states.

A second reason for the widespread use of special governments is found in constitutional and statutory restrictions on local government fiscal affairs. A common claim

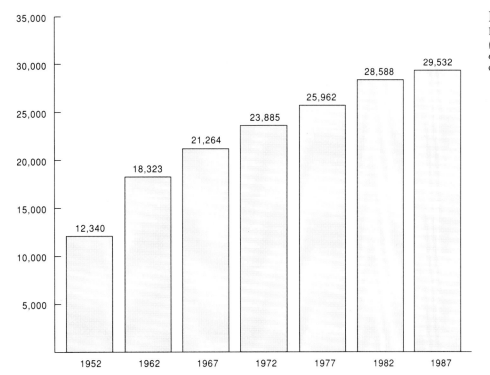

Figure 16.2
Nonschool special districts.
(Adapted from U.S. Bureau of the Census, 1987 Census of Governments.)

has been made that the creation of special districts enabled the legislature and local governments to elude constitutional limitations on bonded indebtedness. Thus, when counties or cities were already bonded to capacity, a special government with its own bonding limitations could incur new debt to provide a new function. This argument may have had merit in some states. For example, the Illinois Constitution of 1870 did not give counties or townships the powers of special assessment or of establishing differential taxing areas, thereby limiting their availability as an alternative to special districts.[9] In California, state law encouraged special districts by making it possible for them to issue general obligation bonds with the approval of a simple majority while general local governments were required by the constitution to obtain a two-thirds vote of approval.[10] In other states, however, the argument of limitations on bonded indebtedness lacked credibility. In many states, the limitations applied only to general obligation bonds while most bonds issued by special districts were revenue bonds that imposed no general obligation.

Perhaps a more persuasive fiscal argument for creating new districts had to do with financing through user charges. Over half of the special districts rely solely on nonproperty taxes, and it is likely that many of those that have property-taxing authority use their powers to tax property only as a last resort. In any case, user charges are the most dominant form of funding special district activities, a feature approved by officials of general governments who were wary of assuming financial responsibility

2. Fiscal restrictions on general governments

Availability of user fees

with their limited tax base. To them, the idea of providing a service supported completely by user charges, separate and apart from the general government, had considerable appeal. The rationale is widespread in local government that those who use a service ought to pay for it.

3. Flexibility of boundaries

The ability to delineate a flexible boundary to encompass territory not common to any particular general government has also been a reason for the growth in new districts. Only about one-fourth of the special districts have boundaries the same as those of a general government. That leaves some 21,000 with boundaries tailored to meet the particular requirements of the clientele and the service. Unique boundaries are necessary in instances where a service is required within a portion of a city, in an area consisting of several cities, in an area overlapping state boundaries, or in an area considered to be metropolitan.

Chicago offers several examples. By 1911, seven small districts had been created to provide parks for neighborhoods within the boundaries of Chicago; by 1930, this had grown to 19. Obviously the city of Chicago was initially too large a jurisdiction to meet the particular needs of neighborhood areas. However, by 1934, the parks were consolidated with three larger ones, and Chicago had a city-wide park system.[11] Most of the library districts in Cook County served single municipalities, but several of them were required to include several cities to provide a sufficient revenue and client base to support libraries. Problems that transcend the boundaries of all political subdivisions in a metropolitan area have been solved with districts covering the entire area. An example of an area-wide district is the Metropolitan Sanitary District of Greater Chicago. In the late 1800s, sewers and rivers were polluting the wells and endangering the water supply. In 1889, the Illinois legislature passed a special law creating the Chicago Sanitary District to solve the metro-wide pollution and water supply problems. The district diverted sewage away from Lake Michigan and channeled the drainage into the Illinois River running south, thus reversing the flow of the Chicago River out of Lake Michigan instead of into it.[12]

Another multi-jurisdictional special district is the Golden Gate Bridge and Highway District which includes one city-county (San Francisco), four entire counties, and part of another.[13] Bi-state special districts include the Breaks Interstate Park Commission of Virginia and Kentucky; the Tennessee-Missouri Bridge Commission; the Delaware River and Bay Authority of Delaware and New Jersey; the Maine-New Hampshire Interstate Bridge Authority, and the huge Port Authority of New York and New Jersey. The Niagara Falls Bridge Commission is an international district involving Canada and New York. Of the 28,588 special districts counted in 1982 by the Census Bureau, 2,670 were multi-county in character, with 219 involving five or more counties.

4. Desire for separate government

A fourth cause for the increased use of special districts is the parochial interest of those supporting a particular service. John Bollens calls this "unadorned self interest." Those who provide the impetus for initiating the new district are particularly interested in securing that specific service in their area. As the "parenting group," they want their child nurtured without unnecessary competition or distractions from other services provided by the general governments. To assure continued control of the service, they opt for the special district because it offers the isolation that enables them to give their particular support, and that guarantees them that they will get the benefits they want from the user fee or taxes they pay. In Bollens's words, it is "the desire of local residents to realize a return on tax money collected in their area."[14] By keeping the function separate from the general government, supporters are able to protect it from the prioritization process involved when a government must provide a number of services within the constraints of limited resources. Standing alone, the need and value of a function of the special district is not measured against the need and value of other services competing for a share of the general fund. A special district guarantees the level of funding, unaffected by the needs of general governments.

Not only does the special district escape the scrutiny and prioritization of the budgeting process, but it also avoids the politics of the general government. Citizens of the jurisdiction are all pressing different demands that must be balanced by public officials who may have priorities of their own. In the course of a year, various functional departments of the general government are called upon to interact in the provision of the whole array of services. Governing boards, responding to citizen pressures, are constantly adjusting and readjusting, thereby maintaining a constant level of political activity affecting departmental decisions. This is not to suggest that the special districts aren't plagued with political conflict. However, it is greatly simplified when confined to a single function.

Fifth, the federal and state governments have encouraged the use of special districts. Federal authorities, interested primarily in achieving some specific national objective, have favored use of the special district to avoid becoming entangled in the complications of general governments. In the 1930s, President Franklin Roosevelt wrote to governors to encourage them to secure passage of laws for the creation of new public corporations empowered to deliver services. Also in the 1930s, the U.S. Bureau of Reclamation adopted a policy of dealing only with irrigation districts that were incorporated as local units of government.[15] Special water districts were encouraged by federal financing channeled through the Farmers Home Administration and by the availability of FHA technicians to help plan the districts.[16] Drainage districts were revived after World War II by new federal water policies and more federal funds.[17] In 1936, the U.S. Department of Agriculture urged states to adopt a standard state soil conservation districts law that called for soil conservation programs administered through autonomous soil conservation districts.[18] Hospital construction funds made available by the passage of the Hill-Burton Act in 1946 encouraged the formation of hospital districts.[19] Mass transit districts were also encouraged since privately owned facilities could not receive public funds. So districts were created as convenient mechanisms for obtaining grants from higher levels of government.[20] States joined the federal government in encouraging the use of special districts by constantly passing new legislation authorizing their use instead of delegating more powers to the general governments.

Bollens points out the importance of federal and state professional functional specialists in expanding usage of special districts. Wary of general government politics, professionals interested in a particular service preferred to see it administered by professionals using professional standards. From their point of view, they saw the special district as a convenient means for accomplishing the task of providing a service

5. Use of special districts encouraged

efficiently and effectively, with a minimum of political interference. When asked, they recommended serious consideration of the neater, more focused special district.[21]

6. Attitudes of general governing boards

Finally, a sixth factor in the extensive use of special districts is based on the attitudes of the governing boards of general governments. Since the majority of these boards are lay people, the addition of another function to their government would merely mean more responsibility and more conflict. And since the financing of the new service was proposed with a balanced income and outgo, no new resources would become available to the local government if it assumed control of the service. Therefore, new services were not often greeted with open arms by the governing boards. Of course, if a professional manager were involved in the general government, the mood was likely different. Aware of the implications of fragmentation of local services, a professional manager would be more inclined to favor unification of all service delivery within the area. Nevertheless, local governing boards were often relieved to find pressure for a service released by the creation of a separate entity. Evidence of this may be seen in the hundreds of special districts approved by the governing boards of counties when, if they chose, they could have denied approval and forced eventual merging of the service into the county or other government.

Problems of Special Governments

Many professional administrators and students of government have expressed alarm over the constant growth in the number of special districts. While temporarily solving problems and offering services, special districts are seen as hazardous to the health of local government in the long run.

1. Many fall short of efficiency

First, they question the efficiency and effectiveness of creating new governments that are duplicative in their use of technical skills, equipment, and buildings. Special districts involved in services relating to the community infrastructure, such as bridges, roads, conservation, irrigation, drainage, sewage disposal, and sanitation, all utilize engineering expertise and similar types of heavy equipment. When each district purchases these resources individually, they may end up paying more for smaller quantities and under-utilizing certain services and equipment, resulting in costlier service delivery than could be offered by a larger general government. Also, the proprietory attitude that goes with ownership often stifles a free exchange of resources among local governments.

2. Reliance on user charges

Special districts are also criticized on fiscal grounds. Since heavy reliance is placed on the imposition of user charges to finance special district services, a high degree of regressivity is built into the revenue system since all customers, rich or poor, are required to pay equally for the service. In response to this argument, it may be pointed out that local residents may have been confronted with the choice of financing a service with user charges or having no service at all, in which case they chose the lesser of evils. Another fiscal criticism is that many special districts are not empowered to issue general obligation bonds but only revenue bonds. Because revenue bonds are not based on the "full faith and credit" of the community, interest rates on revenue bonds tend to be higher. The difference of one or two percentage points on interest can run into millions of dollars of added tax burden. Also, the creation of a special district to manage a popular community service can deprive the general government of an opportunity to make profits for reducing the tax burdens of taxpayers. It is not uncommon for some community services financed by user charges, such as garbage collection, water distribution, or electricity, to accrue profits that help meet other costs in general governments—costs that must be paid by many of the same taxpayers involved in the special district.

The lack of political responsiveness and accountability is another common criticism of special districts. Special districts are remote from the electorate, whether the governing board members are elected by the people or appointed by some governing body or public official. Because special districts seldom sponsor romantic and exciting services, they attract very limited media coverage. With little publicity, special district officials and activities are relatively unknown to the citizens and consumers of services. Many times, people are totally unaware of the existence of the special district providing them with services, believing that the city or the county is managing a water system, garbage collection, or mass transit. Mayors, councilors, county commissioners, township supervisors, and town selectmen often receive complaints about special government services over which they have no control.

3. Lack of accountability

Political accountability is easily lost when citizens are served by a pyramid of governments that may include the state, the county, a township, a school district, and five or six special districts. Many of the officials are elected but unknown; others are appointed and out of direct reach of the ballot box. A dissatisfied citizen may be shuttled from one government to another and from one official to another in search of someone willing to assume ultimate responsibility for mismanagement, waste, or simple incompetence. (See table 16.3.)

Speculation about visibility is transformed into figures when elections are held for special district governing board members, if there is an election. Voter turnout for special district elections are in the 10–25 percent range more often than not. An Oregon report on special district turnout indicated that the 10–25 percent range looked excellent when compared to a median turnout of four percent of the eligible voters in Oregon.[22] Some special districts have more to be concerned about than citizen apathy. In California, a dearth of candidates to serve on governing boards has resulted in widespread appointments and cancellations of elections.[23] Absent citizen awareness and involvement, special districts are freed from the tug of accountability in the management of governments sometimes employing thousands of people and handling millions of dollars. One of the original arguments for creating a special district was the desire for direct, grassroots control of the service to be performed. "Yet," an ACIR report stated, "one can question the degree of grassroots control that exists in the light of sparse voting . . ."[24]

Finally, special districts institutionalize political resistance to change. General consensus exists among advocates of government reorganization that many special districts have outlived their usefulness and should be merged into larger units or into general governments. In its report, *Modernizing Local Government,* the Committee on Economic Development proposed the abolition of all self-governing special districts in rural areas and transfer of their functions to strengthened county governments.[25] The committee, in *Reshaping Government in Metropolitan Areas,* advocated a reorganization of urban services that left little room for special districts.[26] Despite this call

4. Resist change

Table 16.3 The Challenge to a Good Citizen in LaGrange, Illinois:
Special Districts Add to Electoral Duties

Government	Boards and Officials
United States	Presidential electors
United States	2 U.S. Senators chosen at large
United States	1 Congressmember from district
State of Illinois	Governor, Lt. Governor, Secretary of State, Attorney General, Treasurer and Comptroller elected
State of Illinois	Supreme Court, appellate court, circuit court judges elected
State of Illinois	For legislature: 1 senator and 1 house member per district
Cook County	15 Commissioners: 10 elected in Chicago; 5 elected in rest of county
Forest Reserve District	Governed by county commission acting as Forest Reserve Board ex-officio
Cook County TB Sanitarium District	Board of five appointed by president of Cook County Commission with approval of Commission
DesPlaines Mosquito Abatement District	Board of five appointed by president of Cook County Commission with approval of Commission
Metro Sanitary District of Greater Chicago	Board of nine trustees elected at large
West Suburban Mass Transit District	Representative appointed by village president of LaGrange
LaGrange Park District	Board of five members elected at large
Lyons Township	Governed by board of four trustees and a supervisor all elected at large, plus clerk, assessor, collector, and highway commissioner also elected at large
College District of DuPage	Board of seven trustees elected at large
Lyons Twp. High School District	Board of seven elected at large
Elementary School Districts 105 and 102	Board of seven elected at large
South Cook County Soil and Water Conservation District	Board of five members elected by landowners or landoccupiers
LaGrange	Board of six trustees and village president elected at large

for reshaping the role of special governments, little has been achieved outside of the extensive consolidation of school districts. Consolidation and reorganization have been successfully resisted even in cases where clear evidence points out high levels of inefficiency, lack of effectiveness, and inadequate fiscal resources. However, many special districts continue because a few beneficiaries of the district have gained a position of political strength that can be used to resist reform. Though apathetic citizens may not provide a base of political power for the district hierarchy, the governing boards, professionals, and contractors have a vested interest to protect. Any alteration of the status of the district, whether consolidation with a neighboring district or a merger with a general government, will cast doubt over the future roles of the present hierarchy. This doubt becomes the springboard for opposition to any change.

Special districts may be generally criticized by structural reformers, but the opinions are by no means unanimous. After a comprehensive analysis of the pattern of special districts in Cook County and Chicago, Donald Stetzer concluded, "The evidence suggests that the advantages outweigh the disadvantages, for the districts enjoy substantial support and evidently are meeting the needs and fulfilling the goals of Cook County citizens."[27]

John C. Bollens, after a nationwide review of special districts, offered a series of recommendations to minimize the adverse impacts of special districts. He advocated absorption of the special district by the general government whenever boundaries were coterminous; changing constitutions and laws to permit general governments flexibility to take over services; converting smaller districts into subcounty service areas; increasing state supervision and reporting; broadening county control over special districts; requiring greater uniformity in organization and procedures; and merging single-function districts into multi-function districts where the same area of service was involved.[28]

Reform recommended

Endnotes

1. John C. Bollens, *Special District Governments in the United States* (Berkeley: University of California Press, 1957), p. 1.

2. Donald Foster Stetzer, *Special Districts in Cook County* (Chicago: University of Chicago, 1975), p. 161.

3. Ibid., pp. 12–13.

4. Ibid.

5. Will Baughman, "Special Districts in California," *The Tax Digest,* Vol. XXII, No. 7 (July 1944): 235 as cited in *Special Districts or Special Dynasties?* (Berkeley: Institute for Self Government, 1970), p. 5.

6. See William H. Cape, Leon B. Graves, and Burton M. Michaels, *Government by Special Districts* (Lawrence: The University of Kansas, 1969).

7. U.S. Advisory Commission on Intergovernmental Relations, *Profile of County Government* (Washington: Government Printing Office, 1972), p. 40.

8. U.S. Department of Commerce, *1987 Census of Governments, Governmental Organization* Vol. 1 (Washington: Government Printing Office, 1988), p. vi.

9. Stetzer, *Special Districts in Cook County,* p. 123.

10. *Special Districts or Special Dynasties?*, p. 11.

11. Stetzer, *Special Districts in Cook County,* pp. 88, 100.

12. Ibid., pp. 60–63.

13. Bollens, *Special District Governments,* p. 27.

14. Ibid., p. 15.

15. Cape, Graves, and Michaels, *Government by Special Districts,* p. 32.

16. Ibid., p. 63.

17. Ibid., p. 95.

18. Ibid., p. 115.

19. Ibid., p. 209.

20. Stetzer, *Special Districts in Cook County,* p. 113.

21. Bollens, *Special District Governments,* p. 12.

22. Cited in *Special Districts or Special Dynasties?,* p. 20.

23. Ibid., pp. 20–23.

24. U.S. Advisory Commission on Intergovernmental Relations, *The Problem of Special Districts in American Government* A-22 (Washington: Government Printing Office, 1964), p. 67.

25. Committee for Economic Development, *Modernizing Local Government* (New York: CED, 1966), p. 42.

26. See Committee for Economic Development, *Reshaping Government in Metropolitan Areas* (New York: CED, 1970).

27. Stetzer, *Special Districts in Cook County,* p. 156.

28. Bollens, *Special District Governments,* pp. 247–263.

CHAPTER 17

LOCAL GOVERNMENT V: METROPOLITICS

Areas of Common Interests but Uncommon Governments

America becomes Metropolitan

The metropolitan centers of America were created and shaped in response to the values, concerns, needs, and aspirations of the people who converged at the various geographic points to pursue the economic, social, or political "American dream."

Over the past two centuries the demographic face of America has witnessed two major urbanizing currents, one external and one internal. One current drifted across the Atlantic, bringing the peoples of other countries to flesh out the barren frontiers and to man the machines in the industrializing urban centers. Another current carried the progeny of pioneers from the mechanizing farms into the centers of population to engage in manufacturing, retailing, finance, public service, and numerous other pursuits.

External and internal currents of urbanization

At first, the urban newcomers huddled around the downtown core of economic activities so they could walk to their jobs and to the amenities of city life. As they continued to pour into the cities, the infrastructures and tools of governance strained to accommodate the mounting demands for services. Political bosses appeared to fill the leadership vacuum, draw together power, apply it to deliver the services, and somehow keep the feeble city governments from collapsing during the years of crisis. Soon, they were displaced by reformers who, stressing management skills and a professional civil service, made cities relatively manageable.

All the while, the influx of people grew from a current to a torrent as the rapidly changing economy continued to offer a plethora of new and better opportunities. Cities became congested masses of humanity. Aided by the automobile, better streets, and government-guaranteed home loans, the urbanites began to suburbanize by spilling out

Title photo: A symbol of intergovernmental cooperation in metropolitan areas is the Los Angeles County Hall of Administration. By providing county municipalities with services under the Lakewood Plan, the county has helped at least 35 new cities avoid heavy capital investments in duplicate facilities. (Title photo courtesy of Los Angeles County)

Suburbanization and fragmentation

of the municipal boundaries into the spacious but unorganized fringe areas. Saddled with archaic and cumbersome annexation laws, the central cities were unable to keep their boundaries and jurisdiction moving out as rapidly as the suburbanites. In some cases, the need of municipal services in the suburbs was met by urbanized townships and counties but most suburbanites felt more comfortable when they controlled their own municipalities and special districts. Hence, governments sprouted throughout the metropolitan area in response to the service needs of each new suburban settlement.

Central cities decline as suburbs grow

By the 1930s, the outward migration started to change the balance between central cities and suburbs. During the decade of the thirties, central cities as a whole gained only five percent, whereas the suburbs increased 14 percent. Strong urbanization trends kept most central cities growing, though much slower than the suburbs. During the 1960s, some of America's major central cities started to decline in population even though all central cities as a category continued to grow. Between 1970 and 1980, however, 52 of the nation's 85 largest central cities experienced population declines. Where central city growth did occur, it was usually due to annexation of adjacent suburbs or consolidation of governments. Without earlier annexations or consolidations, more cities in the Midwest, South, and West would have experienced population declines along with those in other sections of the country. As central cities declined and suburban cities grew, population densities shifted. Between 1970 and 1980, only 19 of the 85 largest central cities increased in density.[1]

The outward push of the population from the central core city has been so strong that more than half of all metropolitan area population is now located *outside* the corporate boundaries of the central cities. In 1990 more than five times as many Bostonians live outside Boston's city limits as lived inside—3,209,534 to 574,283. Although St. Louis can rightfully claim more than 2,444,099 as the population of its metropolitan area, the incorporated city of St. Louis contains only 396,685, a 12 percent decline from 1980. In even more striking contrast, the San Francisco–Oakland–San Jose area numbers more than 6,253,311 in population, but San Francisco proper can claim only 723,959 residents (see figure 17.1).

More and more, the metropolis is being divided into one complex set of governments for the place of work of its citizens and another complex set of governments for their place of residence, with intricate overlapping and intertwining of the two. Because the government of metropolitan areas constitutes a special problem distinct from city government as such, this chapter gives separate treatment to developments and trends in a field that might well be called *metropolitics.*

Defining the metropolitan area

The metropolitan phenomena were too significant to neglect even though they lacked governmental unity. The conglomerates of governments were called *metropolitan districts* and first appeared in the 1920 census. By 1980, 318 standard metropolitan statistical areas (SMSAs) were counted, containing 170 million persons, or 76 percent of the national population. The 1990 census revealed continued swelling of the metropolitan population to 193 million or 77.6 percent. In seven states on the east coast more than 90 percent of the population lived in metropolitan areas in 1987.[2] The terminology used by the U.S. Census Bureau for reporting metropolitan area information has changed from time to time, with the latest coming after the 1980 census. The term *standard* was dropped and new *metropolitan statistical areas* (MSAs) were defined as any county containing a central city or contiguous cities of 50,000 or more people, plus all adjacent counties metropolitan in nature, and economically and socially inte-

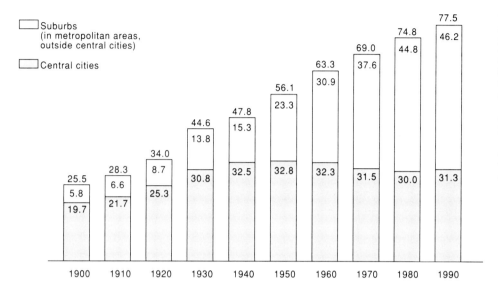

Figure 17.1
Percent of U.S. population living in metropolitan areas and in their central cities and suburbs 1900–1990. (Metropolitan areas as defined at each census since 1910. Data for 1900–1940 exclude Alaska and Hawaii.) Source: U.S. Bureau of the Census, *1990 Census Profile,* "Metropolitan Areas and Cities," September, 1991.

grated with the central county. Using this definition, 353 MSAs were identified by 1990. Of this number 71 surpassed 1,000,000 in population (Primary Metropolitan Statistical Areas) and 20 were "Consolidated Metropolitan Statistical Areas (CMSAs), which include two or more contiguous PMSAs.[3]

Causes of Suburbanization

What were the values, needs, concerns, and aspirations that motivated millions to forsake the central city to carve new urban settlements out of the metropolitan hinterlands?

First, the central city became an undesirable place in which to live and caused an outward push for many central city residents. Smoke, dirt, and noise combined to encourage inhabitants to seek a more healthful environment. Ethnocentricity became a factor as blacks, Hispanics, and immigrants crowded near the white neighborhoods. Then congestion brought with it derelicts and dependents who huddled in alleys and streets, sometimes threatening lives and property. Crime rates grew; services became minimal; governance became difficult. All of these factors challenged the values of urbanites, created concerns, and motivated them to seek the peace of the suburbs.   *1. Central city "push"*

A second factor explaining the suburban movement is the pull of the many desirable features of the suburban life. Clean air, peaceful streets, and more space were important expectations, as well as the hope for lower taxes and better government. At least their taxes would go for services they would use and the government would be more easily influenced by their desires.   *2. Suburban "pull"*

Another factor was the mass production of automobiles at a price that middle-class families could afford. As long as travel was restricted to carriages, suburbanites could only live a mile or two from the work place. The speedy automobile added miles to the livable periphery of central cities.   *3. Affordable autos*

4. Streets and highways

A fourth factor was the rapid expansion of streets and highways with the financial assistance of federal and state governments. As boggy roads gave way to wide hard-surfaced boulevards, the feasible distance for suburbanites extended even farther into the fringe areas. Throughways and beltlines, facilitated by computer operated signals, enabled commuters to live as far as 30 or 40 miles from downtown.

5. Federal home mortgages

Fifth, the federal government contributed to dispersion of the urban population by providing loan guarantees for families wishing to move out of central city rental units into a home of their own in the suburbs. Small down payments and easy terms put new homes within the reach of millions.

6. Personal income increases

Sixth, as the economic plant of the United States continued to expand and mature, more and more urbanites found their paychecks increasing, enabling them to buy the automobiles, pay for the gas, and make down payments on homes. As family incomes continued to rise faster than the cost of products, more families were financially able to afford suburban living.

7. The beltline

A seventh cause of suburbanization of recent origin has been the *beltline*. As highways improved through the decades, more and more of the country's shipping business was shifted from the fixed railroad lines to the flexible trucking industry. When the beltlines appeared as a part of the interstate system, thousands of businesses left the high-tax, confining central cities, taking their jobs with them. As the jobs moved into suburbs transversed by the high-speed roadways, people followed.

Problems of Governing Metropolitan Areas

Fragmentation of Government

Over fifty years ago when Charles E. Merriam made his frequently quoted statement that "the adequate organization of modern metropolitan areas is one of the great unsolved problems in modern politics,"[4] he might well have added that the situation would get worse without much hope of getting better. Twenty years later, in reporting the publication of Robert C. Wood's book *1400 Governments,* which gave a bleak picture of local government in the New York metropolitan region, *The New York Times* headlined its story with the words: "EXPERT PREDICTS REGIONAL CHAOS WITHIN 25 YEARS; More Urban Sprawl, Noise, Traffic, Air Pollution, and Blight Foreseen; AREA DISUNITY BLAMED; Study Discounts Possibility of Accord Among 1,467 Local Governments."[5] While the New York region provides the outstanding example of the impact of the modern population explosion on traditional local governmental structure, it is by no means alone in its situation. The 1950 census report revealed that for the first time more than half of the people of the United States lived within *metropolitan areas;* and by 1990, the metropolitan majority had risen to 77.6 percent. The 1990 census revealed that 90 percent of the decade's national growth took place in metropolitan areas. The government of these metropolitan areas frequently came

Governmental chaos

to be described in such terms as "scrambled eggs," "hopeless chaos," and "political disintegration," because each metropolis is governed not as a single area but as a strange proliferation of autonomous counties, cities, townships, and special districts. (See figure 17.2.)

One of the few things that seems forever stationary in this day of metropolitan population movements is the political boundary line. No metropolis (or state) has seen

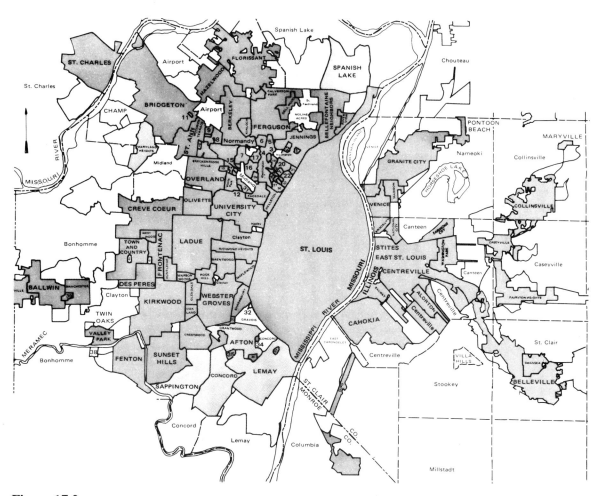

Figure 17.2
Governmental fragmentation in the St. Louis metropolitan area.
(Source: Advisory Commission on Intergovernmental Relations, Improving Urban America: A Challenge to Federalism *(Washington, D.C.: Government Printing Office, 1976), p. 164).*

fit to create a single unit of government capable of governing an entire urban community. Rather than 353 units of local government for the 353 metropolitan areas, there was a total of over 31,924 separate units of government in existence within these metropolitan areas in 1987. The American metropolis may not be the *best* governed area imaginable, but it may well be the *most* governed, from a numerical standpoint.

If the New York area is reported separately from the governmental units in northeastern New Jersey and Nassau and Suffolk Counties, the Chicago area has the largest number of units, with 1,194. In the top twenty metropolitan areas the number of separate units of government averages 452. In short, the statistical picture is one of

Table 17.1 Governmental Fragmentation

Top 20 SMSAs by Number of Local Governments			
Chicago	1,194	Detroit	345
Philadelphia	867	Boston	337
Pittsburgh	739	San Francisco-Oakland	331
St. Louis	663	Indianapolis	326
Houston	622	Omaha	305
Minneapolis-St. Paul	424	Kansas City	297
Dallas-Ft. Worth	392	Newark	279
Nassau-Suffolk	369	Allentown-Bethlehem	279
Denver-Boulder	356	Los Angeles	276
New York	352	Cincinnati	276

Source: Bureau of the Census, Local Government Employment in Selected Metropolitan Areas and Large Counties, *1983.*

Rampant fragmentation

extreme fragmentation of local government for all but a handful of metropolitan areas, with an average of approximately 90 governments per area. The trend is in the direction of even greater complexity and multiplication of units of government, particularly in the case of special districts and suburban cities. (See table 17.1.)

What have been the effects of the suburban movement upon government of the metropolitan area? What happens when cities spread out like volcanic lava, consuming the countryside and rendering their boundary lines unrealistic? Political problems of the first magnitude have resulted. An early comparative study of 112 metropolitan surveys revealed a striking similarity in the governmental consequences that seem to occur almost universally in the wake of the metropolitan explosion.[6]

Split administration of functions

The illogical administrative split-up of clearly metropolitan-wide functions of government constitutes a serious problem. This is perhaps the most universal characteristic of metropolitanism, as indicated by the number of separate units of government "required" to govern 353 metropolitan areas. A typical metropolitan area of some 90 units of government most likely would include several counties, 15 townships, 25 municipalities, 15 school districts, 25 special districts, four federally supported planning districts, and one regional council. It requires no Solomon to point out that disease, crime, and fire are no respecters of political boundary lines. Yet what metropolitan area has had the minimum wisdom or vision to create a government with the metropolitan-wide authority necessary to cope with metropolitan-wide problems? A few cities have made progress in this direction, but the progress has been painfully limited. Metropolitan area water supply, police and fire protection, street and park systems "just growed," like the immortal Topsy. The result has been scores of police departments or water supply systems in a single urban area. Without authority to guide the progress of the whole urban region, unified policy formulation and execution becomes impossible.

Fiscal Resources Vary

One of the most serious and visible results of the uncontrolled suburban movement is the financial disadvantage suffered by the central city. While more and more of the city's people move outside the city limits and out of the city tax collector's reach, the cost of government for the central city has shown no tendency either to decrease or remain stationary. Complicating this trend are the suburbanites who escape city taxes and continue to burden the city's traffic and parking problems, use the city's streets and parks, and frequently receive many other city services without charge. This places an inequitable burden on one group of metropolitan taxpayers. Bond issues for various public works, voted and paid for by the central city dwellers, are more often than not equally beneficial to suburban residents who enjoy all privileges except the dubious one of sharing the costs. The blighted sections of metropolitan areas, while paying few taxes, provide costly problems of public health, crime control, fire protection, slum clearance, and the like. These areas are usually located within the central city and never in the wealthier suburbs most able to finance such services. *Suburbanities use central city services*

Even suburbia is no longer uniformly wealthy, if it ever was. Some have begun to write about "the other suburbia" of the 1990s—heavily segregated minorities in poor suburbs without some of the redeeming features of core cities, such as mass transit and organized political power. Ford Heights, Illinois (formerly East Chicago Heights), is one of the poorest suburbs in America, and there are similar ones in the other major metropolitan areas.[7] *Growing poverty in some suburbs*

An additional thorn in the flesh of the central city is the fact that it suffers a serious loss of revenue from state taxes shared with cities on the basis of population, because a large portion of its daytime population cannot be counted. For purposes of figuring the city's share of such taxes, where a person sleeps is more important than where he or she works. The central cities' local tax burden is usually considerably greater than that of the suburbs, even though central city expenditures for education are less than in the suburbs, both on per-capita and per-pupil bases.

Computations of expenditures made in the 85 largest SMSAs revealed that central cities had general expenditures of $1,291 per capita in 1981, as compared to $980 for the surrounding area. Noneducation expenditures accounted for the major portion of the gap, with $882 being spent in central cities as compared to $521 outside of the central cities. Despite the widening expenditure gap between central cities and their suburbs between 1957 and 1981, the gap in per capita taxes was narrowed, primarily due to increased federal and state aid to central cities.[8] (See table 17.2). *Wide spending gap*

Unequal Services

Another governmental problem common to most metropolitan areas is the existence of unequal services in different sections of the same metropolitan area. For cities in the early stage of metropolitanism, the suburbanites suffer most in this respect. Although they have more room, fresh air, and quiet, they also frequently find the multiple menace of inadequate sewage disposal, fire protection, police protection, and water supply, to name only a few. Before its metropolitan consolidation, suburban Nashville provided good examples—more than 150,000 of them—of metropolitan residents who received almost no municipal services, even having competitive, private enterprise fire and police departments that served only paid-up subscribers.

In older metropolitan areas where suburban communities have been separately incorporated for many years, the overall result is much the same. Some of the suburban communities may well pride themselves on having the finest and most efficient city

Table 17.2 Comparisons of Central Cities and Suburbs

85 Largest SMSAs		
	CC	**Suburbs**
Black	21.4%	5.5%
Households with children under 18	33.1%	41.3%
Households with persons 65 and over	22.7%	19.7%
Per capita Average income	$ 6,972	$ 7,989
Household Average income	$14,601	$20,270
Per capita Government expenditure	$ 1,291	$ 980
Per capita Education expenditure	$ 410	$ 460
Per capita Non-education expenditures	$ 882	$ 521
Per capita Local taxes	$ 475	$ 383
Per capita Property taxes	$ 332	$ 315
Per capita Nonproperty taxes	$ 143	$ 64
State aid	$ 430	$ 365
Federal aid	$ 185	$ 64

Source: U.S. Advisory Commission on Intergovernmental Relations, Fiscal Disparities: Central Cities & Suburbs, 1981 *(Washington, D.C.: Government Printing Office, 1984).*

government of the whole area. This fine record is frequently possible, however, only because low-value property has been excluded from the boundaries of such cities, re- *Underprivileged pockets* sulting in unwanted and underprivileged pockets of the metropolitan community being left to their own inadequate resources. Metropolitan dispersion clearly tends to result in an unhealthy difference in the quality of governmental services within a given metropolitan area.

The inequality of government services can be traced partially to the different needs of central city residents as compared to those in the suburbs. As indicated earlier, living in the suburbs has a price tag for transportation, housing, and other costs. People who can't afford the price tag, such as the unemployed, underemployed, and retirees, must remain in the central city and look to the city government for many social services. On the other hand, suburbanites, having escaped responsibility for financing programs for social dependents, can invest heavily in services for themselves, such as education, clean streets, trimmed trees, libraries, and spacious parks.

Weakening Democratic Control

The dispersed condition of metropolitan government results in a weakening of citizen control over local government in the metropolitan area as a whole and in the central city in particular. In a maze of 90 governments, the metropolitan citizen in search of accountability encounters a number of questions. Which official or unit of government *Who is to blame?* is to receive the credit or blame for good or poor public service? Will the bewildered citizen blame the county, the central city, the suburban cities, or the many special districts for sluggish commuter traffic? Who gets blamed for an ineffective attack on an epidemic, for gangland-type crimes in various parts of the area, or for the low water pressure in the network of 40 different water supply systems? It becomes virtually impossible to place the credit or blame for the respective deeds or misdeeds of their many governments. Democratic control by the people of the area as a whole has been dispersed and dissipated.

Prior to the exodus of the middle class to the suburbs, the middle-class leaders redesigned the central city government to conform to the reform ideology. To break the grip of the corrupt bosses, the electoral system was changed so that city officials were chosen in nonpartisan, at large elections held separately from the partisan state and national elections. Unable to relate to this new nonpartisan system, many citizens dropped out of the active electorate because they could not function effectively without a political reference point. After securing these reforms that left many of the lower socioeconomic groups alienated from city affairs, the middle class moved to the suburbs. Only through the prodigious efforts of some political leaders, particularly blacks and Hispanics, have some of the reformed cities been able to reestablish links with those functionally disenfranchised by the reform movement. However, in many cities, the chasm between the governed and the government remains.

Left reform governments behind

Fragmentation of government in metropolitan areas not only results in financial inequalities, unequal services, and weaker democratic control, but the existence of numerous legally independent governments provides parochial interests with a political base from which they can wage war against the rest of the metropolitan area. Many of the unsolved problems in metro areas go begging for solution because municipalities, counties, and townships, and special districts weigh every proposal in terms of their own immediate self-interest rather than the long-term benefits that may accrue to the metropolitan area as a whole. Having a legal existence, these local governments hold a strong, fortified position on the high ground. Making up the first line of the fighting regiment in each entity are the elected boards, government employees, and the suppliers and contractors serving the entity. Only proposals that can benefit every entity escape the veto, meaning that all suggestions to equalize taxes and services, or to create metro-wide entities to achieve that end, are doomed because shifting of benefits and burdens would be inevitable.

Beneficiaries of fragmentation

Demographic Balkanization

Finally, fragmentation has made possible the Balkanization of economic, social, political, and cultural differences in the metropolitan area, producing virtually insurmountable cleavages. The most pronounced cultural gap—or social distance—exists between the central city and the suburbs. Central cities are melting pots of minorities, while suburban cities tend to be predominantly white; central cities shelter a loose concept of family, while the suburbanites nurture the conventional family; central city dwellers earn less money and count the poor and unemployed among their numbers, while suburbanites are fully-employed, middle- and upper-income; central cities are burdened with a disproportionate share of the uneducated and drop-outs, while the suburbs are overflowing with college degrees and professionals; central city dwellers are basically renters with very little in personal possessions, while suburbanites own homes flanked with spacious green lots. These contrasting characteristics result in a conflict of political and policy orientations, with central cities being Democratic and favoring social

Pockets of parochialism

programs to meet their needs and many suburbanites being Republican and opposed to high-cost social efforts. The political consequences of these differences are significant when proposals for unified action by central cities and suburbs are made to achieve order in metroland.

In Defense of Fragmentation

Challenge existence of ills

A strong group of dissenting voices, disagreeing with the diagnoses of metropolitan ills, has arisen to question even the existence of metropolitan problems as such. At the outset, Vincent Ostrom and others questioned the assumption "that the multiplicity of political units in a metropolitan area is essentially a pathological phenomenon."[9] Meyerson and Banfield disagreed sharply with the view that the American city is in a state of crisis, and contend that, contrary to the common view of blight, congestion, and ineffective government, the American metropolis is one of the great achievements of all time.[10] James M. Banovetz expressed strong doubt that the core city subsidizes the suburbs because of fragmentation, and even doubts that serious problems of subsidies exist.[11] One of the most extreme attacks on metropolitan reform advocates was made by Charles Adrian, who accused them of "almost total lack of concern with the political process and the probable ignorance . . . of the fact that a democratic public is a 'satisficing' public and not one concerned with optimum economy."[12] Adrian accused the metropolitan survey authors of making the false assumptions that "efficiency and economy are the highest political values held by the American homeowner," that "the core city of a metropolitan area must 'expand or die,' " and that "a metropolitan area is a monolithic interest—a single community."[13] Some argue that the international analogy and/or the market analogy provide(s) a better explanation for metropolitan fragmentation, which is accepted and implicitly endorsed as a natural result of diversity.[14]

These dissenting voices suggest that all too often the evils of fragmentation are presented with "wailing and gnashing of teeth" while the advantages of governmental diversity are totally neglected. From their point of view, if these governmental entities didn't serve some beneficial purpose for the people, they would never have been created in the first place.

A Vehicle for Services

Incorporation often necessary

The incorporation of a sprawling suburb into a municipal entity provided residents with a vehicle for the provision of services unavailable beyond the city's boundaries. In some cases, the suburbs were actually several miles from the central city and the central city was not prepared to annex extensive tracts of land to reach the pockets of development scattered over the countryside, nor was it prepared financially to extend water, sewer, garbage, bus, or other services to these distant enclaves. Thus, even to many of the central city fathers, incorporation was a wise course for suburbs. In this respect, incorporation of suburban settlements to provide services could hardly be termed an urban phenomenon. Thousands of cities were incorporated across America for the very same reason.

More Efficient, Responsive Service Delivery

Contrary to common folklore, bigger is not necessarily more efficient when it comes to city governments, and many municipal services actually cost more as the size of the city increases. Though it could be argued that small suburbs falling in the 10,000 to 30,000 population range hardly achieve economies of scale, many suburbs are large enough to professionally staff a whole array of municipal services. Also, the middle-class ethic supports the use of professional management skills to a greater degree than the culturally diverse central city. The influence of a dissatisfied suburbanite on a government serving 50,000 people is much more likely to be felt than the influence of a central city dweller on a government serving 500,000 people. The neighborhood movement within central cities attests to the frustration felt by many citizens as they try to impact services and policies. New York's partial breakup of services into districts is an admission that smaller units of governance can be helpful in efficient, responsive delivery systems.

Smaller cities responsive

A Revalidation of Pluralism

While service considerations may have been a motivation for the establishment of many governmental entities, the desire to insulate the value system of the white middle class was certainly reflected in zoning ordinances and building codes of many other suburban cities. As the middle class observed the value systems being brought to central cities by the various immigrations, they felt threatened and chose to seek an environment more supportive of their life style. In doing so, they asserted their right to move freely in society, to use state laws to incorporate municipalities, and to develop communities in which the values they held dear were shared by those of like mind. Rather than being homogenized into a mass urban culture, they chose their own version of pluralism and the right to be different from those in the central cities. Here again, this motivation is not necessarily a central city–suburb phenomenon. Millions of Americans have moved from one neighborhood to another, from one city to another, from one state to another, motivated by the desire to preserve the values they treasure.

Asserted right to move freely

The Issue of Obligation

By abandoning the social costs of the central city and by raising legal barriers to avoid a sharing of those costs, suburbanites have declared that they are not obligated, just because of geographic happenstance, to pay these central city costs anymore than the residents of Chadron, Nebraska. They are thereby forcing an urban nation to determine whether these social costs are obligations of the central city, the metropolitan area, the state that fathers governmental entities, or the nation as a whole. The question of obligation is even more complex today than it was 30 years ago since many suburbanites hold their jobs as well as own their homes in the suburbs and seldom go into the city. Furthermore, many suburbanites have never gone through the central city-to-suburb cycle but have come to their suburb directly from Chadron, Nebraska. They are not obligated to a central city by a fact of former residence or by fact of present employment. The creation of legal entities in the suburbs is forcing policymakers to clarify the issues involved in forcing suburbanites to reassume political and financial liability for central cities.

Does the suburbanite owe?

Reality of metropolitan problems

The worth of these arguments notwithstanding, the reality of metropolitan problems has come from the outpouring of literature on such subjects as air pollution, water shortage, stream pollution, traffic and parking congestion, mass transit dilemmas, and the host of problems related to racial and economic ghettos. It is scarcely conceivable that one could read the major books and reports on urban transportation without concluding that this is a *real* metropolitan problem clearly related to governmental fragmentation.[15] Similarly, the recent floodtide of anguished appraisals of neighborhood racial segregation patterns, in relation to the political segregation of "white power" suburban units of government from "black power" core-city units, would seem to illustrate the reality of metropolitan problems. It may well be that the skeptics' real unhappiness is with the proposed remedies, and that their tendency to downgrade the problems is a result of overreacting against what they consider to be unrealistic dogmas of metropolitan reform, so commonly rejected by the voters.

Remedies for Metropolitan Ills

It may be said concerning remedies proposed for the various problems of governing metropolitan areas that "many are called but few are chosen." Metropolitan reformers have in recent years proposed many solutions to these problems; the more important of these proposals are summarized here, including the experience and prospects for each.

Annexing Adjacent Territory

Annexation of the surrounding urbanized territory by the central city is the most commonly proposed remedy, unless the territory has already been incorporated as separate municipalities. It was the method used by the nation's great cities to achieve their present size. The case for annexation is strong, from the viewpoint of both the suburbs and the central city: expensive public works, improvements, and services could be provided at lower cost than by the suburb alone; property values would rise; fire insurance rates would be lower; voting privileges in central city elections could be secured; the city's census standing would be higher; the base for financing municipal government would be broadened; and the city would bring about a suburban development consistent with its own development. For both city and suburban residents advantages result from functioning as one community, such as the capacity to make a unified attack on the metropolitan problems of disease, crime, slums, and juvenile delinquency.

The early logical approach

In spite of the compelling logic of the arguments, it has been virtually impossible for the larger cities to keep pace by means of annexation with population growth on the margin of the city. Opposition to annexation is almost always strong in the suburbs, based on several arguments: taxes would be increased; the government of the central city is corrupt or incompetent; new services would be long delayed in arriving, if they arrive at all; and annexation is a nefarious scheme of the power-grabbing politicians and tax collectors in the city hall.

If the suburb to be annexed is already incorporated, the opposition may be exceedingly strong because of greater community spirit and unwillingness to lose name, identity, and independence. Once a city is surrounded by separately incorporated satellite cities, the chances of annexation are slim. Boston, for example, has never been able to annex Brookline, Newton, and Milton. The suburban cities of Pasadena and Long Beach and even wholly surrounded Beverly Hills have been successful down through the years in resisting all efforts to be incorporated into the city of Los Angeles. More recent developments in metropolitan areas are equally discouraging to proponents of annexation except in cases where the metropolitan core cities are surrounded for the most part by unincorporated territory. Minneapolis became completely encircled by incorporated cities between 1940 and 1950; Pittsburgh is surrounded by 190 municipalities, and Detroit by 87. As long as each individual suburb remains the master of its fate concerning annexation, requiring a majority vote before coming under the jurisdiction of the central city, annexation must be considered a thing of the past for the older metropolitan areas.

Slim chances of annexing incorporated suburbs

A study by Thomas Dye[16] of factors associated with successful annexation in urban areas indicates that "social class distance" between the city and its surrounding suburbs is one of the more important variables. Thus, central cities with larger proportions of middle-class residents were more successful in annexing the middle-class suburbs than were the central cities with smaller proportions of middle-class residents. Manager governments were significantly more successful in annexation than nonmanager governments, perhaps harmonizing better with a suburban preference for "antiseptic, non-partisan, professionalized municipal government." The age of the settlement proved to be an important variable, with older urbanized areas having greater immobility of boundaries than younger ones. Surprisingly, the ease or difficulty of the legal procedure for annexation does not in itself provide an explanation for differences in success and failure in annexation. Similarly, the size of the urbanized area was not an important variable.

Annexing and social distance

The U.S. Supreme Court ruled annexation to be a voting rights violation in Canton, Mississippi, in 1971, and in Petersburg, Virginia, in 1973. In 1975, the Court held that a city could alter its racial composition by annexing predominantly white suburbs as long as there is a legitimate governmental motive and blacks enjoy a proportionate share of political power in the enlarged city.[17] To add the emotional racial issue to the already complex political problem simply makes it even more difficult to achieve annexation.

In spite of the successful annexations in many metropolitan areas, the fact remains that the central core cities of most of the older and larger metropolitan areas are finding it necessary to look to devices other than annexation to secure metropolitan political integration. If separate suburban incorporation could be avoided, annexation might play a surprisingly important role in the structuring of the future government for the new and presently emerging metropolis. After the straitjacket of incorporated satellite cities has been wrapped around the core cities, however, they are forced to turn from annexation to a variety of alternative proposals.

Not a central city solution

Extraterritorial Powers

When annexation seems out of the question, a municipality is sometimes granted the right to exercise certain powers outside the city limits. Such extraterritorial powers have been sustained by the courts on the ground that they are essential to effective use of the intraterritorial powers granted to the city. The device takes such forms as the inspection of all sources of milk supply for a central city, even though the milkshed may extend many miles in all directions outside the boundaries of the city; the control of land platting outside the boundaries of the city; the control of contagious diseases for a certain number of miles beyond the corporate limits; the regulation of undesirable trades; and the suppression of houses of prostitution within a certain distance of the city. As a permanent device for furnishing integrated government to the whole metropolitan community, extraterritorial power has important limitations. The problem of financing such activities in an equitable manner is perplexing. Furthermore, the exercise of governmental power over persons having no control over the government is not conducive to cooperation over the long run.

Intergovernmental Cooperation

Lakewood Plan still strong

Probably the most widely used means of coordination in metropolitan areas is that of intergovernmental arrangements for municipal activities. The prevalence of contractual and informal agreements probably can be attributed to the failure to obtain fundamental change in the structure of government of the area or disturbance of political alignments. Local governments in California have made wide use of intergovernmental agreements, especially for county provision of service to cities. Los Angeles County, for example, has close to 1,500 contracts calling for a wide range of services to the 84 municipalities in the county. One aspect of this procedure is the Lakewood Plan, named for that city of 75,000 that in 1954 was the first to contract for a whole package of services rather than contracting on a piecemeal basis. The Lakewood Plan, or the *contract cities plan* as other cities prefer to call it, has been adopted by 35 of the 38 cities incorporated in Los Angeles County since 1954. The package of services is not the same for each city, with some tendency for older cities to begin to perform certain services for themselves. One of the more recent contracts called for 46 Los Angeles County sheriff's deputies to patrol the northern part of the city of Long Beach (pop. 420,000), for three years while the city hired and trained new officers of its own. It was the first "full-service city" in California to contract a portion of the city to outside service deliverers, and was estimated to save Long Beach $50,000 in the first year of the contract.[18]

Councils of government

During the 1960s and 1970s, Councils of Governments (COGs) became popular in metropolitan areas as a mechanism through which representatives of the various governments in the metro area could meet to discuss and study common problems. COGs are not governments; they do not have legal standing under state law, nor do they deliver any services. They are cooperative organizations, many with staffs that study and report on metropolitan problems. Some of the earliest ones organized were the Supervisors Inter-County Committee (Detroit, 1954), the Metropolitan Regional Council (New York, 1956), and the Metropolitan Washington (D.C.) Council of Governments (1957). The Association of Bay Area Governments (ABAG) was organized in the San Francisco area in 1961 and moved vigorously into the field of regional planning. The Council of Governments was given a boost by the U.S. Housing and Urban Development Act of 1965 which authorized financial assistance for planning. From a modest beginning of only 12 in 1965, the number of councils of governments rose steadily to more than 500 by 1990, excluding those with a non-metropolitan focus. The COG is praised as the wave of the future by its advocates, but is viewed by its opponents as a toothless tiger or, even worse, a protector of the inadequate status quo. It has been said that a COG can be anything from an Elk's lodge to a metropolitan government. Despite the inherent weakness of voluntarism and the malapportioned structure of COG favoring the small suburban governments, they seem destined to become a common institutional addition to the metropolitan scene even though federal funding cuts in the 1980s threaten their vigor.

COGs as toothless tigers

Restructuring Metropolitan Areas

When proposals for overcoming fragmentation of governments in metropolitan areas move from cooperation to restructuring, entire community power structures that include local officials, public employees, economic interests, and taxpayers are threatened and opposition becomes more determined. Nevertheless, examples of successful restructuring can be found to offer hope to those who feel restructuring is the only long-range solution to metropolitan problems.

The Federated Metropolis

One option is a type of metropolitan government that might be termed *federal*, in that there is a formal division of powers between a central government and the constituent municipalities. Based on a rough analogy to the relationship between the national government and the states, the larger unit of government performs area-wide functions—those that transcend municipal boundaries, while the component municipalities continue to perform the purely local functions. The *federated metropolis* covers the entire metropolitan area. In cases where the area coincides generally with the boundaries of a county, some plans provide for the county to become the central federated government. Functions retained by the existing municipalities might include fire protection, police protection, garbage disposal, and similar activities more local in character, although the difficulty of defining "purely local" is quite obvious. In a day when it has become increasingly unrealistic to attempt a division between national and state functions, and between state and local functions, any further subdivisions of local functions into those that are "area-wide" and those that are purely local would seem to be moving against the stream of government history.

Two-level government

For many years, the city of London, having a two-tiered government consisting of a county council and several metropolitan boroughs, was the only metropolitan government properly characterized as municipal federalism. In 1953, Toronto became the second metropolis to make use of the federal principle by uniting with its several suburbs in a federated city. In spite of several failures to secure adoption in the United States, the idea of metropolitan federation is still alive, primarily because of the highly publicized Toronto experience. The Municipality of Metropolitan Toronto was created by the provincial parliament in 1953 and given jurisdiction over several area-wide

The Toronto experience

functions, both in the city of Toronto and in its 12 suburban satellite cities. The federation was a compromise between complete amalgamation (annexation), proposed by the city of Toronto, and complete independence as defended vehemently by the suburban cities. The result was to leave the 13 cities in charge of such activities as police, fire, health, library, and welfare services, while creating a new metropolitan level of government to handle water supply, sewage disposal, housing, education, arterial highways, metropolitan parks, and overall planning.

In 1957, the 13 local police forces were taken over by the metropolitan government, causing some critics to say that metropolitan federation is merely "disguised annexation." After a study in 1965, the provincial government reduced the 13 constituent municipalities to six and moved welfare and education to the Metro government. Defenders of the federation principle contend that the merger to six cities has strengthened the federation because they are now of sufficient size, strength, and resources to become permanent, viable political units. Metropolitan Toronto has been widely publicized for an outstanding record of accomplishment in such activities as highways, rapid transit, water supply and sewerage, and regional planning. Undoubtedly, Toronto will continue to be an interesting testing ground for bold innovation in metropolitics, although it is important to remember that the restructuring was legislatively imposed from above, and not adopted by ballot at the grassroots level.

Partial federation in Dade County

The voters of Miami and Dade County in 1957 narrowly adopted a two-tiered form of metropolitan government which incorporates, to a limited degree, the principle of federation. The heart of the Dade County "Metro" plan is the retention of the existing municipalities (Miami plus 27 suburban cities) for the performance of "purely local" activities, with the allocation of authority to Dade County for those governmental activities that are "essentially metropolitan" in nature. During its first five years of existence, while receiving nationwide acclaim as a civic pacemaker, it was repeatedly fighting off the attacks of anti-Metro forces in the form of a multitude of lawsuits and three county-wide referendums which would have gutted the new structure. The tenure of the first two county managers was short; the first was dismissed in 1961 and the second in 1964. In addition to political battles it has had financial ones, stemming from the fact that it has many of the obligations of a city, but only the taxing power of a county. It has become the largest council-manager government in the nation. In technical terms, Dade County's Metro is more nearly a "municipalized county" than it is a federation of municipalities, since the cities as such are not represented on the board of commissioners. But whatever the classification, this "great bold venture in modern government," as second Metro Manager McNayr once called it, has offered a strong ray of hope to many other American metropolises.

The Unified Metropolis

With the passage of the Metropolitan Winnipeg Act by the provincial legislature in 1960, Manitoba took its first step toward the eventual consolidation of 12 municipalities in the Winnipeg metropolitan area of 600,000 people. Initially, the metropolitan corporation assumed the functions of planning, zoning, building regulations, assessment of property, the zoo, distribution of water, sewage disposal, public transportation, major parks, civil defense, mosquito abatement, and weed control. Council members

Winnipeg consolidates area

for the government were elected in ten districts, with the districts crossing the boundaries of municipalities. In 1972, the next step was taken by the provincial legislature and the preexisting structure was abolished in favor of 50 electoral wards and one central government for the metropolitan area.[19] Councilors served on the governing board of "unicity" as well as "community councils" in various parts of the city to ensure essential community services were being delivered.

The Municipalized County

In certain counties political pressure from unserved suburban groups opposed to annexation and from reform groups discouraged in their annexation efforts resulted in what might be called a *municipalized county*. In spite of the county's legal position as an administrative district of the state and created to perform state functions, many states have begun to grant counties authority to provide services traditionally considered municipal in type. Probably the best known example of a county performing a multiplicity of municipal functions is Los Angeles County, as mentioned previously; it has more functions than the city of Los Angeles and a budget exceeding that of the city. Among its many urban functions are street improvements, street lighting, sanitation, fire protection, police protection, library service, public parks, and regional planning. Montgomery County, Maryland, with a council–manager form of government, is serving as the *de facto* municipal government for most of the 580,000 residents of the rapidly growing northwest sector of the metropolitan area of Washington, D.C.

County performing municipal services

Expansion of county functions evokes much less opposition than annexation or city-county consolidation. This fact undoubtedly explains the rapid advances in many states in the direction of transforming the urban county into a unit of metropolitan government. The one serious weakness of the movement to expand the county's functions is the fact that the county, as it is commonly organized, is still suited to the rural conditions of the horse-and-buggy era rather than to the task of administering municipal functions. Its limited powers, numerous elective officials, and its cumbersome and impotent governing body are scarcely designed to facilitate effective and efficient performance of the heavy responsibilities of metropolitan government. Many students of government feel, however, that it might be made suitable for local government in urban regions by drastic structural changes, such as the provision for a single county executive and the establishment of a county legislative body that is both representative and responsible.

City-County Separation

A few cities in the United States have resorted to city-county separation to achieve partial unification. It eliminates one of the layers of government under which the city resident must live and pay taxes, and it is considered a viable option where a large central city represents a substantial part of the county. City-county separation involves removal of the city's territory from the jurisdiction of the county, consolidating the city and county functions within the city limits, and restricting the services and costs of the county government to the residue of the former county. The four outstanding examples are Baltimore (1851), San Francisco (1856), St. Louis (1875), and Denver (1903). Judicial interpretations of the state constitutions resulted in varying degrees of consolidation of city and county functions in each case.

Rural resists separation

City–county separation is always strongly resisted by the rural portions of the county that are to become the doughnut-shaped "rump" county. The impoverished remains of the county may find it necessary to unite with surrounding counties in the face of operating a suburban and rural government without sufficient tax resources. On the other hand, city-county separation usually seriously complicates the future expansion of the city, because enlargement of the city-county's boundaries is much more difficult than extension of the single city's corporate limits.

City-County Consolidation

Merging governments

Under city-county consolidation, the city limits are extended to coincide with the county boundaries and the two governments are consolidated, leaving no troublesome remnant county as in city-county separation. It eliminates duplicate sets of officers for city and county functions and overlapping jurisdiction between city and county. Twenty-five cities have adopted some form of city-county consolidation.

The advantages of consolidating county and city governments in metropolitan areas include the taxpayers' benefit from eliminating one layer of government, the voters' benefit from the shorter ballot, more simplified structure of local government, and administrative improvements resulting from metropolitan-wide jurisdiction. This last benefit, governmental integration of the whole metropolitan area, cannot be claimed in all cases of city-county consolidation. The largest metropolitan areas spill over into more than one county as well as into neighboring states, so that consolidation with a single county would not encompass the whole urban area. Another difficulty of the consolidated city-county is the need for future annexation to keep pace with the suburban movement. This would necessitate detaching territory from adjacent counties, which would generally require jumping constitutional hurdles and working political miracles.

Consolidations still occurring

Political scientists on several occasions have pronounced city-county consolidation to be a thing of the past, only to see it resurrected as a serious proposal in some major city. The mergers of Baton Rouge and East Baton Rouge Parish in Louisiana in 1947, Nashville and Davidson County in 1962, and Jacksonville and Duval County in 1967 were each declared by skeptics to be rare accidents of metropolitan reform, and not really a serious option for most cities. Yet such major consolidations as Indianapolis-Marion County, Columbus-Muscogee County (Georgia), Lexington-Fayette County (Kentucky), and Savanna-Chatham County, all occurring since the 1967 Jacksonville merger, make it clear that it is still a viable issue in metropolitan areas in the United States.

Nashville-Davidson County

Voters of Nashville and Davidson County adopted a charter in June 1962, consolidating the city and county governments into a single metropolitan government. Four years earlier, a similar proposal had been rejected by the suburban and rural voters of the county. However, an ambitious annexation drive by the city of Nashville in 1960 caused many suburbanites to look at city-county consolidation in a more favorable light, and the tide turned in favor of "Metro." The unique feature of the Nashville plan is an expandable urban services district, beginning initially with the core city's boundaries, but expanding with the urban growth and the extension of the full complement of urban services, and with a tax rate corresponding to the higher level of services. All persons are in the "general services district," and receive and pay for all area-wide

Table 17.3 City-County Consolidations

By Legislative Action

New Orleans-Orleans Parish, Louisiana	1805
Boston-Suffolk County, Massachusetts	1821
Philadelphia-Philadelphia County, Pennsylvania	1854
San Francisco-San Francisco County	1856
New York-New York County, New York	1874
New York and Brooklyn-Queens and Richmond Counties, New York	1898
Honolulu-Honolulu County, Hawaii	1907
Indianapolis-Marion County, Indiana	1969

By Referendum

Baton Rouge-East Baton Rouge Parish, Louisiana	1947
Hampton-Elizabeth City County, Virginia	1952
Newport News-Warwick County, Va.	1958
Nashville-Davidson County, Tennessee (defeated in 1958)	1962
Virginia Beach-Princess Anne County, Virginia	1962
South Norfolk-Norfolk County, Virginia	1962
Jacksonville-Duval county, Florida (defeated in 1935)	1967
Juneau-Greater Juneau Borough, Alaska	1969
Carson City-Ormsby County, Nevada	1969
Columbus-Muscogee County, Georgia (defeated in 1962)	1970
Sitka-Greater Sitka Borough, Alaska	1971
Suffolk-Nansemond County, Virginia	1972
Lexington-Fayette County, Kentucky	1972
Savannah-Chatham County, Georgia	1973
Anchorage-Greater Anchorage Borough, Alaska	1975
Butte-Silver Bow County, Montana	1977
Anaconda-Deer Lodge, Montana	1977
Houma-Terebonne Parish	1984

In addition to these listed, Baltimore, San Francisco, St. Louis, Denver, and many Virginia cities have achieved some of the same results as consolidation by means of city-county separation. (Source: Adapted from The American County *37 (February 1972): 14–15, with additions from* County News, *periodical published by the National Association of Counties, and* The Municipal Yearbook 1979 *and* The Municipal Yearbook 1984 *(Washington, D.C.: International City Management Association).)*

services of the metropolitan government. All duplicate city and county departments, boards, executives, and legislative bodies are merged into single, metropolitan counterparts. Architects of the plan contend that it has the benefits of unified government for the entire metropolitan area (533 square miles), without the inflexibilities of previous city-county mergers with respect to the problem of governing the developing suburban fringe and the more stable rural areas. The early favorable appraisals of the Nashville Metro approach have provided hope to many of the medium-sized and smaller metropolitan areas located entirely within single counties.[20]

Jacksonville-Duval merge

Voters in the city of Jacksonville, Florida, and Duval County adopted a consolidation plan in 1967 that was patterned in many ways after the Nashville plan. After a series of financial and political crises in city and county government, a study commission recommended to the community and the Duval legislative delegation a Blueprint for Improvement. The delegation adopted a city-county consolidation charter, subject to voter approval by a single majority vote. The proponents, in addition to having the normal "good-government" allies, were joined by a significant number of labor and black leaders, and the charter was adopted by a decisive two-to-one majority.

*State legislature merges
Indianapolis area*

The first city-county consolidation in a northern metropolitan area in this century was approved by the Indiana General Assembly in 1969 for Indianapolis and Marion County. More intriguing than the name chosen for the consolidated government (UNIGOV), was its establishment by the state legislature *without a referendum*. Although this was a sharp departure from traditional state ground rules for consolidation, concessions to political expediency were made by continuing the separate existence of incorporated satellite cities, townships, and most county offices. Several factors made UNIGOV possible: (1) strong Republican party control of the appropriate state and local governmental offices necessary to push the legislation through; (2) the convergence of partisan self-interest, traditional political attitudes and practices in Indiana, and general support of business, civic, and governmental reform groups; (3) vigorous and effective political leadership of Mayor Richard Lugar; (4) mass media support; and (5) shrewd political concessions in structuring the new government—a large 29-member council, preservation of special-service and taxing districts, and of suburban, city, and most county officers.[21] UNIGOV moved to permanent status in 1972, with an overwhelming Republican majority of offices. Five black council members were elected, very close to what the county population ratio would call for, but doubtless a smaller percentage than would be expected if Indianapolis had not consolidated with the county. In the only other modern consolidation by state legislative mandate (Las Vegas and Clark County in 1975), the Nevada Supreme Court overturned it as unconstitutional.

Functional Consolidation

Obstacles to city-county consolidation that have been common to the great majority of consolidation referenda efforts, have caused many cities to resort to a more gradual approach—consolidating single functions common to both city and county governments without a complete political and territorial merger. Functional consolidation in-

Sharing a function

volves the performance by one unit of local government of an activity such as public health or sewage disposal, previously performed by two or more overlapping units. It may be brought about either by state action, permissive or mandatory, that reallocates the functions of local government, or by some form of contractual arrangement between the local governmental jurisdictions. One of the better-known examples of functional consolidation is the extensive plan for redistribution of functions between Atlanta and Fulton County. Functional consolidation is sometimes called the *fabian* or *gradual approach* to eventual city-county consolidation, rather than the frontal attack. However, it is also possible for a piecemeal solution to one or two of the more pressing problems to slow down or to delay indefinitely city-county consolidation.

Portland's new approach

The Portland, Oregon, metropolitan area launched a new approach to regional government in 1979 that combines elements of several different approaches to metropolitan coordination. Called the Metropolitan Service District (MSD), it encompasses three counties and has a popularly elected executive and 12-member council representing the people directly and not just units of government. It has the potential to provide metropolitan aspects of water supply, parks and recreation, transportation, social services planning and coordination, corrections, and cultural activities. Following popular defeat of city-county consolidation for Multnomah County and Portland in 1976, the new Portland proposal reached the ballot and was adopted in 1978 by a 55 percent majority. The new government replaced the existing regional planning agency. Funded by a payroll tax, MSD continues the planning function and has been delegated responsibility for solid waste and the metropolitan zoo.

Special Districts

One of the more popular piecemeal approaches to the problems of metropolitan government is the creation of special districts, distinct from other units of government, that have boundary lines drawn to coincide with the boundaries of the problem or problems to be solved. Special metropolitan districts are popular for a number of reasons, discussed in greater detail in the preceding chapter. Experience with this device has demonstrated the ease with which seemingly insurmountable political boundary lines may be crossed. Districts meet relatively little resistance from politicians because they eliminate no jobs and usually do not disturb the organization's grip on the city government. So far as the suburban politicians are concerned, such authorities are exceedingly popular because they lessen the pressure for annexation to the core city.

Flexible boundaries solve metro problems

Special districts are frequently created for financial reasons, such as equalizing the tax burden over an area wider than that of existing units, or enabling a unit of government to evade established tax or debt limits. In the latter case, existing units of government in a metropolitan area may already be up to their tax and debt limits, so that the only local means of providing additional revenue to finance a desired service is to establish a new unit of government. There seems to be a growing willingness on the part of state legislatures to give special districts the power to exercise a number of functions, thus permitting multipurpose special districts. Some of its proponents hope that it might gradually evolve into a general area-wide government by adding functions as the failure of the smaller units of government becomes apparent. The special district has many critics, primarily of its low level of citizen participation and accountability, causing some to refer to special districts as "invisible government".

Attacking Fiscal Disparities

Because municipal boundaries serve to corral taxable resources, some cities in a metropolitan area may attract extensive industrial and commercial development—and taxable resources—while other cities starve. Recognizing the growing disparity in the tax bases of governments in the Minneapolis-St. Paul metropolitan area, the Minnesota legislature passed a Fiscal Disparities Act to pool new commercial/industrial property valuation for sharing by all governments in the area. Under the program, 60 percent of the growth remained under local control but 40 percent of the new valuation was pooled and distributed on the basis of indices that suggested need. Statistics compiled by the Twin Cities Citizen League, an independent research and educational organization, revealed that the valuation in the pool grew from $137 million (6.7 percent) of the metro commercial industrial valuation in 1975 to $884 million (22.8 percent) by 1983. According to the Citizens League, if the law had not been passed, the ratio between the municipality with the highest per capita commercial industrial valuation and the lowest would have been 13–1. With the law, it has been held to 4.7–1. The central cities of St. Paul and Minneapolis were the primary beneficiaries of the program.[22]

Minneapolis-St. Paul pioneer valuation sharing

The Politics of Metropolitics

Fragmentation as a political problem

In many respects, the champions in the vanguard of metropolitan reorganization are of the same cut as the reformers that arose in the corrupt cities to quash boss rule. Government was to be designed in accordance with the latest principles of efficient administration and conducted according to the edicts of sound management. Thus, when they arrived at the metropolitan maze, they quickly detected the chaos, mismanagement, and waste arising out of a pluralistic governmental structure, seemingly accountable to everyone and no one at the same time. To any intelligent human being, from a vantage point of disinterest, the solutions were simple and obvious. Yet, after more than 50 years of hard labor in the vineyards of reform, metropolitan reformers have barely bottled enough to mark a festive victory, should one occur. It seems that the solutions that are politically acceptable solve few problems, yet those that are effective are politically unacceptable. The backward look certainly does not offer much encouragement to advocates of some kind of area-wide approach to governing the metropolis.

For every advocate of reform, there are at least five opponents ready to fight to the last suburban trench. As indicated earlier, suburbanites are suburbanites for several reasons but one principal reason has been to erect the legal wall of incorporation between them and the social ills of central city. Efforts to recapture them and saddle them with burdens they moved to escape is certain to meet with resistance.

Central cities not always for merger

Central city residents aren't always that interested in being unequally yoked with the suburbs, either. If money is poured into renovating the downtown, the costs will eventually surface in higher rents or higher taxes, neither of which they want. Also, the black leadership of central cities has waited for decades to gain a more formidable role in city affairs. They are not about to start consolidating with white suburbs that will once again give whites dominance of central city politics.

Political parties have a stake in avoiding structural reorganization. Central cities are as much Democratic strongholds as many suburbs are Republican fortresses. A fragmented metropolitan area permits each to master a share of the hill whereas consolidation would threaten both of them.

As indicated earlier, the beneficiaries of the numerous governments also oppose restructuring. The holders of public office in all of the governments commanding resources, those who draw their paychecks from special districts or municipalities, and those who sell goods and services to area governments all represent special interests that are quickly mobilized when uncertainty threatens the status quo.

Political agenda must be addressed

The aspirations of these many beneficiaries of the present metropolitan chaos clearly make restructuring a political rather than a management decision. Before significant reform can be achieved, the political agenda must be addressed. On that agenda are such matters as the readjustment of financial responsibilities, the future role of minorities in new governments, and the protection of all legitimate interests in the new system of governance. In a number of restructuring efforts, these issues were dealt with at the same time as negative factors, such as threats of annexation or corruption in government, propelled citizens toward consolidation.

Occasionally, forces outside of the metropolitan area were mustered to accomplish the task. Most notably, this was the case in Toronto, Indianapolis, Minneapolis, and Winnipeg where state or provincial legislatures took charge. However, states are reticent to use authority to override expressions of local pluralism. After 30 years of legislative reapportionment, a significant change in the attitudes of most state legislatures toward metropolitan problems has failed to appear. Help is not likely to come in the 1990s, either. While a number of federal agencies, such as the Department of Housing and Urban Development and the Advisory Commission on Intergovernmental Relations, sympathize with the metropolitan riddle, huge federal deficits coupled with a philosophy of solving local problems at home have dampened any new federal initiatives.

Circumstances suggest that metropolitan restructuring will continue along the path established in the last few decades—slow incremental change, with an occasional burst of success attributable to unique local circumstances. As long as water runs out of the tap, the sewer lines remain open, and the bus comes on time, the apathetic citizen who is suspicious of change will not respond to a call to arms to meet a crisis he or she does not perceive.

Intergovernmental muddling-through

Apart from the intimidating array of political factors militating against major restructuring of the metropolis to achieve area-wide governance at the sub-national or sub-state level, there is the even more intimidating "megalopolis" that is no longer just a "megatrend" in the distant future. Area-wide formal government for one metropolitan community becomes many times more difficult to achieve when the community is "Yorkadelphia," "Boswash," "DFW City," or even "Global City." When two or more major metropolitan areas grow together, the politics of achieving regional governance moves to an extremely high level of difficulty. Only a correspondingly high level of crisis is likely to pierce that kind of political sound barrier. This new urban globalization trend was discussed in chapter 3.

The challenge of governing "Boswash"

An unusual macro view of the problems of governing U.S. metropolitan areas has been taken by John Kincaid who, after comparing the "consolidation school" and the "diversity school," concludes that the time may be right to revive the "international" and "market" analogies of metropolitan politics. The new yearning for ethnic autonomy so fiercely demonstrated in Eastern Europe and the former Soviet Union in the early 1990s may well support Kincaid's call for theories of governance "that accomodate the desires for individual freedom and local self-government," and not merely "mechanisms of multi-jurisdictional government." This is, of course, the classic question of federalism.[23]

International and market analogies of metropolitics

Endnotes

1. U.S. Advisory Commission on Intergovernmental Relations, *Fiscal Disparities* (Washington: Government Printing Office, 1984), pp. 5–6.

2. They are New Jersey (100%), Massachusetts (96%), Maryland (93%), Connecticut (92%), Rhode Island (91%), Florida (91%), and New York (90%). Adapted from U.S. Bureau of the Census, *1987 Census of Governments,* Vol. 1, "Government Organization," pp. 36–38.

3. *The Municipal Year Book,* 1992 (Washington, D.C.: International City Management Association, 1992), p. xiii.

4. In Merriam's preface to Victor Jones, *Metropolitan Government* (Chicago: University of Chicago Press, 1942), p. ix.

5. *New York Times,* July 17, 1961. Wood's volume, published by the Harvard University Press, is one of nine resulting from the New York Metropolitan Regional Study.

6. See Daniel R. Grant, "General Metropolitan Surveys: A Summary," *Metropolitan Surveys: A Digest* (New York: Government Affairs Foundation, 1958), pp. 1–24.

7. "The Other Suburbia," *Newsweek,* June 26, 1989, pp. 22–24.

8. U.S. Advisory Commission on Intergovernmental Relations, *Fiscal Disparities,* pp. 12–15.

9. Vincent Ostrom, Charles Tiebout, and Robert Warren, "The Organization of Metropolitan Areas: A Theoretical Inquiry," *American Political Science Review* 55 (December 1961): 831.

10. Martin Meyerson and Edward C. Banfield, *Boston: The Job Ahead* (Cambridge, Mass.: Harvard University Press, 1966), p. 2.

11. "Metropolitan Subsidies—an Appraisal," *Public Administration Review* 25 (December 1965): 297–301.

12. Charles R. Adrian, "Metropology: Folklore and Field Research," *Public Administration Review* 21 (Summer 1961): 148–149.

13. *Ibid,* pp. 149, 150, 152.

14. John Kincaid, "Metropolitan Governance: Reviving International and Market Analogies," *Intergovernmental Perspective,* 15 (Spring, 1989), pp. 23–27.

15. See the U.S. Advisory Commission on Intergovernmental Relations, *Improving Urban America: A Challenge to Federalism* (Washington: U.S. Government Printing Office, 1976).

16. Thomas R. Dye, "Urban Political Integration: Conditions Associated with Annexation in American Cities," *Midwest Journal of Political Science* 8 (November 1964): 430–446.

17. *City of Richmond* v. *United States,* 422 U.S. 358 (1975).

18. John L. Larkin, "Public Safety Clashes with Public Oversight," *Public Administration Times,* 14 (March 1, 1991).

19. Thomas J. Plunkett, unpublished paper, 1972, prepared for City of Winnipeg.

20. For an analysis of the sources of support for and opposition to the Nashville Metro proposal, see Brett W. Hawkins, *Nashville Metro: The Politics of City-County Consolidation* (Nashville: Vanderbilt University Press, 1966). See also David A. Booth, *Metropolitics: The Nashville Consolidation* (East Lansing: Institute for Community Development and Services, Michigan State University, 1963); Daniel R. Grant, "A Comparison of Predictions and Experience with Nashville 'Metro', " *Urban Affairs Quarterly* 1 (September 1965): 34–54; and "Metropolitics and Professional Political Leadership: The Case of Nashville," *Annals of the American Academy of Political and Social Science* 353 (May 1964): 72–83.

21. George L. Willis in *County News,* June 16, 1972, p. 14.

22. Gary T. Johnson, "Tax Base Sharing and Fiscal Disparities: A Retrospective," *Municipal Management* (Fall 1984): 67–70.

23. John Kincaid, "Metropolitan Governance: Reviving International and Market Analogies," *Intergovernmental Perspective,* 15 (Spring 1989), p. 27.

FINANCE

CHAPTER 18

Meeting State Needs with Limited Resources

Voters have often found it unwise to learn about government finance from the "economy candidate" who runs for governor for the first time. The glib promises of greatly increased governmental services without corresponding increases in state taxes simply brand the candidate as one of two things—a deceiver or an ignoramus. Many a victorious gubernatorial candidate in recent history has faced the prospect of new taxes or an unbalanced budget immediately upon taking office. The reelection campaign speeches by an incumbent about financing state government are amazingly different after spending a term learning about state finance in the rigorous school of hard knocks.

As indicated in chapter 13, state and local financial relationships have become so integrated in recent decades that they can only be considered in tandem. States not only prescribe local debt limitations, accounting procedures, and auditing standards, but they also share revenue, provide grants-in-aid, assume local programs, and assist in local revenue collection. Much of the intergovernmental assistance moving from states to political subdivisions is aimed at assisting local governments in carrying out state-mandated functions, such as education, law enforcement, and health. Thus, financially and functionally, states and their local governments are engaged in joint efforts of raising the revenue to deliver services to citizens. Because of this close relationship, this chapter will include references to both levels of government.

State-local finances interrelated

Expenditures—Meeting the Needs

When all spending by all governments—federal, state, and local—is considered, close to half of it is spent by state and local governments. When national defense spending is removed from the total, the federal government actually spends less than the total for state and local governments.

Although there can be no doubt about the great increase in state and local expenditures, it is incorrect to assume this high rate of increase is proof of waste and extravagance. The increase in population and the decrease in the purchasing power of the dollar must be credited, at least partially, for causing increased expenditures. In-

Reasons for expenditure increases

Title photo: Almost all states now use the "executive" budget process in which the governor and his budget advisors establish program and fiscal priorities for presentation to the legislature.

Figure 18.1
General expenditure of
state governments, by
function: 1990.
*(Bureau of the Census,
State Government
Finances, 1990.)*

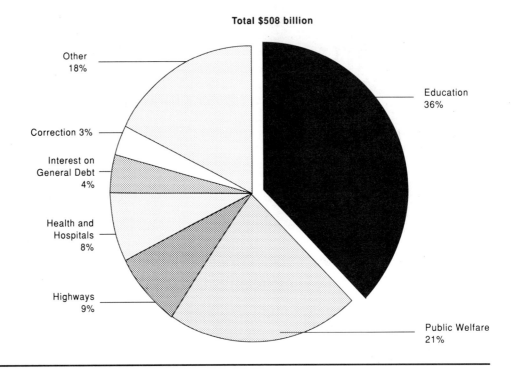

Total $508 billion

Other 18%

Correction 3%

Interest on General Debt 4%

Health and Hospitals 8%

Highways 9%

Education 36%

Public Welfare 21%

flation makes it especially hazardous to compare annual statistics on public expenditures. When *constant dollars* are used rather than *current dollars,* the percentage increase in expenditures during the past decade is reduced sharply. Much of the increase, however, must be attributed to expansion of state and local functions through steadily broadening old services and provision of new services.

Major spending categories

For what is the money spent? At the state level, the functions of education, highways, health care, and public welfare account for close to three-fourths of annual expenditures. Until recent years, the predominance of the cost of education over all other functions of government was primarily observed at the local government level. State and local governments spend more for education than for highways, public welfare, and health and hospitals combined. Functions next in financial importance to all of the aforementioned are police protection, sanitation and sewerage, natural resources, housing and urban renewal, fire protection, and parks and recreation, each accounting for one to three percent of state and local expenditures (Figure 18.1).

Education payrolls a major cost

What part of state and local expenditures goes for salaries and wages of government employees? Payrolls for public school teachers and other employees in the field of education account for more than 50 percent of all state and local expenditures for personal service. The gubernatorial candidate who promises to improve the financial status of school teachers is biting off a very sizable hunk of the total budget for state and local government. By the same token, the candidate who criticizes the "wasteful expenditure of vast sums of the taxpayers' hard-earned money" is very likely to be revealing ignorance concerning the objects of state and local expenditures.

Considering policy differences

One of the significant areas political science research has focused on is comparative state politics, emphasizing the differences in state policy outputs and the search for factors that can explain these differences. This kind of research is a response to criticism of preoccupation with the inputs of the political system—public opinion, voting, pressure groups, party politics, etc., and neglect of explaining specific results of the political process. Among other measures of policy outputs used in this research is the level of state expenditures for various functions. The early results by Dye, Hofferbert, and others seemed to show that the socioeconomic characteristics of states—personal wealth, urbanization, industrialization, and education—were far more influential than political traits, such as voter turnout, interparty competition, and the quality of legislative apportionment.[1] This appeared to be upsetting to political scientists, especially to those who have long argued that political variables—features of the political system— have a great deal to do with the nature of state policies. As a result, a controversy has ensued over the relative importance of political versus socioeconomic variables. Sharkansky, employing a larger concept of state politics, has discovered that certain political variables are more significant than some socioeconomic variables in their correlation to policy measures. In particular, the character of previous state expenditure decisions and the proportion of spending responsibilities assigned to state (as opposed to local) governments are found to be highly influential determinants of current state expenditures.[2] The state political culture, as discussed in chapter 3, would also influence spending priorities.

Financial Planning—The Budget Process

A budget is simply a financial plan, and the budgetary process is simply the process of preparing that financial plan. It is the process through which priorities are established and the available resources are apportioned among competing demands and needs. If there is any single document that reflects the intentions of a government, it is the budget. It is the major device through which leaders in government plan and ultimately decide which facilities and services should be provided and when.

Budget sets priorities

    With the exception of only two or three states, the initial budget is now proposed under the supervision of the governor. Performing this critical task for the governor is an office of the budget or a division of budget in a larger department of administration. A typical budget cycle begins some months before the forthcoming legislative session when the governor meets with the budget staff to discuss general policies to be incorporated in the proposed budget. On the basis of this conference, the budget staff prepares a memo, outlining the ground rules to be used by the various departments of government in preparing their proposed budgets to the executive budget office. Departments then prepare their requests, which almost always exceed available resources and perhaps even their own expectations. The requests are sent to the office of budget and a schedule of preliminary budget hearings is made by the budget office to hear agency explanations of the requests. After the hearings, the budget office compiles the requests into a preliminary budget. Through this process, which requires several months, the budget office is communicating with the governor's office to forewarn the office of detectable trends. Once the tentative budget is put together, departments may be advised of the decisions of the budget office so opportunity is provided to communicate

The executive budget cycle

Figure 18.2

Year-end balances as a percentage of expenditures. *(Source: Marcia Howard, "Fiscal Survey of the States," National Governors Association-National Assn. of State Budget Officers (April, 1991).)*

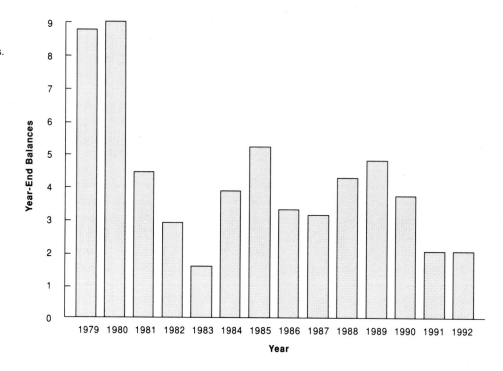

objections, if any, directly to the governor before the document wins the governor's final stamp of approval. After the departmental appeals are heard, the spending portion of the budget is finalized.

Problems in estimating income

Estimating state income for the budget period represents the other half of the budgeting process. For the 32 states that have instituted annual budgets, this is simpler than for the 18 states that must predict two years into the future for biennial budgets.[3]

1. National economy

While some state revenue structures are more responsive to economic change than others, the performance of the national economy is still the major determinant for state revenue. The economic roller coaster in the 1980s and 1990s caught many states short, and tax increases poured out of the legislative process to shore up sagging income. The ending balances in state treasuries headed downward (Figure 18.2).

"It's like flying in a dense fog without radar," Charles Connor, legislative budget analyst in New Hampshire, commented about budgeting in times of economic uncertainty.[4]

In states relying heavily on oil taxes, the international economy reaches deep into budget pockets when prices drop and tax revenues disappear. This happened in the 1980s and early 1990s, leaving Alaska, Louisiana, New Mexico, North Dakota, Oklahoma and Texas scrambling for new millions to balance budgets. In Alaska, 90 percent of the state general fund came from oil revenue; in Louisiana mineral resources accounted for 42 percent; and in Texas, 26 percent.[5]

2. Earmarking limits options

Earmarking of tax revenues for specific functions also impairs the ability of budget balancers. Because this income can only be spent on the designated function, such as gas tax revenue for highways, it really represents a budget within a budget, calling for a balancing of income and spending in the functional area involved. When significant portions of state revenue are dedicated, estimates for the remaining general fund become even more difficult, requiring a higher degree of precision. The practice of earmarking has a very natural origin in the desire of a pressure group to secure with certainty more money for a particular function, for example, to designate that all revenue from the gasoline tax be spent for highway purposes. It is also the only way, on occasions, to make a tax increase acceptable to the public. Although states earmark taxes for everything from Confederate pensions (Louisiana and Texas) to sick fishermen (Alaska), the bulk of earmarked revenue goes to education, highways, and welfare. Lawmakers have begun to recognize the handicaps of earmarking and have slowly removed earmarking restrictions. While 51 percent of state tax collections were earmarked as of 1954, this figure had fallen to 23 percent in 1988, where it seems to have stabilized. At the high end, Alabama, Montana, Tennessee and Utah earmark over 50 percent of their revenues, while at the low end Rhode Island earmarks only five percent.[6]

In recent years, state budget makers have been forced to comply with orders from federal courts that have had tremendous impact on expenditures. A series of decisions applying the "cruel and unusual" punishment provision of the Eighth Amendment to conditions in prisons and jails resulted in billions of dollars in new costs for expanded corrections facilities. A former warden estimated that compliance would cost $5 million for some counties and up to $1 billion for some states.[7] Another series of federal court decisions mandated deinstitutionalization of the mentally retarded, resulting in billions more for group homes and staff services. In 1985, the U.S. Supreme Court reversed an earlier decision and ruled that state and local governments had to comply with the overtime provisions in the Fair Labor Standards Act. This decision resulted in scores of lawsuits brought by employees against state and local governments to obtain backpay for past employment practices.[8] In 1990, the U.S. Supreme Court decided in *Missouri v. Jenkins* that a federal judge could directly impose a tax to implement a program for dealing with racial discrimination in schools.[9]

3. Mandates and court orders

Congress has joined the federal courts in adding to the fiscal burdens of state and local governments. With a huge federal income tax cut in 1981, coupled with budget-cutting schemes, the federal government has shifted the fiscal burden of many new programs to state and local governments. "The money ran out, but the activism didn't," observed Professor David R. Beam of Illinois Institute of Technology.[10] As an example, in 1990, observers counted 20 additional requirements from Washington that topped over $15 billion over five years.[11]

Another budgetary uncertainty is the level of federal grants to states. Almost all states now require that federal funds be appropriated by the legislature in order to be spent by the executive agencies. While some federal cutbacks simply mean a proportionate reduction of programs, cutbacks in programs of high state priority will require replacement with state funds. Obviously, the variables to be considered by revenue estimators require the latest in economic indicators as well as a fairly reliable Ouija board and a crystal ball. With Congress in continuous session and most state legislatures on restricted schedules, unexpected changes in grant programs can occur at any time and create immediate dilemmas for state budget makers—especially those on biennial cycles.

4. Federal grants vary

5. Deficit spending limited

Unlike the federal government, state constitutions do not permit extensive deficit spending. Consequently, almost all governors are required to propose a budget in which the expenditures and the income balance. To cope with the changing income, states have resorted to several techniques to avoid deficits. Two-thirds of the states have *rainy day funds* as reserves to be used in a fiscal crisis. Unfortunately, tight state budgets have prevented the diversion of sufficient moneys into these funds to meet the kinds of shortfalls states have been experiencing.[12] Several states have enacted temporary contingency taxes that would be triggered into action in the event revenue fell below a certain level before the budget period was over.[13] A number of states linked spending plans to income by authorizing certain expenditures only if sufficient revenues were available. Some states have resorted to one-time revenue windfalls, such as speeding up the collection of taxes, deferring capital expenditures, and changing accounting systems.[14]

Budget goes to legislature

After the proposed expenditures and estimates of income are approved by the governor, the budget moves from the executive to the legislative branch of government where it must be processed in the same manner as other laws are enacted. The budget is introduced as bills for appropriations, usually prepared under the supervision of the executive budget office. In about half of the states, the budget is introduced as a single bill; in the remaining half, it appears as multiple bills, running as high as 450 in Arkansas. Once introduced, the bills are referred to appropriate legislative committees where the agencies of government appear to defend their requests and often ask for a restoration of funds cut by the governor's budget office.

More spending proposals appear

Many bills affecting the budget enter the legislative process without going through the budget office. Legislative members and committees often introduce proposals for spending that tend to unbalance the executive budget and force a reduction in the governor's proposals, an increase in taxes, or a rejection of the proposals. Almost all legislatures require the preparation of cost estimates in the form of fiscal notes for measures that incur state expense. In addition to the new spending proposals are other bills that impact the budget picture. For example, legislative members or committees often propose alterations in the tax system that would result in losses of state income. If these are passed, replacement revenues must be adopted or expenditures reduced. To keep abreast of all these fiscal variables in the decentralized legislative committee

Computers monitor fiscal impacts

system, over half the states use computers to keep up with legislative activity. As the adjournment date approaches, the computer printouts invariably inform legislators that expenditures exceed expected income and politically hazardous adjustments must be made before they can go home. Usually, some of the last bills to be passed by a legislative session pertain to appropriations and revenue.

Legislatures make minor changes

After the legislature has completed its work, the bills making up the expenditures and revenue of the state budget appear at the governor's office as passed by the legislature. Though some changes have been made to reflect the preferences of the legislature, these are usually not significant unless the process involved a governor of one party and a legislature of the opposite party. Even in those cases, governors' budgets maintain a remarkable degree of integrity because of the wide consensus that exists for present spending patterns and the incremental nature of handling budgets. The governor approves or disapproves the measures affecting the budget along with the other legislation crossing the executive desk. Almost all states continue to use the July 1–June 30 fiscal year (or biennium) even though the federal government starts its fiscal year on October 1.

Since the governor is accountable for the preparation of the initial budget, there is little question that he or she must bear a major share of the responsibility for state finances. However, the budget as proposed must be enacted into law by the legislative branch of the government. Since both branches are involved, it is technically incorrect to claim that "the governor raised the taxes" or "the governor spent too much money," thereby implying that budgets are adopted in some way other than the legislative process.

Who is to blame for spending?

As budgets continued to grow year after year, state policymakers searched for new budgeting techniques that would apply more stringent standards to expenditures and, hopefully, retard spending. The new techniques have had varying degrees of success from state to state. On the whole, however, states found that the size of budgets was determined more by culture and politics than by the number of printouts a computer could produce.

Though numerous constitutions and statutes had provisions that restricted the taxing and spending powers of states for decades, the adoption of Proposition 13 in California early in 1978 caught national attention because it seemed to signal a shift in the fiscal winds. Hailed as a "taxpayers' revolt," the proposition cut back local property taxes and required a two-thirds vote of the legislature to enact new taxes. Despite its early success, the revolt did not grow into an immediate national conflagration and, by 1987, it was pronounced dead by *U.S. News and World Report* when major tax-cutting initiatives were turned down in four states.[15] Of the 11 revenue-limiting measures on state ballots in 1990, only one in Oregon was approved by the voters.[16] Of all the states, Oregon made the strongest stand against the revolt when voters refused to approve property tax cutbacks in the elections of 1978, 1980, 1982, and 1984. A property tax limitation was finally passed in 1990. Undaunted by the single Oregon victory in 1990, advocates of limitations continued their drive with a flurry of proposals in around 10 states in 1992. So, the anti-tax movement remains very much alive in the 1990s. During the post-Proposition 13 era, around 20 states adopted some kind of tax and spending limits, but legislatures were free to alter the limitations in eight of the states by a simple majority. Nevertheless, in most of the remaining states the requirement for a two-thirds vote of the legislature or voter approval to adopt new tax measures or alter expenditure limitations could spell budgetary problems.[17]

Revolts against spending

While the tax revolt resulted in the adoption of restrictions in less than one half of the states, its impact on the taxing and spending policies of state and local governments was nationwide. Following the defeat of a number of revenue-cutting proposals in 1984, John Shannon, assistant director of the Advisory Commission on Intergovernmental Relations, observed that the losses occurred because the tax revolt had achieved its goal of "slowing state and local spending."[18] When Proposition 13 was finally upheld by the U.S. Supreme Court in 1992, it received only faint praise by Justice Blackmun, whose majority opinion stated "no matter how unfair or unwise" it might be, it was "not palpably arbitrary."

Revolts slow spending

Raising the Revenue with Nontax Sources

Taxes are a last resort

All state and local revenue does not come from taxes. The anti-tax political environment enveloping governments has spurred rare ingenuity from time to time in designing methods for obtaining revenue without increasing taxes. In some jurisdictions, use of taxes has become somewhat of a last resort when all else fails.

1. Licensing

Licensing represents one area in which state and local governments use police powers to raise revenue. Under the police power, states are permitted to enact laws and regulations to protect the health, welfare, morals, and public safety of society. To protect society properly, many activities are regulated through the issuance of licenses for which there is a charge, often intended to raise revenue as well as cover the cost of administering the licensing program. For example, states may charge $10 for issuing a driver's license and deposit it in the general fund for routine appropriations. In many states, the automobile registration fee is intended to raise money for maintaining streets and highways. Probably all states dedicate the receipts from hunting and fishing licenses to finance game and wildlife programs, and thus relieve the general fund of that burden. On the local level, the licensing of private establishments handling alcoholic beverages is a source of revenue for many cities, towns, counties, and townships.

2. User charges

User charges, or service fees, are a significant source of funds, more so for local governments than the states. User charges may be distinguished from license fees in that licensing is the raising of money through the use of the police power, whereas user charges are determined by the particular service rendered and usually intended to merely finance the particular service rather than raise revenue to relieve general appropriations. For example, many local governments engage in garbage collection and charge a monthly fee for such collection. Other activities involving user charges include toll roads and bridges, school tuition, water distribution, parking meters, inspection fees, bus and subway fares, sheriff's fees for serving court papers, green fees, issuance of birth certificates, campsite fees, and numerous other charges made by public agencies for the provision of specific services.

Local services rely on user fees

With restricted taxing authority and options, many local governments have turned to user fees to pay for numerous local services. As a matter of fact, user fees are the fastest growing sources for local governments. User fees have several advantages—probably the most important one is that it is a revenue tool local governments can use. It also discourages waste, such as would be the case if some services were free. Supporters claim that it is only fair that those who benefit from a service pay for it when that service benefits only the recipient and does not achieve a socially desirable objective.

Disadvantages of user fees

User fees also have several disadvantages. If widely used by a government, they can contribute to a regressive revenue system that bears heavily on low-income groups. They may prohibit the use of public facilities that ought to be available to everyone, regardless of income levels. User fees are not deductible from federal income taxes whereas general taxes are, thereby forcing citizens in high user fee jurisdictions to pay a higher federal tax than citizens in lower user fee areas. Finally, user fees, being easy for policy-makers to impose without fear of political reprisal, disguise actual tax burdens by confusing the revenue picture seen by voters.

Proprietary activities, comparable to private business, produce revenue for a good many states and local governments. Some of the activities falling under the user fee category could also be included as proprietary ventures, such as local government-owned, government-operated agencies providing electricity, water, garbage collection, toll bridges and highways, and many others. However, activities more like private business operations include the wholesaling and retailing of alcoholic beverages through state and local stores, an activity now involving governments in more than one-third of the states. States that have been endowed with public ownership of valuable natural resources have been able to sell and lease mineral rights and timber. North and South Dakota have ventured boldly into the private sector, with South Dakota operating a cement plant and North Dakota milling flour and managing a state-owned bank.

3. Proprietary activities

While fascinating, the socialistic ventures of the northern plains have not stirred the imagination of state revenue raisers quite as much as the most recent proprietary state activity—operating lotteries. Beginning with New Hampshire in 1964, 34 states had adopted this fund-raising technique by 1992. Though the rage for lotteries may be new to most people, historians are fully familiar with the widespread use of lotteries in colonial times.

Lotteries become a rage

In 1612, the Virginia Company of England was permitted to stage a lottery to raise funds for developing the Virginia colony in America. At one time or another, all 13 colonies operated lotteries, many of which were used for roads, canals, bridges, and other improvements. Education was also a major beneficiary of lottery receipts. The founding of Columbia University (as King's College) was made possible by a lottery; Yale, Harvard, Dartmouth, Brown, William and Mary, and Union all shared in lottery receipts during colonial times. This early contagion of gambling fever even struck George Washington and Benjamin Franklin, both of whom were lottery sponsors. Lotteries eventually fell into disrepute, however, first among the Quakers of Pennsylvania and then among other members of the clergy. Pennsylvania and Massachusetts outlawed them in 1833 and were soon followed by many other states by 1840. The scandals of the Louisiana State Lottery in 1891 buttressed the arguments of opponents that lotteries led only to graft and corruption.[19]

Lotteries in colonial era

Whether or not the state's climate or terrain inculcates a yen for gambling has not yet been researched, but New Hampshire, active in colonial lotteries, was also the leader in initiating the revival of state-sponsored gambling. To overcome public resistance, a number of the state lotteries have dedicated receipts to education. Schools in New Hampshire have obtained over $50 million in lottery receipts since 1964. Several states deposit the receipts into the state general fund; Arizona and Massachusetts share with local governments; Pennsylvania earmarks for the elderly; and Colorado and Vermont use some funds for capital expenditures.[20]

New Hampshire sets trend

After deducting the payout for winners and management expenses, states realize around 40 percent of the gross receipts as profits. Even though state annual gross receipts may run into the millions and top $18 billion nationwide, lottery receipts still represent only 2.6 percent of the average state's tax income.[21]

Federal grants are another nontax source of revenue for state and local governments and they represent a significant contribution to state budgets. The proportion of state and local revenue coming from federal aid increased sharply during the 1960s

4. Federal grants

and 1970s, but began to decline in the 1980s as huge federal deficits reduced available federal funds. During the decade of the 1980s, federal contribution to state and local spending declined from 24.4 percent to 16.8 percent.[22]

Try block grants
In spite of the popularity of federal aid among state and local officials, the proliferation of categorical grants and federal restrictions spurred the Reagan administration to propose alterations in distribution of the federal treasury. Motivated by the dual goals of reducing state dependence on federal funds and giving states more latitude in using federal funds, the administration cut back a number of grant programs and sought to group categorical grants into larger block grants, whereby states could establish their own priorities for spending. President Bush continued the effort to consolidate grants into more general categories. Only limited success was achieved in the block grant effort since interest groups benefitting from the categorical grants resisted changes.

5. Borrowing
A fifth nonrevenue source is borrowing through bonded indebtedness. Borrowing is often necessary because large governmental capital expenditures cannot be paid off in a single budget year. During the first few decades of the nation's history, state constitutions imposed no limits upon the debt which the legislature might incur. Legislative abuses of this financial liberty brought some states to the brink of disaster and led the people to adopt constitutional clauses restricting the borrowing power. The numerous defaults of the 1840s, for example, constituted sufficient evidence to the people of legislative ineptitude. Within a 15-year period, 19 states incorporated restrictive borrowing clauses in their constitutions. Several of the provisions were cited in chapter 5.

Avoiding borrowing limitations
In spite of the state constitutional limitations on borrowing and on total debt, state and local indebtedness has been increasing steadily. Increases have been made possible through a number of techniques. The creation of new units of government in the form of special districts and/or authorities provided new bonding authority to fund many specific services. Some forms of bonding, such as revenue bonds, are not included in the limitations, thereby constituting an open end. In some states, voters approved amendments to constitutions, granting exceptions to the general bonding limitations. As an example, the voters in the tax revolt state of California have been voting to bypass their own limitations with new bond issues to finance veterans' loans, school facilities, water treatment, waste sites, water distribution systems, senior citizen centers, and other programs. Because many local government services are proportionately more capital intensive than state services, local debt is almost double that of states.

Public borrowing is usually accomplished through the issuance of bonds which may be for terms of ten to 40 years. Longer terms are discouraged because the interest to be paid over such periods becomes excessively burdensome, and because it is unwise to have bonded indebtedness beyond the life of the improvement.

Types of bonds
The two major classifications continue to be general obligation and revenue bonds. Under general obligation (GO) bonds, the government pledges its total revenue capacity to repayment, thus constituting a constitutional lien on the property of taxpayers. Revenue bonds are retired only from the revenues of a particular governmental enterprise, such as city water department charges, the toll road fees, or dormitory room rents. Because general obligation bonds are more secure to the lender, they attract a

lower interest rate, resulting in less cost to the taxpayers. However, bonding limitations have prevented widespread use of general obligation bonds and have forced greater reliance on revenue bonds. As recently as 1972, general obligation bonds were being used slightly more than revenue bonds, but by the mid-1980s revenue bonds had taken a strong lead.

Among the recent trends in state and local debt is the creation of state *bond banks* to assist local governments in managing debt. With a state bond bank, local governments plan to pool their bond issues through the bond bank, which then offers a large combined issue. With the state involved, marketing costs are reduced, interest rates are lower, and more bidders are attracted.[23]

Lease-purchase and lease-back arrangements have also become more common as a method for obtaining new buildings without incurring direct debt. Under this practice, a state building authority is created, or perhaps a private entrepreneur is contacted, to construct a building and receive annual rentals though the appropriations process. The annual lease payments include sufficient funds to pay the debt involved in construction with the understanding that the building becomes government property at the end of the lease period.

Leasing to avoid debt

Another trend in state and local debt that has caused concern at the federal level is the use of state and local bonding to raise funds for private enterprises. Federal budget-makers are concerned because the interest earned on state and local bonds is exempt from the federal income tax. Consequently, the more bonds that are issued by state and local governments, the less revenue appears at the U.S. Treasury. The tax exemption makes the bonds attractive to buyers as a way to avoid income taxes. They are willing to lend their money at a lower interest rate because they can gain it back in lower federal income taxes. The U.S. Treasury Department estimates an annual revenue loss of over $30 billion in tax-exempt interest.[24] The bonds have been used for building housing developments, constructing business buildings, paying for private pollution control, and numerous activities heretofore considered private in nature.[25] By offering tax-exempt industrial development bonds, state and local governments can attract industries and offer inducements to stimulate economic activity, all at the expense of the federal treasury. When Congress passed the 1986 Tax Reform Act, it added restrictions to state and local use of tax-exempt bonds. Two years later, the U.S. Supreme Court said there was no constitutional reason Congress couldn't tax interest earned from the bonds.[26]

Curb abuse of bonds

Tax Only If All Else Fails

The financial interrelationships of the state and local tax systems must function within the context of federal fiscal policies. Inevitably, state and local governments must adapt and adjust to the federal tax structure. This adaptation can be seen in the tax patterns that exist at the three levels of government. State and local governments use a variety of taxes—property, general sales and gross receipts, motor fuels, income, motor vehicles, alcoholic beverages, tobacco, corporation franchises, estate, and inheritance. When the three levels of government are considered separately, state government leans heavily upon three big tax sources—general sales, income, and motor fuel taxes—which account for more than three-fourths of state tax collections. The federal government

Tax patterns vary

relies on one big revenue producer: nearly 90 percent of federal tax collections come from the income tax (individual and corporation). Local governments also rely heavily on one tax—close to 75 percent of local tax collections are derived from the property tax.

Problems in federalizing income taxes

States that use the income tax have found that constant vigilance is required to protect their tax base. For the convenience of taxpayers and auditors, many states have federalized their income tax, meaning that they have substantially adopted the federal tax rules as their tax rules. In fact, several states have gone so far as to accept the whole federal tax base by applying their own tax rates to federal taxable income as defined by federal rules. The system is convenient and neat until the federal government changes the rules. Federal tax legislation in 1982 provides a case in point. By permitting federal taxpayers a rapid depreciation of investments, states using the federal tax base stood to lose millions of dollars in revenue. In 1986, it was an opposite scenario. In the Tax Reform Act, Congress eliminated loopholes and increased adjusted gross income, resulting in new gains for those states with income taxes piggybacked on the federal system.[27] This inconvenience of merging tax bases suggests that those who wish to piggyback must sometimes be content to go where the pig goes.

State-federal cooperation in taxing

Generally speaking, relationships between the state and federal governments in the area of tax administration have been cordial. Federal-state cooperation in administering income taxes began in 1931 when state officials were permitted to review federal tax returns to check compliance of their own taxpayers. Almost all income tax states have followed Minnesota's lead of 1957 in signing an agreement of coordination with the Internal Revenue Service. Today, state and federal governments exchange computer tapes to crosscheck filers and inform each other of completed audits and fraudulent returns. Exchange of information is not confined to income taxes, but most activity is in that area because it is a significant revenue source for both governments. States have been the principal beneficiaries of the exchanges.[28] Legislation in the early 1970s offered the services of the U.S. Treasury in collecting state income taxes for states but this proposal has not been implemented.

1. Federal limitations in state taxation

Before considering some of the more significant taxes at the state and local levels, it is important to note some of the restrictions, both federal and state, that limit the taxing power of state legislatures. The federal Constitution prohibits states, without the consent of Congress, from levying tonnage duties or placing duties on imports or exports. By implication, it prohibits a state from using its taxing power to evade constitutional restrictions. Thus, a state may not use its taxing power to impair the obligation of a contract or to violate the equal protection of law and due process clauses of the Fourteenth Amendment.

2. State constitutions limit taxes

Many state constitutions restrict the taxing power far more than does the federal Constitution. Some place a maximum limit on the rate of taxation, especially property taxation. Many have tax uniformity clauses which, if strictly interpreted, mean more than merely fair play and equity in taxation throughout the state, requiring that all property be taxed at a uniform rate. Some constitutions may prohibit certain taxes, such as the income or sales tax, or they may limit the rate of tax. A number of these restrictive constitutional provisions grew out of the tax revolts of the 1970s and 1980s.

3. Tax capacity

The tax capacity of the state is also a limiting factor when it comes to raising revenue. Computations designed to measure tax capacity have been made on a con-

Table 18.1 States Ranked by Tax Effort

High Tax Effort States				Low Tax Effort States		
State	**Effort**	**Above National Average**		**State**	**Effort**	**Below National Average**
New York	152	+52		New Hampshire	66	−34
Alaska	127	+27		Nevada	69	−31
Wisconsin	119	+19		Florida	82	−18
Iowa	113	+13		Tennessee	83	−17
Hawaii	112	+12		Alabama	84	−16
Michigan	112	+12		Arkansas	84	−16
Minnesota	112	+12		Delaware	84	−16
Maryland	108	+ 8		Missouri	86	−14
Utah	106	+ 6		Kentucky	88	−12
Maine	105	+ 5		Texas	88	−12
Kansas	104	+ 4		West Virginia	88	−12
Rhode Island	104	+ 4		Colorado	89	−11
Illinois	102	+ 2		Georgia	89	−11
Montana	102	+ 2		Oklahoma	89	−11
Washington	102	+ 2		Louisiana	90	−10
New Jersey	101	+ 1		Connecticut	90	−10
Vermont	100			Virginia	91	− 9
				North Dakota	91	− 9
				Idaho	93	− 7
				North Carolina	93	− 7
				Indiana	93	− 7
				California	94	− 6
				Massachusetts	94	− 6
				Mississippi	94	− 6
				Wyoming	94	− 6
				South Dakota	95	− 5
				Arizona	96	− 4
				South Carolina	96	− 4
				Ohio	97	− 3
				Pennsylvania	97	− 3
				Nebraska	98	− 2
				New Mexico	99	− 1
				Oregon	99	− 1

Tax effort is the ratio of a state's actual tax collections to its tax capacity. The relative index of tax effort is created by dividing each state's tax effort by the average for all states. The index for the U.S. average is 100. Source: ACIR, 1988 State Fiscal Capacity and Effort, M–170, August 1990.

tinuing basis by the Advisory Commission on Intergovernmental Relations and reveal both the ability of states to raise taxes and the effort they are applying to their tax program (Table 18.1).[29]

The gaps between tax capacity and tax effort clearly demonstrate that a state's political, cultural, and historical traditions have significant impact on the will to tax and spend in the public sector. In some states, apparently, legislatures not able to handle the conflict involved in revenue-raising surrender to interest groups that resist taxation.

4. Culture and politics

In other states, where people support public services, legislatures move forward in reflecting the tax policies supported by the political culture of the state. Studies of lobbying organizations rank business groups high on influence at the state legislature, meaning that legislatures must overcome a definite anti-spending bias in order to pass tax legislation. The influence of the business lobby partially explains why income taxes are significant revenue producers in only one-fourth of the states, while sales and excise taxes are the mainstay of state revenue in most states. In any event, the politics of taxing and spending are much more important in the design of the state's ultimate tax pattern than are the capacity to pay, state constitutions, or federal restrictions.

5. Interstate competition

Competition among states is also a factor that is taken into account by legislative finance and taxation committees. An expanding economic base is seen by most states as a partial solution to the state's problems, whatever they might be. As a result, states are constantly seeking to outmaneuver each other in offering new inducements to attract businesses and industries. Maintaining a tax structure favorable to economic activity, then, becomes an important objective, if not a fervent holy crusade, for many state policy-makers. An argument against raising the sales tax may be that the neighboring states are already one percent lower; an argument against income taxes may be that this will discourage corporate executives from locating in the state; an argument against the cigarette tax is that bootleggers will take over the business; and an argument against gas hikes alleges that motorists will fill their vehicles on the other side of the state line.

Qualities of sound taxation

Regardless of the level of government, there are certain qualities or principles of sound taxation that have been recommended by tax specialists through the years for consideration in evaluating revenue proposals.

Taxpayers forewarned

Certainty. One desirable quality of a tax is that the burden is determined by a fixed formula that forewarns the taxpayer of the amount that will be expected when the tax is due. This quality was touted as a result of the capricious tax collecting systems in medieval and Biblical days when collectors extorted as much as they thought they could get from the victim. Almost all taxes now have a quality of certainty except property taxes, which involve enough variables to leave some doubt. Even for property taxes, changes are usually small and incremental.

Should be easy to pay

Convenient. Payment of the tax should be convenient and not create hardship on the taxpayer. Sales taxes are convenient to pay because a little is paid at each transaction; income tax withholding has made that tax convenient; various excise taxes are convenient because they are paid upon purchase. Property taxes fail to meet this test in cases where the taxing governments expect an annual or semi-annual payment. Many urban dwellers are not as aware of this inconvenience as farmers because the property tax payments of urban dwellers are included in their monthly rent or mortgage payments, whereas farmers pay in lump sums.

Low cost administration

Economical to administer. This quality says that administrative costs should not devour too much of the revenue. However, there is no standard by which administrators determine whether the tax has become too expensive to collect. Sales and income tax administrative costs may be as little as one percent whereas property tax administration may cost three percent. Under these circumstances, is the property tax economical to collect? There is hardly a tax left that is not economical to collect unless it exists in a small taxing jurisdiction where an economy of scale is impossible to achieve.

Equitable. The burden of the tax should impact taxpayers in similar circumstances in a similar fashion. A tax with numerous exemptions and special benefits, such as the income tax, may result in so many loopholes that two people or two corporations earning the same amount of money will pay vastly differing tax bills. The property tax is often attacked on the principle of equity since varying practices in assessing will result in owners of property of comparable value paying differing amounts of taxes in the same taxing jurisdiction.

Treating taxpayers equally

Ability-to-pay. Adam Smith, writing in the *Wealth of Nations* around the time of the American Revolution, proposed the principle that citizens ought to share in the public burden in proportion to their ability to pay. A tax that conforms to this principle is called a *progressive tax* in that the burden will fall most heavily on those most able to pay, such as in the case of income taxes using a graduated tax rate. A tax that fails to achieve this principle is called a *regressive tax,* the burden of which falls most heavily on those least able to pay. The sales tax is often used as an example of regressive taxation. Property taxes are often regressive as well, particularly when the owner of the property, say a farmer, gets no crop, loses money, and still pays property taxes.

Progressive vs. regressive taxation

In 1991, an organization called Citizens for Tax Justice released a report criticizing the state and local tax structure as being regressive, with people in the lowest income categories paying the highest percentage of income in taxes (Table 18.2).

In defense of state and local governments, *State Legislatures* magazine pointed out that the federal government dominated the use of the progressive income tax, interstate competition restrained state taxation, and discussions of tax fairness must take into account the manner in which revenue is spent.[30]

Benefits-received. Contrary to the principles of *ability-to-pay, benefits-received* advocates argue that those who receive the benefits of government ought to pay for them. The best example of this principle can be seen in many states where gasoline taxes, paid by vehicle operators, are earmarked for highways, which are used by the vehicle operators. At one time, the property tax was assumed to be based on the *benefits-received* principle. However, the degrees of property ownership have become so disparate in the past century that there is only a limited relationship between ownership of property and such public programs as education, health, and welfare.

Taxing users of services

Simplicity. Taxpayers should understand the tax system sufficiently so they can judge its conformance to the tax principles in which they believe. At present, the sales tax and excise taxes would reflect the quality of simplicity but both the state income tax and local property tax fall tragically short. When taxes become so complicated that voters are no longer sure of their equitableness, then taxpayer resistance and revolts can be expected as a response.

Easy to understand

Table 18.2 Regressivity in State and Local Taxes

| | State and Local Taxes in 1991 as Shares of Income for Families of 4 | |
	Income	Tax as a percentage of income
Lowest 20%	$ 12,700	13.8
Second 20%	26,800	10.9
Middle 20%	39,100	10.0
Fourth 20%	54,000	9.5
Next 15%	82,200	9.2
Next 4%	184,400	8.7
Top 1%	875,200	7.6

From A Far Cry From Fair, *Citizens for Tax Justice, April 1991.*

Politics and tax principles

The emphasis given to these principles in adoption of tax policies is the product of politics. Usually, individuals and organizations appearing before legislative committees argue for a principle that will shift the burden of taxation to other segments of society. The upper-income groups will resist the taxes based on the *ability-to-pay* and argue strenuously for *benefits-received* taxation. Representatives of lower income groups will argue just the opposite, knowing full well that the opposite will benefit them. Whether a state has a tax structure based on *ability-to-pay* or *benefits-received* will be determined by the political power of the various economic groups in the budget making and adopting processes. Principles may sound like unchanging measurements of sound taxation but their application will still be determined by the political process.

Taxes defined

Taxes are compulsory contributions exacted by the government for public purposes. While the federal and local governments depend heavily on single taxes for raising revenue, states have a more diversified revenue picture.

Property taxes

As recently as the period immediately preceding World War I, the general property tax was the principal source of revenue for state and local governments. It accounted for more than one-half of all state revenue and virtually all local revenue. The general property tax has dropped almost completely out of the picture as a source of revenue for state governments, producing less than two percent of total state tax collections in the 1990s. Many states have abandoned it altogether. On the other hand, the property tax remains the major tax source for local governments, accounting for around 75 percent of local tax revenues in the 1990s. Dependence on property tax varies considerably from state to state, ranging from less than 40 percent of local tax revenue in Alabama all the way to 99.2 percent of local taxes in New Hampshire. Regionally, property taxes are of most importance in local finance in the New England states, and they are least used in the southern states.[31]

Classes of property taxed

Four classes of property are subject to taxation, though not in all states. (1) *Real estate* is a class that includes land, buildings, and all permanent attachments thereto. (2) *Tangible personal property* includes items that have value because of their immediate utility, such as tractors, store inventories, household goods, and equipment. (3) *Intangible personal property* includes items that represent value, such as stocks, bonds, savings accounts, and bank accounts. (4) *Public utilities,* which consist of all the first three categories, constitute a class of their own because most states assess them at the state level while the first three groups are assessed locally.

Many states have given up on taxing intangible personal property because it is so difficult to identify within the taxing district, making it easy to escape. Some states have repealed taxes on all tangible personal property because it consumed a good deal of assessing time for the amount of tax yield involved; it required invasion of the privacy of homes; much of it was lost when owners moved it from one taxing jurisdiction to another; many valuable items, such as coin and gun collections, were never fairly assessed; and, in some cases, the tax was an undue burden on certain kinds of businesses or occupations. Other states have sought to make the tangible personal property tax more fair by exempting livestock, farm equipment, business inventories, and other categories.

Personal property tax administration difficult

The property taxation process begins when a local official is designated as the assessor and determines the value of property in the jurisdiction, whether it be a town, township, municipality, or county. Since the property tax is an *ad valorem* tax (meaning *by value*), the assessor's task is to determine what the property would be worth if a willing seller were selling it to a willing buyer in a normal transaction.

Property tax based on value

Once the assessor has used appraisal skills to arrive at a value, a "level of assessment" is applied. Less than half of the states apply the tax to full value.[32] While some states may use a standard level of assessment, such as 20 percent, for all property, other states may establish different levels of assessment for different classes of property. Also affecting the tax base are such items as the homestead exemption which may provide that the first $5,000 in value be exempt. After considering the various rules peculiar to the state, the appropriate level of assessment is applied to the full value and the resultant figure is called *taxable valuation.*

Apply level of assessment

While the assessor is busy valuing the property tax base, government boards and budget boards of local governments are determining the amount of taxes that will be required to finance their activities for the ensuing year. Ultimately, they end up with a levy measured by the *mill* (1/1000th of a dollar). In many states, the county government compiles the various budget levies and collects the property tax for the smaller political subdivisions. The levies for the various governments are converted into a unified tax bill that is sent to the taxpayer. When the taxpayer sends payment, the receipts are divided and distributed to the governments on the basis of their original levies. (See table 18.3.)

Budgets determine mill rates

The property of multistate public utilities, such as power, gas, telephone, and railroad companies, is assessed by a state authority, often applying complex formulas that include systemwide earnings, stock, and bond value, and original cost depreciated. States have often used the formula that resulted in the largest amount of revenue. Railroads particularly suffered from discriminatory property taxation by states and finally persuaded Congress to enact legislation that prohibited states from taxing railroads at higher rates than local commercial properties. Prior to this legislation, state and local taxes would sometimes be greater than a railroad's net operating income.

Most states handle utility assessment

Once the full value of the interstate firm is determined, an appropriate share is claimed for the state and is apportioned out to the taxing jurisdictions for inclusion in the local tax base. Several states have forsaken this complex system for a more simple *gross receipts* tax.

Table 18.3 Levying the Property Tax

Full value of Darrell Johnson's residence as determined by the assessor	$120,000
Level of assessment used in the jurisdiction	20%
Taxable valuation	$ 24,000

Levies determined by the budgets of various taxing governments overlapping Darrell's residence

a. Grover County	25 mills	
b. Edlung Township	8 mills	
c. School District #74	40 mills	
d. Various other districts	14 mills	.087 mills
	Total taxes	$ 2,088.00

Why the property tax survives

  The property tax has survived years of condemnation for a number of reasons. First, and perhaps most important, it is a tax that is in place and now in use. Budget-makers like it because it provides a relatively stable source of income. In some specific circumstances, it can be justified on the "benefits-received" principle, such as use for farm-to-market roads. Finally, it is the only tax that gets at current appreciation in property values.

Property tax ranked least fair

  Criticisms of the property tax have accumulated through the years until it consistently ranks as the least fair in the annual public opinion poll taken by the Advisory Commission on Intergovernmental Relations. Much of the criticism originates in assessing practices. Many jurisdictions are still functioning with elected assessors who unavoidably interject politics into the appraisals and who lack the training demanded by the job. Even when appointed professionals are used, true value is a matter of judgment that, when applied to varying types of property, can result in a considerable range of assessments. Inclinations of assessors are to better approximate true value for houses in the lower ranges, say $90,000 and less, than in the houses valued around $250,000 or $500,000. The reasons for this practice are twofold. First, large homes are not sold as often, providing less of a guide as to the market. Second, considering the doubt involved, large homes tend to be occupied by influential citizens who know the problems in placing values on large houses.

1. Unfair assessments

2. Property tax regressive

  For many owners, property taxes are regressive, especially for lower income people with fixed incomes. One tax study claimed that the property tax burden ranged from 5.58 percent of income for the lowest income families to 3.76 percent for the highest income families.[33] Responding to this criticism, a number of states provide homestead exemptions and circuitbreakers for the elderly and the low income. The homestead exemption provides that the property tax not be imposed on the first $5,000 or $10,000 of value, or whatever level is determined by law or ordinance. The circuitbreaker places a maximum tax, usually figured as a percentage of income.[34]

3. Discourages improvements

  Property taxes discourage renovation of housing, retooling of factories, and rehabilitation of businesses because improvements increase value and increases in value will increase taxes. Thus, the reward for improvement is more taxes. Some jurisdictions have sought to overcome this disadvantage by exempting improvements for a period of years, such as occurs in enterprise zones designated in depressed sections of cities.

A few jurisdictions, such as the Pennsylvania cities of Pittsburgh and Harrisburg, have been shifting emphasis of the property tax away from the building to the landsite.

The incidence of the property tax, even when professionally assessed, does not fall equally. Some taxpayers, such as businesses, are able to shift their burden to consumers, and others, such as farmers, have to absorb it as a cost of production.

4. Uneven burden

When the property tax is imposed through a public referendum, it is possible for majorities of people who own little property to approve ever-increasing tax burdens for the minorities who may own a disproportionate share of property.

5. Unfair imposition

In most states, certain properties owned by charitable and religious organizations are exempt, thereby shifting costs of fire and police services to the remaining property owners. Decades of developing loopholes have left the property tax complex, violating the principle of simplicity. Lump sum payments of the tax have also made it inconvenient to pay.

6. Exemptions

Some measures have been adopted to better the administration of the property tax, including the improvement of recruitment and training of personnel, the development of procedures that can be applied to achieve uniform results, and the supervision of local assessments by the state revenue department or board of equalization.

Improving administration

Since it was first enacted on a statewide basis in West Virginia in 1921, the general sales tax has developed rapidly as a source of revenue. It is now one of the major revenue producers at the state level. Yielding heavily along with state income taxes, the sales tax produced over one-fourth of the state revenue in the early 1990s. It is used in almost all states and, because of its broad base, the sales tax is one of the first taxes to be raised or its base adjusted to meet emergency revenue shortfalls. Local governments in many states are permitted to levy sales taxes, further increasing the total tax rate.

Sales tax a major revenue source

The sales tax has become prominent in state tax systems in spite of its acknowledged regressivity because it meets the tests of certainty, convenience, and simplicity, and it represents somewhat of a compromise between benefits received and ability to pay. Because these qualities disguise its impact, a sales tax increase results in little resistance, thereby making it politically popular. Its regressivity is often reduced by exempting food and prescription drugs. As an alternative to exemptions, four states provide a per capita credit on state income taxes to offset sales taxes paid.

Sales tax popular

Forty-six states levy a corporate income tax and 44 levy an individual income tax, producing over one-fourth of the state-collected revenue. Although Virginia had an income tax as early as 1843, it was not until Wisconsin adopted it in 1911 that it proved administratively workable at the state level. Most state income taxes using a graduated rate schedule are progressive, thereby usually meeting the test of ability to pay. State income taxes with modest rate structures, or with exemptions and deductions beneficial to higher income groups, may actually be regressive in incidence. All states require withholding for each pay period and meet the convenience test. Many state income tax systems begin with the federal income tax base and change it in response to the political pressures in the particular state. Several states, most notably Nebraska,

Income tax

Using federal tax base

Rhode Island, North Dakota, and Vermont, simplify their state income taxes by levying a percentage of federal income taxes paid. This practice accepts the federal tax base, with whatever exemptions and deductions (many of which are called loopholes) have been adopted by Congress.

A major argument in favor of the state income tax is that it is the most progressive of the taxes available to states. However, only about ten states have demonstrated the political will required to impose a healthy rate structure to the base. State-by-state comparisons are very difficult since the tax bases and the ranges within tax brackets vary considerably. Thus, the actual rates are only part of the picture.

Income tax goes with the economy

Another benefit, at least to the state tax collectors, is that a graduated income tax will respond gingerly to an expanding economy. In fact, it can grow faster than the economy, making unpopular increases in rates unnecessary when the economy is growing. During the years of double-digit inflation, income tax collections escalated even beyond economic growth, resulting in a revenue windfall for states. An angry public forced a number of states to restrict the inflationary impact on the income tax by indexing tax obligations to a stable measurement, such as the U.S. Consumer Price Index (CPI).

Arguments against state income taxes

Income taxes have been restrained in most states by the presence of the highly graduated federal income tax and the political opposition of influential high-income citizens. The tax is attacked as a penalty for hard work and a disincentive for economic expansion. It is also argued that the state income tax complicates the tax structure because it usually deviates to some degree from federal income tax rules. This violates the rule of simplicity and makes compliance confusing.

Highway user taxes

Even though they are technically excise taxes, taxes on gasoline and automobiles are often called *highway user taxes* because in most of the states they are earmarked for use in highway construction and maintenance. States add their levies to the tax levied by the federal government for its highway grant-in-aid programs. All or a portion of the motor vehicle registration fees, discussed under licensing revenue, may also be fed into the highway user fund along with excise taxes on other fuels and vehicle-related purchases.

Taxing offensive conduct

States have had few qualms about levying *sumptuary taxes,* those levies aimed at regulating personal conduct that offends the public morals. Liquor, beer, and tobacco taxes fall in this category, although here again they could be classified as excise taxes. These taxes are levied by the state at the wholesale level and require wholesalers to pay the taxes on merchandise distributed to retailers. Dealing with only a few wholesalers makes the tax simple for the state to administer. The tax is recovered by the retailer by addition to the ultimate sale price to the consumers. Since each state varies its tax rate on alcoholic beverages by the type of drink and volume of alcohol, attempts to compare tax rates in this area are frustrating. Because of the mounting proof that cigarette smoking is a serious health hazard, this sumptuary tax will continue to rise in the 1990s as it becomes more offensive to public morals.

Death taxes

Death taxes, including *estate, inheritance,* and *gift,* are imposed in some combination to some degree in every state except Nevada. Extensive use of death taxes can be attributed in part to the incentive plan provided by the federal government in 1924 which in effect penalized any state not taxing inheritances. Congress amended the federal inheritance tax in 1921 to permit deductions to be made from the federal tax up to 80 percent, if the state collected such a tax. Florida had no inheritance or estate tax for many years, much to the unhappiness of neighboring states that were losing wealthy retired residents to Florida. However, in 1930 it finally levied an estate tax to claim the revenue that would otherwise go to the federal government. Estate taxes are imposed on the property of the deceased before distribution to heirs; inheritance taxes fall on individuals who receive property from an estate; gift taxes are imposed on property given away in anticipation of death.

Severance taxes loomed into prominence with the energy crisis of the 1970s and became particularly significant for the states with gas, oil, and coal reserves. In Alaska, Wyoming, Louisiana, New Mexico, Oklahoma, Texas, North Dakota and Montana, severance taxes constituted over 12 percent of the state revenue before the drop in oil prices in 1986. Seeing an opportunity to import tax revenue, these energy-rich states all imposed significant taxes on the practice of severing minerals from the soil. Montana's 30 percent severance tax on coal was challenged as an undue burden on interstate commerce but the U.S. Supreme Court sustained the state's levy in *Commonwealth Edison Co. v. Montana,* No. 80–851. Protesting the high Montana tax, Senator David Durenberger of Minnesota, representing a consumer state, threatened federal limitations on state severance taxes. Seizing the opportunity to use energy resources as a means of exporting tax burdens may be attractive to states as long as production and income remain steady. However, when oil prices skidded from $43 per barrel to less than $15, states with heavy oil taxes were forced to scramble for new revenues to fill the shortfall. For each $1 drop in the worldwide oil price, Texas lost $40 million annually. Thus, the drop cost Texas over a billion dollars annually.

Taxing use of natural resources

In addition to coal and oil, severance taxes are levied on iron ore, forest products, phosphates, copper, nickel, salt, cement, uranium, and a host of other minerals.

Severance taxes are imposed by one of two methods. They are either measured by the *unit,* such as by the ton or by the barrel, or they may be measured by *value,* such as ten percent of market. The unit system has the disadvantage of requiring periodic adjustment to keep up with changing values. The value system is workable when the product involved is being purchased in a relatively competitive market involving several buyers and sellers. Unless a genuine market exists, however, prices may be artificially depressed to limit tax liability.

Imposing severance taxes

There is no business tax as such, but states have devised a variety of taxes on business operations in addition to the property and income taxes paid by many businesses. Special taxes may be levied on incorporation or entry into the state based on a variety of measures. Some sort of franchise tax is collected in every state but it cannot compare in importance with the various consumer taxes.

Special taxes for special operations

Because of their bookkeeping systems, insurance companies may end up with very little liability under the state corporate income taxes. Hence, many states substitute a tax on the gross premiums collected on insurance policies sold in the state. Cooperative ownership also poses tax problems since earnings are apportioned to various participating customers. Unique tax policies may be tailored to capture revenue from

Figure 18.3
General Revenue of State
Governments, by Source:
1990.
*(Source: Bureau of the
Census,* State Government
Finances, 1990.*)*

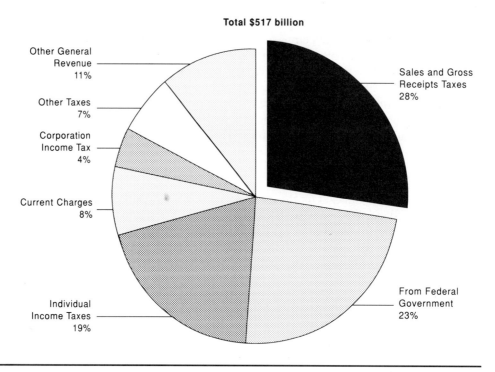

Total $517 billion

Other General Revenue 11%

Other Taxes 7%

Corporation Income Tax 4%

Current Charges 8%

Individual Income Taxes 19%

Sales and Gross Receipts Taxes 28%

From Federal Government 23%

---

this form of economic activity. Banks and similar financial institutions also have unique internal accounting systems that may encourage states to impose something other than a corporate income tax. Rural cooperatives providing electrical, telephone, or water services may be taxed in some fashion suited to the objectives of the state in regard to these services. Usually, the tax burden is kept light to facilitate their use in the state.

*States strive to export
burden*

With some dozen or so taxes available for use, each state has designed a tax structure that is unique. Whenever possible, states have used taxes that export the burden to taxpayers in other states. This has been particularly true about the energy-rich states, but it has also been true in regard to corporate income taxes in states with industries that service the entire nation. Because a number of states have been successful in exporting significant amounts of their taxes to out-of-state payers, computations of per capita tax burdens can be misleading.

Exportation of the tax burden has strained relations among more than just a few states. Sales and use tax laws have occasionally resulted in double taxation on purchases made in one state and used in another; personal income taxes are often imposed to capture revenue from large numbers of out-of-state residents who commute into the state to work. A case in point is the conflict that erupted over Oregon's efforts to tax thousands of Washingtonians who commuted to Portland to work. In retaliation, Washington authorized local governments to impose an excise tax on out-of-staters for police, fire, and other local services.

*Congress takes up
discrimination*

When the corporate community complained to Congress in the 1960s about the burdensome and often discriminatory taxation of state governments, a bill was drafted to nationalize collection of state income and sales taxes on the basis of uniform systems. State tax officials tied the hearings up for months until they could formulate a Multistate Tax Compact to demonstrate a willingness to deal with interstate tax problems without federal interference. Less than half of the states participate in the Compact and abide by its directives. As a consequence, the opportunity to export tax burdens still prevails.

The desire to import revenue is one factor explaining variations in state tax systems. Another factor appears to be the date a particular tax was adopted.[35] The states that first used the income tax, such as Delaware, Oregon, New York, and Wisconsin, continue to rely on it for a major portion of income; states that first adopted sales taxes, found in the South and Midwest, continue to stress this source for revenue.

Tradition and taxes

Political parties seem to have had little impact on tax structures. As Professor Susan B. Hansen has pointed out, parties have varying degrees of significance in the policy process from state to state; divided governments have muted party roles; and some state constitutions have limited revenue options.[36] Perhaps even more constraining than party preferences is the political culture of the state. Regardless of party affiliation, if a majority of the legislators are imbued with doctrines of the state's political culture, they will tend to behave similarly.

Impact of parties

The proximity of state and local governments to the electorate has been a major influence on taxing and spending policies. Tax revolts, though not occurring in every state, sharpened sensitivities and forced all policy-makers to note carefully the nuances of public opinion. With taxpayers literally looking over their shoulders, budget proposers must be prepared to justify every increase. If anything more than a modest operating balance appears in the state or local coffers, politicians respond to the political climate by instantly insisting on tax cuts or refunds, making it even more difficult to develop long-term coherent financial programming. Because of the fiscal flexibility at the federal level, protected by distance from the taxpayers, Washington responds at a much lower stress level between problem and solution than do states. As the federal government continues to curtail state and local aid, and as the sluggish economy fails to produce new revenues, a new level of state and local statesmanship will be required to deal with fiscal affairs in the highly politicized atmosphere of the 1990s.[37]

Taxing close to home

Endnotes

1. For a brief review of this literature, see Ira Sharkansky, *Regionalism in American Politics* (Indianapolis: The Bobbs-Merrill Co., 1970), pp. 180–181.

2. Ira Sharkansky, *Spending in the American States* (Chicago: Rand McNally, 1968); see also the review of new developments in policy analysis research by Stuart S. Nagel, ed., *Improving Policy Analysis* (Beverly Hills, Calif.: Sage Publications, Inc., 1980).

3. National Association of State Budget Officers, *Budgeting Processes in the States, 1989* (Washington, D.C., 1989).

4. Ronald K. Snell, "Deep Weeds: Dismal Outlook for 1991," *State Legislature* 17 (February, 1991): 15.

5. Rob Gurwitt, "Balancing Budgets in an Energy Bust," *Governing* 1 (March, 1988): 61–64.

6. Ronald K. Snell, "Earmarking State Tax Revenues," *Intergovernmental Perspective* (Fall, 1990): 12–16.

7. Linda Harriman and Jeffrey D. Straussman, "Do Judges Determine Budget Decisions? Federal Court Decision in Prison Reform and State Spending for Corrections," *Public Administration Review* 43 (July/August 1983): 343.

8. Bradford. E. Southworth. "Fair labor, fair wages." *State Government News* 34 (February, 1991): 20–22.

9. Gary Enos, "Court-ordered tax hikes upheld," *City & State* 7 (April 23, 1990): 1, 49.

10. Jacqueline Calmes, "Bricks Without Straw: The Complaints Go On But Congress Keeps Mandating," *Governing* 1 (September, 1988): 21.

11. Martha Fabricius, "More Dictates from the Feds," *State Legislatures* 17 (February, 1991): 5.

12. See Steve D. Gold, *Preparing for the Next Recession: Rainy Day Funds and Other Tools for States,* a monograph (Denver: National Conference of State Legislatures, 1983), pp. 1–9.

13. Ibid., pp. 10–12.

14. Ibid., pp. 12–15.

15. Richard Alm, "The Tax Rebellion Runs Out of Steam," *U.S. News and World Report,* November 19, 1984.

16. Rodd Zolkos, "Oregon officials strapped in tax straitjacket," *City & State* 8 (February 11, 1991): 13.

17. See Rochelle L. Stanfield, "The Taxpayers' Revolt is Alive or Dead in the Water—Take Your Pick," *National Journal,* December 10, 1983. Also see Marcia A. Howard, *State Tax and Expenditure Limitations* (National Association of Budget Officers, Washington, DC, 1988).

18. Alm, "The Tax Rebellion."

19. This historical summary of lotteries is based on Leon W. Anderson, *To This Day* (Canaan, N.H.: Phoenix Publishing, 1981), pp. 283–287, and Ernest E. Blanche, "Lotteries Yesterday, Today, and Tomorrow," *The Annals of the American Academy* (May 1950), pp. 71–74.

20. Elaine S. Knapp, "Lotteries Raise Cash for States," *State Government News* 26 (June 1983): 4.

21. Steven D. Gold, "Lotteries: Still Small Change," *State Legislatures* 15 (July 1989): 14–15.

22. Hal Hovey, "State and Local Tax Policy: Looking Ahead," *Intergovernmental Perspective* (Fall, 1990): 6.

23. David S. Kidwell and Robert J. Rogowski, "Bond Banks: A State Assistance Program that Helps Reduce New Issue Borrowing Costs," *Public Administration Review* 43 (March/April 1983): 109.

24. Penelope Lemove, "Bond Issuers Reconsider Their Strategies," *Governing* 1 (June, 1988): 60.

25. Kenneth J. Kirkland, *Debt Policy and Management for States: Issues and Approaches,* a monograph (Denver: National Conference of State Legislatures, n.d.), p. 3.

26. Virginia Rutledge, "Disaster areas need tax-exempt bonds," *City & State* 6 (November 6, 1989): 7.

27. Neil R. Peirce, "Tax Windfall for 34 States May Spark Uproar," *The National Journal* (December 20, 1986): 3090.

28. George F. Berak, *Financing Government In a Federal System* (Washington: The Brookings Institution, 1980): 35, 45.

29. Advisory Commission on Intergovernmental Relations, *1988 State Fiscal Capacity and Effort* M–170 (Washington, D.C.: Government Printing Office, 1990).

30. "Progressive Taxes are Hard to Build," *State Legislatures* 17 (August 1991): 8.

31. Steven D. Gold, *Local Sales and Income Taxes,* a monograph (Denver: National Conference of State Legislatures, 1982), pp. 8–9. Also, see U.S. Department of Commerce, Bureau of the Census, *Government Finances: 1988–89* (Washington, D.C.: Government Printing Office, 1990).

32. Julie Bennett, "Upgraded tax-assessment plans stem appeals, cut revenue loss," *City & State* 7 (September 24, 1990): GM6.

33. Tax Foundation, Special report: *Tax Burden by Income Class* (Washington, D.C., Tax Foundation, 1989): 16.

34. For a discussion of property tax relief measures in the states, see Robert D. Ebel and James Ortbal, "Direct Residential Property Tax Relief," *Intergovernmental Perspective* 15 (Spring 1989): 9–14.

35. See Clara Penniman, "The Politics of Taxation," in *Politics in the American States,* 2d ed., ed. Herbert Jacobs and Kenneth N. Vines (Boston: Little, Brown and Co., 1971), p. 553.

36. Susan B. Hansen, "Extraction: The Politics of State Taxation," *Politics in the American States,* 4th ed., ed. Virginia Gray, Herbert Jacobs, and Kenneth N. Vines (Boston: Little. Brown and Co., 1981), pp. 428–430.

37. See Jeffrey L. Katz, "State Tax Politics, 1990: No Place to Hide," *Governing* 3 (June, 1990): 29–33.

CHAPTER 19

POLICY PROBLEMS OF THE '90S

Confronting states in the decade of the 1990s is an array of critical problems testing the metal of leadership, challenging the adequacy of political institutions, and trying the foresight of the citizenry. Each of these policy problems is viewed differently by each state. What one state will adjudge to be of critical importance another will disregard as secondary. These variations in policy perceptions are rooted in the uniqueness of each state.

Factors influencing perceptions

Factors influencing these perceptions are numerous. In chapter 3, five factors were discussed. History, we noted, still colored the design of political institutions, provisions in state constitutions, and responses to contemporary problems. Geography harbored a distinct combination of lands and resources that affected policies and governance. The variety and dimensions of economic forces dictated the form of many state policies and the mix of competing groups in the policy process. Then we noted that the distribution and composition of the population varied from state to state. Finally, the political cultures of states represented a peculiar mix of attitudes and expectations of government that shaped policy perceptions and outcomes.

In chapters 7 and 8, we observed the variations that exist among states when it comes to political party competition and interest groups. These forces also color the context within which legislative and executive policy proposals are conceived and brought forth. In chapter 9, we stressed the uniqueness of each legislative process since it was influenced differently by the state's executive branch, political party system, pressure groups, and legislative constituencies.

Dynamics of personalities

The factors of uniqueness often go beyond these few categories defined by observation and research. Policy problems and their solutions may become part of a state's agenda simply on the strength of personal leadership in the governor's office, a respected administrator in the bureaucracy, a dynamic legislative leader, or even some private organization. Not only people but events, such as a natural disaster or a gang shooting, may also create agenda items of importance.

Title photo: Among the many policy problems confronting state and local governments in the 1990s will be the development of adequate water supplies. (Photo courtesy of the Metropolitan Water Reclamation District of Greater Chicago.)

Sometimes, the existence of a major problem may be generally recognized but there may be some doubt as to who should deal with the problem. On some occasions, the private sector may be pushing a problem into the public sector for solution. On the other hand, the public sector leadership may have a policy of "privatizing" as many problems as possible.

When the Founding Fathers created the federal system, they thought they had divided the public problems into two categories—those to be solved by the national government and the remainder to be solved by the states. However, with the evolution of the intergovernmental system discussed in chapter 2, the states and the national government now share just about every problem on the public agenda. However, it may take several years—or even decades—before it becomes clear as to which level of government ought to take the lead role. All the while, neither level is sure on which agenda the problem should appear. At present, it is difficult to know for sure who is really in charge of AIDS, garbage, child and spouse abuse, homelessness, and numerous other issues.

Most problems now intergovernmental

The policy problems discussed in this chapter will include those in which the role of states is unavoidable. In the limited space available, only those were selected that promise to become more serious and more controversial in the 1990s. No attempt is being made to discuss them in order of importance because importance will be a matter of judgment of the citizens and policy-makers of the states.

The High Cost of Growing Old

The rapid progress in medical discoveries and technologies is giving Americans ever-increasing years of life expectancy. Rumors and myths notwithstanding, for most seniors the majority of these additional years will be spent in good health and normal activity. As we consider the problems of the elderly, it is imperative to keep in mind that it is untrue that vast numbers of the elderly suffer from inadequate income, ill health, loneliness, above-average crime, and other social or economic problems. It is true, however, that the elderly experience some of these problems in greater proportion than the nonelderly but not as seriously as the general public believes.[1] Only about five percent of the elderly end up in nursing homes or other institutions. If disabled, most of the elderly are cared for in their homes by relatives and friends.[2]

Most elderly independent

Though the vast majority remain self-sufficient, the growing ranks of elderly are funneling larger and larger numbers into costly elderly support programs and institutions. The very elderly—those most likely to require public support—will continue to grow disproportionately into the next century (Figure 19.1).

As census data indicates a growing number of dependent elderly in the decades ahead, changes in the family unit indicate that the public sector will be expected to assume more of the responsibility for care in the future. The increase in the number of working women, high divorce rates, distances from family members, and declining fertility rates all suggest that families will not be available to care for elderly members.

Growing old without families

The program bearing the brunt of this changing demographic and social pattern is Medicaid, a medical care program for needy persons financed jointly by the state and federal governments. Though intended to be a program for the poor rather than the elderly, close to 40 percent of the annual Medicaid budget goes to persons aged 65 and over.

Figure 19.1
Actual and projected
increase in the 85+
population: 1900–2050.
*Sources: U.S. Bureau of the
Census. "America in
Transition: An Aging
Society," by Cynthia M.
Taeuber.* Current
Population Reports *Series
P-23, No. 128 (September
1983). U.S. Bureau of the
Census. "Projections of the
Population of the United
States, by Age, Sex, and
Race: 1988 to 2080," by
Gregory Spencer.* Current
Population Reports *Series
P-25, No. 1018 (January
1989). U.S. Census Bureau.
Compilation by Pam Tobey
for* The Washington Post,
June 10, 1985.

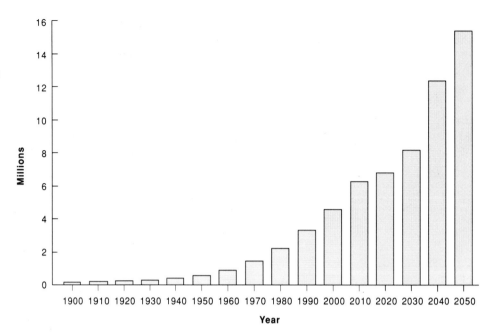

*Nursing homes use up
savings*

The elderly are eligible for Medicaid if they are poor, something that often happens when confinement in a nursing home is necessary for a long period of time. The majority of nursing home patients enter as paying customers but, with care running from $20,000 to $30,000 annually, life savings quickly evaporate. Within a year or two, most of the elderly find themselves in poverty and look to Medicaid to pay for their continued stay.[3] Around one-half of the nation's nursing home patients are on Medicaid.

As Medicaid costs for the elderly keep mounting, both the federal and state governments are maneuvering to shift costs and otherwise reduce the impact of the problem. In the 1980s, the states rejected a federal proposal to limit the federal share and leave the states to pick up the rest of the costs. Most states have launched programs intended to help the elderly remain in their own homes. Home meals and home health care are common. To reduce the cost of living, states offer a variety of property tax "circuit-breakers" and income tax exemptions.[4] Oregon pioneered foster care for the disabled elderly and pays caretakers for providing a home.[5]

As governments cast about for solutions, little hope is in sight for fiscal relief. Without question, one of the challenges to states in the 1990s is preserving the dignity of the elderly in the face of mounting costs.

Health Care: Who Can Afford It?

*U.S. has quality
medicine*

The quality of medical care in the United States is perhaps without parallel anywhere in the world. The number of professional practitioners is constantly rising, even though the distribution between urban and rural areas continues to be unbalanced. New pro-

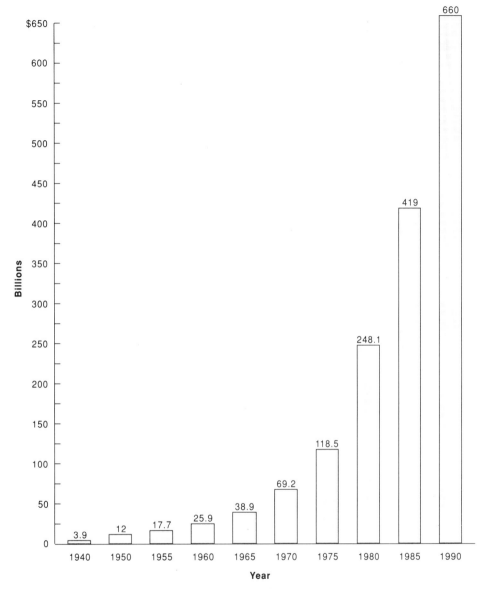

Figure 19.2
National health expenditures, 1940–1990. *(Source: © 1990 The Council of State Governments. Reprinted with permission from* State Government News *(May, 1990).)*

cedures have eliminated or simplified surgery and new discoveries in drugs have resulted in remarkable control of life-threatening conditions. Institutions have the latest in high technology and ample space, in some cases surpluses of both. While the capacity for good medical care has increased dramatically, the cost of buying into that system has put medical care beyond the reach of millions of Americans (Figure 19.2).

Since 1970, health spending as a percentage of gross domestic product in the United States has exceeded that of all industrialized countries. Costs in the United States even outrun the cost of care in those countries with socialized medicine which

Health care costs excessive

is so roundly denounced as wasteful and inefficient.[6] At the beginning of the 1990s, national health expenditures were running an estimated $660 billion—and growing. The $2,600 spent for every man, woman, and child was 50 percent more than what was being spent in Canada.[7]

Cite causes of problem

Joseph Califano, Jr., Secretary of Health, Education, and Welfare in the Carter Administration, attributes these mounting costs to a number of factors. Hospitals are overbuilt, with only 60 percent of the beds being used. Doctors are ordering many unnecessary medical procedures, such as coronary bypasses, Cesarean deliveries, hysterectomies, and the like. Medical malpractice insurance has forced doctors to add the cost of premiums to their fees. Insurance adds almost $600 per baby in New York and $450 in Oregon.[8]

In some states, insurance premium increases are condoned and may be encouraged by members of the medical profession who are strategically located on insurance and institutional boards where fees are set. Increases can also be blamed on the people who have good insurance coverage at their place of employment and are unconcerned about mounting medical costs as long as their bills are covered by insurance. (On average, only five percent of hospital care is paid out-of-pocket by the patient.)[9] Without a complaining constituency, pressure for restraining medical costs is minimized.

Many cannot afford insurance

To cope with medical needs, most people turn to insurance for their protection. If they are not fortunate enough to be covered at work, they pay $300 to $400 per month for individual family plans. For part-time employees or those working at a minimum wage, this cost is an unmanageable portion of the family budget and they forego insurance. It is estimated that around 35 million Americans do not have medical insurance. For them, health is a daily gamble.

Two-thirds of the uninsured are employed, dependents of uninsured employees, or self-employed. They are involved in businesses that are too small to offer health insurance, either because the firms are not economically capable or the cost of insurance for a small group is excessively high.[10]

States mandating coverage

While trying to gain control of the spiraling costs on the one hand, states are adding to the problem on the other. Many states have passed legislation ordering insurance companies to include in their policies the services of optometrists, chiropractors, podiatrists, mental health professionals, and other practitioners. Every such addition increases the ultimate cost of insurance policies.[11] To reduce the cost of medical insurance for small companies or the uninsured, some state legislatures are considering stripping down these mandates on policies and authorizing policies that provide the most basic of health care services. Of course, the interest groups and professionals who supported the original mandates resist such changes.

Helping the uninsurable

In addition to those who cannot afford insurance is a group of citizens considered to be uninsurable by insurance companies. They suffer from pre-existing disqualifying chronic conditions. To assist the uninsurables, half of the states have formed special "risk pools" to provide insurance, even though the premiums may be high. The premiums paid, however, are not sufficient to finance the risk so the pools are often subsidized by state revenues or levies on insurance companies.[12]

Those who need medical treatment and have no insurance are forced to use up their limited personal resources. Once these resources are depleted, they are eligible for Medicaid. As the decade of the '90s began, 24 million Americans (10 percent of the population) were receiving assistance through Medicaid. The cost of Medicaid was estimated to quadruple from $12.5 billion in 1970 to $50 billion in 1994.[13] Under the Medicaid program, the federal government mandates minimum coverage but leaves some coverage options to the individual states. As a consequence, disparities exist among the state programs. In some states, certain care is authorized that is denied in other states. Because of these variations, and deficiencies in coverage, millions of poor people are not able to buy insurance or obtain Medicaid. Their medical expenses, if they dare to incur any, are absorbed by the providers of the treatment. These costs then become overhead and are charged to the patients who can pay.

Burden falls on Medicaid

Mounting medical costs have forced a number of states into programs of health care cost containment. In some cases, the efforts arise out of the state's responsibilities for Medicaid administration; in other cases, public pressure has forced states to take action. As examples, Alaska created a Medicaid Rate Commission to determine payment rates for all health care facilities in the state; California created the office of negotiator to receive bids and negotiate health care costs with vendors; the Connecticut Commission on Hospitals and Health Care annually reviews and approves hospital capital expenditures and budgets; and the Maryland Health Services Cost Review Commission sets and reviews rates for various hospitals. Business coalitions have been springing up to protest the increasing medical costs reflected in the medical and hospital insurance premiums they pay for their employees. These coalitions are patrolling the halls of state government, proposing various policies and methods by which states can curb the tide of medical bills. As an example, a Michigan coalition not only included Ford, Chrysler, Dow Chemical, and Kellogg, but it also had representatives of the AFL-CIO and the United Auto Workers.[14] The Arizona Coalition for Cost Effective Quality Health Care represents 1,000 companies throughout the state.[15]

States try cost containment

As states battle the normal trends toward higher and higher medical costs, the spread of AIDS promises to accelerate Medicaid costs. Statistics indicate that the disease is spreading more rapidly among low income people, most of whom will require long-term hospitalization and expensive medication at public expense.[16]

AIDS impacts Medicaid

The prognosis is not good for medical care in the United States. Expenses will continue to climb. Employers will seek ways to avoid the excessive costs of insuring employees. More and more people will find America's quality medical care beyond their financial resources. Many simply will not get medical care and experience chronic ailments and premature death.

Fighting Poverty—Sort Of

The Social Security Act of 1935 was perhaps the most significant piece of social legislation adopted in the twentieth century. Even in the 1990s, some 60 years after passage, its provisions continue to serve as the point of reference for many of the intergovernmental social services being provided. It launched four broad thrusts: (1) federal system of old-age and survivors insurance; (2) federal-state systems of unemployment insurance; (3) aid to the states for public assistance to needy persons in specified categories; and (4) aid to states for maternal and child welfare services.

Poverty fight began in 1935

Over the past 60 years, remarkable progress has been made in aiding dependent people as the original Social Security Act has been amended and new programs created. While not yet defeated, poverty among the elderly has declined. In fact, on the average persons over 65 have more resources than those under 65. The retarded and the mentally ill have been liberated from confining institutions and given new opportunities in the least restrictive environments.

Poverty increases for children

In spite of these gains, poverty still haunts millions of Americans. The lack of health care for the needy has already been discussed. While the elderly have gained much economic ground since the 1930s, poverty among children has increased. Aid for families with dependent children (AFDC) has become a major state and federal expenditure. Its magnitude cannot be measured by the cash payments alone but must take into account a large share of the food stamp and Medicaid programs. In the past forty years, AFDC grew from 2.2 million to over 10 million recipients. Because AFDC is the major welfare program, policy-makers who come into office with the belief that high welfare costs are attributable to loafers are stymied when they find that dependent children must become their chief target to save money. To limit the opportunities of

Very few loafers on welfare

able-bodied "loafers" from benefiting from AFDC, for years states refused to make payments when an employable spouse was in the household. However, this cure eventually began to appear worse than the disease since it forced unemployed parents to leave home so their families could receive benefits. Though state after state has at one time or another scrutinized the AFDC rolls, and audits for fraud were conducted regularly by federal administrators, the vast majority of AFDC claims have been found to be legitimate. The nation's largest county, Los Angeles, did report in 1992 that its new mandatory fingerprinting requirement for eligibility to receive welfare benefits, aimed at detecting duplicate requests, saved $5.4 million in six months.

Single-parent families increase AFDC

Increasing AFDC costs cannot be attributed to wholesale fraud. Rather, this particular program is increasing because of the growing number of single-parent families. The number of families consisting of a woman and children rose from 4.1 million in 1960 to around 7 million in the 1980s. The proportion of poor residing in such families has doubled.[17] Many of the single-parent homes are the consequences of divorces, with the man leaving the home and evading parental responsibilities for payment of child support. According to census data, 75 percent of all children in single-parent households receive no support from absent parents.[18] Viewing this as a major defect in AFDC administration, the national government enacted legislation in 1975, and again in the 1980s, to enhance state efforts to force noncustodial parents, married or unmarried, to accept financial responsibility for children. The legislation resulted in the creation of

Governments pursue non-supporting parents

special child support enforcement units, federally-funded and state-administered, to locate delinquent parents. States agreed to aid each other through reciprocal enforcement of support obligations, meaning that a father living in Arizona, sought by Iowa, would be required by Arizona to make support payments as determined in Iowa. The legislation required states to extend their paternal enforcement programs. It permits the interception of federal income tax refunds and portions of unemployment compensation payments going to parents who have been determined liable for dependent children. As the high divorce rate continues, poverty in single-parent families will constitute an increasing challenge to child support collections.

Another response to the growing cost of welfare has been mandatory work programs. In the mid–1980s, around 40 states were requiring work as a condition for some welfare payments, with most of the programs directed at the AFDC category. While modern programs are more sophisticated than the workhouses of the last century, the premise prevails that able-bodied persons ought to perform some useful work in exchange for their benefits. Until recently, federal welfare policies prohibited work requirements attached directly to benefits. However, along with the arrival of the Reagan and Bush administrations came federal income tax cuts and a strong drive to curb public expenditures. In 1988 the Family Support Act was enacted to take effect in 1990. The legislation provided funds for training AFDC clients for jobs with the promise that during the first year of employment they would continue to receive Medicaid coverage and child care allowances. To put the program together, federal and state cooperation was required. Those clients most likely to succeed were targeted to participate. Quotas were established. If they weren't met voluntarily participation would become mandatory or states would lose AFDC money. *Try work programs*

Clients, caseworkers, and taxpayers all welcomed the program as a thrust long overdue. It was hailed as a fundamental breakthrough in welfare with its focus on moving families toward independence instead of continuing cash assistance.[19] Unfortunately, the program is underfunded and will not finance the kind of effort required to reduce significantly the cost of AFDC. Another weakness in the program is the quality of jobs for which training is being provided. Many of the enrolled clients are preparing for low-paying positions that will not support a single breadwinner after Medicaid and child care are withdrawn. Expansion of the concept, both programmatically and financially, will be require in the '90s to meet expectations. *Program falls short*

In the 1980s, another group of needy people appeared on the welfare scene to challenge state and federal governments. Thousands of people without homes were found living in cardboard boxes, makeshift quarters in alleys, under bridges and railways, and on the streets of most major cities. Estimates of their numbers run from 300,000 to three million.[20] One-third of the homeless were families consisting of parents and children; one-fourth suffered a mental illness; and one-third were drug users and alcoholics.[21] A few were individuals with considerable talent who just dropped out of society. *Coping with the homeless*

Apparently the deinstitutionalization of the mentally ill became a tragic experience in poverty for many. Well-wishers managed to get them released to the "least restrictive" environment which turned out to be streets and alleys. During the decades of deinstitutionalization, around 500,000 patients were released from institutions. Initially, 65 percent of the patients went home to families. Today, however, only about one-fourth return home. Many obviously find their niches among the homeless. *Mentally ill among the homeless*

Loss of low cost housing has also been blamed for the increase in homelessness. This may explain the presence of large numbers of families roving the streets. The Neighborhood Reinvestment Corporation, a nonprofit group funded by Congress, is predicting that the number of poor households will grow from 11.9 million in 1983 to 17.2 million by 2003. At the same time, the number of low income rental units will shrink from 12.9 million to 9.4 million.[22] Simple logic suggests that this trend will create thousands of new prospects for street life. *Low-cost housing on decline*

Provide limited funds

After local, state, and federal governments patched together emergency programs for several years, the McKinney Act became law in 1987 to provide aid for the homeless. Appropriations have grown slowly through the years.[23] The McKinney Act meets some of the immediate needs but does not hold out much hope for long-term solutions to the problem of homelessness in the 1990s.

Who should be in charge?

While problems of the poor and dependent beg for solution, controversy persists over the level of government that ought to be assigned primary responsibility for welfare programming and financing. As a result of the crisis in the 1930s, the national government has fallen heir to most welfare programming although considerable sums of state and local money are involved. Also, almost all programs end up being administered by state governments and their political subdivisions. Both the Reagan and Bush administrations have favored shifting more responsibility to states, alleging that those closest to the problem can do the best job of solving it. State and local governments have resisted this devolution, primarily because of the costs involved.

Benefits vary widely

Pointing to the disparity in welfare benefits from state to state, some have proposed that the time has come to vest the national government with prime responsibility and that a national welfare program be uniformly applied across the country. As an example, in the past, California has paid five times the welfare benefits as were being paid in Mississippi. Advocates of a national plan claim that these disparities are enough to attract welfare clients from one state to another, thereby penalizing states offering high benefits.[24] Poverty, the argument goes, is an offshoot of a national economy and, therefore, must be dealt with from the national perspective.

Garbage! Garbage! Who Gets the Garbage?

A number of environmental problems beset the states and the national governments, all of great importance to future generations. Among these are the unsolved challenges of acid rain, the greenhouse effect, oil spills, and air and water pollution. After several decades these issues continue to demand a top position in policy priorities. However, in recent years, the disposal of solid waste has rapidly emerged as an environmental problem of major proportions.

Categorized as solid waste are paper and paperboard, metals, plastics, food wastes, yard wastes, and any number of other products of the throw-away society.

Throwaway garbage increases

As the efficiencies of mass production and new technology have increased, it has become cheaper to throw away packaging and products rather than recycle or conserve. The average American of today generates twice as much garbage as the average American of 1960. Disposable packaging wastes are up 200 percent since 1960. At the same time, landfill fees have remained cheap, making it economical to haul 90 percent of the solid waste generated to the landfills for burial. At the landfill, some waste materials refuse to decay while others generate pollutants that seep into the water table (Figure 19.3).[25]

Close landfills

To head off pollution of underground water, the federal government used its commerce powers to regulate garbage disposal. Through the years, stringent regulations have been evolving from the Environmental Protection Agency for the operation of landfills. The cost of complying with these regulations is making continuance of land-

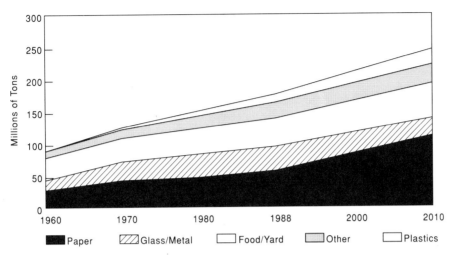

Figure 19.3
Yearly U.S. municipal solid waste generation, 1960–2010. *(Source: Environmental Protection Agency,* Characterization of Municipal Solid Waste in the United States: 1990 Update *(Washington, D.C., 1990).)*

fills economically infeasible for thousands of cities and counties. Some 14,000 landfills were closed over the past decade and experts estimated that another one-third of the remaining 6,500 would be closed by the mid–1990s.[26]

Low-level radioactive waste

Low-level radioactive wastes are another class of garbage that requires special disposal in the throw-away stream. The sources of low-level radioactive waste include not only the nation's 112 commercial nuclear power plants but also companies, universities, hospitals, and medical facilities engaged in research or use of certain wastes. Low-level wastes include uranium, therium, cesium, and other radioactive metals; protective clothing used by workers; and supplies and equipment contaminated from power plants, hospitals, and manufacturers.[27]

Interstate game of hearts

Both categories of garbage—ordinary solid waste and low-level radioactive waste—have resulted in an interstate game of hearts with every state trying to leave the queen of spades with its neighbor. Nevertheless, data collected by the national Solid Waste Management Association indicated that at least 43 states were either importing or exporting some 15 million tons of solid waste annually. New Jersey and New York were responsible for exporting half of it.[28]

Garbage classified as interstate commerce

The political implications of becoming one of the nation's "dumpgrounds" soon became apparent as citizens of one state after another objected to the development of landfills for disposal of garbage—especially anything radioactive—for other states. In response to public pressures, legislatures have passed measures to outlaw the importation of garbage. Federal courts have overruled such legislation on the grounds that garbage is another item of interstate commerce protected by the U.S. Constitution.

Fees will finance disposal

According to one estimate, the cost of complying with the federal regulations will triple waste management budgets as state and local governments generate documentation and site monitoring for the Environmental Protection Agency.[29] The national government deems solid waste as sufficiently a national problem to regulate but not sufficiently national to warrant federal money. Without federal assistance and limited state resources, the fiscal impact will be borne largely by the generators of the waste and will be paid through garbage pickup fees or dumping fees at landfills.

Move to reduce volume of garbage

To curb the growing garbage pile, states and local governments are adopting laws and ordinances to reduce the need for landfill space. Since a good share of landfill material consists of lawn clippings, special collection sites or containers are being used to divert them to composting. Recycling goals have been set by over half of the states to reduce solid waste from 25 to 50 percent by the mid-1990s.[30] Though a popular concept, recycled material faces stiff competition in the marketplace and may not be as much an economical solution as an ecological solution. As of 1990, only 11 percent of the solid waste stream in the United States was being recycled as compared to Japan, where recycling took 43 percent.[31]

Intergovernmental solution

The solutions to the solid waste problems in the United States will evolve out of the intergovernmental character of the federal system. The national government will establish standards to be met by states and local governments. Eventually, the federal government will, as circumstances require, compel interstate cooperation to provide the disposal sites necessary. State and local governments will be required to implement programs to meet the standards and sort out financing techniques that will be politically acceptable.

Return of the Water Wars

Without water, humans, animals, and plants would all perish in a short time. Because abundant water is critical to the continuation of an abundant life, control of water resources has been a source of controversy since the early epochs of man. While water was naturally plentiful in the eastern states, as the wagon trains moved west into the semi-arid and arid sections of the United States, concern over the adequacy of water escalated. Many a range war erupted over the control of a stream of flowing water as sheep and cattle owners realized the very existence of their empires rested on the availability of water. Today, mayors of major metropolitan centers see water as a critical ingredient in future growth. States are enviously looking across their borders to their well-supplied neighbors. All the while, those who have water are moving to protect it from diversion.

Indians have water rights

State laws, however, do not constitute the last word on water rights. Indians have claims to water based on federal law, which supersedes water grants made under state laws. In 1908, the U.S. Supreme Court affirmed the rights of Indians to water by halting upstream diversions that were depriving Indians of sufficient water to irrigate pastures and farmland on the reservations.[32] Then in the 1960s, the Court quantified the amount of water to which Indians were entitled by holding that they had the right to as much as was necessary to irrigate the acreage on the reservation.[33] The dimensions of the problems involved with Indian water rights vary from state to state. In Arizona, where Indian reservations constitute 27 percent of the state, there have been estimates that Indian tribes are entitled to five times more water than is available in the entire state.[34] Major conflicts exist in over 60 water basins involving more than 100 Indian communities throughout western United States, with the outcomes affecting urban growth in Tucson, Salt Lake City, Albuquerque, and Reno; energy development in the San Juan and Powder River basins; and agriculture in Arizona, California, Nevada, and Washington.[35]

Problems of water ownership are compounded by growing shortages. The surface water supply is inadequate, forcing heavier usage of groundwater for industrial, commercial, and domestic purposes. At least one-fourth of all groundwater withdrawals can be termed *overdraft,* that is, usage that will not be replaced by natural replenishment processes. One-half of this overdraft occurs in the six states overlying the huge Ogallala Aquifer—Nebraska, Kansas, Colorado, Oklahoma, New Mexico, and Texas.[36] Groundwater represents a major source of all water for many arid and semi-arid states— 27 percent in Colorado, 33 percent in Idaho, 40 percent in California, and 60 percent in Arizona. Even Arkansas and Mississippi obtain half of their supply from groundwater. Almost 50 percent of the nation's population uses groundwater for domestic purposes, and it is the primary source of drinking water in Massachusetts, New York, New Jersey, Maryland, and Florida.[37]

Overdrafting groundwater

To restrict the usage of water, over 30 states have inaugurated requirements that water users obtain permits from the state before drawing surface or groundwater. To deal with limited water supplies, permits are often prioritized, giving preference to uses the state considers more important.

Dole out permits

To deal with interstate water management, many states have entered into compacts with neighbors. Providing the institutional framework, interstate compacts either (1) comprehensively plan and manage water resources of a basin through a single governmental entity, or (2) divide the water of a basin among member states for management as the states see fit. The Delaware River Basin Compact, involving Delaware, New Jersey, New York, and Pennsylvania, is an example of the total management compact, while the Colorado River Compact, involving seven western states, is of the allocation variety.[38] The $3.5 billion Central Arizona Project, designed to carry 3,000 cubic feet per second across two-thirds of Arizona, will take much of Arizona's allocation in the 1990s to Phoenix and Tucson to relieve the Ogallala Aquifer.

Use compacts to manage water

The genius of civil engineering is being employed in some states to move large quantities of water between river basins. Metropolitan Boston is receiving an interbasin water transfer from the Connecticut River. Another example is the California State Water Project that transfers water for the Feather River system in northern California into the Sacramento River and then to southern California by aqueduct. Hydrologists have also been studying interbasin transfers from the Missouri River basin to supplement the drawdown occurring in the states over the Ogallala Aquifer.[39]

Move water between basins

As the demand for water increases and the supply remains erratic, states are fighting each other for larger shares of the interstate streams flowing in or near them. When South Dakota offered to sell a share of its water rights on the Missouri River to move coal in a slurry pipeline, downstream states filed suit and halted the sale. When the U.S. Corps of Engineers proposed to maintain high flows from the dwindling water supply behind upper Missouri dams, Montana and the Dakotas challenged the Corps' authority in federal courts. While the upper Missouri River states continued to contest with downstream states, the Great Lakes states and provinces were becoming alarmed by rumors that Great Lakes water was being proposed to meet water shortages in the arid Southwest. Leaders from the Great Lakes states, Ontario and Quebec signed a Great Lakes Charter pledging a united front against water diversion plans.

States fight over water

States guard water supplies

When California was in the midst of an extended drought, a Los Angeles County official proposed piping water from the Columbia and Snake rivers to parched Southern California. The proposal was greeted unsympathetically by the governors of the affected states. Besides, U.S. Senator Steven D. Symms of Idaho had taken care of future diversion plans by attaching a specific prohibition to the 1986 Water Resources Development Act. The Symms amendment required unanimous agreement by the seven governors before diversion could take place.[40]

While states are very involved in water management, control of navigable streams and interstate water supplies will rest substantially with the federal government and its agencies. Nevertheless, state leaders, responding to constituent needs, will continue to maximize state power and influence in securing adequate water supplies for all users. After considerable conflict, major decisions will be made in the 1990s as water shortages become more pressing.

Economic Development—The Game of Interstate Larceny

States fight for jobs

In a competition that has turned into aggressive "hardball," all 50 states are now engaged in open warfare for new jobs and new economic activity. Stealing companies from neighboring states with tax giveaways and cheap money has become a standard practice in the name of economic development.

Starting with New York, Mississippi, and South Carolina in the 1940s, all states are now committing more and more public resources to subsidizing private enterprise. The advent of computers, satellites, and fast transportation have not only made industry mobile but also provided new options in strategically locating divisions of companies anywhere in the world.[41]

Economic development agencies

Somewhere in the governmental structure of every state is an agency—perhaps several—commissioned to manage the state's drive for new businesses. Among its duties is coordination of the total economic development resources of the government, providing information to prospective businesses, offering technical advice, arranging for financial assistance, planning overseas trade missions and marketing, conducting research and promotion, and preparing presentations for any executive willing to listen.

Local giveaways

Partners in this relentless pursuit of new business are the local governments that consider themselves prime sites for new business activity. On the local level, they offer additional incentives—startup capital, industrial sites, low taxes, liberal zoning, and free municipal services. And they're not above stealing business from each other when given the opportunity.

Offer tax concessions

Tax concessions have always been at the top of every state checklist for enticing companies. What started out years ago as a modest offer of a property tax waiver for inventories in transit has turned into a full-blown giveaway of corporate income taxes, sales taxes and property taxes. When one state raises the bid with one or more new concessions, most other states fall in line like dominoes—or develop a competitive alternative (Figure 19.4).

Provide venture capital

When most states successfully neutralized each other with tax concessions, the competition sharpened and turned to venture capital and bonding. To provide low-cost loans or grants, states have offered packages involving revenue bonds, general obligation bonds, state tax monies, and even pension funds.

Figure 19.4
"If you'll relocate in Nebraska, we'll waive income taxes, sales taxes, and property taxes for five years and provide you with free utilities."

At one time, the economic development attack teams sponsored recruiting banquets in major cities, with invitations going to the leading prospects in the area. The director of the state economic development agency would then present the wonders of doing business in Homestate with a multimedia production. However, with the increasing competition, more important players were called in—not only the secretary of commerce but also the governor. Today, the governor is expected to commit days of a busy schedule making the economic development "pitch" and calling on major business prospects for one-on-one presentations.

Governors make "pitch"

Competition is earnest and sometimes bitter. When General Motors let it be known that it was looking for a site for its new Saturn plant, the governors of seven midwestern states appeared on a television talk show to participate in a public bidding match for the plant. None of the contestants won—it went to Tennessee. Pennsylvania gave Volkswagen a $40 million loan and made $30 million in rail and highway improvements. Ten years later, Volkswagen closed the plant and left the country, with repayment of the loan to begin in 1998. To get the Toyota plant, Kentucky and its local governments put up over $100,000 in incentives for every one of the 3,000 jobs created. To keep Sears in Illinois, the State of Illinois offered a package worth $178 million.[42]

One reporter on the war between the states for economic development has noted that "companies have learned that they can play states off against one another and are not adverse to doing so in order to better their bottom line."[43] The game is getting so good that even the home-based businesses are announcing intentions to move out of the state unless tax concessions are offered.

Play states against each other

According to another writer, Dennis O. Grady, this predatory interstate competition is not in the best interests of the citizenry. "The beneficiaries," he alleges, "are the stockholders of the corporations receiving the tax breaks, free land, and cheap credit."[44]

States giving away tax base

Disadvantages in the escalating economic development conflict are serious. States end up giving away tax revenue sorely needed for education, infrastructure, social services, and other programs. States have become victims of clever exploitation by private companies seeking to maximize gains at public expense. While new companies gain the breaks, most of the in-state companies continue paying their fair share of the tax burden. States are finding that private enterprise isn't free anymore and economic development is one game that is becoming very expensive.

Education: Much Rhetoric, Few Solutions

Once upon a time, American free public education was hailed as the foundation of a free democracy that enabled millions of immigrant children to share in the social, economic, and political opportunities of a maturing nation. What once commanded the enthusiastic support of parents has become a battleground over sex education, secular humanism, rampant drugs, quality of instruction, racism, violence, and stagnation. While some parents are taking their children out of the public schools, others are moving to communities with quality education and still others are wondering about the future of public education as we know it.

Public education in question

According to one writer who summed up a U.S. Department of Education report:

> Most American elementary and high school students' performances are low and not improving. Most students are unable to think through problems on their own, show only modest performance in reading, mathematics, science, history, and civics, and few demonstrate those skills we usually associate with the ability to function in more demanding jobs in the workplace or the capability to do college work.[45]

Investment up; results down

This indictment follows at least one decade of concentrated effort at reform and the continued annual expenditure of one-third of all state and local revenue. As total expenditures in actual dollars have climbed steadily over the past 20 years, the scholastic aptitude test (SAT) scores have declined.

Local control through districts

School districts are governed by boards of citizens elected in nonpartisan elections, commonly held at times other than general elections. Consisting of from five to 15 members, the boards administer the schools through professional education administrators who prepare budgets, plan staffing, screen prospective teachers, recommend courses of study, and carry out specific board policies. The amount of authority exercised by the superintendents will vary with the orientations of board members and the amount of confidence and trust the boards place in their judgment.

States strive for uniformity

Through the years, states have reflected a commitment to uniformity in quality education by enacting laws designed to bring schools into uniformity. Local school boards may approve school curricula but state law will prescribe the minimum requirements; they may select the teachers but state law will dictate their educational requirements and certification; boards may adopt the schedule of school athletic events but state laws may prohibit competition during weekdays; boards may approve budgets but laws may prescribe the mill levies, accounting procedures, and fund administration.

School districts receive more than mandates and regulations from state legislatures. They are also the beneficiaries of financial support. During the 1920s, states developed an awareness of the increasing differences in the property valuation from school district to school district. Since property valuation is regarded as a measurement of available revenue from property taxes, these disparities meant that children in schools with high property valuations were getting a better education than children in schools with lower valuations. To ameliorate these disparities, states began to adopt *equalization* and *foundation* programs under which state funds were provided to districts, with larger amounts going to help districts with low valuations.

Equalizing educational resources

Even though some progress had been made, wide disparities still existed in many states. By the 1970s, some reformers decided to bypass the state legislative process and seek relief in the courts. When the California Supreme Court ruled disparities in property valuation to be a violation of that state's equal protection clause, hope grew that the U.S. Supreme Court would follow suit. However, the Court ruled in *San Antonio Independent School District v. Rodriguez* that the equal protection clause in the Fourteenth Amendment of the U.S. Constitution did not apply. With no ruling to be applied nationwide, those seeking reform returned to the state courts to renew challenges, one state at a time. In the 1970s and 1980s, state supreme courts found education finance systems in ten states unconstitutional. However, during the same time period, courts in 13 states found the finance systems acceptable. With no clear judicial mandate in sight, funding remains a major unresolved issue in most states.

Equality not achieved

Courts mired in funding issues

Federal interest in primary and secondary education has been sporadic at best. Proposals to provide federal aid to education prior to 1965 were frequent but never given serious consideration. Education lobbyists considered the appropriation of federal funds in the Elementary and Secondary Education Act of 1965 as a major breakthrough. They hoped it was a sign of a new growing federal commitment but they were destined to be disappointed. The level of federal support has remained around seven percent of costs for the past 30 years. During the administrations of Presidents Reagan and Bush, both presidents strongly supported numerous education reforms but neither proposed increased federal appropriations. Early in his administration, President Bush dramatized his desire to be known as the "education president" by summoning all governors to an education summit in Charlottesville, Virginia. Here the president and the governors issued a joint statement calling for clear national performance goals.[46]

Federal support minimal

As long ago as the 1970s, clouds began to gather on the education horizon and signs of an approaching storm appeared. Throughout the decade, parents and educators watched with growing alarm a ten-year decline in the scores of high school seniors taking standardized tests and the mounting evidence that many young people were graduating with basic learning deficiencies in reading, writing, and arithmetic. Researchers were finding that teachers were coming into education from the lower academic levels in colleges. Horror stories began to appear to attest to the presence of classroom teachers who were themselves functionally illiterate and unequal to the challenges of teaching others. Many teachers were found to be suffering from psychological burnout and were marking time until retirement.

Crisis began developing in 1970s

The storm that began brewing in the 1970s was finally unleashed in the 1980s as numerous reports poured out of national "blue ribbon" committees, questioning the

Reports of the 1980s

adequacy of primary and secondary education. Practically unanimous in deploring the condition of education, they warned of a nation "at risk" by pointing out perceived weaknesses and often charging that the declining quality of teachers was to blame for deteriorating academic standards. Unfortunately for policy-makers, the reports failed to reflect a consensus on either the problems or the solutions. Some called for more federal financial assistance; others focused on the need for a more stringent curriculum; still others called for programs to attract and improve good teachers. As a result, the national dialogue over improving primary and secondary education was, in many ways, incoherent. One professional called the variety of commission reports "a potluck supper" in which the delectables fell into three categories: " . . . wholesome main courses for which no recipe is given; gourmet dishes of extravagant cost; and enticing desserts that, once tested, turn out to be nothing but sugar and air."[47]

Parents opt for private education

Widespread and systematic criticism of public education gave impetus to advocates of private education. Many parents, including a considerable number of evangelicals, became dissatisfied with the lack of discipline, hallway violence, drug abuse, poor standards, uneven quality of instruction, and "morally neutral" teaching. Even without financial incentives, they began supporting private education, much of it with a religious flavor.

In response to this growing interest in private education, proposals such as education vouchers and tuition tax credit gained public support. The voucher system would break up the monopoly of education by providing parents with vouchers that could be used to pay for education in public or private schools, whichever they chose.

Propose open enrollment

Another proposal that surfaced to help students escape mediocre schools was "open enrollment," a system in which students could attend whichever public school they wished. Started by Minnesota in 1987, the program has spread to other states, notably Arkansas, Iowa, Nebraska, and Ohio.[48] For many people opposed to education vouchers and tuition tax credits, the arguments against open enrollment are the same— a few mobile students will benefit while the economically deprived will be stuck with mediocrity. Even so, a public opinion poll indicated that well over half of the adults favored the free choice approach.[49]. A comparative analysis of private and public schools produced persuasive evidence that "market-driven" schools offered such advantages that the choice system should be made available to force public schools to respond to a market as is the case in private schools.[50]

Political conflicts in 1990s

Though the initial impact of the commission reports has been absorbed by the educational institutions, political conflict over education will continue unabated through the 1990s. A variety of competing ideas and groups are still on the field, ready to defend or champion their causes. Public opinion supports prayer in schools, merit pay for teachers, tougher discipline, voucher payments, tax credits, and teacher competency testing. If they can't have religious values taught in schools or theories of evolution modified, parents of strong evangelical convictions will continue to open their own schools. A determined band of civil libertarians, on the other hand, will resist every threat to separation of church and state, whether it be religious observances in schools or subtle plans to obviate the traditional interpretation of the First Amendment. Educators and their organizations will resist proposals that threaten their professional well being and that of the public school system. With this array of proponents and opponents harboring deep convictions, the struggle over the fate of public education will tax the institutions of federal, state, and local governments well into the next century.

Orphans at Birth: America's 'At Risk' Children

Children living in poverty increased over 20 percent in the 1980s, primarily because of the increasing number of single-parent homes. The number of children living in such homes has tripled since 1950. The school dropout rate ranges from 40 to 50 percent in many cities. Every year, 375,000 babies are born having already been exposed to drugs.[51] Every 90 minutes, a young person commits suicide, making suicide the third leading cause of death among teenagers.[52] Between 700,000 and 800,000 verified cases of child abuse are registered annually, with over 1,000 children dying from abuse.[53] The number of children in out-of-home foster care has been steadily increasing while the number of available foster homes has been decreasing.[54]

Children increasingly "at risk"

These and other statistics paint a dark picture for children in the 1990s. But these are more than statistics—they are reflections of chronic underlying forces that are shaping the circumstances in which children struggle toward adulthood.

Perhaps the leading cause of the increasing number of children at risk is the breakup and decline of the parenting entity charged with protecting and nurturing children. Families are no longer what they used to be. In fact, the U.S. Census Bureau struggles constantly with the definition of "family" due to the fragmentation of traditional families and the new unstructured relationships seeking the identity of a family.

Family life disappearing

In 1970, 40 percent of the American households fit a traditional two-parent definition. By the end of the 1980s, this had shrunk to 27 percent. Increasing in numbers have been the single parent families and partnerships of both heterosexual and homosexual preferences.[55] The safety net of the extended family has vanished. No longer are uncles, aunts, cousins, or grandparents conveniently available to shore up failures in the parenting process. They live hundreds of miles away.

The decline of the parenting entity can readily be seen in the statistics that show a dramatic increase in the number of parents working. Many parents have new priorities that compete with their parenting activities. With both parents working, many times out of choice rather than necessity, they trade off activities with children for opportunities to improve their standard of living. Children are not receiving the parental guidance they need and are often required to fend for themselves many hours of the day. This increases their social isolation, their autonomy, and their own decision-making, often at ages too young to cope.

More parents working

Some researchers claim that a number of disturbing behaviors among youths can be linked to the inattention of parents: high levels of drug and alcohol abuse, illegitimate births, and suicide. One researcher claims that the increase in teen-age suicide is a result of social isolation growing out of relaxed and inattentive parenthood.[56] With more hours on their own, children are provided more opportunities to engage in risky activities for which they lack perspective or judgment. They replace the absent parental relationships with peer friendships. In search of acceptance and affection, they join peers in consumption of alcohol, use of drugs, and/or sexual relations.

Consequences of parental neglect

Divorce devastating for children

While the lack of parental interest or support can result in placing children at risk in many ways, divorce is even more devastating for children and has a much greater emotional impact. In a study of 7- to 11-year-olds, children of divorce were found to be twice as likely to require mental health services. In addition, they were more likely to marry as teenagers, become substance abusers, and become sexually active—and pregnant—at earlier ages.[57]

Divorce leaves one parent poor

In addition to the emotional upheaval caused in children by divorce, the remaining single-parent family, most often headed by the mother, is left in economic straits. One parent is suddenly responsible for the duties of two—earning the income as well as caring for the family. For many, this is an impossible assignment and poverty strikes. Almost half of the single-parent families live in poverty and are forced to turn to public support. Meanwhile, the departing spouse—usually the man—finds his standard of living improved, especially because he neglects his responsibility to continue financial support for the children. For this reason, the federal and state governments have teamed up in aggressive programs to intercept money going to men who are delinquent in their child support payments.[58]

Poverty impacts outlook

Growing up in poverty, often on welfare, children develop a self-image of low esteem. Emotionally scarred by the rejection of one parent, they are forced to join the work force at an early age and forego many experiences associated with growing up. Their school work suffers; sometimes they just drop out. Under-educated, they create new lifetime obstacles for themselves. In many cases, the experiences at home are so negative, children simply run away, believing life could be no worse out in the unknown.

Can't reverse trend

If broken relationships and declining parental roles are the root causes of children at risk, then the solutions must necessarily be directed at re-establishing relationships and parental roles. However, this is easier stated than achieved. The determination of adults to pursue their own goals is seldom changed by discussion of the consequences of their actions. The divorce rate will continue to be high; the two working parents family will become more common; the abuse and poverty cycle will continue; the extended family will never be restored.

Governments provide programs

Because the government cannot control these private decisions, it must turn to treating the consequences and lessening the shock on children. In any case, the solutions are always second-best. Where child abuse and neglect become obvious, the federal, state, and local governments seek to provide foster homes and alternative living opportunities. Where poverty strikes the single-parent home, the intergovernmental triad provides financial aid for families with dependent children and programs to help families become self-sufficient. Where both parents must necessarily work, all levels of government have moved to provide child care.

Treat family as unit

Many state governments have initiated programs that go beyond children at risk and seek to aid families at risk. They believe that many of the problems of individual children begin in families that are at risk. Hopefully, by keeping the family unit together, the best interests of the children will be served. Under this concept, counseling and other services are provided to the family as a unit.

Effectively dealing with the problems of children at risk will continue to be a challenge in the 1990s—and long into the future. When a highway deteriorates, the problem is obvious and the solution simple. But when a family deteriorates, or children become at risk, government is hard pressed to restore relationships or overcome years of trauma with a simple solution.

Government can't replace family

Conclusion

This brief description of some of the critical problems confronting state and local governments is not inclusive. Numerous other problems will all command the attention of future policy-makers. Whether or not state governments are adequately structured and policy positions are competently staffed to cope with problems of this magnitude remains to be seen. The political turmoil involved in raising the revenue to begin coping with these problems is foreboding, at least at the outset of the 1990s. Without revenue, solutions become remote.

As these problems beg for solution, public opinion is becoming less supportive of the public sector. In fact, there is reason to believe that alienation and cynicism is widespread. Without public support, governments in democratic societies cannot act with vigor or effectiveness. The policy problems of the 1990s are indeed challenges that will test the metal of leadership, challenge the adequacy of political institutions, and try the foresight of the citizenry.

Opinion turns against government

Endnotes

1. Henry J. Aaron, "When Is a Burden Not a Burden? The Elderly in America," *The Brookings Review* (Summer, 1986): 17–24.

2. Alice M. Rivlin and Joshua M. Wiener et al., "Who Should Pay for Long-Term Care for the Elderly?" *The Brookings Review* (Summer, 1988): 3–4.

3. Phillip Keisling, "Protection from Catastrophe," *The Washington Monthly* (November 1983): 41.

4. Corina Eckl, "Aging America: No. 1 Problem of the 21st Century?" *State Legislatures* 16 (July 1990): 40.

5. Julie Rovner, "No Help From Congress On A Near-Term Solution for Long-Term Care," *Governing* 3 (June 1990): 26.

6. David L. Wilson, "Trends in the Health Service Industry," *National Journal* 22 (September 29, 1990): 2361.

7. Joseph A. Califano, Jr., "Ways to Cut America's Health Bill," *State Government News* 33 (May 1991): 12.

8. Ibid., p. 13.

9. Paul Feldstein, "The Financing and Delivery of Medical Services," *The Journal of the State Legislative Leaders Foundation* 2 (Winter 1991): 4.

10. Penelope Lemov, "Health Insurance For All: A Possible Dream," *Governing* 3 (November 1990): 57.

11. Julie Kosterliz, "States Increasing Their Regulation of Health Plans' Benefits, Eligibility Rules," *National Journal* 17 (December 21, 1985): 2913–2915.

12. Lemov, p. 58.

13. Dennis Farney and Joe Davidson, "States Grow Restive About Picking Up the Tab for Social Programs Mandated by Washington," *The Wall Street Journal* (September 14, 1989): A26.

14. See *Summary of Health Care Cost Containment Approaches: United States,* a monograph (Bismarck, N.D.: N.D. State Health Department, 1984).

15. Linda E. Demkovich, "Businesses Drive to Curb Medical Costs Without Much Help from Government," *National Journal* 16 (August 11, 1984): 1508–1510.

16. Tony Hutchison, "The Medicaid Budget Tangle," *State Legislatures* 16 (March 1990): 17.

17. Henry J. Aaron, "Six Welfare Questions Still Searching for Answers," *The Brookings Review* (Fall, 1984): 14.

18. See Carolyn Royce Kastner and Lawrence R. Young. *A Guide to State Child Support and Paternity Laws* (Denver: National Conference of State Legislatures, October 1981), p. iv.

19. Jo Anne B. Barnhart, "The Family Support Act: Public Assistance for the 1990s," *Intergovernmental Perspective* (Spring, 1991): 13. For a brief and balanced commentary on welfare reform in New Jersey, Michigan, and Connecticut, *see Public Administration Times* 15 (May 1, 1992), pp. 6–7.

20. Susan J. Smith, "New Thinking About the Homeless: Prevention, Not Cure," *Governing* 1 (February 1988): 26.

21. Ilene Grossman, "Homelessness," Trends Analysis Project Report from the Midwestern Office of the Council of State Governments (February 1988): 1.

22. Smith, p. 26.

23. Lee Walker, "A Problem in State-Federal Relations," *The Journal of State Government* 63 (January-March 1990): 16.

24. See Paul E. Peterson and Mark C. Rom, "The Case for a National Welfare Standard," *The Brookings Review* (Winter, 1988).

25. Joe Kraus, "Changing Considerations for Waste Disposal," a Trend Analysis Project Report, Council of State Governments, February 1988.

26. H. Lee Murphy, "Landfills can't bury problems of dwindling space, stiff rules," *City & State* (June 18, 1990), GM4.

27. Paul Furgia, "Hot Stuff," *Governing* 2 (November 1989): 50, 52.

28. Todd Sloane, "Brother, can you spare a landfill?" *City & State* (July 1990): 31.

29. Megan Seacord, "Feds Tell States Where to Put It," *State Legislatures* 16 (May/June 1990): 27.

30. Special compilation, "State Budgets for Recycling," *Recycling Times* (January 29, 1991): 6.

31. Cited by Christian Turner and Dayna Ashley, *Developing Recycling Markets and Industries* (Denver: National Conference of State Legislatures, 1990): 2.

32. *Winters* v. *United States,* 207 U.S. 564 (1908).

33. *Arizona* v. *California,* 373 U.S. 546 (1963).

34. Larry B. Morandi and Greg H. Lazarus, "Water Resources Management: Issues and Policy Options (Denver: National Conference of State Legislatures, November 1982), p. 26.

35. Rob Stern, "Indian Water Rights Battles Continue," *State Government News* 27 (June 1984): 7.

36. Morandi and Lazarus, *Water Resources Management,* p. 16.

37. Ibid., p. 20.

38. See Morandi and Lazarus, pp. 77–91, for a detailed account.

39. Morandi and Lazarus, pp. 110–112.

40. Joe Bower, "Golden State's neighbors pull plug on water plan," *City & State* (July 2, 1990): 3, 40.

41. Bruce A. Williams, "Regulation and Economic Development," *Politics in the American States,* 5th ed., Virginia Gray, Herbert Jacob, & Robert Albritton, eds. (Glenview, IL: Scott Foresman, 1990): 485.

42. See Rodd Zolkos, "High-stakes incentives race runs out of gas," *City & State* (July 30, 1990): 3.

43. Ilene Grossman, "States battle to attract jobs," *State Government News* 30 (December 1987): 11.

44. Dennis O. Grady, "State Economic Development Incentives: Why Do Businesses Compete?" *State & Local Government Review* 19 (Fall, 1987): 93.

45. Julie Lays, "Educating Eddie," *State Legislatures* 17 (April 1991): 20, citing the *National Assessment of Educational Progress.*

46. National Governors' Association, "Governors, Bush Agree to Set Education Goals," *Governors' Weekly Bulletin* 23 (September 29, 1989): 1.

47. Paul E. Peterson, "Did the Education Commissions Say Anything?," *The Brookings Review* 2 (Winter 1983): 6.

48. Julie Lays, p. 21.

49. Cited by Lillian Kinnel, "Parents and Students Seek School Choice," *Comparative Politics Newsletter* 11 (February 1990): 4; and also by Joe Nathan, "Expanding educational options," *State Government News* 32 (August 1989): 12.

50. John E. Chubb and Terry M. Moe, "Politics, Markets and the Organization of Schools," *American Political Science Review* 82 (December 1988): 1065–1087.

51. Statement of the National Coalition for an Urban Children's Agenda, published by a coalition of ten organizations. No date. Copies obtainable from National Association of State Boards of Education, 1012 Cameron Street, Alexandria, VA 22314.

52. Julie Lays, "Too Young To Die," *State Legislatures* 12 (November/December 1986): 18–19.

53. Tommy Neal, "Child Abuse: Our National Scandal," *State Legislatures* 16 (May/June 1990): 20.

54. Laura Kliewer Foster, "Foster care system facing crisis," *Midwesterner* (April 1991): 1.

55. "Deciding How to Define 'Family' Is Upcoming Issue," *State Legislatures* 15 (October 1989): 5.

56. James S. Coleman, "Families and Schools," *Educational Research* 16 (August/ September 1987): 35.

57. Michael W. Kirst, Milbrey McLaughlin and Diane Massell, "Rethinking Children's Policy: Implications for Educational Administration," *Preparing Schools for the 1990s,* an essay collection (New York, Metropolitan Life, 1991), p. 39.

58. Mark Weston and Charles Brackey, "Getting Parents To Pay Up," *State Legislatures* 13 (April 1987): 28.

Index